# American Environmental Leaders

## Volume II

# American Environmental Leaders
## From Colonial Times to the Present

Volume II
M–Z

Anne Becher
Joseph Richey

Grey House Publishing

|                          |                      |
|--------------------------|----------------------|
| PUBLISHER:               | Leslie Mackenzie     |
| EDITORIAL DIRECTOR:      | Laura Mars-Proietti  |
| EDITORIAL ASSISTANT:     | Jael Bridgemahon     |
| MARKETING DIRECTOR:      | Jessica Moody        |
| AUTHORS:                 | Anne Becher          |
|                          | Joseph Richey        |
| COPYEDITOR:              | Elaine Alibrandi     |
| COMPOSITION & DESIGN:    | ATLIS Systems        |

Grey House Publishing, Inc.
185 Millerton Road
Millerton, NY 12546
518.789.8700
FAX 518.789.0545
www.greyhouse.com
e-mail: books @greyhouse.com

While every effort has been made to ensure the reliability of the information presented in this publication, Grey House Publishing neither guarantees the accuracy of the data contained herein nor assumes any responsibility for errors, omissions or discrepancies. Grey House accepts no payment for listing; inclusion in the publication of any organization, agency, institution, publication, service or individual does not imply endorsement of the editors or publisher.

Errors brought to the attention of the publisher and verified to the satisfaction of the publisher will be corrected in future editions.

Except by express prior written permission of the Copyright Proprietor no part of this work may be copied by any means of publication or communication now known or developed hereafter including, but not limited to, use in any directory or compilation or other print publication, in any information storage and retrieval system, in any other electronic device, or in any visual or audio-visual device or product.

This publication is an original and creative work, copyrighted by Grey House Publishing, Inc. and is fully protected by all applicable copyright laws, as well as by laws covering misappropriation, trade secrets and unfair competition.

Grey House has added value to the underlying factual material through one or more of the following efforts: unique and original selection; expression; arrangement; coordination; and classification.

Grey House Publishing, Inc. will defend its rights in this publication.

Copyright © 2008 by Grey House Publishing, Inc.
All rights reserved. No part of this publication may be reproduced, stored in a retrieval system, or transmitted, in any form or by any means, electronic, mechanical, photocopying, recording, or otherwise, except for the inclusion of brief quotations in a review, without prior permission in writing from the publishers.

Publisher's Cataloging-In-Publication Data
(Prepared by The Donohue Group, Inc.)

Becher, Anne. American environmental leaders : colonial times to the present / Anne
   Becher, Joseph Richey. — 2nd ed.
     2 v. : ill. ; 28 cm.
   Includes bibliographical references and index.
   Content: v. 1. A-L — v. 2. M-Z.
   ISBN: 978-1-59237-119-8

1. Environmentalists—United States—Biography. I. Richey, Joseph. II. Title.
GE55 .B43 2008
363.7/0092/273

DUST STORM DISASTER
   Words and Music by Woody Guthrie
   TRO-© Copyright 1960 (Renewed) 1963 (Renewed) Ludlow Music, Inc., New York, NY.
   Used by permission.

ROLL ON, COLUMBIA
   Words by Woody Guthrie
   Music based on GOODNIGHT, IRENE by Huddie Ledbetter and John A. Lomax
   TRO-© Copyright 1936 (Renewed) 1957 (Renewed) and 1963 (Renewed)
   Ludlow Music, Inc., New York, NY. Used by permission.

THIS LAND IS YOUR LAND
   Words and Music by Woody Guthrie
   TRO-© Copyright 1956 (Renewed) 1958 (Renewed) 1970 (Renewed) 1972
   (Renewed) Ludlow Music, Inc., New York, NY. Used by permission.

SAILING DOWN MY GOLDEN RIVER
   Words and Music by Pete Seeger
   TRO-© Copyright 1971 (Renewed) Melody Trails, Inc., New York, NY. Used by permission.

DIRTY STREAM
   Written by Pete Seeger
   Published by SANGA MUSIC, INC. Administered by The Royalty Network. Used by permission.

## Table of Contents

**Volume I**

List of American Environmental Leaders, vii

Preface, xiii

Acknowledgments, xv

Introduction, xix

Biographical Profiles A–L, 1

**Volume II**

List of American Environmental Leaders, vii

Biographical Profiles M–Z, 499

Key Documents, 897

Timeline, 1003

List of Leaders by Occupation/Focus, 1015

Index, 1025

About the Authors, 1051

# List of American Environmental Leaders

## Volume I
Abbey, Edward, 3
Ackerman, Diane, 4
Adams, Ansel, 6
Adams, Henry, 8
Adams, John Hamilton, 10
Adams, John Quincy, 12
Addams, Jane, 13
Albright, Horace, 15
Alston, Dana, 17
Amidon, Elias, and Elizabeth Roberts, 19
Anderson, Adrienne, 21
Anderson, Ray, 25
Andrus, Cecil, 27
Anthony, Carl, 29
Audubon, John James, 31
Austin, Mary, 33
Ausubel, Kenny, 36
Ayres, Richard, 38
Babbitt, Bruce, 43
Bahouth, Peter, 44
Bailey, Florence Augusta Merriam, 46
Ball, Betty, and Gary Ball, 48
Balog, James D., 51
Bari, Judi, 52
Bartlett, Albert, 55
Bartram, John, and William Bartram, 58
Bates, Marston, 60
Bauer, Catherine, 61
Bavaria, Joan, 63
Bean, Michael, 65
Beattie, Mollie, 67
Beebe, C. William, 69
Begley, Ed, Jr., 71
Bennett, Hugh Hammond, 73
Benyus, Janine, 76
Berg, Peter, 74
Berle, Peter, 78
Berry, Friar Thomas, 80
Berry, Wendell, 82
Bertell, Rosalie, 84
Bien, Amos, 86
Bierstadt, Albert, 89
Bingham, Eula, 91
Bixby, Kevin, 93
Blackgoat, Roberta, 94
Blaeloch, Janine, 96
Bloomberg, Michael, 98
Bookchin, Murray, 100
Boulding, Kenneth, 102
Bramble, Barbara, 104
Brand, Stewart, 107
Brandborg, Stewart, 109
Bresette, Walt, 113
Brower, David, 115
Brown, Janet, 118
Brown, Lester, 119
Brown, Michael, 122
Browner, Carol, 124
Bullard, Robert D., 126
Burroughs, John, 129
Butcher, Devereux, 131
Cade, Thomas, 135
Caldwell, Lynton, 137
Callicott, J. Baird, 139
Carhart, Arthur, 141
Carlton, Jasper, 143
Carr, Archie, 145
Carr, Marjorie Harris, 148
Carson, Rachel, 150
Carter, Jimmy, 152
Carter, Majora, 155
Carver, George Washington, 157
Castillo, Aurora, 159
Catlin, George, 160
Caudill, Harry, 162
Chafee, John, 164
Chapman, Frank, 166
Chappell, Kate, and Tom Chappell, 167
Chase, Robin, 170
Chávez, César, 172
Chavis, Benjamin, 174
Chief Sealth (Seattle), 734
Christy, Elizabeth, 176
Cizik, Richard, 178
Clawson, Marion, 179
Cobb, John B., Jr., 181
Colborn, Theo, 183
Colby, William, 186
Cole, Thomas, 188

# List of American Environmental Leaders

Collom, Jack, 190
Commoner, Barry, 192
Connett, Ellen, and Paul Connett, 194
Conway, Stuart, 197
Cook, Richard A., 198
Cooper, James Fenimore, 201
Costle, Douglas, 202
Cowles, Henry, 204
Cox, Paul, 206
Craighead, Frank, and John Craighead, 208
Cronon, William, 211
Daly, Herman, 215
Darley, Julian and Celine Fanny Rich, 217
Darling, Jay Norwood "Ding", 220
David, Laurie Ellen, 224
Dawson, Richard, 226
DeBonis, Jeff, 228
Desser, Christina Louise, 231
Devall, Bill, 233
Devoto, Bernard, 234
DiCaprio, Leonardo, 236
Dilg, Will, 238
Dingell, John, Jr., 239
Dittmar, Hank, 241
Dombeck, Michael, 244
Donovan, Richard, 246
Douglas, Marjory Stoneman, 249
Douglas, William Orville, 251
Dowie, Mark, 253
Downing, Andrew Jackson, 255
Drayton, William, 257
Drury, Newton, 259
Dubos, René, 262
Dunlap, Louise, 264
Durning, Alan, 265
Dutcher, William, 267
Dyer, Polly, 270
Earle, Sylvia, 275
Edge, Rosalie, 277
Ehrenfeld, David, 279
Ehrlich, Anne, and Paul Ehrlich, 281
Eisner, Thomas, 284
Ellis, Juliet, 286
Elton, Charles S., 288
Emerson, Ralph Waldo, 290
Figueroa, Rogelio, 295
Fontenot, Willie, 296
Foreman, Dave, 299

Fossey, Dian, 302
Franklin, Jerry, 304
Frome, Michael, 306
Fuller, Buckminster, 309
Fuller, Kathryn, 312
Futrell, J. William, 314
Gagliano, Sherwood M., 319
Geisel, Theodor (Dr. Seuss), 320
Gelbspan, Ross, 323
Gibbs, Lois, 325
Gleason, Henry Allan, 327
Gold, Lou, 329
Golten, Robert, 331
Goodman, Paul, 333
Gore, Albert, Jr., 335
Gottlieb, Robert, 338
Gould, Stephen Jay, 341
Gray, Asa, 343
Grinnell, George Bird, 345
Grogan, Pete, 347
Grossman, Richard L., 349
Gussow, Joan Dye, 352
Guthrie, Woody, 354
Gutiérrez, Juana Beatriz, 357
Hair, Jay, 363
Hamilton, Alice, 365
Hansen, James E., 367
Hardin, Garrett, 370
Harrelson, Woody, 372
Harry, Debra, 374
Harvey, Dorothy Webster, 376
Hawken, Paul, 379
Hayes, Denis, 382
Hayes, Randy, 383
Hays, Samuel P., 385
Henderson, Hazel, 387
Hermach, Tim, 390
Hill, Julia Butterfly, 392
Hoagland, Edward, 395
Hornaday, William Temple, 397
House, Donna, 399
Huerta, Dolores, 402
Ickes, Harold, 409
Ingram, Helen, 411
Jackson, Henry, 415
Jackson, Wes, 417
Jacobson, Michael, 419
Janzen, Daniel H., 421

Jensen, Derrick, 424
Johnson, Glenn S., 425
Johnson, Hazel, 428
Johnson, Lady Bird (Claudia Alta), 431
Johnson, Robert Underwood, 433
Jones, Van, 435
Jontz, Jim, 437
Jordan, Chris, 439
Jukofsky, Diane, 441
Kamp, Dick, 445
Kane, Hal, 446
Katz, Daniel, 449
Kaufman, Hugh, 451
Kellert, Stephen, 453
Kendall, Henry, 456
Kennedy, Robert F., Jr., 457
Kingsolver, Barbara, 460
Kratt, Chris, and Martin Kratt, 461
Krupp, Fred, 463
LaBudde, Samuel, 469
LaDuke, Winona, 471
Lammers, Owen, 473
Lappé, Frances Moore, 475
Leopold, Aldo, 478
Lindbergh, Anne Morrow, and Charles
   Augustus Lindbergh, 480
Littletree, Alicia, 482
Lopez, Barry, 484
Louv, Richard, 486
Lovejoy, Thomas, 488
Lovins, Amory, and Hunter Lovins, 490
Luce, Benjamin, 492
Lyons, Oren, 494

## Volume II
MacKaye, Benton, 499
Mader, Ron, 500
Mander, Jerry, 503
Mann, Michael E., 505
Manning, Richard, 507
Marsh, George Perkins, 510
Marshall, Robert, 512
Marston, Betsy, and Ed Marston, 514
Martínez, Dennis, 516
Mather, Stephen, 519
Matthiessen, Peter, 521
McCloskey, Michael, 523
McDonough, William, 525

McDowell, Mary, 528
McHarg, Ian, 530
McKibben, Bill, 532
McPhee, John, 534
Meadows, Donella H., 536
Meany, Edmond, 538
Merchant, Carolyn, 540
Merculieff, Ilarion (Larry), 542
Miller, Laura, 545
Mills, Enos, 546
Mills, Stephanie, 548
Mitchell, George J., 550
Mittermeier, Russell, 553
Montague, Peter, 554
Moses, Marion, 556
Moss, Cynthia, 558
Moss, Doug, 560
Muir, John, 562
Mumford, Lewis, 565
Murie, Mardy, and Olaus Murie, 568
Muskie, Edmund, 570
Nabhan, Gary, 575
Nader, Ralph, 577
Nagel, Carlos, 579
Nash, Roderick, 581
Nearing, Helen, and Scott Nearing, 584
Needleman, Herbert, 586
Nelson, Gaylord, 588
Nelson, Willie, 590
Newman, Nell, 591
Nickels, Greg, 594
Norton, Bryan, 596
Noss, Reed, 598
Odum, Eugene, 603
Oliver, Mary, 605
Olmsted, Frederick Law, Jr., 609
Olmsted, Frederick Law, Sr., 607
Olson, Molly Harriss, 610
Olson, Sigurd, 612
Orr, David, 615
Osborn, Fairfield, 616
Owings, Margaret, 618
Packard, Steve, 623
Palmer, Paula, 625
Parkman, Francis, 627
Peacock, Doug, 629
Perkins, Jane, 631
Peterson, Roger Tory, 633

# LIST OF AMERICAN ENVIRONMENTAL LEADERS

Peterson, Russell, 635
Pinchot, Gifford, 637
Plotkin, Mark, 639
Pollan, Michael, 642
Popper, Deborah, and Frank Popper, 643
Postel, Sandra, 647
Pough, Richard, 649
Powell, John Wesley, 652
Pritchard, Paul C., 654
Pryor, Cynthia, 657
Pulido, Laura, 658
Raven, Peter, 663
Red Cloud, Henry, 665
Reilly, William K., 667
Reisner, Marc, 669
Reynolds, Michael, 670
Richards, Ellen Swallow, 673
Rifkin, Jeremy, 675
Ringo, Jerome C., 677
Ritter, Bill, Jr., 679
Robbins, John, 682
Robin, Vicki, 684
Rockefeller, John D., Jr., 686
Rockefeller, Laurance, 689
Rodale, Robert, 691
Rolfes, Anne, 693
Rolston, Holmes, III, 695
Roosevelt, Franklin D., 697
Roosevelt, Theodore, 699
Rosenfeld, Arthur H., 702
Roszak, Theodore, 703
Ruether, Rosemary Radford, 705
Safina, Carl, 709
Sagan, Carl, 712
Sale, Kirkpatrick, 714
Sandoval, Arturo, 716
Sanjour, William, 718
Sargent, Charles Sprague, 719
Sawhill, John, 721
Schlickeisen, Rodger, 724
Schneider, Stephen, 725
Schultes, Richard Evans, 728
Schurz, Carl, 730
Schwarzenegger, Arnold, 732
Seeger, Pete, 736
Selikoff, Irving, 738
Seo, Danny, 740
Sessions, George, 742

Seton, Ernest Thompson, 743
Shabecoff, Philip, 746
Shapiro, Andrew L., 748
Shuey, Chris, 750
Silkwood, Karen, 753
Sive, David, 754
Smith, Rocky, 757
Sneed, Cathrine, 758
Snyder, Gary, 760
Soleri, Paolo, 762
Solomon, Susan, 765
Soulé, Michael, 766
Speth, James Gustave, 769
Standing Bear, Chief Luther, 771
Steel, William, 773
Stegner, Wallace, 775
Steingraber, Sandra, 776
Stone, Christopher, 779
Stone-Manning, Tracy, 780
Subra, Wilma, 783
Suckling, Kierán, 785
Susanka, Sarah, 787
Swearingen, Terri, 789
Tall, JoAnn, 795
Tamminen, Terry, 797
Tchozewski, D. Chet, 799
Tewa, Debby, 802
Thompson, Chief Tommy Kuni, 804
Thoreau, Henry David, 806
Thorne, Oakleigh, II, 809
Thorpe, Grace, 812
Tidwell, Michael, 814
Tokar, Brian, 817
Tompkins, Douglas, 819
Toor, Will, 821
Turner, Frederick Jackson, 823
Turner, Ted, 824
Udall, Morris, 829
Udall, Stewart, 831
Vogt, William, 837
Walter, Martin, 841
Warburton, Barbara, 843
Waring, George, 844
Warshall, Peter, 846
Watson, Paul, 848
Waxman, Henry, 850
Werbach, Adam, 852
Whealy, Diane, and Kent Whealy, 854

White, Gilbert F., 857
White, Lynn, Jr., 859
Whitman, Walt, 861
Willcox, Louisa, 864
Wille, Chris, 866
Williams, Terry Tempest, 868
Wilson, Diane, 871
Wilson, Edward O., 872

Winter, Paul, 874
Wolf, Hazel, 877
Wolke, Howie, 879
Woodwell, George, 881
Worster, Donald, 883
Yard, Robert Sterling, 889
Zahniser, Howard, 893
Zwick, David, 895

White, Gilbert F., 857
White, Lynn, Jr., 859
Whitman, Walt, 861
Willcox, Louisa, 864
Wille, Chris, 866
Williams, Terry Tempest, 868
Wilson, Diane, 871
Wilson, Edward O., 872

Winter, Paul, 874
Wolf, Hazel, 877
Wolke, Howie, 879
Woodwell, George, 881
Worster, Donald, 883
Yard, Robert Sterling, 889
Zahniser, Howard, 893
Zwick, David, 895

# American Environmental Leaders

## Volume II

# American Environmental Leaders

From Colonial Times to the Present

M

## MacKaye, Benton
(March 6, 1879–December 11, 1976)
Regional Planner

Regional planner Benton MacKaye, a cofounder of the Wilderness Society (TWS), was the primary force behind the Appalachian Trail, built during the 1920s and 1930s to link a 2,000-mile corridor of mountain wilderness stretching from Maine to Georgia. He was a leader among regional planners, issuing perennial reminders in his writings and group discussions that planners should work toward improved habitability of the earth, which MacKaye, following his mentor Patrick Geddes, called "geotechnics."

Benton MacKaye was born on March 6, 1879, in Stamford, Connecticut, one of five children whose father, Steele MacKaye, was a well-known actor, director, and playwright. The family moved frequently throughout the northeastern United States but established a fixed summer home in the village of Shirley Center, Massachusetts, in the late 1880s. Steele MacKaye organized summer pageants, writing original plays and directing local actors for performances in the Shirley Center town hall. As a child, MacKaye was exposed to the best of urban centers: while living in Washington, D.C., he visited the Smithsonian Institution frequently and met personally such renowned explorers as Adm. Robert Peary and Major JOHN WESLEY POWELL. He also benefited from rural Shirley Center: he spent his teenage summers on mini-"expeditions" modeled after those of Peary and Powell, assiduously mapping forests, charting the course of the Squannacook River, and observing birds within a four-mile radius of his home. These childhood experiences were later to form the base for MacKaye's belief that for a healthy civilization, humans must have access to three types of environs: urban, rural, and "primeval" or wilderness.

MacKaye studied forestry at Harvard University, earning his B.A. in 1900 and his A.M. in 1905. He worked for GIFFORD PINCHOT's U.S. Forest Service for the first 13 years of his career, surveying forested areas in New England and the South to be incorporated into the National Forest system. Thanks to one of his reports, 30,000 acres of land in the White Mountains became the first parcel in the White Mountain National Forest. During the remainder of his career, he also served as forester or planner for several other government agencies, including the Department of Labor, the Geological Survey, the Bureau of Indian Affairs, and the Tennessee Valley Authority. He also taught at the Harvard Forest School for many years. But it was as a member of independent organizations and intellectual groups that MacKaye distinguished himself.

During the early part of the 1900s, MacKaye developed a plan for what would blossom as the Appalachian Trail. The article he wrote for the *Journal of the American Institute of Architects* in 1921, "An Appalachian Trail: A Project in Regional Planning," proposed a 2,000-mile trail along the mountainous wilderness belt between Maine and Georgia. MacKaye suggested that the trail be constructed and maintained by local or regional groups and that the government protect the area in its wild state. The idea caught on almost immediately, and branches of the new Appalachian Trail Club formed to build their segments of the trail. By 1937, the trail was completed, and in 1938 the federal government moved to protect it.

MacKaye worked with a group of regional planners during the 1920s who called themselves the Regional Planning Association of America (RPAA). They criticized what they felt were the overdeveloped urban centers of the time, whose thirst and hunger were like tentacles reaching out and depleting nearby rural areas. Inspired by the Garden Cities movement of England, they proposed industrialized yet park-filled cities of a moderate size that would exemplify geo-technics or improved habitability. A 1925 issue of *Survey Graphic* magazine featured the ideas of RPAA members and left its indelible print on the fields of regional planning and urban design. Fifty-one years later, RPAA member LEWIS MUMFORD called the articles an accurate diagnosis of "the disorders of random metropolitan congestion and suburban scattering."

Despite being far ahead of their time in that respect, in another aspect the group neglected to foresee a problem with their all-out promotion of the automobile. The private car was seen by the RPAA school as a useful vehicle that could quickly carry urban inhabitants to rural and primeval settings. MacKaye proposed, in a 1931 article for *Harpers*, the "townless highway," which was basically the prototype for the modern freeway. What none of the RPAA planners foresaw, wrote Mumford in his 1976 tribute to MacKaye, was that the automobile would "wreck our far more efficient railroad system and in many areas completely wipe out virtually all public transportation, with all its useful auxiliary services—telegraph offices, taxis, baggage and regular freight deliveries."

In 1935, MacKaye, along with seven other proponents of wilderness protection, co-founded the Wilderness Society. All of the co-founders, who included ROBERT MARSHALL, Harvey Broome, Harold Anderson, ALDO LEOPOLD, Ernest Oberholtzer, Bernard Frank, and ROBERT STERLING YARD, concurred that wilderness was an important antidote to increasingly inhumane and uninhabitable large urban areas. MacKaye served as president of the Wilderness Society from 1945 to 1950 and then as honorary president from 1950 until his death. His long life afforded him the enjoyment of seeing TWS grow from a tiny, underfunded fledgling organization to one of the most influential conservation lobbies in the United States.

MacKaye spent his many sabbaticals between government jobs and writing projects in Shirley Center. It was there that he spent his final years, under the affectionate care of his friends and especially his next-door neighbor, Lucy Johnson. He died at the age of 97, on December 11, 1976, in Lucy Johnson's Shirley Center home.

### BIBLIOGRAPHY

Anderson, Larry, *Benton MacKaye: Conservationist, Planner, and Creator of the Appalachian Trail*, 2008; Bryant, Paul T., ed., *From Geography to Geotechnics*, 1968; MacKaye, Benton, *Expedition Nine: A Return to a Region*, 1969; Mumford, Lewis, Stuart Chase, George Marshall, Paul H. Oehser, Frederick Gutheim, Harley B. Holden, Paul T. Bryant, Robert M. Howes, and C.J.S. Durham, "Benton MacKaye: A Tribute," *Living Wilderness*, 1976; Oehser, Paul H., "On Benton MacKaye's Centenary," *Living Wilderness*, 1979.

## Mader, Ron

(November 8, 1963– )
Journalist, Web Publisher

Ron Mader is an environmental journalist specializing in ecotourism and sustainable development in Latin America as well as the Mexico–United States borderlands. Mader created the expansive "Planeta.com: Global Journal of Practical Ecotourism" (www.planeta.com) in 1995. This was the Web's first site focusing on

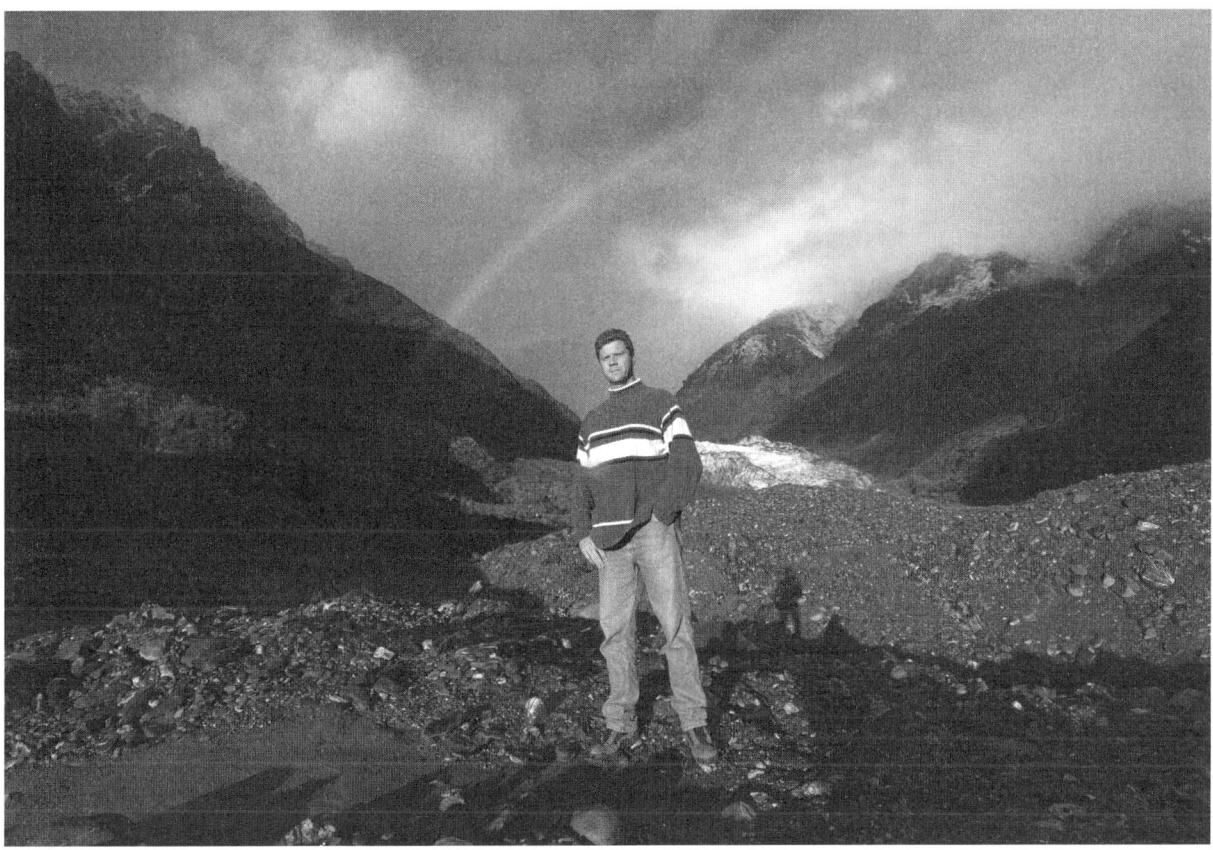
Ron Mader (Photograph by Tom Walter/Flow Photography)

ecotourism and responsible travel. It has won numerous awards and has served as an online workshop for those working toward sustainability around the world.

Ronald Earl Mader was born in Fort Wayne, Indiana, on November 8, 1963. He became interested in travel and the environment as a child thanks to his parents—both schoolteachers—who took Ron and his older siblings, John Carl and Cheryl Barbara, on cross-country treks, visiting national parks and heritage sites in the United States. In Fort Wayne, Mader was an active member of the Fort Wayne Astronomical Society and a radio broadcaster, producing a book review program ("Page 35") for radio station WBNI. Mader studied telecommunications and film studies at Indiana University–Bloomington, graduating with a B.A. in 1986.

After graduation, Mader relocated to Los Angeles, California, where he attempted to sell his own movie scripts. Finding real life—and the stories he was hearing from Central America and Mexico—more interesting than his fictional work, he decided to refashion his career by improving international journalism and news coverage from the Americas. In 1988 Mader moved to Austin, Texas, and began studies at the University of Texas at Austin, where he earned a master's degree from the Institute of Latin American Studies in 1990. As Mader recounted in a 1999 interview, "I knew how to communicate but I didn't know what to say. Refocusing my career in Texas provided me with the impetus to make an impact in how U.S. citizens could improve their understanding of events and issues in Latin America." Mader's early focus on ecotourism would blossom again a few years later.

Mader worked first as a reporter and editor for the *Mexico City News* (1992–1993) and then forged a successful freelance career, focusing on the U.S.-Mexico border, Mexico, and ecotourism in Latin America in general. He has written stories about economic and environmental problems and their potential solutions for such publications as *Transitions Abroad*, *Texas Environmental News*, *Honduras This Week*, *Mexico City News*, and *South American Explorer*.

Mader is best known in the tourism profession for Planeta.com, which includes in-depth information written by experts worldwide on sustainable development (economic development that can continue for generations and that empowers local communities), ecotourism (tourism that provides material assistance to conservation projects, empowers local communities, and is capable of sustaining itself financially), and environmental conservation. The site is a rich, continuously updated source of information for students, researchers, travelers, and businesspeople looking for like-minded contacts.

Planeta.com creates incentives for communication, opportunities for conversation, and rewards for participation among travelers and locals who share a vision of eco-friendly, people-friendly, and place-friendly travel. Mader spotlights what is local across the globe and models what Mader calls "decentralized communications," encouraging engaged direct conversation among all the players or stakeholders working toward responsible travel and ecotourism. Playing the role of a communication catalyst since its inception, Planeta.com provided an example of how Web 1 and later Web 2.0 communication could empower readers to generate their own content in the form of announcements, essays, travel features, photography and video.

Planeta.com has hosted 20 on-lne conferences since 2000. The discussion with the greatest number of participants was the "Sustainable Development of Ecotourism Web Conference, conducted on-line as a precursor to the 2002 World Ecotourism Summit. More than 900 people registered for the discussion. Other noted e-conferences include "Ethical Marketing of Ecotourism," "Financing Sustainable Tourism," "Food, Health, and Building Communities," and "Tourism and Climate Change."

In 2001 Planeta.com launched the Colibrí Ecotourism Award to highlight those working in Mexico. The award is announced to coincide with World Environment Day, June 5. Mader says that awards highlight best practices and offer benchmarks that others can follow.

Mader's work has received recognition and awards from *Outside* Magazine, the *Dallas Morning News*, the *Miami Herald*, and most recently the Mexican government, which awarded Mader the Lente de Plata (Silver Lens) award for the web site's exhaustive coverage of Mexican ecotourism and environmental travel options.

In addition to his on-line work, Mader has written two ecotourism-oriented guidebooks, *Mexico: Adventures in Nature* (1998) and *Honduras: Adventures in Nature* (coauthored with James D. Gollin, 1998). These books, which emphasize the natural history–oriented destinations within each country, offer information about the history, culture, economy, and ecology of the respective nation and instruct visitors on how to keep their impact as positive as possible. Mader contributed several chapters to the *Responsible Travel Handbook* (2006), published by *Transitions Abroad*.

Mader lives in Oaxaca City and works as a correspondent for *Transitions Abroad*. In Oaxaca Mader co-created the Oaxaca Options speaker series and annual Rural Tourism Fairs which showcase Oaxaca's cultural and biological diversity. For Mader, working on the ground is as important as writing, as he believes environmental leadership needs practical application to be meaningful.

Mader is active on the lecture/conference circuit, having keynoted at the 2007 Ecotourism New Zealand Conference and presented at the World Ecotourism Summit (2002). He also has led workshops for indigenous tourism leaders, sharing lessons learned on using the Web to communicate points of view that are often left out of mass media.

**BIBLIOGRAPHY**
"An interview with Ron Mader of Planeta.com," www.practicalenvironmentalist.com/organizations-we-like/an-interview-with-ron-mader-of-planetacom. htm#more-535; Mader, Ron, "Bypassing the Power Structure (in Mexico)," *Forbes*, 1997; Mader, Ron, "Latin America's New Ecotourism," *Honduras This Week*, 1999; "Planeta.com: Global Journal of Practical Ecotourism," www.planeta.com; "Ron Mader's Home Page on Mexico Connect," www.mexconnect.com/mex_/trave/rmader/ronhome.html.

# Mander, Jerry
(May 1, 1936– )
Writer, Advertising Executive

Jerry Mander is a renowned advocate for ecological and social causes, including native rights. He is well known for his marketing work—he spent 15 years as a successful marketer, ultimately serving only nonprofit social groups—and has been described by the *Wall Street Journal* as "the Ralph Nader of advertising." Mander is the author of *Four Arguments for the Elimination of Television* (1978) and *In the Absence of the Sacred: The Failure of Technology and the Survival of the Indian Nations* (1991), among other influential books. Through the International Forum on Globalization, an orgnaization he co-founded in 1994, Mander continues to fight both the encroachment of technology in society and economic and industrial globalization.

Jerry Mander was born on May 1, 1936, in New York City to Jewish immigrants from eastern Europe. Although he was urged by his parents to take over his father's business in the garment industry, Mander found himself drawn to the flash and glamour of the marketing field, leading him to obtain a B.S. in economics from Wharton School of Business at the University of Pennsylvania in 1958. In 1959, he concluded his studies with an M.S. in economics from Columbia Graduate Business School.

During 1961 and 1962, Mander worked as assistant director of the San Francisco International Film Festival. In 1962, he formed Jerry Mander & Associates, a public relations firm of which he was president until 1965, when he joined a celebrated advertising company that became Freeman, Mander, and Gossage. As president and partner of the firm, Mander spearheaded its many successful campaigns for environmental and social advocacy groups, including the Sierra Club. Freeman, Mander, and Gossage authored such successful campaigns that Robert Glatzer of *New Advertising* credited the ads with "starting the whole ecology boom." The advertisements were characterized by "coupons" that could be torn out and mailed to political leaders. The most notable campaigns were instrumental in keeping dams out of the Grand Canyon and establishing, among other preserves, Redwood National Park.

In 1967, Mander wrote *The Great International Paper Airplane Book* with George Dippel and Howard Gossage. A simple account of the first Scientific American International Paper Airplane Contest, the book includes pseudoadvertisements written by Mander. The accusations that Mander and company were subtly undermining U.S. production of supersonic transport aircraft (SSTs) may have risen from the fact that an ad for the contest with cynical references to the SST appears on a page facing a real Lockheed ad advocating SST production. A U.S. SST was never built.

Conflicted interests became more apparent with the success of Mander's social campaigns, and large corporations such as auto manufacturers dissolved their accounts with the firm. The absurdity of the tenets and goals of marketing pressed hard on Mander, and the firm dissolved in the summer of 1972. That same year, he worked to create Public Interest Communications (PIC), the country's first nonprofit advertising agency. PIC catered exclusively to community, environmental, and social action groups and launched successful, albeit unprofitable, campaigns. In 1974 Mander took a leave from advertising to address his growing concern with the problems of marketing, and especially with television.

In 1978 Mander completed *Four Arguments for the Elimination of Television*. This potent critique of a widespread and readily accepted medium asserts that television is intrinsically dangerous. Mander's marketing experience gave him a deft understanding of how corporations use the power of television as a homogenizing force. He argues that television invades individual and mass consciousness and is so viciously harmful to personal sanity and health that it must be abolished.

For the next decade Mander worked on a book to follow *Four Arguments*, while continuing to advocate and work for many ecological and social action groups. Since 1980, he has been senior fellow at the Public Media Center, a group that has campaigned for Sierra Club, Greenpeace, Planned Parenthood, Friends of the Earth, and others. Mander continued to be influenced by his increasing ties with activist groups and especially by the struggles of Native American peoples. In 1991 his book, *In the Absence of the Sacred: The Failure of Technology and the Survival of the Indian Nations*, was published. The book grapples with two related issues, the flaws of technological society and native people's struggles against its encroachment. The critique of technological society revolves around a more widespread application of the attitude that Mander presented in *Four Arguments*. In this book, technology and the mechanization of society are accused of provoking depression, alienation, and social atrocities in modern society. The book discusses the subjugation of native populations around the world and the assault waged against them by technological society.

Mander subsequently cofounded the International Forum on Globalization (IFG), an organization of activists and writers worldwide who provide analyses and critiques of the impact of globalization on culture, society, politics, and the environment, through teach-ins and conferences and many publications. Mander has edited two books about globalization. *The Case Against the Global Economy: And for a Turn Toward the Local* (co-edited with Edward Goldsmith, 1996), consists of 43 essays that decry economic and industrial globalization and explain how international agreements such as the North American Free Trade Agreement and the General Agreement on Tariffs and Trade have led to stepped-up plundering of natural resources and disregard for human rights, especially in poor countries. *Paradigm Wars: Indigenous Peoples' Resistance to Globalization* (co-edited with Victoria Tauli-Corpuz, 2006) includes 28 articles about indigenous rights and resistence to exploitation of their lands.

The 2007 *Manifesto on Global Economic Transitions*, edited by Mander and co-signed by more than 50 world scientists and environmental and social justice activists, describes the impending ecological, social and economic breakdowns the world faces, due to the end of cheap energy, depletion of the "commons" (fresh water, clean air, biodiversity, fertile soil, etc.), and climate change, and warns that a worldwide technological "fix" is not the solution—there is none available yet, and if one were to be developed, it would be at great cost. Rather, communities worldwide should devise and improve their local systems for food, transportation, and manufacturing, and make sure that these are sustainable. The *Manifesto* is available for free download at www.ifg.org/pdf/manifesto.pdf.

Mander contributes articles to periodicals including *The Nation*, *City Magazine*, *San Francisco Chronicle*, and others.

BIBLIOGRAPHY

"International Forum on Globalization," www.ifg.org/; Mander, Jerry, "The Dark Side of Globalization: What the Media Are Missing," *The Nation*, 1996; Mander, Jerry, "Internet: The Illusion of Empowerment," *Whole Earth Review*, 1998; Mander, Jerry, *In the Absence of the Sacred: The Failure of Technology and the Survival of the Indian Nations*, 1991; Mander, Jerry, and Edward Goldsmith, eds., *The Case Against The Global Economy: And for A Turn Toward The Local*, 1996.

## Mann, Michael E.

(December 28, 1965– )
Climatologist, Geophysics Professor

Michael Mann is a climate scientist who has had a significant impact on global warming science and public policy. He teaches at Pennsylvania State University's Meteorology and Geosciences departments, and is the author of more than 100 peer-reviewed and edited publications. He also is the Director of the Penn State Earth System Science Center. Mann is a lead author of the "Observed Climate Variability and Change" chapter in the UN's Intergovernmental Panel on Climate Change's (IPCC) Third Scientific Assessment Report (TAR) of 2001. He is most closely associated with a graph that was published therein called "the hockey stick." Mann has testified before the U.S. Congress, and served as an advisor to government and non-government policymakers. He is a regular media commentator appearing in major print, radio, television, and internet media outlets.

Michael Evan Mann was born in Amherst, Massachusetts on December 28, 1965. He was curious about the natural world even as a young child. While pursuing a Ph.D. in theoretical physics, he decided to instead apply his training and knowledge to the societally critical scientific topic of climate change. He holds a double A.B. from the University of California-Berkeley in applied math and physics, an M.S. in physics from Yale University, and a Ph.D. from Yale University in geology and geophysics. He taught in the Environmental Sciences Department at the University of Virginia from 1999 to 2005 before taking his posts at Penn State. Mann is married to Lorraine Santy, and has a daughter, Megan, who was born in 2005.

In the late 1990s, Mann and his colleagues Raymond S. Bradley and Malcolm K. Hughes plotted the aforementioned "hockey stick" graph that details variations in the temperature of Earth's northern hemisphere over the last 1,000 years, leading to the declaration that the 1990s were the warmest decade in the past millennium. For the 850 years preceding the use of temperature-measuring equipment, the authors used evidence of variations in temperature from proxy sources such as tree rings, glacial layers, coral, ocean and lake sediments, and historical documents. The graph was dubbed the "hockey

Michael Mann has tapped the information contained in such natural archives as tree rings, ice cores and coral reefs to distinguish between ordinary temperature changes and those produced by global warming. (Photograph by Tom Cogill)

stick" by scientist Jerry Mahlman because of its shape: a sharp, blade-like rise in temperatures during the second half of the 20th century at the end of an otherwise less variable 950-year shaft-like trajectory.

The graph makes a compelling visual case for the unprecedented, human induced recent warming of Earth through the emission of greenhouse gases since the Industrial Revolution. A version of the graph appeared in AL GORE's Oscar-winning documentary *An Inconvenient Truth* (2006). However, despite Mann's statement in 2005 that "I am not myself familiar with any scientific document that has been more comprehensively reviewed than the TAR," the hockey stick became a lightning rod of controversy among global warming skeptics, including Joe Barton, a Republican who represents Texas's 6th congressional district. The oil and gas industries have featured among his top five campaign contributors in the past three election cycles (2004, 2006, and 2008).

In 2005, Barton chaired the House Energy and Commerce Committee. After reading a front page article in *The Wall Street Journal* on February 14, 2005 critiquing the math used for the "hockey stick" graph, he sent letters making several inquiries of Mann, Bradley, Hughes, the NSF, and the IPCC. Mann complied thoroughly and graciously. The Canadian researchers cited in the critical WSJ article, Steven McIntyre, a mining industry executive, and Ross McKitrick, an economist, have no formal training in climate science, and the original publication where their critique appeared, *Energy & Environment*, is a policy journal that is not subject to scientific peer review.

As early as 2003, Mann reported in testimony before Congress that more than a dozen independent research groups had reconstructed the average temperature of the Northern Hemisphere going back 1,000 years, and all agreed that the warming in the late 20th century is unprecedented and can not be explained without the contribution from anthropogenic influences. In 2006, a panel from the National Research Council concluded that the Mann-Bradley-Hughes research was likely to be true, and the IPCC's 2007 Fourth Assessment Report flatly states that "warming of the [Earth's] climate system is unequivocal."

Mann is one of the founders of RealClimate.org. Launched in December 2004, the website states that it is "a commentary site on climate science by working climate scientists for the interested public and journalists, [which aims] to provide a quick response to developing stories and the context sometimes missing in mainstream commentary. The discussion here is restricted to scientific topics." *Time* magazine's April 28, 2008 Special Environment Issue named Real Climate one of the top 15 environmental websites.

In 2007, Mann was the co-recipient of the Nobel Peace Prize along with the several hundred colleagues who constitute the IPCC. A member of the National Academy of Science, he has been an organizing committee chair for their "Frontiers of Science" and has served in other panels. He was editor of the *Journal of Climate* from 2000-2002, and in 2002 was named by *Scientific American* as one of the 50 leading visionaries in science and technology.

Like Dr. JAMES HANSEN of NASA's Goddard Institute, this brilliant scientist and diligent academic has been thrust into an environmental leadership position while trying to understand and make known processes that are destroying humanity and our home planet. Like Hansen, Mann is a true public intellectual whose timely, rigorous scientific posts energize grassroots movements seeking to break through the gridlock in Congress and elsewhere preventing the greening of public policy.

**BIBLIOGRAPHY:**
"A Bid to Chill Thinking," *The Washington Post*, July 22, 2005; Kancler, Erik, "The Man Behind the Hockey Stick," *Mother Jones*, April 18, 2005; Peterson, Britt, "Committed to Climate Change," www.SeedMagazine.com, April 18, 2006; Ignatius, David; Mooney, Chris, "Mann Hunt," *The American Prospect* web only, www.prospect.org/cs/articles?articleId=9932, July 5, 2005; Michael Mann's letter to Joe Barton, Chairman, House Committee on Energy and Commerce, July 15, 2005 in response to Barton's letter of June 23, 2005; www.met.psu.edu/dept/faculty/mann.htm; www.realclimate.org; www.opensecrets.org.

## Manning, Richard
(February 7, 1951– )
Journalist, Author

Montana-based author Richard Manning has written about many important environmental issues pertaining to the western landscape and follows his convictions beyond his writing and into his daily life. While working as a reporter, he became one of the first journalists in the Northwest to undertake a major investigative report on the logging business and wrote a series critical of the timber industry that ended up costing him his job. He and his wife designed and built an environmentally sensitive house in western Montana using place-conscious methods and materials such as timber framing, an on-demand water heater, earth-sheltering, and a composting toilet. He chronicles the entire building process in *A Good House: Building a Life on the Land* (1993); he has also written books about his timber industry investigations, the land use history of native prairies, and the threat of mining to a Montana river.

Richard Dale Manning was born on February 7, 1951, in Flint, Michigan. He lived there until the age of five and then lived briefly in Tennessee and Ohio before returning at the age of ten to Alpena, Michigan, the hometown of his parents. Manning did well in school, earning a scholarship at the University of Michigan, where he enrolled in 1969. He originally intended to become a doctor but became involved in antiwar activism and ended up studying political science. When the draft ended in 1973, he left school, 12 credit hours short of a degree.

From 1974 to 1976, Manning worked as news director of a radio station in Alpena and then worked for two years as a reporter with the *Alpena News*. He moved west in 1978, and for the next six years he held reporting and editorial positions at three papers in southern Idaho. Then, drawn to the quiet mountains of Montana, Manning and his wife and young son moved to Missoula, where he took the position of political reporter with the *Missoulian*, one of the largest papers in the state. He reported on state politics and county government for about three years, until early 1988, when he took a new assignment as the environmental reporter.

Manning began working on a series of stories about the two dominant timber corporations logging in western Montana forests, Plum Creek International and Champion. Realizing that no one outside of these corporations knew how hard they were logging their land, Manning went to great lengths to uncover the truth of the situation. The two timber companies, reacting to economic and political trends in the 1980s, had abandoned sustained yield harvesting and begun massive clear-cutting. The ponderosa pine and western larch in Montana's northern Rockies were being liquidated at breakneck speed, destroying the natural systems in the forests and streams and threatening the long-term health of the local economy. When questioned by Manning, officials at Champion admitted that in less than a decade they had already cut lands that they had said would take 30 years to harvest.

Manning submitted his series, which exposed these findings, in late May, expecting after a week of editing that they would be in print. But the series, the most intense effort of Manning's reporting career, met with balking from *Missoulian* management, who wanted to avoid controversy. Finally, nearly six months after he wrote it, the series went to print. During the week of its publication, Manning's marriage of 17 years ended in divorce. The following year was an unsettling time for him: Branded at work as a troublemaker, he found it hard to get straightforward responses from his superiors. His editor eventually confronted him, saying he was becoming too passionate and that he would be taken off the environmental beat. Having joined the newspaper profession because he believed its duty was to foment debate and "raise hell," Manning could no longer endure what he called corporate journalism, and rather than accept a different position, he quit. After Manning left the paper, his timber series won a C. B. Blethen Award for investigative journalism, which the *Missoulian* accepted. Without a job for the first time since he was 13, Manning embarked on a new freelance writing career. He started by recounting the story of his timber industry investigations and their impact on his life in his book *Last Stand: Logging, Journalism, and the Case for Humility*, which was published in 1991.

By early 1991, Manning had remarried and sought to establish his life with his new wife, Tracy, by building a house. Manning chronicled the story of designing and building their environmentally conscious home in *A Good House: Building a Life on the Land* (1993). He writes of his realization that building anything is an imposition on the land, though he and his wife planned every detail so as to minimize negative impact. They built on a south-facing slope, which allowed them to use passive solar heating and "earth-sheltering," with three sides of the house semiburied and insulated by the hill. Manning designed the house using timber framing—a system of supporting the house with large upright posts and beams, which is less wasteful than using smaller planks like two-by-fours. To conserve water, they installed a composting toilet, which uses less than a pint to flush, as opposed to five gallons per flush used by conventional toilets. This also allows the drain water from the rest of the house to be filtered and reused on the garden. In all, the house cost $50,000 to build and measured 1,200 square feet, much less than the median home size in the United States, which was 1,905 square feet in the late 1990s. In *A Good House* Manning argues that conservation cannot coexist with this trend toward expansion and that frugality must be built into daily life.

Manning's third book, published in 1995, studies one of the most disrespected biomes in the country—the native prairies of the Great Plains. *Grassland: The History, Biology, Politics, and Promise of the American Prairie* explores the history of this country's grasslands, from settlement to the slaughter of bison, to the farming and overgrazing that continue to deplete the soil. Manning advocates a massive restoration, including reintroducing bison as a more sustainable alternative to cattle, tearing out barbed-wire fences, and adapting agriculture to more natural methods. His next project was *One Round River: The Curse of Gold and the Fight for the Big Blackfoot* (1997), a book about the threat of a cyanide heap–leach gold mine on Montana's Blackfoot River, known to many as the river featured in Norman Maclean's *A River Runs Through It* (1976). Manning's book exposes the absurdity of mining the deposit, which is one of the lowest-grade ores ever considered for mining on such a massive scale: It would leach as little as one ounce of gold from 60 tons of ore. The mine would leave a hole in the earth more than a mile in diameter and would require pumping and rerouting 15.8 million gallons of water each day, diverting water from creeks, springs, wetlands, and ponds in a 100-square-mile area. Manning takes the title for the book from an essay by ALDO LEOPOLD, who encouraged viewing a river as a cycle, not a straight line that can wash away pollution forever.

Manning published two books in 2000: *Food's Frontier*, an account of sustainable agriculture in the developing world, and *Inside Passage*, the case for a natural economy in the coastal temperate rain forests. His 2004 book *Against the Grain* was lauded by DEBORAH POPPER as "an important book…Manning points the way to restored humanity and for ecosystems: a counteragriculture of food rather than food products. Diversify what gets planted, raised and eaten…"

Manning founded two Internet-based bioregional news services that compile environmental articles from regional newspapers: "Tidepool" (now called "Sightline Daily", now affiliated with ALAN DURNING'S Sightline Institute in Seattle) covers the Pacific Northwest coastal forests, and "HeadwatersNews" (now a service of the University of Montana's Center for the Rocky Mountain West) serves the Rocky Mountain region.

Manning's work has won much recognition. In 1989 he received the Audubon Society Journalism Award, in 1993 he won the R. J. Margolis Award for environmental reporting, and his work has won three C. B. Blethen Awards for investigative journalism. He and his wife, the executive director of the Clark Fork Coalition, live in the home they built near Lolo, Montana.

**BIBLIOGRAPHY**

Connors, Philip, "One Round River: The Curse of Gold and the Fight for the Big Blackfoot," *The Nation*, 1998; "Headwaters," headwatersnews.org; Manning, Richard, *A Good House: Building a Life on the Land*, 1993; Manning, Richard, *Last Stand: Logging, Journalism, and the Case for Humility*, 1991; Schildgen, Bob, "Grassland: The History, Biology, Politics, and Promise of the American Prairie," *Sierra*, 1996; "Tidepool," tidepool.org.

## Marsh, George Perkins
(March 15, 1801–July 23, 1882)
Scholar

George Perkins Marsh was a man of extraordinarily broad intellect, renowned in such fields as linguistics, philology, and etymology. During his long life, among other activities, he invented glass instruments, mined a marble quarry, served as Vermont's railroad commissioner, helped write the *Oxford English Dictionary*, bred sheep, and served for two terms in the U.S. Congress. But history esteems him most highly for his seminal contributions to the environmental sciences. Marsh was an avid student of the land, especially how human activity altered it. His book *Man and Nature, or Physical Geography as Modified by Human Action* (1864) made a deep impact on thinking about land use when he wrote it, and even today is considered an important primer.

George Perkins Marsh was born on March 15, 1801, in Woodstock, Vermont. By the age of five he had memorized an encyclopedia; then he went on to study Greek and Latin. At the age of eight, his eyes gave out, and he began to spend more time outside. He befriended nature, discovering a fantastic world of nonhuman beings. His father assiduously taught him the names of all the local trees and natural landmarks. Marsh developed powerful oral comprehension skills: because he was not able to read himself for several years, he had to learn from hearing others read to him. When he turned 15, Marsh entered Dartmouth College, where he immediately distinguished himself as the most brilliant student there. Graduating at the age of 19 in 1820, Marsh continued on to become a lawyer in 1825. But the legal field did not entirely satisfy his wide-reaching curiosity, and Marsh dabbled in a host of additional fields. He learned 20 languages, writing a book about Icelandic grammar. He collaborated with the authors of the *Oxford English Dictionary* and produced

George Perkins Marsh (Library of Congress, Prints & Photographs Division, LC-USZ62-109923)

two volumes on the history and etymology of the English language.

Marsh was elected to the U.S. Congress in 1840. What most captured his interest during his two terms in Washington, D.C., was the debate about how to spend the enormous bequest to the government by James Smithson. Smithson had specified that he wanted the money spent on increasing and disseminating knowledge throughout the United States, and Marsh proposed that it be used to found a research institution and museum. The Smithsonian Institution owes its existence to Marsh's proposal, and Marsh also collected many of its early biological specimens.

Marsh first ventured into environmental sciences when he studied the decline of freshwater fish in Vermont's streams and rivers in 1857. Contamination by factories and mills and disruption of water flow by dams were obvious problems. But Marsh delved further, and highlighted other, more subtle issues. He saw that deforestation and careless cultivation denuded the land and that when it rained, floods were more likely to occur. The floods had several damaging consequences: they filled the waterways with sediment, which altered their courses and covered spawning grounds with silt. Without forests, there was less precipitation, and a reduced stream flow elevated the temperature of the water. This complicated explanation is reflective of modern ecological analysis, but it was innovative and totally unique in Marsh's time.

Marsh proposed a solution for Vermont's problem as well. After his experience in government, he had little faith that policy changes would improve the situation. Instead, he urged private landowners to protect their own forests and farmland. If good, accessible scientific knowledge spread throughout the populace, and individual enterprise prevailed, he thought this would be the most effective response.

Marsh had been sent as minister first to Greece from 1849 to 1854 and then, by President Lincoln, to Italy in 1861. There, in addition to performing his ministerial duties, he wrote *Man and Nature*. This book contained a sort of environmental history of certain areas of the world, recounting how human activity had altered each one. The Sahara Desert, for example, was created when humans' livestock deforested northern Africa; overgrazing was also the culprit in creating the arid Provence and Dauphiné regions of France. In the United States, this was not ancient history; Marsh's home state of Vermont had the highest rate of deforestation and soil erosion. In addition, Marsh traced the causes of natural disasters and was able to conclude that in each case, the behind-the-scenes culprit was human activity—usually deforestation. Marsh's conclusion was that human activity was inherently destructive to nature. His moral to the story: the earth was not given to humans to consume and waste, but rather to use with care.

Upon its release in 1864, the book was greeted with acclaim both in the United States and in Europe, where Marsh was still living. European foresters heeded the book's recommendations, but Americans still did not seem fully ready to begin conserving their vast resources. In fact, some land speculators even turned around Marsh's description of the deforestation-desertification relationship, claiming to potential buyers that the West would become more humid and lush if new landowners planted enough trees!

Marsh died in Vallambrosa, Italy, on July 23, 1882. His ideas experienced a revival in the mid-1900s, with an international conference, "Man's Role in Changing the Face of the Earth," at Princeton University in 1955 and the reissue of *Man and Nature* by Harvard University Press in 1965.

**BIBLIOGRAPHY**

Lowenthal, David, *George Perkins Marsh: Prophet of Conservation*, 2000; Lowenthal, David, *George Perkins Marsh: Versatile Vermonter*, 1958; Marsh, George Perkins, *Man and Nature*, David Lowenthal, ed., 1965; Marsh, George Perkins, *So Great a Vision: the Conservation Writings of George Perkins Marsh*, Stephan C. Trombulak, ed., 2001; Strong, Douglas, *Dreamers & Defenders: American Conservationists*, 1988.

# Marshall, Robert

(June 2, 1901–November 11, 1939)
Forester, Cofounder of the Wilderness Society

Intrepid mountaineer and professional forester Robert Marshall fought tirelessly during his short life for conservation of wilderness in its wildest state. During his two years as recreation director for the U.S. Forest Service, he restricted roads and development from some 14 million acres of national forest land; as the Bureau of Indian Affairs forestry director, he created 16 wilderness areas on Indian reservations. The Wilderness Society (TWS), which he cofounded, still leads the pack of conservation organizations on lobbying for new protected areas and environmental legislation. Marshall's deep personal love for wild places was complemented by a firm commitment to social justice. Marshall believed that too much time in the city would wear down the human spirit and that everyone—even society's poorest—deserved time in the wilderness to replenish.

Robert Marshall was born on June 2, 1901, into a liberal, privileged New York family. His father was a well-known constitutional lawyer who frequently came to the defense of oppressed minorities and lobbied lawmakers to preserve Adirondack forests. The Marshall family spent summers at their cabin on Lower Saranac Lake in the Adirondacks, and it was there that young Robert grew to love mountains and mountaineering. The family's private guide led Robert and his brothers up all 46 Adirondack peaks over 4,000 feet. Robert quickly overtook his guide, hiking 30 to 40 miles and climbing as many as 16 mountains per day.

In an attempt to combine his love for mountains with a profession, Marshall studied forestry at Syracuse University, earning a bachelor's degree in 1924. He then went on for a master's degree in forestry at Harvard University (1925). His thesis experiment at the Harvard Forest in Petersham, Massachusetts, taught him that selective cutting (cutting only certain trees) rather than clear-cutting (cutting all trees in a given area) led to healthier and more diverse secondary growth. Immediately after graduation, Marshall went to work for the U.S. Forest Service in the Montana Rockies, where he stayed for three years, until 1928. Marshall had the opportunity to meet a diverse group of westerners during these years, including poor, unemployed men who would sign on to fight fires in national forests when needed. Hearing their hard luck stories was real-world proof to Marshall of the cruelty of the modern industrial world's cutthroat capitalist exploitation.

When Marshall returned to the East Coast to continue his education, he studied plant physiology at Johns Hopkins and became active in the school's Liberal Club. Marshall was one of the first who combined his liberal politics with conservationism. He joined GIFFORD PINCHOT and other veteran foresters in signing "A Letter to Foresters," which criticized the forest industry's destructive clear-cutting practices and proposed a greater degree of control of the forest industry. It urged the creation of more public forests, a cause that Marshall would continue working toward during the rest of his life.

Marshall took a break from Washington in 1930–1931 and traveled to the Arctic village of Wiseman, Alaska. After studying the inhabitants of Wiseman, Marshall concluded that people were happier and more fulfilled in such a frontier environment than in any urban setting. His description of the colorful individuals and their lifestyle became *Arctic Village* (1933). For a book published during the Depression, when the general public could not afford to buy books, *Arctic Village* was considered a best-seller. True to his social commitment, Marshall split the royalties with the inhabitants of Wiseman.

During the 1930s, Marshall worked at the U.S. Forest Service and at the Bureau of Indian Affairs (BIA) forest service, always pushing for greater protection of wilderness and more public ownership of forests. His management style included much fieldwork, with at least half of his time spent roaming wild places in question. While at the BIA, Marshall felt that he was able to have vastly more useful interactions with Native Americans when he was hiking around their reservations than as another white official talking at them in a meeting hall. Marshall worked toward preserving wilderness on Indian reservations and usually argued against plans for new roads cutting through them. A precursor to ecotourism advocates, Marshall felt that Indian-guided wilderness trips would contribute more to reservation economies than would one-shot clear-cutting or mining projects.

When in 1937 Marshall transferred to the U.S. Forest Service and became its recreation director, he worked hard to establish more public forests and keep existing national forest lands roadless and undeveloped. Although he advocated grand-scale recreation, he felt that the country's national forests should be free of motorized transportation and concessions such as hotels or lodges and stores, in order to preserve wilderness in a state as wild as possible and to assure accessibility for all economic classes. Whenever civil rights issues arose, he was quick to respond; Marshall fought against segregated campsites in the South and resorts that discriminated against minorities. In 1935 Marshall's strong beliefs and effective work earned him an accusation by New York congressman Hamilton Fish of being a communist. This was followed up in 1938 and 1939 with his inclusion on a list of government employees contributing to communism. Marshall was self-confident enough to brush off these attacks, but several of his colleagues lost their jobs and had their careers ruined by the House Un-American Affairs Committee.

Along with BENTON MACKAYE, Harvey Broome, Harold Anderson, ALDO LEOPOLD, Ernest Oberholtzer, Bernard Frank, and ROBERT STERLING YARD, Marshall was a cofounder in 1935 of the Wilderness Society (TWS). During its first years it was a humble operation funded almost in entirety by Marshall, but TWS has since grown to be one of the most active and influential conservation organizations in the nation.

Marshall died in the prime of his career, on November 11, 1939, at the age of 38, during an overnight train ride from Washington, D.C., to New York. His $1.5 million fortune was left in three equal parts to social advocacy organizations, civil liberties organizations, and TWS. Two years after his death, the Bob Marshall Wilderness Complex in northwest Montana was created and named for him. With the addition of the contiguous Great Bear and Scapegoat wilderness areas in the 1970s, the 1.5-million-acre Bob Marshall Wilderness Complex became the largest roadless area in the United States.

**BIBLIOGRAPHY**

Brown, Phil, *Bob Marshall in the Adirondacks: Writings of a Pioneering Peak-Bagger, Pond-Hopper, and Wilderness Preservationist*, 2006; Fox, Stephen, *John Muir and His Legacy: The American Conservation Movement*, 1981; Glover, James M., *A Wilderness Original: The Life of Bob Marshall*, 1986; Gottlieb, Robert, *Forcing the Spring: The Transformation of the American Environmental Movement*, 1993; Heacox, Kim, *Visions of a Wild America: Pioneers of Preservation*, 1996; Marshall, Robert, *Alaska Wilderness*, 1970; Marshall, Robert, *The People's Forests*, 1933.

## Marston, Betsy, and Ed Marston
(July 6, 1940– ; April 25, 1940– )
Writers, Editors, Publishers

For 19 years, Ed and Betsy Marston served as publisher and editor, respectively, of *High Country News* (HCN), a highly respected biweekly newspaper specializing in western environmental issues.

Elizabeth (Betsy) Avice Pilat was born on July 6, 1940, in New York City to Oliver and Alice Avice Pilat. She was brought up in a literary household; her father was a New York City newspaperman and wrote ten books, mostly political biographies. She attended the University of Delaware, earning a B.A. in English in 1962, and the Graduate School of Journalism at Columbia University, where she earned an M.S. in 1963.

Edwin Herman Marston was born on April 25, 1940, in Brooklyn, New York, and grew up in Queens, New York. He says that his earliest memories are of wanting to be a journalist, long before he knew what a journalist was. But as he grew older, he decided he needed a more dependable income than he thought journalism could provide, so he went into the sciences. He graduated from City College of New York in 1962 with a B.S. in physics and earned his Ph.D. in physics in 1968 from the State University of New York at Stony Brook.

The Marstons met in 1961, at City College of New York, where Betsy was spending a year away from the University of Delaware and where both wrote for the student newspaper. They were married in 1966. Betsy became the first woman anchor on a New York television news program, for public television station WNET, winning an Emmy award for her three-part documentary on singer Paul Robeson in 1974. Ed was an assistant professor of physics at Queens College from 1968 to 1971 and an associate professor at Ramapo College in Mahwah, New Jersey, from 1971 to 1974. In 1976, he wrote the textbook *The Dynamic Environment: Water, Transportation, and Energy*, based on a physics course that he taught that used physics to describe how urban areas worked—how water flowed into a city, how oil flowed through the trans-Alaska pipeline, how elevators limited the height of skyscrapers.

By 1974 the couple had two small children, Wendy and David, and were tired of spending so little time with them because they worked such long hours. They decided to take a year off and retreat to their Colorado mountain cabin near the small town of Paonia. But after a month of their vacation, they realized they were "failures at leisure," and so they began working: Ed wrote environmental impact statements for local land management agencies, and Betsy made candles, mostly for fun. Two months later, after realizing that they needed more intellectual stimulation to be happy, they started a local weekly newspaper, *The North Fork Times*. Despite the suspicion of local people about the radical politics of these urban dropouts, the paper quickly rose to become the county paper of record. The Marstons published it for six years before selling it in December 1980. They then took off enough time to build a passive solar home and then founded another paper, the biweekly *Western Colorado Report*, which focused on how the boom in energy development was affecting the small towns of western Colorado. When oil prices plummeted in 1983, and the boom went bust, the paper's readership dropped precipitously.

Just as they were wondering what to do with the ailing *Western Colorado Report*, the Marstons heard that *High Country News* (HCN), which was published out of Lander, Wyoming, needed a new staff. HCN had been founded in 1970 by wildlife biologist, teacher, and fifth-generation Wyoming rancher Tom Bell, who was outraged by the destruction being wreaked on his beloved western lands by ranchers, miners, loggers, politicians, and government bureaucrats. Bell edited the 16-page tabloid for four years, then passed it on to a series of professional journalists who shared his environmental passion and gave the paper a national reputation for reliable, in-depth reporting. Its few but devoted subscribers were so loyal that on the several occasions when the paper was threatened with bankruptcy, they sent unsolicited donations amounting to thousands of dollars to keep it afloat. When all three staffers quit the paper in 1983, the board of the nonprofit paper chose the Marstons to take the reins. An intern hauled the archives, the photo file, the mailing list, and an addressing machine from Lander to a former church in downtown Paonia, and the Marstons merged their *Western Colorado Report* subscription list with that of HCN and started their crash course in western politics and land and resource management.

The paper's network of freelancers continued to send in high-quality stories; the first scoop the Marstons published was a 1984 story by Tom Wolf about how the Glen Canyon Dam had almost collapsed when, during the 1983 flood year, the Colorado River ate away at the dam's core and spillway channels. The Bureau of Reclamation later acknowledged the veracity of the story and released photos that showed how close the dam was to breaking apart. Every two years the paper published a four-issue series that delved deep into a problem. The 1986 series, "Western Water Made Simple," examined the Columbia, Missouri, and Colorado Rivers and their various development projects. It received a prestigious George Polk award for environmental reporting and was published in book form by Island Press in 1987, as was a 1988 series on the resurgence of extractive industries, entitled *Reopening the Western Frontier*.

Even though the Marstons themselves are liberal environmentalists, and the paper is known for its environmental advocacy, the Marstons do recognize that in the West, where most nonurban residents live directly or indirectly off the land, strong local communities are as important as protected public lands. The Marstons feel that condominium development and rural sprawl pose threats, much like the decades-long impacts created by subsidized extractive industries. HCN features include views from the many sides of every debate, and for this reason the paper's readership has expanded to include not only environmentalists but also high-level decision makers, reporters looking for story ideas, and western miners, loggers, and ranchers.

When they first took on HCN, the Marstons believed that the paper's number of subscribers would never rise to more than a few thousand. The ten states covered by HCN—Washington, Oregon, Idaho, Montana, Wyoming, Utah, Colorado, Nevada, Arizona, and New Mexico—are now the fastest-growing region in the United States. By 2008, there were 25,000 subscribers to the paper, and the paper is generally regarded as an important regional institution. Columns and essays by HCN writers are offered to other newspapers through the Writers on the Range syndicated column service, currently subscribed to by some 50 newspapers throughout the west. The paper also operates a web site (www.hcn.org) with an easily accessible archive of seven of the paper's 30 years, recordings of HCN's former radio show on real audio, the current issue, and an on-line newsletter. The paper became a nonprofit foundation in its first home in Wyoming; it is the primary project of the High Country Foundation. Thirty seven percent of the paper's operating costs are from subscriptions, and 48 percent more comes from contributions and foundation support. While the Marstons produced the paper, more than 200 interns spent a few months in Paonia to learn the western environmental beat. Since 1998, interns have been paid. Many of these interns now freelance for HCN or other news media throughout the country or are engaged in other environmentally oriented activities.

Ed Marston has written a 35,000-word memoir for *Colorado: 1870–2000*, which features photographs taken of Colorado landmarks by two great photographers, W. H. Jackson, who lived in the nineteenth century, and John Fielder, who works in the present. Ed Marston is very active in his local community: he has redeveloped several downtown buildings in Paonia, Colorado, he serves on the board of the Colorado Watershed Assembly and the Paonia Chamber of Commerce, and he is an elected board member of the Delta-Montrose Electric Association. He was a John S. Knight Journalism Fellow at Stanford University for the academic year 1990–1991. Betsy Marston edits the *High Country News* Writers on the Range syndicated column service and is an elected member of the Delta County School Board.

The Marstons live on a mesa just outside Paonia.

**BIBLIOGRAPHY**

Burkhead, Rebecca, "Watching the West, The Duo Who Keep High Country News Aloft," *Columbia Journalism Review*, 1993; "High Country News," www.hcn.org; Hill, David, "High Country News: Small Paper, Strong Voice," *Washington Journalism Review*, 1989; Jackson, William Henry, John Fielder, and Ed Marston, *Colorado: 1870–2000*, 1999; Marston, Betsy, "The Little Paper that Could," *High Country News*, 1995; Marston, Ed, ed., *Reopening the Western Frontier*, 1989; Marston, Ed, ed., *Western Water Made Simple*, 1987.

## Martínez, Dennis

(August 10, 1941– )
Restoration Ecologist, Ethnoecologist

Dennis Martínez has been involved with restoration ecology since 1969—before the field of restoration ecology had even formally come into existence. Martínez is of O'odham, Chicano, and Anglo heritage and has been adopted by the Pretty Weasel Family of the Whistling Water Clan, Absorooka Tribe at Crow Agency, Montana. He melds western science, native cultural practices, and traditional ecological knowledge in his work, recognizing that all are necessary for successful ecological restoration. He specializes in North American temperate forest, desert mountain, and tropical dry forest ecosystems. Martínez assists traditional communities in Canada, Mexico, and the United States (including Hawai'i) with the ecological restoration of their tribal land bases and ancestral lands and the renewal of their traditional relationships with the land.

Dennis Martínez was born on August 10, 1941, on a ranch near Selma, California, in the San Joaquin Valley. He was raised by his grandparents and grew up hunting and fishing in the Sierra Nevada mountains. Even as a child, he noticed negative changes in the San Joaquin Valley caused by the area's increased population and urban development. Before he left the area for college, the salmon disappeared from the San Joaquin River, deer populations crashed, groundwater sources dried up, and wetlands with their native waterfowl were lost. Martínez studied at the University of California at Berkeley, receiving his B.A. in history and philosophy of science (Darwinian evolution) in 1976.

Martínez began doing landscaping work in the San Francisco Bay area in 1969. After meeting a Pomo Indian elder and learning from him about traditional uses of native plants, Martínez became very interested in incorporating these plants into his landscaping projects. In 1975, David Amme, Don Cook, and later, David Kaplow, along with Martínez launched a nonprofit group, Design Associates Working with Nature (DAWN). The first major restoration contractor on the West Coast, DAWN pioneered the use of little-known native species in its restoration projects. DAWN worked in public parks, U.S. military lands, and plots owned by such conservation groups as The Nature Conservancy and the Audubon Society, in an attempt to replicate the ecosystems that existed before European colonists changed the California landscape.

In the decades since then, Martínez has worked as a contractor or consultant on scores of ecological restoration projects. He works primarily with indigenous people to restore the landscape that their ancestors had inhabited without depleting for thousands of years. Traditional indigenous cultures of North America influenced the ecological structure, composition, and function of their habitat by selective harvesting of useful plants and animals and by regular light burnings. What European colonists considered "virgin wilderness" was in many cases actually more like a carefully tended plant and animal reserve. Martínez has come to recognize that ecological restoration and the restoration of traditional caregiving relationships with the land go hand-in-hand, and he has worked with many traditional communities on both of these aspects. From 1989 to 1990, he worked with the Ya-ka-ama ("Our Land") Indian Development and Education Corporation's project as nursery manager and tribal liaison, servicing more than 20 rancherias and reservations in five California counties. From 1987 to 1992, he helped design a restoration plan for 7,000 acres of ancestral lands for the Sinkyone Intertribal Wilderness Council, which had been clear-cut by Georgia Pacific lumber company. The Takelma Intertribal Project, which he currently cocoordinates with Takelma/Siletz elder Agnes Pilgrim, is a collaborative effort among the local indigenous community, the U.S. Forest Service, and scientists from the Pacific Northwest Forest Experimental Station and Oregon State University. The project strives to restore the precontact cultural landscape of oak/pine savanna, maintain it with regular light burns, and preserve and restore culturally significant plants and animals as cultural and natural resources. The local indigenous community celebrated its First Rites Salmon Homecoming Thanksgiving ceremony in May 1994 for the first time in 150 years and has continued to celebrate it annually.

The Hawai'ian island reserve of Kaho'olawe, which is sacred to native Hawai'ians and in ancient times was an important departure and arrival point for boats to other islands of Polynesia, was ecologically devastated by the goats that Captain Cook left there and then later was bombed by the U.S. Navy for 50 years. Martínez has consulted for the Kaho'olawe Island Reserve Commission, a state office responsible for the restoration of the dry tropical forest ecosystem, focusing on the cultural and spiritual aspects of ecological restoration. Another of his consulting projects is with the Mountain Maidu of the northern Sierra Nevada in California, who have a contract with the Pluma National Forest, focusing on cultural landscape restoration.

Martínez emphasizes that restoration work can take many years before it can be considered completed. For instance, the restoration of tallgrass prairie at the University of Wisconsin's arboretum, the Curtis Prairie, after 60 years boasts only half of the species that grew in the precontact tallgrass prairie. An attempt begun in 1850 to restore the full species composition of a meadow in England is just now reaching completion.

Martínez has been a member of the Society for Ecological Restoration (SER) since 1989 and has served two terms on its International Board of Directors. He has been cochair of its Science and Policy working group and serves on the Peer Training working group and the International Awards committee. He founded the Indigenous People's Restoration Network

(IPRN) Working Group in 1995. He has succeeded in integrating the issue of cultural survival for Native peoples into the programs and annual meetings of SER, negotiating an internationally acceptable definition of "ecological restoration.". He has been steadfast about reminding his restorationist colleagues that national laws governing land management and protection of indigenous cultural resources are inadequate and the National Forest Management Act does not "recognize American Indian natural resource management practices as having a role in forest planning. Traditional elders are not consulted.... There is no First Amendment constitutional protection for sacred sites lacking obvious artifacts or structures.... Landscape change is ignored in the delineation of tribal cultural resource areas." Martínez has defended burial and village sites sacred to indigenous peoples from development and has acted as a liaison between Indian people and government land agencies during negotiations about the protection of cultural resources.

In response to this problem, the IPRN shares traditional ecological knowledge (TEK) with colleagues in the ecological restoration field, and with indigenous communities themselves. IPRN offered several training workshops from 2001 till 2004, for Native and non-Native forest workers in restoration forestry and First Nation historical forest management practices. Martinez and the IPRN has been instrumental in assuring the inclusion of Native people and TEK in restoration conferences worldwide.

In addition to his work with SER, Martínez is a member of the Traditional Knowledge Council of the American Indian Science and Engineering Society and of the Karuk Tribal Team for Cultural Resource Protection. With Judith Vergun, he is cochair of the Oregon State University Pacific NorthWest Traditional Ecological Knowledge Project. He has served as member of the advisory council, board, or steering committee of the following organizations: Baca Institute of Ethnobotany, the Institute for Sustainable Forestry, the Cultural Conservancy, Black Mesa Permaculture Project, the Indigenous Permaculture Center, the Kaho'olawe Island Reserve Commission, Earth Legacy, Sombra Buena Organic Forest Products (based in Honduras), and Native American Food Systems Project. He is a member of the Alliance of Forest Workers and Harvesters. SER recognized Martínez in 1997 with its John Rieger Service Award for his substantial contribution to ecological restoration. Martínez speaks widely, at tribal and nontribal conferences, and has published articles in a number of journals and books, including a Forest Service publication on special forest products and an Environmental Protection Agency publication called "This Place Called Home: Tools for Sustainable Communities."

Martínez resides in an intentional community in the Klamath Mountains near Glendale, Oregon, called Mountain Grove Center for New Education. The community sustains itself in part through selective thinning of high-quality hardwood timber and small-diameter softwoods, milling them locally to add value to the commercial product. The community's aquatic ecosystems have been restored to the point that native coho salmon have begun to return after a long absence. Martínez earns part of his income from working in the woods as a vegetation surveyor, seed collector, restoration contractor, nursery grower of native plants, and restoration thinner and logger.

## BIBLIOGRAPHY

Ausubel Kenny with J.P. Harpgnies, *Nature's Operating Instructions: the true biotechnologies*, 2004; Ford, Jesse and Dennis Martínez, "Traditional Ecological Knowledge and Wisdom," *Ecological Applications*, 2000; "Indigenous Peoples' Restoration Network," www.ser.org/iprn; Martínez, Dennis, "Salmon Homecoming," *Intricate Homeland*, 2000; Martínez, Dennis, and Jesse Ford, *Ecological Applications* (Special Invited Feature on Traditional Ecological Knowledge), 2000; Posey, Darrell, *Cultural and Spiritual Values of Biodiversity*, 2000.

## Mather, Stephen
(July 4, 1867–January 22, 1930)
National Park Service Director

Stephen Mather was the first director of the burgeoning U.S. National Park Service from 1915 to 1929 and is remembered for improving, enlarging, and consolidating the country's national parks. With a team including assistant HORACE ALBRIGHT and publicist ROBERT STERLING YARD, Mather convinced Congress to create a National Park Service, transformed inaccessible and unknown national parks into attractions that the public began to visit in droves, reformed the chaotic concessions system, and doubled the acreage conserved as national parks and monuments. A millionaire, Mather never hesitated to donate his own money if not enough federal or private money was allotted for a particular national parks cause.

Stephen Tyng Mather was born on July 4, 1867, in San Francisco, California. His mother, English-born Bertha Jemima Walker, had followed her husband, Joseph Mather, when he traveled west for his Gold Rush accounting job. She never liked California and left her husband and children for the East Coast when Mather was six years old. Mather stayed in California, spending free time on horseback and camping trips in the state's vast wilderness, until he graduated with a degree in journalism from the University of California at Berkeley in 1887. After graduation, Mather traveled east to see his mother and began working as a journalist at the New York *Sun*. He spent five years writing for the *Sun* before marrying Jane Thacker Floy in 1893 and entering the borax mining business with his father.

Borax, a water-softening chemical found in quantity in California and Nevada, was little known and little used until Mather got into the business. In order to create a market for borax, Mather, as the Pacific Coast Borax Company's publicity manager, paid anyone who had a letter about one of the many wonders of borax published in a small-town newspaper or women's magazine. This campaign resulted in 800 published letters in 250 publications in 33 states. Borax became a household word, and Mather, eventually a co-owner of the company, became a millionaire.

Like many wealthy Americans at the dawn of the twentieth century, Mather and his family visited Europe and marveled at the luxury and comfort of visitors' lodgings and services in Europe's mountain parks. Disappointed with the quality of facilities in national parks in the United States, Mather fired off a disgruntled letter to Secretary of the Interior Franklin Lane. Secretary Lane was just then wondering whom he could hire to improve the parks on the shoestring budget his department had for the job. Lane invited Mather to take the job and improve the parks as he saw fit. Mather felt ready to move out of industry and into conservation; it has been said that he felt it was time to give something back to the earth since up until that point he had been taking so much from it. So in 1915 he accepted the invitation and became assistant secretary of the interior in charge of national parks.

Mather approached his new job with the same entrepreneurial spirit that had earned him his millions from borax. He hired an able assistant, Horace Albright, who was to accompany him during his entire tenure with the parks and would succeed him after his resignation in 1929. Mather and Albright made a checklist and got to work. They immediately identified the need for greater public interest in the national parks. Mather and his publicity assistant, Robert Sterling Yard, placed over 1,000 magazine articles extolling the national parks and had photo-filled brochures about the parks sent to the country's wealthiest citizens and power elite, including all members of Congress. Within a year, most members of

Congress knew much more about the parks, and many had visited them personally, some on trips for influential people that were organized by Mather. In 1916, Congress passed the National Park Service Act, which created the National Park Service as a bureau of the U.S. Department of the Interior. Under this act, all parks would fall under the jurisdiction of the National Park Service, which would facilitate administration and coordination.

Another major task on the checklist was to ease travel and lodging in the parks so that more people would be able to visit. Once World War I began and U.S. tourism in Europe ceased, more Americans wanted to visit their own national parks. At that point, arriving at most existing parks was a daunting task. The automobile was still a modern contraption, so roads to and within the parks were either nonexistent or in terrible condition. Rail connections to the parks were also scarce, and once passengers got off in the towns nearest the parks, it was hard to find transportation and guides to the parks. Mather campaigned successfully to award concessions to only one company per park or area of park, a system that resulted in more orderly, reliable transportation and lodgings but earned him enemies among those who lost their right to work in the park.

Some approaches by Mather to popularize the national parks and please visitors included tactics that today would be prohibited, such as building a tunnel through a giant sequoia tree, public feeding of the bears in Yellowstone, and heaving bonfires off Yosemite Falls. Current critics of the Mather legacy complain that he built too many roads through areas that should have been left more remote. Mather did have strict ideas of what was acceptable, however. When a Glacier National Park concessionaire did not dismantle a sawmill on time after building a new lodge, Mather lost patience. He invited his daughter and a large party of visitors to observe as he personally dynamited the sawmill.

Mather's personal charisma was a key ingredient to his success in raising interest and funds for the parks. He charmed potential patrons on the dozens of exploratory pack trips he organized for them. Congressmen and wealthy conservationists were impressed both by the scenery to which he escorted them and by his energy and his vision. He always invited the wives of these individuals, knowing that once the men returned to their jobs they would forget about their trip but that the women would remember and remind them to follow up on their commitments.

Mather was also a skillful personnel manager, identifying talented parks employees, encouraging them to seek posts where their gifts would be of use, and often offering generous gifts or loans to help them reach their potential.

In addition to his work on behalf of national parks and monuments, Mather encouraged the growth of the state park movement. His vision included a state park for every 100 miles of state highway. This would allow cross-country motorists to camp in a different beautiful place every night and would also serve as a pressure valve for the National Park Service. Senators and congressmen could be pushy about having their particular local attraction declared a national park, and Mather felt that many of these attractions did not deserve the stature of national park but should be conserved under some designation.

After 14 whirlwind years of nonstop work on behalf of the national parks, criss-crossing the country repeatedly and at breakneck speed, Mather suffered a stroke in 1928. He resigned from his post as director of the National Park Service in 1929 and died of a second stroke in Brookline, Massachusetts, on January 25, 1930. He has been memorialized with a Mount Mather in Alaska, the Mather Memorial Highway in Mount Rainier National Park, and the Mather Memorial Arboretum at the University of California.

**BIBLIOGRAPHY**

Albright, Horace M., *The Birth of the National Park System: The Founding Years, 1913–1933*,

1985; Albright, Horace M., and Marian Albright Schenck, *Creating the National Park Service: the Missing Years*, 1999; Fox, Stephen, *The American Conservation Movement: John Muir and His Legacy*, 1986; Hartzog, George B., *Battling for the National Park Service*, 1988; Mackintosh, Barry, *The National Parks: Shaping the System*, 1991; Sellers, Richard West, *Preserving Nature in the National Parks: a History*, 1997; Shankland, Robert, *Steve Mather of the National Parks*, 1970; Wirth, Conrad L., *Parks, Politics and the People*, 1980.

# Matthiessen, Peter
(May 22, 1927– )
Writer

Peter Matthiessen has forged a subgenre of outdoor adventure writing by covering unexplored territories, wildlife, and native peoples as far away from contemporary modern life and its accoutrements as he could find them. Author of more than 20 books, his fictional and nonfictional accounts of the Amazon, East Africa, the Miskito Coast, and the Himalayas are found, respectively, in his most famous works: *At Play in the Fields of the Lord* (1965), *The Tree Where Man Was Born* (1972), *Far Tortuga* (1975), and *The Snow Leopard* (1978), which won a National Book Award. While Matthiessen describes himself as "a generalist," his eye and ear for details in the natural world have helped him produce lasting work in American literature and have made him a standard bearer for creative nature writers.

With ancestry dating back to seventeenth-century Danish whaling captain Matthies the Fortunate, Peter Matthiessen was born the fortunate son of Elizabeth Carey and Erard A. Matthiessen on May 22, 1927, in New York City. From his earliest days, in a house overlooking the Hudson River, or in his family's Fifth Avenue apartment across from Central Park, or visiting his family's vacation home on Fishers Island off Long Island, Matthiessen had privileged access to untamed woods, the sea, and the city. His life as a man, in addition to his life as a writer, is marked by his rejection of the amenities of affluence and his quest for an unmediated experience with nature.

As a boy, Matthiessen and his younger brother collected snakes, and they earned their sea legs early on deep-sea fishing trips off Montauk, which instilled him with a lifelong love of the ocean. After a tour in the United States Navy at Pearl Harbor (1945 to 1947), Matthiessen attended the Sorbonne at the University of Paris (1948 to 1949) and received a B.A. in English from Yale University in 1950. While he was still in college, his fiction writing was already gaining attention at the *Atlantic Monthly* and Farrar, Straus publishers. He married Patricia Southgate in 1951 and moved to France, where, along with writers William Styron, George Plimpton, and Ben Bradley, he cofounded the *Paris Review* in 1953. Parisian notoriety aside, Matthiessen's early novels did not earn him much acclaim or money, so he returned to Long Island to work as a commercial fisherman to support his family and his writing career. He later relates how idyllic it was for him to return to the ocean after several years of urban high life. But during this period, his wanderlust overcame him, and his marriage disintegrated. He set out to visit every wildlife reserve in the United States for a book on the state of the country's endangered wildlife. This project showed Matthiessen how his writing could serve both as a warning about species on the brink of extinction and an homage to species already gone (the great auk, the passenger pigeon, the near extinction of the bison). The descriptive power of his writing was nationally recognized in the resulting book, *Wildlife in America* (1959).

*Wildlife in America* also put Matthiessen "on the map" in another sense. A growing rate of extinction further motivated his quest to commune with most endangered species before they disappeared and to seek out, as he told *Buzzworm* in 1993, the wild "people and places that still have their own integrity." He seized opportunities that took him far from the familiarity of his Long Island home. The *New Yorker* magazine underwrote five months of trekking in South America between Tierra del Fuego and Lima, Peru, for articles later yielding the book, *The Cloud Forest: A Chronicle of the South American Wilderness* (1961). But as would be the case with other journalistic projects, he would reserve the best writing for his novels. Matthiessen has compared his nonfiction writing to cabinetmaking, that is, the crafting of something utilitarian, while he says his novels are the work of artistry, like fine sculpture. *At Play in the Fields of the Lord* (1965) is set in the Amazon and involves the fate of the fictitious Niaruna tribe after the intervention of Christian missionaries. The book reflects Matthiessen's distrust for Western civilization's effects on the preindustrial people left in the world. The research that Matthiessen did for *New Yorker* pieces about turtling off the Miskito Coast of Honduras resulted in his greatest novel, *Far Tortuga* (1975), which some critics have acclaimed as second to *Moby Dick* among U.S. sea novels.

With the Harvard-Peabody expedition in 1961, Matthiessen moved to a remote corner of New Guinea to live with the aboriginal Kurelu people, believed to be the last Stone Age culture. Matthiessen's account of this experience, *Under the Mountain Wall: A Chronicle of Two Seasons in the Stone Age* (1962), decries the inevitable loss of culture to the industrial juggernaut of the twentieth century. Later in the 1960s he went to live with the East African Hazda, a tribe whose graceful integration into what otherwise could be described as a harsh, uninviting environment fascinated Matthiessen enormously. The Hazda mythologize that man climbed down from the baobab tree, and it was this folktale that inspired Matthiessen to write *The Tree Where Man Was Born* (1972). Of his fascination for "the small people," the Eskimos, sherpas, and pygmies he has written about, he told *New York Times Magazine* in 1990, "I just love being with people who know the wilderness and wild things so well. They're not the least bit sentimental about it, the way conservationists and naturalists are." His interest in the non-Westernized indigenous peoples is also part of his life-long study of the ease with which certain tribes coexist with nature.

Matthiessen continued to write books about animals after the publication of *Wildlife in America*. These included *Shorebirds of North America* (1967), reprinted as *The Wind Birds* in 1973; *Sand River* (1981), which focused on the large game left in the East African Selous Game Reserve; and his award-winning nonfiction work, *The Snow Leopard* (1978), written after trekking the Crystal Mountain in northwestern Nepal. *The Snow Leopard* is similar to his previous books in that he kept a copious journal and wrote as he traveled through a remote region of the world in search of endangered species and cultures, but he did not see the snow leopard even once. Instead, he had a chance encounter with a high-altitude solitary monk, Buddhist teacher Shey Gompa, at the Crystal Monastery. In this book, Matthiessen's philosophical discourse achieves greater heights, charting his own spiritual journey.

Matthiessen's latest nonfiction work has focused on the Arctic and the Antarctic. He wrote a series of articles for the New York Review of Books on the Arctic Refuge, the indigenous people who live there, and the struggle to defend it from oil exploration. *End of the Earth: Voyages to Antarctica* (2003) recounts the voyages of 18th and 19th century explorers together along with his own two trips there, in search of the emperor penguin. His most recent literary project is a trilogy based on the murder of a Florida farmer and hunter Edward Watson (*Killing Mister Watson*, 1990; *Lost Man's River*, 1997; and *Bone by Bone*, 1999), which Matthiessen in 2008 reworked and published as a single, three-part work, *Shadow Country: A New Rendering of the Watson Legend*.

As far-ranging and adventurous as Matthiessen has been with his writing, he has been equally adventurous internally. After the death of his second wife, Deborah Love, from cancer in 1972, Matthiessen began sitting zazen, and after years of practice and study, he was ordained a sensei (teacher of Zen). Appropriately, his Zen Buddhist name is Muryo, meaning "Without Boundaries." When he is not on the road, he lives in Sagaponack, Long Island, New York, with his wife since 1980, Maria Eckhart, an editor at *Conde Naste Traveler*. Matthiessen is a member of the American Academy and Institute of Arts and Letters; the New York Zoological Society, for which he served as trustee from 1965 to 1978; and the American Academy of Arts and Sciences. He was also elected to the Global 500 Honour Roll, United Nations Environment Program.

### BIBLIOGRAPHY
Dowie, William, *Peter Matthiessen*, 1991; Houy, Deborah, "A Moment with Peter Matthiessen," *Buzzworm*, 1993; Iyer, Pico, "The Laureate of the Wild," *Time*, 1993; Matthiessen, Peter, *The Peter Matthiessen Reader: Non-fiction 1959–1991*, ed. McKay Jenkins, 1999; Trip, Gabriel, "The Nature of Peter Matthiessen," *New York Times Magazine*, 1990; Tredinnick, Mark, *The Land's Wild Music: encounters with Barry Lopez, Peter Matthiessen, Terry Tempest Williams, and James Galvin*, 2005.

## McCloskey, Michael
(April 26, 1934– )
Executive Director and Chair of the Board of the Sierra Club

Michael McCloskey was executive director of the Sierra Club from 1969 to 1985 and chairman of the board of directors of the Sierra Club from 1985 to 1999. He was instrumental in bringing about the organization's transformation from a 17,000-member excursion-focused club to one of the largest, most influential conservation and advocacy groups in the United States.

John Michael McCloskey was born on April 26, 1934, to John Clement and Agnes Margaret Studer McCloskey in Eugene, Oregon. He spent his youth learning to hike and climb in the Three Sisters Primitive Area of western Oregon, which was virtually an extension of his backyard. In his book *The History of the Sierra Club*, Michael Cohen writes that McCloskey "had learned the true spiritual value of an old-growth forest while reveling in the forests, being swallowed up in the green wilderness." McCloskey went away to college at Harvard University, secure in his knowledge that the wild places he had grown up in would never disappear. He earned a bachelor's degree in 1956 and then spent several years in the army before returning to Oregon in the late 1950s, only to find that a large amount of his favorite forests and wilderness areas simply did not exist anymore.

McCloskey had returned to Oregon to study law at the University of Oregon and while he was completing a law degree, he jumped headlong into the local conservation movement. In his final year of law school, he found that environmental issues in the Pacific Northwest had grown to the point that the outdoor groups were in desperate need of staff assistance to link together all of the various activists and campaigns. Regional conservation groups began to raise money to hire a staff person, and the Sierra Club, based in San Francisco (having no staff outside of San Francisco at the time), agreed to match whatever funds were raised. The money was raised, and in 1961 McCloskey began to represent numerous conservation groups in the Northwest, including the Sierra Club. He kept this job for four years, spending more than half of his time on the road, working to organize isolated conservation groups, encouraging them, and providing successful strategic models for them to emulate.

In 1965, McCloskey married Maxine Mugg Johnson, an important conservationist in her own right, who worked for the protection of marine mammals. They moved to San Francisco and McCloskey began to begin work as assistant to the president of the Sierra Club, Will Siri. McCloskey had already proven that he was overqualified for such a position, and it was not long before he was assigned to create a new conservation department whose sole purpose would be to focus on organizing the Sierra Club's conservation activities. McCloskey served as conservation director from 1966 to 1969, during which time the Sierra Club was fighting for the preservation of the Grand Canyon and for the creation of a Redwood National Park, as well as for a new national park in Washington's Northern Cascades.

McCloskey became executive director of the Sierra Club in 1969 and served in this position until 1985. Then he became chairman of the Sierra Club in Washington, D.C., a position he occupied until his retirement in 1999. During McCloskey's tenure as executive director, the Sierra Club grew dramatically. Both the club's membership and its net worth increased fivefold. When McCloskey started with the organization in 1961, the Sierra Club had a membership of 17,000, most of whom joined because they enjoyed going on the outings sponsored by the club. By 1982, the Sierra Club had grown to include nearly 300,000 members and had become much more organized and results-oriented. In an interview in a 1982 *Sierra* magazine, McCloskey talks about the Sierra Club's overarching philosophy and how the club has been able to maintain a common philosophy considering the growth it has undergone and the diversity of members it has attracted. There is, he believes, a philosophy that binds Sierra Club members together. What it boils down to is a "respect for the needs of future generations, of other creatures and of the processes that make life on the planet possible." It was this respect that allowed the Sierra Club to address such issues as pollution, energy, population growth, urban planning, economics, and transportation under McCloskey's leadership.

A 1996 memo of McCloskey's received significant attention in the United States. The memo, entitled "The Limits of Collaboration," was designed to "spur discussion" among the Sierra Club's board of directors, but it ended up being published in *High Country News* and *Harper's Magazine*. In the memo, McCloskey questioned the true effectiveness of collaborative decision making in resource management, which at that time was coming into vogue as a management strategy. He argued that while collaborative, community-based management does empower the communities doing the managing, it also disenfranchises the significant urban constituency of large environmental organizations such as the Sierra Club. McCloskey also argued against the effectiveness of the consensus decision-making aspect of collaboration, stating that "only ideas of the lowest common denominator survive." "The public and the environment," in his opinion, "deserve better." This opinion of his is in direct opposition to the opinion of many environmentalists who believe that consensus-based decision making plays an important part in environmental policy decisions. Another opinion, published by the *Duke Environmental Law and Policy Forum* in 1999 that generated debate within the environmental movement was that social equity and sustainable development are mutually exclusive, and that the definition of "sustainability" is so vague that it cannot help communities seeking to achieve it.

McCloskey taught courses on the management of advocacy organizations and on international environmental policy at the University of Michigan's School of Natural Resources and the Environment from 1988 until 2000. He retired from the Sierra Club in 1999. His 2005 memoir *In the Thick of It* provides an insider's account of the Club's accomplishments and diverse internal debates.

Michael McCloskey has received several important awards for his conservation work. Among these were the JOHN MUIR Award from the Sierra Club in 1979, being named to the UN Environmental Program Global 500 Honor Roll in 1992, and Lifetime Achievement Awards from the Wilderness Foundation in 1998 and the Public Land Law Conference in 2006.

### BIBLIOGRAPHY

Cohen, Michael P., *The History of The Sierra Club 1892–1970*, 1988; Glendin, Frances, "A Talk with Mike McCloskey, Executive Director of the Sierra Club," *Sierra*, 1982; McCloskey, John Michael, *In the Thick of It: My Life in the Sierra Club*, 2005; McCloskey, Michael, "The Limits of Collaboration," *Harper's Magazine*, 1996.

## McDonough, William

(February 20, 1951– )
Architect, Designer

William McDonough is an internationally recognized designer and architect whose design of the headquarters of the Environmental Defense Fund (EDF) in 1985 helped launch the "green" building movement. Designer of products ranging from athletic shoes to recyclable carpeting, and eloquent proponent of the "cradle to cradle" model for sustainable design and production, McDonough has expanded the idea of environmental design from buildings to products to manufacturing processes.

William McDonough was born on February 20, 1951, in Tokyo, Japan, the son of Bari and James E. McDonough, a U.S. executive with Seagram's. He was raised in Hong Kong. After receiving his undergraduate degree from Dartmouth College in 1973, he worked in Jordan for a year as a planning consultant. McDonough returned to the United States to attend Yale, but after receiving his architecture degree in 1976, he once again went overseas, this time to pursue an interest in energy-efficient building. He is recognized as having designed one of the first solar-heated homes in Ireland. His early exposure to the architecture of Asia and the Middle East had a lasting influence on McDonough. Impressed by native dwellings that responded to the landscape and climate, such as the energy-efficient Bedouin tent, he aimed for a similar harmony between building and environment. Among his professional influences, McDonough cites Joseph Paxton, Louis Sullivan, Frank Lloyd Wright, and Mies van der Rohe. He also admits to being inspired by idea people from a broad cross section of disciplines, from BUCKMINSTER FULLER to organic gardening entrepreneur ROBERT RODALE.

McDonough joined Davis, Brody and Associates in New York in 1977; he represented the firm in a joint venture, working in the office of Jacquelin Robertson. In 1981 he founded the firm now called William McDonough + Partners. He developed a design approach based on the premise that an architect should consider not only the needs of the client but also the needs of the surrounding landscape and of the people who will use the building. The firm's guiding principles—best summed up as above all, do minimum harm—formed the foundation of McDonough's philosophy, fully expressed in the "Hannover Principles" he wrote with partner Michael Braungart almost twenty years later.

One of McDonough's early projects was designing the headquarters of the Environmental Defense Fund in New York in 1985. Concerned about the "sick building" syndrome that was widespread in tightly sealed buildings built in the energy-conscious 1970s, the EDF specified that its headquarters be designed for optimal indoor air quality. The building featured what would become McDonough's basic building blocks: minimal use of toxic materials and maximum use of natural light. McDonough more than met his goal of improving indoor air quality; the building provided a fresh air exchange six times the national standard. The EDF building is generally recognized as one of the innovative designs that sparked the "green architecture" movement.

McDonough was often frustrated in his attempts to use safe building materials because of the dearth of suitable products such as nontoxic paints and adhesives. He realized that "green architecture" could not develop without a similar "greening" of industry. Materials, products, even manufacturing and building processes needed to be created with environmental considerations in mind—in short, industry would have to be reengineered from the bottom up. In 1995, McDonough formed a sister company, McDonough Braungart Design Chemistry, to address this need. With his partner, German chemist Michael Braungart, McDonough has designed many nontoxic, recyclable, or biodegradable products, including cosmetics, toys, food containers, athletic shoes, upholstery fabric, and carpeting. McDonough has also served as a consultant to major companies, including Ciba Geigy, Unilever, Monsanto, Ford Motor Company, and IBM, working with them to improve their products and manufacturing processes.

In 1992, McDonough participated in the UN Conference on Environment and Development (also known as the Earth Summit) in Rio de Janeiro, Brazil, where he represented the American Institute of Architects (AIA). McDonough moved his company from New York to Charlottesville, Virginia, in 1994 when he became the "Green Dean" of the School of Architecture at University of Virginia. He remained Dean for four years until 1998.

At the same time, McDonough remained active though his two companies: McDonough Braungart Design Chemistry (MBDC), which works with clients to "create products and systems that contribute to economic, social, and environmental prosperity," and his architectural firm, William McDonough + Partners. The *Business Week* Architectural Record Award for the best corporate headquarters was awarded to McDonough in 1998 for his design of Gap Inc.'s new headquarters in San Bruno, California. In addition to his customary use of low toxicity materials and abundant natural lighting, McDonough used design features—such as a sound buffer of soil, native grasses, and wildflowers on the roof—to create a healthy working environment for employees. The headquarters showcases McDonough's ability to design buildings that are not only environmentally friendly, but also people friendly.

Other McDonough + Partners projects of the 1990s included Nike's European headquarters, Coffee Creek Center (a pedestrian-oriented development) in Chesterton, Indiana, the Herman Miller "Greenhouse" factory and offices in Holland, Michigan, and the Joseph

Lewis Center for Environmental Studies at Oberlin College in Oberlin, Ohio. McDonough designed the Oberlin center as a teaching tool for students that demonstrates practical solutions to environmental problems, such as using an artificial wetlands to filter waste water. The center received both a *Chicago Atheneum* American Architecture Award and an AIA Committee on Architecture for Education Honor Award in 1999. Current projects include the Museum of Life and the Environment on the Catawba River in York County, South Carolina, the American University School of Internationa Service in Washington, D.C., and the Frito-Lay Distribution Center in Henrietta, New York.

McDonough, known as an eloquent and impassioned speaker, has been praised as a visionary and criticized as a utopian. McDonough's philosophy of sustainability, written with Micael Braungart, is outlined in a set of guidelines proposed for the city of Hannover, Germany, host of EXPO 2000. The nine principles range from the ineffable "Respect relationships between spirit and matter" to the practical "Create safe objects of long-term value." McDonough believes that the twenty-first century will bring a new industrial revolution in which business, not governmental regulation, will be the driving force for environmental progress. Braungart and McDonough have collaborated on *Cradle to Cradle* (2002), which sets out their vision for "remaking the way we make things"—production that doesn't simply use resources but that rather lends some ecological benefit to the world. The book itself is a model for this type of design, it is made of plastic resin and inorganic fillers, and can be recycled wherever polypropylene can be processed.

McDonough stepped down from his position of dean at the University of Virginia School of Architecture in 1999, but he continues to teach in the business school there as a visiting professor, and teaches as well at the school of civil and environmental engineering at Stanford University. McDonough has served on the board of Second Nature, a nonprofit organization in Boston that helps higher education institutions incorporate environmental sustainability into their curriculum.

From 1993 to 1996, McDonough served as adviser to the President's Council on Sustainable Development. In 1999, he received the only Presidential Award for Sustainable Design ever awarded to an individual, and was named one of *Time* magazine's "Heroes for the Planet." *Time* recognized McDonough as a "Hero of the Environment" again in 2007, along with Braungart. In 2003 he was given the U.S. EPA Presidential Green Chemistry Challenge Award, and in 2004, the National Design Award.

McDonough lives in Charlottesville, Virginia, with his wife, Michelle, and children, Drew and Ava.

**BIBLIOGRAPHY**

Braungart, Michael, and William McDonough, "The Next Industrial Revolution," *Atlantic Monthly*, 1998; "The Hannover Principles: Design for Sustainability," www.mcdonough.com/principles.pdf; Klimint, Stephen, "Green Giant," *Planning*, 1999; Lacayo, Richard, "Heroes of the Environment: William McDonough and Michael Braungart," *Time*, 2007; "MBDC." www.mbdc.com, "McDonough + Partners: Architects and Community Design," www.mcdonoughpartners.com; Rosenblatt, Roger, "The Man Who Wants Buildings to Love Kids," *Time*, 1999, "William A. McDonough, FAIA," www. mcdonough.com.

## McDowell, Mary
(November 30, 1854–October 14, 1936)
Settlement Worker, Garbage Activist

Known affectionately as Chicago's "Garbage Lady," Mary McDowell was a leader in the settlement movement in Chicago and was instrumental in cleaning up the city's garbage and sewers. She led the University of Chicago Settlement, located in "Packingtown," one of Chicago's poorest neighborhoods. She was active in many of the Progressive movement's issues, including union organizing, literacy campaigns, justice for African Americans, and fair housing, and was eventually appointed commissioner of public welfare. For her work with the least powerful of Chicago's citizens, Mary McDowell was dubbed the "Angel of the Stockyards."

Mary McDowell was born on November 30, 1854, in Cincinnati, Ohio, to Jane and Malcolm McDowell. When she was seven, the Union army called her father into service, and McDowell developed a keen identification with President Lincoln and the cause of abolition. One biographer suggests her lifelong interest in the rights of African Americans stemmed from her experiences during the Civil War. When McDowell's father returned from the war, he moved the family to Chicago. Malcolm McDowell started a successful steel foundry, and the McDowells became prominent Chicago citizens. McDowell had her first experience with social work during the great Chicago fire of 1871. She helped people evacuate the city and then organized and distributed relief supplies. Rutherford B. Hayes, then the governor of Ohio, was an old friend of the McDowell family, and he delivered his state's aid directly to the McDowell home. In the early 1880s the McDowells moved to Evanston, Illinois, where Mary met Frances Willard, leader of the Woman's Christian Temperance Union. McDowell became a close friend of Willard and worked as a state organizer for the Young Woman's Christian Temperance Union.

From left to right: Julia Lathrop, Jane Addams, and Mary McDowell on Capitol Hill, 1913. (Library of Congress, Prints & Photographs Division, LC-USZ62-50050)

In 1890, McDowell went to work with JANE ADDAMS at Hull House in Chicago. The settlement movement aimed to combat urban poverty on a neighborhood level. Settlement houses were centers where people could seek education, childcare, help in gaining employment, and housing aid. The workers were mostly middle-class Progressive reformers and in many ways were the first professional social workers in the United States. Though McDowell only taught kindergarten at Hull House for a few months, it was to prove a turning point in her life. In 1894, the new Department of Sociology at the University of Chicago decided to found a new settlement, and Addams recommended McDowell for the position of head resident. McDowell accepted the position, moved into the University of Chicago Settlement, and remained there for the rest of her life. The settlement was "back of the yards," in the neighborhood nearest the meat packing yards. The situation in Packingtown was dismal: makeshift, overcrowded housing; massive unemployment; and utter lack of sanitation facilities. McDowell's arrival in the community was greeted with suspicion. There had been a massive, violent meat packers' strike a few months earlier, and many workers thought McDowell was a spy, sent by plant owners to identify labor leaders. McDowell eventually earned the trust of her neighbors through hard work and effective advocacy. She founded the area's first kindergarten, organized a successful neighborhood cleanup campaign, and fought for and won public bathing facilities. She was given the nickname "Fighting Mary" for her labor organizing. McDowell helped organize one of the first women's unions, the Women's Trade Union League of Chicago, and actively supported the workers during the packing strike of 1904. McDowell published articles in the local press in support of the strikers and helped raise money; she is credited with helping maintain the peace. The plant owners brought in African American replacement workers, and McDowell intervened to stop the strikers from carrying out reprisals, which would have taken the form of lynch mobs.

McDowell also led the fight for a safer, healthier environment. Packingtown was bordered on one side by the meat plants, on another by the city's vast, open garbage pits, and on the third side by an arm of the Chicago River called Bubbly Creek because of its high content of carbonic acid gas. The combination of these factors and the overcrowded, impoverished living conditions created serious health hazards. McDowell organized for years to get the city to clean up and cover the river and did make headway, though modern waste treatment facilities were not built during her lifetime.

McDowell was more successful with garbage. The municipal garbage dump bordering Packingtown was an exhausted clay mine, owned by a powerful alderman who charged private haulers a hefty dumping fee. The alderman used his influence to block any efforts to improve sanitation at the dump. McDowell's first success was to get the city to extend garbage collection services to her neighborhood. But this failed to alter the pollution of the pits themselves. McDowell began a huge press campaign to generate public support and political pressure. In 1911, a supporter financed McDowell's trip to Europe, where she researched the disposal methods of large cities in England, France, Holland, and Germany, cities with better sanitation programs than Chicago. She gathered information that could be useful in a public relations campaign and on her return began speaking to numerous groups around the city. Mass meetings were organized throughout Chicago, women's clubs began organizing garbage committees, and the city council began to take notice. In 1913, the first modern garbage reduction plant was built, in which greases were extracted from the garbage and resold for a number of commercial purposes. The open dumps were closed, ending a significant threat to the health of Packingtown.

McDowell continued her work in the settlement throughout her life and saw a number of achievements. She was instrumental in generating the publicity that pushed Pres. THEODORE ROOSEVELT and the U.S. Congress to enact inspection regulations at the packing plants. She helped create networks of parks and community gardens. In 1923 she was appointed commissioner of public welfare by Mayor William Dever, in which capacity she set up a Bureau of Employment and lobbied for a permanent Housing Commission. McDowell's work earned her the respect of her neighbors, Chicago's political machine, and the profession of social work. She died on October 14, 1936. The University of Chicago Settlement was renamed the Mary McDowell Settlement in her honor.

**BIBLIOGRAPHY**
Breton, Mary Joy, *Women Pioneers for the Environment*, 2000; Davis, Allen, *Spearheads for Reform*, 1967; Taylor, Lea, "The Social Settlement and Civic Responsibility—The Life Work of Mary McDowell and Graham Taylor," *Social Service Review*, 1954; Wade, Louise, "Mary E. McDowell, Angel of the Stockyards," www.kentlaw.edu/ilhs/mcdowell.html; Wilson, Howard, *Mary McDowell: Neighbor*, 1928.

## McHarg, Ian
(November 20, 1920–March 5, 2001)
Landscape Architect, Environmental Urban Planner

Ian McHarg was a landscape architect and environmental urban planner. His famous book *Design with Nature*, released in 1969, called for ecologically sensitive urban planning and for the recognition that humans can and must create cities that exist in harmony with nature. McHarg brought ecological awareness to urban planning and landscape architecture, and was responsible for elevating both of these fields to national prominence, in both the political and social spheres.

Son of John Lennox and Harriet Bain McHarg, Ian Lennox McHarg was born on November 20, 1920, in Clydebank, Scotland. He spent his childhood living in between examples of two very different types of human occupation of land. The large, smoking city of Glasgow was only ten miles to the east of his home. The blast furnace flames lighting the eastern horizon at night made a lasting impression on him. To the west were countryside and the Firth of Clyde, with its estuary opening into the Atlantic Ocean. In the introduction to *Design with Nature* McHarg writes, "During all of my childhood and youth there were two clear paths from my home, the one penetrating further and further to the city and ending in Glasgow, the other moving deeper into the countryside to the final wilderness of the Western Highlands and the Islands." According to McHarg, the career he eventually pursued was a response to the simple choice laid out for him in his childhood: beautiful countryside or city? He chose both. He discovered landscape architecture at the age of 16 and saw in it the opportunity to provide for those who lived in cities the positive experiences he had found in nature.

In 1939, McHarg entered the British Army, eventually serving as an officer with the Second Independent Parachute Brigade Group in Italy for two years beginning in 1943. After World War II, McHarg spent four years at Harvard University in Cambridge, Massachusetts, studying landscape architecture. He earned his bachelor's degree in 1949, a master's in landscape architecture in 1950, and a master's in city planning in 1951. In 1947, McHarg married Pauline Crena de Longh. They would have two sons together. In 1950, McHarg took his new family back to Scotland. He was "determined to practice my faith upon that environment of drudgery that is Clydeside." He worked as a planner for the Scotland Department of Health from 1950 to 1954. During this time, he discovered that he had contracted pulmonary tuberculosis. He spent the first six months of his convalescence in a hospital on the outskirts of Edinburgh, a hopeless and horrible experience for him. After six months, he transferred to a Swiss sanatorium for British parachutists, where he recovered. For the next half year, he hiked the Swiss countryside, an experience that impressed upon him the healing powers of the natural world, not just for the spirit, but for the flesh as well.

In 1954, McHarg was invited to join the faculty at the University of Pennsylvania, where he established the Department of Landscape Architecture and Regional Planning. McHarg remained at the University of Pennsylvania full-time for the next 32 years, serving as department chair from 1960 until 1986, when he retired.

In the late 1960s, Russell Train, then head of the Conservation Foundation (he would later become head of the Environmental Protection Agency during the Nixon administration), approached McHarg and requested that he write a book on the ecological aspects of urban planning. McHarg accepted and spent one year of his life producing *Design with Nature*, which was published in 1969. This book was extremely well received and reviewed. It was reprinted four times in its first year alone and has become the book of authority for the design and planning professions, as well as for students of ecology. When *Design with Nature* was published, there was no legislation requiring an ecological understanding of areas to be developed (the role environmental impact statements fulfill today). As McHarg wrote in his autobiography, *A Quest for Life*, published in 1996, "The book contributed to the efflorescence of environmental legislation. Moreover, it has increasing relevance for countries only now confronting the crisis of the environment and the need for ecological planning."

In *Design with Nature*, McHarg pioneered layered mapping techniques that were the precursor to the geographic information systems (GIS) used in much of modern mapping. McHarg created a system whereby all of the different physical attributes of a site—soil, drainage, vegetation, groundwater—are recorded on separate, transparent maps that are laid over one another to determine which areas are most suitable for development, and what type of development should be pursued. His book explains that the dynamic processes of nature should be considered in the design process and that "changes to parts of the system affect the entire system." *Design with Nature*, which has been described as "almost a book of poetry," is still required reading in many universities' departments of landscape architecture. It was nominated for a National Book Award in 1971.

In 1963, McHarg helped to create the firm Wallace-McHarg, Roberts and Todd, architects, landscape architects, and planners in Philadelphia. The firm grew to include offices in Los Angeles, Miami, Denver, and San Francisco. Through this firm, McHarg was involved in such projects as a 1962 plan for four contiguous Maryland river valleys, in which it was proposed, for the first time, that development rights be transferred in order to preserve a landscape. He also helped to design the 600-acre Pardisan Environmental Park outside of Tehran, Iran, in 1976. Fee disputes over this project led to McHarg's leaving the firm.

McHarg maintained a busy schedule after his retirement. He was a visiting professor at the University of California, Berkeley, in 1986 and 1987 and at Pennsylvania State University and Harvard in 1994. In 1996, he published his autobiography, *A Quest for Life*. And in 1998 he released *To Heal the Earth: Selected Writings of Ian L. McHarg*, a compilation of some of his most important writings. In 1977, three years after the death of his first wife, McHarg married Carol Anne Smyser, with whom he had two sons. McHarg received numerous awards for his accomplishments, including the Bradford Williams Medal of American Society of Landscape Architects, 1968; an outstanding achievement award from Harvard University, 1992; the Thomas Jefferson Medal from the University of Virginia, 1995; the Pioneer Award from the American Institution of Certified Planners, 1997; and the Japan Prize, given to scientists who have made original and outstanding contributions to science and technology, in 2000.

McHarg died on March 5, 2001, of pulmonary disease.

**BIBLIOGRAPHY**
Cohen, William J., "Ian McHarg's Triumph," *Planning*, 2001; Holden, Constance, "Ian McHarg: Champion for Design with Nature," *Landscape Architecture*, 1977; Knack, Ruth, "Utopia!" *Planning*, 1997; Landecker, Heidi, "In Search of an Arbiter," *Landscape Architecture*, 1990; McHarg, Ian L., *Design with Nature*, 1969; McHarg, Ian L., *A Quest for Life*, 1996; Revkin, Andrew C., "Ian McHarg, 80, Architect Who Valued a Site's Natural Features, *New York Times*, 2001.

## McKibben, Bill
(December 8, 1960– )
Writer

Bill McKibben came to prominence as an environmental writer with the 1989 publication of his groundbreaking book, *The End of Nature*. His overriding concerns have been rampant consumerism, the disruption in our current culture of our traditionally intimate relationship with nature, and most recently, global warming. McKibben's writing has been lauded for its clarity and eloquence; he offers advice for change and personal expressions of hope for the future of humanity and the natural world.

William Ernest McKibben was born in Palo Alto, California, on December 8, 1960, and reared in Lexington, Massachusetts. His parents, Gordon McKibben and Margaret Hayes McKibben, were both journalists for the *Boston Globe*. Throughout his childhood, young McKibben envisioned himself as "a newspaperman" and at Harvard University became president of the student newspaper, *The Crimson*.

McKibben graduated with a B.A. in 1982 and went to work for the *New Yorker*, whose editor, William Shawn, had admired McKibben's college journalism. At the *New Yorker*, he wrote hundreds of articles, primarily "Talk of the Town" stories, as well as longer, general-interest features and humorous fiction. In

Bill McKibben stands in front of solar panels as he talks to students on a field trip. (AP Images/Toby Talbot)

1987, when William Shawn was forced to resign, McKibben quit the *New Yorker* to become a freelance magazine writer and to work on his first book.

*The End of Nature* was published in 1989 and became an almost instant bestseller. Dire, alarming, and provocative, it was the first book written for the general public about global warming. In addition to becoming a source of great controversy it gave McKibben a reputation as a prophet of ecological doom. He warned of imminent global disaster, basing his ideas on scientific evidence about the greenhouse effect. With clarity, precision, and universally praised eloquence, he outlined the implications to the environment of the industrial world's proliferation of methane and carbon dioxide, which prevent heat from escaping the atmosphere, causing the earth's temperatures to increase, the polar ice caps to melt, oceans to rise, and droughts to occur.

Noting that our ecological problems are "huge and growing," McKibben called for radical solutions, notably ending the use of machines that burn oil and coal. He eschewed traditional answers, such as planting more trees to absorb carbon monoxide, describing them as too little too late and even misguided, when the solutions must come by changing our consumerist way of life.

Almost two decades after the publication of *The End of Nature*, McKibben began organizing an activist response to the progression of global warming and dearth of public and official response to it. During the summer of 2006, he helped lead a five-day walk across the state of Vermont to demand action, and in 2007 he founded stepitup07.org, to demand that Congress enact curbs on carbon emissions that would limit them by 80 percent by the year 2050. One thousand four hundred communities in every state of the U.S. held demonstrations on April 14, 2007—the largest collective protest about climate change in history. McKibben published *Fight Global Warming Now* after the day of protest, as a guide to help people with effective environmental activism in their communities.

How humans live, particularly we Americans who use most of the earth's resources, is an ongoing thread through McKibben's writings. In 1992, with *The Age of Missing Information*, he examined the causes of human indifference toward the environment, the twin culprits of conspicuous consumption and television, "our main information source." To make his case, McKibben taped 103 television channels during a 24-hour time span, then watched every hour of every channel. He found that the endless blast of information from sports, weather, and news channels; shows about people and comedy; MTV and its imitators; and so on are not only empty of content but exacerbate the boredom we already fear. He followed his television blitzkrieg with a week alone in the mountains. The "three rarest commodities" of contemporary life are "solitude, silence and darkness," he wrote. Quiet contemplation in the midst of nature allows one to become observant, refreshed, and content and to hear "natural broadcasts... sense the presence of the divine... that has marked human beings in every culture as far back as anthropologists can go."

In 1995, McKibben published *Hope Human and Wild: True Stories of Living Lightly on the Earth*, a nuts-and-bolts, everyday specifics of three locales: Curitiba, a mountain city in Brazil; Kerala, a community in India; and his own home in the Adirondack Mountains of New York, where he found enormous environmental and social progress thanks to human imagination and prudent government. This book was an attempt to "convince myself and others that it is not completely pie-in-the-sky to imagine there could be other ways to conduct ourselves... The point of the book is to counter despair," he told Michael Coffey of *Publishers Weekly* in 1995.

McKibben tackled issues of overpopulation in 1998 with *Maybe One: A Personal and Environmental Argument for Single Child Families*. In this book he tries to persuade Americans to consider reducing strain on the earth's resources by having just one child. "When we think of overpopulation, we usually think first of the developing world... [b]ut... we fool ourselves when we think of population as a brown problem," he wrote. He listed statistics showing, for example, that one "American uses seventy times the energy of a Bangladeshi, fifty times that of a Malagasy, twenty times that of a Costa Rican... During the next decade, India and China will each add to the planet about ten times as many people as will the United States... [but] the 57.5 million northerners... added during this decade will add more greenhouse gases to the atmosphere than the roughly 900 million southerners."

McKibben's *Deep Economy: The Wealth of Communities and the Durable Future* (2007) argues that "bigger" can no longer be equated with "better" and that there is great value in developing local food, energy-generation capacity, and culture.

Between publication of his major books, McKibben has produced several smaller ones, including *The Comforting Whirlwind: God, Job and the Scale of Creation* (1994), in which he challenged current thinking about the environmental crisis through a reading of the book of Job; *Hundred Dollar Holiday: The Case for a More Joyful Christmas* (1998) with tips on simplifying the frenzied materialist holiday against "those relentless commercial forces" and returning it to a time of fellowship with each other and the natural world; *Long Distance: A Year of Living Strenuously* (2000) about a year-long elite-level training for endurance competitions; *Enough* (2003) about the perils of genetic engineering; and *Wandering Home* (2005) tracing a solo hiking trip through New England.

McKibben continues to contribute articles to a wide range of publications, including the *Atlantic*, the *New York Review of Books*, the *New York Times*, *Natural History*, *Outside*, *Rolling Stone*, *Esquire*, *Audubon*, and many others. He is the recipient of Guggenheim and Lyndhurst Fellowships, and won the 2000 Lannan Prize for nonfiction. He is a board member of *Grist* magazine and a scholar-in-residence at Middlebury College. With his wife, writer Sue Halpern, and daughter, Sophie, he lives in Ripton, Vermont.

**BIBLIOGRAPHY**
Coffey, Michael, "Bill McKibben: Environmental Hope in Conservative Times," *Publishers Weekly*, 1995; Official site for Bill McKibben: Author—Educator—Environmentalist," www.billmckibben.com.

## McPhee, John
(March 8, 1931– )
Writer

John McPhee is a Pulitzer prize-winning reporter and a writer of creative nonfiction whose focus on the interactions and relationships between people and the natural world has been instructive and revealing. He is not an editorialist, and his environmentally focused books do not preach any kind of message. Rather, his works such as *Encounters with the Archdruid* (1972), *Coming into the Country* (1977), and *The Control of Nature* (1989) simply present the characters of the people and of the land they live in and allow readers to draw their own conclusions.

John Angus McPhee was born on March 8, 1931, in Princeton, New Jersey. He was the youngest child born to Harry Roemer McPhee and Mary Ziegler McPhee. His father, a physician, was a specialist in sports medicine and was the regular physician for Princeton University's athletic teams. McPhee grew up watching Princeton's various athletic teams practice and became, despite his small stature, an accomplished athlete himself. Throughout his childhood, McPhee spent his summer months at Keewaydin Camp in Vermont, a place he would later refer to as the most important educational institution he attended. He attended Princeton High School, where he was active in sports and where his skills as a writer began to take shape. He remembers his English teacher, Olive McKee, as having a considerable influence on him.

McPhee graduated from Princeton High School in 1948, at the age of 17. He had already been accepted into Princeton University, but his mother, believing that he needed another year to mature, sent him to Deerfield Academy in Massachusetts. At Deerfield, McPhee studied under the guidance of the headmaster, Frank L. Boyden, who many years later was the subject of McPhee's book, *The Headmaster* (1966). McPhee entered Princeton University in 1949. At Princeton, he studied English and appeared as the regular teenage panelist on the radio and television quiz show, *Twenty Questions*. He graduated from Princeton with a B.A. in English in 1953. He satisfied his senior thesis requirement by submitting an unpublished novel, *Skimmer Burns*. In doing so, he set a precedent for future students in the Princeton English Department. McPhee spent his next year in England, doing postgraduate work at Cambridge University. He studied literature and in his spare time toured with a basketball team that played against teams from schools such as Oxford and the London School of Economics.

Returning to the United States in 1954, McPhee settled for a short time in New York City in an attempt to establish himself as a freelance writer. Biographer Michael Pearson quotes McPhee about this period of his life: "I didn't rule out anything as a younger writer. I tried everything." McPhee wrote speeches and articles for W. R. Grace and Company in New York City. He wrote short stories and sold several television scripts to a popular show of the time, "Robert Montgomery Presents." In 1957, McPhee became a reporter for *Time*. For five years, he wrote the magazine's "Show Business" column and also produced nine cover stories on such celebrities as Joan Baez and Barbara Streisand. He continued selling articles to various periodicals, and in 1963, the *New Yorker* purchased "Basketball and Beefeaters," an account of his experiences playing basketball in England. McPhee sold another article to the *New Yorker* two years later. Entitled "A Sense of Where You Are," the article was about Princeton basketball star and general All-American hero, Bill Bradley. The article was published in book form in 1965 and was praised by critics for its clarity and its capacity to inspire without preaching.

Soon after the publication of *A Sense of Where You Are*, McPhee accepted a position as a staff writer with the *New Yorker*, which he still occupies today. Since 1974, McPhee has also been the Ferris Professor of Journalism at Princeton University.

McPhee has written more than 30 books on a wide variety of subjects, many of them addressing, in one form or another, the natural world and the people who live in and around it. In *Encounters with the Archdruid* (1972), he tags along with environmentalist DAVID BROWER in a series of three confrontations/discussions with an exploration geologist, a dam builder, and a developer. In these encounters, McPhee draws no conclusions of his own but presents the "characters" with all of their complexities and allows readers to choose sides for themselves. Another book of his that focuses on the natural world, *Coming into the Country* (1977), is perhaps his most popular environmentally focused work. Its plot line focuses on a search for a new Alaskan capital to replace Juneau. According, again, to Michael Pearson, this book asks questions about the type of self-confidence and skill that exists among the human dwellers of this daunting landscape. It asks, "Will this survive, especially if the wild country is lost or even tamed into more civilized parks?" As in *Encounters with the Archdruid*, McPhee does not answer this question for himself. He allows his subjects to decide. And the answers are never simple or clear, if only because McPhee provides so many different points of view.

In another book, *The Control of Nature* (1989), McPhee examines the relationships between humans and the natural world in three different parts of the world: the Mississippi River, an Icelandic volcano, and the San Gabriel Mountains of southern California. He portrays three scenarios in which humans attempt to force uncooperative nature to comply with their demands. Along the Mississippi, humans attempt to prevent the totally natural shift of the river out of its current bed and on to a different course. In Iceland, people fight the eruption of a volcano with fire hoses in an attempt to save the commercially valuable harbor on the island of Heimaey. And in southern California, suburbanites, against all common sense, occupy hillsides prone to massive mud slides. McPhee has also produced a series of four books about American geology. Called *Annals of the Former World*, the series is composed of *Basin and Range* (1981), *In Suspect Terrain* (1983), *Rising from the Plains* (1986), and *Assembling California* (1993). These books describe McPhee's tours of the United States with professional geologists and are considered by many the most ambitious of McPhee's work. They provide a perspective into the dramatically short period of time humans have occupied the planet by presenting humans as but a minor character in the vast history of earth. They were re-published as a tetrology in 1998 and McPhee was awarded the Pulitzer Prize for this work in 1999. McPhee's most recent works include *The Founding Fish* (2002), dedicated to the natural history of *Alosa sapidissima* (shad) and its place in American history, and *Uncommon Carriers* (2006), sketches of men who haul freight via truck, train, and ocean tankers.

While the majority of McPhee's books focus on the natural world, he has written on a variety of other subjects such as tennis, oranges, and Russian art. He has received many awards for his writings, in addition to his 1999 Pulitzer Prize: the American Academy of Arts and Letters Award in Literature, the Woodrow Wilson Award from Princeton University in 1982, the JOHN WESLEY POWELL Award from the United States Geological Survey in 1988, the John Burroughs Medal in 1990. McPhee lives in Princeton, New Jersey, with his wife, Yolanda Whitman, whom he married in 1972. He has four grown children from a previous marriage: Laura, Sarah, Jenny, and Martha, as well as four stepchildren: Cole, Andrew, Katherine, and Vanessa Harrop.

**BIBLIOGRAPHY**
Hamilton, Joan, "An Encounter with John McPhee," *Sierra*, 1990; "John McPhee," *Contemporary Authors Online*, 2007; "John McPhee Home Page," www.johnmcphee.com; Pearson, Michael, *John McPhee*, 1997.

## Meadows, Donella H.
(1941–February 6, 2001)
Founder and Director of the Sustainability Institute, Writer

A self-proclaimed grassroots worker, Donella H. Meadows arose as a voice for environmental consciousness in the early 1970s with the publication of *The Limits to Growth*, a slim yet controversial book that sold nine million copies and linked population and economic growth with the environment. With that publication, her reputation as an advocate for sustainable systems flourished. Founder and director of the Sustainability Institute, the prolific Meadows also wrote a range of magazine and earth-friendly articles—the most visible being her syndicated column, "The Global Citizen." In addition to her writing, Meadows taught environmental studies at Dartmouth College and lived on a small farm where she practices sustainable agriculture.

Often labeled professionally as a systems analyst and international coordinator of management systems, the multifaceted yet independent and private Donella "Dana" Hager Meadows defied any convenient categorizing and preferred not to publicize her personal history. Instead she chose to rechannel any attention that came her way toward the ideas she considered vital both to the welfare of the environment and its resources and to human communities and the human spirit. What is open knowledge about Meadows's personal life is that she was born in 1941 in Elgin, Illinois, graduated from Caroleton College in 1963, received her Ph.D. in biophysics from Harvard University in 1968, and was married to Dennis L. Meadows, professor of systems policy and social science research and former director of the Institute for Policy and Social Research at the University of New Hampshire.

Together with Dennis Meadows and Jorgen Randers, policy analyst and president emeritus of the Norwegian School of Management, "Dana" Meadows was the lead writer of the 1972 book *The Limits to Growth*, the 1992 update *Beyond the Limits: Confronting Global Collapse, Envisioning a Sustainable Future*, and the update published in 2004, *The Limits to Growth: the 30-year update*.

While working together at the Massachusetts Institute of Technology (MIT) in the late 1960s and early 1970s, the three researchers developed computer models, based on the exponential concept of doubling, that demonstrate a range of future scenarios for our global economy. *The Limits to Growth* presented 12 computer graphs, from the most negative case predicting an exhaustion of nonrenewable resources and hence the deterioration of human life, to the most optimistic case promoting a European sustainable standard of living. Twenty years later in *Beyond the Limits*, the authors again used computer models to restate their concerns, with graphs showing a growing world population stripping food supplies and natural resources by 2100. Thirty years later, Dennis Meadows and Randers used updated computer models to show that we have overshot Earth's capacity to sustain us, but suggestions for changes of means of production and use of resources are given.

In 1985—between work on *The Limits to Growth* and *Beyond the Limits*—Donella Meadows, along with photographer Jenny Robinson, published *The Electronic Oracle: Computer Models and Social Decisions*, a critical look at computer modeling as a method for social, economic, and political analysis. Then in 1991 Meadows authored *The Global Citizen*, a collection of personal stories, research experiences, and environmental insights. This book gave its title, tone, and format to her weekly opinion column—a column that the Context Institute called "one of the most reliable places we know for holistic and humane commentary on world affairs." Meadows's articles also appeared in *Amicus Journal, Earth Island Journal*, and *Organic Gardening* and *Whole Earth*, where she was a contributing editor.

Regardless of the format, Dana Meadows tenaciously worked to counter the "religion" of consumption and growth in hopes of turning the tide toward moderation and sustainability. Indeed, as a writer she might be compared with RACHEL CARSON for her natural prose style that combined readability with scientific discourse to convey a futuristic warning. Similarly, Meadows uses her prose with its snappy journalistic style as a venue to temper scientific theories with a positive vision. Indeed, while she was compelled by the predictability of her computer model calculations that forecast a dubious future of depleted earth resources, she also believed we all have the responsibility to make informed choices. Consequently in her later work she allowed spirituality to influence her mindset, which had previously been focused solely by scientific method. For Meadows, therefore, sustainability took on an encompassing meaning—a meaning that she clarified at a roundtable discussion of environmentalists conducted by *The Amicus Journal* as the "protection of the environment, social justice, and all of the other issues... [getting off] growth and productivity and quantitativeness and reductionism, into wholeness and wellness and living with limits."

Despite her persistent fight for sustainability, in a 1996 interview with *Social Justice* Meadows admitted that she was "disheartened to hear the political debate just talk about growth, growth, growth, growth and to hear nobody stand up and challenge them." Meadows's seemingly indefatigable desire for action led to the development of the Sustainability Institute—"a think-do tank"—which sponsors people, programs, and initiatives targeted toward raising awareness about the consequences of our lifestyle decisions. A Pew Scholar in Conservation and Environment and a MacArthur Fellow, Dana Meadows lived the life she professed, from farming organically to driving a gas-electric hybrid car. One of her last projects was an environmental studies textbook written, naturally, from a systems perspective.

Meadows died at the age of 59 of bacterial meningitis in Lebanon, New Hampshire. An archive of her writings, including 15 years of Global Citizen weekly columns, is available on-line through the website of the Sustainability Institute, www.sustainer.org.

### BIBLIOGRAPHY

"Environmental Futures," *The Amicus Journal*, 1995; Meadows, Donella H., "The Global Citizen: A Column by Donella Meadows," www.pcdf.org/meadows; Saxon, Wolfgang, "Donella Meadows, 59, Autor, and Advocate for Environment," *New York Times*, 2001; "Sustainability Institute," www.sustainer.org; Walljasper, Jay, "Rethinking the Left," *Social Justice*, 1996.

## Meany, Edmond

(December 28, 1862–April 22, 1935)
Historian, President of the Washington Mountaineers

Edmond Meany became the president of the Washington Mountaineers in 1907, one year after its inception, and held that position until his death in 1935. Meany was the backbone and inspiration of the burgeoning outdoors club that still combines outdoors expeditions with conservationist activism. After the Sierra Club, no outdoors group has had a greater impact on wilderness recreation in the American West than the Mountaineers.

Edmond Stephen Meany was born on December 28, 1862, in East Saginaw, Michigan. His family moved to Washington while he was still a teenager. During the summer of 1880, Meany's father drowned while working on a steamer on the Skagit River. Meany, not yet 18, was left as the primary supporter of his mother, sister, and baby brother. In the years that followed, Meany operated a small dairy, pasturing cows on grass that grew along the sides of Seattle's unpaved streets, delivered newspapers, kept books for a grocer, and worked as a janitor both at his church and at the only bank in town.

Showing promise and determination, Meany entered the University of Washington and graduated in 1885 at the top of his class.

He became a reporter at the *Seattle Press* and was promoted to city editor. In 1889–1890, the *Seattle Press* sponsored the Press Exploratory Expedition into Washington's Olympic Range; the explorers thought enough of Meany to name a mountain after him. He would later get the chance to climb his namesake peak on the first Mountaineers outing.

In 1891, Meany was elected to the state legislature and was instrumental in securing land in northern Seattle for the current University of Washington campus. The decision to move the university was controversial, as the original campus was conveniently located in downtown Seattle. Despite its panoramic views of the Cascades to the east, the Olympics to the west, and Mount Rainier to the south, the new campus was some distance out of the city, at the very end of a streetcar line. After serving for two sessions in the state legislature, Meany became the registrar at the university before becoming a history lecturer. In 1897, he was appointed as head of the history department, and in 1906, he became the managing editor of the *Washington Historical Quarterly;* he held both positions for the rest of his life.

Though not included among the charter members of the Mountaineers (founded in 1906), Mcany joined just after the charter rolls closed. The Mountaineers offered an ideal combination of his major interests: aboriginal legends, Northwest history, and outdoor recreation. Meany quickly became a popular member of the club, speaking at monthly meetings and sharing his considerable knowledge of native lore. He succeeded the club's first president, Henry Landes, in 1907 and helped outline the club's mission, which remains the same almost a century later:

> To explore and study the mountains, forests and water courses of the Northwest and beyond; to gather into permanent form the history and traditions of these regions and explorations; to preserve by example, teaching and the encouragement of protective legislation or otherwise the beauty of the natural environment; to make expeditions and provide educational opportunities in fulfillment of the above purposes; to encourage a spirit of good fellowship among all lovers of outdoor life.

Meany took his role as president very seriously and set very high standards of conduct for club activities. He established standards of mountaineering ethics that prioritized group safety and minimized the impact of environmental degradation caused by large groups in mountainous and wilderness areas. These mountaineering ethics made the Mountaineers' concern for the outdoors among the foremost among outdoors groups in the nation. During Meany's leadership, the Mountaineers formed its own legislative committee to concentrate specifically on preservation issues in both the national and state arenas.

Meany was also an affable and amiable leader. He was a frequent participant in campfire entertainment on outings, telling stories of the early explorers in the Northwest, or from native mythology, or reciting his own poetry. Meany's pleasant attention to all members, old or new, made him a beloved figure the club could rally behind during its formative years. Originally just an outdoors exploration club, the Mountaineers, under Meany, expanded into rock climbing, skiing, snowshoeing, and even theater performances. Nevertheless, conservation remained a primary mission for Meany. Writing in the Mountaineers' 1910 annual, Meany postulated: "This is a new country. It abounds in a fabulous wealth of scenic beauty. It is possible to so conserve parts of that wealth that it may be enjoyed by countless generations through the centuries to come."

Meany was also a devout Christian. He always led the Sunday morning worship service on club outings. Meany bought land at the eastern end of the Stampede Tunnel, adjacent to the Northern Pacific Railroad tracks, and donated it to the club for the purpose of building a ski lodge. The Meany Ski Hut was built on this land, the sole proviso from its benefactor being that the hut be closed on Easter Sundays for religious observation.

Meany died on April 22, 1935, of a stroke, just before he was to give a lecture at the University of Washington. He was survived by his wife, Sarah Elizabeth Ward of Seattle, whom he married in 1889, and two of their four children.

**BIBLIOGRAPHY**

"Edmond S. Meany," www.washington.edu/research/showcase/1894a.html; Frykman, George, *Seattle's Historian and Promoter: The Life of Edmond Stephen Meany*, 1998; Gowen, Herbert H., "Meany, the Road Maker," *Washington Historical Quarterly*, 1935; Kjeldsen, Jim, *The Mountaineers: A History*, 1998; McMahon, Edward, "Professor Meany as I Knew Him," *Washington Historical Quarterly*, 1935; Sieg, Lee Paul, "Edmond S. Meany: The Value of a Man," *Washington Historical Quarterly*, 1935; Todd, Ronald, "A Selected Bibliography of the Writings of Edmond Stephen Meany," *Washington Historical Quarterly*, 1935; Warren, James, "History of Edmond Meany," *Seattle Post-Intelligencer*, 1984.

## Merchant, Carolyn

(July 12, 1936– )
Professor, Author, Environmental Historian

As a professor of environmental history and the author of several classics of environmental theory, Carolyn Merchant has broadened society's awareness of how humans and their natural environment impact each other. In her pathbreaking book, *The Death of Nature: Women, Ecology, and the Scientific Revolution* (1980), Merchant elucidated the emerging concept of "ecofeminism" and helped bring it into wide usage in environmental discourse. By delineating age-old connections between women and nature and exposing the forces that have oppressed them both, she offered a gender-based perspective as a new context for interpretation of environmental values and interactions. In *The Death of Nature* and other books, Merchant also provides historical analyses of the expansion of power over nature by social institutions, and in doing so, she puts into perspective current arguments over the importance of environmentalism and suggests guidelines for a future sustainable partnership with the natural world.

Carolyn Merchant was born on July 12, 1936, in Rochester, New York, the daughter of George and Elizabeth (Barnes) Merchant. She attended Vassar College, graduating with a bachelor's degree in 1958. She earned a master's degree four years later in 1962, from the University of Wisconsin at Madison, where she also earned her Ph.D. in 1967. Beginning in 1969, Merchant taught as a lecturer at the University of San Francisco, becoming an assistant professor of history of science in 1974, and staying until 1978. The following year she became an assistant professor at the University of California at Berkeley (UCB), and one year later she was promoted to associate professor of environmental history, philosophy, and ethics.

Intrigued by the interactions between humans and their natural environment over time, Merchant focused her research on American environmental and cultural history within the larger contexts of philosophy and the history of science. In examining the relationship of certain ideas to cultural trends, Merchant began looking into the women's and ecology movements and eventually recast her field of study to encompass the historical roots of both. The culmination of these scholarly investigations was *The Death of Nature: Women, Ecology, and the Scientific Revolution* (1980). Merchant emphasizes the age-old association between women and nature and explores these historical connections in light of the exploitation that has left both women and the environment oppressed by culture and the economy. She undertakes a critical reassessment of the scientific revolution in the book and demonstrates how scientific progress has contributed to the domination of both women and nature. Though the term *ecofeminism* had been around since the mid-1970s, it was not until the publication of trailblazing books such as *The Death of Nature* that the connection between feminist and ecological ideas became a popular framework for interpreting interactions between humans and the environment. New dialogues arose as people began to look at contemporary views of nature and society through a gender-based perspective, leading to new analyses of arguments about the causes of environmental degradation. For example, patriarchal parenting roles were examined and implicated in the way that some boys, as they grow up, come to want control over their environment, and people's differing outlooks on the natural world now took on gendered explanations. Merchant's book helped to establish ecofeminism as an intellectual movement and helped it develop into new approaches to action.

In a later book, *Radical Ecology: The Search for a Livable World* (1992), Merchant discusses another new concept—radical ecology—that she sees as an ethic that seeks fundamental changes in the way society and its institutions relate to nature and the environment. An offshoot of social ecology, which Merchant describes as the interactions among people and the various political and social customs that shape their views of nature and its resources, radical ecology urges new patterns of thought, challenges the political and economic order, and supports social movements in the restoration and protection of the environment. In *Radical Ecology*, Merchant discusses how other concepts such as deep ecology, ecofeminism, sustainable development, and green politics fit into the definition of radical ecology and shows how, by presenting alternative views, it raises public consciousness and exposes some of the social and scientific assumptions that underlie the mainstream environmental movement.

Her next book, *Earthcare: Women and the Environment*, was published in 1995. It is a collection of essays that brings together a comprehensive summary of 15 years of Merchant's work. The range of essays provides a good balance between the scholarly and the practical. Some deal with the various definitions of ecofeminism and how they depict the factors that curtail the advancement of women and the protection of the environment. Others give examples of how women have participated in the conservation movement through history and up to the present. She concludes the collection by extending the hope that humans can be equal partners with nature rather than trying to control it and that diversity as well as biodiversity should be valued.

Merchant's research into the interactions between nature and culture includes *Green Versus Gold: Sources in California's Environmental History* (1998), which she edited. It is an investigation of California's environmental history: from the American Indians who lived there, to the gold rush, logging, cattle ranching, water use, and urbanization. She brought together documents from California's ecological history along with other primary sources and interpretive essays to illuminate the state's ongoing struggle between environment and economy.

*Reinventing Nature: The Fate of Nature in Western Culture* (2004) is an examination of the different concepts of "Eden" through history: some have seen it as a state that has been in continual decline due to human degradation of it; others have seen Eden as something that can only be achieved through explicit attempts to create it.

Merchant's work has helped put the contemporary disharmony over environmentalism into useful context and has provided guidelines for policy reassessment. Her research has been recognized and encouraged widely—in 1984 she was awarded a Fulbright senior scholarship in Sweden, in 1991 she was the ecofeminist scholar at Murdoch University in western Australia, and she has also received fellowships from the Center for Advanced Study in the Behavioral Sciences at Stanford University, the American Council of Learned Societies, and the Guggenheim Foundation. She has served on the executive committees of the American Society for Environmental History and the History of Science Society and has served on the advisory boards of *Environmental History Review*, *Environmental Ethics*, *International Journal of Ecoforestry*, and the Association for the Study of Literature and the Environment. She has written and edited several reference volumes: *The Columbia Guide to American Environmental History* (2002, 2007), *Major Problems in American Environmental History* (1993, 2005), and the three-volume *Encyclopedia of World Environmental History*, (2004). Merchant received the Career Achievement Award from the UCB College of Natural Resources in 2008. She continues to teach at UCB and lives in Berkeley, California.

### BIBLIOGRAPHY

"Carolyn Merchant," ecnr.berkeley.edu/facPage/dispFP.php?I=617; Gottlieb, Robert, *Forcing the Spring*, 1993; Kaufman, Polly Welts, "Earthcare: Women and the Environment," *Pacific Historical Review*, 1997; Merchant, Carolyn, *The Death of Nature: Women, Ecology, and the Scientific Revolution*, 1980; Merchant, Carolyn, *Earthcare: Women and the Environment*, 1995; Merchant, Carolyn, *Radical Ecology: The Search for a Livable World*, 1992; Merchant, Carolyn, ed., *Green Versus Gold: Sources in California's Environmental History*, 1998; Mills, Stephanie, "The Death of Nature: Women, Ecology and the Scientific Revolution," *Whole Earth Review*, 1996.

## Merculieff, Ilarion (Larry)

Aleut Elder, Founder of the International Bering Sea Forum and The Alaska Indigenous Peoples' Council for Marine Mammals

Aleut elder Ilarion (Larry) Merculieff leads native organizations into areas of scientific research, community wellness, and political efforts to conserve lands, aquatic life, and ancient ways of survival. He has been instrumental in achieving legal, cultural, and economic victories for Aleuts and other indigenous peoples beginning in 1968. His primary missions are to protect Alaska's environment, subsistence rights, the Bering Sea, and restoration of "Original Teachings" and "Laws for Living" throughout the world. Merculieff also has the role of transmitting what he learns from indigenous wisdom-holders to young people and internationally. He brings highly sophisticated and advanced insights and information from the Aleut culture and wisdomkeepers of many traditions, to environmental policy makers and the general public throughout the Western Hemisphere.

Ilarion (Larry) Merculieff (Aleut) grew up on the Pribilof Islands in the Bering Sea, 500 miles from mainland Alaska. Ilarion, or Larry as he was called, held natural leadership skills. At the age of four, he was given his tra-

Larry Merculieff (Photograph by Roy Corral)

ditional name, Kuuyux, which is a name given to one person in each lifetime. This name, stemming from a 10,000-year-old culture, means "extension," like an arm extending out from the body, or "bridge" from ancient to modern times. When he was 18 years old, the leaders of his village asked him to be their representative in Washington, D.C., to implement provisions of the Fur Seal Act of 1966. This Act eliminated the total control that the U.S. Government held over the Aleuts and granted the right to vote in state and federal elections. But most formative for Merculieff have been his traditional upbringing and the sacred ceremonies in which he participates with people of many traditions, including the Maori, Hopi, Mapuche, Mayan, and Stony Elders whose wisdom continually informs him.

The Aleut people are known as people of the sea lion. During Merculieff's lifetime, 80 percent of the sea lions vanished. He saw sea lions feed on northern fur seal pups, more than ever in living memory; rapidly declining populations of northern fur seals, seabirds, sea otters, and crabs; and lived through the subsequent tribe-wide effect of this on St. Paul Island. Over a ten-year period, he estimates that as much as 70 percent of the young men between the ages 17 and 27 years old were lost to incarceration for felony crimes, accidental death to due to alcohol, murder, domestic violence, and suicide. Prior to this time, these things did not occur.(on such a scale) Larry Merculieff points to the fact that the relationship between older, more experienced sea lion hunters and the young men was effectively severed because the older hunters, being self-regulating, cut down their hunting significantly. In an effort to convoke cultural and community wellness, Merculieff led a successful campaign and the largest subsistence rights march in Alaska's history to regain Alaskan Native fishing rights in traditional fishing areas along state controlled rivers. Later he led a successful four-year effort to gain federal and international recognition of the rights of Alaska's coastal peoples to take halibut for subsistence purposes. His leadership and negotiation skills among various communities and professions, among tribal officials, scientists, federal and state government, environmentalists, and youth leaders have made Larry Merculieff a busy man during turbulent times in the Bering Sea and throughout Alaska and the world.

As Coordinator of the Bering Sea Council of Elders, he worked with Alaska Native elders from seven regions of Alaska who focused on the health of the Bering Sea ecosystem and the coastal and river cultures who depend on the Bering Sea. These elders have asked him to pursue funding for a grand gathering of elders who want to share their concerns about these changing times with the younger generations.

Merculieff is a principal co-founder of the Alaska Forum on the Environment, Alaska Oceans Network, International Bering Sea Forum and The Alaska Indigenous Peoples' Council for Marine Mammals. From 1990 to 1994 he was City Manager of the City of St. Paul, Alaska. In 1994, Merculieff served as chairperson of the Alaska Chapter of The Nature Conservancy, and became principal advocate for the establishment of the Pribilof Islands National Maritime Wildlife Refuge. He directed Environmental Programs for the Alaska Inter-Tribal Council in 1998, and served as Director of Public Policy and Advocacy for the Rural Alaska Community Action Program (2000-2003). Most recently, Merculieff served as a principal United States representative on the North American Steering Committee that conducted the Convening of Indigenous Peoples for the Healing of Mother Earth and Restoration of Original Teachings in Chiapas, Mexico, in March 2008.

Merculieff's writing is published in such magazines as *Cultural Survival*, *YES*, *RED INK*, and *First Alaskans*, and was featured in the "American Heroes" section of the *National Wildlife* magazine. He received the Alaska Native Writers on the Environment Award, Buffet Finalist Award for Indigenous Leadership, Rasmuson Foundation award for Creative Non-Fiction, and the Environmental Excellence Award for lifetime achievements.

Merculieff is currently an independent consultant and the volunteer Deputy Director of the Alaska Native Science Commission. He is now speaking, in a multi-state tour, to educate the general public on climate change and ocean acidification. He lives in Anchorage, Alaska.

## Bibliography

Merculieff, Larry, Eco-Arts Festival, Boulder, Colorado, September, 2007, www.democraticing.org; Klaver, Ellen, interview with Larry Merculieff, November 13, 2007; Climate data to be gathered from Natives in Alaska and Russia (mp3 audio) Alaska Public Telecommunications, May 2006; Holleman, Mary Beth, "Hot Passion for a Cold Ecosystem," National Wildlife Federation, 1996.

# Miller, Laura

(November 18, 1958– )
Mayor of Dallas, TX, Co-founder of Texas Clean Air Cities Coalition

As mayor of Dallas, Laura Miller co-founded and led the Texas Clean Air Cities Coalition in August 2006 to oppose a proposal by energy company TXU to build 11 new coal-fired power plants across Texas. The coalition, which included more than 20 Texas cities and counties, opposed the "fast-tracking" of several of the proposed power plants, which was facilitated by Texas Governor Rick Perry through an executive order signed in 2006. Miller and the coalition also opposed the plants on the grounds they would further deteriorate air quality in Central and North Texas. Miller and the coalition planned to intervene in the permit hearings on each of the plants conducted by the Texas Commission on Environmental Quality. Ultimately, such intervention became unnecessary as a state district court in Austin ruled that Perry lacked the authority to issue the executive order facilitating fast-tracking of the permitting process for the plants, and because plans for the majority of the plants were dropped after private equity firms KKR, Texas Pacific Group and Goldman Sachs purchased TXU (now Oncor Electric Delivery, Luminant, and TXU Energy) in 2007. Miller's work and battle against TXU is the subject of the Alpheus Media documentary film *Fighting Goliath: The Texas Coal Wars*, narrated by Robert Redford and directed by Mat Hames and George Sledge.

Laura Miller was born on November 18, 1958, in Baltimore and lived in Concord, Massachusetts, as a child. Her parents divorced when she was 11. A few years later, Miller moved with her father to Connecticut and graduated from Rippowam High School in Stamford. As a student at Rippowam, Miller founded Students With A Purpose, a group to raise money to pay for cleaning supplies to keep the school's water fountains clean. The group sold pickles at lunch and bagels during breakfast to raise the funds it needed.

After graduating from high school, Miller attended the University of Wisconsin-Madison. While in college, Miller was named one of America's "Top 10 College Women" by *Glamour* magazine.

Miller first came to Dallas as part of a summer internship program through the university, and was assigned to work for the Style section of the now-defunct *Dallas Times Herald*.

After graduating from college, Miller worked at *The Miami Herald* and traveled Europe as a free-lance writer for a year. After a year abroad, Miller was hired by *The Dallas Morning News* as an investigative reporter. Her work included an exposé on NCAA recruiting violations.

While at the *Morning News*, Miller was set up with state legislator and lawyer Steve Wolens, a Democratic state representative, on a blind date by former Dallas County Commissioner Chris Semos. After leaving Texas and working briefly at the *New York Daily News*, Miller returned to Dallas, married Wolens, and was hired as metro columnist for the *Dallas Times-Herald*.

After her tenure at the *Times-Herald*, Miller worked at *D* magazine and was a columnist for the *Dallas Observer*, an alternative weekly newspaper. During her time with the *Observer*, Miller became a frequent and outspoken critic of Dallas city government. Her criticism of city government ultimately turned into a desire to work for change, and Miller decided to run for Dallas City Council.

Miller was elected to the Dallas City Council representing District 3 in 1998. Shortly after taking office, she was diagnosed with breast cancer, from which she eventually made a full recovery.

In 2001, after popular Dallas Mayor Ron Kirk announced he would resign to seek the

Democratic Party's nomination for a U.S. Senate seat from Texas, Miller entered the race for Kirk's unexpired term, and was elected mayor of Dallas in 2002.

During her tenure as mayor, Miller led the charge to pass an ordinance prohibiting discrimination on the basis of sexual orientation for city employees, and worked for the construction of a $23 million homeless assistance center, and the continued redevelopment of downtown Dallas. As mayor, Miller also fought for and won approval of a strengthened smoking ban for Dallas. In 2007, Miller elected not to seek another term as mayor.

In April of 2008, Poulsbo, Washington-based Summit Energy hired Miller to handle public relations for a project that would result in the construction of a coal gasification plant in Texas. The plant was proposed as an integrated gasification combined cycle coal plant, which pollutes less than traditional coal plants. Upon accepting the position with Summit, Miller resigned from leading the Texas Clean Air Cities Coalition.

Miller and Wolens have two daughters, Alex and Lily, and a son, Max.

### BIBLIOGRAPHY

Nelson, Colleen McCain, "Miller's intensity doesn't waver from childhood to motherhood," *The Dallas Morning News*, February 10, 2002; Official biography, City of Dallas, www.dallascityhall.com/pdf/mcc/LauraMillerBiography.pdf; Souder, Elizabeth, "Miller batting for coal: Ex-Mayor doing PR for firm wanting to build lower-polluting plant," *The Dallas Morning News*, April 1, 2008; Schulte, Bret, "A Texas Mess Over Coal; Proposed plants have stirred a clean-air uproar," *U.S. News & World Report*, November 26, 2006; "Film Highlights Former Mayor's Coal Fight, CBS 11 TV, Dallas, cbs11tv.com/entertainment/Laura.Miller.Movie.2.627518.html.

## Mills, Enos
(April 22, 1870–September 21, 1922)
Naturalist, Conservationist

Mountaineer and naturalist Enos Mills is remembered as the "Father of Rocky Mountain National Park." From age 14 he roamed the Colorado mountains and guided visitors in forests below Longs Peak. A chance meeting with JOHN MUIR in 1889 led Mills to a career as a nature writer and conservationist. He authored 16 books, including *Wild Life on the Rockies* (1909) and *Your National Parks* (1917), which along with his public speaking tours taught a postfrontier generation to revere wild places. He lobbied for almost a decade to have the federal government establish a national park to protect the Rocky Mountains. His original vision called for a park along the crest of the Rockies from Wyoming to New Mexico. In 1915, Congress protected a small fraction of that with the establishment of Rocky Mountain National Park, which now includes 400 square miles of land near Estes Park in northern Colorado.

Born outside Pleasanton, Kansas, on April 22, 1870, Enos Abijah Mills grew up in a Quaker farm family. His parents, Enos and Ann (Lamb) Mills, were originally from Indiana but had traveled west, mining in the Rockies before homesteading in Kansas. A sickly child, Mills often missed school but read widely on his own. At age 14 he was sent to visit relatives in Colorado with hopes of improving his health. Mills stayed with his uncle, the Reverend Elkanah Lamb, at his ranch at the base of 14,255-feet-high Longs Peak. The Lamb family guided people up the mountain and led Mills on his first ascent.

Mountain air and a better diet improved Mills's health immediately. Within a year he had built a small cabin homestead across the valley from the Lamb Ranch. Taking seasonal jobs around the West, he traveled as far away as Butte, Montana, where he started as a toolboy in the copper mines. On a trip to San Francisco in 1889, Mills was walking along the beach in Golden Gate Park when by chance he met the famous mountain man and wilderness writer John Muir. Muir encouraged Mills to share his strong interest in nature by writing for magazines. Mills began to document his treks, keeping journals and carrying an Eastman Kodak pocket camera. Soon he was publishing quick-paced, inspirational essays in national magazines such as *Harper's* and *Saturday Evening Post*. He would write 16 books and take more than 15,000 photographs during his lifetime.

In 1902 Mills bought the Lamb Ranch from his uncle. Changing its name to the Longs Peak Inn, he used it to develop his Trail School, a guide service offering nature walks popular with visitors of all ages. He soon expanded the inn's facilities, designing furniture and buildings to fit the surroundings while adding modern amenities such as steam heat and telephones. Around 1906 he became the official Colorado snow observer, measuring wind speeds and snow depths for the state Department of Agriculture. At the same time he took a more active stance in the national environmental conservation movement, joining others in the fight to preserve Niagara Falls in 1906.

The growing threat to nature in other areas of the country, and the conservationist response to it, alerted Mills to the urgency of protecting the best parts of the Rocky Mountains. Mills envisioned a huge park preserve that would stretch along the mountain crest from Wyoming to New Mexico. Persuading legislators to create even a smaller version of this park turned into a seven-year fight. Mills wrote hundreds of letters and lectured around the country, emphasizing the importance of protecting natural areas from settlement. He learned valuable lessons in politics while lobbying with Muir against the damming of California's Hetch Hetchy Valley. Although they lost the fight, the struggle tested Mills's activism and gave him experience in Washington. He also won a minor battle. To balance the Hetch Hetchy verdict, the Wilson administration gave the country something Muir, Mills, and other preservationists had been requesting for several years: a separate National Park Service within the Department of the Interior, whose sole role was to create and protect national parks. This was a great improvement over the previous arrangement, in which many separate entities shared the administration of the parks, and there had been no effective coordination.

Mills's sometimes ferocious and always untiring activism finally bore fruit. In 1915 an Act of Congress signed by Pres. Woodrow Wilson set aside 358.5 square miles of land, near the heart of Colorado, to be preserved and protected as a national park. The *Denver Post* praised Mills's "single-handed" efforts and gave him sole credit for the park's creation.

Mills's travels had yielded another success as well. At a lecture in Cleveland, Ohio, a young woman named Esther Burnell was swayed by Mills's words and in time decided to visit the Longs Peak Inn. After completing college, in 1916 she homesteaded near Estes Park and started working for the curmudgeonly Mills as his secretary. She married him in 1918. Their daughter, Enda, was born during a snowstorm the next year.

Mills believed passionately that nature was a necessary adjunct to civilization, teaching that "wilderness is the safety zone of the world." The park that exists because of his vision now draws more than three million visitors a year. On September 21, 1922, Mills died suddenly at age 52 of an unknown illness, at his home in Colorado. His homestead cabin, now on the National Register of Historic Places, is maintained by his descendants as an informal museum dedicated to Mills's life and work.

### BIBLIOGRAPHY

Drummond, Alexander A., *Enos Mills: Citizen of Nature*, 1995; "Enos Mills Cabin," www.home.earthlink.net/~enosmillscbn/index.htm; McKibben, Bill, "Hero of the Wilderness," *New York Review of Books*, 1989; Mills, Enos and James H Pickering, *Enos Mill's Colorado*, 2005; Mills, Enos, *Radiant Days: Writings by Enos Mills*, 1994; Mills, Enos, John Fielder, and T. A. Barron, *Rocky Mountain National Park: A 100 Year Perspective*, 1995; Mills, Ester Burnell and Hildegarde Hawthorne, *Enos A. Mills of the Rockies*, 2001; Stansfield, John, *Enos Mills: Rocky Mountain Naturalist*, 2005; Wild, Peter, *Enos Mills*, 1979.

## Mills, Stephanie

(September 11, 1948– )
Bioregionalist, Writer

Stephanie Mills's well-known commencement address at Mills College in 1969, in which she dramatically extolled the virtues of population control, catapulted her into the limelight literally overnight, and she has been active as an organizer, editor, and author ever since. Her current focus is on bioregionalism, a philosophy that is based on the idea that humans should become familiar with the natural processes of the land upon which they live, and having achieved an appreciation for the land, act appropriately towards it.

Stephanie Mills was born on September 11, 1948, in Berkeley, California, to Robert and Edith Mills. She spent her childhood in the city she refers to in her memoir, *Whatever Happened to Ecology?* as "Anywhere, USA." The rest of us refer to it as Phoenix, Arizona. Due to the suburban nature of the Phoenix area, Mills does not feel as if she grew up in the desert. But in spite of the generic immediate scenery of her childhood, the desert landscape of Arizona instilled in her an appreciation for vast open spaces, the preciousness of water, and the desert's native plants and animals.

Mills attended Mills College in Oakland, California, where she witnessed first hand the fervor and passion of the antiwar movement. For a variety of reasons, however, she did not participate. She saw one of the shortcomings of the student movement as its not being comprehensive enough. The "war against the planet," the degradation of the environment, was being ignored, and Mills was an ambivalent, apolitical participator in the generation-wide effort of the 1960s to (as she puts it), "Fix It and Realize the Ideal." In college, Mills had an environmental epiphany while reading *The Place No One Knew: Glen Canyon of the Colorado*, which was published by the Sierra Club in 1963 and contains photographs by Eliot Porter of pre-dam Glen Canyon. This book, coupled with the marijuana she was using at the time she read it, connected her to the threats facing planet Earth and inspired a desire to preserve all remaining intact wilderness. As student speaker at her 1969 commencement, Mills spoke about the problem of overpopulation, stating that she was "terribly saddened that the most humane thing for me to do is to have no children at all." Her speech, "The Future Is A Cruel Hoax," received quite a bit of attention in the national media. It was widely reprinted and catapulted her to celebrity status.

After her graduation, Mills began a career of activism, writing and editing in the San Francisco Bay area. She worked as a Planned Parenthood campus organizer, as editor in chief of *Earth Times*, and as a conference coordinator for her alma mater, Mills College, during the years between 1969 and 1974. She then went to Georgia for a year and worked as a writer for a birth control center. Returning to San Francisco in 1975, Mills took a position as director of outings program with DAVID BROWER's Friends of the Earth. She remembers the staff as being outgoing and volatile. It was, she says, "maddeningly unbureaucratic and refreshingly nonprofessional. It really couldn't afford to be otherwise." She moved up to director of membership development, a fundraising position that she herself claims she was not very good at. She kept the job because she liked the company, and her "big break" came when she was offered the editorship of Friends of the Earth's main publication, *Not Man Apart*. She edited the journal for the years of 1977 and 1978, in the process coming to a realization that the hierarchical structure of Friends of the Earth and other similar organizations rendered them ineffective, incapable of producing a fundamental change in culture. At this point she became curious about the potential of bioregional organizations.

Bioregionalism focuses on natural history in an attempt to address that which is wild and native and to help humans achieve a "sense of place." It teaches people to really know where they live, to recognize native plants and animals, to understand local weather patterns, and to have an appreciation for such overlooked features as soil, wildflowers, fire, and moon cycles. In an article for *Sierra*, Mills writes, "Only by alighting—and staying put—do we stand a chance of finding out who we are, where we are, and what we are going to do about it."

After leaving Friends of the Earth, Mills helped to plan a conference called "Technology: Over the Invisible Line?" that took place in 1979. Technology became a major interest area for Mills, who would go on to make significant intellectual contributions to the debate on a highly technologized world. Immediately after the conference, Mills took a position with the journal *Coevolution Quarterly* as an assistant editor, and in 1981, she was invited to guest-edit a special issue on bioregions. After this issue's success, she became a full editor of the magazine, which was later renamed *Whole Earth*. She remained in this position for two years, until 1982, when she became editor in chief and research director for California Tomorrow, a nonprofit organization dedicated to helping to build a society in which diversity of race, culture, and language are embraced as our greatest strengths. Then, from 1983 to 1984 she acted as director of development for World College West in San Rafael, California.

In 1984, Mills moved to northwest Lower Michigan and dedicated herself to freelance writing, publishing articles in such periodicals as *Sierra*, *Orion* and *Whole Earth Review*. She has written four books, including her memoir *Whatever Happened to Ecology?* (1989); the two-part *In Service of the Wild* (1995), whose first part describes the ecological restoration of her farm in Michigan's Upper Peninsula, and whose second part tells five other land restoration stories, among them that of ALDO LEOPOLD and his "shack" and the Nature Conservancy's restoration of savanna and prairie in northern Illinois. Her 2002 *Epicurean Simplicity* celebrates the simple life and *Tough Little Beauties* (2007) is a varied collection of her essays. Mills also contributed to and edited *In Praise of Nature* (1990), a collection of reviews and excerpts from many of the best books about nature and humans in nature. *In Praise of Nature* is built around five essays, "Earth," "Air," "Fire," "Water," and "Spirit" and contains work from such authors as HERMAN DALY and PAUL EHRLICH. *Turning Away from Technology: A Vision for the 21st Century* (1997) collects the proceedings of two historic MegaTechnology conferences held in 1993 and 1994, and presents 50 prominent thinkers' ideas on the negative impacts of technology. She is currently at work on a biography of Robert Swann, a World War II pacifist who pioneer decentralist economic alternatives such as community land trusts.

Mills continues to be active in various environmental and activist organizations. She was vice president of Earth First! Foundation for three years, from 1986 until 1989, and she works with the Traverse Area Community Currency Corporation, which issues a local currency. In recent years she has taught as an adjunct professor at Grand Valley State University's Northwest Michigan campus. She travels frequently to read from her books, give formal lectures, and less formal talks. She has begun to incorporate the subject of Peak Oil into her reflections from the podium.

In 1987, she received an award from Friends of the United Nations Environment Program, in 1992, was named an *Utne Reader* visionary, and in 2008 she was named Great Lakes Bioneer of the Year.

Mills lives in Maple City, Michigan. She is divorced and has no children, just as she promised in her commencement address.

### BIBLIOGRAPHY

Baker, Will, "Whatever Happened to Ecology?," *Whole Earth Review*, 1991; Mills, Stephanie, "The Future Is A Cruel Hoax," in *American Earth: Environmental Writing Since Thoreau*, edited by Bill McKibben, 2008; Mills, Stephanie, "The Journey Home," *Sierra*, 1997; Mills, Stephanie, *Whatever Happened to Ecology?* 1989; "Stephanie Mills: Author, Speaker, Bioregionalist," www.smillswriter.com.

## Mitchell, George J.

(August 20, 1933– )
U.S. Attorney, U. S. Senator from Maine, Diplomat

A former senator from Maine, George Mitchell often led the fight to pass key environmental legislation throughout his lengthy career in politics. A consensus builder on the Committee on Environment and Public Works for 14 years, he championed the first major acid rain bill, Superfund toxic waste cleanup, and the reauthorization of the Clean Air Act, among other important pieces of legislation. Appointed Senate majority leader in 1988, he authored the book *World On Fire* (1990), which focused on the greenhouse effect. Since his retirement in 1995, Mitchell has held leadership roles in the quest to solve other problems, and is best known for his role in negotiating a historic peace agreement in Northern Ireland (1998) and bringing to light the use of steroids by Major League Baseball players (2007).

George John Mitchell was born on August 20, 1933, in Waterville, Maine, to working-class parents George and Mary (Saad) Mitchell. Mitchell spent his youth in Waterville. After receiving his bachelor's degree from Bowdoin College in 1954, he entered the military and served as an officer in the United States Army Counterintelligence Corps until 1956. He married Sally Heath in 1959. They had one daughter, Andrea. In 1960 he earned a law degree from Georgetown University. An attorney in government and private practice for much of the 1960s and 1970s, he served as a trial lawyer in the Antitrust Division of the Justice Department for two years.

He then made a life-changing move, taking a position in Washington, D.C., as executive assistant to Maine's senior congressman, Sen. EDMUND MUSKIE, who became Mitchell's most important political mentor. Muskie was a known conservationist and political powerhouse; Mitchell never forgot his influence. Though he returned to private law practice in Maine in 1965, he remained active in the Maine Democratic Party. In 1968 and 1972, Mitchell served as deputy director for Muskie's vice presidential and presidential campaigns. Mitchell made an unsuccessful run for governor of Maine in 1974, but his political advancement was not slowed. In 1977, he was appointed U.S. attorney for the state of Maine, after Muskie had recommended him to Pres. JIMMY CARTER. Both Muskie and Carter were pleased with Mitchell's performance, and in 1979, the president appointed Mitchell to a newly created U.S. district court judgeship in Bangor, Maine.

Mitchell's star continued to rise. In 1980, when Muskie was named U.S. secretary of state, he recommended that Mitchell fill the remaining two years of his congressional term. Gov. Joseph Brennan appointed Mitchell to the post, beginning his 14-year career in the Senate. Senator Muskie had been working on legislation pertaining to windfall profits tax, waste treatment costs, veterans' education, and approval of the Strategic Arms Limitation Talks (SALT) II treaty. Senator Mitchell was thrust into committee work, eventually serving on the Environment and Public Works, Finance, Veterans Affairs, Governmental Affairs, and Senate Democratic Steering Committees. Among Mitchell's first tasks was working with Sen. William Cohen to achieve the passage of the Maine Indian Lands Claim settlement of 1980.

In 1982, the state of Maine faced a new threat. Growing concern about waste materials from nuclear power plants led to numerous studies on long-term storage options. One federal report suggested that parts of Maine could act as radioactive waste repositories. Citing the state's faultline geology, Mitchell successfully fought this plan. His constituents were pleased. That same year, Mitchell won his first Senate race with 61 percent of the vote.

Other major legislation championed by Mitchell included the Clean Water Act, passed in 1987. Mitchell worked to override Pres. Ronald Reagan's veto of the act, criticizing the president for his failure to keep his promises about funding clean water programs. The Clean Water Act was a highpoint in Mitchell's congressional record. Three years later, he worked to expand the landmark legislation. A 1990 amendment provided financial resources to small communities for upgrading waste treatment facilities and dealing with runoff or nonpoint-source pollution. After being re-elected by a landslide 81 percent of the vote in 1988, Mitchell authored the nation's first oil spill prevention and cleanup bill, the Oil Pollution Act of 1990. The act preserved the right of states to regulate standards for oil transport more strictly than federal law.

Mitchell was instrumental in the 1990 passage of the Clean Air Act, which he brought to the floor and pushed until it was signed into law. The original Clean Air Act, passed in 1970, had aimed at obvious sources of pollution; the 1990 law was aimed at invisible pollutants and the secondary effects of cleanup technologies, such as acid rain caused by high-stack chimneys. While preparing for the Clean Air Act fight, Mitchell put his research on the environment to good use by writing a book about pollution's effects on the atmosphere. *World On Fire*, published in 1990, described the new "greenhouse effect" and suggested new policies to slow the process of global warming. *New York Times* book reviewer Tom Yulesman wrote that the book was significant in that it reflected "how concern for the environment [by politicians] has deepended since the time when Ronald Reagan declared that trees are a major source of air pollution."

Mitchell had also inherited Senator Muskie's files on the Superfund legislation, which established a Hazardous Substance Response

Trust Fund from fees on oil and chemical industries. The fund paid for certain losses resulting from releases of hazardous chemicals. The new Comprehensive Environmental Response Compensation and Liability Act also defined "hazardous substances" more clearly than had been previously outlined in the Clean Air Act, the Clean Water Act (1972), the Solid Waste Disposal Act (1965), and the Toxic Substances Control Act (1976). Mitchell's work on this and other legislation earned him the Wilderness Society's prestigious Ansel Adams Award in 1994. Among other achievements, he counted successes in the areas of childcare, affordable housing, civil rights, campaign finance reform, and universal health care.

Mitchell also accumulated political bonuses. In late 1984 he was appointed chairman of the Democratic Senatorial Campaign Committee and led the Democrats in gaining 11 seats and majority control of the Senate. He was then appointed to the Select Committee on the Iran-Contra Affair in 1987, from which he reminded Oliver North that "God does not take sides in American politics." His performance during the Iran-Contra hearings helped him win the post of Senate majority leader in 1988, succeeding Robert Byrd.

In March 1994, George Mitchell announced his decision to retire from the Senate at the end of his term, after six years of being voted the "most respected member" of that organization. A month later, when Justice Harry A. Blackmun retired from the U.S. Supreme Court, Mitchell quickly became Pres. Bill Clinton's top choice to replace the exiting justice. Though Mitchell turned down the nomination, he found other ways to serve the president. He remained active in international politics, becoming special adviser to the president and the secretary of state for economic initiatives in Ireland in 1995. He compiled the Mitchell Report, released on January 24, 1996, which called for a phasing-out of guerilla weapons in Northern Ireland in addition to elections prior to the opening of peace talks. After serving as moderator for more than 22 months, Mitchell's mission was eventually completed on April 12, 1998, with the signing of a multilateral peace agreement, approved by public referendum. His efforts won him a nomination for the 1998 Nobel Peace Prize, the Presidential Medal of Freedom in 1999, and the 1998 Liberty Medal from the National Constitution Center.

In 1999, Mitchell founded the Senator George J. Mitchell Scholarship Research Institute, which has provided more than $1.6 million in funds for worthy Maine students. Bowdoin College also serves as repository for the senator's papers.

In 2006, Mitchell was asked by Major League Baseball Commissioner Bud Selig to head up an investigation of steroid use by major league baseball players. Mitchell's report, released in December of 2007, included the names of 89 players, for whom it found evidence of steroid use, including many all-stars and most valuable players.

**BIBLIOGRAPHY**

Blumenthal, Stanley, "The Wisdom of George Mitchell," *New Yorker*, 1994; Mitchell, George J., *Making Peace*, 1999; Mitchell, George J., *World on Fire*, 1990; "The Mitchell Institute," www.mitchellinstitute.org; Power, Samantha, "George Mitchell," *Time*, 2008.

## Mittermeier, Russell
(November 8, 1949– )
Zoologist, President of Conservation International

Russell Mittermeier is an internationally recognized expert on primates and reptiles. Since the mid-1970s he has been a proponent of conservation worldwide. As president of Conservation International (CI), a nongovernmental organization that facilitates conservation in the most biodiverse regions of the world, Mittermeier acts as an influential advocate of biodiversity preservation.

Russell Alan Mittermeier was born on November 8, 1949, in Bronx, New York. His mother stimulated his interest in the natural world by taking him to the Bronx Zoo and the American Museum of Natural History and allowed him to assemble a collection of pet reptiles and amphibians. By the age of six, Mittermeier had decided to become a jungle explorer.

Mittermeier studied at Dartmouth College and was given the opportunity to spend his senior year in Central America, with a fellowship to study monkeys. He was a member of Phi Beta Kappa and graduated *summa cum laude* from Dartmouth in 1971. Continuing on to Harvard University, Mittermeier earned an M.A. (1973) and a Ph.D. (1977), both in biological anthropology. His doctoral research took place in Surinam, one of the most biodiverse rain forests in the world. Mittermeier developed a great familiarity with and affection for Surinam's flora and fauna, as well as for its Maroon people, rain forest–dwelling descendants of escaped slaves who, according to a *Time* profile of Mittermeier, say that the forest goes "to the heart of our society."

Mittermeier's extensive travels in Surinam, Madagascar, and other poor tropical countries convinced him that poverty is the greatest culprit in environmental destruction. The land that poor people must farm is often unsuitable for agriculture, and cultivation results in erosion of soil and sometimes, on steep slopes, devastating landslides. When the best agricultural land is claimed by wealthier owners, poor people must colonize forested areas to grow their food. And when economies are designed so that small-scale subsistence farming does not even produce enough food for families, farmers who live near forests resort to poaching or selling lumber. Mittermeier has worked with several international conservation organizations that collaborate with local governments and nonprofit organizations to promote environmental conservation. Since 1976, he has served the conservation movement in a variety of capacities, ranging from conservation associate at the New York Zoological Society (1976–1977), to consultant for the World Conservation Union (since 1983), to chairperson of the World Bank Task Force of Biological Diversity (1988). Other organizations he has worked with include the World Wildlife Fund–U.S., the World Health Organization, and conservationist organizations in Peru and Brazil.

Since 1989, Mittermeier has been president of Conservation International (CI), which focuses its efforts on areas of the world that harbor the most biodiversity. CI concentrates on three types of biodiverse regions. Global Biodiversity Hotspots (see biodiversityhotspots.org) are the 34 areas of the world that are most biodiverse but are threatened by human activity, Wilderness Areas are rich like the biodiversity hotspots but are of a minimum size of 10,000 square kilometers, with fewer than 5 humans per square kilometer, and retain original vegetation in at least 70 percent of their area. CI has identified 37 areas that fulfill these requirements, and Mittermeier profiled them in the book he co-wrote with his wife Cristina Goettsch and atricio Robles Gil in *Wilderness: Earth's Last Wild Places* (2002). The final area of focus for CI is Oceans and Seascapes—CI works in three of these rich yet endangered marine areas. CI's goals are to save species, conserve landscapes and seascapes, empower local communities to use their natural resources effectively and responsibly, and to develop a conservation ethic.

In addition to his work with CI, Mittermeier has been an adjunct professor at the State University of New York at Stony Brook since 1977, is a scientific fellow of the New York Zoological Society, and a member of the Linnean Society of London. He has written several books and over 200 scholarly papers.

BIBLIOGRAPHY

Conniff, Richard, "Primate Central: Counting Species has Long Been a Feathery Obsession, but Now a World-Renowned Conservation Biologist Wants Globetrotters to Pursue Other Finds…," *Audubon*, 2007; "Conservation International," www.conservation.org; Mittermeier, Russell, *Lemurs of Madagascar*, 1994; Mittermeier, Russell, *Primate Conservation in the Tropical Rain Forest*, 1987; Mittermeier, Russell, *Pantanal: South America's Wetland Jewel*, 2006; Rosenblatt, Roger, "Into the Woods," *Time*, 1998.

## Montague, Peter
(November 6, 1938– )
Director of the Environmental Research Foundation, Editor of *Rachel's Environmental and Health Weekly*

Peter Montague has been providing solid, understandable, scientific information about the effects of toxic substances on human health since 1980, when he founded the Environmental Research Foundation (ERF). He edits a weekly newsletter entitled *Rachel's Environmental and Health Weekly*, which covers technical issues that are either ignored, censored, or just poorly treated by the mass media. It is sent for free by e-mail to more than 10,000 subscribers, with the goal, according to the ERF mission statement, of "helping people find the information they need to fight for environmental justice in their own communities." Montague is a strong proponent of the precautionary principle—"a lens for decision-making" through which we should ask, before making any decision, "How can we minimize harm to the environment and human health?"

Peter Montague was born on November 6, 1938, in Westport, Connecticut, with what he calls a "justice gene" that he says has always prevented him from just sitting back and watching bullies picking on other people, men abusing women, humans taking advantage of nonhumans. His earliest concern about environmental problems came during the late 1950s, after reading a newspaper article about radioactive fallout coating the northeastern United States, fogging film at the Eastman Kodak plant in Rochester, New York. He tried to research radioactivity, but the two books he found at his local library were impossible for him to understand. Rather than abandoning the topic, he taught himself the science he needed to understand it and began to follow the issue in the news. During the early 1960s, Montague was impressed that biologist BARRY COMMONER, through his scientific research on radioactive fallout and his ability to clearly communicate its danger, was able to convince Pres. Kennedy to sign an above-ground atomic test ban treaty with the Soviet Union in 1963.

Montague earned a B.A. in journalism at the University of the Americas in Mexico City in 1962 and then obtained an M.A. in English at Indiana University, Bloomington, in 1967 and a Ph.D. in American studies in 1971 from the University of New Mexico (UNM). In 1971, he cofounded the Southwest Research and Information Center (SRIC), a small public interest research organization based in Albuquerque, New Mexico, that focuses on local and regional environmental problems. From 1974 to 1979, he and Katherine Montague edited its monthly publication, *The Workbook*, a rich source of information about environmental, social, and consumer problems "aimed at helping people gain access to vital information that can help them assert control over their own lives," according to its mission statement.

During the environmental awakening following the first Earth Day in 1970, university administrators asked Montague—by then well known locally for his environmental activism—to teach a course on the environment. His environmental courses for the School of Architecture and Planning at UNM, which he taught until leaving New Mexico in 1979, transformed students into environmental investigators. They chose "really bad ideas" of government and industry, he recounted to David Case of TomPaine.com, and then would immerse themselves in research, emerging with enough information to challenge policy makers and experts. Their strategy was often to "clog the toilet," to focus on the waste disposal processes of these projects. This had particular relevance for nuclear power plants: without a safe way of disposing their radioactive waste, they had difficulty winning public support for continued operation.

While teaching at UNM, Montague bolstered his scientific knowledge through frequent conversations with a fellow activist and physicist friend, Charles Hyder. After years of daily, informal tutoring sessions, Montague had gained much knowledge about many scientific issues pertaining to the environment. He published many articles and several books during this period, including *Mercury*, cowritten with Katherine Montague and published by the Sierra Club in 1971.

In 1979, Montague moved to Princeton University in New Jersey, where he worked first as a research fellow for its School of Engineering/Applied Science Center for Energy and Environmental Studies and then as project administrator for the school's Hazardous Waste Research Program. These positions allowed him to research the generation and disposal of hazardous materials in New Jersey, including radioactive and hazardous waste. The university suffered from a conflict of interest, however, because it was the recipient of large donations from many of the corporations with the most serious records for contamination in the state. In December 1983, the university discontinued the Hazardous Waste Research Program and transferred Montague to work on computer support and network development.

Concurrently with his work for Princeton, Montague set up the Environmental Research Foundation, through which he hoped to provide community activists with important technical information about environmental and health matters that usually remained the domain of a small, elite community of "experts." ERF's first project was an on-line database, the Remote Access Chemical Hazards Electronic Library, which was called RACHEL (as in RACHEL CARSON). Montague edited RACHEL and, beginning in 1986, the weekly newsletter *Rachel's Hazardous Waste News*. These resources were offered to hazardous waste activists who needed solid scientific information that was written in a style accessible to nonscientists.

In December 1990, Montague left Princeton, and the following month he took a position with the Washington, D.C.–based Greenpeace USA toxics campaign as a senior research analyst. His role was to provide research support to ten community organizers and grassroots campaigners who worked with citizen activist groups fighting hazardous waste incinerators. He stayed with Greenpeace for one year before going to work full time for the Environmental Research Foundation in 1992, at its new Annapolis, Maryland–based headquarters.

ERF developed a web site (www.rachel.org) that offers an extensive conference calendar, links to thousands of environmental organizations throughout the world, and a searchable archive of ERF's hundreds of reports and newsletters, many available in Spanish. The newsletter continues to be a major focus of Montague, who writes or edits every weekly issue. Renamed *Rachel's Environmental and Health Weekly* to reflect a broader focus, it is now published electronically. Each issue, distributed for free to a subscriber list of more than 10,000, takes a specific issue pertaining to environment and public health and synthesizes important findings for readers who are not experts.

The Precaution Reporter, ERF's second weekly publication, distributed on-line to 1,000 subscribers since 2005, tracks precaution as a lens for decision-making worldwide.

ERF's primary goal of empowering citizen activists with easily understood scientific knowledge furthers its complementary goal: that grassroots action be "the effective lever for change in our neighborhoods and that informed citizens are the essential backbone of a strong democracy and a healthy environment."

In addition to his writings for *Rachel's*, Montague has written and edited more than 130 papers, journal articles, book chapters, and books. He has served on the board of directors of the SRIC and that of Sustainable America, a coalition of economic development organizations. He was awarded the Joe A. Callaway Award for Civic Courage from the Shafeek Nader Trust for the Community Interest in December 1996. Montague resides in Annapolis, Maryland.

### BIBLIOGRAPHY

"Environmental Research Foundation," www.rachel.org/; "Southwest Research and Information Center," www.sric.org; "TOMPAINE.com: "Peter Montague: A Common Sense Civic Hero," www.tompaine.com/Archive/scontent/3005.html.

## Moses, Marion

(January 24, 1936– )
Physician, Founder of the Pesticide Education Center

Founder of the Pesticide Education Center, Marion Moses is a physician and advocate for health and justice for farmworkers. She began working with CÉSAR CHÁVEZ, DOLORES HUERTA, and the United Farm Workers (UFS) in the 1960s and went to medical school to gain knowledge that could be useful in their struggle. She is an acknowledged scientific expert on the health effects of pesticide exposure and an active part of the struggle against environmental racism.

Marion Moses was born on January 24, 1936, in Wheeling, West Virginia. She graduated from Georgetown University in 1957 with a B.S.N. and from Columbia University in 1960 with an M.A. in nursing education. In 1964 she was living in Berkeley, California, when she became interested in the plight of farmworkers. She joined Citizens for Farm Labor, a group working to publicize the workers' cause, and reactivated the University of California's Student Committee on Agricultural Labor. For five years she volunteered as a nurse with the United Farm Workers in Delano, California. This was a vital period in the organization's history, the height of the grape boycott and strikes, and Moses was a key participant in this struggle. The workers were striking for better wages and working conditions, including better health and safety regulations. At this time there was no requirement for sanitary facilities in the fields and no protection against pesticide exposure. Moses decided to pursue a medical degree in order to become a more effective advocate on these issues. She received an M.D. from Temple University in 1976 and completed her residency in internal medicine at the University of Colorado Medical Center in 1977. She completed a residency in occupational medicine at Mount Sinai Medical Center in New York City in 1980 and was board certified by the American College of Preventive Medicine and Public Health in 1980.

Moses returned to work with the farmworkers as the medical director of the National Farm Workers Health Group, a post she held from 1983 to 1986. In 1988 César Chávez held a widely publicized hunger strike to call attention to a new grape boycott, this time focused primarily on the issue of worker exposure to pesticides. Moses was one of the attending physicians during his fast. Her work with the UFW makes Moses's views on the effects of pesticide exposure particularly compelling. In the mainstream media, this issue is often described from the point of view of consumers, fearful of the trace residues left by pesticide use in the fields. Moses emphasizes that agricultural workers have far more to fear and are much more vulnerable than the average American consumer. Workers are subject to doses many times larger than those of consumers and experience exposure over a more prolonged period. Moses puts the issue of pesticide safety into an international context. Multinational corporations produce and use pesticides to produce crops as cheaply as possible, at the expense of the health of farmworkers. These corporations work hand in hand with the U.S. Department of Agriculture, which subsidizes research in chemical means of production, at the expense of research into organic methods. And farmworkers, the least powerful actors in the agricultural field, pay for these subsidies with higher cancer rates and neurodevelopmental problems among their children.

In 1988 Moses founded the Pesticide Education Center to increase awareness of the dangers of pesticides among workers and consumers. The center's mission is "to educate consumers to make more informed choices to protect themselves, their families, their pets, their neighbors, and the environment from toxic pesticides." The center collects the results of recent research into the health effects of pesticides and produces educational materials, including the video *Harvest of Sorrow* and Moses's 1995 book *Designer Poisons*. In 1990 Moses led a landmark study, funded with a $500,000 appropriation from Congress, to assess the danger pesticides pose to farmworkers. The study will follow the same group of workers for many years, in the hopes of gathering definitive epidemiological evidence about the effects of exposure. Increased risk of cancer and other disease is notoriously hard to prove. Each pesticide is chemically unique, and it is difficult to demonstrate an undeniable link between a particular pesticide and a particular instance of disease. Moses's work aims to establish this link, by thoroughly documenting every aspect of the workers' daily environment, over a prolonged period of study.

In 1991 Moses served on the National Advisory Committee of the First National People of Color Environmental Summit, which played a pivotal role in making the concerns of people of color heard in mainstream environmental organizations. Moses has also been active as an adviser to the Environmental Protection Agency (EPA), serving on a number of committees, including the Toxic Substances Advisory Committee and the National Advisory Committee of the Pesticide Farm Safety Center. In April 1999, Moses led a walkout by environmental groups of another committee, the EPA's Tolerance Reassessment Advisory Committee. Moses, representing the Pesticide Education Center, joined Consumer's Union, Natural Resources Defense Council, Farmworker Justice Fund, and other national groups in resigning in protest of what they saw as the Clinton administration's capitulation to the chemical industry. Moses continues to direct the Pesticide Education Center in San Francisco, California.

### BIBLIOGRAPHY

Newton, David, *Environmental Justice*, 1996; "Pesticide Education Center," www.pesticides.org; Ruttenberg, Danya, "Interview with Dr. Marion Moses," *Sojourner*, 1999.

## Moss, Cynthia
(1940– )
Conservationist, Co-founder and Director of Amboseli Elephant Research Project

Elephant researcher and conservationist, Cynthia Moss is the director of the Amboseli Elephant Research Project (AERP), which she co-founded in 1972. In her 40 years of experience working with these enormous mammals, Moss has made a significant contribution to human knowledge of the lives of elephants, in particular the social behavior and family dynamics of wild African elephants. She has researched the same population of wild elephants since the early 1970s and has studied and come to know the unique personalities of over 2,000 elephants in her career. Her research provided insight into the structure of elephant families and tribes as well as mating, response to the death of another elephant, and the upbringing of young elephants. Her focus on elephants' complex social relationships, intelligence, and communication systems has given her the status of one of the leading authorities on elephants. Through her continued research and outreach activities, she strives to ensure the protection of elephants in their natural habitat.

Born in Ossining, New York, Moss enjoyed wildlife and horseback riding as a child, but never envisioned a future of studying wild elephants in Africa. She attended Smith University in Massachusetts and graduated in 1962 with a bachelor's degree in philosophy. In 1964 she took a job as a theater researcher and reporter for *Newsweek* magazine in New York City. She first encountered wild elephants while traveling to the Lake Manyara National Park in East Africa in 1967. This experience had a profound influence on Moss, and she moved to Africa the following year to work with the elephant population in Tanzania as a research assistant to elephant expert, Dr. Iain Douglas-Hamilton. When the project ended, she stayed in Africa, studying elephants and other mammals.

Four years after moving to Africa, Cynthia Moss co-founded the Amboseli Elephant Research Project (AERP), with fellow elephant conservationist Harvey Croze. This project, set in the Amboseli National Park in southern Kenya, provided researchers the opportunity to study the tribe in a natural setting of 150 square miles on protected land, safe from poachers and other human threats. After securing long-term funding from the African Wildlife Foundation in 1975, Moss was able to devote full-time effort to this project and related conservation efforts. Under Moss' direction, the AERP has become one of the longest-running research projects of wild mammals, and the Amboseli elephant population, has become one of the longest-studied populations of free-roaming elephants in the world. While most other elephant populations in Africa have decreased drastically, the Amboseli tribe has grown from 400 to over 1,500 elephants since the beginning of the AERP.

The ivory trade and the dramatically increasing human population in Africa pose problems for elephants' survival in their natural habitat. Between1979 and 1989, the total elephant population in Africa decreased by more than half due to poaching, and the number of elephants in Kenya dropped by 80 percent. During the 1980s Moss worked to get the African elephant endangered status and lobbied for an international ban on ivory trade, which was passed in 1990 at the Convention on International Trade in Endangered Species (CITES).

Moss' current research efforts continue to focus on ensuring the African elephant's survival in the wild. She works to provide Kenyans with deeper understanding and appreciation of elephants. The AERP is part of the local economy by putting money back into the local community through ecotourism and employment. The Project also organized a compensation system so that local farmers would be given money in the rare event that an elephant killed one of their animals. Other conservation activities include advocating for the welfare of elephants with a position statement on the harmful effects of the use of elephants in the circus.

The African Elephant Conservation Trust, AERP's first independent operating base in the United States, was developed in 1999. Two years later, in 2001, Moss established the Amboseli Trust for Elephants (ATE), a non-profit organization, in both the USA and Kenya, that focuses on conservation of elephants in the context of the local ecosystem through knowledge and awareness. The Trust organizes and funds the AERP research activities. In conjunction with research, the ATE also promotes community education, training, and awareness to promote African elephants' welfare and conservation.

Cynthia Moss currently serves as President of the Board of Trustees and Chairperson of the ATE, and directs the AERP in Kenya. Her research has provided humans with insight into the intelligence and social behavior of elephants, and she has brought her knowledge and passion into popular culture with several television documentaries and books.

**BIBLIOGRAPHY**

Amboseli Trust for Elephants, www.elephanttrust.org; Moss, Cynthia (actor), *Echo and Other Elephants: Enchanting Stories of an Elephant Family*, Closed- captioned, Color, DVD-Video, Subtitled, NTSC, 2008; Moss, Cynthia, *Elephant Memories: Thirteen Years in the Life of an Elephant Family*, 2000; Moss, Cynthia, *Little Big Ears: The Story of Ely*, 1997; Moss, Cynthia, *Echo of the Elephants: The Story of an Elephant Family*, 1994; Moss, Cynthia, *Portraits in the Wild: Behavior Studies of East African Mammals, Second Ed.*, 1982; Pringle, Laurence, *Elephant Woman: Cynthia Moss Explores the World of Elephants*, 1997.

## Moss, Doug
(November 13, 1952– )
Editor and Publisher

Doug Moss is the founder, publisher, and executive editor of *E The Environmental Magazine*, the nation's leading independent, bimonthly magazine devoted to the environment.

Born in Norwalk, Connecticut, on November 13, 1952, Douglas Edward Moss grew up catching frogs and fishing in local ponds but traces his environmentalism to an event that occurred much later. While living in New Haven, Connecticut, after graduating with a degree in marketing from Babson College in 1974, Moss one day watched a television report about the clubbing of baby harp seals. Moss, a business forms salesman who had no history of political activity, was outraged. His first impulse was to call the television station and complain, but then he realized the television was only the messenger, so instead he joined a local antifur group. When he found that he enjoyed activism, he began running with a local community of left-of-center intellectuals and activists. Moss started to spend his free time on such activities as gathering signatures on petitions for BARRY COMMONER's 1980 candidacy for president and the successful Norwalk nuclear freeze referendum of 1982.

In 1979, Moss left Burroughs Corporation, whose forms he had been selling since 1974, and started his own company, Douglas Forms. Most of his clients were magazines, and from his work producing renewal forms for them, he learned more about the business end of publishing. Moss and a few other members of the local chapter of Friends of Animals, which he had helped found, decided to publish an animal rights magazine. In late 1979 the first issue of *Animals' Agenda* appeared.

After nine years of publishing *Animals' Agenda*, Moss tired of the narrow range of issues covered by the animal rights' movement.

Doug Moss (Photograph by Jeanne Licari)

He and his wife, Deborah Kamlani, decided to move on. It was the summer of 1988, which Moss now refers to as the "greenhouse summer" because it was so hot that scientists' predictions of global warming were beginning to seem more real to the American public. In a 1999 interview, Moss recalled that while he and Kamlani ate breakfast in a Westport, Connecticut deli one hot morning, they read a *New York Times* article about the medical waste washing up on New Jersey beaches. Global warming, contaminated oceans, and other related issues triggered the idea to use their publishing skills in a new nonprofit venture. Moss and Kamlani decided to leave *Animals' Agenda* and put their publishing experience to use on a new, independent magazine that would focus on a broad range of environmental topics.

*E The Environmental Magazine* incubated during 1988 and 1989, and its first issue appeared on newsstands in December 1989 with a January/February 1990 cover date. It got an early boost from two events that mobilized the public on environmental issues: the now infamous April 1989 *Exxon Valdez* spill in Prince William Sound and the 20th anniversary of Earth Day on April 21, 1990. Unbeknownst to Moss, Kamlani, and cofounder Leslie Pardue, two more environmental magazines were being inaugurated at the same time, *Buzzworm* and *Garbage*. For several years, there was enough momentum in the new environmental movement that the market supported all three magazines. By the mid-1990s, however, *Buzzworm* and *Garbage* both had folded.

*E* serves as a bimonthly "clearinghouse" for environmental information, according to its mission statement, providing information that is both accessible for the general public and detailed enough to be of use to serious environmentalists. One unique and very useful feature of the magazine is that almost all of its articles end with contact addresses and phone numbers for reader follow-up. Its departments include news, commentary, and interviews with such environmental leaders as environmental justice specialist Dr. ROBERT BULLARD and biotech expert JEREMY RIFKIN. The magazine's Green Living section features consumer and health shorts, travel options, and recommendations for greener earning and spending.

Moss's business and marketing training have contributed to *E*'s survival. Knowing that publishing ventures suffer a notoriously low profit margin, Moss founded the nonprofit corporation Earth Action Network to solicit grant support for *E*. The first few years were slim for *E*, and Moss and Kamlani took out personal home equity and business loans to kick start the magazine. But thanks to a 1997–1998 debt resolution campaign, several foundations stepped in to help retire *E*'s debt.

Since then, the magazine has fared well but is still a struggle, Moss says. Foundations don't tend to fund media projects, even though Al Gore's *An Inconvenient Truth*, a "media project if there ever was one," says Moss, "should be evidence of the incredible change power of media." *E* currently has a circulation of 50,000, sold primarily through subscriptions but also on newsstands and in bookstores across the country. *E* maintains an active website, emagazine.com, which showcases the magazine's content, provides weekly news and commentary in addition, and which enjoys between 400,000 and 600,000 monthly visitors.

*E* also syndicates its content widely to other magazines, newspapers and websites, and its editors appear on many a radio and television program, promoting the magazine's content as each issue is published.

In 2004, *E* published its first of two books. *Feeling the Heat: Dispatches from the Frontlines of Climate Change* profiles actual world "hot spots" where people are already coping with the consequences of climatic disruption. The book was an expansion of an earlier *E* cover story and was favorably reviewed in many venues, including the *New York Review of Books*.

*E*'s second book, *Green Living: The* E *Magazine Handbook for Living Lightly on the Earth* (2005), is a comprehensive guide to the environmental lifestyle. From recycling to rainforest protection, *Green Living* introduces readers to broad categories of issues, and features a compendium of green products and services, from organic foods to non-toxic cleaners to eco-travel options. Like *E* itself, the book is loaded with contact information so readers can conduct further research or join activist efforts. In 2006, *Green Living* served as the basis for a double-page spread in *Parade* magazine (34 million readers) entitled "Make Your Household Healthy."

In late 2003 *E* introduced *EarthTalk*, a nationally syndicated weekly Q&A column that is distributed free, and by request only, to over 1,600 newspapers, magazines and websites with a collective circulation reach of 70 million readers. The column is also posted by some highly trafficked websites, including MSNBC.com and the *New York Times'* About.com. *EarthTalk* answers reader-submitted questions on a wide range of environmental topics, ranging from "Did global warming cause Hurricane Katrina or make its impact worse?" to "Where can I recycle my plastic CD jewel cases?" *EarthTalk* is an effort to reach beyond "the choir" of committed environmentalists and offer highly useful information to sympathetic but uninformed people shown in poll after poll to be ready and even eager for "green" information. In 2009, Plume, *Green Living*'s publisher, will publish a "best of" *EarthTalk* book.

Moss and Kamlani live in Westport, Connecticut, with their two sons, Tim and Jeff.

**BIBLIOGRAPHY**
Booker, Vonetta, "The Staying Power of *E*," *Fairfield County Weekly*, 1999; "*E Magazine*," www.emagazine.com; Sledge, Anne, "*E Magazine* Remains True to Its Eclectic Roots," *Fairfield County Business Journal*, 1999.

## Muir, John
(April 21, 1838–December 24, 1914)
Writer, Naturalist, First President of the Sierra Club

Bearded, long-haired John Muir was America's prototypical wild man, happiest when he was wandering wild lands. He is remembered for his passionate writings in defense of the wilderness, his untiring fight for their preservation, and his role as founding president of the Sierra Club.

Born on the North Sea coast in Dunbar, Scotland, on April 21, 1838, John Muir emigrated with his family to Portage, Wisconsin, in 1849, in pursuit of religious freedom. His father was a preacher for the evangelical Disciples of Christ branch of Christianity. The Muir children and their mother tended the farm. The father had a strict approach to child rearing: he prohibited his eight children from singing or reading anything besides the Bible, even from eating a balanced diet and keeping the house comfortably warm in winter. The Muir children were nurtured by their mother, however, who loved nature and art. All of the Muir children, especially John, became avid naturalists. Whereas their father subscribed to a religion based on fear, John and his siblings recognized God in every natural and beautiful place.

Muir borrowed books from neighbors to read by kerosene lamp in the dark of night; he also spent nights tinkering in his workshop, inventing clocks, barometers, hydrometers, and more fanciful apparatuses, such as a bed that dumped out the sleeper when it was time to wake up and a desk that rotated books around in a circle so that each could be studied the same amount of time. These inventions eventually provided Muir with a way to escape the oppressive family farm. Young John Muir traveled to Madison to exhibit his inventions at the 1860 Wisconsin state fair. There he became a star and decided to stay in Madison and attend the University of Wisconsin. Muir studied botany and geology until 1863, when he fled to Canada to avoid conscription for the Civil War. After a factory accident in Canada that left him temporarily blind, he reevaluated his life plans and decided to abandon his work with machinery and factories. In 1867, he began a 1,000-mile walk through the post–Civil War countryside, walking 25 miles a day, sleeping outside where he could, penniless most of the time, but feeling rich in freedom. Throughout his walk he col-

John Muir (right) and President Theodore Roosevelt on Glacier Point, Yosemite Valley, California, in 1903. (Library of Congress, Prints & Photographs Division, LC-USZC4-4698)

lected botanical specimens, drawing and studying them. Eventually he boarded a steamer for California and from the docks in San Francisco he walked to Yosemite Valley.

The dramatic mountains and waterfalls and lush flower-filled valleys of Yosemite enchanted Muir. He stayed in the area for ten years, working first as a farmhand and shepherd, and later at a sawmill cutting fallen logs for tourist cabins. His home consisted of an 8-foot by 6-foot extension of the top floor of the sawmill, hanging over a river. It was packed with his botanical collections and his notes. During his free time, he hiked through Yosemite's wilderness, becoming more and more interested in the geological phenomena that formed it. Over time, Muir developed a theory that ran counter to the accepted explanation of how Yosemite had been formed—that earthquakes were responsible for the jagged mountainscape. Muir came to believe that a glacier had gradually carved out the valley, leaving the granite protrusions Half Dome and El Capitan. Muir described his ideas to the

A section of Muir Glacier, Alaska. (Library of Congress, Prints & Photographs Division, LC-USZ62-61822)

tourists he guided through Yosemite, and his theories traveled by word of mouth. Eventually he was persuaded to write them down in the first of his many articles for national magazines ("Yosemite Glaciers," published in *New York Daily Tribune*, 1871). Today, geologists accept his theory but make two amendments: that there were two glaciers rather than one and that water too was important in carving the valley.

While Muir was intensely interested in the natural history of Yosemite, he became also increasingly concerned about its preservation. During the late 1800s, loggers and ranchers were rapidly exploiting California's forests, clear-cutting huge stands of the state's unique ancient redwoods. Vast tracts of primary forest were in the hands of a small group of wealthy owners, who were eager to make as much money as quickly as possible by exploiting their land. Muir began to spend his winters writing articles promoting preservation of beautiful natural areas. He favored the creation of national parks that would set aside spectacular sites like Yosemite, protecting them forever from development. In his vision, they would be reserves to replenish the spirit of an American people who, Muir predicted, would need more contact with nature as urban areas grew more crowded and frenetic. He believed that when tourists visited natural areas, the beauty and peace of nature would transform them into preservationists. Through his writings, Muir succeeded in persuading politicians to establish numerous national parks, including Yosemite in 1890 and Mount Rainier in 1899.

When University of California professors Henry Senger and William Armes decided in 1892 to found the Sierra Club to work for conservation, they asked Muir to attend the first meeting. Although Muir was shy and feared social occasions, he believed so deeply in the cause that he did attend the meeting and accepted a nomination to serve as the Sierra Club's first president.

Muir became so well known through his writing and Sierra Club activism that Pres. THEODORE ROOSEVELT asked him to be his personal guide through Yosemite during a 1903 tour of the West. The two men spent three entire days hiking together, and Roosevelt left California convinced of Muir's preservationist vision.

Muir's final preservationist battle was against a dam that would flood the Hetch Hetchy meadows just outside of Yosemite. In his arguments for their preservation, he compared them to cathedrals and churches and claimed that "no holier temple has ever been consecrated by the heart of man" (*The Yosemite*, 1988). Despite a fierce and energetic battle, in which he collaborated with Sierra Club member WILLIAM COLBY and *Century* editor ROBERT UNDERWOOD JOHNSON, the fight to preserve Hetch Hetchy was lost in 1913, and the valley now lies under a reservoir that collects water for San Francisco.

Muir was married to Louisa Strenzel and for over 30 years lived on her family's farm in Martinez, California. They raised wine grapes and fruit trees and, thanks to Muir's hard work and shrewd business sense, quickly became quite wealthy. The couple had two daughters, Annie and Helen, both of whom, as adults, accompanied Muir on mountaineering expeditions. Louisa was a quiet yet strong presence in the household. She helped Muir with all of his writings and, throughout their marriage, always encouraged him to take time off from the farm and explore the natural wonders that inspired his awe. Louisa Muir died in 1905. On December 24, 1914, shortly after the Hetch Hetchy defeat, John Muir died of pneumonia.

**BIBLIOGRAPHY**

Cohen, Michael P., *The Pathless Way: John Muir and the American Wilderness*, 1984; Ehrlich, Gretel, *John Muir: Nature's Visionary*, 2000; Fox, Stephen, *The American Conservation Movement: John Muir and His Legacy*, 1986; Muir, John, *My First Summer in the Sierra*, 1988; Muir, John, *The Story of My Boyhood and Youth*, 1965; Muir, John, *A Thousand Mile Walk to the Gulf*, 1981; Nash, Roderick, *Wilderness and the American Mind*, Revised Edition, 1973; Wilkins, Thurman, *John Muir: Apostle of Nature*, 1995; Strong, Douglas H., *Dreamers & Defenders: American Conservationists*, 1988; Wolfe, Linnie Marsh, *Son of the Wilderness: The Life of John Muir*, 1945; Worster, Donald, *A Passion for Nature: The Life of John Muir*, 2008.

## Mumford, Lewis
(October 19, 1895–January 26, 1990)
Social Philosopher, Urban Planner

Lewis Mumford's interests ranged from history to fine arts and literary criticism, but he is best known for his contributions to the fields of urban planning and architecture. The author of more than 30 books, Mumford believed that the modern obsession with technology obscured those human values that created great civilizations and that unplanned growth and mechanization contributed to the breakdown of biological, social, and personal well-being.

Lewis Charles Mumford was born on October 19, 1895, in Flushing, Queens, New York, the illegitimate son of a German Protestant, Elvina Baron Mumford, and Lewis Charles Mack, a Jewish businessman, whom the boy never met. Nor did he meet the man whose name he carried, John Mumford, an Englishman his mother had married briefly 12 years before his birth.

Mumford's mother kept a boardinghouse in Manhattan. "I was a child of the city. New York exerted a greater and more constant influence on me than did my family," he wrote in his autobiography, *Sketches from Life*. The teeming, diverse, energetic New York of his childhood was home to more than a million foreign-born immigrants. Every weekend, his grandfather took Mumford on long walks throughout the city, "saunters [that] furnished the esthetic background of my childhood," he wrote.

In 1909, Mumford entered Stuyvesant High School to prepare for an engineering career, but by 1912, upon enrolling in City College of New York, he had decided to become a writer. At 20, Mumford discovered the works of Patrick Geddes, who would be his greatest influence and who shaped the young man's future as a social philosopher and urban planner. Geddes was an early environmentalist, a Scottish botanist who used his scientific training to help revitalize and rehabilitate the choking, grimy slums of industrial Edinburgh. Following Geddes's pattern, Mumford made long, solitary explorations of New York, studying its streets, neighborhoods, buildings, bridges, and geology. Reading Geddes's University of London Extension Lectures, Mumford learned to take notes as he walked, recording city life and its supporting activities and, as if in the wilderness, noting where the city's humanistic ecosystems were disrupted.

In 1917, Mumford and Geddes began corresponding; they did not meet until 1923.

Geddes's ideas about using the past to design future cities inspired Mumford, who came to believe that "the city is an age-old instrument of human culture, essential to its further development." History and antiquity would inform Mumford's theory of "organic planning," in which he cited cities of medieval Europe and other eras as models of situations where physical layout gave rise to cultural growth, artistic expression, and human contact. "When one considers the amount of space and fine building given to Pompeii's temples... markets... law courts... public baths...stadium... theatre... one realizes that American towns... do not, except in very rare cases, have anything like this kind of civic equipment, even in makeshift form," he wrote in *Technics and Civilization* (1934), one of four volumes of his Renewal of Life Series. Mumford described organic planning as embracing the myriad processes by which a city evolves historically, each generation building on the accomplishments of the previous.

In 1920, after a year in the navy and a stint on the staff of the literary magazine *Fortnightly Dial*, Mumford went to London as acting editor of *Sociological Review*. This move was to "mold the rest of my life," he wrote, for there he met Victor Branford, a financier and Geddes collaborator. Branford's interpretations of science and art and the role of religion as the binding element of human communities would form a crux of Mumford's later thoughts.

Mumford left London in 1921 to marry Sophia Wittenberg. His first book, *The Story of Utopias*, published in 1922, emphasized the role of artists of all disciplines in the process of social transformation. His notion of artists' responsibility for the reconstruction of our inner and outer worlds was a step beyond Geddes's belief that a systematic sociology must be linked to the good life. Mumford wrote that artists could contribute to social reform by suggesting images of a more balanced, spiritually satisfying life, which could be integrated into the plans of regional surveyors. Like Geddes, Mumford advocated festivals and pageants, such as those of the Middle Ages, to celebrate and understand the city's diverse history. The *Story of Utopias* was followed in 1924 by *Sticks and Stones*, his first book about architecture and the architect's role as artist-reformer.

Meanwhile, Mumford joined three great American planners—Clarence Stein, Henry Wright, and BENTON MACKAYE—to form the Regional Planning Association of America (RPAA), which attempted to stop unplanned urban growth and restore human scale to cities. RPAA proposed small satellite cities—suburbs—separated from a parent city by open space. Mumford moved into an RPAA-planned community in Sunnyside, Queens, which featured clustered buildings and a large common garden. He helped plan Radburn, a community in Fairlawn, New Jersey, and served in various other urban development organizations, including the New York Housing and Regional Planning Commission. While Mumford was involved in the RPAA, he met CATHERINE BAUER, who would later become well known as a planner and advocate of improved housing for poor people.

*The Golden Day*, a discussion of the utilitarian, "timekeeper" culture brought to American shores by Protestant settlers, was published in 1926, the same year Mumford helped found and edit *The American Caravan*, a periodical dedicated to the works of emerging writers. He also produced a biography of Herman Melville.

Although he had never received a college degree, Mumford began a part-time visiting professorship at Dartmouth College in 1929 and soon became a popular lecturer and teacher, with appointments at Stanford University (where he helped design the humanities program), the University of Pennsylvania, and the Massachusetts Institute of Technology, among others. He was appointed to the New York City Board of Higher Education.

In 1931, Mumford joined the *New Yorker* magazine staff with his column "The Sky

Line," which he wrote until 1963. He challenged readers to consider the costs to people of politically motivated urban projects and spoke out against industrialists, promises of "progress," and what he called "the myth of the machine." He attacked "bigger-is-better" proponents and led bitter campaigns against the policies—such as building a railroad through Washington Square—of then New York commissioner of public works Robert Moses. Through "The Sky Line," Mumford battled developers and skyscrapers, which he labeled "elegant monuments to nothingness." Most of his fights were lost, but thanks to Mumford's outspoken courage, such areas as preservation, social issues, and urban development could no longer be the sole, secret purview of planners and politicians but became public issues, matter for community dialogue.

After World War II, Mumford came out against proliferation of the atomic bomb. In the 1960s, he protested against U.S involvement in the war in Vietnam. But across time, he became increasingly despairing about the dehumanization and desocialization born of mechanization and industrialism: unemployment, isolation, invisibility of the individual, dissolution of families and communities, the future of children and the natural environment, the pollution of air and water.

Mumford won the National Book Award for *The City in History* in 1962, the Presidential Medal of Freedom in 1964, the National Medal for Literature in 1972, the French Prix Mondial del Duca in 1976, and many other awards, including the honorary Knight Commander of the British Empire in 1977. Although he never completed his college education, he was awarded an honorary LL.D. from the University of Edinburgh in 1965 and an honorary doctorate of architecture from the University of Rome in 1967.

His final book, *Sketches from Life* (1982), chronicled Mumford's early years into the 1930s and was nominated for an American Book Award. In 1986, Mumford was awarded the National Medal of Arts. He was overjoyed to be recognized as an artist. Yet, according to biographer Donald Miller, it was bittersweet. With old age, Miller wrote, Mumford "was frustrated, sometimes to the point of anger, that he would no longer…do any good in the world. 'Resignation would be easier' [he said], 'if the world at large were in a more hopeful state.'"

Mumford and his wife, Sophia, had two children: a son, Geddes, born in 1925, and a daughter, Alison, born in 1935. Geddes Mumford was killed in combat during World War II and was memorialized by his father in a 1947 biography titled *Green Memories.*

Lewis Mumford died on January 26, 1990, at the age of 95 at his home in Amenia, New York.

**BIBLIOGRAPHY**

Hughes, Thomas P., and Agatha C., eds., *Lewis Mumford: Public Intellectual*, 1990; Luccarelli, Mark, *Lewis Mumford and the Ecological Region,: the Politics of Planning*, 1995; Miller, Donald L., *Lewis Mumford: A Life*, 1989; Miller, Donald L., *The Lewis Mumford Reader*, 1986; Mumford, Lewis, *The City in History*, 1961; Mumford, Lewis, *The Culture of Cities*, 1938; Mumford, Lewis, *Sketches from Life: The Early Years*, 1982; Mumford, Lewis, *The Story of Utopias*, 1922; Wojtowicz, Robert, *Sidewalk Critic: Lewis Mumford's Writings on New York*, 2000.

## Murie, Mardy, and Olaus Murie
(August 18, 1902–October 19, 2003; March 1, 1889–October 21, 1963)
Conservation Activist; Wildlife Ecologist, Naturalist, Cofounder of the Wilderness Society

Arguably the "first family" of Alaskan wilderness, Olaus and Mardy Murie were highly influential players in the interwar wilderness movement that culminated in the 1964 passage of the Wilderness Act. The focus of their own work was the preservation of Alaska's wild lands. As a member of the U.S. Biological Survey, Olaus Murie conducted pioneering wildlife studies, predominantly in Alaska and Wyoming. Once they married, Mardy frequently joined him on his wilderness expeditions. After the death of Olaus in 1963, Mardy continued the work they had begun together, joining the Governing Council of the Wilderness Society and working for the protection of wild Alaska.

Olaus Johan Murie was born in Moorhead, Nebraska, on March 1, 1889, the son of Norwegian immigrants. His father died when he was quite young, leaving his mother to care for him and his brother, Martin, and his half-brother, Adolph. Murie spent much of his childhood picking potatoes, working on truck farms, and delivering milk to help make ends meet at home. Growing up in natural surroundings led to his early interest in the environment and conservation. One of his early influences was ERNEST THOMPSON SETON, whose books in the local library Murie nearly wore out from avid reading. Following Seton's example, Murie sketched and painted the animals he observed on his wanderings. He studied biology at Fargo College in North Dakota and later zoology at Pacific University in Oregon, where he received a B.A. in 1912. Murie worked as a conservation officer for the Oregon State Game and Fish Department. Within two years, he was hired as a field mammal curator for a Carnegie Museum of Natural History expedition to Canada. It would be the first of his many trips to the northern wilds.

After serving as a balloonist and observer in World War I, Murie joined the U.S. Biological Survey and hunted predators in the Olympic Peninsula in Washington during the winter of 1916–1917. Whereas his contemporary, ALDO LEOPOLD, was an avid predator hunter as a young man, Murie seemed to lack such enthusiasm. His record that winter was exceptionally poor: two bobcats, one cougar, and no wolves killed. His future wife, Mardy, would later say that he never believed strongly in predator control. His criticisms of the predator control policy, however, were mild at first. Writing to his superior from Alaska in 1923, Murie hinted that predators might not represent such a problem as was believed. "I have a theory," he wrote, "that a certain amount of preying on caribou by wolves is beneficial to the herd, that the best animals survive and the vigor of the herd is maintained." Such views were well ahead of their time and practically heresy in their day. Accordingly, Murie tempered his criticisms so as not to jeopardize his job. Over the years, however, Murie became an increasingly vocal opponent of predator control, believing that predators played a crucial role in maintaining balance in the ecosystem.

In 1920, Murie was sent to Alaska and northern Canada to conduct the first "life history" of the caribou in that region. Accompanied by his brother Adolph, Murie conducted studies on a variety of wildlife, including waterfowl, bears, and especially elk. While in Alaska in 1924, Murie met Margaret Elizabeth Thomas, soon to be his lifelong partner for his future wilderness studies.

Margaret Elizabeth Thomas—fondly called the Grandmother of the Conservation Movement—was born August 18, 1902, in Seattle, but she spent her childhood in Fairbanks, Alaska. In 1924, she was the first woman to graduate from the University of Alaska at

Margaret "Mardy" Murie on her porch in Grand Teton National Park as the sun sets in Jackson, Wyoming, June 29, 2002. (AP Images/Laura Rauch)

Fairbanks. That same year, she married Olaus and joined him on many of his wilderness expeditions. Their honeymoon was a dogsled caribou research expedition that covered some 500 miles of Alaska's Brooks Range. Subsequent trips included their three children: Martin (named for Olaus's brother who died during the 1922 influenza epidemic), Joanne, and Donald. The Murie family's adventures are described in Mardy Murie's book, *Two in the Far North*.

In 1926, the couple moved to Jackson Hole, Wyoming to study elk. They built a cabin, and from this home base, Olaus Murie wrote the works that his fame rests on: about wilderness preservation and the delicate ecological balance of the wild and human intervention in it. In a 1927 study in Wyoming, Murie concluded that the decline in the elk population in the region was a result of a reduction in their natural predators. Because predators were not keeping elk populations in check, elk numbers ballooned until the animals were forced to stray from their normal feeding patterns in order to find food. Murie demonstrated that the bushes the elk had started to feed on were ripping their mouths (a disease called soremouth), causing fatal infections. Murie's findings and his appeals against the slaughter of predatory animals were instrumental (along with Aldo Leopold's later assessments) in the reversal of previous predator control policies.

Called "Mr. Wilderness" by the *Washington Post*, Murie, along with BENTON MACKAYE, ROBERT MARSHALL, and several others, cofounded the Wilderness Society in 1935. Murie served as a member of the society's council, beginning in 1937, and as a director from

1945 until his death. In that capacity, Murie was a leading member of the conservation movement's lobbying for the congressional protection of the nation's wilderness areas. He was awarded the Audubon Medal of the National Audubon Society in 1959 and the John Muir Award of the Sierra Club shortly before his death. Olaus Murie died on October 21, 1963, in Jackson Hole, just months before the passage of the Wilderness Act in 1964, the realization of his life's work.

Mardy Murie attended the signing of the Wilderness Act by Pres. Lyndon Johnson, in her late husband's stead. Working with her husband before his death and independently once she was a widow, Mardy Murie wrote letters and articles, traveled and lectured, and promoted wilderness preservation to the public and the government. After the Wilderness Act, she continued to push for wilderness preservation, especially in Alaska. She played a significant role in the 1980 passage of the Alaska National Interest Lands Conservation Act, the greatest land preservation act in U.S. history. Testifying for this act, Murie said: "I am testifying as an emotional woman and I would like to ask you, gentlemen, what's wrong with emotion? Beauty is a resource in and of itself… I hope the United States of America is not so rich that she can afford to let these wildernesses pass by, or so poor she cannot afford to keep them."

Murie also served on the Council of the Wilderness Society, received an honorary doctorate from the University of Alaska and the prestigious Audubon Medal, and was named an honorary park ranger by the National Park Service. She was also on the founding board of the Teton Science School. Her most recent award, in 1998, was the Presidential Medal of Freedom, which Pres. Bill Clinton bestowed on her for her lifetime service to conservation.

On September 16, 1998, the Murie Center was formally opened with a gathering of some of the nation's top conservation leaders on Mardy Murie's front porch. Mardie Murie died five years later at her home, on October 19, 2003. The Murie Center is dedicated to continuing to carry out the Murie legacy of land conservation and wilderness protection through the development and implementation of innovative strategies.

**BIBLIOGRAPHY**

Glover, James M. "Thinking like a Wolverine: The Ecological Evolution of Olaus Murie," *Environmental Review*, 1989; "Murie Center," www.muriecenter.org; Murie, Adolph, *A Naturalist in Alaska*, 1961; Murie, Olaus, *The Elk of North America*, 1951; Murie, Olaus (finished by Mardy Murie), *Wapiti Wilderness*, 1966.

## Muskie, Edmund
(March 28, 1914–March 26, 1996)
U.S. Senator from Maine

Edmund Muskie served as a member of the Maine state legislature from 1946 to 1951, as governor of Maine from 1955 to 1959, and as U.S. senator from Maine from 1959 to 1980. As senator, he sponsored the Clean Air Act of 1963, the Water Quality Act of 1965, and a 1967 act that authorized more than 400 million dollars for pollution control. He served as chairman of the Environment and Public Works Subcommittee on Environmental Pollution and was a supporter of the 1966 Model Cities Act.

The second child of Stephen and Josephine Muskie, Edmund Sixtus Muskie was born on March 28, 1914, in Rumford, Maine. His father had emigrated to the United States from Poland in 1903 to escape the oppressive environment of his home country. Muskie's mother was from a large Polish family in Buffalo, New York. In his book, *Journeys* (1972), Muskie remembers his childhood as being "as healthy and happy a childhood and family life as a boy could wish." He pursued the bulk of his interests out-of-doors. He fished, hunted, and played baseball and football, and in winter he skied. The natural environment of Maine had a lasting impact on him. "My journey towards a place in the environmental sun," he writes in *Journeys*, "began in my backyard, in the environment of the place I was born and raised."

While studying at Bates College in Lewiston, Maine, Muskie became interested in politics, finding that his sensibilities were more in alignment with the New Deal philosophy of the recently elected president, FRANKLIN D. ROOSEVELT, than with the traditionally Republican views of most residents of Maine. Muskie graduated *cum laude* from Bates College in 1936. He received a scholarship to Cornell University Law School and received his LL.B. degree in 1939. He was admitted to the Massachusetts bar in 1939 and to the Maine bar in 1940.

In 1940, Muskie moved to the small town of Waterville, Maine, and practiced law for a short period of time before enlisting in the naval reserve in 1942. He served as an engineering officer on destroyer escorts in both the Pacific and Atlantic theaters of operation in World War II and was released to inactive duty in 1945. He returned to Waterville to revive his law practice and to become active in the Maine Democratic Party. In 1946, Muskie was elected to the Maine House of Representatives. He was elected to three consecutive terms. In 1948, during his second term, Muskie was chosen to be the Democratic minority leader. In 1951, in the middle of his third term, Muskie resigned from the Maine House of Representatives to become district director of the Maine Office of Price Stabilization, a position he occupied for just one year before becoming a Democratic national committeeman in 1952.

In 1954, Muskie decided to run for governor. According to Muskie's biographer David Nevin, he ran not so much out of a strong personal desire as out of a sense of responsibility. He was simply the only possibility for the Maine Democratic Party, and when he won, he was probably even more surprised than the Republicans were. He served two terms as governor, working during both terms with a state legislature that was predominantly (four to one) Republican. However, due to his tact and skills in politics and consensus building, he was able to steer his economic and educational programs through the legislature. He also pushed for legislation that created a state program for the building of water treatment plants and that established a classification system for improving the quality of Maine's streams and rivers.

Muskie decided not to seek a third term as governor in 1958. Instead, he ran for the U.S. Senate, defeating the Republican incumbent, Frederick G. Payne, by a wide margin. He was the first Democrat ever to be elected to the Senate by the state of Maine and kept his seat from 1959 until 1980. Muskie was instrumental in bringing about some of the most important environmental legislation in the history of the United States. In a short piece written for *Commonweal*, Abigail McCarthy quotes political commentator Mark Shields, "Before he [Muskie] began his work, there were no national laws and international agreements governing the quality of the country's air and water." Muskie responded to this dearth of environmental legislation, earning himself the nickname "Mr. Clean" for his efforts. He was the chief sponsor and floor manager of the Clean Air Act of 1963 and the Water Quality Act of 1965, and in 1967 he sponsored a $428,300,000 authorization for pollution control efforts. He supported Pres. Lyndon Johnson's Model Cities Act of 1966, which provided $1.2 billion to improve housing, recreation areas, education, and health in economically depressed urban areas throughout the United States. Muskie served as chairman of the Environment and Public Works Subcommittee on Environmental Pollution, and he was the Senate Budget Committee's first chairman from 1974 to 1980, in which post he developed a complex system for tracking federal spending.

In 1968, Muskie gained national prominence as the running mate in Hubert Humphrey's unsuccessful bid for the presidency. Throughout the campaign, Muskie was described as being Humphrey's greatest asset. In 1972, Muskie entered the presidential race himself. He did not, however, receive the Democratic nomination. In 1980, he resigned his position as senator to serve as Pres. JIMMY CARTER's secretary of state in the final year of the Carter administration.

After Carter failed to be reelected in the 1980 presidential election, Muskie practiced law in Washington. In 1986, he served on an investigative board, headed by Sen. John G. Tower, which examined the role of President Reagan's National Security Council staff in the Iran-Contra "arms for hostages" affair. He also served on a delegation that traveled to Vietnam to explore the lifting of the U.S. trade embargo with that country and chaired the Center for National Policy, a Democratic think tank. He died of a heart attack on March 26, 1996, after being treated at Georgetown University Hospital for a blocked artery in his leg. He was survived by his wife of 48 years, Jane, and five grown children.

**BIBLIOGRAPHY**

Lippman, Theo and Donald C. Hansen, *Muskie*, 1971; McCarthy, Abigail, "Edmund S. Muskie: Let Us Now Praise Honorable Men," *Commonweal*, 1996; Muskie, Edmund S., *Journeys*, 1972; Nevin, David, *Muskie of Maine*, 1972; Ross, James Gardner, *As Maine Goes... : The Early Years of Edmund Muskie*, 1986.

# American Environmental Leaders

From Colonial Times to the Present

**N**

## Nabhan, Gary
(March 17, 1952– )
Ethnobiologist, Agricultural and Desert Ecologist, Nature Writer

Gary Nabhan is an award-wining writer and conservationist whose wide-ranging, prolific work has explored such connections as those between cultural diversity and biological diversity, between people and desert wildlife, between wild and cultivated plants, and between poetry and natural science. His second book, *Gathering the Desert* (1985), received the JOHN BURROUGHS Medal for nature writing. The MacArthur Foundation gave him a "genius" fellowship in 1990, the same year he received a Pew Scholarship on Conservation and Environment. Sicily honored him in 1991 with the Premio Gaia Award for his contributions to "a culture of the environment." One of Nabhan's main interests over the years has been food—regional traditions for growing and preparing it, and the role and importance of pollinators in its production. Definitely a specialist in the Southwest, Nabhan has focused his research and writing on the Sonoran Desert region of northwestern Mexico and the southwestern U.S.

Gary Paul Nabhan was born on March 17, 1952, in Gary, Indiana, one of three children of Theodore and Jerri Nabhan. Lake Michigan's Indiana Dunes, tucked among the wasteland of steel mills and power plants, provided Nabhan's early introduction to the wild outdoors, as recounted in *The Geography of Childhood: Why Children Need Wild Places* (1994), a book he coauthored with longtime friend Stephen Trimble. His Lebanese family and community also set the stage for his interest and success in cross-cultural work. After a short stint at Cornell College, Nabhan attended Prescott College in Arizona, where he graduated in 1975 with a liberal arts degree that combined regional American literature and environmental biology. His postgraduate work at the University of Arizona, Tucson, resulted in a M.S. degree in plant sciences in 1978 and a Ph.D. in arid lands resources in 1983 and in a continuing love for the desert and its peoples.

Gary Paul Nabhan (Copyright © 2007, Gary Nabhan. All rights reserved.)

As a graduate student, Nabhan started collecting seeds from Native American farmers, first as a job for the U.S. Department of Agriculture (USDA) seed bank and then to help a nutrition project introducing vegetable gardening on the Tohono O'odham (Papago) reservation. Organizers learned that while broccoli and spinach were hard to promote, seeds of corn, beans, and squash varieties that their grandparents had grown were often requested—they thrived under desert growing conditions, and the O'odham already had names, recipes, and good memories of them. As Nabhan helped grow native seeds for redistribution, he realized these crops were worth saving not only for the genes they might add to future modern hybrids, but because they still had cultural value in their present form. His first book, *The Desert Smells like Rain: A Naturalist in Papago Indian Country* (1982), is a "sensitive and compassionate portrayal" (according to Rep. MORRIS UDALL) of the Indian people he worked with at this time.

In 1983, Nabhan cofounded Native Seeds/SEARCH, a nonprofit group that has expanded the seed-saving efforts to include Native peoples throughout the southwest and to promote the use of native crops and wild foods. The essays in *Enduring Seeds: Native American Agriculture and Wild Plant Conservation* (1989) and *Cultures of Habitat: On Nature, Culture and Story* (1997) chronicle some of the important projects started by Nabhan and Native Seeds/SEARCH. Nabhan has been especially involved in a program to publicize the benefits of traditional desert plant foods in preventing type 2 diabetes, particularly among high-risk indigenous populations. His interest in studying one of the few areas where wild chiles grow in the United States recently led to its designation as a protected botanical area.

In 1986, Nabhan became assistant director of the Desert Botanical Garden in Phoenix. His projects there included establishing a hands-on ethnobotanical trail; creating a database of endangered, useful plants found along the U.S.-Mexico border; and editing a book still widely used, *Desert Wildflowers: A Guide for Identifying, Locating and Enjoying Arizona Wildflowers and Cactus Blossoms* (1988). Nabhan's research projects took him to Organ Pipe Cactus National Monument, where he met his second wife, park naturalist Caroline Wilson. With Wilson he coauthored *Canyons of Color: Utah's Slickrock Wildlands* (1995). His work at this borderland monument, and an association with Conservation International, led to Mexican regulations to stop wholesale destruction of ironwood trees that are used for imitation Seri Indian artwork and to make mesquite charcoal. Nabhan helped form the Ironwood Alliance, a binational coalition that monitors ironwood tree protection efforts and successfully lobbied for the protection of the Ironwood Forest, a 129,000-acre site near Tucson that received national monument status in 2000.

In 1991, Nabhan moved to Tucson to become writer-in-residence at the Arizona-Sonora Desert Museum, where he edited a collection of natural history essays, *Counting Sheep: Twenty Ways of Seeing Desert Bighorn* (1993). He also finished writing an account of his 1990 Franciscan pilgrimage to Assisi, *Songbirds, Truffles, and Wolves: An American Naturalist in Italy* (1993). Once he became director of science at the Arizona-Sonora Desert Museum, Nabhan cofounded the museum's "Forgotten Pollinator" (later called the "Migratory Pollinator") campaign to raise awareness on the vital but little-appreciated interdependence of plants and the animals that help them reproduce. This project included the book *The Forgotten Pollinators* (1996) that Nabhan cowrote with Stephen L. Buchmann. Another book, *Desert Legends: Re-storying the Sonoran Borderland* (1994), provides some of the basis for another museum program, the Sense of Place Project, which works with small communities on both sides of the U.S.-Mexico border to document, preserve, and celebrate the region's cultural and ecological heritage. In the spring of 2000, Nabhan organized a successful 250-mile cross-country, cross-border, cross-cultural Desert Walk to raise money for Native American internships, to heighten awareness about the epidemic of diabetes among Native American communities, and to promote intergenerational cultural exchanges among the Seri, Tohono O'odham, and Yoeme—an unusual event, yet perhaps typical of Nabhan's thinking.

Nabhan's most recent research and conservation focus, which he initiated in 2004, has been with the "Renewing America's Food Traditions" consortium. He has written or edited several books on food—including *Renewing the Food Traditions of Chile Pepper Nation* (2008), and *Arab/American: Landscape, Culture and Cuisine in Two Deserts* (2008), *Renewing the Food Traditions of Salmon Nation* (2006), and *Tequila!: A Natural and Cultural History* (with Ana Guadalupe Valenzuela Zapata, 2004).

Nabhan taught at Northern Arizona University from 1998 until 2008, and directed the Center for Sustainable Environments, a research center specializing in the sustainable use of natural resources on the Colorado Plateau. In 2008 he accepted a position as a Research Social Scientist at the Southwest Center of the University of Arizona in Tempe. Nabhan has served on a number of non-profit organization boards, including the Orion Society, Seed Savers Exchange, the Amazon Conservation Team, and the Radius of Arab-American Writers.

Nabhan lives in Arizona and travels and lectures frequently. When at home, he tries to eat as much locally-produced food as possible: he gathers wild plant foods and raises heirloom vegetables, field crops and fruit, and raises Navajo-Churro sheep and Black Spanish turkeys.

**BIBLIOGRAPHY**

"Arizona-Sonora Desert Museum," www.desertmuseum.org; Erickson, Jim, "Biologist Nabhan Leaving Desert," *Arizona Daily Star*, 2000; Goldstein, Carol, "Gary Nabhan: Native Seeds," *Omni*, 1994; "Native Seeds/SEARCH," www.nativeseeds.org; "Official Site: Gary Nabhan," www.garynabhan.com.

## Nader, Ralph

(February 27, 1934– )
Public Interest Lawyer, Founder of Numerous Public Interest Organizations

Thanks to the tireless efforts of consumer advocate Ralph Nader, the United States is a safer place. Automobiles in the United States now have mandatory seat belts, industrial air polluters must conform to the standards of the Clean Air Act, and the Occupational Safety and Health Administration oversees safer and healthier U.S. workplaces. In 1969, Nader founded the Center for Study of Responsive Law, which monitors government regulatory agencies to ensure that they are working honestly and effectively. He has founded numerous other organizations to watch over the government or lobby Congress, including the Public Interest Research Groups (PIRGs) and Public Citizen.

Ralph Nader was born on February 27, 1934, in Winsted, Connecticut, to parents who had emigrated in 1912 from Lebanon. As a child, Nader listened closely to his family's dinner table conversations about social injustice. From an early age he showed an inclination toward law. He spent free time watching trials at Winsted's town hall, and his recreational reading was the *Congressional Record*. As a student at Princeton University, he became an activist, protesting the spraying of the campus trees with the pesticide dichlordiphenyltrichlor (DDT). He studied law at Harvard University, where a research project on automobile safety initiated his career in consumer advocacy.

Nader was able to continue his work on the topic of auto safety as a staff consultant for Daniel Patrick Moynihan, who was then President Johnson's assistant secretary of labor. Nader's 1964 "Report on the Context, Condition and Recommended Direction of Federal

Activity in Highway Safety" was converted into the widely read *Unsafe at Any Speed* (1965). That book deserves much of the credit for the 1966 passage of the National Traffic and Motor Vehicle Safety Act, which mandated seat belts and forced the car industry to install collapsible steering columns and padded dashboards. Nader and his cause gained further public attention when he sued General Motors in the mid-1960s for invasion of privacy. General Motors, threatened by Nader's research, had been making harrassing phone calls to him and sending seductive women his way to lure him into compromising situations. General Motors agreed to pay $425,000 to Nader in order to settle the suit, a sum 30 times more than any previous invasion-of-privacy settlement.

Nader used his settlement money to found a network of watchdog and consumer activist organizations. His energetic teams of lawyers and researchers, nicknamed "Nader's Raiders," produced stacks of reports incriminating big business for various social and environmental ills. They documented the lack of effectiveness of company-run workplace hazard policies; these documents became important ammunition in the fight for the Occupational Safety and Health Act (OSH Act; 1970). Once the OSH Act was passed, Nader's Raiders discovered and publicized key problems that the Occupational Safety and Health Administration—the federal agency created by the OSH Act—would have to respond to, such as cancer epidemics in certain chemical plants and the black lung disease in coal mines. The studies by Nader's Raiders of the industrial sources of air pollution aided the passage of the Clean Air Act of 1970.

Nader's Raiders worked through the organizations he founded, such as the Center for Study of Responsive Law, a Washington, D.C.–based nonprofit watchdog that monitors government regulatory agencies, and both Public Citizen and the U.S. Public Interest Research Group (U.S. PIRG), membership groups for concerned consumers. In 1970, Nader exhorted the students of the University of Oregon to form their own student consumer activist organization. They founded the Oregon Student Public Interest Research Group, which was the first of many student affiliates to U.S. PIRG. The PIRGs, funded by students, with student volunteers and professional staffs in each state where they exist, continue to promote environmental legislation at a statewide level.

Nader continues to direct Public Citizen, leading it on diverse research campaigns that address consumer abuse. He is a frequent speaker on college campuses. In his talks, he reminds his listeners that unless monitored by private citizens and the government, industry will exploit its workers and the public and pollute the environment. To ensure that business is not given free rein to abuse and destroy, Nader recommends that people pay close attention to its activities and join organizations that can mobilize quickly in response to problems. Nader has been recognized by *Life Magazine* as one of the 100 most influential people of the twentieth century. He has run for president in every presidential election since 1996.

**BIBLIOGRAPHY**

DeLeon, David, *Leaders from the 1960s*, 1994; Gottlieb, Robert, *Forcing the Spring*, 1993; Nader, Ralph, "Beyond Politics as Usual," (audio recording produced by Alternative Radio), 1996; Nader, Ralph, "Corporate Power: Profits before People," (audio recording produced by Alternative Radio), 1994; "Public Citizen," www.citizen.org; "U.S. PIRG," www.uspirg.org.

# Nagel, Carlos

(February 7, 1931– )
Cultural and Environmental Organizer

Carlos Nagel has been a leader in the effort to create an environmentally, economically, and socially sustainable future for the region encompassing northern Mexico and the U.S. borderlands. Nagel believes that in the same way that a healthy environment depends on diversity, a healthy social dynamic thrives on a diversity of perspectives, and he has thus devoted his career to building bridges between cultures. He works to encourage community participation in the process of ecosystem management, bringing together researchers, nongovernmental organizations, representatives of the local communities, and members of the Tohono O'odham Nation and other Native American groups to discuss regional land use issues and increase local awareness of the environment. He founded Friends of Pronatura, an organization that promotes the conservation of the natural and cultural diversity in Mexico and the U.S. borderlands, and is also a founding member and has served as president of the board of the International Sonoran Desert Alliance, an organization that helps foster cross-cultural dialogue regarding ecological, economic, and social issues.

Carlos Nagel was born on February 7, 1931, in Argentina and came to New York with his family as an adolescent. After serving in the U.S. military from 1952 to 1954 in Korea, he attended the University of Washington, earning a B.A. in 1958 in museum administration. Beginning in 1959, Nagel worked for nine years as superintendent of the National Institutes of Health Primate Ecology research facility in Puerto Rico. As administrator, he worked closely with the ecologists who carried out the scientific population dynamics research, and he introduced innovative participatory management techniques. His supervisor, mentor, and friend during his years at the research facility was Carl Koford, who contributed greatly to Nagel's environmental awareness. Nagel later described this period as a time when, without his knowing it, he was being injected with the "antibody" of ecological consciousness—cultivating an appreciation of healthy, diverse ecosystems that came to permeate his outlook on the world.

In 1968 he was named assistant director of the Oakland Museum in California and stayed for one year, leaving in 1969 to become director of the Museums of New Mexico in Santa Fe. In 1974 he was asked to join the Arizona-Sonora Desert Museum in Tucson to establish a comprehensive binational environmental program with Mexico. He left the museum in 1978 to create the Cultural Exchange Service, a consultant service specializing in cross-cultural communications that seeks to find common ground among individuals with different orientations in businesses, environmental groups, and civic organizations.

One of Nagel's best-known achievements began to take shape in 1985, when he and a group of environmentally concerned Tucson residents began looking for a way to help support Pronatura, the premier national conservation organization in Mexico. When the Tucson group approached Pronatura to ask what they could do, the founders of the organization suggested a kind of "reverse imperialism," with the creation of a U.S. branch of the Mexico-based organization. With that, Nagel and the others founded the nonprofit Friends of Pronatura to assist its Mexican counterpart in promoting education, research, and information dissemination on environmental issues affecting southwestern North America. After its inception, FPN worked extensively on U.S.-Mexico borderland issues and supported several of the six chapters of Pronatura in Mexico with grants and publicity campaigns in the United States.

In 1988, Friends of Pronatura received a grant from the U.S. Man and the Biosphere Program (U.S. MAB), a project designed to promote ecosystem management programs that incorporate sustainable development, to document global change and biological diversity through monitoring and scientific research, and to organize regional and international cooperation in the effort to resolve complex issues of multipurpose land use. U.S. MAB uses United Nations Educational, Scientific and Cultural Organization (UNESCO)–designated biosphere reserves as sites for implementing management plans, conducting research, and bringing together cooperating institutions. The grant provided to Friends of Pronatura allowed the group to study applications of the biosphere reserve concept in the region. As president of FPN, Nagel used the opportunity to put one of his strongest beliefs to use: that just as the health of an ecosystem stems from its biological diversity, the health of a social environment is promoted by a diversity of opinions, viewpoints, attitudes, feelings, and actions. During the following year, Nagel successfully expanded the discussions on the biosphere reserve to include leaders of the Tohono O'odham and local communities, state and local governments, and nongovernmental organizations. This effort fostered a new willingness to use the biosphere reserve concept as a structure for empowering diverse parties to maintain dialogue and cooperate in addressing shared problems. For example, Nagel planned a symposium to discuss protection of the Pinacate, an ecologically fragile area in northwest Sonora, Mexico. The gathering, held in Hermosillo, Sonora, in 1988, included researchers, representatives from nongovernmental organizations, community members, and members of the Tohono O'odham, a Native American nation whose traditional homelands encompassed much of the area. This was the first time the O'odham were consulted and given an opportunity to express their views on the region, which included sites of critical importance to their culture, history, and identity.

To continue to nurture international relationships and to increase local awareness about the need to protect the western Sonora Desert border region, another forum on land use was held in 1992 in Ajo, Arizona. About 200 people attended from all over the region, including federal, state, county, and tribal government officials; business leaders; and members of the O'odham Nation. The group tackled many complex issues, including the potential environmental and socioeconomic effects of the North American Free Trade Agreement and how to expand and improve communication among agencies and citizens regarding the biosphere reserve concept. As a result of the positive response from the conference, Nagel collaborated with the Sonoran Institute, an organization devoted to community-based conservation, to forge an alliance called the International Sonoran Desert Alliance (ISDA), made up of individuals from the United States, Mexico, and the Tohono O'odham Nation. ISDA has since grown into a large network, and in 1994 it was incorporated as a nonprofit organization in Arizona, and its first board of directors was elected. In 1998 Nagel joined the board of ISDA and in 1999 was elected president. He has also served on the boards of directors of the Sonoran Institute, the Development Center for Appropriate Technology, and the Yonosé Foundation in Tucson.

Nagel's work has involved him in other groups as well. He is a founding member of the following organizations: Environmental Committee of the Arizona-Mexico/Sonora-Arizona Commissions, the Arizona-Mexico Border Health Foundation, and Hands Across the Border (a school exchange program that has involved over 6,000 Sonoran and Arizona students each year since 1982). He has also served as vice president of the board for the Center for Studies of Deserts and Oceans (in Puerto Peñasco, Sonora). He also presents seminars on a broad spectrum of topics ranging from intercultural issues to the relations between the environment and business.

In 1998 the Arizona-Sonora Desert Museum presented Nagel with its Sixth Annual Luminaria Award for his work to increase public knowledge and appreciation for the environment, particularly the Sonoran Desert. In 2007, the Sonoran Institute presented him with the Cele Peterson Award for his more than 30 years of service to the community of Tucson. Nagel is unmarried, his partner since 1978 having died in 1999; he has five adopted children. He lives in Tucson, Arizona.

### BIBLIOGRAPHY
Faulkner, Tina, "Community-Based Groups Set the Agenda for Conservation of the Colorado River Delta," *Borderlines*, 1999; Nagel, Carlos, "Commentary," *Natural Resources Journal*, 1993; "Pronatura," www.pronatura.org.mx; Williams, Florence, "On the Borderline," *High Country News*, 1994.

## Nash, Roderick
(January 7, 1939– )
Environmental Historian and Ethicist

Roderick Nash's seminal work, *Wilderness and the American Mind* (1967), is considered a classic study of how the concept of wilderness has shaped the American character. Nash, a professor of history and environmental studies (now retired), successfully bridged the gap between academic discourse and popular literature on the environment. He brought a new voice to the debate over wilderness—that of the historian. His exploration of wilderness as an intellectual idea led the way toward a new consideration of the role of philosophy and ethics in the field of environmentalism. *Wilderness and the American Mind* continues to be widely read; now in its fourth edition, it has remained in print for more than 40 years. Nash has become a well-known and highly respected spokesman for wilderness preservation and environmental education.

Roderick Frazier Nash was born January 7, 1939, in New York City. He is the son of Jay B. Nash, a professor, and Emma (Frazier) Nash. Nash graduated *magna cum laude* with a degree in history and literature from Harvard University in 1960. He pursued graduate studies at the University of Wisconsin, earning his M.A. in 1961 and his Ph.D. in 1964. He taught history at Dartmouth College from 1964 to 1966 before moving to the University of California at Santa Barbara (UCSB) as an assistant professor in the history department. In 1970, he founded UCSB's Department of Environmental Studies; he served as chair of the department for six years.

Nash began his writing career as an academic historian, specializing in intellectual and social history. He soon zeroed in on the subject that would prove to be his forte: the idea of wilderness. His academic background gave him an as yet unexplored perspective from which to examine the subject of wilderness. The mid-1960s were fraught with political battles over what exactly constitutes a wilderness and what uses were consistent with a wilderness designation. Nash removed the discussion from the highly emotional political arena and brought it into the intellectual realm: wilderness as a social construct in the minds of Americans. Although it was written originally as his Ph.D. dissertation, *Wilderness and the American Mind* gained an audience and an influence that extended well beyond academia. He was invited to appear on television and in Public Broadcasting Service (PBS) and National Geographic documentaries, and he was interviewed in popular magazines.

In the 1970s, Nash wrote many articles for the general public on why wilderness should be valued. "What Is Wilderness and Why Do We Need it?" appeared in the *Daily Idahoan* in Moscow, Idaho, in 1976; it and others were widely reprinted in newspapers, magazines, and textbooks. During this period, Nash also received several grants from the Rockefeller Foundation to research environmental issues. Although he was drawn more and more into the environmental arena, Nash continued to write on other aspects of American history. *The Nervous Generation* (1970) and *From These Beginnings* (1973) focused on the social, intellectual, and biographical elements of American history. In 1973, a revised edition of *Wilderness and the American Mind* was issued. The new edition reflected the evolution of Nash's thought since the original publication. The first edition began with the preconceived ideas of wilderness that immigrants to the United States brought with them from the Old World—attitudes that had been drawn, in turn, from the Judeo-Christian depiction of nature in the Bible. The revised edition looked beyond the Western historical tradition and a purely intellectual idea of nature. In the preface, Nash delved into prehistory to explore the intuitive meaning of wilderness as perceived by early man.

Underlying Nash's evolving philosophy is a fundamental belief that in the United States, understanding of the environment must start with an understanding of the role of wilderness in the nation's imagination. In a 1989 documentary in the PBS series *The American Experience*, he restated the premise he first presented in *Wilderness and the American Mind*. "If there was one thing that shaped our character and culture, one single factor you could point to, it would be wild country." The United States, he claimed, based its national identity on wilderness just as Europe based its on a shared history full of intellectual and artistic traditions. Wilderness made the United States fundamentally different from Europe. Nash traced the transformation of this perception of wilderness from an essentially negative attitude in the early years of the United States to the positive attitude held two hundred years later. Through skillful use of historical examples, Nash conveyed how Puritans saw the wilderness as a hostile wasteland and moral vacuum capable of sucking all the humanity out of man, while later generations came to see it as a benign spiritual force that soothed the often dangerously overstimulated modern mind.

By 1989, Nash had developed an environmental philosophy that centered on the ethics of the human-nature relationship. In *The Rights of Nature: A History of Environmental Ethics*, Nash demonstrates that the concept in the United States of who—or even what—warrants ethical and legal consideration has changed radically from the days of the founding fathers; the circle of inclusion has gradually expanded from White males only to encompass females, Blacks, and other disenfranchised groups. Nash argues that extending legal and ethical rights to all living species—even plants and trees—is a logical extension of our liberal tradition. This book is also considered foundational in the field.

Nash's influence has been felt not only through his writing but also through his teaching. The infamous Santa Barbara Oil Spill of January 28, 1969 inspired Nash not only to pen the "Santa Barbara Declaration of Environmental Rights," which focused on the rights of the environment, which Nash read for network television, but also to establish, with other faculty members at UCSB, the first teach-in about the environment and new environmental studies interdisciplinary major, which students welcomed as an option that seemed especially relevant to them. Many of Nash's graduate students in UCSB's environmental studies program have become environmental writers. One of these was Calvin Martin, author of *Keepers of the Game*, which won the American Historical Association's

Beveridge Award in 1978. Nash's role as a leader in the field of environmentalism was recognized in 1974 when he was selected by the American Academy of Achievement as "one of forty giants of accomplishment from America's great fields of endeavor." The Charles A. Lindbergh Fund named him a Lindbergh Fellow in 1982 for advocating a balance between technological progress and environmental preservation. In 1988, he received the William G. Anderson Award of the American Alliance for Health, Physical Education, and Recreation to honor the contributions he had made to the field of outdoor recreation. Nash has served as a consultant to many government agencies and nongovernmental organizations, including the National Park Service, *National Geographic*, the U.S. Forest Service, the state of Alaska, and the Rockefeller Foundation. He has been associated in a leadership role with various environmental organizations and publications, including the Sierra Club, Friends of the Earth, the Yosemite Institute, *Environmental Ethics*, and *Journal of Environmental Education*.

As an environmental leader at the beginning of the twenty-first century, Nash has often been asked what he thinks the future holds for planet earth. In articles and interviews, he remains unabashedly optimistic about the future, having faith in nature's ability to restore balance. He envisions population "islands" surrounded by undeveloped land and a generation of children brought up with an ethic of sustainability. Nash believes such changes can come about through a new model of environmental education that embraces the study of both the humanities, such as ethics and philosophy, and the sciences.

Although a native New Yorker—he likes to say that he lived for 18 years with a view of a brick wall—Nash became a backcountry enthusiast. After serving as a fishing guide in Ontario and Wyoming in the mid-1950s, he became one of the first professional river guides in the country, running the Snake River in Grand Teton National Park. Over the next 30 years, Nash developed into an experienced riverboatman, running the Colorado River through the Grand Canyon over 50 times and performing first descents of rivers in California, Alaska, and Peru. Nash co-wrote with Robert Collins a guide to the best whitewater rafting spots in the West in 1978, *The Big Drops: Ten Legendary Rapids of the American West*.

Retired from UCSB since 1993, Nash has maintained an active intellectual presence in the field of environmental literature through his book reviews, which appear frequently in such publications as *American Historical Review*, *New England Quarterly*, and *Journal of American History*. Nash and his wife, Lindamel Murray, live in Santa Barbara, California, and Crested Butte, Colorado. He has two grown daughters, Laura and Jennifer.

**BIBLIOGRAPHY**

Murphy, Pat, "Roderick Nash: Environmental Disciple," Environmental News Network (http://www.enn.com), 2000; Nash, Roderick, interview, *Environmental History*, 2007, www.historycooperative.org/journals/eh/12.2/nash.html; Nash, Roderick, *The Rights of Nature: A History of Environmental Ethics*, 1989; Nash, Roderick, *Wilderness and the American Mind*, 1967; Public Broadcasting System, "The Wilderness Idea: John Muir, Gifford Pinchot, and the First Great Battle for Wilderness," (video recording) 1989; "Rod Nash, Author, Professor of Environmental Studies," *Lands of Brighter Destiny: The Public Lands of the American West*, Elizabeth Darby Junkin, ed., 1986.

## Nearing, Helen, and Scott Nearing
(February 23, 1904–September 17, 1995; August 6, 1883–August 24, 1983)
Writers, Founders of Back-to-the-land Movement

Helen and Scott Nearing have been described as the grandparents of the back-to-the-land movement. Following Scott Nearing's controversial and subversive academic career, in which he was fired from every university he worked for because of his radical views, the Nearings moved to a farm in Vermont, where they farmed organically and lived simply for 19 years. Then Helen and Scott Nearing moved to Maine, where they did the same thing until their deaths at the ages of 91 and 100, respectively. They were prolific and influential writers, whose books addressed all manner of social issues and whose ideas inspired many others to return to the land, and to live "the good life," the title of their best-known book.

Scott Nearing (Library of Congress, Prints & Photographs Division, LC-USZ62-82851)

The oldest of six children, Scott Nearing was born on August 6, 1883, in the company town of Morris Run, Pennsylvania, to Louis and Minnie Zabriski Nearing. Scott's grandfather, Winfield Scott Nearing, supervised the Morris Run Coal Company with a union-busting iron hand (he earned the nickname Czar Nearing of Morris Run). Scott's father operated the company fruit and vegetable store. In 1898, when Scott was 15 years old, his family moved to Philadelphia, and he enrolled in Central Manual Training High School. He decided not to enroll in the more academic Central High School, because he sought a practical education, one that combined both theory and practice. He graduated from high school in 1901 and entered the University of Pennsylvania Law School. Scott did not enjoy studying law, as Steve Sherman writes in *A Scott Nearing Reader, The Good Life in Bad Times:* "It was increasingly clear that anything having to do with the gathering of unseemly amounts of money, and defending it as lawyers were trained to do, nettled him." He decided to turn his attention to the social sciences.

In 1903, Nearing entered the Wharton School at the University of Pennsylvania, where he studied economics and oratory at Temple College (now Temple University). He received a B.S. in economics from the Wharton School and a Bachelor of Oratory from Temple College in 1905. That same year, he began work as secretary of the Pennsylvania Child Labor Commission, a position he held until 1907. In 1908, Scott married Nellie Marguerite Seeds. They would later separate in 1925. Nearing earned a Ph.D. in economics at the Wharton School in 1909. He taught economics at the Wharton School as an instructor from 1906 to 1914, before being promoted to assistant professor in 1914. He also taught economics at Swarthmore College from 1908 to 1913.

In 1915, in a nationally publicized academic freedom case, Nearing was dismissed from the Wharton School for his vocal opposition to child labor. The University of Pennsylvania was under pressure to silence Nearing. Powerful textile manufacturers, who employed large numbers of children, exercised a significant degree of control over the amount of state funding the university received, and in the interest of retaining that funding, the University of Pennsylvania fired Nearing after nine years of employment. For the next two years, from 1915 to 1917, Nearing worked at the University of Toledo as a professor of social science and dean of the Colleges of Arts and Sciences. He was fired from the University of Toledo for vocalizing his pacifist views, and he was indicted by a federal grand jury for writing a pamphlet entitled "The Great Madness," which spoke out against U.S. involvement in World War I. He went to trial in 1919 and was acquitted of all charges. In 1917, Nearing became an instructor at the Rand School of Social Science in New York and joined the Socialist Party. He ran for Congress on the Socialist Party ticket in 1918, but lost.

During this period of his life, Nearing was writing copiously. Between 1917 and 1937, he published more than 30 books and pamphlets, including *The Menace of Militarism* (1917), *Dollar Diplomacy: A Study in American Imperialism* (1925), *Whither China? An Economic Interpretation of Recent Events in the Far East* (1927), *Black America* (1929), and *War: Organized Destruction and Mass Murder by Civilized Nations* (1931). He also joined the Communist Party in 1927, only to be expelled three years later after publishing *The Twilight of Empire* (1930), a history of imperialism that challenged the party's official text, *Imperialism*, written by Lenin. In 1929, Scott met Helen Knothe.

Helen Knothe was born February 23, 1904, in New York City to Frank and Maria Obreen Knothe. In a 1994 interview with *Whole Earth Review*, she described her family as "rather out of the ordinary... They were intellectuals, they were musical, they were artistic." Her parents, both vegetarians, were interested in eastern religions and were "quite philanthropic." Helen began studying the violin as a child, and by the time she was 17 she faced a choice: stay in the United States and go to college (Vassar or Wellesley) or travel to Europe and study the violin. She chose Europe. Not only was she a developing concert violinist, she was also a student and practitioner of eastern philosophies. She spent the years 1921 to 1925 with Krishnamurti, an important Hindu spiritual leader. Helen then spent several years traveling around Australia before moving back to the United States permanently. She met Scott Nearing in 1929; their first date was spent admiring fall foliage in New Jersey.

By 1931, Scott Nearing had been separated from his first wife for six years. He and Helen moved to New York together, where they attempted to piece together a living in the impoverished Great Depression economy. In 1932, they decided that if they were going to be poor, they might as well be poor somewhere where they could at least grow their own food, so they bought a farm near Jamaica, Vermont. They refurbished the farmhouse and rejuvenated the soil through natural, organic means. They lived off of what they produced and sold maple syrup and sugar to pay the taxes. During the winters, they traveled extensively, visiting places such as Germany, Russia, Austria, and Spain. Scott used these trips to gather material for his books, which he continued to produce at a rapid pace.

It was at their Vermont homestead that the couple developed their four-four-four daily schedule. They would spend four hours of each day gardening or otherwise working to provide for their basic needs. They would spend four hours undertaking professional activities (Scott Nearing eventually wrote a total of 50 books, six of them co-authored with Helen). And they would spend four hours working in service to their community, fulfilling their obligations as members of the human race. In 1947, after the death of Scott's first wife, Helen and Scott were married. By the early 1950s, hundreds of visitors were visiting the Nearing farm each year. This popularity, along with the development of a nearby ski resort, impelled the Nearings to move once more in search of solitude. In 1951, they purchased a house in Harborside, Maine.

In Maine, they continued to farm (their cash crop was blueberries rather than maple syrup and sugar), and they wrote what is perhaps their best known work, *Living the Good Life* (1954). This book became a bestseller in the early 1960s with the dawning of the back-to-the-land movement, and the Nearings became mentors for those seeking to escape the materialism and corruption that was becoming prevalent as the United States was beset by racial and social injustices.

In 1972, at the age of 90, Scott Nearing wrote his autobiography, *The Making of a Radical*, and he and Helen began constructing a new stone house, which they finished in 1976. In 1973, Scott Nearing received an honorary degree from the Wharton School of Economics, the institution that had fired him 58 years earlier. He died in 1983, just a few weeks after his one hundredth birthday, purposefully fasting to death. In her *Whole Earth Review* interview, Helen Nearing describes the experience of losing her husband in this way as being completely natural, saying "I wish more people could go as readily and easily and unaffected as he was…. He was a model for me in his living and in his going." Helen Nearing continued to live and farm in Maine. She also continued to write, publishing *Simple Food for the Good Life* in 1985 and *Loving and Leaving the Good Life* in 1992. She died in a car accident in 1995 at the age of 91.

### BIBLIOGRAPHY

Cole, John N., "Scott Nearing's Ninety-Three-Year Plan," *Horticulture*, 1976; Johnson, Linnea, "Legendary Homesteaders, H. and S. Nearing," *Mother Earth News*, 2003; Nearing, Helen, *Loving and Leaving the Good Life*, 1992; Nearing, Scott, *The Making of a Radical*, 1972; Sherman, Steve, *A Scott Nearing Reader: The Good Life in Bad Times*, 1989; Simon, Tami, "The View from Ninety," *Whole Earth Review*, 1994.

## Needleman, Herbert

(December 13, 1927– )
Pediatrician, Lead Researcher

Author of a 1979 study proving a link between low-level lead exposure and impaired mental function, Herbert Needleman has been a long-time advocate for reducing lead levels in the environment. Needleman's work intensified the growing momentum to enforce stricter regulation of lead. Because his findings so clearly showed the need to eliminate the possibility of lead exposure, Needleman became a target for the already-ailing lead industry and had to defend his research from industry-planted complaints. Levels of lead in children's bloodstreams have fallen by 75 percent since 1979, thanks to Needleman's research and the national concern and activism it has spurred.

Herbert Needleman was born on December 13, 1927, in Philadelphia. He graduated from Muhlenberg College with a B.S. in 1948 and earned his M.D. from the University of Pennsylvania in 1952. In order to finance his studies while in medical school, he worked as a laborer at a DuPont chemical plant, where he encountered firsthand the toxic effects of lead. He noticed that one older group of workers kept to themselves and behaved oddly, and when he asked about them, Needleman was told they were from "the house of butterflies." Years before, more than 300 workers had suffered acute lead poisoning at the plant. Four of them died, and others were permanently disabled and unable to return to work. While the group Needleman had noticed was still able to work, they suffered lasting neurological damage, including a tendency to gesture at imaginary insects.

Needleman next encountered lead poisoning in 1957, while completing a pediatric residency at an inner-city hospital in Philadelphia. Needleman diagnosed a three-year-old girl with lead poisoning, acquired from the lead paint on the walls of her family's home. A paint chip as small as a dime can result in acute symptoms, and the girl had probably eaten a small piece. When lead enters the bloodstream, the body mistakes it for calcium. In much of the body this substitution causes no obvious harm, but in the brain, lead causes small blood vessels to leak, resulting in swelling and pressure. The child had classic symptoms of lead poisoning, and Needleman told her mother she could not bring the girl back to their house, because a second exposure would almost certainly cause catastrophic damage. The mother told Needleman that any other house they could afford to rent would also have lead paint. Needleman realized that the problem of lead exposure extended beyond his medical skills. Lead was ever present in the environment, not only in paint but also in gasoline, automobile exhaust, and the pipes that carried drinking water. The solution would have to be political as well as scientific.

In 1974, while teaching at Harvard Medical School, Needleman began a study of the effects of low-level lead exposure on children's behavior and intelligence. Needleman compared groups of children with low and high levels of lead exposure, correlating their intelligence quotients (IQs), educational achievements, and teachers' blind evaluations of their behavioral characteristics. His research demonstrated a clear, direct link between chronic, low levels of lead exposure and impaired mental function. The students with higher lead exposure showed consistently lower IQ scores, weaker academic performance, and higher negative behavior ratings. Needleman published his findings in 1979, at a time when the lead industry was already feeling regulatory pressure. In 1977, lead had been banned from household paint, and the Occupational Safety and Health Act of 1978 contained new, stricter monitoring of lead in the workplace. Needleman's work earned him an influential voice as an adviser to the Environmental Protection Agency (EPA), which phased in a ban on leaded gasoline during the 1980s. The Centers for Disease Control, too, issued stricter guidelines for what could be considered safe lead blood levels.

In 1981, Needleman met Dr. Claire Ernhart while both were serving as consultants to the EPA during revisions to the Clean Air Act. Ernhart, a developmental psychologist who received substantial grant money from the lead industry, charged that Needleman's 1979 study was flawed and that he should therefore be disqualified as an adviser to the government. A panel of outside experts reexamined Needleman's work and confirmed his findings. In 1991, Ernhart again challenged Needleman's study, bringing formal charges of scientific misconduct in a letter to the National Institutes of Health. Needleman was investigated over a period of three years, before being formally cleared of all charges in 1994.

In 1990, Needleman founded the Alliance to End Childhood Lead Poisoning, a public interest group devoted to developing comprehensive strategies to end lead poisoning. The alliance's mission is "to frame the national agenda, formulate innovative approaches, and bring critical resources to bear—scientific and technical knowledge, law and public policy, economic forces, national allies, and community organizations and leaders—to prevent childhood lead poisoning." One way in which this organization have worked has been to return to the Homewood area of Pittsburgh where Needleman first studied the problem, and help families whose homes were painted with lead-based paint, cover the outer walls with aluminum siding.

Needleman continues to research the consequences of lead poisoning. A study published in 2000, in which Needleman looked at the lives of those with high levels of lead as children, revealed that as they grew older they were more likely to continue to have behavioral problems, and that between 11 and 38 percent of delinquency can be attributed to high lead exposure.

Needleman has also been active in efforts to reduce exposure to pesticides, many of which lead to brain damage and other neurological impairment, and has performed research on the risk of exposure to lead through dental amalgam fillings.

Needleman's work has contributed to a dramatic reduction in the lead hazard in the United States. Levels of lead in children's blood fell by more than 75 percent during the 20 years following the publication of his 1979 study, and his advocacy played no small role in the reduction. For his tenacious and courageous work, Needleman has garnered many awards. In 1992, he was awarded the National Wildlife Federation's Conservation Achievement Award, in 1995 the Heinz Award in the Environment, in 2003 the Prince Mahidol Award, in 2004 the Rachel Carson Award for Integrity in Science from the Center for Science in the Public Interest, and in 2006, the Distinguished Investigator Award from the Neurotoxicology Speciality of the Society of Toxicology. Needleman is a pediatrician and child psychiatrist at the University of Pittsburgh Medical Center.

**BIBLIOGRAPHY**
"Alliance to End Childhood Lead Poisoning," http://www.aeclp.org; "Dr. Herbert Needleman," The Heinz Awards www.awards.heinz.org; Lewis, Thomas, "The Difficult Quest of Herbert Needleman," *National Wildlife*, 1995; Rosner, David and Gerald Markowitz, "Standing Up to the Lead Industry: An Interview with Herbert Needleman," *Public Health Reports*, 2005.

## Nelson, Gaylord
(June 4, 1916–July 3, 2005)
Governor of Wisconsin, U.S. Senator from Wisconsin

Wisconsin native Gaylord Nelson spent 32 years of his life as a Democratic politician, including ten years as a state senator, four years as Wisconsin's governor, and 18 years in the U.S. Senate. During his career he led the fight to pass such landmark environmental legislation as the Clean Air Act, the National Pesticide Control Act, the Water Quality Act, the Natural Lakes Preservation Act, and the Wild Rivers Act, but he was perhaps best known as the father of Earth Day.

Born on June 4, 1916, Gaylord Nelson attributes his deeply ingrained environmentalism to his upbringing in the small town of Clear Lake, Wisconsin. Clear Lake was surrounded by lakes and marshes, which Nelson explored throughout his boyhood. After being inspired by a visiting politician, Nelson undertook his first political project: asking the town council to line the roads that led into town with elm trees. The council declined to take on the project, but Nelson did not lose his interest in politics. Nelson earned a bachelor's degree at San Jose State College in California in 1939 and graduated from the University of Wisconsin law school in 1942. Immediately he was drafted into the military and served for the remainder of World War II. Upon his return to civilian life, Nelson married Carrie Lee and was elected to Wisconsin's state senate, an office he retained for ten years.

When Nelson was elected governor in 1958, he reread one of his favorite books, ALDO LEOPOLD's *Sand County Almanac*, which urged a view of nature as a community that we humans must respect and conserve. Nelson convinced the state legislature to set aside $50 million to buy and conserve wildlands in the state. During his governorship, Wisconsin became the first state to regulate the use of the harmful, nonbiodegradable laundry detergents that were polluting lakes and rivers. The state also passed strict laws against trash dumping and littering.

Nelson was elected U.S. senator in 1962, bringing a previously nonexistent environmental consciousness to Congress. He successfully convinced Pres. John F. Kennedy to undertake a national conservation tour during the summer of 1963. With 80 reporters signed up for the trip, Nelson thought the tour would be a giant success and would awaken the American public to environmental problems. However, newspaper editors were not interested, and the tour went completely unpublicized. Still, Nelson continued his work quietly.

After a visit to Santa Barbara, California, where he witnessed the destruction wrought by a huge oil spill, an idea occurred to him. He was familiar with the "teach-ins" that were being organized around the Vietnam War and issued a call for a country-wide environmental teach-in. Once the idea caught on, he enlisted Harvard Law student DENIS HAYES to coordinate the event. Earth Day, April 22, 1970, was celebrated at 2,000 colleges and 10,000 elementary and secondary schools by 20 million Americans, who spent the day picking up trash, dredging rivers, closing streets to cars, and a variety of other activities. Public enthusiasm for Earth Day carried a lot of weight with Nelson's colleagues in Washington. President Nixon had dedicated his 1970 State of the Union speech to the cause of environmentalism, and in the decade following Earth Day, much environmental legislation was passed, including the Water Quality Act, the National Pesticide Control Act, the Clean Air Act, the Natural Lakes Preservation Act, and the Wild Rivers Act. Nelson took a leadership role in the passage of much of this legislation.

Nelson left public office in 1980 and went to work for the Wilderness Society, which his intellectual mentor Aldo Leopold had helped found. Nelson was the honorary chair of the 1990 Earth Day and won the Conservationist of the Year award from the National Wildlife Federation and the United Nations Environmental Program's Environmental Leadership Award.

Nelson died on July 3, 2005, of cardioascular failure.

**BIBLIOGRAPHY**

Christofferson, Bill, *The man from Clear Lake: Earth Day Founder Gaylord Nelson*, 2004; "Joint Resolution to Designate April 22, 1990 as Earth Day and to Set Aside the Day for Public Activities Promoting Preservation of the Global Environment," Public Law 101-186, 1989; Motavalli, Jim, "Founding Father: Gaylord Nelson on Earth Day's Past, Present and Future," *E Magazine*, 1995; Mowrey, Mark, and Tim Redmond, *Not in Our Back Yard*, 1993; Schneider, Keith, "Gaylord A. Nelson, Founder of Earth Day, is Dead at 89," *New York Times*, 2005Shulman, Jeffrey, and Teresa Rodgers, *Gaylord Nelson: A Day for the Earth*, 1992.

## Nelson, Willie
(April 30, 1933– )
Singer, Songwriter

Willie Nelson is a country singer who, in his later career, has worked tirelessly and enthusiastically to raise money for family farms, alternative fuels and animal rights. He is the founder of Farm Aid and BioWillie, and repeatedly lends his voice and iconic status to environmental causes.

Willie Hugh Nelson was born on April 30, 1933, in Abbott, Texas. His parents lived with his grandparents in a tiny cotton farming community. All the cotton planted in Abbott was picked, processed and milled within a fifty-mile radius, instilling in Nelson, at an extremely young age, the value of the family farm and local production. Before the second grade, Nelson was picking cotton alone. Nelson's grandfather had bought him a guitar by the time Willie was six, and in Nelson's own words, sent him "out into the world with a profession that would last a lifetime." Nelson's sister Bobbie began playing the piano, and the two embarked on their lifelong musical partnership that continues today. After high school, Nelson worked as a tree trimmer in East Texas, then, in lieu of the draft, spent nine months in the air force. He was discharged for medical reasons, and, wishing to pursue music, returned to Abbott where he met his first wife, Martha. The pair relocated frequently over the next few years before settling in Nashville. Nelson quickly became a very popular songwriter. Patsy Cline's 1962 recording of Nelson's "Crazy" is considered one of the greatest records of all time, with its gentle lyrics, country twang and Cline's unmistakable, impeccable vocals.

Nevertheless, Nelson's own career didn't take off until he moved to Austin in the late 1960s and began playing a more rock-influenced style of country, with hints of jazz and swing. Throughout the 1970s, Willie Nelson became the most popular figure in country music. He partnered up with various musicians, including Waylon Jennings in 1976, for country music's first platinum album, *Wanted: The Outlaws!* This "outlaw" brand of country, as opposed to what was coming out of Nashville, became Nelson's trademark, along with that of many other country singers like Jennings, Merle Haggard, Kris Kristofferson, and Johnny Cash. Undoubtedly, Nelson's individualism and outlaw tendencies provided the framework through which he turned his interests to the environment.

In 1985, Nelson, along with musicians Neil Young and John Mellencamp, began Farm Aid, an annual benefit concert to raise money for family farms. The idea was spawned by a comment Bob Dylan made at Live Aid earlier in the same year, wondering aloud if any kind of similar event could be held for America's family farms. The concert has gone on each year since (except 1988 and 1991), drawing numerous, widely famous acts, with all the proceeds going to the preservation and subsidization of family farms. Farm Aid became its own, year-round organization that, along with its preservation work, strives to increase public awareness about the importance of family farms. Nelson, Mellencamp, Young and Dave Matthews make up the board of directors.

Nelson has also been an outspoken advocate of biodiesel. In 2005, he and several other partners formed Willie Nelson Biodiesel, also known as "BioWillie," a company that markets and brings biodiesel to truck stops throughout the South. On April 1, 2006, Nelson and actor Morgan Freeman broke ground on Willie's Place at Carl's Corner, Texas—a truck stop and biodiesel processing plant that processes more than two million gallons of biodiesel per year. The fuel is made primarily from soybean oil and can be used in any engine that runs on traditional diesel. In August 2007, Nelson released his book *On the "Clean" Road Again: Biodiesel and the Fu-*

*ture of the Family Farm*, in which he promotes biodiesel as not only a cleaner source of alternative fuel but also as a way to save the American family farm. Nelson recounts the days before Prohibition in which the American farmer was responsible for the production of ethanol, the main source of automotive fuel. As biodiesel can be made from a variety of sustainable crops, the "idea of the American farmer growing our fuel" would simultaneously alleviate our dependence on foreign oil, while kick-starting the struggling agricultural economy.

Willie Nelson is a generous supporter of political and humanitarian campaigns. With the Society for Animal Protective Legislation, Willie lobbied for passage of the American Horse Slaughter Prevention Act. He adopts horses from Habitat for Horses. Willie Nelson's Country Peach Cobbler Ice Cream sends all Nelson's proceeds to Farm Aid. Kinky Friedman, as a candidate for Governor of Texas in 2006, promised Nelson a job as head of a new Texas Energy Commission for his work with alternative fuels.

Along with his tireless work at benefits, organizations, foundations and concerts, Nelson established the Willie Nelson Peace Research Institute in 2007. The Institute's mandate is the belief in the "Promise of Peace on Earth in Our Lifetime as the Birthright of Our Global Human Family." The Institute invites you to record or video the song "A Peaceful Solution" (written by Nelson and his daughter Amy) to give away to the world. Anyone is free to record the song, and the song will be featured on the Willie Nelson Peace Research Institute website.

Nelson currently owns a ranch in Luck, Texas, with his fifth wife, Annie. He is the father of nine children.

**BIBLIOGRAPHY**
Nelson, Willie, with Shrake, Bud, *Willie: An Autobiography*, 2000; Nelson, Willie, with Pipkin, Turk, *The Tao of Willie: A Guide to the Happiness in Your Heart*, 2006; Nelson, Willie, *On the "Clean" Road Again: Biodiesel and the Future of the Family Farm*, 2007; www.benjerry.com; www.habitatforhorses.org; www.willienelson.com; www.willienelsonpri.com.

# Newman, Nell
(1959– )
Writer, Co-founder and President of Newman's Own Organics

Organic food executive Nell Newman entered the food industry with the help of her father's successful food label, Newman's Own. Paul Newman's brand was equally well known for foods such as salad dressings, sauces, and popcorn, and donating all its post-tax profits to charity. In 1993, Nell Newman co-founded Newman's Own Organics, as a division of Newman's Own, to promote the mainstream appeal of organic food products. Newman's Own Organics then became an independent company in late 2000.

The daughter of actor Paul Newman and actress Joanne Woodward, Nell grew up in rural Connecticut where her family grew fruits and vegetables, raised chickens, and fished in nearby rivers. Her mother taught Nell to cook using fresh, natural foods from their gardens, and her father taught her to fish. Nell was interested in birds from an early age. Even as a

Nell Newman (Photograph courtesy of Nikki Brooks Photography)

child, she was saddened to watch the peregrine falcon population decrease to near extinction as a result of a synthetic pesticide, DDT, which interfered with the birds' ability to successfully reproduce. She went on to study human ecology at the College of the Atlantic in Bar Harbor, Maine, working to return peregrine falcons to their natural habitat. After graduating with her bachelor's degree, Nell worked for New York's Environmental Defense Fund. She then moved to California and spent two and a half years working at the Ventana Wilderness Sanctuary. Her next position was fundraising for the Santa Cruz Predatory Bird Research Group. Frustrated by lack of funding for long-term predatory bird studies, Nell began to look for other ways to have a positive impact on the environment.

As a longtime advocate of organic foods, Nell began to channel her energy into increasing public awareness of the benefits of organic farming for a more sustainable environment. She thought that consumers should know about their food in terms of where it comes from and how it is produced. With a family connection in the food industry, she developed the idea for an organic division of Newman's Own in 1992. After serving her family an organic Thanksgiving dinner that same year, her father was sold on the idea and agreed to support her. Initially hesitant to introduce organic foods into his company, her father, like many Americans, associated the term "organic" with dense, tasteless, bland foods. However, after the meal Nell prepared, which included all of his favorite traditional Thanksgiving foods, Paul Newman agreed to loan her and her business partner, Peter Meehan, the start-up funds for Newman's Own Organics, which they repaid one year later. The original slogan was "Great tasting products that just happen to be organic."

In selecting products, Nell aimed to create organic products that are familiar to the mainstream public. She wanted to modernize the image of organic foods. The first product offered by Newman's Own Organics was organic pretzels, followed by organic chocolate bars. The majority of the company's products are snack foods including several different types of cookies such as Fig Newmans, popcorn, soy crisps, and dried fruit. Olive oil and balsamic vinegar, pet food, mints, tea, and fair trade coffee are also offered. Each item is packaged with distinctive labeling, featuring Nell and "Pa" Newman, and has an amusing, and sometimes outlandish story about the qualities or origins of the product. In actuality, the organic ingredients used come from farms that have not used pesticides or artificial fertilizers for three or more years. Newman's Own Organics products are certified organic and nutritional information is available for all products on the company's website.

While maintaining the integrity of her company's organic foods, Nell strives to find a balance between taste and the necessities of operating a business. The company's vision is to be part of the organic food industry by producing consumer products, as well as supporting organizations with similar objectives. Paul Newman gives away all his royalties after taxes from Newman's Own Organics to education and charitable organizations. Since 1982 he has donated more than $200 million to charities worldwide.

Currently, Nell Newman lives in a solar-powered house in Santa Cruz and serves as the President of Newman's Own Organics. Not straying far from her roots in rural Connecticut, she keeps chickens and grows her own produce. She also drives a sports car, surfs, and shops at local farmer's markets. In 2003 Nell Newman further shared her passion for environmentally conscious living with her book, *The Newman's Own Organics Guide to a Good Life: Simple Measures That Benefit You and the Place You Live*. The guide includes chapters on food, transportation, energy and water, communication, money and investing, shopping, pets, and cleaning.

**BIBLIOGRAPHY**

D'Agnese, Joseph and Newman, Nell, *The Newman's Own Organics Guide to a Good Life: Simple Measures That Benefit You and the Place You Live*, 2003; Gordon, Wendy, "A Conversation with Nell Newman," *The Green Guide, National Geographic*, May/June 2003; www.newmansownorganics.com.

## Nickels, Greg

(August 7, 1955– )
Mayor of Seattle, Washington

As Mayor of Seattle, Greg Nickels initiated rapid, environmentally conscious changes to the city's public transportation, waste management and carbon footprint. In response to the federal government's refusal to sign the Kyoto Protocol, Nickels led a nationwide coalition of mayors promising to curb their respective city's greenhouse gas emissions to Kyoto Protocol standards. With his maverick sensibilities and independent thinking, Nickels has successfully pushed an environmental agenda both in Seattle and across the nation.

Greg Nickels was born on August 7, 1955 in Chicago to Kathie and Bob Nickels. The family moved to Seattle in 1961. The oldest of six siblings, Nickels attended Seattle Preparatory School and then the University of Washington before dropping out to pursue his passion for public service. At the age of 18, he interned for Senator Warren G. Magnuson in Washington D.C. Nickels returned to Seattle the next year, landing work in the city's purchasing department. In 1979, at the age of 23, he became Norm Rice's Legislative Assistant, working intimately with Rice and learning a great deal from the future mayor. In 1987, following eight years of Rice's tutelage, Nickels became the youngest person ever elected to the King County Council. It was here Nickels began to realize his potential as a candidate for change. Nickels, re-elected three times to the Council, and as chair of the Seattle/King County Board of Health from 1996-2001, took on the tobacco industry's advertising campaigns aimed at children. The Marlboro Man was banned from various parts of Seattle, and graphically violent video games were removed from the Seattle Center. It was also here Nickels began cementing his dedication to the environment and his national advocacy work toward a safer, healthier and environmentally friendly public transportation system.

On January 1, 2002, Nickels became the 51st mayor of Seattle. Upon taking office, Nickels immediately launched his 100-Day Agenda, to rapidly put into action his "get it done" list, while maintaining records of the city's accomplishments and setbacks. Nickels has framed his entire mayorship around four main priorities:

> Get Seattle Moving
> Keep Our Neighborhoods Safe
> Create Jobs and Opportunity for All
> Build Strong Families and Healthy Communities

Under these general guidelines, Nickels has improved upon Seattle in a variety of ways. But it is through his innovative work with transportation and climate disruption that Nickels has become respected nationally.

Under Nickels, Sound Transit, the greater Seattle/Puget Sound area's public transportation system, expanded its light rail and streetcar system. A long-awaited fifteen-mile connection from downtown Seattle to the SeaTac Airport is under construction. The upgraded streetcar system will carry hundreds of thousands of new riders and is being funded, primarily, from new property taxes. In 2003, Nickels was named Chair of the Transportation and Communications Committee of the U.S. Conference of Mayors. Likewise, he was a founding member and continues to serve on Sound Transit's Board of Directors. Nickels has been invaluable in advocating for Seattle's government vehicles to run on alternative fuels and biodiesel. In 2006, more than 600,000 gallons of B20, a blend of 20 percent biodiesel and 80 percent ultra-low sulfur diesel, was used by city vehicles. Garbage and recycling trucks are being converted to low-emission exhaust systems, and more segments of Seattle's award-winning urban bike system are scheduled to be built in conjunc-

Mayor Greg Nickels (left) with Anthony Magda at a Clean and Green Seattle event in 2002. (Photograph courtesy Seattle Municipal Archives)

tion with new public transportation routes. Furthermore, with his "Bridging the Gap" initiative, Nickels has provided funds for improvements to continue in the future. The funding package, based on property, business and parking taxes, will provide about $540 million over nine years to continue maintenance and improvements on bridges, streets, viaducts, overpasses, corridors and various stations.

On February 16, 2005, without the support of the United States, the Kyoto Protocol was ratified into law by 141 industrialized nations. The essential doctrine of the Kyoto Protocol states that greenhouse gas emissions must be reduced to 7 percent below 1990 levels by the year 2012. After a snowless 2004/2005 winter in the areas surrounding Seattle, Nickels directly realized the grave necessity of dealing with global warming. A snowpack, Nickels states, "is essential for water and power throughout the summer." "I issued a challenge to mayors across America to join with me in taking local action to try and meet the spirit and letter of the Kyoto accords while our federal government was failing to act." On March 30, 2005, Nickels, along with eight other mayors representing more than three million citizens, issued the challenge to more than 800 other mayors to join the U.S. Mayors Climate Protection Agreement. Through Nickels's leadership, the U.S. Conference of Mayors unanimously passed the Agreement on June 13, 2005. The Agreement provides methods and guidelines to meet the standards set by the Kyoto Protocol. The number of mayors adopting the Agreement continues to increase.

During Nickels's tenure as Mayor, Seattle increased its recycling capacity, even making the recycling of food scrap mandatory in

2009. Whereas the nation recycles about 30 percent of its trash, Seattle recycles 44 percent, and the city has set goals of 60 percent by 2012, and 72 percent by 2025.

Greg Nickels, his wife Sharon, and their two children, Jacob and Carey live in West Seattle.

**BIBLIOGRAPHY**

Little, Amanda Griscom, *City City Bang Bang: An interview with Seattle Mayor Greg Nickels on his pro-Kyoto cities initiative*, 2005; Cornwall, Warren, "Seattle reports milestone in cutting emissions," *Seattle Times*, 2007; www.seattle.gov/mayor/; www.gregnickels.com/.

## Norton, Bryan
(July 19, 1944– )
Philosopher

Author of numerous works on ethics and the environment, Bryan Norton is an influential voice in the fields of environmental policy and philosophy. Much of his work has been directed at showing that environmentalism, as a movement, is more philosophically coherent and politically unified than is usually credited, an argument made most clearly in his book *Toward Unity among Environmentalists*. In particular, Norton has argued that philosophical differences among environmentalists should not be allowed to interfere in efforts to effect change. Norton's work aims to unite theory and action, through his writings, through his role as a consultant to government agencies and through work with environmental groups.

Bryan Norton was born on July 19, 1944, in Marshall, Michigan, where his family ran a farm. Norton later credited his love of nature to his early years on the farm. He studied government and philosophy at the University of Michigan in the 1960s, where he absorbed the value of social activism. He graduated with a B.A. in 1966 and stayed at the university to earn a Ph.D. in philosophy in 1970. He published his first book, *Linguistic Frameworks and Ontology*, in 1977 while teaching at the University of South Florida in Sarasota.

Norton's professional interest in environmentalism began in 1981, when he was invited by the University of Maryland's Center for Philosophy and Public Policy to study the Endangered Species Act of 1973. The study was funded in part by the National Science Foundation's Ethics and Values in Science and Technology Program. Norton began looking at the act during the heyday of the snail darter controversy. The case was one of the first to test the power of the Endangered Species Act, when a population of the obscure, endangered fish was found in the Tennessee River where a large dam project was in development. The battle between environmentalists and the powerful Tennessee Valley Authority received national press coverage and focused attention on the question of whether all species deserve unlimited protection to exist. (The case eventually drew to a close without a clear victory on either side, when a population of snail darters was found on another branch of the Tennessee River.) While reviewing this and other cases, Norton became interested in a question that was to hold his attention for much of the next decade: On what philosophical grounds can one argue for the preservation of biological diversity? Norton's first consideration of the question was published in *Why Preserve Natural Variety?* (1987), a book that was the direct result of his work at the University of Maryland. The book examines the various rationales behind the

Endangered Species Act and reviews a number of pressing practical concerns, such as how to prioritize species for protection, when time and resources are limited. Should we, for example, focus on those species that are most at risk for immediate extinction, even if these efforts might be futile, or should we instead focus our efforts on less critical cases, where species might be kept from reaching near-extinction?

*Toward Unity among Environmentalists* (1991) attempts to step back from these debates and find a solution to what Norton calls "the environmentalists' dilemma" of reconciling human-centered arguments for environmental protection with demands that species and ecosystems be protected for themselves. During 1985 and 1986, Norton was the Gilbert White Fellow at Resources for the Future, where he studied a variety of environmental organizations. His research convinced him that environmentalists need a more thoroughgoing discussion of values. He argues that environmental debates are often structured on a false dichotomy between utilitarian approaches, which call for environmental protection on the basis of economic value, and moral or ethical approaches, which argue that biodiversity is intrinsically valuable apart from human needs. Norton bridges this gap with a policy-centered approach, focusing on unity of purpose and action rather than differences in ideas. He foregrounds the context of environmental debates to show that while humans are ever-present, we are just one part of the larger picture, dependent upon the very ecosystems we seek to preserve. In the epilogue to the book, he writes, "We must value nature from our point of view *in a total context* which includes our cultural history and our natural history. Nature must be valued, from the ecological-evolutionary viewpoint of environmentalists, in its full contemporary complexity and in its largest temporal dynamic."

Norton has gone on to develop his ideas in numerous essays and further books, including the edited collections *Ecosystem Health* (1992), with Benjamin Haskell and Robert Costanza, and *Ethics on the Ark* (1995), with Michael Hutchins, Elizabeth Stevens, and Terry Maple. The latter collection came out of a workshop held in Atlanta, Georgia, in March 1992, that brought wildlife conservationists, biologists, philosophers, animal rights activists, and zoo professionals together to explore differences among individuals and groups and to come to consensus wherever possible to make policy recommendations for the role of zoos in wildlife preservation. His latest books have been devoted to the concept of sustainability. *Sustainability: A Philosophy of Adaptive Ecosystem Management* (2002), discusses the importance of language and framework in productive communication about environmental protection. Not only is it of importance to use common definitions of terms, but the discourse must allow for open participation and mutual respect between all participants. *Searching for Sustainability: Interdisciplinary Essays in the Philosophy of Conservation Biology* (2003) includes 27 essays that Norton has written, examining sustainability from a variety of perspectives. Again, Norton maintains the importance of those from different disciplines (economists, philosophers, biologists, etc.) finding common language and evaluative criteria with which to discuss the problem.

Norton works to put his ideas into action, facilitating practical efforts at environmental conservation today by collaborating with the U.S. Environmental Protection Agency, the U.S. Army's Environmental Policy Institute, the U.S. Forest Service's Global Change Program, and Zoo Atlanta. Norton has served on the editorial boards of *Environmental Ethics*, *Environmental Values*, *Ethics and the Environment*, and *Ecosystem Health*. He is distinguished professor of philosophy at Georgia Institute of Technology in Atlanta, Georgia.

**BIBLIOGRAPHY**

"Bryan Norton," Georgia Institute of Technology, www.spp.gatech.edu/faculty/bnorton.php; Kim,

Ke Chung, and Robert Weaver, *Biodiversity and Landscapes*, 1994; Preston, Christopher, "Epistemology and Intrinsic Values: Norton and Callicott's Critiques of Rolston," *Environmental Ethics*, 1998; Steverson, Brian, "Contextualism and Norton's Convergence Hypothesis," *Environmental Ethics*, 1995.

## Noss, Reed
(June 23, 1952– )
Ecologist, Conservation Biologist

Reed Noss has been a prominent leader in the fields of conservation biology and conservation planning and in the effort to raise awareness of the value and present decline of global biodiversity. His own career has paralleled the advent of the mission-oriented approach toward science, and he has advanced and promoted large-scale ecosystem management and protection. He has authored and edited numerous books, journal articles, and research publications, and has served as a consultant, adviser, and professor for universities, nonprofit organizations, government agencies, and private firms.

Reed Frederick Noss was born in Dayton, Ohio, on June 23, 1952, the son of James F. and Margaret J. Noss. At a young age, he experienced and learned to treasure natural areas around his home only to see them destroyed by development. This, in turn, sparked a personal and professional interest in conservation. Noss graduated from the School of Education at the University of Dayton, Ohio, in 1975 with a B.S. He then began graduate study in outdoor education at Antioch College in Yellow Springs, Ohio, before moving on to the University of Tennessee in Knoxville and receiving an M.S. in ecology in 1979. He then worked several years for the Ohio Department of Natural Resources, followed by a year with the Florida Natural Areas Inventory (a project of The Nature Conservancy). He earned his Ph.D. in wildlife ecology from the School of Forest Resources and Conservation at the University of Florida in 1988.

While working toward his doctorate in Florida, Noss conducted community-level studies and surveys of endangered and threatened species, including the red-cockaded woodpecker and gopher tortoise. Noss also developed a proposal for establishing a state-wide network of core reserves, connecting corridors, and buffer zones in Florida. While this effort in conservation planning was considered radical at the time, it was later revised and now serves as the base for the conservation land acquisition program in Florida and a model for large-scale ecosystem preservation in other places as well.

After receiving his doctorate, Reed Noss took on a variety of positions, first as a project director for the U.S. Environmental Protection Agency, then as an independent researcher, adviser, and consultant. His career has centered on efforts to protect ecosystems on large scales, enhance existing preserves of wildlands, and educate people of the importance of biodiversity and the value of conservation planning. Noss has had an atypical career in the sense that he has spent much of his professional life as an independent consultant, although he has also worked in academia, for Oregon State University, University of Oregon, and the University of Idaho, , and currently he is an endowed professor at the University of Central Florida. He has also worked on behalf of such nonprofit organizations as the World Wildlife Fund and The Nature Conservancy and government agencies such as the National Biological Service, U.S. Bureau of Land Management, and the U.S. Forest Service.

Noss's work examines the benefits of approaching conservation from a larger scale rather than species-by-species, explores the vital relationship between species and habitat, and promotes the protection and restoration of native biodiversity and ecological integrity. His case studies have identified and assessed core reserves, movement corridors, and at-risk areas in Ohio, Florida, the Blue Mountains of Oregon and Washington, as well as in such ecosystems as the Greater North Cascades, the Greater Yellowstone, the Utah/Wyoming Rockies, and the Klamath/Siskiyou Mountains of Oregon and Northern California. Noss has also performed as a consultant and adviser outside of the country, specifically in Chile and Nicaragua.

In 1991, Noss cofounded with DAVE FOREMAN (a founder of Earth First!) the Wildlands Project, an organization that specifically advocates a connected network of wildlands reserves through conservation science. Promoting the mission-oriented approach of conservation biology and planning, Noss served as science director for the group through 1996 and then again from 2002 until 2004.

In 1993, he was named the editor of *Conservation Biology*, the journal of the Society for Conservation Biology, a position he held until 1997. He is still a consulting editor for the journal. Over his career, Noss has published more than 260 scientific and semitechnical papers and been a regular contributor and peer reviewer for journals such as *Ecology*, *Ecological Applications*, Biological Conservation, and *Journal of Wildlife Management*, as well as *Conservation Biology*. His articles and reports stress the value of keystone species, including large carnivores, in maintaining ecosystem and bioregional health, as well as the crucial role of wildlife corridors and connectivity in maintaining biodiversity and healthy wildlife populations. In 1993, Noss was awarded a three-year Pew Fellowship in Conservation and the Environment. He was recently recognized by Thomson Scientific's "ISI highlycited.com" as one of the 500 most often cited authors in all fields.

His first book, *Saving Nature's Legacy*, coauthored with Allen Cooperrider, was published in 1994. Derived from an instructional series the two men conducted for the U.S. Bureau of Land Management, the book provides guidelines on setting conservation priorities, inventorying biodiversity, and establishing and monitoring reserve networks. The book specifically defines conservation biology as "science in the service of conservation" with the "fundamental belief... that biodiversity is *good* and should be conserved." It notes the growth of the field of conservation biology as a direct response to the decline of biodiversity and differentiates it from traditional fields of science in that it is "cross-disciplinary and depends on the interaction of many different fields (e.g., geography, economics, political science in addition to wildlife biology, forestry, ecology)." *Saving Nature's Legacy* (1995) received the annual Conservation Community Award for Outstanding Achievement in the Field of Publications from the Natural Resources Council of America. In 1995, Noss received the Edward T. LaRoe Memorial Award, the highest award of the Society for Conservation Biology.

Noss's *The Science of Conservation Planning*, coauthored by Michael A. O'Connell and Dennis Murphy, was published in 1997. It focuses on the successful management of Habitat Conservation Plans as laid out in the Endangered Species Act. His third book, *The Redwoods Forest: History, Ecology, and Conservation of the Coastal Redwoods*, which he edited and to which he contributed several chapters, was published in 1999. Noss has written or edited numerous other books since then. With co-editors David Maehr and Jeffrey Larkin, he shared the Wildlife Society's Outstanding Edited Book Publication Award for *Large Mammal Restoration*, published in

2001. Noss is currently working on a book for Island Press on the ecology, biogeography, and ecological and cultural history of the grasslands of the southern United States.

Noss served as president of the Society for Conservation Biology from 1999 until 2001 and is a member of its Board of Governors. He has founded and is president of two private institutes. The Conservation Planning Institute, headquartered in Corvallis, Oregon, works to identify and implement priority areas for conservation of biodiversity. The Florida Institute for Conservation Science is a think tank and research institute that focuses on critical issues in conservation, restoration, land use, and regional planning, chiefly in the southeastern U.S., and adjacent regions.

Noss has directed research in the Rocky Mountains, Florida, the Pacific Northwest, and California. He promotes systematic, multicriteria conservation planning, at regional to continental scales. At the University of Central Florida, he directs the Science and Planning in Conservation Ecology (SPICE) lab and works on a variety of projects with his students that range from detailed studies of the ecology of endangered species to planning and management of wildland-urban interface and the protection, restoration, and management of ecosystems. He was elected a Fellow of the American Association for the Advancement of Science in 2001, and a Scientific Fellow of the Wildlife Conservation Society in 1999.

Reed Noss lives with his wife, Myra Noss and their children in Central Florida.

## BIBLIOGRAPHY

"Conservation Planning Institute," www.conservationplanninginstitute.org; "Florida Institute for Conservation Science," www.flconservationscience.org; Noss, Reed F., *A Citizen's Guide to Ecosystem Management* (booklet published by the Biodiversity Legal Foundation), 1999; Noss, Reed F., "A Regional Landscape Approach to Maintain Diversity," *Bioscience*, 1983; Noss, Reed F., "Values are a Good Thing in Conservation Biology," *Conservation Biology*, 2007; Noss, Reed F., and Allen Y. Cooperrider, *Saving Nature's Legacy*, 1994; Noss, Reed F., and Dennis D. Murphy, "Species and Habitat Are Inseparable," *Conservation Biology*, 1995; Soulé, Michael, and Reed Noss, "Rewilding and Biodiversity," *Wild Earth*, 1998.

# American Environmental Leaders

From Colonial Times to the Present

## Odum, Eugene
(September 17, 1913–August 10, 2002)
Ecologist

Eugene Odum is known worldwide among ecologists for his groundbreaking *Fundamentals of Ecology*, the first textbook on ecosystem ecology and the only one for ten years after its publication in 1953. Odum is unquestionably the father of modern ecology; as a result of his dogged quest to develop a discipline that studies the biological and physical components of the natural world as a system, *ecology* has become a household word.

Eugene Pleasants Odum was born in Lake Sunapee, New Hampshire, on September 17, 1913, the first of two sons of Howard and Anna Louise (Kranz) Odum. As a young boy he moved to Chapel Hill, North Carolina, and spent hours in the expansive wilderness that surrounded the small southern town. The young Odum would wake early and disappear into the woods to watch birds. At first he was interested in different species of birds, then he began to wonder about birds and their environment, and eventually, he became more and more interested in the whole environment, or ecosystem, itself. Odum pursued his interest in college, receiving a bachelor's degree in biology in 1934 and a master's in 1936, both from the University of North Carolina at Chapel Hill.

Odum left his beloved southern home in 1936 to pursue a doctoral degree in zoology at the University of Illinois. During graduate school, Odum began developing his idea of ecology as an integrative science that includes not only the study of the biological aspects of a community but also its physical, chemical, and geographic components. Ecology, he believed, was much more than a subdiscipline of biology. He graduated in 1939, and after a yearlong stint as a resident biologist at the Edmund Niles Huyck Preserve near Albany, New York, he returned to the South to pursue an academic career that would lead to the development of a new discipline of science.

Professor Eugene Odum (right) and his brother, Professor Howard Odum, at a press conference on September 23, 1987, after receiving their Crafoord Prize. (AP Images/Borg Thuresson)

Odum became an assistant professor of zoology at the University of Georgia, Athens, in 1940. He made $1,800 a year, which at that time was enough to support himself and his young wife, Martha, who was an artist. His career was interrupted during World War II when he was called upon to teach anatomy and physiology to nurses and premedical students. In 1945, he and his colleagues in the biology and zoology departments held a meeting to discuss what courses undergraduate students should be required to take for their major. Odum suggested ecology. "They looked at me like, what's that?" Odum recalled. He took the question as a challenge, and the young assistant professor set out to establish the principles upon which a scientific discipline of ecology could be established.

Five years later, Odum articulated the principles he had developed in a textbook, *Fundamentals of Ecology*, so that ecology could be taught to students in the same fashion that biology or physics or chemistry is taught. The only problem was that universities did not yet offer courses on ecology. Without much of a market for his book, Odum had a difficult time getting it published. When he was finally successful in 1953, it became the only published textbook on ecology, and for the first several years the book was in print, very few copies sold. Then in the early 1970s, when environmental consciousness began to develop in the United States, sales of his book increased dramatically. The book continues to be used worldwide.

Back in Georgia, Odum was successful in integrating ecology courses into the university curriculum; in 1951, he also began an ecology research program at the Savannah River Atomic Energy Site in Aiken, South Carolina. The site has become the Savannah River Ecology Laboratory, and the 300-square-mile area is now a national environmental research park. In 1954, Odum led the way in establishing the University of Georgia's Marine Institute on Sapelo Island to study Georgia's coastal marsh ecosystem, and in 1961, he became the founding director of the university's Institute of Ecology. He served in that capacity until 1984.

Throughout his distinguished career, Odum wrote extensively on ecosystem ecology, with 12 books and countless journal papers to his credit. His *Ecology* book series, first published in 1963, has been printed in five editions; the 1997 edition was *Ecology: A Bridge between Science and Society*. His last book was *Ecological Vignettes: Ecological Approaches to Dealing with Human Predicaments*, published in 1998. As reflected in its title, Odum became interested in the impact of human beings on ecosystems, which he termed *human ecology*.

In *Ecology: Our Endangered Life Support System* (1993), Odum argued for the extension of market economics to include ecosystem services. Market economics was not sustainable, he said, because it was based on the increasing consumption of goods with no monetary cost calculated in for the air, water, and soil that are used or destroyed to produce the goods. Odum believed that in order to solve our environmental problems, the emerging discipline of human ecology needed to include not only the natural sciences, but the social sciences and humanities as well. "Science alone will not solve any of our problems," Odum said. "Science can help, but it's not going to save the world from environmental deterioration because the problems and solutions deal with people and the non-science disciplines."

Using an analogy from ecology, Odum argued that as a society, we have developed beyond the "pioneer" stage of development, when survival depends on producing numerous offspring, to a "mature" stage of development, in which maintenance of the quality of life is more important than growth in size. As in any ecosystem, growth beyond a certain level requires very high maintenance and begins to produce diminishing returns. "We now suffer from too many good things," said Odum. "We have to change somewhat the way we live."

Odum received numerous awards throughout his career, including three prestigious international honors: the Institut de la Vie Prize from the French government in 1975; the Tyler Ecology Award, presented at the White House by Pres. JIMMY CARTER in 1977; and the Crafoord Prize from the Royal Swedish Academy of Science in 1987. The Crafoord is considered the Nobel Prize of ecology. Odum shared two of these awards with his brother, Howard T. Odum, a professor of environmental engineering at the University of Florida and an ecosystem ecologist. Odum received honorary degrees from the Hofstra University, Ferum College, the University of North Carolina–Asheville, Universidad del Valle in Guatemala, the Ohio State University, and Universidad San Francisco de Quito in Ecuador.

Odum retired as a professor in 1984, but continued to be involved in the development of ecology at the College of the Environment of the University of Georgia until his death of an apparent heart attack while tending his garden on August 10, 2002.

### BIBLIOGRAPHY

Chaffin, Tom, "Father Ecology Marches On," *Georgia Magazine*, 1998; Edwards, Lorraine, "Father of Ecology," *Georgia Journal*, 1983; Ezzard, Martha, "Ecologist Odum Still Planting Ideas," *Atlanta Journal*, 1998; Gunderson, Lance, Carl Folke, Michelle Lee, and C.S. Holling, "In Memory of Mavericks, *Conservation Ecology*, 2002; Meyers, J. Michael and David W. Johnston, "In Memoriam: Eugene Pleasants Odum, 1913-2002," *The Auk*, 2003; Shearer, Lee, "Father of Ecosystem Ecology," *Athens Magazine*, 1996; Williams, Phil, "Eugene Odum: An Ecologist's Life" (video produced by University of Georgia), 1997.

## Oliver, Mary
(September 10, 1935– )
Poet, Nature Writer

Mary Oliver is one of the most respected contemporary American writers. Her poems are couched in a deep awareness of nature that seeks not to romanticize the natural world but rather to find understanding and universal wisdom within its cycles and predator/prey relationship. Oliver believes that solitude and a sense of mystery are the two key ingredients for a poet and is infamous for her daily walks, which she considers part of the poetic process.

Born September 10, 1935, in Maple Heights, Ohio, a semi-rural suburb of Cleveland, Oliver grew up spending most of her time outdoors, walking and reading. About her childhood, Oliver said, in a 1992 interview for the *Christian Science Monitor*, "I grew up in a small town in Ohio.... It was pastoral, it was nice, it was an extended family. I don't know why I felt such affinity with the natural world except that it was available to me, that's the first thing. It was right there. And for whatever reasons, I felt those first important connections, those first experiences being made with the natural world rather than with the social world."

As a teenager and an admirer of the poet Edna St. Vincent Millay, Oliver wrote a letter to Millay's sister and was invited to live for a time in Millay's old house helping to sort through the deceased poet's papers. After graduating from the local high school, she went on to attend both Ohio State University and Vassar College but did not receive a degree at either school.

Oliver published her first collection of poems, *No Voyage and Other Poems*, in 1963. On the strength of her poetry itself, Oliver became the Chair of the Writing Department of the Fine Arts Work Center, Provincetown, Massachusetts, from 1972-1973. In the 1980s Oliver was teaching at Case Western Reserve University and published *American Primitive* in 1984, for which she won the Pulitzer Prize for Poetry. In 1986 she was the Poet in Residence at Bucknell University. In 1991 she was the Margaret Banister Writer in Residence at Sweet Briar College in Virginia. She then went to Bennington, Vermont, where she held the position of the Catharine Osgood Foster Chair for Distinguished Teaching until 2001.

Oliver has authored more than a dozen books of poetry, including *New and Selected Poems* (1992) which won the National Book Award, and *House Light* (1990) which won the Christopher Award and the L. L. Winship/PEN New England Award. Her poetry has been included in the yearly anthology *The Best American Poetry* twice.

> **Little Summer Poem Touching the Subject of Faith**
>
> Every summer
> I listen and look
> under the sun's brass and even
> into the moonlight, but I can't hear
>
> anything, I can't see anything—
> not the pale roots digging down, nor the green
>     stalks muscling up,
> nor the leaves
> deepening their damp pleats,
>
> nor the tassels making,
> nor the shucks, nor the cobs.
> And still,
> every day,
>
> the leafy fields
> grow taller and thicker—
> green gowns lofting up in the night,
> showered with silk.
>
> And so, every summer,
> I fail as a witness, seeing nothing—
> I am deaf too
> to the tick of the leaves,
>
> the tapping of downwardness from the banyan
>     feet—
> all of it
> happening
> beyond any seeable proof, or hearable hum.
>
> And, therefore, let the immeasurable come.
> Let the unknowable touch the buckle of my spine.
> Let the wind turn in the trees,
> and the mystery hidden in the dirt
>
> swing through the air.
> How could I look at anything in this world
> and tremble, and grip my hands over my heart?
> What should I fear?
>
> One morning
> in the leafy green ocean
> the honeycomb of the corn's beautiful body
> is sure to be there.

From *West Wind: Poems and Prose Poems*, by Mary Oliver. Published by Houghton Mifflin Co., Boston. Copyright 1997 by Mary Oliver. Reprinted by permission.

She has received the American Academy of Arts & Letters Award, a Lannan Literary Award, the Poetry Society of America's Shelley Memorial Prize and Alice Fay di Castagnola Award, as well as fellowships from the Guggenheim Foundation and the National Endowment for the Arts.

Oliver's poetry is greatly influenced by Walt Whitman, Henry David Thoreau, and William Blake. Her poems are filled with her observations of nature, gathered on her daily walks. In *Women's Review of Books*, Maxine Kumin describes Oliver as an 'indefatigable guide to the natural world.'

In Janet McNew's essay, 'Mary Oliver and the Tradition of Romantic Nature Poetry,' McNew states:

> Oliver remains faithful to her attachment to nature. Instead of forsaking the natural for supernatural eternity, her poems follow the cycles of the seasons to image loss and the possibility for renewal. These vast natural cycles, which usually symbolize traps and prison houses for the romantic visionary, are strangely consoling for Oliver. Wedding her close to them holds her close to the deepest mysteries she knows, those of natural transformation. ...
> from *Contemporary Literature* 30:1 (Spring 1989)

Poet Stanley Kunitz has said of Oliver's poetry, "Her special gift is to connect us with our sources in the natural world, its beauties and terrors and mysteries and consolations."

Oliver lives and writes in Provincetown, Massachusetts.

### BIBLIOGRAPHY

www.poets.org/poet.php/prmPID/265; http://mclibrary.nhmccd.edu/lit/olive6.html; www.clevelandartsprize.org/lit_1979.htm; www.poetryfoundation.org/archive/poet.html?id=5130; www.english.uiuc.edu/maps/poets/m_r/oliver/about.htm; archive.uua.org/pressroom/mediakit/ga/MaryOliverBio.pdf; www.ohioana-authors.org/oliver/index.php.

## Olmsted, Frederick Law, Sr.
(April 26, 1822–August 28, 1903)
Landscape Architect

Frederick Law Olmsted Sr. designed Central Park in New York City and many other city parks, in an attempt to humanize and make more healthy the expanding industrialized urban centers of the mid-nineteenth century. He was also a respected journalist and social thinker; he served as general secretary of the U.S. Sanitary Commission, the agency in charge of health services for soldiers during the Civil War; and he helped inspire the National Park Service and the U.S. Forest Service.

Frederick Law Olmsted Sr. was born on April 26, 1822, in Hartford, Connecticut, a city that his ancestors had helped found seven generations before. He had relatives throughout the region and from a very early age was allowed to explore the countryside surrounding Hartford. When he was nine years old, he took his six-year-old brother on a journey by foot to visit an aunt and an uncle 16 miles away. His parents also took their eight children on many long trips by horse-drawn cart through rural New England. Olmsted attended country schools until he was a teenager, at which time he boarded with clergymen who tutored him privately.

After a few false starts in careers that did not suit him (business, the merchant marine, farming), Olmsted began to travel and write. In 1850, he toured England and parts of continental Europe on foot to explore agriculture and landscape architecture, and in 1852 he published the book, *Walks and Talks of an American Farmer in England*. Next, he took three long investigative trips through the American South, publishing his observations of slavery and its effects on the South in serial form in the *New York Daily Times*. (In 1861, these were collected in a three-volume set called *The Cotton Kingdom*.)

Olmsted became widely recognized as an influential progressive thinker and was of-

Frederick Law Olmsted, Sr. (Library of Congress, Prints & Photographs Division, LC-USZ62-36895)

fered the position of superintendent of Central Park in New York City in 1857. Olmsted saw the post as an opportunity to improve public health in an increasingly dirty and crowded city, especially for the poor, who were not able to escape the city as the wealthier classes could. Central Park, at that time a squatter's settlement in the rural area of Manhattan, was in the process of being developed as a recreational area, and the park's board of commissioners held a contest for a park design. Prominent architect Calvert Vaux invited Olmsted to collaborate on a design, and they won the competition. Vaux and Olmsted devoted the next four years to the park's construction. During this period, in 1859, Olmsted married his late brother's widow, Mary, and adopted her three children. In 1861 Olmsted had to take a leave of absence from landscape architecture in order to direct the U.S. Sanitary Commission, which attended the wounded soldiers of the U.S. Civil War. He stayed with that post until 1863 and was lauded for his skill in organizing his employees in the brand new field of sanitation.

After his stint with the Sanitary Commission, Olmsted moved his family to California, where he managed a mining estate. Having been previously depleted of all its gold, the mine failed. While in California, however, Olmsted visited and was deeply impressed by the Yosemite Valley. He was appointed to Yosemite's Board of Commissioners, which convinced California's congress to declare Yosemite a state park in 1864. Twenty-six years later, in 1890, Yosemite became a national park. Olmsted used two justifications to argue for the protection of Yosemite: the tourism it would attract would be good business, and the government should purchase the land before the wealthy elite did, in order to assure access to it for all citizens.

Upon his return to New York in 1865, he and Vaux became partners and were contracted to design several more parks, including Brooklyn's Prospect Park, Washington and Jackson Parks in Chicago, and Seaside Park in Bridgeport, Connecticut. In all, he and his partners (Vaux, until 1872; then later his stepson, John C. Olmsted; his son, FREDERICK LAW OLMSTED JR.; Charles Eliot; and Henry Codman) designed some 80 public parks and 13 college grounds. In each case, the Olmsted approach was to humanize the area and make it a healthier place to live. The design for the Riverside subdivision of Chicago, for example, included streets that followed natural curves in the land and left the most attractive areas of the site as commons, where neighbors could recreate together. Olmsted and Vaux were called to Buffalo to help that growing city avoid the hygiene problems faced by other cities. Their solution included over 600 acres of new tree-filled parks that served both as recreation grounds and buffers between neighborhoods. When in 1881 Boston city officials asked Olmsted's firm to help with the pestilent Back Bay area, a flood-prone marsh filled with the sewage from Boston's suburbs, which drained into the Charles River, Olmsted designed a system of parks to surround Back Bay and protect it from pollution and at the same time to protect nearby neighborhoods from flooding. The Capitol area of Washington, D.C., was another Olmsted project; he landscaped the grounds with an eye for shade and year-round greenery and proposed the marble staircase and terrace addition to the capitol that distinguishes it today.

Another of Olmsted's accomplishments of the 1880s was the protection of Niagara Falls from industrial development and a tourist-oriented sprawl right up to the river's banks. Olmsted's organizational skills helped convince the New York and Ontario governments to found a binational park around the falls in 1883. Olmsted and Vaux were hired to landscape the new park in 1886.

Olmsted became interested in forestry in the early 1890s while designing Biltmore, the Vanderbilt family's large country estate in Asheville, North Carolina. When young GIFFORD PINCHOT approached Olmsted in 1892 to ask to manage the estate's forests according to the scientific forestry principles he had just studied in Europe, Olmsted gave his consent. Olmsted later supported Pinchot in his quest to establish a national Division of Forestry to manage the nation's national forests. For this support, Olmsted is credited for providing impetus for the establishment of the U.S. Forest Service.

Although Olmsted paid close attention to recreational and health considerations in his designs, his private clients often cut corners in the implementation, in order to cut cost. Olmsted also spent years fighting with commissioners and regulatory committees, because his designs did not conform to all of the rules of the day. This adversity took a toll on his physical and emotional health, but his inherent idealism gave him the strength he needed to continue until his retirement in 1895. Olmsted died on August 28, 1903, in Waverly, Massachusetts.

### BIBLIOGRAPHY

Beveridge, Charles E., *Frederick Law Olmsted: Designing the American Landscape*, 1995; Fein, Albert, *Frederick Law Olmsted and the American Environmental Tradition*, 1972; Roper, Laura Wood. *FLO: A Biography of Frederick Law Olmsted*, 1973; Rybczynski, Witold, *A Clearing in the Distance: Frederick Law Olmsted and America in the nineteenth century*, 1999; Stevenson, Elizabeth, *Park Maker: A Life of Frederick Law Olmsted*, 1977; Strong, Douglas H., *Dreamers and Defenders: American Conservationists*, 1988.

## Olmsted, Frederick Law, Jr.
(July 24, 1870–December 25, 1957)
Landscape Architect

Primed by FREDERICK LAW OLMSTED SR., who was not only Frederick Law Olmsted Jr.'s father but also the father of landscape architecture, Frederick Law Olmsted Jr. was an important landscape architect himself. He is also remembered as an effective public servant and a dedicated conservationist.

Henry Perkins Olmsted was born on July 24, 1870, in New York City and was immediately nicknamed "Boy." His father decided early on that this son would eventually take over his prestigious landscape architecture firm, and so when "Boy" was four years old, his father had the child's name changed to Frederick Law Olmsted Jr. Sharing a name would aid continuity in the family business, Olmsted Sr. believed. The young Olmsted grew up steeped in landscape architecture. His father worked at home, and prominent people in the field often visited. There were maps and surveys all over the house. Olmsted Jr. was once found scanning a map of New York City while sleepwalking.

Olmsted Jr.'s apprenticeship with his father began early. At the age of 16, he accompanied his father to California, to help with the design of Stanford University. He attended Harvard University and supplemented his education there with piles of landscape architecture readings heaped on by his father. Upon graduation in 1894, Olmsted Jr. accompanied his father to Biltmore, the country estate of the Vanderbilt family. This was to be the last major project of Olmsted Sr. and the first for Olmsted Jr.

When senility claimed Olmsted Sr., Olmsted Jr. joined his stepbrother, John Olmsted, as a partner in the family firm. His major early assignment was to continue the work in Washington, D.C., begun by his father in the 1880s. As a member of the Senate Park Commission, Olmsted designed the grounds of the White House, the Jefferson Memorial, the Washington Monument, the Shrine of the Immaculate Conception, the National Arboretum, and Lafayette and Rock Creek Parks. Indeed the parklike appearance of much of Washington, D.C., today is due in great part to two generations of the Olmsted aesthetic.

Olmsted's firm also drew up the plans for numerous suburban developments and cities and towns, including Rochester, New York; Boulder, Colorado; New Haven, Connecticut; and Pittsburgh, Pennsylvania. He helped found the American Society of Landscape Architects and the American Institute of Planners.

In addition to his work on urban planning and city parks, Olmsted also was an advocate of national parks. He campaigned actively against the Hetch Hetchy dam that submerged an area compared by JOHN MUIR to the world's most inspiring cathedrals. He also worked with Horace McFarland of the American Civic Association to draft an unsuccessful bill to create a national park bureau in 1910.

Six years later, Olmsted collaborated with STEPHEN MATHER, director of the national parks, to write the National Park Service Act. Olmsted's contribution consisted of the policy statement for the new National Park Service: "To conserve the scenery and the natural and historic objects and the wildlife... and to provide for the enjoyment of same in such manner and by such means as will leave them unimpaired for the enjoyment of future generations." Thanks to powerful lobbying by Mather and his team, this bill made it through Congress and was signed by President Wilson in 1916.

Olmsted stood up for the parks in the early 1920s when various bills were introduced to Congress to allow livestock grazing within parks or construction in national parks of dams for hydroelectricity or irrigation. He, along with Mather and National Park Association director ROBERT STERLING YARD, successfully lobbied the Senate against these bills.

Olmsted helped further park development in 1928 when he drew up a master state park plan for California. The plan recommended parks in redwood groves, coastal and desert areas, in the mountains, and at historic sites. California voters then approved a bond issue to raise six million dollars to start purchasing land for state parks. Olmsted was invited to serve on the Yosemite Planning and Policy Committee, which he did from 1928 to 1956. Olmsted's entry in the *Dictionary of American Biography* comments that this must have seemed to Olmsted Jr. a satisfying post, given that Olmsted Sr. had been the first commissioner of the park in 1864, and its protection as a park has generally been attributed to him.

As a gift for his 83rd birthday, a group of Olmsted's friends bought and dedicated the Frederick Law Olmsted Redwood Grove in the Prairie Creek Redwoods State Park in Humboldt County, California. Olmsted died in Malibu, California, on December 25, 1957. Olmsted and his wife, Sarah, had one daughter, Charlotte.

### BIBLIOGRAPHY

Fein, Albert, *Frederick Law Olmsted and the American Environmental Tradition*, 1972; "Frederick Law Olmsted," *Dictionary of American Biography, Supplement VI*, 1980; "Frederick Law Olmsted, 1870–1957, An Appreciation of the Man and His Works, Landscape Architecture," *Landscape Architecture*, 1958; Roper, Laura Wood, *FLO: A Biography of Frederick Law Olmsted*, 1973.

## Olson, Molly Harriss

(July 11, 1960– )
Sustainability Consultant

Sustainability expert Molly Harriss Olson has worked with the Great Barrier Reef Marine Park Authority, the World Conservation Union (IUCN), Wildlife Australia, Greenpeace, and the Natural Step (TNS) to promote conservation and sustainability. She served as inaugural executive director of President Clinton's Council on Sustainable Development, and currently she directs the Australian company Eco Futures Pty Ltd. to develop innovative strategies to accelerate the adoption of sustainable practices and facilitate collaboration among leaders in business, government, and civic organizations on achieving a sustainable society.

Molly Harriss Olson was born on July 11, 1960, in Alliance Nebraska, and moved with her family at an early age to Palo Alto, California. Her mother, who was very interested in Native Americans, told stories to young Olson about the strong connections Native Americans had with the earth. Her father, who loved his work as a music teacher, provided her with an example of how one could make a living by pursuing a passion. Molly Olson's own passion for nature started early with a keen interest in kelp beds, coral reefs, and scuba diving. As a teenager, she learned to dive in Pacific Grove, California, not far from her home, and that passion eventually took her to the Great Barrier Reef and Australia.

Olson pursued Environmental Studies at the University of California at Santa Cruz (UCSC). During a summer internship in Washington, D.C., Olson studied the Alaska Native Claims Settlement Act and realized that economics would have more to bear on the future of this magnificent area than its ecological significance. Upon her return to UCSC the next fall, Olson added economics to her study program. In 1982 she graduated from UCSC with a joint B.A. degree in economics and environmental studies. Her honors thesis, which she researched in Australia, was entitled "The Great Barrier Reef: A Legal and Economic Analysis." The paper was all about sustainability long before the term came into vogue.

Continuing her education, Olson became a Bates resident scholar at Yale University's School of Forestry and Environmental Studies, earning a master's degree in environmental policy there in 1985. At the same time that she was becoming more interested in sustainability and how it benefited conservation efforts, she remained interested in coral reef habitat, especially the Great Barrier Reef. During the late 1980s, Olson authored a number of reports on conservation in Australia for the Australian government, local communities, and the World Conservation Union, and she edited *Wildlife Australia* magazine. Olson headed Greenpeace's Ocean Ecology department from Australia, leading campaigns on the famous Greenpeace vessel, *The Rainbow Warrior*. She conducted scientific research on the Great Barrier Reef and served as a delegate to numerous international meetings and negotiations. As a member of the IUCN's Commission on Parks and Protected Areas, Olson helped organize the IUCN's General Assembly in Perth in 1990. By 1991, Olson had become an adviser to the environmental minister of Australia and conducted a major review of the Australian government's funding for the environment.

During the first Clinton campaign for U.S. president, Olson returned to the United States to serve as deputy national coordinator of Environmentalists for Clinton-Gore, 1992, setting up committees of prominent pro-Clinton environmentalists in every state. Upon the victory of the Clinton-Gore team, Olson was appointed executive director of the President's Council on Sustainable Development (PCSD), a 25-member council whose distinguished members represented industry, government, and environmental, labor, and civil rights organizations. The council worked for three years to develop a national strategy for sustainable development, articulated in the 1996 publication *Sustainable America: A New Consensus*. The goals addressed the interdependent issues of health, environment, economic prosperity, equity, conservation, stewardship, sustainable communities, civic engagement, population, international responsibility, and education and were accompanied by policy recommendations and indicators of progress. Before completing her work at the PCSD, Olson ensured that an implementation phase for the report would follow. This implementation culminated with a national town meeting with

Vice President AL GORE in April 1999. The council disbanded in September 1999.

Continuing to use her expertise in sustainability, in 1995 Olson became the first executive director of the U.S. branch of the Natural Step, an international nonprofit educational organization that promotes sustainability for corporations, organizations, and individuals. The Natural Step, which was founded in 1992 by Swedish oncologist Karl-Henrick Robèrt and brought to the United States by environmental industrialist PAUL HAWKEN, cites scientific principles and laws in defining how societies must function if they are to be sustainable. Olson's work during her two years at the Natural Step attracted the attention of the World Economic Forum, which in 1995 selected her for its Global Leaders for Tomorrow Program, comprising leaders born after 1950 who have distinguished themselves as recognized leaders in the world community.

Currently, Olson and her husband, Australian environmental leader Philip Toyne, direct an Australian international policy firm, Eco Futures Pty Ltd., which advises business, government, and civic leaders on strategies for achieving sustainability. She travels and speaks worldwide, and has sat on the boards of a number of Australian and international environmental organizations. Olson and Toyne live on a farm in the village of Gundaroo, New South Wales, with their son, Atticus, and Toyne's son, Jamie.

BIBLIOGRAPHY

"EcoFutures," www.ecofutures.com; "The Natural Step," www.naturalstep.org/; Olson, Molly Harriss, "Accepting the Sustainable Development Challenge," *Willamette Law Review*, 1995; Olson, Molly Harriss, "Shaping a Path to Sustainability," *UNEP Our Planet*, 1996; The President's Council on Sustainable Development, *Sustainable America: A New Consensus for the Future*, 1996.

## Olson, Sigurd

(April 4, 1899–January 13, 1982)
Nature Writer, President of the National Parks Association, Conservationist

Sigurd Olson was a nature writer and activist whose contemplative essays celebrated the beauty and spiritual nature of wilderness, with a particular focus on the lake country of northern Minnesota. He held several influential positions in the national conservation movement throughout the 1950s and 1960s, serving as president of the National Parks Association and the Wilderness Society Council. In 1962, he was appointed consultant to Secretary of the Interior STEWART UDALL; in this capacity, he was instrumental in crafting the Wilderness Act of 1964. He was also a key figure in the establishment of the Boundary Waters Canoe Area Wilderness along the Minnesota-Ontario border.

Sigurd Ferdinand Olson was born to the Reverend Lawrence J. and Ida May (Cedarholm) Olson in Humboldt Park, Illinois, on April 4, 1899. His parents were both Scandinavian immigrants: His father was from Sweden, his mother from Denmark. They moved to Wisconsin when Sigurd was seven and his brother Kenneth was 11. His family settled in Ashland, Wisconsin, in 1912. Olson was fascinated by nature from an early age and spent much time in such solitary pursuits as fishing, trapping, and hunting. Olson attended Northland College in Ashland for two years. In the fall of 1918, he transferred to the University of Wisconsin at Madison not long before Congress lowered the age of draft eligibility to 18. Olson immediately joined the Students Army Training Corps, but he served for only eight weeks before the armistice was signed. He returned to the University of Wisconsin and graduated in 1920 with a degree in animal husbandry. Olson found the agriculture courses dry, a far cry from the romance and beauty he had experienced on the farm; nevertheless, he accepted a job teaching high school agricultural classes in northern Minnesota. Although Olson was to continue in the field of education for 27 years, he found teaching unfulfilling. He spent every weekend camping in the woods or canoeing on the region's many lakes, forming a deep attachment to the area known as "canoe country." His first extended canoe trip also yielded his first published writing, an article for the *Milwaukee Journal*.

Olson spent summers working on the Uhrenholdt farm near Seely, Wisconsin. He married Elizabeth Uhrenholdt, the farmer's daughter, in 1921. Olson sought to join his academic and outdoor interests through a career as a field geologist. He enrolled in a graduate program in geology at the University of Wisconsin but became disillusioned as he realized that most geologists were employed by mining companies, whose devastation he had seen firsthand in the iron ore region of northern Minnesota. After one semester, he left the university and took a job as a high school biology teacher in Ely, Minnesota, in the midst of his beloved "canoe country." Olson's sons, Sigurd T. and Robert K., were born in Ely in 1923 and 1925, respectively. Again, he changed his focus—this time embarking on the study of ecology. The Olsons soon moved to Champaign, Illinois, so that he could attend the University of Illinois. At a time when predators were seen as pests and wolves were the target of predator control programs, Olson set about investigating the role wolves play in an ecosystem; his thesis on timber wolves is considered a pioneering work in the field. Olson received his master's degree in ecology in 1932.

Upon his return to Ely, Olson began teaching full-time at Ely Community College. He later became dean of the college, a position he held for 11 years. Throughout his academic career, Olson continued writing nature essays, despite active discouragement from agents and editors, who assured him they would never sell. Persevering, Olson sold a few articles and wrote a syndicated newspaper column for a brief period before World War II. He eventually came to the attention of Alfred Knopf, who expressed interest in publishing a set of Olson's essays. *The Singing Wilderness* was published in 1956 and appeared on the *New York Times* bestseller list. Olson went on to publish seven more books over the next 24 years.

Olson deliberately wrote in a simple, nonintellectual style so that he could reach a wide range of readers. He appealed to rural sportsmen because he enjoyed hunting and fishing and to conservationists because he advocated wilderness preservation. His personal philosophy—espoused throughout his work but most apparent in such later works as *Reflections from the North Country*—centered on the idea that modern man retains a racial memory of the wilderness, to which the human spirit responds. Olson believed that without a life that allows an intuitive, receptive response to nature, individuals—and thus communities—suffer. The solution, according to Olson, lies in a human ecology that addresses the need to preserve wilderness as well as the need to provide economic sustainability.

The success of his first book allowed Olson to resign as dean of Ely Community College. Realizing that his fledgling writing career would not support him, Olson accepted a position as spokesman for the movement to protect the Quetico-Superior area from road and dam building and increased air traffic. He gained national recognition for his success in a high-profile campaign to ban aircraft in the wilderness. Olson helped negotiate an international treaty governing management of the area along the Minnesota-Ontario border that was later to become the Boundary Waters Canoe Area Wilderness.

Olson went on to serve as the president of the National Parks Association from 1953 to 1958 and as president of the Wilderness Society Council from 1963 to 1968. As a member of the secretary of the interior's Advisory Committee on Conservation from 1960 to 1966, he advised Secretary Stewart Udall on wilderness and national parks issues. His work had a direct influence on the creation and passage of the Wilderness Bill in 1964. He was elected to the Izaak Walton League Hall of Fame in 1963.

Olson's efforts to bridge the divide between conservationists and rural people dependent upon resource extraction sometimes led to conflict. His belief in hunting as a legitimate means of getting close to nature was harshly criticized by his fellow conservationists. They also pressured him to accept nothing less than full wilderness protection for the Boundary Waters Canoe Area. On the other hand, his rural supporters in northern Minnesota accused him of hypocrisy for failing to advocate logging in the wilderness area. At one point, he was hanged in effigy in his hometown of Ely.

Olson became a trustee of Northland College in 1970 and continued an active involvement with the college until his death 12 years later. The Sigurd Olson Environmental Institute was founded in 1972 to serve as the environmental outreach program of the college. The institute works with government agencies, businesses, and citizens on both sides of the U.S.-Canadian border to address environmental problems affecting the Quetico-Superior region. In 1974, Olson was awarded the John Burroughs Medal, the highest honor in nature writing. He received the Robert Marshall Award of the Wilderness Society in 1981.

When he was 80 years old, Olson underwent surgery for cancer of the colon; the surgery, although successful, left him in a weakened condition. He still had enough internal strength, however, to refuse the U.S. Department of the Interior's Conservation Service Award, as a protest against the department's receptivity to oil and gas exploration under the new secretary, James Watt. On January 13, 1982, Olson suffered a fatal heart attack while snowshoeing near his home in Ely. His final written words, later discovered on a sheet of paper left in his typewriter, were: "A new adventure is coming up and I'm sure it will be a good one."

Ten years after Olson's death, the Sigurd Olson Environmental Institute established the Sigurd F. Olson Nature Writing Award, given biennially to recognize writing that both conveys the spirit of the north and raises awareness about the need to preserve wilderness for future generations. In 1998, Olson's sons donated the family cabin near Ely, Minnesota, to the newly created Listening Point Foundation. The cabin is the center of a wilderness education program that carries on the author's ecological philosophy. The preservation of the 26-acre property on Burntside Lake fulfills Olson's wish, as expressed in his book *Listening Point*, that it be "a place reserved for vistas and dreams and long thoughts." The 100th anniversary of Olson's birth was recognized with a U.S. Senate tribute by Sen. Russ Feingold of Wisconsin on August 3, 1999.

**BIBLIOGRAPHY**

Backes, David, *A Wilderness Within: The Life of Sigurd F. Olson*, 1997; Darland, Robert, "In Speaking Out for Wilderness Protection, He Sent a Powerful Message," *National Wildlife*, 2000; Olson, Sigurd, *Reflections from the North Country*, 1976; Olson, Sigurd, *The Singing Wilderness*, 1956; "Sigurd F. Olson Home Page," www.uwm.edu/Dept/JMC/Olson/; "Two to Remember [Conservationists Sigurd Olson and Aldo Leopold]," *Field & Stream*, 1998.

## Orr, David

(January 10, 1944- )
Environmental Studies Professor, Writer

David Orr, chair and professor of environmental studies at Oberlin College in Ohio, is an influential figure in educational reform, and how an emphasis on the environment can help. He has written prolifically on topics including the responsibility of educational institutions to promote "ecological literacy" (an understanding of how humans fit into the earth's ecological web) and how architectural design on college campuses can affect the success of environmental curricula.

David Wesley Orr was born on January 10, 1944, in Des Moines, Iowa, and was raised in New Wilmington, Pennsylvania. He studied history at Westminster College in New Wilmington, receiving his B.A. in 1965. He earned an M.A. from Michigan State University in 1966 and a Ph.D. in international relations from the University of Pennsylvania in 1973. Orr taught at the University of North Carolina at Chapel Hill and has been on the faculty of Oberlin College since 1990, where he is the Paul Sears Distinguished Professor of Environmental Studies and Politics.

Orr's first book, which he coedited with Marvin Soroos in 1979, was entitled *The Global Predicament: Ecological Perspectives on World Order*. It is a collection of essays on topics such as growth and development from an ecological perspective, food alternatives for the future, resource scarcity, and environmental management of such international resources as oceans.

Orr's work has focused on educational reform and how ecological design can contribute to it. He believes that the current ecological crisis is in part a result of the shortcomings of the educational system. Rather than teaching students to respect the interconnectedness of life, which might have prevented much of the environmental destruction we now have to deal with, students in traditional institutions have been taught to compartmentalize life. They have been encouraged to separate themselves from the rest of the ecological web, separate their emotions from their intellects, and separate practice from theory. Although colleges and universities are pumping out some of the best-informed graduates in their history, the students nonetheless lack many areas of knowledge and, most of all, ecological wisdom.

Instead of preparing students to compete in a global economy, which is what most academic institutions currently see as their mission, Orr advocates teaching students to work to make life on earth more environmentally and socially sustainable. He believes that colleges should become models of sustainability and earth stewardship. In his 1994 book, revised in 2004, *Earth in Mind: On Education, Environment and the Human Prospect*, Orr advocates a new ratings system for colleges that would include such criteria as consumption/discards per student, management policy on waste, recycling, purchasing, landscaping, energy use, and how graduates contribute to helping the world become more sustainable.

Orr spent the late 1990s overseeing the Adam Joseph Lewis Center for Environmental Studies building project at Oberlin College, designed by WILLIAM MCDONOUGH of William McDonough and Partners. The building is entirely solar-powered, and purifies all of its own wastewater. In addition, the building itself provides a hands-on laboratory experience for the students who study in it. Orr shared recommendations for those embarking on similar building projects in his 1999 article entitled "The Architecture of Science" for *Conservation Biology*. Students and faculty should participate in the design process along with the architects and engineers. The building should reflect an environmental ethic in terms of what materials are used, how energy-efficient it is, and how alternative sources of energy power it. Building data such as energy performance, energy production, water quality, indoor air quality, and emissions should be on display on site. The *New York Times* described this building as "remarkable" and the U.S. Department of Energy included it in its list of 30 "milestone buildings" of the 20th Century. Orr describes the project in two subsequent books: *The Nature of Design* (2002), and *Design on the Edge: The Making of a High Performance Building* (2006).

Orr is the education "Conservation in Context" editor for *Conservation Biology* and serves on the editorial advisory board of *Orion Nature Quarterly*. His articles frequently expand on situations he encounters at Oberlin, such as proposals for new campus car garages or the college's electronic communication network. He examines them from the perspective of well-known ecological thinkers such as GARRETT HARDIN or WENDELL BERRY and draws parallels with similar phenomena worldwide. Orr also has critiqued recent well-publicized challenges to the environmental movement with reviews that point out the inconsistencies and fallacies of such antienvironmentalist books as *A Moment on Earth* (1995) by Gregg Easterbrook and Martin Lewis's *Green Delusions* (1992).

Orr has received numerous awards for his work. He was awarded a National Conservation Achievement Award by the National Wildlife Federation in 1993, a Lyndhurst Prize in 1992 "to recognize the educational, cultural, and charitable activities of particular individuals of exceptional talent, character, and moral vision," the Benton Box Award from Clemson University for his work in environmental education (1995), a Bioneers Award in 2003, and was named an "Environmental Hero" by *Interiors and Sources* magazine in 2004. He serves on the boards of a number of environmentally-oriented organizations.

Orr lives in Oberlin, Ohio.

#### BIBLIOGRAPHY
"David W. Orr," www.davidworr.com; McDaniel, Carl, *Wisdom for a livable planet: the visionary work of Terri Swearingen, Dave Foreman, Wes Jackson, Helena Norberg-Hodge, Werner Fornos, Herman Daly, Stephen Schneider, and David Orr*, 2005; Orr, David W., *Design on the Edge: The Making of a High Performance Building*, 2006; Orr, David W., *Earth In Mind: On Education, Environment, and the Human Prospect*, 1994; Orr, David W., *Ecological Literacy: Education and the Transition to a Postmodern World*, 1992; Orr, David W., *The Nature of Design*, 2002 Orr, David W., and David J. Eagen, *The Campus and Environmental Responsibility*, 1992.

## Osborn, Fairfield
(January 15, 1887–September 16, 1969)
Writer, Founder of the Conservation Foundation, President of the New York Zoological Society

Fairfield Osborn alerted readers of the mid-twentieth century to the dangers of unbridled population growth and consumption of natural resources through his popular books *Our Plundered Planet* (1948) and *The Limits of the Earth* (1953). Through the New York Zoological Society (NYZS), which he headed for almost 30 years, Osborn helped found the Conservation Foundation, an organization that served as a research and policy institute on natural resource issues.

Henry Fairfield Osborn Jr. was born in Princeton, New Jersey, on January 15, 1887, to Henry Fairfield and Lucretia (Perry) Osborn. His father was a well-known biology professor at Princeton and Columbia Universities, president of the American Museum of Natural History, and a founder and president of the Bronx Zoo. Young "Fair" Osborn grew up in a world of wealth and social prestige and early in his life demonstrated an abiding interest in the natural world. He was allowed to keep his own private menagerie at his family's Madison Avenue brownstone and took one of his pets, a nocturnal flying squirrel, to school with him every day, curled up in his pocket. Osborn atttended Groton School in Groton, Connecticut, and Princeton University, where he earned an A.B. in 1909. He spent one year at Trinity College, Cambridge University, for graduate study in 1909–1910. After his formal education, he spent a few years working in the San Francisco freight yards and laying railroad track in Nevada. In 1914, he married Marjorie Mary Lamond, with whom he would have three daughters and enjoy a long marriage.

After service in the American Expeditionary Force during World War I, Osborn spent the first two decades of his professional life working in business: for Union Oil Company, as treasurer for a label-making company, and then as a partner in the Redmond and Company investment banking firm. He retired from business in 1935.

Despite his immersion in the business world, his heart had remained with animals. In 1922, he had been named a trustee of the New York Zoological Society, which ran the Bronx Zoo and Coney Island's New York aquarium. He served as the treasurer of the NYZS executive board from 1923 to 1935, and as secretary from 1935 to 1940. When he became president of the NYZS in 1940, a position he would hold until just before his death in 1969, "the zoo began to change," recounted LAURANCE ROCKEFELLER, a friend of Osborn and co–board member of the NYZS, in an elegy to Osborn published in *Reader's Digest.*

Osborn, who still maintained a deep love for animals and reportedly was able to detect signs of poor emotional and physical health before even the zookeepers could, did away with cages whenever possible and placed animals instead in open areas that recreated as best as possible their natural habitats. His intuitive approach increased survival rates for gorillas, which until then usually died in captivity. He advised that zookeepers give gorilla babies more physical affection, that they hold and embrace them. According to Rockefeller, survival rates turned around after that. Osborn also raised millions of dollars for the NYZS from his many affluent friends. His *New York Times* obituary reported that "he could go to the very affluent and, without batting an eye, ask for a million dollars for zoo and aquarium improvements; he said that if he asked for a million dollars he was confident he would 'get at least $25,000.'"

At the same time that Osborn devoted himself to improving the welfare of captive animals and the public's ability to learn from and enjoy them, he tried to raise awareness of worsening environmental conditions worldwide. He wrote *Our Plundered Planet* in 1948 about a war that Osborn says in the introduction to the book could potentially result in far more destruction than the recently ended World War II: man's war against nature. The book decries the rampant destruction of the natural environment by an ever-increasing, hungry population and presents "only one solution: Man must recognize the necessity of cooperating with nature. He must temper his demands and use and conserve the natural living resources of this earth in a manner that alone can provide for the continuation of civilization." If the population rate increase did not slow, and people did not amend their relationship with the earth, he warned, "Nature holds the trump card." His next book, *The Limits of the Earth*, published in 1953, provided further information about the devastating impact on water, agriculture, and other life-sustaining resources. Both books, written for nonspecialists, were translated into several languages, and as the first such warnings sounded, they inspired many to join efforts to work toward population control and conservation of natural resources. Osborn served on the Conservation Advisory Committee of the U.S. Department of the Interior from 1950 to 1957 and on the Planning Committee of the Economic and Social Council of the United Nations.

Following the publication of *Our Plundered Planet*, Osborn and other colleagues at the NYZS founded the Conservation Foundation in 1948, a research institute that produced books, reports, and films about natural resources, flood control, and endangered species. Osborn served as the organization's first president until 1962 and then became chairman of its board. The Conservation Foundation was originally part of the NYZS, but affiliated with the World Wildlife Fund (WWF) in 1985 and in 1990 was formally consolidated with the WWF.

Osborn is also known for his work with conservation philanthropist Laurance Rockefeller to establish the Jackson Hole Wildlife Park near Moran, Wyoming, on land owned by the Rockefeller family. Together they founded the Jackson Hole Biological Station to facilitate studies by NYZS biologists there.

Osborn received many awards and honors during his life, including the Medal of Honor from the THEODORE ROOSEVELT Memorial Association in 1949, another Medal of Honor from the city of New York in 1960, and the Gold Medal of the New York Zoological Society in 1966. He continued working actively with the New York Zoological Society and the Conservation Foundation until shortly before his death. Osborn died in New York City on September 16, 1969, after a series of strokes.

**BIBLIOGRAPHY**

Bridges, William, *A Gathering of Animals: An Unconventional History of the New York Zoological Society*, 1974; "Fairfield Osborn, the Zoo's No. 1 Showman, Dies," *New York Times*, 1969; Goddard, Donald, ed., *Saving Wildlife: A Century of Conservation*, 1995; Rockefeller, Laurance, "My Most Unforgettable Character," *The Reader's Digest*, 1972; Stroud, Richard, *National Leaders of American Conservation*, 1985.

## Owings, Margaret

(April 29, 1913–January 21, 1999)
Artist, Founder of Friends of the Sea Otter

An artist with a profound appreciation of nature, Margaret Owings fought to protect the wildlife and wild habitat in her home state of California and became known as the leader of a broad range of environmental causes. While serving as a commissioner of the California State Parks Commission, she led a successful opposition to the construction of a freeway through Pacific Creek Redwoods State Park. She crusaded for some of the threatened species that lived near her, waging battles to eradicate both bounty and sport hunting of mountain lions in the state and founding Friends of the Sea Otter, an organization committed to protecting the California sea otter and its habitat. Owings also established the Rachel Carson Memorial Fund shortly after RACHEL CARSON's death, to ensure that her work to educate the public about hazardous chemicals would continue.

Margaret Wentworth was born on April 29, 1913, in Berkeley, California, to Frank W. and Jean (Pond) Wentworth. She was aware of the natural world from a very early age and enjoyed spending time in the family's rock and live oak garden as she grew up. Her father was a trustee at Mills College where she later went to school, graduating with a bachelor's degree in art in 1934. She completed postgraduate work in art at the Fogg Museum at Harvard University in 1935. From her formal training in art she gained greater sensitivity to life and the natural world, and found that for her, art and nature seemed to go hand-in-hand. She married Malcolm Millard in 1937 and later had a daughter with him. Her marriage took her to Chicago for ten years, then to Carmel, California, before it ended in divorce. At about this time, in 1947, she became interested in environmental activism and joined the Point Lobos League, a small group of people who opposed the mining of sand from a beautiful beach and the construction of a housing development on the coast south of Carmel. The group garnered support and raised funds and was then able to buy a mile and a half stretch of coastline and preserve it as a state park. Many years later Owings still looked back on the group's accomplishment with satisfaction.

On December 30, 1953, she married Nathaniel Owings, a founding partner in Skidmore, Owings & Merrill, one of the country's preeminent architectural firms. Nathaniel Owings undertook plans to design and build a house for them in Big Sur on the coast of California, on a site projecting out from a cliff and affording striking views of the ocean and mountains around it. He built the house in accordance with their desire to live in a structure that had an active presence on the landscape while still respecting the character of the land and its delicate ecology.

By this time, Margaret Owings was becoming well known as an artist, and her paintings had been featured in one-woman shows at the Santa Barbara Museum of Art (1940) and the Stanford Art Gallery (1951). She and Nathaniel continued to work on their spectacular cliff-top house at Big Sur, but they were both increasingly drawn to the landscape and people of New Mexico, particularly near the Rio Grande valley. Together they started building an adobe farmhouse there in 1956, with high-walled courtyards, ancient woodwork, and a studio for Owings to paint in. The couple moved seasonally between the two houses for the next 30 or so years until Nathaniel Owings's death in 1984.

In 1962, Owings was dismayed when a mountain lion was killed for bounty near their Big Sur home. Since the late 1800s, hunter had killed thousands of mountain lions for rewards, following the view that fewer mountain lions meant more deer, cattle, and sheep. Owings opposed the practice and began a crusade to stop it, enlisting such famous conservationists as Rachel Carson and ANSEL ADAMS to speak with her in front of legislative committees. In 1963 the state legislature abolished the mountain lion bounty, though they could still be legally hunted for sport. But after several years, when concerns were raised over continuing declines in the mountain lion population, Owings again came to their defense, promoting a moratorium on all hunting of the animal. In 1971 she succeeded, and sport hunting of mountain lions was abolished in California.

By now, Owings was dedicating more and more of her time to conservation causes and had begun serving as a commissioner on the California State Parks Commission in 1963, a position she held until 1969. During that time she led a campaign to prevent the construction of a freeway through prime alluvial flats in Pacific Creek Redwoods State Park, site of the world's tallest trees. Also in 1963, Owings attended the ceremony for Rachel Carson when she received the Audubon Medal for her book *Silent Spring*. At the time, Carson was dying of cancer and remarked that she worried that no one would carry on her work after she was gone. Owings took those words to heart and resolved to keep Carson's legacy alive. Shortly after Carson's death in April 1964, Owings raised $14,000 and founded the Rachel Carson Memorial Fund, administered by the National Audubon Society (now administered by Environmental Defense), to continue Carson's work of combating toxins in the environment.

Out of the broad spectrum of environmental concerns in which Owings was active, she is probably best known for her work with the California sea otter, a threatened marine mammal that she was fond of watching from her cliff-top home at Big Sur. She championed their cause in 1968 by cofounding the Friends of the Sea Otter organization with Dr. Jim Mattison, at a time when the southern sea otter population numbered about 650. In the early days of the organization, it operated on a volunteer basis, and often the meetings were held in the Owingses' home. Through sheer determination, Owings, who served as president from its beginning until the early 1990s, kept the group functioning—rallying scientists, other conservationists, and educators; speaking to legislators both in Sacramento and Washington, D.C.; and helping to establish environmental policy to protect the sea otter. Friends of the Sea Otter has now grown to 4,600 members in 45 states and 13 countries, and the southern sea otter population has grown in number and range and now includes about 2,400 otters along the central California coast.

Owings filled many other roles as well. She was a trustee of Defenders of Wildlife (1969–1974), a board member with the National Parks Foundation (1968–1969), the first woman to be a board member of the African Wildlife Leadership Foundation (1968–1976), and a trustee of the Environmental Defense Fund (1972–1982, then as an honorary trustee). She was recognized with many awards and citations, including the prestigious National Audubon Society Medal in 1983 and the United Nations Environmental Program's Gold Medal Award in 1988. In 1993 she received an honorary doctorate from Mills College, and in 1998 the National Audubon Society named her one of the top 100 most influential conservationists of the century.

Before she died, Owings spent months compiling a collection of her artwork and writings, which she put together into a book titled *Voice from the Sea: Reflections of Wildlife and Wilderness* (1998). The book covers five decades of her writing and emphasizes her lifetime commitment to wildlife conservation. She died of heart failure at her home in Big Sur, California, on January 21, 1999.

**BIBLIOGRAPHY**

Goldberger, Paul, "Revisiting Big Sur's Wild Bird," *Architectural Digest*, 1996; LaBastille, Anne, "The Crusader of Big Sur," *Living Wilderness*, 1980; Saxon, Wolfgang, "Margaret W. Owings, 85, Defender of Wild Creatures," 1999; Valtin, Tom, "Margaret Owings," *Environmental Defense Fund Newsletter*, 1986.

# American Environmental Leaders

From Colonial Times to the Present

## Packard, Steve

(March 28, 1943– )
Restoration Ecologist, Organizer

Through a combination of sheer determination and rare vision, Steve Packard has succeeded in restoring tallgrass prairie, savanna, and oak woodland communities in the midwestern United States—some of the rarest and least-understood ecosystems in the country. While he has had little formal training in biology, he has a talent for finding new and effective approaches to restoration ecology using common sense and intuition. His unorthodox methods initially ruffled feathers in the academic world, yet his years of work along the North Branch of the Chicago River have produced beautiful results, turning weedy remnants into rich native prairies and savannas. Part of his secret lies in his ability to inspire groups of people to help with the physically and intellectually demanding work of restoring degraded land—he created a whole network of volunteers that came to serve as a model for a new kind of organized environmental activism.

Stephen Packard was born on March 28, 1943, in Worcester, Massachusetts. His father was a self-made businessman who had grown up in the slums of Worcester. His mother overcame physical handicaps to develop great spiritual strength and generosity. Steve was the oldest of seven children and even as a young child had a love of nature in his blood. In 1952 his family moved from industrial Worcester to rural Shrewsbury, Massachusetts, and he was able to further develop his consuming interest in the natural world. His fourth-grade teacher had an enlightening influence on him, and he spent many hours with her and her husband, learning about nature's wild things. As a sixth grader he turned his backyard into a nature center, putting up bird feeders and transplanting trees.

He went to Harvard in 1961—the first from his family to attend college—but rebellious tendencies made him restless, and he left after two years. He moved to New York City, where he spent a year in a community of artist and filmmakers, then returned to Harvard to finish his degree in social psychology and anthropology, graduating in 1966. For the next few years he was absorbed in antiwar, civil rights, and related movements. He joined a newsreel collective, which made propaganda films for activist groups, and this eventually took him to Chicago. When the antiwar movement subsided, he was 30 years old and at a loss. At this point, he turned back to the passion of his youth—nature. He came across a ROGER TORY PETERSON guide to wildflowers and decided to learn all the flowers in the Chicago area. This led him to seek out wild places, and what he found were many degraded remnant prairie sites along the North Branch of the Chicago River. His interest in nature fully reawakened, he took a job in 1975 (for $95 a week) with the Illinois Environmental Council, a fledgling lobbying group, and committed himself to saving what was left of the prairies. The experience he gained from his activist days served him well; he had a thorough understanding of politics and a flair for organizing people and keeping them involved. This was the beginning of the North Branch Prairie Project—later renamed the North Branch Restoration Project—whose goal was to restore sites as closely as possible to the condition they were in when European settlers found them.

Many obstacles were in the way of the North Branch project. The land the volunteers wanted to save belonged to the Forest Preserve District, whose administrators were reluctant at first to let a band of volunteers help manage their sites. Also, the prairie sites themselves were in very poor shape—filled with trash and overrun with brush that had long ago choked out the native prairie species in many areas. Packard was left to decide what to plant and how to convince the Forest Preserve District to give his group increasing responsibility. With a little political finesse, lots of determination, and some common sense, the group was soon able to begin their experiment. They cleared brush by hand and attempted many plantings, not knowing at first what would work and what would not. And although it took years to see results, they did not give up.

By 1979 Packard was working as a field representative for the Natural Land Institute, a private, nonprofit environmental group. He also continued working in all his spare time on the North Branch Restoration Project, which was starting to show progress. He and his volunteers had made some headway clearing brush but were now ready for a more natural method of brush control—fire. Their proposal for controlled burning was met with even more bureaucratic balking, but they did succeed in gaining the necessary permits, and they quickly found fire to be an effective and irreplaceable tool. The techniques used have paid off. Twenty years after their project began, native flowers again bloom by the hundreds of thousands on the North Branch prairies and savannas, and birds and other species that had abandoned the area have returned.

Part of the legacy of Packard's early work is that he challenged rigid academic views. Without formal scientific training he was able to take a more open-minded approach to find innovative solutions. His efforts have encouraged recognition of the important contribution restoration practitioners have made through in-the-field experimentation. Also, the success of the North Branch Restoration Project awakened others in the conservation world to the ability of volunteers to take on major responsibilities. At the Illinois Nature Conservancy, where Packard worked from 1983 to 1998, he established a Volunteer Stewardship Network. It has since grown to 8,000 volunteers on 202 Illinois restoration sites. The network has come to serve as a model for similar work in many other states and countries. The Chicago Audubon Society recognized him for his role in setting up the Network with its 1983 Protector of the Environment award.

Starting in the mid-1980s he broadened his focus to include building a culture of conservation for the Chicago region. A 13-county metropolitan area with over eight million people, the Chicago region paradoxically harbors the greatest concentration of biodiversity in the midwestern United States. He designed and organized a massive collaboration, the Chicago Region Biodiversity Council (also known as the "Chicago Wilderness Consortium"). It now includes 200 public and private agencies with many scores of scientists, hundreds of land management and education professionals, and thousands of volunteers working to protect and restore 225,000 acres of core natural areas such as corporate campuses, rights-of-way, golf courses, and wooded neighborhoods, as well as protected areas such as state parks and county preserves. The goal is to build a positive relationship between people and nature in an advanced metropolitan culture. Chicago Wilderness has been described as a model for the planet, an important one considering the shift of the world's populations to cities. Currently Packard remains active with Chicago Wilderness, Chicago Audubon, and its Urban Habitat program. He resides in Chicago.

**BIBLIOGRAPHY**

"Chicago Wilderness," www.chicagowilderness. org; "Chicago Audubon Society," www. chicagoaudubon.org; Packard, Stephen, "Rediscovering the Tallgrass Savannas of Illinois," *Proceedings of the Tenth North American Prairie Conference*, Denton, Texas, 1986; Packard, Stephen, "Restoring Oak Ecosystems," *Restoration & Management Notes*, 1993; Packard, Stephen, and John Balaban, "Restoring the Herb Layer in a Degraded Bur Oak 'Closed" Savanna," in *Proceedings of the North American Conference of Savannas and Barrens*, James S. Fralish,

Roger C. Anderson, John E. Ebinger, and Robert Szafoni, eds., 1994; Packard, Stephen, and Cornelia F. Mutel, eds., *The Tallgrass Restoration Handbook: For Prairies, Savannas, and Woodlands*, 1997; Stevens, William K., *Miracle under the Oaks: The Revival of Nature in America*, 1995.

## Palmer, Paula
(June 8, 1948– )
Sociologist, Executive Director of Global Response

Sociologist and writer Paula Palmer lends her pen to the environmental causes of indigenous peoples throughout the world. Unlike conservationists who see humans as innately destructive of "wilderness," Palmer recognizes that traditional indigenous cultures have refined ways of living on the land without destroying valuable ecosystems. Palmer's career—working with indigenous and Afro-Caribbean residents of the Talamanca Coast of Costa Rica and, since 1996, directing Global Response, an urgent action network that responds to environmental crises affecting indigenous people—has been devoted to helping indigenous people carry out their own goals for a continued sustainable lifestyle.

Born in Valparaiso, Indiana, on June 8, 1948, Palmer studied at Valparaiso University; at the University of Colorado–Boulder, where she received a B.A. in English literature in 1970; and at Michigan State University, where she earned an M.A. in sociology in 1989. During her undergraduate years, Palmer edited a civil rights newspaper and worked in the student movement to end the war in Vietnam. A 1973 backpacking trip to Costa Rica became a turning point in her life. Via train and boat, she made her way to the roadless Talamanca region, intending only to spend a short time there. It was rainy season—there was little to do besides play with the village children and listen to elders tell stories. She became fascinated with the history of the English-speaking Black villagers, who had come to Costa Rica from the Caribbean islands during the 1800s. When they invited her to stay and establish an

Paula Palmer (Photograph by Mary Hey)

English-language school to carry on their cultural traditions, she eagerly accepted.

Since there were no textbooks for her to use, Palmer decided to make her own. She tape-recorded and transcribed interviews with the oldest people in the coastal villages, asking them to talk about every aspect of their lives. These transcripts became the children's reading primers. As villagers became more involved in remembering and thinking about their history as a unique people, they encouraged Palmer to put their recollections together in a book. *What Happen* (1977; rev. ed., 1993) has become Costa Rica's classic oral history of Talamanca's Afro-Caribbean community.

Palmer went on to two other major writing projects in Talamanca. As director of the Talamanca Community Research Project, she taught high school students how to do oral history research; her indigenous and Afro-Caribbean students became authors of articles that Palmer published in a series of magazines called *Nuestra Talamanca Ayer y Hoy*. Costa Rica's Ministry of Education later reprinted these magazines as a textbook about the unique cultures of Talamanca. In a region that lacked electricity, telephones, and paved roads, the magazines generated community pride and increased appreciation and cooperation among Talamanca's different ethnic groups. Young people learned to value the traditional knowledge and skills that sustained their communities as well as the natural resources of the forests and the sea.

With two indigenous coauthors, Juanita Sánchez and Gloria Mayorga, Palmer also published *Taking Care of Sibö's Gifts*, an oral history of the KéköLdi Indigenous Reserve in Talamanca. This book is a product of a method of sociology called Participatory Action Research (PAR), in which a researcher helps members of a community analyze their own culture, history, economy, and ecology and then use what they learned when making decisions about their future. As a result of their research with Palmer, the Kekoldi indigenous community began a project to breed endangered green iguanas and opened a community center where elders teach their language and their traditional knowledge and practices to young people. Once they saw that outsiders were interested in their culture, they began to lead educational tours through parts of their forest home. As a result of this work, the Kekoldi people were awarded the Richard Evans Schultes prize for ethnobotany and biodiversity conservation.

Palmer returned to the United States in 1993 and settled in Boulder, Colorado. She became the environment and health editor of the American Indian quarterly *Winds of Change*. She also taught courses in the Environmental Studies Department of the Naropa University. Since 1996 she has served as executive director of Global Response, an international network for environmental action and education that helps communities around the world organize effective campaigns to stop or prevent environmental destruction. At the request of local communities, Global Response publishes action alerts that describe specific environmental threats. Global Response members—adults, teens, and children—are asked to write letters to specific officials, urging them to make environmentally sound decisions. The organization has a history of successful campaigns for environmental justice and environmental protection. For Palmer, it is a way to create a world community of ordinary citizens, young and old, who work together to preserve the health and abundance of life on earth.

**BIBLIOGRAPHY**

"Global Response," www.globalresponse.org; Palmer, Paula, "Breathing Life into the Struggle for Indigenous Peoples' Rights," *Peacework*, 2007; Palmer, Paula, "Empowering Indigenous Peoples to Preserve Their Forests and Cultures," *The Forum for Advancing Basic Education and Literacy*, 1994; Palmer, Paula, "The Pen is Mightier than the Sword: Global Environmental Justice, One Letter at a Time" in *Power, Justice and the Environment: a critical appraisal of the Environmental Justice movement*, David Pellow and Robert Brulle, eds., 2005; Palmer, Paula, "We Can Survive and Prosper," *Cultural Survival Quarterly*, 1992; Palmer, Paula, *What Happen: A folk history of Costa Rica's Talamanca Coast*, 1979; Palmer, Paula, and Corrine Glesne, *Coastal Talamanca: A Cultural and Ecological Guide*, 1993; Palmer, Paula, Juanita Sánchez, and Gloria Mayorga, *Taking Care of Sibo's Gifts: An Environmental Treatise from Costa Rica's KéköLdi Indigenous Reserve*, 1993.

## Parkman, Francis
(September 16, 1823–November 8, 1893)
Historian

Author of *The Oregon Trail* and the seven-volume *France and England in North America*, Francis Parkman chronicled the early history of the colonization of the northern United States and Canada and created a vivid description of the wilderness encountered by the early settlers. Parkman was an avid outdoorsman and naturalist, as well as an expert on the cultivation of roses. He was an early advocate for the preservation of nature, particularly the great tracts of unspoiled forest in the West, and created through his writing an appreciation for the importance of the wilderness in the United States and the lives of its citizens.

Francis Parkman was born on September 16, 1823, on Boston's Beacon Hill, to a life of privilege. His parents were both from prominent New England families, and from his mother's family Parkman inherited enough money that he never had to earn his own living. He was a frail child and at age eight was sent to live with his maternal grandfather, Nathaniel Hall. Hall had retired to the country near Medford, Massachusetts, and while in his care Parkman learned the joys of a life in the woods. During the four years he lived in Medford, Parkman explored the wilderness of the Middlesex Fells, which bordered his grandfather's land, and became a close and enthusiastic observer of nature. When his family considered him sufficiently strong, Parkman was returned to Boston, where he went to preparatory school before entering Harvard in 1840. There he studied with the historian Jared Sparks, who helped inspire the project that was to be Parkman's life work: the history of the French and Indian wars in New England.

Francis Parkman (Library of Congress, Prints & Photographs Division, LC-USZ61-97)

Parkman graduated from Harvard in 1844 and went on to take a law degree in 1846. Parkman had no intention of practicing law, however, and while at Harvard began publishing prose sketches in *Knickerbocker*, covering historical topics and his adventures in the White Mountains. In 1846 Parkman set out for a journey to the West with his cousin Quincy Shaw, the journey chronicled in *The Oregon Trail*. Parkman undertook the trip in part to observe Native Americans, who were central in his history of New England, but with whom he had had little direct experience. With Shaw and Henry Chatillon, a guide they met in Missouri, Parkman journeyed across the eastern half of the Oregon Trail and part of the Santa Fe Trail. In Wyoming they met a band of Oglala Sioux. Parkman stayed several weeks in the company of the Indians and was deeply affected by the experience. He saw in the Oglala Sioux both a model for the way the wilderness tests and molds men and a reflection of the racist stereotypes of the time. *The Oregon Trail* is marred by Parkman's racist comments on the inferiority of Native Americans, though Parkman also later argued for more equitable treatment of native peoples as the United States expanded its borders westward. The principal drama of the book is that of the masculine adventurer, testing himself in the wilds, mastering the obstacles of the land through strength and bravery, and conquering wildlife with his trusty rifle. Like THEODORE ROOSEVELT, who read and admired *The Oregon Trail*, Parkman wished to preserve nature so that men could continue to prove their manhood through hunting.

Upon returning from his journey, Parkman's always-precarious health completely collapsed. He was stricken with arthritis, and his eyesight nearly failed. For much of the rest of his life he wrote through dictation. In spite of these obstacles, Parkman began publishing *The Oregon Trail* in serial form in *Knickerbocker* in 1847 and in book form in 1849. He then set to work on the pieces of *France and England in North America*, which he called "a history of the forest," because the main subject of the work is the encounter of French, English, and Native Americans with the forests of New England. Parkman's history is filled with close description of the forest and detailed accounts of the adventures of soldiers and trackers during the disputes over control of Canada and the northern United States. Parkman knew the land forms, plants, and animals of his setting, and his work preserves a record of the experiences of the European settlers as they met the frightening, foreign wilderness of North America. One of Parkman's contributions to the creation of an environmentalist sentiment in the United States is his recognition that this wilderness was not an enemy to be conquered, but a treasure worth preserving. For Parkman, the wilderness played a crucial role in developing the strength of the nation and its people, through testing and molding the national character, and *France and England in North America* records both the events of the early chapters of North American history and Parkman's love of nature.

The completion of this history took most of the rest of Parkman's life, concluding with the last volume, *A Half-Century of Conflict*, in 1892. Parkman also wrote numerous other works, including essays in support of CARL SCHURZ's policies of forest preservation. Parkman witnessed the disappearance of ancient forests in New England and hoped that similar destruction could be avoided in the West. Parkman was a good naturalist: He understood that destroying forests affected all parts of the surrounding ecosystem and wrote detailed descriptions of the delicate balance among land, water, plants, and animals. Parkman also became heavily involved in horticulture, particularly of roses and lilies. His 1866 *Book of Roses* was for many years considered the definitive work on the subject of rose cultivation. Parkman was appointed professor of horticulture at Harvard and served as president of the Massachusetts Horticultural Society. He died on November 8, 1893, of peritonitis, at his home in Brookline, Massachusetts.

### Bibliography

Gale, Robert, *Francis Parkman*, 1973; Jacobs, Wilbur, *Francis Parkman, Historian as Hero: The Formative Years*, 1992; Jacobs, Wilbur, "Francis Parkman—Naturalist—Environmental Savant," *Pacific Historical Review*, 1992; Jacobs, Wilbur, "Lessons from the Master—Francis Parkman, Historian as Hero of the Early American West," *Journal of the West*, 1997; Townsend, Kim, "Francis Parkman and the Male Tradition," *American Quarterly*, 1986.

## Peacock, Doug
(April 5, 1942– )
Naturalist, War Veteran, Outdoorsman, Hayduke

Naturalist, bear expert, war veteran, and consummate outdoorsman, Doug Peacock is the author of four books and numerous articles on wilderness and conservation. His memoir, *Grizzly Years: In Search of the American Wilderness* (1990), chronicles his war experience in Vietnam and subsequent encounters with grizzly bears in the backcountry of the American West. Based on fourteen years of close observation and first-hand experience with grizzlies, the book solidified his reputation as a leading authority on bear behavior. His second memoir, *Walking It Off: A Veteran's Chronicle of War and Wilderness* (2005), recounts his close and sometimes complicated friendship with author EDWARD ABBEY. A fierce defender of wilderness, Peacock remains an inspirational figure in the American environmental movement.

Doug Peacock was born on April 5, 1942, in Alma, Michigan, to Marion and Kathryn Peacock. The son of a Boy Scouts leader, Doug spent a lot of time in the woods as a boy. He studied archeology and philosophy at the University of Michigan before volunteering for the military draft in 1965. Peacock served two tours of duty in Vietnam as a Green Beret medic. Upon his release from the Army in 1968, he returned to the U.S. a disillusioned war veteran, seeking refuge and solitude in remote wilderness areas of the West. It was there, in the backcountry of Wyoming and Montana, that he developed his fascination and passion for grizzlies.

In 1969, Peacock was introduced to Edward Abbey, beginning a close friendship that would last for two decades until Abbey's death in 1989. Together, they conceived acts of sabotage against logging operations, land development activities, and other destructive invasions of the wilderness. This practice of sabotage in the name of wilderness protection would come to be known as "monkey wrenching," and would eventually lead to the formation of the environmental group, *Earth First!* Peacock would gain notoriety as the model for George Washington Hayduke, a character in Abbey's 1975 novel, *The Monkey Wrench Gang*.

Peacock credits grizzly bears with saving his life in the troubled years following his return from Vietnam. Helping him to heal the psychological wounds of war, grizzlies taught him the virtues of humility, respect for life, and tolerance for other beings. Being in grizzly country makes us acutely aware of our ancient fear of falling prey, he explains, an awareness that has guided the development of human intelligence throughout our evolution as a species. "I know this feeling as a beautiful fear," Doug writes. "No other creature on the continent instills this most mnemonic and useful of human dreads: the origi-

Doug Peacock and Elk (Photograph by Andrea Peacock)

nal shudder." This primeval fear forces a basic humility that serves as the basis for human reason and rational thought. Peacock believes that our own viable survival as a species depends upon preserving and maintaining the conditions of wild nature under which we evolved. For this reason, he believes the fates of bears and humans are linked.

Peacock currently lives in Montana with his wife Andrea, with whom he co-authored *The Essential Grizzly: The Mingled Fates of Men and Bears* (2006). He has two children, Laurel and Colin, from a previous marriage. Doug continues to write and lecture, visiting schools to speak about conservation and the need to preserve wilderness. In 2007, he was awarded a Guggenheim Fellowship. Doug is a board trustee of Round River Conservation Studies, a nonprofit organization dedicated to international conservation research and education. Through his association with Round River, Peacock has worked with the Taku River Tlingit First Nation in British Columbia to help protect its traditional territory, an area that includes millions of acres of wilderness. He is currently working on a project he calls "Repatriation," a personal and archeological consideration of North America's earliest inhabitants and the implications for modern man. A friend and mentor of many writers and activists, Peacock continues to serve as a spiritual adviser for the environmental movement. Doug remains passionately devoted to the defense of grizzly bears and saving what remains of the planet's wild lands. "I'm a defender of wild causes," he says. "All of 'em. Anyplace."

**BIBLIOGRAPHY**
Chamberlain, Ted, "Doug Peacock: Veteran of the Grizzly Wars," *National Geographic Adventure*, 2000; Martin, Robert E., "Doug Peacock's Environmental Call to Arms," *Review Magazine*, 2006; Peacock, Andrea and Doug, *The Essential Grizzly: The Mingled Fates of Men and Bears*, 2006; Peacock, Doug, *Grizzly Years: In Search of the American Wilderness*, 1990; Peacock, Doug, *Walking It Off: A Veteran's Chronicle of War and Wilderness*, 2005.

## Perkins, Jane
(April 18, 1948– )
Environment and Labor Organizer

During her career, Jane Perkins has worked both as a labor organizer and as an environmental activist. She worked within the American Federation of Labor–Congress of Industrial Organizations (AFL-CIO) as its liaison to the environmental movement, and was instrumental to the formation of a "Blue-Green Alliance." Her mission was to bridge the perceived gap between labor and environmentalists, defining goals that both camps could support in a quest for a healthy environment and economically secure workers.

Jane Perkins was born in Pottsville, Pennsylvania, on April 18, 1948. From an early age she learned of the hazards of unsafe work environments and the potential of unions to make a difference in the lives of workers. Both of her grandfathers contracted black lung disease and died in their forties as a consequence of working in coal mines without protection. Her mother sewed piece goods in factories and was a member of the International Ladies Garment Workers Union. She participated in several strikes both as a striking worker and a scabbing worker, crossing the picket lines to substitute for strikers. Watching her mother in these difficult situations made a deep impression on Perkins.

Perkins was the first member of her family to attend college. She earned a B.A. in humanities from Pennsylvania State University in 1971. After being unfairly fired from her first job after college and feeling firsthand the frustration of injustice without union representation, Perkins sought work in the labor movement. She took a job as business agent in the Harrisburg office of the Pennsylvania Social Services Union, a local of the Service Employee's International Union (SEIU). She spent six years helping workers negotiate contracts, handling grievances and arbitration, and organizing new workers, before moving on to assume the elected office of secretary-treasurer of the union local.

The Three Mile Island nuclear power plant accident in 1979 was the catalyst for Perkins's transformation into an environmentalist. She and other family members were evacuated from their Harrisburg, Pennsylvania, homes when the power plant melted down. Because of her activity in the labor movement, Perkins immediately sensed the dilemma for those concerned with both environmental safety and job security. A well-known labor activist by this time, Perkins was invited by the local environmental group Three Mile Island Alert to represent the voice of labor within their group. Perkins agreed to join and soon organized the ad hoc Greater Harrisburg Labor Committee for Safe Energy and Full Employment, which in turn organized a labor march on the issue in Harrisburg. Perkins's work on the march caused problems for her with some unions. She was accused of causing dissension within the labor movement and faced internal union charges. Other unions, notably the Machinists' Union, the United Mine Workers, and the Furniture Workers, had come out against nuclear power and supported Perkins during the controversy.

The nuclear accident and her burgeoning environmentalism propelled Perkins into politics. In 1981 she was elected to Harrisburg's city council, where she created and chaired an ad hoc Three Mile Island committee, as well as presiding over committees dealing with other city affairs. She ran for state senate as a Democratic candidate in 1984, on a platform of fair taxes, personal integrity, and government spending priorities. Although she lost the election, she was endorsed by farmers', citizens', labor, women's, consumers', and environmental groups. The year 1985 took her to Washington, D.C., where she served as the first director of the New Populist Forum (now called Democrats 2000), which was founded by Iowa senator Tom Harkin, Texas agricultural commissioner Jim Hightower, and Illinois congressman Lane Evans. This organization serves as a bridge for debate between political progressives and conservative populists and as a network for progressive populists elected to office.

By this point in her career, Perkins was recognized as an expert in organizing people, motivating them to participate in projects and activities, solving organization-wide problem issues, and doing this all with limited budgetary resources. The newly reorganized environmental organization Friends of the Earth (FOE) recruited her in 1991 to repair its ailing management systems, eliminate its debt, and iron out problems with its recent merger with the Environmental Policy Institute and the Oceanic Society. After helping FOE reorganize and refocus, Perkins spent one year as a private-sector consultant and then two more as a consultant to the AFL-CIO. In 1997 she joined the staff of the AFL-CIO, where she worked until 2002 as its environmental liaison.

Perkins's mission at the AFL-CIO was to help the labor movement integrate the goal of a healthy environment with its advocacy for workers. She assembled a group of labor activists and environmentalists interested in the goal, the Blue-Green Working Group, and they slowly developed a set of principles for collaboration on emissions issues. After five years of negotiations, in February of 2002, a two-page agreement was reached, and four years later, in 2006, the Blue/Green Alliance was born, representing more than three million unionized workers and led by United Steelworkers of America the Sierra Club. Perkins is widely credited for initiating the contacts and the work that brought the Blue/Green Alliance to life.

**BIBLIOGRAPHY**

"AFL-CIO," www.aflcio.org/home.htm; Dougherty, Laurie, "Between the Devil and the Deep Blue Sea: Workers in the Global Environment," *Dollars and Sense Magazine*, 1999; Harwood, Jon, "Perkins Seeks Water-bond Review," *Evening News*, 1983; "Jane Perkins Is Selected Woman of Year," *The (Harrisburg) Patriot*, 1983; Moberg, David, "Brothers and Sisters Greens and Labor: It's a Coalition That Gives Corporate Polluters Fits," *Sierra*, 1999; Perkins, Jane, "Recognizing and Attacking Environmental Racism," *Clearinghouse Review*, 1992.

## Peterson, Roger Tory

(August 28, 1908–July 28, 1996)
Ornithologist, Painter, Writer

Bird-watchers and other nature enthusiasts all over the world know Roger Tory Peterson as the inventor of field guides. By simplifying the techniques used in the field, he made bird identification accessible to everyone, not just scientists and museum curators. Birding became a hobby and a passion for millions, awakening them to the natural world. Peterson was active in many ornithological and conservation organizations and is well known for his paintings of birds and other wildlife.

Born on August 28, 1908, in Jamestown, New York, Roger Tory Peterson was the son of European immigrants. His parents both came to the United States as young children, his mother from what was then eastern Germany and his father from Sweden. He grew up roaming the fields and hills around his home, often neglecting household chores. A dreamy thinker, he did not fit in well at school and was nicknamed "Bugs Peterson" because of his affinity for everything from snakes to skunks. But at the age of 11 he found inspiration. His seventh-grade teacher, who was interested in birds, started a Junior Audubon Club in which she passed out pamphlets on birds and had the children color on bird sketches. Peterson was hooked. He began bird-watching in the field and painting birds instead of doing homework.

Peterson's first job after high school was at Union Furniture Company, painting Chinese scenes on expensive lacquered cabinets, a job that allowed him some creativity and a chance to keep painting. He could not afford college, but after a few years he did move to New York City to study art at the National Academy of Design for three years. Later, from 1931 to 1934, he worked as a teacher in the science department at the Rivers School in Brookline, Massachusetts. It was there that he developed the idea that would change the course of nature study forever.

*Roger Tory Peterson at his studio in Old Lyme, Connecticut. (AP Images/Bob Child)*

He had decided to reinvent bird identification in the field and began by simply combining his two loves: bird-watching and painting. The tradition for anyone studying birds up until this point was to head to the fields with a shotgun. Identifying birds in a less destructive way was not easy. "Bird guides" at the time were either hefty scientific texts or skimpy leaflets with little helpful information. Peterson's goal was a marriage of the two: a small, lightweight guide, organized to show birds as they appear in the field; sometimes distant, sometimes aloft, sometimes in poor light. This could be done by observing "field marks": easy to spot characteristics that distinguish one species from another. Peterson did all the illustrations and descriptions himself, a painstaking labor of love met with huge skepticism from publishers. Five turned him down before Houghton Mifflin, in 1934, prompted by *Bird Lore* editor WILLIAM VOGT, cautiously printed 2,000 copies, insisting that Peterson receive only half a share of royalties. They need not have worried. The print run sold out in one week and launched what is today a multibillion-dollar industry. The original book, *Peterson's Field Guide to Eastern Birds*, has never been out of print. The original book expanded into a whole series of over 45 guides that help nature enthusiasts identify anything from butterflies to seashells, from reptiles to mammals, from minerals to the weather, all of which he edited until his death.

It is hard today to appreciate what a brilliant and influential idea Peterson had with his field guide. The impact of the original book and all the field guides that have followed has been tremendous. At the time of publication it brought a new awareness of birds and their world. People began to value birds as soon as they could name them, identify them, and enjoy them. And consequently people began to care about habitat and the destruction of it. Many credit Peterson for paving the way for the environmental movement because he got people to pay attention to what they were seeing.

Following the success of his field guide, Peterson served as education director for the National Audubon Society and art editor for *Audubon Magazine* from 1934 to 1943. In 1936 he married his first wife, Mildred Washington; though they shared a passion for the natural world, their marriage was turbulent and ended after six years. Very shortly after that he married his second wife, Barbara Coulter, in 1943. The same year Peterson was drafted into the Army Corps of Engineers, stationed near Washington, D.C., where he served until 1945. During this time, he and Barbara had two sons, Tory and Lee.

After his army term Peterson continued writing and editing field guides, working on paintings, and photographing and filming birds all over the world. He remained involved in many organizations and agencies until the time of his death. He was art director for the National Wildlife Federation's conservation stamp program from 1946 to 1975 and served on the board of directors of various agencies such as the National Audubon Society, the World Wildlife Fund, and Hawk Mountain Sanctuary Association. He gave the keynote address and was a panelist at the Earth Care Conference at the United Nations in New York in 1975 and gave numerous lectures throughout the country emphasizing all phases of conservation from wildlife preservation to pollution and population control. In 1964 he addressed a U.S. Senate investigative committee hearing on dichlordiphenyltrichlor (DDT), recommending that it be banned and lobbying for strict control on all new chemicals.

After 33 years together, his marriage to Barbara crumbled apart. They were divorced in 1976, and once again Peterson quickly remarried, this time to Virginia Westervelt.

By the end of his career he had accumulated many honors and awards, including the Audubon Conservation Medal from the National Audubon Society, the Gold Medal from the World Wildlife Fund, and in 1980 the Presidential Medal of Freedom, and he was twice nominated for the Nobel Peace Prize. Roger Tory Peterson died at 87 years of age in his home in Old Lyme, Connecticut, on July 28, 1996.

## BIBLIOGRAPHY

Devlin, John C., and Grace Naismith, *The World of Roger Tory Peterson*, 1977; Drennan, Susan, "In Memoriam: Roger Tory Peterson, 1908-1996," *The Auk*, 1998; Gordon, John Steele, "Inventing the Bird Business," *American Heritage*, 1996; Graham, Frank, Jr., "Field Guide for America: Roger Tory Peterson Taught This Country to See Its Birds—and Much More," *Audubon*, 1996; Leo, John, "He Was a Natural," *U.S. News and World Report*, 1996; Zinsser, William, "A Field Guide to Roger Tory Peterson," *Audubon*, 1992.

## Peterson, Russell

(October 3, 1916– )
Governor of Delaware, President of National Audubon Society

Russell Peterson defies conventional stereotypes—he has been a nearly lifelong Republican and has worked for the chemical industry, yet he is widely recognized as a powerful and influential proponent of environmental causes. As governor of Delaware he enacted strict legislation protecting the state's coastline from development by the oil industry, despite the billions of dollars of rapid industrial growth it would provide. Following his term as governor, he held a succession of high-level appointed positions in state and federal administrations and nonprofit organizations, including chairman of the President's Council on Environmental Quality and president of the National Audubon Society. In each position, he worked his way to the forefront of the environmental movement, always battling industry's resistance to change and promoting a belief that a healthy environment leads to a healthy economy.

On October 3, 1916, Russell Wilbur Peterson was born in Portage, Wisconsin, to John Anton and Emma (Anthony) Peterson, the seventh of eight sons. Neither of his parents had any formal education past fifth grade. During his elementary school years Peterson held a number of jobs, delivering newspapers and working in restaurants. In high school he proved his competitive spirit and perseverance on the football and basketball teams. He graduated from high school as president of his class in 1934, in the midst of the Depression. His family was in financial straits and tried to talk him into staying home to help, but he was determined to go to college. He began his studies at the University of Wisconsin in 1934, and by working two or more jobs he paid his way through school. At the end of his junior year in 1937, he married Lillian Turner—a marriage that lasted until her death 57 years later. He graduated the next year with a B.S. in chemistry and immediately entered the university's Ph.D. program in chemistry, receiving his doctorate in 1942.

The DuPont Company offered him a job at their Experimental Station in Wilmington, Delaware, and he accepted. For the next 26 years he worked for DuPont, where he was frequently promoted and eventually groomed for top management. But although his career was flourishing, he grew disillusioned with some of their policies. In 1968 he left DuPont and turned his attention toward civic activism and politics; he quickly became a prominent figure in the local Republican Party. That same year he ran a successful campaign for governor of Delaware, and in January 1969 he was sworn in. Almost immediately he began reforming Delaware's archaic justice system—abolishing the public whipping post and the debtor's prison and introducing concepts such as out-of-prison punishment as an alternative to building more prisons.

Peterson continued to make waves the following year when he unveiled his plan to protect the Delaware coastal zone from industrial development. The coastline had come under serious threat from the planned construction of a Shell Oil refinery, which would likely become the stimulus for a complex of other industrial plants. Governor Peterson issued a moratorium on all new industrial development in Delaware coastal areas, pending a report from his new task force on coastal affairs. Throughout the year while the task force gathered data, there was little public debate on the issue and almost no opposition from heavy industry—probably because they were reassured by Peterson's background as a Republican and former official at DuPont. But when the report came out and Peterson started pushing the Coastal Zone Act, which prohibited all new development on the coast, it was too late for the oil companies to fight it. With the support of the people of Delaware behind it, the state legislature voted for the protection of their coastal areas and the Coastal Zone Act has remained intact, despite frequent assaults from heavy industry.

In 1973, Governor Peterson lost his bid for a second term, which he attributed to a financial problem. Less than ten months later, he was sworn in as chairman of the President's Council on Environmental Quality, intent on continuing his conservation work on a national scale. In his three years on the council, he tackled issues such as nuclear waste and ozone depletion and countered the argument that environmental regulations are bad for the economy. Following his work on the Council of Environmental Quality, he held a number of appointed positions with state and federal administrations, nonprofit organizations, and the United Nations—continuing his dedicated commitment to environmental causes.

In 1979, the National Audubon Society, looking for someone with visibility and political influence, named Peterson as its new president. At the time, the Audubon Society had 350,000 members but had yet to become an effective lobbying force. The organization was operating with a one-million-dollar deficit and lacked a clear organization of its environmental themes. Under Peterson, Audubon showed a 19 percent per year increase in revenue, its membership increased to 550,000, it gained potent political influence, and it launched a major effort toward reaching each of the five goals that define the Audubon Society: conserving plants and animals, fostering careful use of land and water, promoting rational strategies for energy use, protecting life from pollution, and seeking solutions for global problems involving population, resources, and the environment. Peterson strongly believed that overpopulation is the single biggest threat to the global environment and broadened Audubon's focus to global issues. Under his leadership, Audubon established an international program, which played a role in United Nations conferences on the environment, in the World Conservation Union, and in the International Council for Bird Preservation. He also reestablished a youth education program called the Audubon Adventures Club, which introduced millions of schoolchildren to birding and nature study.

In the early 1980s, during President Reagan's first term, with Secretary of State James Watt leading an antienvironment crusade, Peterson was an ideal foil. As a Republican formerly involved with the chemical industry, he was proof against Reagan's and Watt's charge that the environmental movement was a liberal cabal. He participated in the Group of Ten, a gathering of ten leaders of national environmental groups who strategized responses to Reagan's antienvironmental policies.

Peterson left Audubon in 1985 to spend more time writing and speaking about environmental issues. He taught as a visiting professor at Dartmouth College, Carleton College, and the University of Wisconsin–Madison over the next several years and continued to serve on boards of directors for various environmental organizations. He has won many awards, including the Gold Medal from the World Wildlife Fund in 1971, the Audubon Award in 1977, and the Robert Marshall Award from the Wilderness Society in 1984, and was named Conservationist of the Year by the Wildlife Federation in 1972. In the mid-1990s, as Republicans became more and more conservative, Peterson realized there was little he could do to turn the party around, and in October 1996 he became a Democrat. He lives with his second wife, June, in Wilmington, Delaware, where an urban wildlife refuge along the Christina riverfront has been established and named in Peterson's honor.

**BIBLIOGRAPHY**

Gottlieb, Robert, *Forcing the Spring: The Transformation of the American Environmental Movement*, 1993; Graham, Frank, Jr., *The Audubon Ark: A History of the National Audubon Society*, 1990; Holden, Constance, "Peterson Leaving a Changed Audubon Society," *Science*, 1984; Peterson, Russell W., *Rebel with a Conscience*, 1999.

## Pinchot, Gifford

(August 11, 1865–October 4, 1946)
Forester, Founder of U.S. Forest Service

The first professional forester in America, Gifford Pinchot introduced the methods of scientific forest management to the United States. He believed that forests were like crops that, if properly cultivated, would yield a profit and would continue bearing indefinitely. Pinchot became the first director of the U.S. Forest Service, which he established during Pres. THEODORE ROOSEVELT's term in office.

Gifford Pinchot was born on August 11, 1865, in Simsbury, Connecticut. His wealthy parents raised him at their estate, "Grey Towers," in Milford, Pennsylvania, and in France, where he lived between the ages of six and nine. His father, businessman James Pinchot, was one of the few American men at that time concerned about the depletion of the nation's forests. When his son was still a boy, James Pinchot decided that Gifford should do something to solve the problem. Young Pinchot agreed and was happy to follow his father's guidance. Knowing that forestry was a field that Europeans had been practicing for many years, Pinchot's father urged his son to study forestry in Europe. After graduating from Yale with a B.A. in 1889, Pinchot traveled to Germany, where he met the great Prussian forester Detrich Brandis, who became his mentor. Brandis's first recommendation was that Pinchot attend the French National School of Forestry in Nancy, France. After a semester there, Pinchot visited the managed forests of central Europe with Brandis and a group of his students. They saw forestry being practiced in such a way that no part of the tree was wasted, not even the sawdust. There was no clear-cutting; to the contrary, only selected trees were cut, and the direction in which they fell was determined carefully to prevent them from damaging other trees on their way down. This was in clear contrast to the clear-cutting that was then standard forestry practice in the United States. Pinchot returned after 13 months of study, eager to visit the vast forests of the West (he was embarrassed to admit that he had never traveled west of the Allegheny mountains) and to put what he had learned in Europe into practice.

Gifford Pinchot (Library of Congress, Prints & Photographs Division, LC-DIG-npcc-14903)

In 1892, Pinchot was offered a job at Biltmore, the Vanderbilt family's 5,000-acre forested estate in Asheville, North Carolina. The estate had been designed by the eminent landscape architect FREDERICK LAW OLMSTED SR., who along with Vanderbilt was interested in helping Pinchot develop the field of managed forestry in the United States. At Biltmore, Pinchot successfully proved that scientific forest management would fulfill three objectives: the forest would yield a profit to its owner; there would be a constant annual yield of timber that would allow a permanent workforce to remain employed year-round; managed forestry would actually improve the forest rather than degrade it. Pinchot prepared an exhibit for the 1893 Chicago World's Fair that demonstrated these objectives; this was the first of the many publicity campaigns that he undertook to promote managed forestry during his life.

As the country's only trained forester, and as the scion of an elite family who boasted personal friendships with all of the U.S. presidents who served during his lifetime, Pinchot's skills and reputation quickly became known in government circles. When Secretary of the Interior Hoke Smith asked the National Academy of Science in 1896 to make a survey of the country's forests, Pinchot was asked to serve as secretary of the National Forest Commission. The commission, headed by dendrologist CHARLES SPRAGUE SARGENT, spent the summer of 1896 surveying the major forests between Montana and Arizona. Everyone on the commission was concerned about the health of forests in the United States, but there was a major rift about how best to protect them. Sargent and his allies were in favor of a purely preservationist strategy: locking up the forests and employing the military to protect them from destruction. Pinchot believed that forests were a national resource to be managed for a sustained yield. Despite differing opinions, the commission filed a single report recommending that Pres. Grover Cleveland set aside over 21 million acres of forested land. When Cleveland signed them into the national reserve in 1897, westerners reacted angrily, believing that this would set back the economic development of the region. Pinchot learned an important lesson from this experience, that communication with the public would be crucial in raising public support for any further forestry policy.

In 1898, Pinchot became head of a tiny new office in the Department of Agriculture, the Division of Forestry. He invited a small group of his friends and colleagues, mostly classmates from his Yale days, to work with him there. Although the Division of Forestry did not have direct control of the forest reserves, which were held by the Department of the Interior, it offered management advice for state-owned and private forests. As requests for help grew, so did the need for more trained foresters. Pinchot convinced his family in 1900 to endow his alma mater with $150,000 to found the Yale Forestry School and to host summer classes at Grey Towers.

Once Theodore Roosevelt became president in 1901, Pinchot became one of the most influential men in Washington. He was a member of Roosevelt's informal "tennis cabinet," Roosevelt's closest friends and advisers, who were as likely to be found stripped to their shorts and boxing with the president as discussing policy during long walks in the countryside with him. Roosevelt was a committed conservationist, interested both in preserving spectacular sites from any human intervention and in sustainable management of natural resources. Roosevelt trusted Pinchot to the extent that Pinchot wrote most of his conservation speeches, and Roosevelt insisted that Pinchot be allowed to review any policy having to do with natural resources.

Pinchot organized two major conservation conferences during Roosevelt's tenure, both of which served to publicize his approach to conservation. The American Forest Congress in 1905 was organized shortly before a Pinchot-inspired bill arrived in Congress. Influential politicians, lumbermen, miners, stockmen, and railroad executives were invited to discuss the nation's forest policy. The Forestry Division bombarded the national press with press releases proclaiming that if timber-cutting continued at the current rate for another 60 years, all forests in the United States would disappear. A month after the conference, Congress passed a bill consolidating the management of all 86 million acres of U.S. forest reserves and handing them to Pinchot's newly renamed U.S. Forest Service (USFS). The bill allowed the USFS to issue timber-cutting permits and collect usage fees. Under Pinchot's decentralized management plan, rangers in the field were given the power to make arrests, which made illegal cutting easier to control. Three years later, in 1908, Pinchot and Roosevelt organized the Governor's Conservation Conference, intended to make conservation a priority for state governments. Pinchot's ideas permeated the conference. He wrote many of the speeches given by Roosevelt and some of the governors, and he purposely excluded preservationists like Charles Sprague Sargent and JOHN MUIR, whose viewpoints he was not interested in publicizing.

Shortly before Roosevelt left office, Congress began to rebel at what it perceived as too much emphasis on conservation. Under Pinchot's influence, Roosevelt had established 130 new national forests, covering 173 million acres, and had increased funding for the USFS one hundred-fold. In 1907, an amendment was tacked onto an important agriculture appropriations bill that took away the president's power to declare new national forest reserves. Pinchot and Roosevelt responded by declaring 16 million acres of forest reserves in the two weeks before Roosevelt signed the bill.

This sneaky tactic turned politicians against Pinchot. That, plus problems that Pinchot had with a new secretary of the interior, Richard Ballinger, caused President Taft to dismiss Pinchot, then 45 years old, in 1910.

Upon his departure from Washington, Pinchot founded the National Conservation Association, which fought for his approach to conservation.

Pinchot married suffragette Cornelia Bryce in 1915, at the age of 49. She accompanied him through the political career that occupied the rest of his life. During the 1920s and 1930s, Pinchot served as governor of Pennsylvania for two terms and as commissioner and secretary for the Pennyslvania Department of Forests and Waters. Although he was no longer involved formally in Washington, D.C., affairs, Pinchot served as an adviser to many later national parks and national forest officials.

Pinchot died in Milford, Pennsylvania, on October 4, 1946, after a long bout with leukemia.

**BIBLIOGRAPHY**

"Gifford Pinchot," www.phmc.state.pa.us/ppet/pinchot/page1.asp; "Gifford Pinchot—USFS History—Forest History Society," www.foresthistory.org/research/usfscoll/people/Pinchot/Pinchot.html; McGeary, M. Nelson, *Gifford Pinchot: Forester Politician*, 1960; Pinchot, Gifford, *Breaking New Ground*, 1947; Strong, Douglas, *Dreamers & Defenders: American Conservationists*, 1988.

## Plotkin, Mark

(May 21, 1955– )
Ethnobotanist, Founder of Amazon Conservation Team

Ethnobotanist Mark Plotkin is known for his adventures with the indigenous peoples of the Amazon rain forest and his attempts to help them conserve their ecosystem and their way of life. Soon after Plotkin began visiting the Amazon in 1977, he found that young indigenous people were losing interest in their peoples' ancient traditions, attracted instead to Western ways. To combat what he worried would be a tragic loss of knowledge, Plotkin initiated the Shaman's Apprentice Program in the mid-1980s, through which elderly shamans train young tribespeople about traditional healing, legends, music and handicrafts. Now called the Shamans and Apprentices Program, it is one of the projects of the Amazon Conservation Team, which Plotkin co-founded with ethnobotanist Liliana Madrigal in 1995.

Mark J. Plotkin was born on May 21, 1955, in New Orleans, the son of Helene, a schoolteacher, and George, who owned a shoe store in New Orleans's French Quarter. As a boy, his parents took him frequently to the Audubon Zoo, and he was allowed to visit the swamps around New Orleans to collect reptiles. He kept his animals in the basement; his mother moved the washing machine into the kitchen to avoid disturbing her son's basement zoo.

Plotkin entered the University of Pennsylvania in 1973 to study biology but was disappointed when he found that the faculty there focused on molecular and cellular biology. So he dropped out and moved to Cambridge, Massachusetts, where he found a job as curatorial assistant at Harvard's Museum of Comparative Zoology. He took night classes with Harvard's extension program and enrolled in one given by eminent ethnobotanist RICHARD EVANS SCHULTES. As he explains in his colorful memoir *Tales of a Shaman's Apprentice* (1994), watching Schultes's slides and listening to his accounts of decades of Amazon research seduced him. He realized that his dreams of being a jungle explorer could become reality, and from then on he worked to make it happen.

During his undergraduate work at Harvard, Plotkin studied chameleons in Haiti and other lizards in Venezuela, French Guiana, and the island of Guadeloupe. He earned an A.B. degree *cum laude* in 1979 and immediately went on to Yale University's Forestry School for a master's degree in wildlife ecology, which he received in 1981. After that he attended Tufts University and earned a Ph.D. in biological conservation in 1986.

Plotkin took the first of his many trips to South American rain forests in 1977, when he accompanied primatologist and zoologist RUSSELL MITTERMEIER on a search through French Guiana's jungles for the elusive black caiman. Later in 1979, he traveled to Surinam, where he studied how the Saramacca Maroon people—rain forest-dwelling descendants of escaped slaves—used native medicinal plants. Plotkin continues to work primarily in Surinam because of its largely intact forest and because the national forest service is dedicated to conservation.

Convincing native shamans to reveal their knowledge to him about medicinal plants is a skill that Plotkin developed over time. He recalled in a 1989 *Smithsonian* article that at first, the native Tiriós called him *panankiri*, which meant "alien." While crossing a river with a group of Tiriós tribespeople during that first 1982 visit, Plotkin clumsily slipped on a rock and fell into a river, and one shaman continues to call him "white-man-who-fell-on-his-ass." But Plotkin's cheerful, friendly manner, his repeated visits over the years, his respect, his willingness to try even their hallucinogenic preparations, and his sincere interest in plants eventually charmed his shaman hosts, who tell him what they know about each plant and allow him to take botanical samples.

From the beginning, Plotkin knew that countless medicinal plants were powerful healers. He had observed many cures, where the shaman combined spiritual work with potent botanical preparations. Plotkin says he has also experienced several cures first hand. Once shamans cured him of a persistent fungal infection of the skin; on another occasion he was attacked by a swarm of wasps and some crushed bark applied by a shaman made the pain disappear almost immediately; and an old muscular injury was healed with a salve and clouds of smoke from an shaman's pipe. But Plotkin's interest in learning about rain forest medicine and his concern that the knowledge and the forest be conserved have never been motivated solely by a desire to bring powerful medicines back to the United States.

A hallmark of Plotkin's work has always been to insist that rain forest conservation depends upon the survival of the rain forest's indigenous people and their traditions.

Throughout his career he has worked to strengthen the native cultures he has visited. During the 1980s, Plotkin noticed that with each visit to native villages, native culture seemed to be a little less present; Western dress, Walkmans, and outboard motors for their canoes were becoming more and more prevalent. Plotkin became concerned that young people were losing interest in their culture's shamanic traditions and that aging shamans had no one who wanted to inherit their wealth of knowledge. Plotkin quickly realized that individually he was not capable of preserving the knowledge, thirsty for it as he was, since he was just an occasional visitor to many different tribal villages. So, with resources from the World Wildlife Fund, where he worked as plant conservation coordinator from 1985 to 1990, Plotkin initiated the Shaman's Apprentice Program, through which youth from the Tiriós tribe and three others were encouraged to study directly with the elderly shamans.

Plotkin and ethnobotanist Liliana Madrigal founded the Amazon Conservation Team (ACT) to support and further this type of work, which they call "biocultural conservation." This encompasses protecting biodiversity, strengthening tranditional health systems and culture, and prioritizes partnership with indigenous communities and local governments. In short, ACT explains, they "help the keepers of the forest keep the forest." Word has traveled through the Amazon, and tribes are now approaching ACT for support in conserving their bioculture. The Shamans and Apprentices program has trained more than 70 apprentices in Suriname and Colombia

One of ACT's priorities has been to draft cultural maps that define territorial boundaries, resources, and spiritual sites. This is very important evidence for effective land and resource management, and for any legal battles over land that may arise. Local indigenous people are trained to use Global Positioning Systems, and mapping has been completed for 29.5 million acres in the northeast Amazon. ACT collaborated in the creation a 168,000-acre national park in the Colombian Amazon, which is co-managed by local indigenous communities and the Colombian environmental agency.

The work of Plotkin and ACT has received a lot of publicity thanks to the popularity of *Tales of a Shaman's Apprentice*, which has come out in several print editions and been adapted into a children's book, an audiobook, and a video documentary. *Medicine Quest* came out in 2000, with more of a focus on the development of specific medicines from rainforest and ocean species.

Plotkin and Madrigal, live near Washington, D.C. with their two daughters, Gabrielle and Anne.

## Bibliography

"Amazon Conservation Team," www.amazonteam.org; Hallowell, Christopher, "In Search of the Shaman's Vanishing Wisdom," *Time*, 1998; Jackson, Donald Dale, "Searching for Medicinal Wealth in Amazonia," *Smithsonian*, 1989; Plotkin, Mark, *Tales of a Shaman's Apprentice*, 1993; Reed, Susan, "Sorcerer's Apprentice," *People*, 1993; Royte, Elizabeth, "Mark Plotkin," *Smithsonian*, 2005; "The Shaman's Apprentice," www.theshamansapprentice.com.

## Pollan, Michael
(February 6, 1955– )
Food Writer, Environmental Journalist

Michael Pollan is one of the leading thinkers in the politics of food and environmental well-being. He demonstrates how our relationships to food and to the wider biotic world of which we are a part influence our health, communities, farmers, animals and ecosystems. A prolific writer, accomplished editor, and environmentalist, Pollan blends ethics, science, economics and his own experiences to explore these issues with his readers. His books include: *Second Nature: A Gardener's Education* (1991), *A Place of My Own: The Education of an Amateur Builder* (1997), *The Botany of Desire: A Plant's-Eye View of the World* (2001), *The Omnivore's Dilemma: A Natural History of Four Meals* (2006) and *In Defense of Food: An Eater's Manifesto* (2008).

Michael Pollan was born into a literary family on Long Island, New York, February 6, 1955. His mother, Corky, edited books, and his father, Stephen, was a best-selling author. After earning a B.A. in English from Bennington College, Pollan studied at Oxford University, and obtained an M.A. in English Literature from Columbia University. He worked as a reporter and editor with various organizations from 1975 until 1983 when he began as a Senior Editor at *Harper's Magazine*, advancing to Executive Editor. Since 1995, Pollan has been a Contributing Writer for the *New York Times Magazine*. In 2003, he accepted a position as Knight Professor of Journalism at the University of California, Berkeley. His multiple awards include 2000 Reuters-IUCN Global Awards for Environmental Journalism; 2006 California Book Award; 2006 Pioneer of Precaution Award from the Center for Health, Environment & Justice; and the 2007 James Beard Award for Best Writing on Food.

Pollan is fundamentally concerned with our relationship to the more-than-human world. His books and articles reflect on the many meanings of nature and humanity's place on Earth. For example, in *Second Nature*, he rejects the view that wilderness provides the gold-standard for nature and looks to the garden as a place to understand and cultivate responsible relationships with other creatures and the broader biotic world. In *The Botany of Desire*, he explains how humans are not masters over the nonhuman world—using plants to serve our own designs—but are, often, instrumentalized by Earth's flora. In both *The Omnivore's Dilemma* and *In Defense of Food*, he explains how provisioning ourselves in terms of food offers opportunities to know about the complex dynamics driving many environmental dangers, appreciate the interconnections between the human and nonhuman worlds, and deepen our sense of wonder and joy at the sensual pleasures of eating.

In almost all his writings, Pollan implicitly criticizes those environmentalist orientations that understand humans as separate from nature. Pollan sees a co-evolutionary relationship between the two, insisting that we sensitize ourselves more intimately and mindfully to the nonhuman world, and see our well-being as inherently linked to that of nature's well-being. He does this at the most personal level, enabling us to see our own ecological responsibilities and encouraging us to take meaningful actions in the service of both environmental protection and personal well-being. Pollan recognizes that environmental stewardship and the deepening of personal engagement with the world go hand-in-hand.

Pollan brings such interdependence to light by revealing the complexities and consequences of how we provision ourselves. For example, his work on food reveals the dynamics of agricultural commodity chains. He shows, for instance, how industrialized agriculture's heavy reliance on corn—for everything from cattle feed to fast processed food—affects farmers, soil, water and pesticide use. Such effects assume geopolitical proportions as corn-intensive agriculture involves subsidies that disadvantage farmers in the developing world, increases demand for petroleum to grow and transport corn, and contributes to climate change as forests are increasingly converted to agricultural lands. In addition to drawing global connections, Pollan reveals individual and societal ones as he points out the ill health effects of a corn-based, fast food diet.

The accessibility of Pollan's writing has attracted many newcomers to the environmental movement. He leads his readers on a journey through an examined life. He gleans his experience for lessons of how to live ecologically sensitive lives, and asks fundamental personal questions: What is on my plate, and how did it get here? What resounding impacts do my inputs have on our health and planet? How can I meaningfully cultivate the living world around and within me?

These questions inevitably become political. In an interview in 2007 Pollan stated, "You've got three votes a day, and how you cast those votes, we have seen over the last few years, has a tremendous effect.... Consumers are starting to re conccive what it means to be a consumer, and [see] that citizenship is part of consumption." (Grist). Pollan underlines such politics not just with food choices but with decisions about our everyday activities. His work provides meaningful engagement with such enormous challenges such as climate change, fresh water scarcity, soil infertility and loss of biological diversity as well as with societal opportunities to build stronger communities and deepen the human experience.

Pollan currently lives in Berkeley, California, with his wife Judith Belzer and his son Isaac. He teaches graduate courses on environmental journalism at the University of California Berkeley and continues to write.

## BIBLIOGRAPHY

Demory, P., "It's All Storytelling: An Interview with Michael Pollan," *Writing on the Edge*, November 1, 2006; Philpott, T., "Table Talk: A Conversation with Michael Pollan," *Grist.org*, October 12, 2007; Price, C., "How Michael Pollan Ruined My Life: Thinking About Where Our Food Is Coming From," *San Francisco Chronicle*, May 7, 2006; Weinraub, J., "Q & A with Michael Pollan: Think Global, Eat Local," *Washington Post*, June 28, 2006; Pollan, Michael, "The Cornification of Food," Alternative Radio, 2007, www.alternativeradio.org; www.michaelpollan.com.

## Popper, Deborah, and Frank Popper
(August 18, 1947– ; March 26, 1944– )
Cocreators of the Buffalo Commons Concept

Frank and Deborah Popper have brought their knowledge of land use planning and geography to the study of the American Great Plains, where heavy agriculture and extractive industries have exploited the land and led to large population losses. The Poppers first wrote about the Great Plains in 1987 in the magazine *Planning*, where they articulated the concept of the Buffalo Commons, a proposal for restoring large parts of the plains to their pre-settlement state, with bison instead of cattle and native shortgrass instead of cultivated wheat, corn, and cotton. The idea provoked heated responses and sparked a vigorous debate, and the Poppers accomplished in one article what few academics achieve in a lifetime: They caught the attention of the nation and engaged an entire region in a dialogue about its future. From the various responses came new ideas for the Great Plains based on preservation and sustainable industries such as tourism, and many of the Poppers's original proposals, such as more buffalo production, are springing to life on the ground.

Deborah Epstein was born on August 18, 1947, in New York City to Irving (a lawyer) and Fay (Falkowsky) Epstein. She grew up in New York and attended Bryn Mawr College, graduating with a bachelor's degree in history in 1969. In August 1968 she and Frank Popper were married, and they moved to Boston after her graduation. Deborah then took a job as a neighborhood worker in the Boston Model Cities program, a government-funded service that tried to integrate redevelopment of inner city neighborhoods with a wide range of social services and job opportunities. In 1971 the Poppers moved to Chicago, where their children were born: Joanna in 1972 and Nicholas in 1977. Deborah divided her time between her children and library school at Rosary College (now Dominican University) in River Forest, Illinois. She received her master's degree in library science in 1977. She held library positions first in Montgomery County, Maryland, in 1983, and then in Mountainside, New Jersey, from 1984 to 1985. She then began work on a second master's degree from Rutgers University, and in 1986 she began working there too, as a research assistant in the Department of Urban Studies and teaching assistant in the Department of Geography. At Rutgers she completed her master's degree in geography in 1987 and her doctorate in geography in 1992. After teaching at New York University, she is now a full professor of geography at the College of Staten Island/City University of New York, where she has worked since 1994.

Frank J. Popper was born on March 26, 1944, in Chicago, Illinois, to Hans (a physician) and Lina (Billig) Popper. He received his bachelor's degree in psychology from Haverford College, graduating in 1965 with high honors. During the following year he did graduate work at the Massachusetts Institute of Technology and then went to Harvard University to complete his master's degree in public administration, which he received in 1968. He began working that year as a research associate at the Twentieth Century Fund (now the Century Fund) in New York City, staying for one year. He continued his studies at Harvard and earned a Ph.D. there in political science in 1972. In the meantime he had moved to Chicago in 1971 and become a staff associate with the Public Administration Service, where he worked until 1973. At that point he switched to the American Society of Planning Officials (now the American Planning Association), where he worked as a senior research associate until 1974. Between 1975 and 1981 he directed the Twentieth Century Fund's Project on the Politics of State Land-Use Regulation. In 1979 and 1980 he also worked as a senior associate at the Environmental Law Institute in Washington, D.C. He then held a Gilbert White fellowship at Resources for the Future in Washington before becoming an associate professor in what is now the planning department at Rutgers University in New Brunswick, New Jersey, in 1983 and a full professor in 1991. Frank Popper is known for originating the concept of LULUs, or "Locally Unwanted Land Uses," described in a landmark 1981 article in *Planning*, a magazine for urban planners. In that article about the common practice of pariah land uses like building toxic plants in areas where residents are unable to effectively oppose them, he articulated a phenomenon that has become key to the environmental justice movement.

To conservationists, the Poppers are best known for their seminal article in the December 1987 issue of *Planning*, the Poppers wrote "The Great Plains: From Dust to Dust." The fragile semiarid grassland ecosystems of the U.S. Great Plains, which extend from Montana and North Dakota in the north to

Deborah and Frank Popper (Photograph courtesy of Westend Film & TV Produktion)

New Mexico and Texas in the south, had suffered decades of abuse from heavy-handed farming, too many roads, overgrazing, and too many people. The Poppers argued that ecological impoverishment was showing up in declines of farm and ranch economies, increasing dependence on federal subsidies, dropping water tables, rising wind erosion, and long-term depopulation. They suggested that because many rural residents were already giving up trying to make a living from the current agricultural system, the Great Plains could feasibly be restored to early-nineteenth-century conditions, before settlement and overly aggressive agriculture took over. The Poppers called their restoration approach "the Buffalo Commons" and proposed that a federal agency be established to administer the removal of fences, the replanting of native shortgrass prairies, and the restocking of native animals such as bison. The native prairie ecosystem would reestablish itself. The Buffalo Commons would become the world's largest historic and wildlife preservation project.

After the Poppers' article came out, the Associated Press wire service picked up the story, and it was printed in more than 150 newspapers, magazines, and journals, creating a buzz of responses that ranged from supportive interest to outrage. The Poppers were inundated with mail and speaking invitations at a range of forums: planners, environmentalists, farmers, ranchers, local communities, agricultural economists, and businesspeople, among others. Many farm and ranch families in plains communities scorned the Buffalo

Commons, seeing it as a threat to their way of life and an assault on their ancestry. Some of the Poppers' Great Plains appearances required armed guards, and a talk in Montana in 1992 had to be canceled because of death threats. But contrary to many local perceptions, the Poppers were not threatening the forced removal of people living on the Great Plains but instead were offering the Buffalo Commons as a metaphor for the alternative future of a region in economic and ecological decline. Once this point became clear, a dialogue often became possible. The Poppers's idea touched off a national debate on the region's problems. The Buffalo Commons caused policy makers and residents alike to think about economic possibilities for the Great Plains that place more emphasis on preservation and ecotourism and less on agriculture and extraction.

The Poppers still study the region. Deborah Popper's doctoral dissertation explored why some Great Plains counties have maintained stable populations while others have decreased. The Poppers have written numerous journal and newspaper articles exploring the future of the region's rural areas. The Buffalo Commons remains controversial and visionary, but it has shown surprising impact and accuracy. Even just the name they gave to the phenomenon has been important, according to the Poppers in their 2006 article entitled "The Onset of the Buffalo Commons":

> The image of a Buffalo Commons... worked as a way of getting discussions started on alternative ways of inhabiting the rural Great Plains...as a poetic metaphor can stimulate imagination, so too can a regional one. The metaphor's two words, buffalo and commons...provoke images both of the region and how it might look different...The fact that they are not generally used together propels the envisioning, making the listener strive to *give* the term sense... The diversity of images evoked allows a greater building process as each person's individual interpretation reverberates against that of others.

Many of the Poppers' proposals and predictions are materializing across the plains as traditional agriculture continues to decline. In 1992 a coalition of tribes formed the Intertribal Bison Cooperative to reintroduce buffalo as an alternative to cattle and as a culturally significant part of Native American identity. Many cattle ranchers, realizing that buffalo are better adapted to the Great Plains and are more cost-efficient to raise, have switched to bison and prospered. Federal agencies are allowing more buffalo to graze on public lands. The Nature Conservancy, the Sierra Club, and other private groups are buying up plains land, restoring buffalo on it and otherwise promoting buffalo. The Poppers expressed confidence, in their 2006 article, that the 21st century would be a good one for buffalo and for the Buffalo Commons.

In 1997 the Poppers received the American Geographical Society's Paul Vouras Medal for their work. Frank Popper continues his work as a land-use consultant to numerous agencies, corporations, and nonprofit groups and as a teacher in the Rutgers planning department and since 2001 as a visiting professor at Princeton University. He received Rutgers' Presidential Award for distinguished public service in 1997. He has served on the governing boards of various land use and planning councils and on the editorial boards of several journals. He chairs the board of the Great Plains Restoration Council, a nonprofit group in Fort Worth, Texas, that is attempting to create the Buffalo Commons. Deborah Popper continues to teach at the College of Staten Island in the Department of Political Science, Economics, and Philosophy and, since 2001, as a visiting professor at Princeton University. She serves on the governing boards of the American Geographical Society and, with Frank, the National Center for Frontier Communities. She is on the editorial boards of the *Journal of Rural Communities*, and with Frank, the *Online Journal of Rural Research and Policy*. The Poppers live in Highland Park, New Jersey.

**BIBLIOGRAPHY**

"Frank J. Popper: The Edward Bloustein School of Planning and Public Policy," www.policy.rutgers.edu/faculty/popper; "Great Plains Restoration Council," www.gprc.org; Manning, Richard, "The Buffalo Is Coming Back," *Defenders of Wildlife*, 1995–1996; Matthews, Anne, *Where the Buffalo Roam*, 1992, 2002; Popper, Deborah, and Frank Popper, "The Bison Are Coming," *High Country News*, 1998; Popper, Deborah, and Frank Popper, "The Buffalo Commons, Then and Now," *American Geographical Society's Focus*, 1993; Popper, Deborah, and Frank Popper, "The Onset of the Buffalo Commons," *Journal of the West*, 2006; Popper, Deborah, and Frank Popper, "The Reinvention of the American Frontier," *The Amicus Journal*, 1991; Popper, Frank, "Siting LULUs," *Planning*, 1981.

# Postel, Sandra
(1956– )
Founder and Director of the Global Water Policy Project, Author

A leading authority on fresh water usage and conservation, Sandra Postel is founder and director of the Global Water Policy Project in South Hadley, Massachusetts. She is also a visiting senior lecturer at Mount Holyoke College, where she currently directs the Center for the Environment. From 1983 to 1994, she worked with the Worldwatch Institute, where she served as vice president for research and coauthored more than a dozen State of the World reports. A Pew scholar and international lecturer, Postel has authored several books and numerous articles on global water issues. She received media attention for her 1992 book *Last Oasis*, which was adapted for PBS television, and for *Pillar of Sand*, her 1999 book about the challenges and risks of global dependence on irrigated agriculture.

Sandra L. Postel was born in Hollis, New York, in 1956 to Harold and Dorothy Postel. She grew up on the south shore of New York's Long Island. After earning her bachelor's degree in geology and political science at Ohio's Wittenberg University in 1978, she went on to study at Duke University, where she was awarded a Master of Environmental Management degree, with an emphasis on Resource Economics, and Policy, in 1980. At Duke she also gained what she has called the "principal passion" of her life—a compelling interest in water issues.

After leaving Duke, Postel found employment as a natural resources consultant with a private firm in Menlo Park, California, but after three years she moved on to the nonprofit Worldwatch Institute. She began as a researcher and worked her way up to the level of vice president. From 1988 to 1994 she codirected the institute's State of the World annual reports, which have been used as textbooks in nearly 600 U.S. colleges and universities. Her own alma mater recognized her efforts in 1991, when she was awarded the Duke University School of Forestry and Environmental Studies' Distinguished Alumni Award.

Compiling research on the world's water supply, Postel wrote her first book under the Worldwatch imprint. *Last Oasis* (1992) documented a pending shortage in clean, available water and argued for conservation. Noting that several of the world's major rivers, including the Colorado, Nile, and Yellow Rivers, are used up before they reach the ocean, Postel outlined the need for better management and for policies that encourage farms and in-

Sandra Postel (Photograph by Paul Teeling)

dustries to conserve water. The book was still popular five years after publication. It was reprinted and made into a television documentary that aired on PBS in the four-part Cadillac Desert series in 1997–1998. To date, *Last Oasis* has been published in nine languages.

In her second book, *Pillar of Sand* (1999), Postel called for a Blue Revolution. She took on the practice of irrigated farming, noting that 40 percent of the world's food comes from irrigated lands that are increasingly salinized and are dependent on unsustainable rates of water use. She also highlighted the importance of protecting rivers and other freshwater ecosystems, even as human demands for irrigation water increase. She advocates protecting vital ecosystems and using water-thrifty technology, such as drip irrigation, to produce more food with less water. If we cannot irrigate more efficiently and modify our diets to comply with the limits of fresh water, she predicts, our civilization will deteriorate as did the great empires of the past.

Postel's third book, co-authored with Brian Richter, is *Rivers for Life* (2003). It is acclaimed as the first book to synthesize the science of river flow with the policies that determine its management, and it calls for a harmonization of the need for fresh water by humans and natural ecosystems. These ideas were further developed in her 2005 publication for Worldwatch Institute, *Liquid Assets: The Critical Need to Safeguard Freshwater Ecosystems.*

Postel has published more than 100 articles and chapters in popular and scholarly publications, including *Science, Natural History, Environmental Science and Technology, Ecological Applications, The Sciences, American Prospect, Technology Review,* and *Water International.* Her article "Troubled Waters" was included in the 2001 edition of *Best American Science and Nature Writing.* She has written op-ed features for more than 30 newspapers in the United States and abroad, including the *New York Times* and the *Washington Post.* She has also appeared periodically on radio and television, serving as commentator on CNN's *Futurewatch.* LEONARDO DICAPRIO included her in his 2007 documentary *The 11th Hour.*

Postel's voice is especially strong in international water policy. She has served as a consultant to the World Bank and the United Nations Development Program and has addressed the European Parliament on environmental issues. She has served on the board of directors of the International Water Resources Association and the World Future Society and has acted as adviser to the Environmental Media Association and the Global 2000 program founded by Pres. JIMMY CARTER. She has been a council member in the UK-based Forum for the Future and has served as senior adviser to the World Commission on Water.

Postel has lectured at many universities, including Duke, Stanford, the Massachusetts Institute of Technology, and Yale. From 1994 to 1996 she was adjunct professor of international environmental policy at Tufts University in the Fletcher School of Law and Diplomacy. In 1995, just after founding the Global Water Policy Project she was named a Pew scholar in conservation and the environment, promising to work to change the policies that cause depletion and mismanagement of the world's fresh water. She has been awarded two honorary doctor of science degrees. In 2002, *Scientific American* named her one of its "Scientific American 50."

Currently director of the Center for the Environment at Mount Holyoke College as well as of the independent Global Water Policy Project, Postel lives in South Hadley, Massachusetts.

**BIBLIOGRAPHY**

Motavelli, Jim, and Elaine Robbins, "Sandra Postel: The Coming Age of Water Scarcity," *E,* 1998; "Mount Holyoke College: Center for the Environment," www.mtholyokc.cdu/ce; Postel, Sandra, *Last Oasis: Facing Water Scarcity,* 1992; Postel, Sandra, *Pillar of Sand: Can the Irrigation Miracle Last?* 1999; "Sandra Postel and the Global Water Policy Project," www.globalwaterpolicy.org; "Worldwatch Institute," www.worldwatch.org.

## Pough, Richard
(April 19, 1904–June 24, 2003)
Cofounder of the Nature Conservancy

Richard Pough cofounded The Nature Conservancy in 1951 to facilitate the purchase and preservation of ecologically valuable land and was president when the organization made its first acquisition in 1955. His vision—to preserve sanctuaries that represent all existing ecosystems—contrasted with the approach of conservationists at that time, which was to focus on preserving individual endangered species or places of spectacular beauty. Pough went on in 1957 to found the Natural Areas Council, which fomented the creation of local preservationist groups throughout the United States and successfully brokered the purchase or donation of land to be set aside as preserves.

Richard Hooper Pough was born on April 19, 1904, in Brooklyn, New York. His parents, Frances Harvey and Alice (Beckler) Pough, were both graduates of the Massachusetts Institute of Technology (MIT). The family spent summers on Block Island, off of Rhode Island, where Pough developed a passion for birds. At the age of ten, his first summer there, "a sandhill crane landed on the island, and when some hunters shot it I was so upset I ran at them, screaming," he told Frank Graham of *Audubon*. He studied at MIT, where he spent free time birding, and graduated with a B.S. in chemical engineering in 1926. After a year at Harvard University studying Oriental art, Pough obtained a job in Port Arthur, Texas, at a sulfuric acid plant. He worked at night so that he could spend his days birding along the Gulf of Mexico. He later traveled to Europe to study birds and art, then worked at a foundry in St. Louis, and in 1932, with his brother Harold, bought and rebuilt a bankrupt photographic equipment company in Philadelphia.

Pough continued to devote his leisure time to birds. One weekend, he invited the young woman he was courting, Moira Flannery, on a birdwatching expedition. They spent a day on the Jersey shore, during which he was proud to point out the droppings of many different species of birds of prey. As they drove home, Moira pointed at a pile of manure on the streets of Newark and pronounced it "elephant." Indeed, a couple of blocks later they came up behind a troop of elephants walking from a circus train. The couple's affection was sealed, and soon they married.

In the early 1930s, Pough read a study on goshawks that cited data from a large number of the dead birds collected from Hawk Mountain in eastern Pennsylvania. Curious about why there would be so many dead goshawks from that area, he went to investigate and found that hunters came from around the region to shoot hawks as they migrated south along the Kittatinny Ridge. He wrote an article and was invited to talk at a New York City meeting of the Audubon Society and other bird protection groups. Heiress and conservationist ROSALIE EDGE was in the audience, and soon she decided that the only way to stop the slaughter was to buy the mountain and preserve it as a wildlife sanctuary. Pough helped facilitate the deal in 1934.

Audubon Society leaders, with whom he worked on the Hawk Mountain sale, were impressed with Pough and offered him a position on the organization's research staff in 1936. He remained with the Audubon Society for 12 years, focusing on "persecuted species," especially hawks and owls. He was insistent that predator control programs were misguided; "Do away with predators and you destroy the balance of nature," he told the *New Yorker*. Pough was instrumental in prosecuting illegal traffickers of wild bird feathers and strengthening regulations on the use of these feathers by the millinery industry—an issue that the Audubon Society activists had first tackled in the early 1900s and that resurged as plumed hats became popular again in the late 1930s. He was also one of the early voices to decry dichlordiphenyltrichlor (DDT), which was first used during World War II. He told the *New Yorker* in 1945 that "if DDT should ever be used widely and without care, we would have a country without freshwater fish, serpents, frogs, and most of the birds we have now." In 1946, Pough published the first of what would be his three Audubon bird guides (*Audubon Bird Guide*, 1946; *Audubon Water Bird Guide*, 1951; and *Audubon Western Bird Guide*, 1957), concise field guides that show how each bird fits into its ecosystem.

In 1948, Pough became chair of the Department of Conservation and General Ecology of the American Museum of Natural History. He was charged with creating an exhibit called the Hall of North American Forests, the preparation of which allowed him to visit forests throughout the continent. He convinced the museum to buy Great Gull Island off of Connecticut, for sale by the federal government, and to establish a research center for terns there. While at the museum, he also came up with a way to help the Cahow (also known as the Bermuda petrel), birds that were so rare they were thought to be extinct. Cahows were found on the islets off of Bermuda, but they were threatened by larger tropicbirds, which killed the cahows' young and took over their nests. Pough suggested a device that would exclude birds larger than the cahows from entering the nests; the concept was put into practice and proved successful. Pough remained with the museum until 1956, when he was fired for his attempts to involve the museum in conservation battles, including the collaborative conservationist effort to stop the Echo Park Dam in Dinosaur National Monument and another fight against the construction of a highway through Van Cortlandt Park.

During the early 1950s Pough raised funds to buy the Corkscrew Swamp in Florida as one of the Audubon Society's system of private sanctuaries. This and his previous experiences with Great Gull Island and Hawk Mountain had convinced Pough of the efficaciousness of preserving ecologically valuable parcels of land by purchasing them. Neither the Audubon Society nor the museum, however, was interested in adding land acquisition to their missions. Pough began promoting the idea among garden clubs and the Ecologists' Union, and it caught on quickly. He was appointed chair of the Ecologists' Union's Committee on the Preservation of Natural Conditions. He convinced the Ecologists' Union in 1951 to change its name to The Nature Conservancy, the name of a similar organization in Great Britain, and he successfully solicited a donation of $100,000 from Reader's Digest founder Lila A. Wallace to seed a revolving fund that would provide down payment loans to local preservationists who needed to act quickly to buy ecologically desirable land.

Pough became president of The Nature Conservancy in 1953. He served in this capacity until 1956, guiding it through its first purchase of land in 1955, the Sunken Forest on Fire Island, for which ecologist OAKLEIGH THORNE II raised much of the necessary funds. This was the first in what has become the largest privately owned system of nature preserves in the world. Pough urged The Nature Conservancy to remain nonpolitical and steer clear of controversial issues, so that it could focus solely on the purchase of private lands for the purpose of conserving habitats and wildlife that represent the diversity of life on earth.

Pough remained involved with The Nature Conservancy as he founded the Natural Area Council in 1957, an umbrella organization for preservation groups. Kathrine Ordway, heiress of the Minnesota Mining and Manufacturing Company, provided the initial funds for another organization that he founded, the Open Space Institute, which worked to convince wealthy landowners to donate ecologically rich plots of 20 acres or more for preservation. Pough's organizations approached their goal creatively, discouraging large-scale development even when they did not have the funds to purchase entire areas, by "checkerboarding"—buying interspersed plots. Over the years Pough raised millions of dollars and participated in the preservation of thousands of acres of land.

During the late 1960s, Pough participated in the Thorne Ecological Institute's Seminars in Environmental Arts and Sciences. He is credited with convincing Army Corps of Engineers chief William Cassidy to give greater consideration to the environmental impact of its projects. The Corps subsequently established an Environmental Advisory Board, to which Pough was appointed.

Pough served many other conservation organizations as well. He was a member of so many organizations that in 1975 he paid about $1,500 per year in dues alone. He held high-level offices for many of these organizations, including the U.S. section of the International Council for Bird Preservation, World Wildlife Fund–U.S., the Linnean Society, National Parks and Conservation Association, Defenders of Wildlife, the American Ornithologists' Union, Thorne Ecological Institute, and the Association for the Protection of the Adirondacks. He received numerous recognitions and awards, including the silver medal of the Federation of Garden Clubs of New York State, the Conservation Award of American Motors Corporation, the Horace Marden Albright Scenic Preservation Medal of the American Scenic and Historic Preservation Society, the Frances K. Hutchinson Medal of the Garden Club of America, and the National Audubon Society Medal in 1981.

Pough died at his home in Chilmark, Massachusetts on June 24, 2003.

**BIBLIOGRAPHY**

Boyle, Robert, "An Earth-Saving Bulldozer that Runs on Money," *Sports Illustrated*, 1975; "Corner-Cornerer," *New Yorker*, 1954; Graham, Frank, "Dick Pough: Conservation's Ultimate Entrepreneur," *Audubon*, 1984; Graham, Frank, "In Memoriam: Richard H. Pough, 1904-2003," *The Auk*, 2004; Lavietes, Stuart, "Richard Pough, 99 Founder of the Nature Conservancy," *New York Times*, 2003; Stroud, Richard, *National Leaders of American Conservation*, 1985.

## Powell, John Wesley

(March 24, 1834–September 23, 1902)
Explorer, Director of U.S. Geological Survey

Explorer John Wesley Powell made the country's first official surveys of the Rocky Mountain region and is especially remembered as leader of the first river trip through the Grand Canyon. The carefully drawn maps and surveys that his teams produced were the first of the topographic maps that the U.S. Geological Survey is known for today. Powell tried to promote orderly and appropriate settlement of arid western lands by designating certain mineral-rich areas for mining and others, with better access to water, for irrigated agriculture. Today, Powell is cited as one of the original promoters of environmentally appropriate land use.

John Wesley Powell was born on March 24, 1834, in Mount Morris, New York. His father, Joseph Powell, was a Methodist preacher whose strong abolitionist sentiments made the family a target for violent advocates of slavery. Powell was kept home from school to protect him. This seclusion, plus the family's frequent moves—always westward, finally ending up in Illinois—forced Powell to educate himself as he could. While the family lived in Ohio, an elderly neighbor introduced Powell to the marvels of natural history. Inspired, Powell began to rove the land, observing plants and animals and collecting specimens. Once he turned 18 years old, Powell became a country schoolteacher and enrolled at Wheaton College in Illinois. Always more knowledgeable about scientific matters than his professors, Powell also took courses at Oberlin and Jacksonville colleges but never stayed at any school long enough to earn a degree. Powell did exert an influence on academia, however; historians credit him with in-

John Wesley Powell (Library of Congress, Prints & Photographs Division, LC-USZ62-3862)

troducing scientific curricula to college-level education. His teaching jobs suited him well, for they allowed him long vacations for explorations of the midwestern prairies and the Mississippi and Ohio Rivers. Powell joined the Illinois State Natural History Society when he was 20 years old and became its secretary at age 27.

In 1861, Powell joined the Illinois Volunteer Infantry, mobilized for the Civil War. He took a one-week leave of absence in 1862 to marry Emma Dean, who accompanied her new husband to the warfront and stayed with him until the war ended. Major Powell was an enthusiastic, effective military leader but also found time to explore and collect fossils. Powell returned from the war one-armed, having lost his right arm during the Battle of Shiloh.

This handicap did not dissuade him from renewing his natural history work. Powell became a lecturer in geology at Illinois Normal University and was named curator of the Illinois Natural History Museum in 1865. In the summer of 1867, he organized the first of his many expeditions: he took a group of 16 students and amateur naturalists to the Rocky Mountains. The United States Army provided the group with rations, and the Smithsonian Institution lent them equipment in return for data collection. Later expeditions continued to receive support from the Smithsonian and from other academic institutions.

Powell's most famous trip took place in 1869. He and a group of 11 men were the first Whites to descend a 900-mile stretch of the Colorado and Green Rivers. They spent almost three months in the Grand Canyon, victims of wild torrents, nearly starving in the arid heat. Three of their party climbed out of the three-quarter-mile-deep canyon but were killed, just as they reached the canyon's edge, by Indians who mistook them for a band of at-large rapists. When Powell's small ragged group emerged from the canyon at the end of the summer, they became famous, and Powell had no trouble obtaining funds for later expeditions.

Powell's travels through the West convinced him that the arid West was a delicate place that could be ruined if settlement was not planned carefully. The 1862 Homestead Act encouraged westward expansion by granting settlers titles to plots of 160 acres, which they could use as they saw fit. Powell saw the beginnings of a disaster: land inappropriate for agriculture was being ruined by erosion, and the lives and dreams of western immigrants were being broken when farms and ranches failed owing to lack of rain and erosion of topsoil. Powell, named director of the U.S. Geographical and Geological Survey of the Rocky Mountain Region in 1875, recommended officially that no land in the West (except for a few areas in California, Oregon, and Washington) be farmed except when irrigation was possible. Powell's 1878 *Report on the Lands of the Arid Region of the United States* explained his findings and recommendations.

Powell asked Congress to pass bills calling for limits to the size of farms and ranches and for the formation of cooperative irrigation associations. Although his intention was to protect westerners from monopolization by large land-owners and assure community control of irrigation, these ideas scared western landowners, who feared government intrusion.

Yet Powell continued to find favor in Washington. The National Academy of Science asked Congress in 1878 to fund extensive land use surveys of the West, and Congress assented. Powell's friend and colleague, Clarence King, was appointed director of the new U.S. Geological Survey (USGS), and Powell became its director when King died in 1884. Under Powell, the USGS began publishing the topographical maps it still puts out today. It also insisted on applying its scientific findings in land use policy.

After a terrible year for western farmers and ranchers in 1886, in which droughts parched crops and then tremendous blizzards killed livestock, Congress in 1888 passed a bill written by Powell calling for a survey of irrigable lands. In order to prevent wealthy speculators from grabbing all the potentially irrigable lands, Powell also succeeded in blocking grants of titles to all claims filed after the 1888 Irrigation Survey Act. But Powell's success was short-lived. He had alienated many different parties in the West: large landowners who did not like his proposal to limit ranch size, small landowners because Powell had said that only large ranches would be economically viable in arid regions, and real estate speculators, among others. By the early 1890s, Powell's proposals for careful, well-planned land-development had been defeated by his many enemies in the West.

In 1894, Powell retired from the USGS and returned to direct the Smithsonian's Bureau of Ethnology, where he had served as director from 1878 till 1884. As well known as Powell was for his revolutionary ideas on land use, he was also acclaimed for his many studies of North American Indian ethnology. Powell died in Haven, Maine, from a cerebral hemorrhage on September 23, 1902.

**BIBLIOGRAPHY**

Darrah, William, *Powell of the Colorado*, 1951; Dolnick, Edward, *Down the Great Unknown: John Wesley Powell's 1869 Journey of Discovery and Tragedy through the Grand Canyon*, 2002; Stegner, Wallace, *Beyond the Hundredth Meridian: John Wesley Powell and the Second Opening of the West*, 1954; Strong, Douglas, *Dreamers & Defenders: American Conservationists*, 1988; Worster, Donald, *A River Running West: The Life of John Wesley Powell*, 2001.

## Pritchard, Paul C.

(August 27, 1944– )
President of National Parks and Conservation Association, Founder and President of National Park Trust

Paul C. Pritchard has been instrumental in the establishment of more than half of the national parks in the United States and has served as an international adviser on park formation. Founder and first president of the National Park Trust, he also served for 17 years as president of the National Parks and Conservation Association. His achievements in environmental conservation include, among others, creation of the Climate Institute and Friends of China's National Parks and the addition of the Alaskan national parks, as well as extensive writing on the environment. He draws his commitment and energy from the environmental challenges currently facing humanity worldwide. He believes that people "must act both locally and globally, just as we treat our entire bodies with one sense of respect."

Paul C. Pritchard was born on August 27, 1944, in Huntington, West Virginia, son of Eason G. Pritchard and Stella N. Pritchard. His love of nature developed during a boyhood in the hills of Huntington and later on the plains of Kansas City, where nature, he has said, "always seemed essential to our daily life." His family regularly made time for camping, hiking, a flower garden, and Boy Scout activities, and his grandparents' farm provided a classroom in life. He attended the University of Missouri at Columbia, where he earned a B.A. in humanities in 1966. From February 1967 to December 1968, he served as an Intelligence Officer in the United States Army. He returned to college and earned a master's degree in the science of planning from the University of Tennessee, Knoxville, in June 1971.

In 1971, after completing his graduate studies, Pritchard worked for the Office of the Governor of the State of Georgia, first as state transportation coordinator, later as chief of natural resources planning. From that time on, his career increasingly focused on the conservation of natural resources. In 1974, he joined the U.S. Department of Commerce as Pacific region coordinator for the National Oceanic and Atmospheric Administration (NOAA), where he was responsible for preservation grants. There he also supervised research for the five Pacific states and two territories for coastal zone management programs. That responsibility included the funding and creation of the nation's first coastal zone program, in Washington State tidal waters, and of the first estuarine sanctuary at Coos Bay, Oregon.

Pritchard left NOAA and returned to his native Appalachia in 1975 to become the first full-time executive director of the Appalachian Trail Conference, a confederation of over 50 hiking clubs that built the country's first recreation footpath, originally laid out in 1925. Though it is now part of the National Park system, the Appalachian Trail, extending from Maine to Georgia, is still maintained by the conference. During his term as executive director responsible for coordination of trail management, he raised over $1 million for acquisitions and established a citizen membership of some 80,000 members.

From 1977 to 1980, Pritchard was deputy director of the U.S. Department of Interior, overseeing the Bureau of Outdoor Recreation/Heritage Conservation and Recreation Service. Pritchard influenced the National Park system's acquisition of the Alaskan parks, including Denali and Glacier Bay. His dedication to the preservation of the land led him to the National Parks and Conservation Association (NPCA), where he served as president from 1980 through 1996. NPCA is a citizen-supported organization dedicated to protecting and enhancing the National Park system of the United States for present and future generations. Its objectives are realized mainly through public education and outreach. While guiding NPCA, he increased the association's membership from some 23,000 to over 500,000, at the same time expanding its budget to nearly $19 million annually. In 1990, he was instrumental in organizing the first Earth Day March for Parks, which remains an annual NPCA event. At its height, NPCA encouraged the development of more than 1,000 park events around the world, including a Russian march.

In 1983, Pritchard founded the National Park Trust (NPT) to acquire holdings from willing sellers who own land inside national and state parks or refuges. An organization of citizen members, which neither seeks nor accepts federal funds, it is dedicated exclusively to preserving and protecting the country's park lands, wildlife, and historic monuments. State and federal agencies contact the trust with projects that have no federal funding, and NPT selects those it is able to help. It is the only charitable group authorized by

Congress to own an entire unit of the National Park system, the Tallgrass Prairie National Preserve in Kansas.

Concurrent with his work at both NPCA and NPT, Pritchard established the Climate Institute, serving as its founding chairman from 1986 until 1988. He remains a board member and chair emeritus. The institute's mission is to protect the balance between climate and life on earth. It is an international leader, interfacing with scientists and policy leaders concerned with global climate change and protection of the ozone layer. In his work for the institute, he has played a significant role in building cooperation among U.S. environmental organizations, through such groups as the National Resources Council of America, which he chaired from 1987 to 1989.

Author of more than 100 articles on the environment, Pritchard contributed to the NPCA book, *National Parks in Crisis*, published in 1982. He edited the 1985 NPCA book *Views of the Green*, a collection of articles by European and North American park experts on the challenges they were addressing. He was asked to write the definition of national parks for the Houghton-Mifflin *Encyclopedia of the Environment*. An adviser to National Geographic Society Books, he collaborated on two books for the Society: *Enduring Treasures: National Parks of the World* (2000) and *The Making of the National Parks: An American Idea* (2001).

Pritchard has actively supported the development of state heritage programs. During the course of his career, he also has been influential in the acquisition of some 200 National Park Service units, which include national monuments, battlefields, seashores, and historic sites as well as parks. He is a member of the Council of Editorial Advisors of the National Center for Nonprofit Boards. Among his international projects, Pritchard has consulted on national park formation and management for Canada, Ireland, and China. He is a founder of the Friends of China's National Parks, a private group of U.S. citizens. The recipient of numerous awards, in 1986 he was honored as the first American to receive the Albert Schweitzer Prize for Humanitarianism, awarded by Johns Hopkins University and the Alexander Von Humbolt Foundation of Hamburg, Germany.

He currently serves on the Jefferson County, West Virginia, Public Service District Board of Directors. Pritchard lives on a farm near Shepherdstown, West Virginia, with his wife, Susan, and their two youngest sons, Stephen and Christopher. He also has two grown children, Robin and Marcus.

**BIBLIOGRAPHY**

"Park Service Report Finds Agency Ailing," *National Parks*, 1992; "Paul C. Pritchard, President, National Park Trust," www.parktrust.org/paul01.html; Pritchard, Paul C., "U.S. National Parks," *Encyclopedia of the Environment*, Ruth Eblen and William Eblen, eds., 1994; Stroud, Richard, *National Leaders of American Conservation*, 1985.

## Pryor, Cynthia

(December 24, 1951– )
Environmental activist, Founder of Yellow Dog Watershed Preserve

Cynthia Pryor did not set out to be an environmental activist. The executive director of the Yellow Dog Watershed Preserve in Big Bay, Michigan, moved to the tiny community with her husband after retiring from a career in telecommunications. In the mid-1990s, when the wild lands she had made her home were threatened by sulfide mining, she dug in her heels to fight the good fight.

Born on Christmas Eve in 1951, Cynthia Pryor grew up hunting and fishing in Michigan. Some of her earliest memories are of watching home movies of her grandfather fishing along the Yellow Dog River, which runs through approximately fifty miles of Upper Michigan wilderness before flowing into Lake Superior. The river is home to wild trout and sustains moose, wolf, and peregrine falcon populations. It infused young Cynthia with a love for places with the fewest roads on the map.

Pryor's father, an Episcopalian priest, raised his daughter to believe in standing up for what is right, but Pryor did not take this philosophy initially with her into the world. Her mother, a nurse who later moved north into arctic Alaska, used to ask her how she was ever going to save the world working for a phone company. "Who wants to save the world?" she would reply.

In 1993, Cynthia Pryor dropped her career as general manager for Verizon where she oversaw a twelve-state operation. She and her husband bought 250 acres on the plains of the Yellow Dog River and built a home off the grid. Employing wind and solar energy, and cooking on a woodstove, Pryor settled down on the outskirts of the town Big Bay (pop. 250) to live a quiet and reclusive life.

The first disruption of her hermitage was in 1995 when she learned that a large logging operation was planned right along the river. She

Cynthia Pryor (Photograph courtesy of Yellow Dog Watershed Preserve, Inc.)

and a small group of local citizens campaigned and eventually succeeded in having the logging company modify its original plan by taking less than it initially intended and not cutting down old growth.

This small group of people started looking around to see what else was happening in their neighborhood. Thus was born the Yellow Dog Watershed Preserve (YDWP). The little not-for-profit, with no ambitions for taking on large campaigns, spent the next few years purchasing property for wild land easement and educating locals on watershed preservation. They took school children out on the river and people hiking for educational tours.

But in 2002 their operation took on a much larger dimension. The Yellow Dog Plains is five thousand acres of wilderness, rich in minerals such as uranium, gold and silver, with no infrastructure and only one road for timber hauling. Pryor received a phone call from a landowner alerting her to a sudden flurry of new activity. Crews of trucks were spotted going in and out, planes started flying over and several landowners were being approached for possible purchase.

Pryor discovered that the Ford Motor Company, which owns several hundred thousand acres and mineral rights all along northern Michigan, had just sold 456,000 acres of mineral rights to Kennecott Minerals Corporation for the purpose of sulfide mining. In Michigan, land rights and mineral rights are equal. Therefore, a mining company has the full privilege to enter private property and begin exploring and mining.

Led by Pryor, the Yellow Dog Watershed Preserve researched the dangers of mineral sulfide mining. They learned that the U.S. Environmental Protection Agency considers acid mine drainage one of the most serious threats to water quality. They also learned that Michigan's Departments of Environmental Quality (DEQ) and Natural Resources (DNR) had been leasing mineral rights to Kennecott since 1992, without the notifying the public. Worse still, the state of Michigan had no regulations to govern underground mining.

Pryor started "raising heck," notifying news agencies and state legislators. "Living here is a dream come true. To have these folks turn paradise into a parking lot, I couldn't stand for it. Love of this place drives me."

A representative of the National Wildlife Federation who manages the Lake Superior area contacted Pryor and helped Yellow Dog Watershed Preserve forge partnerships with the Huron Mountain Club, a more than a century old landowner's club dedicated to stewardship of the wild lands of Michigan, and the local tribal entity, the Keweenaw Bay Indian Community. Pryor then convinced the then new governor of Michigan, Jennifer Granholm, to look into the issue. The new four-way partnership develops a legislative agenda and proposes statutes on sulfide mining.

Cynthia Pryor lives in Marquette County, Michigan, with her husband Robert. They have three sons.

### BIBLIOGRAPHY

www.savethewildup.org/alerts/?id=458; www.yellowdogwatershed.org/index.htm; www.truthout.org/cgi-bin/artman/exec/view.cgi/59/19335; Personal interview, 02/21/08.

## Pulido, Laura

(January 26, 1962- )
Geographer

Laura Pulido's career has focused on issues of race, social movements, and social justice, especially environmental racism and justice. As a geography professor at the University of Southern California, she studies structures and origins of oppression and how people organize themselves to resist exploitive situations. She describes her research as "very regional," covering the Southwest and southern California in particular. She is active in the Los Angeles community, having served as the Los Angeles city commissioner for the Department of Environmental Affairs. She is also a longtime member of the Labor/Community Strategy Center. Over the last few years she has been involved with labor struggles and has been active in a statewide California network to create a Latino Left.

Laura Pulido was born on January 26, 1962, in Los Angeles, California, to Louis and Berta Pulido. Growing up in Los Angeles, she expected to become a housewife because that was all she saw the women around her doing. She became dissatisfied with her high school and left without graduating but later earned her equivalency diploma. Ambitious and intellectually curious, she became a first-generation college student at Golden West College. She majored in social work, a career path that she had seen other women take, and received her associate's degree in 1983. She then enrolled at California State University at Fresno, still a social work major. However, while at Cal State she took a geography class, and suddenly she was hooked. She was fascinated that the field of study provided her with answers to questions she had always had, questions of society and environment—Why were all the African Americans in Watts and all the Mexicans in East LA? Why were there no forests in LA? What forces were shaping Los Angeles and the lives of its residents?

Pulido changed her major from social work to geography, and she excelled in her studies. After receiving a B.S in 1985, she went to the University of Wisconsin at Madison. Far from home, deep in winter darkness and snow, she was homesick and determined to get back to Los Angeles and "never leave again." However, among the benefits that came from attending the University of Wisconsin was the influence of Dr. Diana Liverman, who urged her to continue her studies in urban planning at the University of California at Los Angeles (UCLA). After receiving her master's degree from Wisconsin in 1987, she enrolled in the doctoral program at UCLA. She received her Ph.D. in urban planning in 1991.

At UCLA Pulido grew to be passionate about politics, especially the issue of racism and how that shapes the city. Rather than studying specific incidents or events as a historian would, she says she looks for a broader understanding of what racism is, what economic exploitation is, and "how the experience is played out on the landscape." For example, the urban structure of Los Angeles has "clean suburban areas and Black and Brown spaces" in the industrial zones. Suburbanization was essentially a massive subsidy for Whites to move out of the city, while nonwhites were refused mortgages and equal housing opportunities even up to 1970. Even now, Pulido says, nonwhites do not choose to live in industrial areas of Los Angeles, but economic forces and racism force them to stay in that area.

This has led her to explore how groups react to oppression and White privilege. The development of a "people of color" identity is crucial in the fight against environmental racism. It empowers people to understand what is going on and why, when their communities are neglected or degraded by government policies. However, just as important as self-concept is the way nonwhites are perceived by the dominant society. She has studied the concept of "ecological legitimacy" in the Ganados de Valle case in New Mexico, in which working-class Hispanos were told by the government that they could no longer graze their sheep on an open field, even after the community came up with a plan to manage the land and maintain their animals. To the New Mexican government land managers, the group's plan lacked "legitimacy" because the people were poor, Hispanos, lacked formal education, and because they had an economic interest in using the land. The New Mexico Department of Fish and Game responded to the interests of hunters and mainstream environmentalists but not those of Ganados de Valle. Pulido's book on this subject, *Environmentalism and Economic Justice: Two Chicano Struggles in the Southwest*, was published by the University of Arizona Press in 1996. The second struggle described in this book is of the United Farm Workers (UFW), led by CÉSAR CHÁVEZ and DOLORES HUERTA, who began their fight to improve health and sanitation conditions for migrant farmworkers in the early 1960s. The book discusses UFW's pesticide campaign from 1967 to 1975.

Pulido's most recent book *Black, Brown, Yellow, and Left: Radical Activism in Los Angeles* (2006) examines the radical political movements of African Americans, Asian Americans, and Chicanos in Los Angeles from 1968 to 1978. "The nation as a whole was in political turmoil," she says. However, history seems to give more attention to the "White Left" movement, neglecting the issues that distinguish the "Left of Color." Black, Yellow, and Brown Power radical movements worked to define and empower people beyond the limits set by White society, through class-based and materialist politics. The book won awards from the Association for Humanist Sociology and the Association of American Geographers.

Currently, Pulido is at work on two projects: Latinos racial identity and position over space and time, and Latino-African American relations in Los Angeles.

She resides in Los Angeles.

### BIBLIOGRAPHY

Pulido, Laura, "A Critical Review of the Methodology of Environmental Racism Research" *Antipode*, 1996; Pulido, Laura, "Development of the 'People of Color' Identity in the Environmental Justice Movement of the Southwestern U.S.," *Socialist Review*, 1998; Pulido, Laura, "Ecological Legitimacy and Cultural Essentialism: Hispano Grazing in the Southwest," *Capitalism, Nature, Socialism*, 1996; "USC College: Faculty: Department of American Studies and Ethnicity: Laura Pulido," www.college.usc.edu/faculty/faculty1003620.html.

# American Environmental Leaders

From Colonial Times to the Present

## Raven, Peter
(June 13, 1936– )
Botanist, President of the Missouri Botanical Garden

A passionate advocate of preserving biodiversity, Peter Raven is a scientist and a highly public activist: in addition to his research and teaching, he spends time making speeches and raising public awareness about the current dangerous rates of extinction of plants and animals. His belief that all the fundamental elements of human life, from growing food to building shelter, have their basis in plant life has led him on a quest to explore and maintain the diversity of the plant world. As president of the Missouri Botanical Garden, he transformed a regional botanical garden suffering from neglect into one of the world's leading research centers specializing in tropical plants. He has become a widely recognized botanist and is credited as the cofounder of the field of coevolution. Among his extensive list of publications is *The Biology of Plants,* first published in 1969 and still a standard introductory botany textbook at colleges and universities across the country.

Peter Hamilton Raven was born in Shanghai, China, on June 13, 1936, the only child of Walter and Isabelle (Breen) Raven. Not long after he was born, his family moved to San Francisco, where Raven grew up. Precocious from the start, Raven's interest in the natural world had him searching for insects in Golden Gate Park at the age of seven. By nine years of age he became a student member of the California Academy of Sciences, the youngest member ever. His scope widened to include plants, and at 12 he joined the Sierra Club and went on plant-collecting expeditions with the club. He attended Catholic school, where he learned Latin and Greek—and continued to find rare and interesting plants. When he was 14 his first scientific paper was published. At 15 he discovered a type of manzanita that botanists had presumed to be extinct. This sub-

Dr. Peter Raven (© Missouri Botanical Garden. Photograph by Michael Jacob)

species, Arctostaphylos hookeri subsp. ravenii, was later named for him.

After high school, Raven entered the University of California at Berkeley, where he received his bachelor's degree in botany in 1957. Recruited by botanists at the University of California at Los Angeles (UCLA) who were impressed with his work, Raven enrolled at UCLA and earned his Ph.D. in plant biology in 1960. During his years as a graduate student, Raven made his first trip to the tropics as an exchange student in in Colombia. After graduate school he took a postdoctoral fellowship at the Natural History Museum in London, then worked for a year at the Rancho Santa Ana Botanic Garden in Claremont, California. Following that he accepted a job as assistant professor at Stanford University, where he taught biology until 1971. While at Stanford, Raven collaborated with PAUL EHRLICH, a population biologist who wrote *The Population Bomb* (1968). Together they worked on unraveling the complexities of plant-insect interactions and described a phenomenon they called co-evolution—a groundbreaking idea that has since gained widespread recognition. In addition to his responsibilities at Stanford, Raven wrote several highly popular textbooks. He had noticed that fewer and fewer botany courses were being taught during the 1960s and wanted to halt this decline and bring the study of plants up to date. His *Biology of Plants* (1969) textbook, co-written with two other biologists, went on to become the best-selling botany textbook in the country.

At the age of 35, Raven was appointed director of the Missouri Botanical Garden in St. Louis, Missouri, in 1971. The oldest botanical garden in the United States, it was little more than a modest ten acres when Raven took over, even though the garden actually controlled a 79-acre estate. Under Raven's directorship, the Missouri Botanical Garden has grown to fill the entire 79 acres with a wide variety of plant life in many magnificent gardens. When Raven came to the Missouri Botanical Garden, the facility had only 85 people on staff, including three scientists with doctorates. It now employs just under 500 people—with about 50 Ph.D. staff scientists, some of whom live overseas and conduct field research, along with a number of other overseas associates. Raven and his staff have formed one of the world's most active centers of botanical research where they work toward a vitally important scientific goal: to catalog as many of the world's remaining tropical plants as possible. The scientists there identify about 200 new plant species every year in a race against the rapid extinction rates that could erase more than one of every four plants from nature within this century. Raven is motivated by his belief that as species disappear, the world becomes less interesting, stable, and prosperous—and he hopes to spread the word that plants have value beyond just beautifying our gardens. For example, the future of agriculture depends in part on the genetic material in the food plants and other organisms currently in existence. Also, certain plants hold potential as antidisease agents. Over one-fourth of the world's prescription medicines contain a plant-derived ingredient, and preserving biodiversity is the only way to protect thousands of other plants that may also have healing properties. Working in the equatorial rain forests of Africa, Asia, and Latin America, the Garden's researchers study and collect plants previously unknown to science. They send specimens back to the garden's herbarium, which now contains over six million specimens, and to the national herbarium that they nourish in a number of different countries. In addition to tropical research, the Garden also hosts the Center for Plant Conservation, a consortium of botanical gardens dedicated to preserving and reintroducing native plant species in the United States.

Raven's success in his growing endeavors has come in part from his talent at networking. Interacting with numerous institutions, giving speeches, lobbying members of Congress—all of his outreach and advocacy efforts have led some to call him an "eco-administrator" or a "biopolitician." Because of his high profile, he has raised public awareness of the importance of preserving tropical rain forests and biodiversity. And he does not stop at discussing the biological consequences of environmental degradation. Believing that rampant consumerism in the Western world, widespread poverty, and Third World debt preclude any easy solutions for preserving the environment, he urges governments and policy makers to take into account the planet's limited resources. The Missouri Botanical Garden has been actively helping poorer countries that contain some of the most critically threatened areas of diversity, providing training and support in making plans for sustainable use of resources.

Raven edited *Nature and Society: The Quest for a Sustainable World* (2000), proceedings of the 1997 Forum on Biodiversity sponsored by the National Academy of Sciences, whose distinguished list of contributors includes E. O. WILSON, DANIEL JANZEN, and THOMAS EISNER.

Peter Raven is a member of many professional organizations, including the national academies of science in about 20 countries. He has written over 500 scientific papers and 19 books. He has received scores of honors and awards, the MacArthur Foundation Fellowship in 1985; the International Prize for Biology, awarded by Japan in 1986; and the National Medal of Science in 2000. In 2008, he shared with environmental biologist Harold Mooney the 500,000 Euro BBVA Foundation Award for Biodiversity Conservation. Raven is also a professor of botany at Washington University in St. Louis. He lives with his wife, Pat, in St. Louis, Missouri.

**BIBLIOGRAPHY**

Beardsley, Tim, "Defender of the Plant Kingdom," *Scientific American*, 1999; Lawren, Bill, "Six Scientists Who May Save the World," *Omni*, 1987; McClintock, Jack, "Peter the Great," *Discover*, 1999; "Missouri Botanical Garden," www.mobot.org; Rosenblatt, Roger, "The World is his Garden, Better Tread Carefully," *Time Magazine*, 1999.

## Red Cloud, Henry
(1960– )
Lakota Renewable Energy Leader

Henry Red Cloud is a leader in both Lakota Nation and in the renewable energy movement. He helped spur higher levels of self-sufficiency and sustainability among the Lakota, revitalizing the local buffalo herd and developing affordable renewable energy sources. He established the Red Cloud Renewable Energy Center in 2007, and his company, Lakota Solar Enterprises, provide a development model for other land-based communities.

Henry Red Cloud was born and raised on the Pine Ridge reservation on February 1, 1960. He is the great-great grandson of Chief Red Cloud, the last of the Lakota warrior chiefs to be captured in 1876, then relocated to the Pine Ridge Reservation in South Dakota. Growing up along the Slim Buttes area of the reservation, young Henry Red Cloud witnessed first-hand the connection between a blighted environment and his blighted people. Unemployment, alcoholism, incarceration were rampant. As a teenager, conditions on the reservation and the legacy of broken agreements with the U.S. government reached a tipping point and Henry Red Cloud saw the American Indian Movement and members of his tribe take up arms in desperation in February 1973 at Wounded Knee, the site of a massacre of over 300 Lakota in 1890. The conflict in 1973 would leave a lasting impression on him. He knew there was a better way to improve living conditions for the Lakota.

In 1996, Red Cloud began his work with Trees, Water, & People, a non-governmental organization that conducts grassroots work on renewable energy, reforestation, and watershed management, as well as looks for ways to economically develop the Pine Ridge

Henry Red Cloud and his son (Photograph courtesy of Henry Red Cloud)

Lakota nation within the traditionally sustainable practices of the Lakota.

After attending workshops on supplemental solar heaters, Red Cloud founded Lakota Solar Enterprises, the first, and one of the few, 100% Native American-owned and -operated renewable energy companies. It provides affordable renewable energy for local residents, and training and employment in the renewable energy field. Red Cloud recognizes capacity for energy being fundamental to alleviating the social and economic hardships faced by many Pine Ridge residents, where winters are harsh and unemployment and poverty rates are high.

In its first decade of operation, Lakota Solar expanded from residential installation of wind turbines and solar electric systems on Pine Ridge to manufacturing a broad array of renewable energy sources on and off Pine Ridge Reservation. Red Cloud also sought to involve other reservations in his renewable energy efforts—Wind River, Rosebud Sioux, White Earth, and Standing Rock reservations.

In 2007 Red Cloud established the Red Cloud Renewable Energy Center to expand on the training, creation, and installation of renewable energy options for Native Americans. Operating as a living/learning site, the Red Cloud Renewable Energy Center has demonstration and training sites for different renewable energy projects including their solar heaters, as well as other sustainability projects including windbreaks, a greenhouse, a garden, and a straw bale office. All of these models showcase various forms of sustainability that are realistic and achievable. Beginning in the summer of 2008, the Red Cloud Renewable Energy Center began hosting Native American students for workshops and training in renewable energy.

In 2008 the Center received funding to install 250 supplemental solar heaters for Northern Plains tribal members. The heaters work by simply drawing cold air from a house through a glass solar box that heats the air, which is then re-circulated back into the house. This reduces monthly heating bills with very little maintenance costs, making this solution economically and environmentally beneficial.

Outside of his work with renewable energy, Red Cloud focuses on general issues of sustainability on Pine Ridge, including providing straw bale wraps for mobile homes that provide low-cost, highly efficient insulation.

With help from Village Earth, a non-governmental organization dedicated to bottom-up sustainable development, Red Cloud and his family hosted the first buffalo herd on their ranch with the intent of breeding the herd and sharing the offspring with other members of the Pine Ridge reservation. From 2004 until 2008 the herd has grown from 15 to 80. Th return of the buffalo on Pine Ridge increases self-sufficiency and sustainability by re-establishing a cultural, educational, and subsistence resource.

By working with what is readily available, Henry Red Cloud bridges the need for economic development, self-sufficiency, and ecological sustainability. He lives on Pine Ridge reservation with his wife, three children, extended family and community. He and his brother Albert continue to conduct Lakota religious ceremonies (sweat lodges and song) to cleanse their people and the land.

**BIBLIOGRAPHY**
Red Cloud, Henry, Personal Conversation, May 29, 2008; Village Earth, www.villageearth.org/pages/Projects/Pine_Ridge/index.php; Trees, Water & People, www.treeswaterpeople.org/tribal/info/tribal_lse.htm; Nebraska Historical Society, www.nebraskahistory.org/lib-arch/research/manuscripts/family/james-redcloud.htm.

## Reilly, William K.
(January 26, 1940– )
Administrator of the Environmental Protection Agency, President of the Conservation Foundation, President of the World Wildlife Fund

Director of the Environmental Protection Agency (EPA) under Pres. George H. W. Bush, William Reilly advocated for environmental issues in an administration never fully committed to protecting the environment. Reilly was the first "professional environmentalist" to serve as the agency's head and helped strengthen the Clean Air Act. He served as a check on others in the administration pushing to weaken environmental regulations, including those who would have stripped away wetlands protection. Before his tenure as EPA head, Reilly worked to promote conservation efforts through a variety of groups, including the President's Council on Environmental Quality and the World Wildlife Fund.

William Kane Reilly was born on January 26, 1940, in Decatur, Illinois. His father's job required the family to move to the Rio Grande Valley of South Texas when he was 10, and then to Fall River, Massachusetts while he was in high school. He graduated from Yale University in 1962 with a B.A. in history and from Harvard Law School with a J.D. in 1965. He served in the United States Army from 1965 to 1966. In 1971 he received an M.S. in urban planning from Columbia University. He served as the associate director of the Urban Policy Center from 1968 to 1970 and as executive director of the Rockefeller Task Force on Land Use and Urban Growth from 1972 to 1973.

Reilly's involvement in environmental policy began in 1970, when he joined the President's Council on Environmental Quality, serving as a senior staff member until 1972. In 1973 he became president of the Conservation Foundation, and in 1985, president of the World Wildlife Fund. One of his most important contributions during this period was to facilitate an alliance of the two groups. World Wildlife Fund had particular expertise in the areas of fieldwork and the natural sciences, while the Conservation Foundation was strong in the areas of social science and policy advocacy; joining the groups made it possible to collaborate on pressing issues of international conservation. The groups at first maintained separate operating structures, but by 1991 they had consolidated as a single organization, under the name World Wildlife Fund, Inc.

In 1988, George H. W. Bush was elected president of the United States, with promises to be the "environmental president." Conservationists cheered when he appointed Reilly to head the Environmental Protection Agency, because Reilly was an active and respected member of the environmentalist community. In the early days of the administration, it looked as though Bush might uphold his campaign commitment. One of Reilly's first acts was to halt development of the Denver Water Board's Two Forks dam project. Environmentalists had fought hard to stop the large project, proposed for the South Platte River west of the Denver metropolitan area, because of its impact on the surrounding canyon and the wildlife in and around the river, but the EPA under President Reagan had approved the dam. In early 1989, Reilly vetoed the project, angering western Republicans, who formed one of Bush's key constituencies. Reilly also helped craft 1989's Clean Air Act, which required tough new standards on sulfur dioxide emissions to reduce acid rain. Reilly's position, though, was difficult. He described himself as "the man in the middle," caught between the environmental movement and corporate and other groups demanding environmental deregulation. Environmentalists felt Bush and Reilly were not tough enough on polluters and criticized weaknesses in the Clean Air Act. Business interests felt the Republican president should be more aggressive in following the footsteps of President Reagan's deregulatory path. Bush felt he was not getting credit for his environmental efforts and gradually moved away from his campaign promises. Though Reilly maintained a close personal relationship with the president, he clashed with other administration officials, including Bush's powerful chief of staff, John Sununu. Reilly's balancing act came apart visibly during the Earth Summit in Rio de Janeiro, Brazil, in 1992. Reilly led the U.S. delegation but was unable to persuade the administration to sign the biodiversity treaty. More than 100 other countries, including U.S. allies Germany, Canada, and Britain, approved the treaty, but Bush refused to sign on the grounds that the standards could cost U.S. jobs. Reilly's conflict with the administration during the summit made national headlines.

Reilly was also at odds with vice president Dan Quayle, who headed the Council on Competitiveness, a group of wealthy corporate leaders pushing for relaxed pollution standards and blocking new EPA regulations. Two key areas of disagreement between Quayle's group and Reilly were relaxed emissions standards in relatively unpolluted areas and weakening wetlands protection in Alaska. During the election of 1992, it looked as though Reilly would lose, as the administration pushed the EPA to approve the council's recommendations. But when President Bush lost the election, Reilly stalled the proposals, citing the likelihood that the Clinton administration would simply reverse any new regulations put into place in the closing days of 1992. Reilly's own assessment of the successes of his tenure at EPA includes efforts to restore the health of Chesapeake Bay, the Great Lakes, and the Gulf of Mexico; strengthening the role of science in the agency; and integration of environmental and economic concerns.

Since leaving the EPA in January 1993, Reilly has testified a number of times in front of Congress, on issues ranging from the elevation of the EPA to cabinet status (2001), to the proposal that the EPA regulate carbon dioxide emissions (2007). He has been active in a number of foundations, corporations, and environmental organizations. He serves on the board of directors of ConocoPhillips Co, and the DuPont Corporation, where he has urged the company to support green initiatives. He is the president and chief executive officer of Aqua International partners, a group that finances water projects in developing nations. He has served on the boards of several conservation organizations, including the World Wildlife Fund, the American Farmland Trust, the David and Lucile Packard Foundation, and the Presidio Trust. Reilly resides in San Francisco.

### Bibliography

Dunne, Nancy, "Business and the Environment: Complacency Breeds Contempt," *Financial Times of London*, 1992; "The Presidio Trust," www.presidiotrust.com; Raeburn, Paul, "Bush's EPA Chief Tells of Last-Minute Efforts to Achieve Green Agenda," *Los Angeles Times*, 1993; Roberts, David, "Getting Fresh: A chat with freshwater experts Peter Gleick and William K. Reilly," 2006, www.grist.org/news/maindish/2006/06/30/roberts/index.html.

## Reisner, Marc
(September 14, 1948–July 21, 2000)
Writer, Consultant

Marc Reisner is known for his nonfiction, environmentally focused books. His most famous, *Cadillac Desert* (1986), dramatizes the environmental degradation brought about in the dry American West by federal dam-building policies and by shortsighted water management. He was also an environmental consultant, advocating practical solutions to managing western water resources.

Marc P. Reisner was born on September 14, 1948, to Konrad and Else Reisner in Minneapolis, Minnesota. His father was a family-service executive and a lawyer, his mother a scriptwriter. He attended Earlham College in Indiana, graduating with a B.A. in 1970. He began his career in 1970 as a scriptwriter for environmental telethons and as an environmental lobbyist. In 1972, he took a position with the Natural Resources Defense Council (NRDC) in New York City as a staff writer. He continued working for the NRDC until 1979, when he became a full-time writer, lecturer, and environmental consultant.

Reisner authored several important, environmentally focused works of nonfiction. He was best known for his first book, *Cadillac Desert: The American West and Its Disappearing Water* (1986), in which he examined the environmental, social, and economic consequences of federal dam-building practices in the American West. The book, which Reisner began researching in 1979 with an Alicia Patterson Journalism Fellowship, describes the competition and dam-building one-upmanship that existed between the Bureau of Reclamation and the Army Corps of Engineers, and the resultant dam building frenzy. Water management in the West, Reisner concluded, has been politically motivated and short sighted and was ecologically unsustainable. *Cadillac Desert* points out the reckless overuse of water resources by city residents and farmers and the polluted waterways and soils that have resulted. It also contains a chapter that recounts the crooked dealings undertaken by Los Angeles County in wresting the water of Owens Lake away from the residents of the Owens Valley and in pumping that water over 200 miles of desert to quench the thirst of Los Angeles's growing suburbs. *Cadillac Desert* was ranked 61st in Modern Library's list of the 100 most notable nonfiction works in English published during the 20th century. It was made into a four-hour Public Broadcasting Service documentary that first aired in 1997.

Reisner's second book also deals with the subject of water in the West. Cowritten with Sarah Bates, *Overtapped Oasis* (1990) is an in-depth analysis of the water allocation network in the American West. The problem, according to Reisner and Bates, is not so much one of a shortage of water as it is of the misallocation and inefficient use of water. This inefficient use is the result of the perplexing array of outdated irrigation practices, federal subsidy programs, state water codes, and resistance to reform. Reisner's third book, *Game Wars: The Undercover Pursuit of Wildlife Poachers* (1991), is also focused on an environmental topic, a U.S. Fish and Wildlife Service agent and his efforts to protect such animals as alligators, walruses, and waterfowl.

After publishing *Cadillac Desert* in 1986, Reisner's views on the culpability of agriculture in the degradation of the western lands changed. Whereas he originally believed that much of the environmental degradation was the fault of farmers and was their responsibility to fix, he later came to believe that agriculture was a more preferable alternative than development (which, he felt, would be the inevitable result if farmers were kicked off of the land). Reisner preferred western farms to western suburbs. To restore balance, he said, three distinct areas need to be reformed: fishery restoration, underground water storage, and decision making. Reisner became an advocate for the free market water trading policies of water banking and the trading of water rights, holding that these policies could be utilized to create additional water supplies without building new dams.

Reisner was consulted by the Institute for Fisheries Resources, assisting in its efforts to remove antiquated and marginally useful dams in California. He was also a consultant to America's Farmland Trust, an organization campaigning to protect California farmland from encroaching development. Reisner originated the Rice Lands Habitat Partnership, which provides incentives to enhance waterfowl habitat on private land. In 1998 he became director of the Vidler Water Company, responsible for furthering the company's interests in wetlands restoration. And in the fall of 1999, he was Distinguished Visiting Professor in the Department of Geology at the University of California at Davis.

Reisner considered himself a writer, a conservationist, a consensus builder, and a deal maker. He received numerous awards for his literary and conservation accomplishments. He received a National Book Critics Circle nomination for *Cadillac Desert* in 1986, and in 1993 he was given the San Francisco Bay Institute annual conservation award. Reisner married Lawrie Mott in 1985, with whom he had two children, Ruthie and Margot. He died of cancer at his home in Marin County, California, on July 21, 2000.

### BIBLIOGRAPHY

Associated Press, "'Cadillac Desert' author dies," *Denver Post*, 2000; Lesniak, James G., ed., *Contemporary Authors*, 1994; Pace, Eric, "Marc Reisner, author on the environment, dies at 51," *New York Times*, 2000; Reisner, Marc, "Western Water and the Limits to Consensus: a Call for Democracy and Bold Decisions," *Chronicle of Community*, 1999.

## Reynolds, Michael

Architect, Designer of Earth Ships, Recycler

Maverick and renegade architect, or rather "biotect," Michael Reynolds builds fully self-sustaining homes almost entirely out of recycled materials. His "Earth Ship" design requires no external utility source other than solar and wind technology. The Earth Ship self-regulates its temperature, harvests and recycles water, and holds a self-contained sewage treatment process. Residents can also grow food

Michael Reynolds on the roof of an "Earthship" he designed and built in Taos, NM. (AP Images/Eric Draper)

indoors year-round. In a time of potential ecological devastation due to human industry, Reynolds believes it is criminally insane to continue building homes, businesses, and cities that rely on an ever-dwindling fuel source and are a major source of pollution.

Born and raised near Louisville, Kentucky, Reynolds graduated from the University of Cincinnati in 1969 with a Bachelor of Architecture. Attempting to avoid the draft, Reynolds moved out to Taos, New Mexico immediately after graduating to pursue his hobby of racing motorcycles. In the early 1970s, he began developing his theories on green architecture. Reynolds said that all of his building philosophies have been a direct response to issues raised in the media. He was first struck by two news programs he saw: one with Walter Cronkite predicting a housing storage due to the massive clear-cutting occurring in the Northwest, and then Charles Kuralt reporting on the incredible amount of beer cans littering the nation's highways. Within two weeks, Reynolds had invented a beer can brick to build houses with. Over time the beer can brick proved to have some faults and Reynolds eventually discovered "the most abundant natural resource—used tires." Tires became his most enduring building material. With the energy crisis of the 1970s in full bloom, Reynolds began utilizing the theories of thermal mass in his building, creating thick walls of dirt-filled tires coated with concrete or adobe that absorb sunlight during the day and release that heat during the night.

Reynolds incorporated new elements into his thinking and housing projects until Earth Ships became completely self-sustaining. The prototypical Earth Ship regulates its own temperature through the laws of thermal mass, passive solar south-facing glass walls, and a sophisticated ventilation system to keep the house from reaching uncomfortably high temperatures. Solar panels and wind turbines run all the electrical components. The house is fitted with an elaborate catch-water and filtration and recycle system. Rainwater is harvested off rooftops and filtered before running through the sinks and showers. The run-off "grey water" supplies indoor gardens, which tend to be a significant part of the interior. From there, the water is channeled into flush toilets. Then, through another filtration process, the now "black water" and sludge enters a solar septic system for final reuse. Minimal wastewater is then released into a leach field that waters outdoor landscaping. All the filtration systems are botanical cells, essentially small gardens that effectively clean water for its next use. By this means, people living in a desert setting, which typically receives only about 8 inches of water a year, can multiply that to 30 inches of precipitation a year through intelligent reuse of their limited water. And they enjoy added value knowing that they are nurturing their environment rather than polluting it through traditional excessive use of water and septic systems. All of Reynolds' houses have nominal utility bills, typically about $100 annually, for propane and Internet and satellite services. Most Earth Ships belie the myth that "off-grid living" requires sacrificing modern amenities.

Among Reynolds' achievements: He built the first Farmers Home Administration's financed solar home in March 1981. He won the Terra Alpha Technology acknowledgment award in 1990, and was nominated for the Chrysler Award for Innovation in Design in 1996. Reynolds has consulted and overseen projects in Bolivia, the Himalayas, Japan, and Venezuela. He traveled to the Andaman and Nicobar Islands in Asia after they were devastated by the 2004 Tsunami, and to Mexico after Hurricane Katrina the following year. He continues to demonstrate his recycled and self-sufficient building techniques as a best practice after natural disasters. Showing people how to provide clean water and electricity in their homes without relying on fragile utility sources is Reynolds' primary mission.

In his adopted state of New Mexico, Reynolds succeeded in changing building code and zoning laws to allow for off-the-grid subdivisions and housing. He developed an educational facility in Taos. Because Reynolds sees environmental degradation as his country's largest threat to national security, he promotes legislation allowing residents to declare their building projects experimental test sites for a state of emergency situation to allow radical and innovative building designs that operate on the principal of carbon neutrality.

"The last 35 years have been the easy and fun part developing the technology," says Reynolds. "The tedious part is getting permission to do it. Seventy-five percent of my time is spent getting permission. If it were the other way around, we would have cities built. What it amounts to is how many people are going to die from heat or cold, lack of water or food, or the chaos from lack of energy? If we don't do something radical immediately we're toast."

The 2006 British documentary *Garbage Warrior*, produced by Rachel Wexler and directed by Oliver Hodge, depicts an unapologetic Reynolds. When he is not abroad where his Earth Ship designs are spreading quickly, Reynolds lives north of Taos, New Mexico with his wife Chris and son Jonah.

**BIBLIOGRAPHY**

Shawna Williams, personal interview, June 25, 2008, Taos, New Mexico; www.garbagewarrior.com/; mebuilding.com/ask_http://www.greenhothe_experts.htm#MichaelR; www.nytimes.com/2008/04/20/magazine/20Build-text.html?pagewanted=2&_r=1; www.earthship.net.

# Richards, Ellen Swallow

(December 3, 1842–March 30, 1911)
Sanitary Chemist

Ellen Swallow Richards is remembered as the first woman to graduate with a science degree from a university in the United States, for her help opening the heavy doors of science to other women, and for her groundbreaking innovations in the fields of urban and industrial sanitation, food safety, nutrition, and water purity. Many branches of the environmental sciences, including ecology, limnology, oceanography, marine biology, and sanitary chemistry, can be traced back to Richards's pioneering work.

Ellen Henrietta Swallow Richards was born on December 3, 1842, on a farm near Dunstable, Massachusetts. As both of her parents were trained as teachers, she studied at home until she was 17 years old, at which time her family moved to Westford, Massachusetts, so she could study at Westford Academy there. After several years of working at her family's small store and caring for her infirm mother, Richards attended the brand-new all-women's Vassar College in New York, from which she graduated in 1870 with a bachelor's degree. Her thirst for learning still strong, she applied to study at the all-male Massachusetts Institute of Technology (MIT). MIT accepted her as a "special student" but would not accept tuition payment from her in order to reserve the option of expelling her should its experiment with a female student not work out. There she studied sanitary chemistry and nutrition, earning a master's degree in 1873. She had actually completed sufficient work for a Ph.D. but was not awarded one because hers would have been the first Ph.D. in chemistry to be granted by MIT, and MIT did not want a woman to earn one before a man.

Despite the ingrained sexism at MIT, Richards found a niche there. She made herself useful to professors, mending broken suspenders when necessary and astounding them with her brilliant observations in almost any field. Together with her professor, William Ripley Nichols, she designed the nation's first water purity tests, some of which are still used today. In the laboratory of her future husband, mineralogy professor Robert Richards, she isolated the rare metal vanadium, a near-impossible feat even for mineralogists. She became an instructor of sanitary chemistry and established a Women's Lab where women trained for science-related careers. With the financial support of the Women's Education Association, she also established the marine biology laboratory in Hyannis, Massachusetts that eventually became Woods Hole.

Late-nineteenth-century cities were dirty and disease ridden, lacking clean air and water, sufficient sewage treatment, and garbage collection. Richards's daily walks to school through the filth of Boston led her to important realizations about transmission of disease and the importance of sanitation and hygiene. Richards urged families and city governments to take responsibility for their environment and pushed especially for greater education for women, who were usually those responsible for household sanitary conditions. At that time, it was widely held that women were not meant to study and that those women who did would get sick and become sterile. Richards felt the opposite, that if women did not learn at least enough to improve hygiene in their homes, their families would get sick. Much of her work from 1880 on was devoted to women and the environment and was supported by two major women's organizations of the time: the Women's Education Association and the Association of Collegiate Alumnae. Richards lectured widely to women's clubs, she taught science through a correspondence program whose students were mostly housewives, and she wrote 18 books, among them *The Chemistry of Cook-*

*ing and Cleaning: A Manual for Housekeepers* (1882); *Food Materials and Their Adulturations* (1886); and *Sanitation in Daily Life* (1907).

Richards became a player in the turn-of-the-century debates on eugenics (the improvement of humanity through controlled breeding) by promoting a counter-approach: "euthenics," which she defined as the improvement of human intelligence and health through an improved environment. The science of euthenics metamorphosed until it became home economics, and today Richards is remembered as the mother of that field.

For several years in the 1880s, Richards worked as chief industrial chemist for the Boston Mutual Manufacturers Fire Insurance Combine, which insured factories. Factories at this time were tinderboxes, and safety precautions were rare. With the support of her friend and employer, the distinguished public figure Edward Atkinson, she drew up new requirements with which factories had to comply in order to take out insurance policies.

Richards was reluctant to marry, since marriage at that time usually entailed the woman's sacrificing her own interests so that she could take care of the household and help her husband. But her suitor, Professor Robert Richards, promised that she could continue her work. She did marry Richards in 1875, and the couple embarked on a plan to make their home into a model showcasing their ideas on healthy environments. The windows were full of green plants to produce oxygen, vents were installed to promote air circulation, and their stove was topped with a hood with a fan—a unique feature in those times.

Why is Ellen Swallow Richards not a household name, given the contributions she made toward public health? Her New England character endowed her with extreme modesty. She almost never allowed herself to be photographed and did not seek press coverage, except to further her projects. Her biographer, Robert Clarke, also points out that her work drew together many fields into a holistic view of the environment at a time when science was fragmenting into many separate microfields.

If Richards felt frustrated at the lack of acceptance of her revolutionary yet common-sense ideas, it never slowed her down. She lectured continuously throughout the United States and Europe during the last third of her life. Richards died on March 30, 1911, at her home in Jamaica Plain, Massachusetts, of heart failure.

**BIBLIOGRAPHY**

Ancker, Jessica Scalzi, *Domesticity, Science, and Social Control: Ellen Swallow Richards and the New England Kitchen*, 1987; Breton, Mary Joy, *Women Pioneers for the Environment*, 1998; Clarke, Robert, *Ellen Swallow: The Woman Who Founded Ecology*, 1973; Cravens, Hamilton, "Establishing the Science of Nutrition at the U.S.D.A.: Ellen Swallow Richards and Her Allies," *Agricultural History*, 1990; Hunt, Caroline, *The Life of Ellen H. Richards*, 1912; Lam, Thomas Kwai, *Science and Culture: Ellen Swallow Richards and Nineteenth Century Nutrional Science*, 1981; Richards, Ellen Swallow, *The Art of Right Living*, 1904; Richards, Ellen Swallow, *Euthenics—The Science of Controllable Environment*, 1910; Stage, Sarah, "Ellen Richards and the Social Significance of the Home Economics Movement," in *Rethinking Home Economics: Women and the History of a Profession*, edited by Stage, Sarah, and Virginia Bramble Vincenti, 1997.

## Rifkin, Jeremy
(January 26, 1945– )
Social Critic, Economist, Author

Through his books, lectures, and television appearances, Jeremy Rifkin has emerged as one of the most conspicuous vocal dissenters of the scientific effort to manipulate and alter the genetic makeup of living organisms through biotechnology. Citing possible deleterious consequences to the environment, Rifkin has raised public awareness of the ecological and moral implications of biotechnology and has mobilized support in a campaign against genetic engineering. As cofounder and director of the Foundation on Economic Trends in Washington, D.C., Rifkin has formed coalitions, organized demonstrations, and initiated lawsuits against institutions that neglect to undertake environmental assessments of the risks involved in their biotechnology research. Criticized by some as "anti-progress," Rifkin believes it is time for society to reshape its ideas about the nature of scientific inquiry and to develop a new philosophy of science and technology that is sophisticated, intelligent, and above all, respectful of living things.

Jeremy Rifkin was born on January 26, 1945, in Denver, Colorado, to Milton and Vivette Rifkin and was raised in a middle-class setting in Chicago. He attended the Wharton School of Finance at the University of Pennsylvania, where he was elected president of his class and became known as a fluent and talented public speaker. He earned his bachelor's degree in 1967 in economics and then went on to graduate studies at the Fletcher School of Law and Diplomacy at Tufts University in Medford, Massachusetts, where he received his master's degree in international affairs in 1968. Through the late 1960s, Rifkin immersed himself in anti–Vietnam War activism, and in 1967 he helped organize the first national rally against the war. Antiwar activism and working in New York City for the Volunteers in Service to America occupied his time until he moved to Washington, D.C., in 1971. At that point he founded the People's Bicentennial Commission to promote alternative bicentennial ceremonies and activities that he hoped would reacquaint the country with revolutionary principles. Rifkin and his organization led protests against large corporations, called for a redistribution of wealth in the United States, and promoted social action.

Jeremy Rifkin (left) and Pierferdinando Casini in a hydrogen-propelled car. (AP Images/Umberto Battaglia)

When the bicentennial festivities died down in 1976, Rifkin redirected his activism efforts toward the business world. He cofounded with Randy Barber the People's Business Commission (renamed the Foundation on Economic Trends in 1977) in Washington, D.C., an organization committed to confronting corporate exploitation and urging reforms that would give workers more autonomy and a larger share of corporate profits. Rifkin's book *Own Your Own Job: Economic Democracy for Working Americans* (1977) expands on the threats posed by multinational corporations to fair labor practices.

Rifkin began gaining a reputation as a skilled popularizer of radical ideas, and he continued to fight for labor unions and union pension funds and for alternatives to the current economic system. He also began examining the implications of scientific research in genetic engineering and manipulation of recombinant deoxyribonucleic acid (DNA), becoming more and more alarmed at the exploitation of life forms through techniques such as cloning and selective breeding. With the discovery of technologies that allowed for gene splicing, chemical companies had begun to isolate genes from one organism and inject them directly into the genetic blueprint of another organism. Proponents claimed it was a quicker, cleaner way to develop new plants with special characteristics such as frost resistance or pesticide-tolerance. But Rifkin worried that biotechnology was outpacing society's ability to assess deleterious consequences to the environment or to identify negative moral or economic impacts, and he began voicing his concerns in his characteristically activist approach, appearing on television programs and speaking in public. With the publication of his best-seller book, *Who Should Play God? The Artificial Creation of Life and What It Means for the Future of the Human Race* (1977), cowritten with Ted Howard, Rifkin emerged as one of the most important opponents of genetic engineering.

Unwilling to accept the biotechnology industry's assurance that it was not technology that was inherently bad, it was how it was used, Rifkin began broadcasting his view that technology is not neutral—it reflects the values of the culture. In the early 1980s, in a challenge to what he believed to be dangerous research in genetic manipulation, Rifkin began a series of lawsuits against the National Institutes of Health (NIH) and the University of California, Berkeley. Concerned over potential environmental hazards, Rifkin opposed the NIH's decision to allow university scientists to conduct experiments that would allow the release of genetically modified bacteria (designed to deter frost formation on potatoes) into the environment. The ensuing legal battles brought unprecedented attention to Rifkin, who continued to take to task biotech industries that neglected to undertake environmental assessments of risks involved in their research. Books that he wrote during this time also reflect his concerns. *Entropy* (1980), cowritten with Ted Howard, rejects the contemporary gospel of progress and places modern world problems such as resource depletion and conservation in the context of entropy—a concept holding that disorder increases to a maximum and leads to an ultimate state of inertia. Rifkin argues that unless modern society realizes that its resources are being unsustainably consumed and adjusts its definition of progress to include conserving resources and protecting the environment, a disastrous decline is bound to take over.

His next book, *Algeny* (1983), cowritten with Nicanor Perlas, became one of his most controversial. The term *algeny* refers to the process by which future scientists will be able to alter every aspect of living things. In this futuristic scenario, Rifkin envisions a time when parents will design their own offspring's genetic composition, a scientific paradigm of control that would replace the natural process of evolution. Sounding the alarm about the unforeseeable dangers inherent in this new technological relationship with nature, *Algeny* pleads for a reevaluation of priorities and a rejection of the notion that "if it can be done, it should be done." The book was well-received by the popular press but drew criticism from many in the scientific community, who felt that Rifkin was "antiprogress" and was ignoring the potential benefits of biotechnology.

Through the latter half of the 1980s, Rifkin's work involved protesting military biological testing labs and establishing a coalition to oppose the U.S. government's decision to issue patents for new animal species created by gene splicing. He also formed the National Coalition Against Surrogacy in opposition of surrogate parenthood, arguing against increasing interference with natural biological reproduction processes. In 1989 he published *Time Wars: The Primary Conflict in Human History*, in which he links environmental devastation to the contemporary preoccupation with speed and competition. With society's attention span narrowed to the moment, there is no framework for thinking about sustainability, says Rifkin, and the frantic pace of modern life consumes resources at such an accelerated rate that nature has no chance to replenish itself.

His next effort to draw attention to unsustainable resource consumption came in his 1992 book *Beyond Beef: The Rise and Fall of the Cattle Culture*, an argument against beef production, which he demonstrates to be one of the world's most flagrant sources of ecosystem degradation. He points out that more grain is grown in the United States to feed cattle than to feed people, that beef production wastes water and energy, and that South American rain forests are destroyed to make room for cattle. In 1995, Rifkin wrote *The End of Work* about the "third" or "informational" revolution and its effect on the labor force—what happens when robotics replace workers in retail, service, industry, agriculture? The less attractive possibilities are that the unemployed turn to crime, or that the government be obliged to expand its welfare system. On the other hand, society could possibly become more community- and service-oriented. This book was still stimulating discussion and debate among social scientists more than 10 years later.

An engaging public speaker and prolific writer, Rifkin continues to advance his ideas publicly, hoping to engage society in a dialogue on issues such as technology and genetic engineering. He and his wife, also a writer and activist, live near Washington, D.C.

**BIBLIOGRAPHY**

"Jeremy Rifkin: The Foundation on Economic Trends," www.foet.org; Otchet, Amy, "Jeremy Rifkin: Fears of a Brave New World," *UNESCO Courier*, 1998; Rifkin, Jeremy, *Biosphere Politics: A New Consciousness for a New Century*, 1991; Stix, Gary, "Dark Prophet of Biogenetics," *Scientific American*, 1997; Windstar Foundation's Choices for a Healthy Environment Speaker Video Series, *Jeremy Rifkin—Global Environmental Security: The Greenhouse Crisis* (video recording), 1989.

# Ringo, Jerome C.

(March 2, 1955– )
Clean Energy Organizer, President of the Apollo Alliance

The president of the Apollo Alliance, a coalition of labor, business, environmental, and community leaders working to catalyze a clean energy revolution that will put millions of Americans to work in a new generation of high-quality, green-collar jobs, Jerome Ringo is also the Immediate Past Chairman for the National Wildlife Federation (NWF). He served a two-year term from April 2005 to April 2007, after having been an elected member of the board since 1996. He was the first African American to head a large environmental organization in the United States, the NWF being the largest with four million members and an $80 million budget. He also was the only African American delegate at the 1998 Global Warming Treaty negotiations in Kyoto, Japan.

Jerome C. Ringo is the third of six children born to Earl Ringo, a postal worker, and Nellie Ringo, a nurse. Ringo grew up in coastal Lake Charles, Louisiana, at the height of the Civil Rights movement, hearing recordings of speeches by Martin Luther King, Jr., whom he

Jerome Ringo (Photograph courtesy of the Apollo Alliance)

considers a role model for life. He and his siblings witnessed the burning of a cross on their front lawn when they were preparing to integrate a previously white school. In the bayous he grew up hunting and fishing for food, and thus began his love of nature which would lead him at sixteen to be the first black ranger in the country's largest Boy Scout camp in Cimarron, New Mexico. He attended Louisiana Technical University and McNeese State University, then going to work instead in the petrochemical industry for 22 years producing gasoline, rocket fuel, and plastics.

While working in the petrochemical industry, Ringo was a union organizer and later became a community organizer. He helped join the forces of workers and nearby residents to find solutions to environmental contamination in the area infamously known as "Cancer Alley." In 1994 he took early retirement and founded the company Progressive Resources, Inc., which focused on improving the quality of life for his fellow Louisianans, especially the state's less wealthy and predominantly black residents. The company strove to fight "toxic terrorism," to borrow a phrase from Atlanta-based environmental justice activist Na'Taki Osborne, making sure the Clean Air and Clear Water Acts, as well as state and local environmental protection laws, were enforced locally in stopping the discharge of chemicals at the plants, while keeping them open and people employed. Ringo has also served with the North Lake Charles Economic Development District, the Calcasieu Estuary Environmental Task Force, the Louisiana Wildlife Federation, and the Coalition to Restore Coastal Louisiana.

Since participating in the Kyoto Protocol negotiations ten years ago, Ringo considers global warming the most important environmental issue of our time. He appeared in Vice President AL GOR's Oscar-winning documentary *An Inconvenient Truth*. In 2005 Ringo and his family experienced global warming first-hand with Hurricane Katrina and then by having to evacuate in the wake of Rita. The unprecedented intensity of these hurricanes was due to warmer waters brought on by global warming. The huge loss in coastal marshes that once buffeted the region also contributed. This is explained in part by the way in which levees were built in the area, not allowing land-replenishing sediment from the Mississippi River to flow through to the bayous. However, global warming also contributed to the rise in sea levels, which is predicted to become catastrophically worse for all the world's heavily populated coastal areas if greenhouse gas emissions are not reduced substantially.

In becoming president of the Apollo Alliance in 2005, whose name is inspired by the Apollo space program and whose mission is to promote clean energy/good job strategies through investments in energy efficiency, clean power, mass transit, next-generation vehicles, and emerging technology, as well as in education and training, Ringo has been able to draw on all his past experiences, strengths, and interests—conservationist, sportsman (he's an avid hunter and angler), community and labor organizer, and entrepreneur. The organization has been endorsed by the AFL-CIO and twenty-two international labor unions including the UAW and UMW, every major environmental organization, over fifty businesses and business leaders such as Mitch Kapor, the founder of Lotus, and hundreds of community-based organizations focused on environmental justice and green-collar jobs. In 2004, Apollo came out with a report showing that investing $300 billion over ten years in clean energy and energy efficiency programs nationwide would create more than three million high-quality, career-track jobs in the green economy, so as to "fight both poverty and pollution," as Apollo partner organization Green for All puts it. In March 2008 Apollo released a first-of-its-kind report called "Green-Collar Jobs in America's Cities," along with a companion piece for state policymakers entitled, "Greener Pathways."

In his capacity as president of the Apollo Alliance, Ringo has given speeches to countless local, national and international audiences, from the U.S. Conference of Mayors to the U.S. Congress, the United Nations, and international religious conventions. He is a member of Newsweek's Environment and Leadership Council, and Ebony Magazine, one of the oldest and most successful African American magazines, named Ringo one of the most influential African Americans in April 2006.

## Bibliography

Hertsgaard, Mark, "Green Grows Grassroots," *The Nation*, July 31, 2006; Kancler, Eric, "The Pioneer: An Interview with Jerome Ringo," *Mother Jones*, April 25, 2005; en.wikipedia.org/wiki/Jerome_Ringo; www.apolloalliance.org; www.kyotoplus.org/programm/referent/ringo.html.

## Ritter, Bill, Jr.

(September 6, 1956– )
Governor of Colorado

Former Denver District Attorney, Bill Ritter was elected Governor of Colorado in 2006 when his home state was at a crossroads: to develop natural gas and oil extraction, or move Colorado's largely energy-based economy toward a cleaner long-term vision. His decision became clear when he established a renewable energy standard as state law within a few months of taking office. His reputation as America's alternative energy Governor has grown since then.

Born on September 6, 1956, in Aurora, Colorado, the sixth of twelve children, young Bill Ritter ran mock trials in the family barn to decide which chickens to eat that week. At thirteen, his father, Bill Sr., abandoned the family for Utah. Bill learned new resourcefulness and grew an adult spiritual backbone provided by his mother and the Catholic Church. His debating skills and academic nature led him to law school, where at the University of Colorado he earned a J.D. in 1981. He began his career under the tutelage of a number of tough-love prosecutors.

In 1988, after winning a high-profile case against a police officer in his hometown of Aurora, Ritter exited stage-east to Africa, on a Catholic mission to help Zambians wrestle

Governor Bill Ritter signs House Bill 1281 and Senate Bill 100 into law on March 27, 2007, at the National Wind Technology Center. (Photograph courtesy of Colorado.gov)

with an enormous public health and environmental crisis. He experienced hope and fear in a new way altogether, writing in his journal: "Hope is not about optimism but the ability to act without the promise of an outcome. Death takes the gloves off."

Returning to Colorado, Ritter quickly ascended the ranks among skilled prosecutors and was selected in 1993 by then-Governor Roy Romer to serve as Denver District Attorney. Ritter was later elected in 1994 and re-elected in 1996 and 2000. His reputation as a principled and fair leader led the Colorado Democratic Party to nominate him as candidate for Governor in 2006. He ran against Republican U.S. Congressman Bob Beauprez, known in some environmental circles as "the elk whisperer" for his penchant for proposing that elk herds move off lands rich in natural gas and oil. Ritter's platform included a New Energy Economy for Colorado. In a largely Republican state, Ritter rode the tide of "the blueing of the American West," and in 2007 he was sworn in as Colorado's 41st Governor.

Governor Bill Ritter wasted no time in moving pre-existing energy corporations operating in Colorado toward cleaner, renewable energy. Building upon a 2004 ballot initiative to require power companies to produce 10 percent renewable energy by 2015, Governor Ritter and a Democratic legislature set a new goal: 20 percent by 2020. His Climate Action Plan for the state aims to reduce greenhouse gas emissions by 80 percent by 2050. To achieve this, conserving energy and producing renewable energy would be key.

Ritter and other appointees like former Executive Director of Environment Colorado, Matt Baker, recognized that energy efficiency begins at home, work, and how we get to work each day. Ritter began tightening the belt on consumption and mandated the greening of state government. Two executive orders cut energy consumption and paper consumption in state facilities by 20 percent by 2012, reduced water consumption by 10 percent, and petroleum products in state vehicles by 25 percent. He urged Coloradoans to increase energy efficiency in new and existing homes. Setting a top-down example, he and his family got their own house in order. The Ritters blew new insulation into the over 100-year-old Governor's Mansion, put up solar panels, and provided compact fluorescent lighting for the Capitol. Ritter enthusiastically signed up Colorado with Google's Climate Savers Computing Initiative, a program with the goal of cutting power consumption by computers in half by 2010, netting $5.5 billion in global energy savings and an annual reduction of 54 million tons of $CO2$ emissions per year.

Production of renewable energy was another priority of the Ritter Administration. In 2007 Governor Ritter inaugurated one of the nation's largest photovoltaic solar plants, taking advantage of southern Colorado's consistent sun. On the eastern plains, three new wind farms began producing enough energy to power 250,000 homes. He also set up the Governor's Energy Office (GEO) to provide incentives for new solar, wind, geothermal and biomass innovation projects. In short order, Ritter doubled the state's renewable energy portfolio.

Speaking on alternative energy resources, Ritter projects, "Colorado is open for business in what will be one of the most important industries of the 21st century."

Ritter's ability to attract investment capital in alternative energy in an otherwise agricultural and ranching state did not go unnoticed by other western states with solar, wind and geothermal resources. ConocoPhillips opened its Global Technology Center as an international hub for alternative-fuels research and development. Danish wind energy developer, Vestas, came to Colorado to build 1,800 wind turbine blades per year and create 650 jobs. The conversion of Colorado's economy to run a cleaner machine, and to create a homegrown educated workforce to run it is and will be an important part of his legacy. In recognition of his environmental fast track, Bill Ritter accepted the Charles H. Percy Award for Public Service on behalf of the Western Governors Association from the Alliance to Save Energy.

He and his first lady, Jeannie, have four children: August, Abe, Sam and Tally.

**BIBLIOGRAPHY**

Colorado: the Official State Web Portal, www.colorado.gov/governor; Interview with Governor Bill Ritter's press Secretary Evan Dreyer, April 21, 2008; Moffeit, Miles, "Former DA Follows His Own Path," *Denver Post*, July 31, 2006; Valenty, Richard, "Energy double play," *Colorado Daily*, March 27, 2007; Salon, www.colorado.gov/governorwww.salon.com/opinion/feature/2006/10/23/muckraker/index1.html.

## Robbins, John
(October 26, 1947– )
Founder of EarthSave International, Author

Best-selling author and lecturer John Robbins promotes a reduction in animal product consumption as a solution to a daunting number of environmental and human health problems and has become a leading advocate for healthy living through a plant-based diet. His meticulously researched *Diet for a New America* (1987) depicts some of the abuses of the meat and dairy industries—from environmental problems such as heavy use of pesticides and unsustainable consumption of water and energy, to the abuse of the animals themselves in their factory living conditions. Robbins more recently has written *The Food Revolution* (2001) and *Healthy at 100* (2007), that further detail how and why a vegetarian diet benefits vegetarians and the planet. Robbins founded EarthSave International, a nonprofit organization that supports healthy food choices, preservation of the environment, and a more compassionate world. An eloquent public speaker, Robbins has received standing ovations at thousands of conferences and speaking engagements worldwide as he continues to explore the link between society's food habits and the health of the planet.

John Robbins was born on October 26, 1947, in Glendale, California, to Irma and Irvine Robbins. His father and his uncle, Burton Baskins, founded Baskin-Robbins, which would one day become the largest ice cream company in the world. John grew up with his two sisters in a mansion in Encino, California, with an ice-cream-cone-shaped swimming pool in the backyard. He spent his summers working at the ice cream plant, and for many years he was groomed for the task of taking over and running the family company. But at the age of 21 Robbins realized that he did not want to make money through a product that contributes to bad health, and he stopped working for Baskin-Robbins. He walked away from his family's fortune and turned down scholarships at Harvard, Stanford, and Yale because he did not want to remain in the company of a privileged few. Instead he enrolled at the University of California at Berkeley in 1965, where he immediately got involved in social activism—joining the free speech, civil-rights, and antiwar movements. He graduated from Berkeley with an individual honors major in the history of political consciousness in 1969. He earned his master's degree in humanistic psychology from Antioch College West in 1976.

Eager to live a life closer to the land, Robbins and his wife, Deo (known as Annette when they met at Berkeley), relocated to a remote island in British Columbia in 1975, where they lived a simple vegetarian lifestyle, growing their own organic vegetables and offering yoga classes. In 1984 Robbins and his wife and son Ocean moved to Santa Cruz, California, where Robbins began working on a book. In 1987 *Diet for New America* was published and became a highly influential bestseller. In the book, Robbins warned that the meat-centered American diet had become profligate, wastefully directing resources toward beef production that could be much more efficiently used on plant crops. For example, production of an average pound of beef in the United States required 2,500 gallons of water (most of which went to irrigate the crops that the animal ate). Up to a hundred times more water was necessary to produce a pound of meat than a pound of wheat. If the people in the United States ate just 10 percent less beef, wrote Robbins, the amount of grain saved would feed 60 million people. Likewise, there was a direct relationship between livestock production and deforestation; of the 260 million acres of forest in the United States that had been razed to grow food for livestock, well over 200 million acres could be returned to forest if the food crops went directly to people instead. Livestock farms also used large quantities of pesticides, artificial hormones, antibiotics, and other toxic chemicals, and the residues invariably ended up in the meat, eggs, or dairy products being produced. Robbins cited studies that indicated that very high percentages of dioxin and other toxic chemical residues in the diets of Americans came from animal-based foods. Other health benefits of a plant-based diet were extolled in the book, such as lower cholesterol, lower blood pressure, and reduced cancer rates. The leading cause of death in the United States was heart disease, warned Robbins, and people with the standard meat-based diet had a 50 percent chance of dying from heart disease, while vegetarians had a 15 percent chance.

Robbins's book attracted a large following and garnered a Pulitzer Prize nomination. Not surprisingly, the National Cattlemen's Association did not agree with the accolades and went on the attack. According to EarthSave, the cattlemen paid $50,000 to the animal science department at Texas A&M University to write a dissenting report that the cattlemen then publicized widely, sending it to television, radio, and print media representatives in advance of Robbins's appearances and interviews. Nonetheless, the book's influence sparked a national reexamination of the impact of food production. In 1992 the WorldWatch Institute issued a landmark report addressing the impact of livestock production on the environment.

As a result of the overwhelming reader response to the book, Robbins founded EarthSave International, a nonprofit organization to support the educational work that *Diet for a New America* began. The group provides education and leadership for a shift toward more healthful and environmentally sound food choices, nonpolluting energy supplies, and sustainable use of natural resources. Robbins served as president of the organization for several years and now continues his involvement as chairman emeritus of its board of directors. In 1994 he received the Rachel Carson Award for his work.

Following *Diet for a New America*, Robbins has written several other books about health—spiritual and physical—and diet. *In Search of Balance* (1991, revised in 1997 and re-titled *The Awakened Heart*) was co-authored with Canadian songwriter Ann Mortifee and is a series of meditations on achieving harmony. *Reclaiming Our Health* (1996) examined conventional medicine and alternatives to it and demonstrated some of the many problems with health care in the United States. *The Food Revolution* (2001) extols the vegan diet and exposes the dangers of eating meat—both for individuals and for the health of the planet.

Robbins has become a widely sought public speaker and has lectured at major conferences sponsored by groups such as the Sierra Club, the Humane Society of the United States, Physicians for Social Responsibility, Oxfam, the United Nations Environmental Program, the United Nations Children's Fund (UNICEF), and other public interest organizations. There is evidence that his views are being accepted—in 1999 the Union of Concerned Scientists reported that eating meat is one of the two most environmentally damaging actions Americans perform (the other is driving cars). Later that year *Time* magazine, usually known for its conventional views, ran a two-page feature article depicting the damage to the environment and human health caused by modern meat production and predicted a collapse of the current meat-centered diet. Robbins even convinced his own father, who suffered from high cholesterol, high blood pressure, and diabetes, to take some of his advice and eat less ice cream.

Robbins currently works with Youth for Environmental Sanity, an organization co-founded by his son Ocean, helping to educate, inspire, and empower youth to become leaders in the movement to create a just and sustainable society. He lives with his wife in Santa Cruz, California.

### Bibliography

Carlin, Peter Ames, "Quitting Cold: Ice Cream Heir John Robbins Gave up Fortune to Follow a Rocky—But More Satisfying—Road," *People*, 1997; Colodny, Mark M., "Just Say 'No' to Ice Cream," *Fortune*, 1990; "EarthSave International," www.earthsave.org; "The Food Revolution," www.foodrevolution.org; Robbins, John, *Diet for a New America*, 1987; Robbins, John, *Reclaiming Our Health*, 1996; "YES! Helping Visionary Young Leaders Build a Better World," www.yesworld.org.

# Robin, Vicki

(July 6, 1945– )
President of the New Road Map Foundation

Vicki Robin is president of the New Road Map Foundation, an all-volunteer educational and charitable organization based in Seattle that champions conscious and practical, satisfying and sustainable alternatives to unabated consumerism—or, as she puts it, "tools for shifting to low-consumption, high-fulfillment lifestyles." She is the coauthor, with Joe Dominguez, of the 1992 book *Your Money or Your Life: Transforming Your Relationship with Money and Achieving Financial Independence*, a longtime best seller that details a nine-step program derived largely from the priceless fiscal education Dominguez received while working as a Wall Street stock analyst. In the Dominguez-Robin lexicon, financial independence is not a fanciful pot of gold at the end of the rainbow, but rather an enrichment of life resulting from conscious consumer choices. Although reducing the impact on the environment of U.S. mainstream society was not the initial motivation for Robin's advocacy of voluntary simplicity, the lifestyle's positive environmental implications became clear to her in the late 1980s, and many of those who choose a simpler lifestyle do so as a way of living in greater harmony with the earth.

Victoria Marie Robin was born on July 6, 1945, in Okmulgee, Oklahoma, to a family that knew both ends of the economic scale. Her mother was frugal from having grown up in a family hit hard by the Depression. But her father was a doctor, so the Robins did not want for money or its spoils. The family moved to Long Island, New York, and Vicki grew up always having what she needed but nonetheless understanding the importance of careful shopping. "Somehow I developed early a passion for experience over stuff," she said. "I learned that the less I spent, the more adventures I could have." For example, during her college years she lived in Europe for a year and a half on money her father had left her to finance her education—attending school in Madrid but taking every opportunity to travel as far north as Norway, as far east as Moscow, as far south as Turkey, and as far west as Portugal. She traveled on third-class train tickets, eating bread and oranges, staying in convents—making her money stretch literally across a continent.

After earning a degree in Spanish from Brown University in 1967, Robin pursued an acting career in New York for a while but became discouraged and took to the road with a $20,000 inheritance. While traveling in Mexico she met Dominguez, whose story intrigued her. Disillusioned by the earn-and-spend treadmill, he had retired from Wall Street at age 31 with a nest egg of $70,000. He had been living on the interest ever since. Although that interest only amounted to about $6,000 a year, Dominguez had determined through many years of tracking and evaluating his expenses that this was just enough for him to lead the life he wanted. Robin recognized the value in Dominguez's approach, and before long she, too, was living according to his definition of financial independence. As she and Dominguez traveled together and eventually settled in the Pacific Northwest, others became interested in Dominguez's strategy, and in 1976 he began giving living room talks, out of which grew the New Road Map Foundation. By 1980, he and Robin were traveling around the country giving seminars. Within five years, there was an audiocassette course, 300,000 copies of which were sold by mail. In 1992 came *Your Money or Your Life*, which to date has sold more than 700,000 copies and been translated into five languages. All proceeds from the book and other New Road Map educational programs are donated to nonprofit groups working toward a sustainable world.

Through the 27 years that Robin lived and worked with Dominguez, who died of cancer in 1997 at age 57, her thinking evolved beyond frugality for its own sake. In 1989 she attended the Globe-scope Pacific Assembly, the first public hearing in the United States on the World Commission on Environment and Development, and heard speaker after speaker say that the single biggest problem facing the world was the level and pattern of consumption in North America. Yet she heard no solutions, no suggestions of hope. "And there I sat, knowing from a decade of public education and two decades of living that, at the individual level, mere consciousness about aligning money and values tended to adjust consumption down by 20 percent and often far more," said Robin. "That's when I linked my chosen way of life with sustainability."

She has made spreading the word her vocation. She is a founding member and trustee of Sustainable Seattle, a voluntary civic network and forum concerned with the long-term cultural, economic, and environmental health and vitality of the Puget Sound region. She is also a founding board member of the Center for the New American Dream, a national organization with the goal of changing the pattern and overall quantity of consumption in the United States, without sacrificing quality of life. She was also a founding member of the Simplicity Forum (www.simplicityforum.org), an alliance of leaders who have committed to "achieving and honoring simple, just and sustainable ways of life." In addition, Robin served on a Task Force on Population and Consumption for the President's Council on Sustainable Development, and in 1994 she delivered testimony on overconsumption to the International Conference on Population and Development PrepCom at the United Nations.

Robin has not simply been preaching to the converted. Having a best-selling book has been her ticket into mainstream America—she has made appearances on *Oprah!* and *Good Morning America* and has been featured in *People* and *Woman's Day*. For those who want to delve deeper, The New Road Map Foundation through its Financial Integrity Program offer the nine-step Your Money or Your Life course (www.yourmoneyoryourlife.org), based on the book and program developed by Dominguez. More than a million people have taken advantage of the course—either in seminar form, through a study group, on-line, in a corporate setting, or in a home-study format. The average reduction in individual or household expenditures, after the course, has been 20 percent.

Robin was instrumental in launching an annual Buy Nothing Day moratorium on the busiest day of commerce each year, the day after Thanksgiving, the kickoff to the holiday shopping season. Her goals in the work may be to help effect deep transformations in U.S. culture, but Robin is not heavyhanded. At one Buy Nothing Day celebration in Seattle, for instance, she dressed as a doctor and dispensed medical advice on a spiritually debilitating malady called "affluenza."

Media coverage of the New Road Map Foundation never fails to note, with all due amazement, that Robin has scaled down her monetary needs to the point where she can live on about $8,500 a year. Robin resides in Seattle.

**BIBLIOGRAPHY**
Berner, Robert, "A Holiday Greeting Networks Won't Air," *Wall Street Journal*, 1997; Dominguez, Joe, and Vicki Robin, *Your Money or Your Life*, Viking, 1992; "New Road Map Foundation," www.newroadmap.org; Oldenburg, Don, "No-Shop Option," *Washington Post*, 1996; Wagenheim, Jeff, "If Money Were No Object," *New Age Journal*, 1990.

## Rockefeller, John D., Jr.
(January 29, 1874–May 11, 1960)
Philanthropist

A generous benefactor for the preservation of historic sites and the conservation of areas of natural beauty, John Davison Rockefeller Jr. took a particular interest in the improvement of the nation's national and state parks. His legacy includes the building of the national park on Mount Desert Island in Maine and substantial contributions to parks and natural areas throughout the United States.

John Davison Rockefeller Jr., the son of John D. Rockefeller, the founder of Standard Oil combine, and Laura Celestia Spelman, was born in Cleveland, Ohio, on January 29, 1874. In spite of the family's enormous wealth, Rockefeller and his three sisters were brought up to expect a life of hard work, religious observance, great financial responsibility, and social service. Both parents were devout Baptists, the elder Rockefeller giving both time and money to his church. Rockefeller's father modeled efficiency, rational organization, and hard work, all qualities that had made him one of the richest men in the world.

The Rockefellers lived in Cleveland and spent summers at Forest Hill, outside Cleveland. It was in Forest Hill and away from the city that the family was happiest. Rockefeller particularly enjoyed his first visit to Yellowstone National Park, when he was 12 years old. He kept a diary of the visit, describing walks and sights. This early experience, no doubt, foreshadowed his future efforts as a friend to the nation's parks.

The family moved to New York City while "JDR Jr.," as he later liked to be called, was still a child. After several years in residential hotels, the Rockefellers finally settled down in a spacious brownstone. Rockefeller attended private schools in New York City and received private tutelage during the family's long visits to Cleveland. He entered Brown University in 1893, where he was popular with his classmates, who called him "Johnny Rock." Having had only his sisters and the son of their caretaker to play with when he was a child, Rockefeller would later confess that his time in college was the happiest of his life. While he was not a great scholar, he worked hard, was elected to Phi Beta Kappa, and graduated in 1897.

Unlike his father, Rockefeller never developed an astuteness for the business world, nor did his father ever press him to do so. After college, Rockefeller performed odd jobs for his father in the New York office of Standard Oil and married Abigail (Abby) Aldrich, daughter of Sen. Nelson W. Aldrich of Rhode Island. Together they had six children, all of whom went on to notable careers.

John D. Rockefeller, Jr. (right) with John D. Rockefeller. (Library of Congress, Prints & Photographs Division, LC-USZ62-48511)

During the first years of the twentieth century, a portion of the ever-increasing Rockefeller fortune was transferred from petroleum into philanthropic projects and other industries requiring a boost in capital. Pleased with Rockefeller's handling of the sale of Mesabe Range iron ore properties to J. P. Morgan in 1901, his father gave him the responsibility of overseeing the management of the Colorado Fuel and Iron Company, in which he owned 40 percent. The labor crisis that resulted in the "Ludlow massacre" represented the most devastating publicity of Rockefeller's life and indicated that the days of unrestricted free enterprise and the industry owners' free hand with their labor force, which had made his father rich, were drawing to a close.

For some time, the management of the Colorado Fuel and Iron Company had attempted at every turn to prevent the unionization of its miners. Nevertheless, the western miners were fully determined to achieve company recognition of their right to bargain collectively. The resulting strike in 1914 led management to close the mines and evict the miners' families from their company-owned homes. Tensions rose and the area around Ludlow, Colorado, quickly became a battleground, into which the state militia were sent in an attempt to preserve the last remnants of a tenuous peace. Skirmishes broke out, and a total of 40 people were killed. One famous, though inaccurate, story involves company thugs and militiamen shooting and killing defenseless women and children, when in reality two women and 11 children crawled into a cave to escape the gunfire and died of suffocation. At the center of the crisis was Rockefeller, who stubbornly supported the management as they tried to treat modern labor problems with brutal, antiquated remedies.

The congressional investigations that followed blamed Rockefeller for the tragedy, and he quickly adopted a more modern policy. Following the recommendations made in a thorough study by Canada's future prime minister and labor relations expert, William Lyon Mackenzie King, Rockefeller went to the mining camps with a plan for employee representation. His willingness to listen and his many informal speeches, in which he emphasized the responsibilities and rights of both labor and management and the necessity for the two to work in harmony, helped to heal the wounds and construct a modified company-union arrangement that lasted until the Great Depression.

After World War I, Rockefeller removed himself completely from the business world and concentrated almost exclusively on public service and philanthropy. In the following years, he would contribute $56 million toward the restoration of Colonial Williamsburg, more than $86 million to schools and colleges, $85 million toward religious causes, and $81 million to medical, charitable, and relief organizations. But it was donations to the nation's national and state parks that captivated his most intense personal interest.

Rockefeller "discovered" Mount Desert Island in Maine when he summered in Bar Harbor with his family in 1908. In 1910, he purchased a summer home in Seal Harbor and began contributing to the associations that sought to preserve Mount Desert Island and surrounding areas. With the help of HORACE ALBRIGHT, field assistant to the director of the National Parks Service, and landscape architect FREDERICK L. OLMSTED, JR., Rockefeller began a campaign to create a national park on Mount Desert Island. During his lifetime he gave Acadia National Park, which encompasses Mount Desert Island, a total of $3.5 million in money, lands, and roads.

By 1924, Rockefeller's contributions to Acadia National Park were well known throughout the National Park Service. He was regarded as a potential benefactor for other parks and was courted by Park Service management. In 1924, Rockefeller and his three eldest sons visited Yellowstone National Park. They were met by Horace Albright, who at that time was the Yellowstone Park Superintendent. Rockefeller and Albright, who would later become director of the National Park Service, established a close relationship. More than 1,300 letters were exchanged between the two from 1924 to 1960 on various issues relating to the improvement and conservation of national and state parks. During that period, Rockefeller donated some $40 million to national and state parks, and funded private protection of such spectacular areas as the Grand Tetons. Rockefeller's son, LAURANCE ROCKEFELLER, would go on to become a well-known funder of conservation projects as well.

John D. Rockefeller Jr.'s business interests provided thousands of jobs during the Great Depression. Having entered into a scheme to redevelop the midtown section of New York at the end of the 1920s, Rockefeller found himself with a long-term lease on a considerable amount of heavily taxed real estate. In spite of the nation's economic woes, Rockefeller forged onward with plans to build skyscrapers that would house several enterprises, including the emerging network radio industry. The grand result of this project was the Rockefeller Center, the construction of which provided employment for thousands and was not completed until after World War II. That the Rockefeller Center would become a major tourist attraction also suggested that the Rockefeller talent for making money had not completely disappeared.

As his talented sons began to take over and Rockefeller slipped into the shadows, he made one last generous gesture with a donation of a $9 million plot of land on the East River of New York in 1946 to the United Nations for its home.

Rockefeller's father died in 1937, but for the rest of his life, he insisted upon being called John D. Rockefeller Jr., because, he said, there would always be only one John D. Rockefeller. He died in Tucson, Arizona, on May 11, 1960.

**BIBLIOGRAPHY**

Ernst, Joseph W., *"Dear Father"/"Dear Son": Correspondence of John D. Rockefeller and John D. Rockefeller, Jr.*, 1994; Ernst, Joseph W., *Worthwhile Places: Correspondence of John D. Rockefeller, Jr. and Horace M. Albright*, 1991; Fosdick, Raymond B., *John D. Rockefeller Jr.: A Portrait*, 1956; Harr, John Ensor and Peter J. Johnson, *The Rockefeller Conscience: An American Family in Public and in Private*, 1991; Newhall, Nancy W., *A Contribution to the Heritage of Every American: The Conservation activities of John D. Rockefeller, Jr.*, 1957; "The Rockefeller Archive Center "JDR Jr. Biographical Sketch," archive.rockefeller.edu/bio/jdrjr.php.

## Rockefeller, Laurance
(May 26, 1910– July 11, 2004)
Philanthropist

Grandson of John D. Rockefeller of Standard Oil fame, Laurance Rockefeller spent his life sharing his passion for all places wild. He donated millions of dollars to environmental causes through the Rockefeller Brothers and LSR Funds and was the driving force behind at least two national parks, one in Vermont and one in the U.S. Virgin Islands. Serving on the national Outdoor Recreation Resources Review Commission (ORRRC) in the 1950s, long before green politics were fashionable, Rockefeller helped shape national policy that protected federal lands in the following decades. He received a Congressional Gold Medal for Conservation in 1991.

Laurance Spelman Rockefeller was born on May 26, 1910, in New York City, the fourth child of JOHN D. ROCKEFELLER JR. and Abby (Aldrich) Rockefeller. He was one of six children in the latest generation of a family known as industrialists and bankers. His patriarchal grandfather John D. Rockefeller was among the barons of the oil industry; his matriarchal grandfather Nelson Aldrich was a senator from Rhode Island. The Rockefellers were encouraged to find work of value, and Laurance chose conservation as his specialty.

Rockefeller's father, John D. Rockefeller Jr., was likely the most generous philanthropist in the history of conservation to that time. The developer of New York's Rockefeller Center, he was deeply involved in the establishment of national parks. Instrumental in the founding and expansion of Grand Teton National Park, he also established Colonial Williamsburg and donated land for the United Nations headquarters. From an early age, Laurance shared his father's interest in conservation and wildlife protection. His love of nature was cultivated through family travels to such places as the Rocky Mountains and the Maine seacoast. In 1924 and 1926, Laurance spent summers in the West, visiting Jackson Hole, Wyoming; Taos, New Mexico; and the Grand Canyon in Arizona. The trips shaped his worldview and sparked a lifelong interest in natural places and Native American traditions.

Like other Rockefellers, Laurance attended Ivy League colleges. He graduated from Princeton University in 1932 with concentrations in economics and philosophy and moved on to Harvard Law School. While there he met Mary Billings French, granddaughter of early Vermont conservationist Frederick Billings. With an eye on marriage and the business world, Laurance decided to leave law school. He and Mary French were married in her hometown of Woodstock, Vermont, in August 1934. In time they would have four children: Laura, Marion, Lucy, and Larry.

Stepping into real-world ventures, Rockefeller assumed his grandfather's seat on the New York Stock Exchange in 1937. Ably forecasting business trends, he participated in the founding of Eastern Airlines. At the same time, he assumed some of his father's conservationist roles. In 1940, he stepped in as president of the Jackson Hole Preserve, a corporation the family had formed to protect scenic values and natural habitats of land it held at the base of Wyoming's Teton Range. He and FAIRFIELD OSBORN, president of the New York Zoological Society, established a biological station on the property to facilitate scientific study of the area's wildlife.

Rockefeller soon found a way to combine his twin interests in nature and business. In 1951, he began to construct Jackson Lake Lodge in what would become part of Grand Teton National Park. The first of Rockefeller's grand resorts, it ignited a storm of controversy. Though Grand Teton was not intended as a wilderness park, nor was it considered an appropriate site for major tourist development. Rockefeller argued that a planned resort would preserve the openness of surrounding land. He answered critics by building the lodge to standards of aesthetic beauty tempered by natural interaction. The resort opened in 1955, giving Rockefeller his first success as a developer. Two years later, in 1957, he received the Horace Marden Albright Scenic Preservation Medal from the American Scenic and Historic Preservation Society for his efforts.

After Grand Teton, Rockefeller moved to the Caribbean and bought a large portion of St. John Island in the U.S. Virgin Islands. There he developed the Caneel Bay Plantation Resort, meant to enhance natural surroundings of coral, beaches, and jungle, for guests to engage in what we now call ecotourism. To maintain the lush habitat that surrounded his property, he donated most of his holdings to the National Park system. In all, he gave the U.S. government more than 5,000 acres on St. John, leading to the establishment of Virgin Islands National Park in 1956. The hotel and the park were dedicated on the same day, December 1, 1956. Rockefeller soon built other hotels with similar environmental aesthetics, including Dorado Beach Hotel in Puerto Rico (1958) and the Mauna Kea Resort in Hawaii (1961).

At the same time he was building grand hotels in the 1950s, Rockefeller served as chairman of the Outdoor Recreation Resources Review Commission, the first sweeping federal review of the American outdoors. It was a time when many of the programs that now protect against pollution and designate federally protected wilderness areas were first proposed. Serving under presidents Eisenhower and Kennedy, Rockefeller orchestrated an assessment of the recreation and conservation needs and desires of the American people, outlining the policies and programs required to meet those needs. Reports issued by the commission laid the framework for nearly all significant environmental legislation of the following three decades.

Rockefeller owned the luxurious Woodstock Inn and Resort in Woodstock, Vermont, listed by *Conde Nast Traveler* as one of the top North American resorts. Together with his wife, he was instrumental in the historic and environmental preservation of Woodstock. Frederick Billings had established a progressive dairy farm and managed forest on the GEORGE PERKINS MARSH farm there. The Rockefellers sustained Billings's mindful forestry practices on the property, which served as their home, and in 1983 established the Billings Farm and Museum to continue the farm's work and to interpret rural Vermont life and history. The farm is now a private nonprofit educational institution within Marsh-Billings-Rockefeller National Historical Park, created in 1992 when the Rockefellers gave the estate lands to the federal government.

Through investments and business ventures, Rockefeller continued to add to the family fortune. In 1969, the Rockefeller-controlled Venrock Associates was established as a venture capital firm. It had noteworthy successes, including seed money investments in Intel Corporation and Apple Computer, among other companies. The money, along with that remaining in family trusts and philanthropic foundations, allowed Rockefeller to give generously to environmental interests. Among his giftees were the Laurance S. Rockefeller Library at the California Institute of Integral Studies; the PBS *Religion and Ethics* series; the Library of Congress *American Memory* series, "The Evolution of the Conservation Movement, 1850–1920"; the state of New York, which was granted funds for the acquisition of the 88-acre Rockwood Hall property on the Hudson River near Mt. Pleasant in November 1998; and the Euan P. McFarlane Environmental Leadership Awards for conservation efforts in the Caribbean.

Rockefeller played an important role in the establishment of such conservation organizations as the Conservation Foundation and the American Conservation Association, Inc. He also served on the board of the Citizens Advisory Committee on Environmental Quality, among hundreds of other board commitments. Through the years he participated on the boards of the National Geographic Society, the National Recreation and Parks Association, regional conservation societies, and the New York Zoological Society, to name just a few.

Premier among all his awards was the Congressional Gold Medal he received in 1991. That year, the medal was given for the first time in honor of contributions to conservation and historic preservation. It rewarded Rockefeller's "driving passion" for nature, recognizing his service as environmental adviser to five consecutive presidents and the millions of dollars he donated to numerous conservation organizations. Rockefeller died on July 11, 2004, at his home in the Hudson River Valley.

**BIBLIOGRAPHY**
Bernstein, Adam "Laurance Rockefeller Dies at 94", *Washington Post*, 2004; Harr, John Ensor, and Peter J. Johnson, *The Rockefeller Conscience: An American Family in Public and in Private*, 1991; Kaufman, Michael T., "Laurance S. Rockefeller, Passionate Conservationist and Investor, Is Dead at 94," *New York Times*, 2004; "The Rockefeller Archive Center, Laurance S. Rockefeller Biographical Sketch," archive.rockefeller.edu/bio/laurance.php; Rockefeller, Mary, and Laurance Rockefeller, "Parks, Plans, and People," *National Geographic*, 1967; Winks, Robin W., *Laurance S. Rockefeller: Catalyst for Conservation*, 1997.

## Rodale, Robert
(March 27, 1930–September 20, 1990)
Organic Agriculture Expert, Publisher, Writer

As the chief executive officer of Rodale Press, which publishes magazines such as *Organic Gardening*, *Prevention*, and *Runner's World*, Robert Rodale came to be known as an innovative promoter of healthy active lifestyles. But his influence went beyond that—he spent a lifetime studying and advocating organic farming, focusing especially on its role in regenerating food production in developing countries. His belief in the importance of organic agriculture led him to write *The Basic Book of Organic Gardening* (1971), a syndicated column titled "Organic Living," and *Save Three Lives* (1991), a book about preventing famine by reestablishing traditional farming techniques. Through the Rodale Institute, a nonprofit educational research organization, and its 300-acre research farm in Pennsylvania, Rodale studied ways to improve devastated agricultural systems in Third World countries; he spent the last few years of his life sharing his knowledge around the globe.

Robert David Rodale was born in New York City on March 27, 1930, to Jerome Irving and Anna (Andrews) Rodale. That same year, his father moved his electrical business from New York to Emmaus, Pennsylvania, and set up the family's residence in Allentown. J. I. Rodale then went on to establish a publishing business, which would eventually become Rodale Press. Increasingly interested in organic farming, J. I. Rodale purchased a 60-acre demonstration farm just outside Emmaus, where he pioneered research and demonstration of organic farming practices.

In 1947 Robert enrolled in Lehigh University in Bethlehem, Pennsylvania, to study English and journalism. Two years later, his father pressed him to lighten his coursework so that he could help out with the family business. Robert agreed, on the condition that he be allowed to go on a trip somewhere first. His father gave him a couple hundred dollars, his mother loaned him her new car, and he spent six weeks driving around rural Mexico by himself. This was his first contact with people in a developing country, and their generosity and the relative simplicity of their lifestyles made a great impact on him. In 1951 he married Ardath Harter, a school counselor, with whom he would eventually have five children: Heather, Heidi, David, Maria, and Anthony. Rodale continued attending Lehigh until 1952, but did not receive a degree until he was awarded an honorary doctorate in 1989.

Rodale was named president of Rodale Press in 1951 and helped his father carry on with his commitment to teach people how to grow better food by cultivating healthier soil and eliminating synthetic chemicals. By 1953, Robert Rodale had taken over as editor and publisher of *Organic Gardening* and *Prevention* magazines. Rodale was always a physical fitness enthusiast and was himself a champion skeet shooter. At the age of 38 he returned to Mexico, this time as a member of the U.S. Olympic skeet shooting team in the 1968 Pan-American games, where he won a gold medal.

In 1971, Ballantine published his book *The Basic Book of Organic Gardening*. That year his father died, and Robert Rodale took over the leadership of Rodale Press entirely. Under his guidance, the family-owned Rodale Press grew into a strong positive force, actively seeking to improve the health of its readers and its workers. Rodale's company employs over a thousand people, and all benefit from the nutritious food offered by its cafeteria and from the well-equipped employee fitness center. In 1983, Rodale Press became one of the first large U.S. companies to implement a no-smoking policy.

Perhaps Rodale's greatest impact has come from his role in promoting environmentally sound farming practices worldwide. *Organic Gardening* has become the largest gardening magazine in the world—providing its readers with the tools, ideas, sources, and information they need to successfully grow anything they choose without chemicals. Rodale was also instrumental in the success of the Rodale Institute: a nonprofit research and service organization (separate from the publishing company) that works with people around the globe to develop profitable food systems that preserve environmental and human health. Its headquarters is a 333-acre experimental farm in Berks County, Pennsylvania. He continually raised concerns over the damaging effects of pesticide use, both to humans and the environment. He once wrote an editorial in *Organic Gardening*, called "Tiptoe Through the Toxic Tulips" (1976), in which he issued a prophetic warning about the harm from combinations of pollutants in the environment. Over 20 years later, researchers are finding exactly that—the toxicity of certain chemicals in combination can be 1,000 times more than any of the combined chemicals alone.

Another of Rodale's passions was preventing famine in Third World countries by developing agricultural systems that can sustain people while replenishing their misused land. In his book *Save Three Lives: A Plan for Famine Prevention*, Rodale points out many problems with established famine relief programs, such as the fact that much of the food sent to famine-stricken countries comes from the surplus crops of rich nations like the United States—and is often inappropriate for people who are starving. The worst problem lies in misguided attempts to help poorer countries "improve" their agricultural practices by bringing in heavy machinery and synthetic chemicals. Methods like these were developed in temperate climates and quickly deplete fragile tropical soils. Also, developing countries are urged to plant cash crops such as corn, cotton, or rice—water-intensive crops that are out of place in arid climates and that displace valuable native crops. Rodale praised many of the indigenous food plants he saw on his travels, plants that are drought resistant, highly nutritious, and resistant to diseases and pests native to the land they evolved in. He proposed a system of home gardens and small farms, which return to the use of native food plants and traditional, organic farming methods. He traveled extensively, particularly in Africa, but also in Mexico and Russia to help put his theories into practice. Before his death, China and Eastern Europe had asked for his help in finding solutions to their food crises.

In 1990, shortly after he finished *Save Three Lives*, Rodale was traveling in the Soviet Union. He was there to develop plans for Russian-language editions of magazines and books on sustainable agriculture. On September 20, 1990, while en route to the Moscow airport, he was killed when the car in which he was riding collided with a bus.

## BIBLIOGRAPHY

Long, Cheryl, "Chemical Combinations 1,000 Times as Deadly!" *Organic Gardening*, 1997; Rodale, Anthony, "Robert Rodale: a Retrospective 1930-1990," www.seedsofchange.com/cutting_edge/robert_rodale.asp; "Robert Rodale Interview" *Whole Earth Review*, 1988; Rodale, Robert, *The Basic Book of Organic Gardening*, 1971; Rodale, Robert, *Save Three Lives: A Plan for Famine Prevention*, 1991; Rodale, Robert, "Tiptoe Through the Toxic Tulips," *Organic Gardening*, 1976; Simson, Maria, "Bob Rodale and Sierra Club Fight World Hunger," *Publishers Weekly*, 1991.

## Rolfes, Anne
(October 22, 1968– )
Air Quality Expert, Founder and Director of the Louisiana Bucket Brigade

Anne Rolfes, founder and director of the Louisiana Bucket Brigade (LABB), an environmental watchdog monitoring oil refineries and chemical plants, had to travel to Africa in order to see the environmental damages of her own home state of Louisiana. Under her supervision, the Louisiana chapter of the Bucket Brigade has been the most successful, prolific and vocal of all the Brigades operating in the country.

Rolfes was born on October 22, 1968, and raised in Lafayette, Louisiana, the only child of a pediatrician and a special education schoolteacher. Lafayette is an oil town and Rolfes grew up very aware of the oil industry, namely its positive presence that was extolled in almost every part of the community, from fair and trade shows to shopping malls named after oil refineries. Rolfes describes her upbringing as mainstream. Her high school and college years were not marked by activism in any way. She credits her mother, who worked in a predominantly African American school, for raising her to be aware of social injustices.

In 1986, Rolfes moved to Boulder to attend the University of Colorado, working on a bachelor's degree in political science. In 1991, with a strong desire to visit Africa for no more reason than to see how another part of the world lived, Rolfes joined the Peace Corps. Though better-suited and trained as a teacher, Rolfes, at the time of her Peace Corps interview, was so heavily under the influence of the Steinbeck novel, *The Grapes of Wrath*, that she spent most of her interview discussing soil quality. Subsequently, she was sent to Togo in West Africa as an agro-forester developing tree nurseries.

In 1994, Rolfes returned to the United States. She started volunteering at food banks in San Francisco and tried to figure out what to do with her life. Reading about the environmental damage caused by Shell Oil in Nigeria, she was reminded of the people in Togo, who ultimately moved her to get involved in activist organizations demanding oil companies be more responsible to the communities that host their refineries. Her first protest actions were staged in front of gas stations around the Bay area, but eventually took her to Benin, Nigeria, where she worked with refugees who had been driven off their land by Shell. It was then that she really began to look homeward, wondering about the paradox of wealth produced by oil companies as well as the environmental damages and the effects on the health of surrounding communities.

Rolfes returned to Louisiana where she had a more familiar understanding of the communities. It was in her hometown of Lafayette that she attended a session with local chemist, WILMA SUBRA, on acquiring "bucket samples" of which among 100 different toxins were in the air. Rolfes saw that working with a tool that could really help regular people understand what they were living with resonated strongly with her.

The Bucket Brigade was originally started in California in 1995 at the behest of famed attorney Edward Masry (Erin Brokovich's lawyer), who hired an environmental engineer to design a low-cost system for community members living near petroleum refineries and chemical plants to be able to collect and test their own air samples. The "bucket," a simple device which collects air samples that can then be sent to a lab for testing of 100 different toxic gases, including benzene, sulfur and vinyl chloride, has become a powerful tool for "fenceline" communities to have leverage against major corporations.

Rolfes began volunteering in communities near petrochemical plants and in 2000 founded the Louisiana Bucket Brigade. In Norco, Louisiana, an already thirty-year-old battle had existed between the Diamond community and the Shell Motiva plant next door. Citizens in Norco linked the exorbitant number of health problems in their community to its proximity to the Shell Motiva plant. Property values sank so low that most people could not sell their homes and leave.

Rolfes entered the fray on fire, having just seen the life-and-death situations created by Shell in Nigeria. Rolfes wanted to raise the profile of the Norco issue to a level that Shell would fear. And in 2002, empowering the community with the bucket, Rolfes succeeded in convincing Shell to buy out residents' houses at fair market value and to install more stringent environmental regulation.

Since then the LABB has gone on to work with communities in St. Bernard Parish near the Chalmette Refinery, New Sarpy, Baton Rouge, Lake Charles, Algiers, and Reserve. In 2003, in response to a petition put out by LABB documenting Louisiana's Department of Environmental Quality's lax enforcement, the EPA Inspector General asked for an investigation of the state's environmental programs. Rolfes led the largest collection of community-gathered air samples in the U.S. and documented hundreds of violations of state and federal air quality standards.

Then came Katrina. Rolfes and the Bucket Brigade faced one of their biggest challenges to date: assisting residents whose homes were among the hardest hit by the flooding of Hurricane Katrina and the Murphy Oil spill. Katrina toppled an oil tank and sent more than one million gallons of crude into nearby homes.

Rolfes continues to monitor the air quality around Norco, suspicious of the good neighbor initiative started by Shell Motiva, which only takes air samples every six days and does not measure sulfur compounds. In 2007 she was awarded the Robert Wood Johnson Foundation award for Community Health Leaders for her work advocating for pollution control, health protections and fair compensation so longtime residents living on or near contaminated areas can relocate.

Currently, Rolfes is working on uniting the communities of Louisiana, one community at a time. She has been working intensely with a neighborhood next to an Exxon Mobile facility, as well as raising the profile of communities around the world affected by Shell, including South Africa, Brazil, the Philippines, Ireland, and Curacao.

**BIBLIOGRAPHY**
Personal interview, April 11, 2008; "Why Stay? Activist Anne Rolfes stays to monitor the long-term environmental impacts," Matthew Penix, *New Orleans City Business*, Feb. 26, 2007; "Group keeps eye on Shell's air-monitoring program," Eliza Strickland. *Louisiana Weekly*. Dec 22, 2003, www.louisianaweekly.com/weekly/news/articlegate.pl?20031222f; "We Want Answers!" Michael Tisserand. *Gambit Weekly*. Nov. 08, 2005, www.bestofneworleans.com/dispatch/2005-11-08/news_feat.php; www.communityhealthleaders.org/leaders/leader/anne_rolfes; www.labucketbrigade.org/about/staff.shtml; www.rpcv.org/pages/sitepage.cfm?id=1801&ref=2.

## Rolston, Holmes, III
(November 19, 1932– )
Environmental Philosopher, Theologian, Founder of *Environmental Ethics*

Holmes Rolston III is widely recognized as the father of environmental ethics as a modern academic discipline. He has devoted his career to the development of a philosophical interpretation of the natural world and is regarded as one of the world's leading scholars on the philosophical, scientific, and religious conceptions of nature. His body of work and his role as a founder of the influential academic journal *Environmental Ethics* have been instrumental in establishing, shaping, and defining the modern discipline of environmental philosophy.

Holmes Rolston III was born in Staunton, Virginia, on November 19, 1932, to Holmes and Mary Winifred (Long) Rolston. He grew up in the Shenandoah Valley, where his father was a rural pastor. Their house had no electricity, and water came from a cistern pump outside and another cistern on a hill behind the house from which water flowed by gravity to the kitchen inside. Rolston's mother had been raised on a farm in Alabama, which Rolston would visit for a month each summer and where he explored the woods and swamps. From a very early age he was deeply immersed in nature.

Rolston studied physics as an undergraduate at Davidson College in Davidson, North Carolina, because physics seemed to him to be the science that would best help him understand nature. During his studies, Rolston became interested in biology after working with an entomologist at Davidson; he began to recognize that physics alone could not explain nature the way he had hoped. While physics sought to address order and universal laws of nature, biology explored the more alluring wild nature. Upon completing his undergraduate degree in 1953, Rolston turned to theology and decided to attend Union Theological Seminary. Once he completed his seminary studies in 1956, Rolston pursued theology and religious studies at the University of Edinburgh, completing his Ph.D. in 1958.

Rolston spent the next ten years as a Presbyterian pastor in rural southwest Virginia. Taking two days off each week, Rolston would spend one hiking the southern Appalachian Mountains and the other sitting in on biology classes at nearby East Tennessee State University. After botany and zoology came geology, mineralogy, and paleontology. During this time, Rolston learned the ecology

Holmes Rolston, III (Photograph courtesy of Holmes Rolston, III)

of the mountain woods and discovered that trees and country places had as much to teach him as the scholars.

While he was developing a passion for the wonders of nature, Rolston became alarmed by how quickly the natural world was being lost to development. The sense of wonder he felt for nature turned to horror as he discovered his favorite forests scarred by clear-cuts, mountains stripped for coal, soils eroded away, and wildlife populations decimated. Rolston worked to preserve Mount Rogers, in southwest Virginia, and Roan Mountain, in northeast Tennessee, and to maintain and relocate the Appalachian Trail so that it passed mainly through undeveloped areas.

In his search for a philosophy of nature to complement his biology, Rolston received his first formal training in philosophy when he entered the philosophy program at the University of Pittsburgh. Struggling for respect in a program that considered the philosophy of nature disreputable, Rolston received a master's degree in the philosophy of science in 1968 and accepted a post at Colorado State University in Fort Collins, where he has remained, and currently holds the prestigious position of University Distinguished Professor.

In 1975, Rolston's essay, "Is There an Ecological Ethic?," published in *Ethics*, provocatively probed questions and issues regarding the potential of nature to have an intrinsic value. While debates on this issue had existed since ALDO LEOPOLD's *Sand County Almanac*, published in 1949, Rolston's essay initiated renewed interest in the debate, which ultimately led to the creation of the refereed journal, *Environmental Ethics*, in 1979. Rolston was a founder of that journal and still serves as the associate editor.

Rolston's 1988 book, *Environmental Ethics: Values in and Duties to the Natural World*, is generally recognized as the best available work in its field. Rolston presents a strong argument for a value-centered ecological ethic. He claims that intrinsic values objectively exist at the species, biotic community, and individual levels in nature and that these values impose on humans certain obligations to species and their ecosystems. This intrinsic value of nature is separate from its instrumental value, the latter motivating humans to conserve the environment for their own benefit. Sometimes the two kinds of values complement each other; sometimes they conflict.

Rolston is a prolific writer, having written six books acclaimed in critical notice in professional journals and the national press, chapters in 100 books, and over 100 articles. His work is published and read the world over and has been translated into many languages. He has also served on the Board of Governors of the Society for Conservation Biology. During the 1997–1998 academic year, Rolston delivered the Gifford Lectures at the University of Edinburgh, which resulted in his book, *Genes, Genesis, and God: Values and Their Origins in Natural and Human History.* Because of his prominent status in environmental philosophy, Rolston is often sought after by conservation and policy groups. He has served as a consultant for more than two dozen such groups, including the U.S. Congress and a presidential commission. He has also been a member of the Working Group on Ethics of the World Conservation Union.

Rolston won two very important prizes during the early years of the 21st century: the 2003 Templeton Prize, which is awarded each year to an individual who has made outstanding progress toward spiritual realities; and Villanova's 2005 Mendel Medal, to scientists who have made outstanding contributions to the ethical and religious dimensions of genetics and science.

In early 2000, Rolston visited Antarctica and while there became the only environmental philosopher to have lectured on all seven continents. Avocationally, he is a backpacker, an accomplished field naturalist, and a respected bryologist.

**BIBLIOGRAPHY**

"Holmes Rolston, III," lamar.colostate.edu/~rolston; Rolston, Holmes, III, "A Philosopher Gone Wild," in Karnos, David D., and Robert G. Shoemaker, eds., *Falling in Love with Wisdom: American Philosophers Talk about Their Calling*, 1993; Preston, Christopher J., and Wayne Ouderkirk, eds., *Nature, Value, Duty: Life on Earth with Holmes Rolston, III.* 2007; Rolston, Holmes, III, *Philosophy Gone Wild: Environmental Ethics*, 1989; Rolston, Holmes, III, *Science and Religion: A Critical Survey*, 1987, new edition 2006; Rolston, Holmes, III, "Values Deep in the Woods," *American Forests*, 1988.

## Roosevelt, Franklin D.

(January 30, 1882–April 12, 1945)
U.S. President

Franklin Delano Roosevelt (FDR), state senator and governor of New York and 32nd president of the United States, is known, in addition for his accomplishments in combating the Great Depression, as a dedicated nature lover and conservationist. During his 12 years as president, he appointed such conservationists to his cabinet as Secretary of the Interior HAROLD ICKES and Soil Conservation Service Director HUGH HAMMOND BENNETT. He established the Civilian Conservation Corps, which gave jobs to two and a half million men in soil erosion prevention, reforestation, and national parks facilities construction.

Franklin Delano Roosevelt was born on January 30, 1882, at his family's Hyde Park estate on the Hudson River in upstate New York. His father, James Roosevelt, was vice president of the Delaware and Hudson Railroad and was 52 years old when Franklin Delano was born. His mother, half the age of her husband, was from a wealthy family that owned the estate across the Hudson River. Roosevelt's patrician heritage allowed for home schooling with tutors and governesses until the age of 14 and frequent trips with his parents to Europe. Isolated from his peers, he spent his free time roaming the estate, tracking rabbits, and shooting birds with a rifle given to him by his grandfather. He amassed a

Franklin D. Roosevelt (Library of Congress, Prints & Photographs Division, LC-DIG-npcc-00318)

collection of 300 specimens, and as a reward for his interest, his grandfather gave him a life membership in the American Museum of Natural History.

Inspired by his fifth cousin, President THEODORE ROOSEVELT, Franklin Delano Roosevelt became interested in politics while studying at Harvard University. He was editor of the *Harvard Crimson* student newspaper and was elected chair of his class. He graduated in 1903 and went on to study law at Columbia University. He married a distant cousin, Anna Eleanor Roosevelt, in 1905. Although FDR had an affair early in the marriage that deeply hurt his wife, Eleanor remained loyal and did much to advance his political career. She also helped cultivate his concern for the plight of the nation's poorest.

Roosevelt's political career commenced in 1911 when he was elected to the New York legislature. As chairman of the Forest, Fish, and Game Committee, he introduced eight bills to regulate fishing and hunting. Another of his bills proposed that tree cutting be restricted even on private land, if it would cause environmental damage. To testify for that bill, Roosevelt called in U.S. Forest Service founder GIFFORD PINCHOT, whose argument in favor of the bill included some visual evidence, two slides of a Chinese valley. The first was a painting, circa 1500, of the verdant valley; the second was a recent photograph showing the same area denuded and desertlike after four centuries of indiscriminate cutting. Roosevelt was quite affected by these images, and historian Stephen Fox cites them as inspiration for his politics. In 1912 he declared that unregulated competition in the environmental arena could lead to total deforestation, which would in turn cause floods, erosion, and more problems. Cooperation within a community could assure that greed would not lead to such abuse. This, Fox states, was the ideological foundation upon which Roosevelt's progressive politics would be built.

Roosevelt did not consider himself a conservationist as such, since most conservationists in those days were hearty big game hunters like his cousin Theodore. In 1921, Roosevelt had been stricken with polio and lost the use of his legs, which restricted him to his specially designed roadster, a wheel chair, or uncomfortable leg braces and crutches. Roosevelt nonetheless had a deep appreciation of the aesthetics of nature. He loved Hyde Park and closely supervised his gardeners. He was a proponent of the managed forestry that Forestry Division chief Gifford Pinchot had introduced during Theodore Roosevelt's presidency and purchased a 1,200-acre degraded farm next to Hyde Park that he had his gardeners reforest in an attempt to regenerate the land.

The conservation policies that Roosevelt implemented when he was elected to his first term as president in 1932 reflected a belief that he shared with Pinchot: that natural resources should provide "the greatest good for the greatest number of people." When he took office, Roosevelt was faced with millions of unemployed people suffering in a severely depressed economy and an increasingly degraded environment. Several top officials in his administration, including two men of his cabinet, helped design projects that would provide jobs and further his idea of conservation. Secretary of Agriculture Henry Wallace, worried about the environmental effects of drought and the dust bowl it was causing, successfully lobbied for legislation that would pay farmers to leave degraded land fallow. Director of the new Soil Conservation Service, Hugh Bennett, set up demonstration projects and instructed tens of thousands of farmers in soil conservation methods. Secretary of the Interior Harold Ickes oversaw Roosevelt's pet project, the Civilian Conservation Corps. It put two and one-half million unemployed men to work at such tasks as reforestation, prevention of soil erosion, flood control, and improving accessibility in national parks and forests. In addition to providing employment, the CCC fostered a love for the outdoors that many of its employees had never before had the opportunity to develop. Roosevelt also initiated the Tennessee Valley Authority (TVA) hydroelectric project, which was seen as a cure-all for that poor and neglected region of the country. The series of dams would create jobs and electric power. Decades later, environmentalists would criticize its environmental impact, but at the time, few found fault with the TVA.

Conservation organizations found Roosevelt and Secretary Ickes eminently open to their concerns. They listened to conservation leaders' arguments for preserving wildlife and acted on those leaders' recommendations to close government lands to duck hunting, to refuse to extend hunting season, and to protect trumpeter swans from an artillery range in Utah. Ickes in particular sympathized with supporters of unspoiled wilderness. He and National Forest supervisor ROBERT MARSHALL worked hard to keep certain areas roadless despite the complaints of Roosevelt, who when asked to keep Olympic National Park free of roads, asked "How would I get in?"

Roosevelt, an immensely popular president, was elected to that office four times. He died shortly after he commenced his fourth term, on April 12, 1945, in Warm Springs, Georgia, of a cerebral hemorrhage.

**BIBLIOGRAPHY**

Black, Brian, "Roosevelt, Franklin D.," *Encyclopedia of Earth*, 2006, www.eoearth.org/article/Roosevelt,_Franklin_D.; Fox, Stephen, *The American Conservation Movement: John Muir and His Legacy*, 1981; Nixon, Edgar B., ed., *Franklin Roosevelt and Conservation, 1911–1945*, 2 volumes, 1957; Riesch-Owen, Anna L., *Conservation under FDR*, 1983; Woolner, David B. and Henry L. Henderson, *FDR and the Environment*, 2005.

## Roosevelt, Theodore

(October 27, 1858–January 6, 1919)
U.S. President

While remembered for his prolific accomplishments during his 30-year political career, conservationists honor Theodore Roosevelt as the first U.S. president with a deep commitment to conserving the country's wild lands. During his tenure as president, Roosevelt established over 50 wildlife refuges, 18 national monuments, and five national parks. Roosevelt was the first president who considered conservation an issue of national import, and he left a legacy that has encouraged the presidents following him to contribute to the national treasury of resources.

Theodore Roosevelt Jr. was born to a prominent New York City family on October 27, 1858. Like many conservationists, his intense interest in nature became apparent early in his childhood. At the age of nine, he opened the Roosevelt Museum of Natural History in an upstairs closet of his family's New York City home. Inspired by his father's role in founding the American Museum of Natural History and the Metropolitan Museum of Art, Roosevelt and his cousins eventually amassed a collection of several hundred animal specimens, most of them shot and stuffed by young Roosevelt himself. A fan of the living as well, the boy packed notebooks with his observations of the fauna he studied at his family's summer home in the country and the animals he saw during extended family voyages to Europe and the Middle East. The notebook he kept during his 11th summer was entitled "About Insects and Fishes, Natural History" and was 40 pages long.

Roosevelt intended to become a professional naturalist, but once he began studying at Harvard University in 1876, he quickly learned that natural history studies there were conducted in laboratories, not outdoors as he had hoped. That disappointment, as well as his romance with Alice Lee, a high-society young woman who was not interested in natural history, led him to switch his major to political economy. But although science would not become his profession, he remained a devoted promoter and protector of the natural world throughout his life.

After graduation from Harvard in 1880 and his marriage later that year to Alice Lee, Roosevelt attended law school at Columbia University and became involved in politics. He joined the Republican Club and in 1881 was elected to the New York State Assembly. During the 1882 Assembly recess he traveled to the Dakota Badlands on a buffalo hunt. The vastness of the West enchanted him, and at the conclusion of his visit he invested in land and a herd of cattle and hired his buffalo hunt guides to tend the ranch for him. After two tragic deaths within two weeks of each other in 1884, that of his mother, preceded by that of his wife in childbirth, Roosevelt retreated to his new ranch, where he spent more than half of the next eight years.

Living in the Dakotas, Roosevelt was an unhappy witness to the rapid disappearance of the buffalo and other large game animals of the West. He shared his concern with GEORGE BIRD GRINNELL, and together the two founded the Boone and Crockett Club in 1887. Others could join by invitation only; one of the prerequisites for membership was to have killed at least one adult male of three separate large game species. This elite club had both social goals (to promote a gentlemanly approach to hunting and provide a community network for themselves) and conservationist ends (to work for the preservation of large game and promote research on the habits of wild game). They were successful in their first major battle, one on behalf of Yellowstone Park, in which they convinced Congress to halt the proposed construction of a railroad spur into the park, to limit tourism concessions there, to protect the forest bordering the park, and to enforce the laws against hunting within the park boundaries.

Roosevelt's boundless energy, powerful network of friends, and impressive intellect combined to make him a national figure by the late 1890s. In 1897 he had been named assistant secretary to the navy, a post he stepped down from in 1898 in order to form the Rough Rider cavalry squad. He was recognized as a war hero after his triumph in Cuba during the Spanish-American War and was elected governor of New York. He was also the father of five children, who were born after he married Edith Kermit Carow in 1886. Roosevelt ran for vice president of the country with William McKinley on the Republican ticket and was elected in 1900. Six months after the inauguration, McKinley was assassinated, and Roosevelt assumed the presidency.

The first speech that Roosevelt gave to Congress as president included a strong conservationist message. Roosevelt—who by this time had renounced hunting—urged Congress to see conservation as an insurance policy for future generations of Americans. Natural resources such as forests, he told Congress, should be "set apart forever, for the use and benefit of our people as a whole and not sacrificed to the shortsighted greed of a few." By the turn of the century, half of the nation's forests had been cut, thousands of tons of topsoil had washed away owing to careless farming methods, and many visible species—including the buffalo and the formerly prolific passenger pigeon—were disappearing.

Roosevelt's aggressive conservation program included setting aside forest reserves and establishing wildlife refuges. Roosevelt worked with forester GIFFORD PINCHOT to establish the U.S. Forest Service and add over 150 million acres to its reserves. This tripled the acreage that all previous presidents together had set aside as reserves. In 1903, at the urging of bird-watchers and ornithologists, he established the first federal wildlife refuge in the nation, Pelican Island in Florida. At this time in history, birds with beautiful feathers were in great danger of extinction because plumes were widely used to adorn women's hats.

While president, Roosevelt personally surveyed the country for potential parks and refuges, exploring natural areas new to him. He toured western wilderness areas extensively and begged JOHN MUIR to guide him through Yosemite in 1903. Muir complied, and the two spent four days together in the park, hiking, camping, and sharing stories and visions for the future of wilderness conservation. Back in Washington, Roosevelt issued a standing invitation to his favorite conservationists and naturalists, many of whom would visit him for long evenings of strategizing and early morning bird-watching expeditions on the White House lawn or at the president's country retreat.

In the ten years he was to live after stepping down from the presidency, Roosevelt continued promoting conservation and indulging in his naturalist avocations. He wrote prolifically and corresponded with his naturalist friends, reviewing their books and discussing the fine points of speciation, a topic he was particularly interested in. On January 6, 1919, at his family's home in Sagamore Hill, New York, Theodore Roosevelt died in his sleep of an arterial thrombosis.

**BIBLIOGRAPHY**

Collins, Michael, *That Damned Cowboy: Theodore Roosevelt and the American West 1883-1898*, 1989; Cutright, Paul Russell, *Theodore Roosevelt: The Making of a Conservationist*, 1985; Fox, Stephen *The American Conservation Movement: John Muir and His Legacy*, 1986; Roosevelt, Theodore, *Diaries of Boyhood and Youth*, 1928; Roosevelt, Theodore, *Hunting Trips of a Ranchman*, 1886; Roosevelt, Theodore, *Theodore Roosevelt: An Autobiography*, 1913; Roosevelt, Theodore, *The Wilderness Hunter*, 1893 ; Roosevelt, Theodore, *Wilderness Writings*, edited by Paul Schullery, 1986; "The American Experience/TR's Legacy/Environment," www.pbs.org/wgbh/amex/tr/envir.html.

## Rosenfeld, Arthur H.
(1926– )
Public Interest Physicist, Energy Efficiency Expert

"Father of energy efficiency" Arthur H. Rosenfeld, Ph.D., left particle physics research to focus on energy conservation in America. He has co-founded several organizations including the American Council for an Energy Efficient Economy (ACEEE) and the Center for Energy and Climate Solutions (CECS). As Senior Advisor to the U.S. Department of Energy Assistant Secretary for Energy Efficiency and Renewable Energy during the 1990s, and as current Energy Commissioner to the State of California, Rosenfeld led the process of energy efficiency throughout its many stages; from observation and the creative process to the development of new appliances, turning knowledge into legislative ideas and setting new building policy standards. He has saved hundreds of billions of dollars for the U.S. as well as resources for future generations.

Arthur Rosenfeld was born in Birmingham, Alabama, in 1926. He earned a bachelor of science at eighteen and his Ph.D. in Physics in 1954 under Nobel Laureate Enrico Fermi at the University of Chicago. Later he joined the Department of Physics at the University of California at Berkeley to explore the subatomic world through particle accelerators. After eighteen years of work, Rosenfeld inherited the leadership of the group from Luis Alvarez in 1973, during the onset of the oil crisis of 1973 when oil-producing nations embargoed the United States, Japan and other western nations and quadruped oil prices in a year. Rosenfeld was among those to provide a solution that came not from the troublesome world of oil but from a more beneficial and valuable source: efficiency. During his research in Switzerland, Dr. Rosenfeld realized that European energy expenditure per capita was half of that in the U.S. with comparable living standards. Europe's dependence on foreign oil had already made it more energy conscious. The Europeans drove smaller cars and turned the lights off more often. Energy was being ill spent in the U.S. Rosenfeld foresaw the enormous advantages for reducing consumption of energy.

In 1975, he founded the Center for Building Science at Lawrence Berkeley National Laboratory (LBNL), where broad ranges of technologies were developed over the following twenty years. Insulation, reflective rooftops, high-frequency ballasts for compact fluorescent lamps, and low-emissivity windows that allow light through but block temperature were conceived and launched. Simple ideas like better use of skylights and removing air duct and fume leaks were proven to be energy savers. Water heaters, air conditioners and refrigerators were re-engineered to save energy. Green standards for buildings were advanced. Eventually, he came up with the modeling software DOE-2, the computer program for energy analysis and building design that has become the tool of choice across the U.S. and other countries like China. Beginning in the 1980s, he shifted his efforts to build upon past engineering successes and push forward new policies and projects.

Dr. Rosenfeld received the Szilard Award for Physics in the Public Interest in 1986, and the Carnot Award for Energy Efficiency from the U.S. Department of Energy in 1993. From 1994-1999 he served as Senior Adviser for the U.S. Department of Energy's Assistant Secretary for Energy Efficiency and Renewable Energy David Garman. Few scientists are able to shift their technical capacities to the most urgent matters of their time and redirect our efforts toward a more energy efficient world. He still conducts research and his students continue to polish ideas in emission trading programs and providing clean water in developing countries. He lives in Sacramento, California, with his wife Roselyn, and he is currently steering California's effort in energy conservation as appointed Engineer/Scientist Commissioner to the California Energy Commission.

**BIBLIOGRAPHY**

*A New Prosperity: Building A Sustainable Energy Future*, the SERI Solar-Conservation Study; The Art of Energy Efficiency: Protecting the Environment with Better Technology, Arthur H. Rosenfeld, Senior Advisor; www.energy.ca.gov/commission/commissioners/rosenfeld_docs/index.html; www.energy.ca.gov/commission/commissioners/rosenfeld.html; www.energy.ca.gov/commission/commissioners/rosenfeld_docs/200010_ROSENFELD_AUTOBIO.PDF; www.lbl.gov/Science-Articles/Archive/rosenfeld-doe-advisor.html; www.alumni.berkeley.edu/calmag/200701/id_power.asp; www.kqed.org/quest/television/view/155; www.nrdc.org/onearth/06spr/ca1.asp.

# Roszak, Theodore
(1933– )
Writer, Professor

Theodore Roszak is an author of nonfiction and fiction whose works explore Western society, its fixation with technology, and the effects this fixation has on human relationships with the natural world. He is critical of science and technology and believes that they have led humans to lose touch with nature and spirituality. His best-known work is *The Making of a Counter Culture*, published in 1969, a book that examines the student protest movement of the 1960s in an attempt to reveal it as a backlash against the technocratic, spiritually lacking society of the 1960s.

Theodore Roszak reveals little about his early life beyond that he was born in 1933 in Chicago, Illinois, to Anton and Blanche Roszak and that his father was a cabinetmaker. Roszak attended the University of California, Los Angeles, receiving a B.A. degree in 1955. He then went to Princeton University and earned a Ph.D. in 1958. After graduating with his doctorate, Roszak became a history instructor at Stanford University, where he remained until 1963. In 1964, he moved to London, England, where he had accepted a position as editor for the pacifist journal, *Peace News*. He returned to the United States in 1965, accepting a history professorship at California State University, Hayward, where he still teaches.

Roszak began publishing in 1966. He is a prolific author, and he has published in journals such as *Atlantic*, *Harper's*, *Nation*, *Utne Reader*, and *New Scientist*. His first book, *The Dissenting Academy*, which he edited, appeared in 1968. It was a collection of critical and controversial essays written by prominent, socially conscious educators, and it established Roszak as an agitator for social and political activism. Roszak is probably best known for his second book, *The Making of a Counter Culture: Reflections on the Technocratic Society and Its Youthful Opposition*, which was published in 1969. It was this book that first used the term "counter culture". In it, Roszak outlined the various influences of such intellectual and social subversives as Timothy Leary, Allan Ginsberg, Herbert Marcuse, and PAUL GOODMAN on the student protest movement. Roszak was critical of science and of scientific ways of viewing the world that do not acknowledge subjective ways of knowing. He stated that the "youthful opposition" was calling for a new culture "in which the non-intellective capacities of the personality—those capacities that take fire from the visionary splendor and the experience of human communion—become the arbiters of the good, the true, and the beautiful." The book was nominated for a National Book Award.

Roszak next compiled two anthologies, editing *Masculine Feminine: Readings in Sexual Mythology and the Liberation of Women* (1969) and *An Anthology of Contemporary Material Useful for Preserving Personal Sanity While Braving the Great Technological Wilderness* (1972). Also in 1972, and as a result of work done on a Guggenheim Fellowship throughout 1971 and 1972, he published *Where the Wasteland Ends: Politics and Transcendence in Post-Industrial Society*, a book in which Roszak criticized not only the technological society of the 1970s, but also the human "mindscape" that could result in the type of society that he found himself inhabiting. He called for a transformation of this "mindscape" and for a return to the lost synergy between humans and nature. In the book's introduction, he explained that he was endeavoring to discover the processes that have caused humans to abandon their religious impulses and to become separated from nature and from a mystical view of the universe. This book also was nominated for a National Book Award.

Roszak has written many other works of nonfiction, exploring the relationships between nature, humans, and the afflicted societies in which they live, including *Unfinished Animal* (1975), *Person/Planet* (1978), *The Cult of Information* (1986), and *The Voice of the Earth: An Exploration in Ecopsychology* (1992). "Ecopsychology" is another term coined by Roszak—referring to the effect the environment has on people, not the other way around. Roszak explored this concept at his Ecology Institute at California State University—Hayward, and explored it further in his other writings. In *The Gendered Atom* (1999) he critiqued traditional science for its overly masculine approach, and proposed that scientists instead embrace qualities of sensitivity, gentleness, compassion and intuition. He wrote about the graying of America in *Longevity Revolution: As Boomers Become Elders* (2001) and his most recent non-fiction book is *World, Beware! American Triumphalism in an Age of Terror* (2005), an interpretation of this country's national and international policies since September 11, 2001.

Roszak has also written several novels. Among these are *Pontifex* (1974), *Bugs* (1981), *Flicker* (1993), *The Memoirs of Elizabeth Frankenstein* (1995), *The Blizzard* (2001), and most recently, *The Devil and Daniel Silverman* (2003). In an interview with Catherine Maclay, Roszak commented that all of his books treat the common theme of "the moral and spiritual dilemmas of living in a society that worships technology." He likened all of industrial civilization to a monster of the Frankenstein variety, stating "All of these monsters are connected with one great thing, and that is our screwed-up relations with the natural world. Science tells us that we can steal the earth's resources, and we can remake Mother Earth into anything we want her to be." In 1996, *Elizabeth Frankenstein* received the James Tiptree Jr. award for literature that reflects an understanding of gender issues.

Although Roszak is an advocate for wilderness protection, he is also a self-professed city slicker. He is not, as he wrote in an article for *New Scientist*, "a hiker, camper, climber, or outdoorsman." He is, he says, unable to meet the wilderness on its own terms. Therefore, he writes, "I simply leave the wilderness alone. It is enough for me to simply know it is there." Roszak retired from California State University—East Bay (formerly Hayward) in 2004, and lives in Berkeley, California, with his wife of 35 years, Betty. They have a grown daughter, Kathryn.

**BIBLIOGRAPHY**

"Eco-Psychology: Jeffrey Mishlove Interviews Theodore Roszak," www.williamjames.com/

transcripts/roszak.htm; Locher, Frances Carol, ed., *Contemporary Authors*, 1979; Maclay, Catherine, "Theodore Roszak: The Monster in the Laboratory," *Publishers Weekly*, 1995; Roszak, Theodore, "The Ecology of Wisdom," *Whole Earth*, 2002; Roszak, Theodore, "Leave the Wilderness Alone," *New Scientist*, 1988.

## Ruether, Rosemary Radford
(November 2, 1936– )
Theologian

Rosemary Radford Ruether is a leading feminist and radical theologian who has written extensively about ecofeminism. Her 1992 book *Gaia and God: An Ecofeminist Theology of Earth Healing* discusses strains of Christian thought that contribute to the destruction of the planet as well as those that offer possibilities for forming a "biophilic" relationship to the environment. Ruether's work shows connections between the patriarchal privileging of men over women and Man over Nature and argues for a new ethic of equality and mutual care.

Rosemary Radford Ruether was born in St. Paul, Minnesota, on November 2, 1936, to a Protestant father and a Catholic mother. The youngest of three daughters, Ruether's early life was spent in the Georgetown area of Washington, D.C. Her father died when she was 12, and the family moved to La Jolla, California, her mother's childhood home. In *Disputed Questions*, an account of her "intellectual and personal journey of faith and action," Ruether describes the Catholicism of her youth as "free-spirited and humanistic," connected to the Jesuit tradition and formed in private rather than parochial Catholic school. Ruether attributes her embrace of radical ideas to her mother's influence, particularly to growing up amid her mother's friends, in a community of mothers and daughters. Having been raised in California and Mexico, Ruether's mother had a respect for people from diverse backgrounds and a belief that she could do or be anything she wanted—and she bequeathed the same to her daughter.

Ruether attended Scripps College in Claremont, California, where she majored in philosophy, studying classics with Prof. Robert Palmer. In 1958 she graduated from Scripps College and married Herman Ruether, a political scientist and cultural historian. She went on to earn an M.A. in ancient history (1960) and a Ph.D. in classics and patristics (1965), both from Claremont Graduate School. Her background in classical history led Ruether to reject religious exclusivism in favor of respect for all religions, seeing connections between all such historically and culturally specific quests for meaning. Ruether's work has been particularly attentive to the Christian roots of anti-Semitism and anti-Islamic prejudice.

After completing her Ph.D., Ruether became increasingly active in the struggle for civil rights, first during the summer of 1965 when she went to Mississippi to work with the Delta Ministry, and later as part of the faculty of the School of Religion at Howard University, where she taught for ten years, beginning in 1966. Ruether lived in Washington, D.C., during the height of the movement against the war in Vietnam. She was arrested numerous times, often with other Catholic radicals. Her participation in the peace movement gave her an awareness of the global structure of social inequality, of the ways in which racism in the United States was linked to and mirrored in global imperialism and capitalism. Ruether developed a particular interest in the politics and theology of Latin America, her mother's ancestral home, and center of the flowering of liberation theology in the 1970s and 1980s. Liberation theology stresses the importance of social justice on earth, rather than fulfillment in heaven, and thus serves as one way for Christians to reimagine the human relationship to the natural world.

Reenvisioning our relationship to nature is linked in Ruether's thought to the need to challenge the dualistic thinking that underpins structures of social dominance. She traces the connections between the Christian valuing of God over man, and man over woman, to the dominance in much Christian thought of humans over animals and heaven over earth. Ruether argues that instead of opposition between these terms, we need to see connection. Rather than placing humankind in dominion over nature, we need to see that we are part of nature, joined to other living things through community and compassion. In *Gaia and God*, Ruether traces the damaging effects of Christian apocalyptic thinking, the belief that the world is destined for destruction. Apocalyptic Christians are prepared to sacrifice the earth as part of the vanquishing of evil, and she cautions environmentalists not to let their more dire predictions reinforce the belief in a coming apocalypse.

Ruether's global consciousness is evident throughout her writings on ecofeminism. In 1996 she edited *Women Healing Earth: Third World Women on Feminism, Religion and Ecology*. She has contributed articles to several collections on ecofeminism, including the 1994 book *Ecotheology: Voices from South and North*, edited by David Hallman. In addition to her interest in ecofeminism and feminist theology, she is known for her work in patristics, the historical and theological roots of anti-Seminitism, the Israeli-Palestinian conflict, the history of women in American religion, and liberation theology. Ruether stresses the importance of linking economic justice to environmental reform and the need to build coalitions between working people throughout the world.

Rosemary Radford Ruether has written or edited more than 30 books and hundreds of articles. She contributes regularly to journals such as *The National Catholic Reporter* and *Sojourners*. She spent 25 years as the Georgia Harkness professor of Applied Theology at Garrett Evangelical Theological Seminary, and is now the Carpenter Professor Emerita of Feminist Theology at Pacific School of Religion and the Graduate Theological Union in California. Ruether is married to political scientist Herman Ruether, and they have three children.

**BIBLIOGRAPHY**

"Boston Collaborative Encyclopedia of Western Theology: Rosemary Radford Ruether," people.bu.edu/wwildman/WeirdWildWeb/courses/mwt/dictionary/mwt_themes_908_ruether.htm; Bouma-Prediger, Steven, *The Greening of Theology: The Ecological Models of Rosemary Radford Ruether, Joseph Sittler, and Jürgen Moltmann*, 1995; Ruether, Rosemary Radford, *Gaia and God: An Ecofeminist Theology of Earth Healing*, 1992; Tardiff, Mary, *At Home in the World: The Letters of Thomas Merton & Rosemary Radford Ruether*, 1995.

# American Environmental Leaders

From Colonial Times to the Present

## Safina, Carl

(May 23, 1955– )
Marine Ecologist, Co-founder and President of Blue Ocean Institute, Writer

One of the first marine ecologists to study seabird behavior out at sea, Carl Safina has contributed to a greater understanding of the complex interactions among sea birds, prey fish, and competing predatory fish. But he is as much a compelling writer and advocate as a research scientist, and he uses his other talents to bring marine conservation problems to public attention, often employing his favorite motto, Fish are wildlife, too. He established the Living Oceans Program for the National Audubon Society in 1990 and for 10 years was its director, spearheading such major campaigns as rewriting federal fisheries law in the United States, attempting to gain international agreements to achieve sustainable fish catches, and pushing legislation that will protect and restore depleted and endangered marine life and marine ecosystems. After years of working with the science and public policy sides of marine conservation, Safina also began looking at the human side of the fishing culture and incorporated this aspect, along with in-depth ecological issues, into his landmark and award-winning book *Song for the Blue Ocean: Encounters along the World's Coasts and beneath the Seas* (1997). That book has been followed by two others. In 2003, Safina co-founded the Blue Ocean Institute, which through science, art, and literature, seeks out new conservation constituencies and develops conservation strategies geared toward people and the ocean.

Carl Safina was born on May 23, 1955, in Brooklyn, New York, and grew up near the ocean on Long Island. His father often took him fishing for striped bass, and he acquired a general fascination with nature. When the woods near his house were bulldozed to make room for more houses, he spent more and more time along the coast, where he could still find a sense of nature. His affinity

Carl Safina (Photograph courtesy of Blue Ocean Institute)

for the ocean stayed with him, and when he entered the State University of New York at Purchase in 1974, he enrolled in biology courses and realized that he could create a career out of the things that interested him. He graduated from Purchase in 1977 with a major in environmental science and went on to graduate school, where he chose to study seabirds so that he could continue to explore coastal habitats. While conducting his research, it became evident to him that fish populations were diminishing, and he started questioning why the conservation movement had made no efforts to protect marine and coastal species. He received his master's degree from Rutgers University in ecology in 1982 and his Ph.D. in 1987. And despite having professors tell him that conservation was for people who were not smart enough to get Ph.D.'s, Safina became determined to make marine conservation a legitimate and well-known issue.

Safina began working for the National Audubon Society in 1980 as a research ecologist, formulating innovative field research projects on the ecology of seabirds and fish populations. While studying the breeding biology of endangered terns in their coastal colonies, he noticed gaps in the knowledge of the birds' biology that could only be filled by observing them at sea. He followed the birds offshore and used sonar to survey prey fish schools; he became one of the first scientists ever to study seabirds as marine animals. His work on the interactions among seabirds, prey fish, and competing predatory fish led up to his doctoral dissertation in ecology, which he completed in 1987 at Rutgers University.

Safina's doctoral research and the work he conducted for the National Audubon Society had him spending many hours at sea, and again he observed what appeared to be marked local declines in sea turtles, sharks, and several fish species. When he looked into the problem—researching the records of fishery management agencies and other literature—he saw that the declines he found in New England waters were just part of a larger trend that extended around the globe. Motivated by an increasing sense of urgency over dwindling marine life and the lack of public awareness of the issue, Safina dropped his research projects and devoted his time to getting marine fish issues onto the wildlife conservation movement's agenda. In 1990, he founded and became director of the Living Oceans Program at the National Audubon Society, a marine conservation program that uses science-based policy analysis, education, and grassroots advocacy to campaign on behalf of marine fish and ocean ecosystems, focusing on fisheries depletion and restoring fish abundance through sustainable fishing. In 1991 Safina accepted an appointment by the U.S. secretary of commerce to the Mid-Atlantic Fisheries Management Council and broke new ground by becoming the only professional conservationist to serve on any of the eight federal fishery management councils. That same year he received the Pew Charitable Trust's prestigious Scholar's Award in Conservation and the Environment. Also in 1991, Safina served as a U.S. delegation member to the International Commission for the Conservation of Atlantic Tunas (ICCAT) and found out from Japanese and U.S. representatives that despite the dangerous declines reported to them by their own scientists, they had no intention of lowering bluefin tuna catch quotas. Spurred to action, Safina wrote a petition to the U.S. government to list the bluefin under the Convention on International Trade in Endangered Species (CITES), an action that would effectively suspend commercial fishing for this species. His efforts increased international awareness of the need for conservation of the bluefin tuna: by 1993, tuna quotas were cut for the first time in a decade, and ICCAT made a historic commitment to cut catch quotas in half by 1995. Safina was appointed deputy chair of the World Conservation Union's Shark Specialist Group in 1993 and brought attention to declining populations of sharks. By 1997, the Living Oceans Program had convinced the U.S. government to heed severe declines in Atlantic sharks and cut commercial catches in half. The program also engaged in major campaigns to ban high seas drift nets and to achieve passage of a new high seas fisheries treaty through the United Nations.

Meanwhile, Safina had also been working on a book that he had always wanted to write—one that summed up his experiences as a fisherman and an ecologist and that also addressed some of the cultural issues of fishing. In 1997 his book, *Song for the Blue Ocean: Encounters along the World's Coasts and beneath the Sea*, was published. In researching the book, he traveled to ten countries on four continents over five years, conducting investigations from small aircraft and commercial fishing vessels and engaging in conversations everywhere he went. He talked to families who depend on the fishing industry for their living, economists, officials from various international maritime commissions, and environmentalists. He also collected sobering evidence regarding the status of underwater wildlife. In the northeastern United States the Atlantic bluefin tuna had declined nearly 90 percent over the previous two decades as a result of overfishing, while hydroelectric dams and logging in the Northwest had almost wiped out the salmon. In the South Pacific, coral reefs are destroyed through fishing practices that use dynamite or cyanide-poisoning and by increasing tourism and development that leads to excess silt and sewage runoff. Though Safina protests unsustainable fishing practices, he admits to eating seafood himself and enjoys marine fishing. And unlike many environmentalists, he places blame not only on the fishers or the loggers but also on the excesses of consumers in developed nations. There is no doubt that humans will continue to depend on the oceans as a source of food, writes Safina, and the answer is not to halt fishing altogether. But he does stipulate that for regional fisheries to survive, new regulations will have to be implemented to allow for recovery of fish populations. *Song for the Blue Ocean* was followed by *Eye of the Albatross: Visions of Hope and Survival* (2002), a chronicle of the life and travels of Amelia, one of these giant seabirds, and glimpses many other types of seabirds and people whose lives intersect with them; and *Voyage of the Turtle: In Pursuit of the Earth's Last Dinosaur* (2006), a natural history of the leatherback and other sea turtles.

In 2003, Safina and colleague Mercédès Lee co-founded the Blue Ocean Institute, which works to inspire a closer relationship with the sea through science, art, and literature. They develop conservation solutions that are compassionate to people as well as to ocean wildlife, and share reliable information that enlightens personal choices, instills hope, and helps restore living abundance in the ocean.

The organization's small staff works with commercial fishermen to reduce "bycatch" (turtles and seabirds inadvertently caught and killed in fishing nets) and to promote more consciousness among consumers and chefs about sustainable seafood purchases. It publishes a quarterly on-line journal of seastories (www.seastories.org) and the Blue Ocean Diary, Safina's journal from his research trips around the world.

Safina has published over 100 scientific and popular articles on ecology and marine conservation, including featured work in *National Geographic* and a new foreword to RACHEL CARSON's *The Sea Around Us*. He has testified at numerous congressional and state hearings and has served on the Smithsonian Institution's Ocean Planet Advisory Board. In 1998 Safina was selected by *Audubon* magazine as one of the top 100 most influential conservationists of the century. In 2000, he received a MacArthur Foundation "Genius" grant. His *Song for the Blue Ocean* was chosen as a *New York Times* Notable Book of the Year, a *Los Angeles Times* Best Nonfiction selection, and a *Library Journal* Best Science Book selection. *Eye of the Albatross* won the John Burroughs Medal for nature writing and was chosen by the National Academies of Science, Engineering and Medicine as the year's best book for communicating science. Safina is also author of *Voyage of the Turtle*. He maintains a blog at www.carlsafina.org.

Safina lives on Long Island, New York, with partner Patricia Paladines and her daughter Alexandra.

**BIBLIOGRAPHY**

"Blue Ocean Institute," www.blueocean.org; Lee, M., and Carl Safina, "Effects of Overfishing on

Marine Biodiversity," *Current: The Journal of Marine Education*, 1995; McKibben, Bill, "The Next Waves," *Interview Magazine*, 1998; Revkin, Andrew, "The Biologist and the Sea: Lessons in Marine-Life Restoration," *New York Times*, 2006; Safina, Carl, "Song for the Swordfish," *Audubon*, 1998; Safina, Carl, "To Save the Earth, Scientists Should Join Policy Debates," *Chronicle of Higher Education*, 1998; Safina, Carl, "The World's Imperiled Fish," *Scientific American*, 1995.

## Sagan, Carl

(November 9, 1934–December 20, 1996)
Astronomer, Television Show Host

Carl Sagan was one of the best-known scientists among the public in the United States and perhaps in the world, recognized for his contributions to our knowledge of Venus and Mars, for his extensive work on Mariner missions of the National Aeronautics and Space Administration (NASA), and for his search for extraterrestrial life. Sagan became a household name to U.S. audiences, starting with regular guest appearances on the popular television talk show, *The Tonight Show*, and on the public television series, *Cosmos*, that he hosted, and continuing with his novel, *Contact* (1985), which was made into a major Hollywood film at the end of his life. Additionally, Sagan was one of the authors of a scientific paper predicting that a "nuclear winter," or severe climate disruption that would threaten all life on the planet, would result from nuclear war. This paper influenced national and international nuclear weapons policy, helping to convince the American public of the necessity to end the cold war and the nuclear arms race.

Carl Sagan was born in Brooklyn, New York, on November 9, 1934, to Rachel Gruber Sagan and Samuel Sagan, a Russian immigrant who worked in a clothing factory. As a young child, Sagan was captivated with stars. He also became a devoted science fiction reader, especially enjoying novels about Mars by Edgar Rice Burroughs. Sagan began studying simple mathematical relationships involving stars and planets at an early age. When his family moved to New Jersey, Sagan entered Rahway High School, where he maintained a strong interest in science, and decided to become a professional astronomer. When he graduated in 1951, he was voted the student most likely to succeed. Sagan attended the University of Chicago, receiving a B.S. in physics in 1955, and then, supported by a National Science Foundation grant, he earned an M.S. in physics in 1956. He was awarded his Ph.D. in astronomy and astrophysics in 1960, also from the University of Chicago.

Beginning in 1960, Sagan became increasingly involved with the National Aeronautics and Space Administration, studying Jupiter, and he was asked to advise the NASA astronauts who would be landing on the moon. Sagan won NASA's Apollo Achievement Award in 1970 and worked on NASA's Pioneer 10 and 11 explorations of Saturn and Jupiter and the Mariner 9 and Viking expeditions to Mars.

Sagan did postdoctoral work at the University of California at Berkeley and in 1962 joined the Smithsonian Astrophysical Observatory in Cambridge, Massachusetts, as an astrophysicist. He taught at Harvard University as an assistant professor. Over the next few years, Sagan conducted significant studies of Mars, which culminated with an article for *National Geographic* magazine. In 1968, Sagan moved to Cornell University in Ithaca, New York, where he would live for the rest of his life. At Cornell, he first served as an associate professor of astronomy at the Center for Radiophysics and Space Research, then was promoted to professor and associate director of the center. In 1977 Sagan became the David Duncan Professor of Astronomy and Space Science at Cornell. By this point in his career, Sagan had contributed more than 200 articles to scientific journals.

Sagan began producing a television series for the Public Broadcasting Service (PBS) entitled *Cosmos* in 1970. Making scientific exploration comprehensible and accessible to television viewers around the world, the series became one of the most popular in PBS history. Sagan became a regular guest on Johnny Carson's *Tonight Show*, bringing astronomy and science into the living rooms of millions of American viewers. In 1973 he published his first book, *The Cosmic Connection*, which was very successful, and he continued writing books that brought science home to the average reader. In 1978 he won a Pulitzer Prize for *The Dragons of Eden* (1977), a book about the evolution of the human brain. Sagan then wrote *Cosmos* (1980), a companion book to the television series, and *Murmurs of Earth: The Voyager Interstellar Records* (1978). Sagan's first novel, *Contact*, was published in 1985 and was made into a major Hollywood film in 1997.

Sagan continued his involvement in space exploration throughout the 1980s and 1990s. He believed it was possible that Jupiter's moon might also have some form of life. Sagan also helped NASA to establish a groundbreaking radio astronomy search program for extraterrestrial life called Communication with Extra-Terrestrial Intelligence (CETI).

Actively involved in politics since graduate school, Sagan participated in student protests against the Vietnam War and was an avid supporter of the Democratic Party. In December 1983 Sagan cowrote an article for *Science* warning against the harmful consequences of nuclear war on the global climate. The article stated that even a limited number of nuclear explosions could severely alter the world's climate, causing a "nuclear winter." Strongly debated among respected scientists worldwide, this article was followed with a number of studies by scientists around the world on the effects of nuclear war as well as other human interference in the world's climate, including global warming. Their findings influenced many countries, institutions, and individuals to avoid the potential for nuclear war and its devastating global environmental consequences. As a result of his antinuclear research, Sagan won the National Committee for a Sane Nuclear Policy (SANE) National Peace Award in 1984, the Kennan Peace Award from SANE/Freeze in 1988, and the Helen Caldicott Leadership Award, presented by Women's Action for Nuclear Disarmament in 1988.

Sagan felt strongly that space exploration was misunderstood by many environmentalists, who opposed space missions such as the Cassini probe to Saturn. In Sagan's view, the space sciences and the life sciences were interdependent. In addition to providing unusual access to weather and meteorological studies that can monitor long-term trends in global warming, space exploration and technology offer unparalleled views of the effects of ozone layer depletion, nuclear winter, deforestation, strip mining, ocean dumping, and other environmental hazards. Sagan felt this was extremely important to furthering our understanding of how to protect the environment on earth.

Sagan was married three times and had three sons and two daughters. In 1994, he was diagnosed with myelodysplasia, a serious bone-marrow disease. Despite his illness, Sagan continued to work on numerous projects. His last book, *The Demon-Haunted World: Science as a Candle in the Dark*, was published in 1995. At the time of his death, Sagan was coproducing a film version of his novel, *Contact*, with his wife, Ann Druyan. Released in 1997, the film received popular and critical acclaim as a testimony to Sagan's enthusiasm for the search for extraterrestrial life. On December 20, 1996, Sagan died at the Fred

Hutchinson Cancer Research Center in Seattle, Washington.

**BIBLIOGRAPHY**

"Carl Sagan Center," www.seti.org/csc; Davidson, Keay and Carl Sagan. *Carl Sagan: A Life*, 1999; Head, Tom, *Conversations with Carl Sagan*, 2005; "The Planetary Society, Who We Are, The Planetary Society," www.planetary.org/about/founders/carl_sagan.html; Poundstone, William, *Carl Sagan: A Life in the Cosmos*, 1999 RP

Turco et al. "Nuclear Winter: Global Consequences of Multiple Nuclear Explosions," *Science*, 1983; Sagan, Carl, *Billions and Billions: Thoughts on Life and Death at the Brink of the Millennium*, 1997; Sagan, Carl, *The Demon-Haunted World: Science as a Candle in the Dark*, 1996; Sagan, Carl, *Pale Blue Dot: A Vision of the Human Future in Space*, 1994; Sagan, Carl, and Ann Druyan, *Shadows of Forgotten Ancestors: A Search for Who We Are*, 1992; Terzian Yervant and Elizabeth M. Bilson, *Carl Sagan's Universe*, 1997.

## Sale, Kirkpatrick
(June 27, 1937– )
Cofounder of the E. F. Schumacher Society, Writer, Bioregionalist

Kirkpatrick Sale has advocated social change throughout his long career as a writer. A cofounder of the E. F. Schumacher Society, he has often voiced discontent with the environmental deterioration caused by large-scale commerce. "Something is deeply wrong with America," he wrote in *Human Scale*, his 1980 book on the problems of modern society, and pointed to our decaying environment, the nuclear threat, urban violence, promiscuity, and increased feelings of alienation as markers of societal illness. A former editor of *The Nation* and a freelance journalist, he is author of eight books on subjects ranging from African culture to the neo-Luddites.

Born in Ithaca, New York, on June 27, 1937, to William M. and Helen (Stearns) Sale, John Kirkpatrick Sale grew up in middle-class postwar prosperity. After graduating from high school, he enrolled at Swarthmore College in 1954, but stayed only one year before moving on to Cornell University, where his father was an English professor. Sale edited the student newspaper, often writing scathing editorials. He graduated in 1958 with a B.A. in history, but journalism was his true calling.

A persuasive writer who was bored with convention, he found work in 1959 as editor of the leftist paper, *The New Leader*. It launched him into the publishing world, where he debated social issues for the next three years. He longed for life experience, however, and in 1961 journeyed to Africa, serving as foreign correspondent to the *Chicago Tribune* and *San Francisco Chronicle*. He went back to New York to marry fellow editor Faith Apfelbaum in mid-1962 and in 1963 returned to Africa, taking a post as lecturer in history at the University of Ghana. He absorbed as much local culture as he could, gathering material that would eventually lead to his book *The Land and People of Ghana* (1972).

Returning to New York in 1965, where he has lived since then, Sale became editor of the *New York Times Magazine*. The late 1960s were heady political times, and he was caught in the fervor of Vietnam protest. The student movement at Cornell drew his attention, and in 1968 he decided to turn freelance in order to write about the new activism. He devoted the next two years of his life to studying the Students for a Democratic Society. The experience, in his own words, "further radicalized" him. Sale's book about the movement, *SDS*, came out in 1973.

Established as an independent thinker and writer, Sale published another political volume, *Power Shift* (1975), then turned his attention to another crisis: the damaged environment. He joined the Small is Beautiful movement, inspired by E. F. Schumacher. Schumacher was a Swiss decentralist who advocated small, sustainable communities in the face of massive industrialism. Sale embraced such ideas and expounded on them in his book *Human Scale* (1980). In 1981 he helped form the E. F. Schumacher Society, which is dedicated to Schumacher's vision. Sale served on its board for several years.

For the next year Sale took on the prestigious role of editor at *The Nation* magazine, but he continued to study bioregionalism, convinced that humans would benefit from a return to the land. He spoke up for geographic understanding and small-scale agriculture as cures for society's excesses. His ideas resonated among environmentalists. *Dwellers in the Land*, his next opus, was published by the Sierra Club in 1985. Sale was intent on documenting the environmental movement in much the same way that he had studied political change. He spent much of the next several years writing a history of the environmental movement in the United States, which culminated in *The Green Revolution*, published in 1993.

Sale has written widely on the damage technology does to modern society. For a time in the mid-1990s, he was even suspected of being the Unabomber. When Ted Kaczynski's manifesto appeared anonymously, Sale gained media attention for suggesting that its author was "rational" and "reasonable." Although he disagreed with violent action against individuals, Sale said the Unabomber was not all wrong. The alienation of modern people and the resulting ill effects on the land were what bioregionalism also sought to cure. *Rebels against the Future* (1995), explored the link between the Luddites, who protested the Industrial Revolution, and the neo-Luddites, who speak out against a technology- and profit-driven society. *The Fire of his Genius: Robert Fulton and the American Dream* (2001) is the biography of the antithesis of a Luddite; Fulton invented the steamboat and then spent the rest of his life trying to popularize another invention, the torpedo (his version more like a landmine).

His most recent book is *After Eden* (2005), which traces our planet's ills to humanity's drive to dominate, rather than to create and celebrate life force. At this point in human evolution, we have such high numbers and powerful tools of destruction that we are on the brink collapse. *After Eden* proposes, as does Sale's previous writings, the best way to avoid the inevitable collapse of this civilization is to scale down, to go local.

Sale co-founded the Middlebury Institute in 2005 to study and promote the idea of secession, as a response to the "excesses of the present American empire." He has also served on boards for the School for Living, Project Work, the PEN American Center (as vice president), and The Learning Alliance. A contributing editor for *The Nation*, he continues to send articles to various publications, including the *Evergreen Review*, *Mother Jones*, *Green Revolution*, and *New Roots*. He has given two of the E. F. Schumacher Society's annual lectures. In addition to his non-fiction writing, Sale has published a book of verse, *Why the Sea is Salt: Poems of Love and Loss* (2001). Sale lives in New York City. He and his wife, Faith, have two children, Rebekah Zoe and Calista Jennings.

**BIBLIOGRAPHY**

"The E. F. Schumacher Society," "www.smallisbeautiful.org; Sale, Kirkpatrick, *After Eden*, 2005; Sale, Kirkpatrick, *The Conquest of Paradise: Christopher Columbus and the Columbian Legacy*, Sale, Kirkpatrick, *Dwellers in the Land: The Bioregional Vision*, 1985; 1990; Sale, Kirkpatrick, *The Fire of his Genius, 2001*; Sale, Kirkpatrick, *Human Scale*, 1980; Sale, Kirkpatrick, *Rebels against the Future: The Luddites and Their War on the Industrial Revolution*, 1995.

# Sandoval, Arturo

(December 3, 1947—)
Base Community Organizer, Founder of VOCES, Inc. and Center of Southwest Culture

Arturo Sandoval works within the Chicano and Latino cultures to promote New Mexican environmental awareness and activism. "By working with ranchers, acequia associations and land-grant heirs, the wilderness movement has been able to find local champions," Sandoval says, "rather than coming in with a top-down approach. These are local people who love these particular places, who know the value of keeping places open."

Sandoval was born December 3, 1947. He was raised in rural northern New Mexico, close to the boundary of the Santa Clara Pueblo on land owned by his family for generations. Young Arturo spent his days hauling water from the community well and helping his grandparents on their ranch, and when the chores were done, playing and hiking in the endless hills and arroyos that surrounded him. Sandoval said it was the landscape that raised him as much as his family and shaped the concern for preserving wilderness spaces in his later work.

In the late 1960s, Sandoval dropped out of college, where he was studying English at the University of New Mexico, and volunteered for the VISTA (Volunteers in Service to America) organization in New Mexico. VISTA was a domestic Peace Corps program dedicated to eradicating poverty. This early volunteer service was formative. Instead of traveling to foreign places where he knew nothing about the people or the land, he worked for fifteen months in a familiar environment—the land-

Arturo Sandoval (Photograph courtesy of Arturo Sandoval)

grant community in Anton Chico, New Mexico, working on issues with his peers.

After his service he returned to UNM where he co-founded a Chicano student group, the United Mexican American Students. This organization was instrumental in starting the Chicano Studies program and Chicano Student Services at UNM. Sandoval also assisted

Mexican janitors and service workers at the university in organizing into a union.

In 1970 he left New Mexico to work as the Western Regional Coordinator of the first Earth Day. Sandoval organized students from across the country to join in public marches, rallies and events across the U.S. to focus public attention on environmental issues. More than 20 million people participated in the first Earth Day.

Less than three months after the first Earth Day, Sandoval was drafted for the Vietnam War. He chose to become a war resistor and refused induction into the U.S. Army. He was tried, convicted and given a three-year prison sentence which was eventually suspended for three years of alternate service. He used his community service probation to initiate two programs, a private foundation offering scholarships to minority students at the UNM medical school, and a regional office for a national Chicano health organization.

This focus on both social and environmental activism would continue to drive Sandoval's work. Sandoval said it became very clear to him at a young age that the issues of social injustices and environmental degradation were the same. "The people who are willing to exploit other people because of skin color are the same people to exploit Mother Nature. I see it as a holistic issue, fighting for civil rights and environmental rights."

After serving his probation term, Sandoval took to journalism, wedding his social activism with a personal desire to write. He served as campaign manager for U.S. Representative Tom Udall (D-NM) during his run for Congress in 1988. After Udall's narrow defeat, Sandoval started his own business, VOCES, Inc., a communications and organizational development consulting firm. His clients have included The Wilderness Society, the Mexicano Land Education and Conservation Trust, Zia Pueblo, The McCune Charitable Foundation, New Mexico Workers' Compensation Department, the City of Gallup, Sawmill Community Land Trust and Hispanic Radio Network.

In 1991, Sandoval started the Center of Southwest Culture, which provides organizational development for nonprofits, cultural and educational programs, and works on sustainable economic development work with communities of color, mostly Latino, and promotes cultural projects between the United States and Mexico.

Among the many boards and commissions that Sandoval has served are the New Mexico Wilderness Alliance, New Mexico Latino Sustainability Institute, 1000 Friends of New Mexico, the Sawmill Community Land Trust, and New Energy Economy. He worked for New Mexico Governor Bill Richardson's "Our Communities, Our Future" task force, and the Game and Fish Department's transition team.

Sandoval has worked on successful environmental campaigns to preserve the Ojito Wilderness, 11,000 acres northwest of Albuquerque; the Otero Mesa, one of the last Chihuahuan grasslands; and Valle Vidal. He is currently advocating in Washington to get wilderness designation for the Sabinoso wilderness area, a 25,000-acre stretch that is one of the last Great Plains ecosystems left in New Mexico. As a founding board member of Rio Grande Return, he is trying to garner agricultural support for farmers along the Rio Grande to keep the green belt along the river healthy and economically prosperous. He is also advancing an ecotourism project to preserve the acequia associations of New Mexico, the traditional irrigation ditch systems.

Sandoval lives in Albuquerque with his wife Clara. They have three children. He is increasingly in demand as a speaker and has given lectures to the Environmental Grant Makers Association, the Grantmakers for Education, and Bioneers.

**BIBLIOGRAPHY**

Personal interview, November 19, 2007; *"Tierra Sagrada*: Our Common Ground," Speech delivered by Arturo Sandoval, April 30, 2004, to the annual conference of the New Mexico

Coalition for a Livable Future; Paskus, Laura, "Going Wild," *Santa Fe Reporter*, June 6, 2007.

## Sanjour, William

(February 19, 1933– )
Hazardous Waste Expert at the Environmental Protection Agency, Whistleblower

An administrator and consultant for the Environmental Protection Agency (EPA) for more than 30 years, William Sanjour played a key role in exposing failures and corruption at the agency. Sanjour helped craft the landmark 1976 Resource Conservation and Recovery Act (RCRA) and called attention to the Carter administration's efforts to weaken it. Sanjour then continued to "blow the whistle" on agency waste, fraud, and abuse. He has fought a number of battles to maintain his position within the EPA, winning important grievances and Department of Labor civil actions. With the help of the National Whistleblower Center, Sanjour won a federal court case blocking a regulation by the Office of Government Ethics that would have limited the ability of whistleblowers to speak to citizens groups on their own time. Sanjour has been an important resource for legislators, journalists, and environmental groups by providing an insider's view of the workings of the EPA.

William Sanjour was born in New York City on February 19, 1933. He served in the United States Army from 1952 to 1954, then studied at the City College of New York, receiving a B.S. in physics in 1958. He earned an M.A. in physics from Columbia University in 1960 and worked for the United States Navy's Center for Naval Analysis as an operations analyst until 1964. From 1964 to 1966 he worked as an operations research analyst for American Cyanamid Corporation, and from 1966 to 1967 he worked for the Chemical Construction Corporation. In 1967 Sanjour joined Ernst & Ernst, a consulting firm in Washington, D.C., where he first began consulting for the EPA. He conducted computer simulations of air pollution emissions, designing a model to achieve maximum pollution reduction with minimum costs. From 1972 to 1974 he continued his work for the EPA as a private consultant.

Sanjour joined the EPA full time in 1974, as a branch chief within the newly created Hazardous Waste Management Division. His branch conducted studies to assess the scope of the hazardous waste problem in the United States. Its studies detailed treatment methods, analyzed health and safety impacts, and documented more than 600 cases of damage caused by hazardous waste. These studies were instrumental in the passage of the Resource Conservation and Recovery Act, the first national hazardous waste management law. In 1978, with the country gripped by inflation spurred by the energy crisis, the Carter administration sought to protect industry from the costs of complying with RCRA. The EPA was neither implementing nor enforcing hazardous waste regulations, and after first attempting to deal with the matter internally, Sanjour went public with claims that the EPA was failing to live up to the letter and spirit of RCRA. In response, the agency transferred Sanjour in 1979 to a position with essentially no duties. Sanjour fought the transfer and won appointment as head of the Hazardous Waste Implementation Branch in 1980, a position he held until 1983. This branch helped regional EPA offices implement RCRA and drafted regulations for the transportation of hazardous waste.

During this period Sanjour continued to speak out on important hazardous waste issues, testifying before Congress and speaking and writing for grassroots environmental groups. During the Reagan administration, Sanjour and fellow EPA whistleblower HUGH KAUFMAN were targeted for their actions, and the EPA tried to silence them. Rita Lavelle, the political appointee in charge of Sanjour's office, was responsible for fabricating an unsatisfactory performance review of Sanjour. He fought the evaluation and won, under the agency's own grievance procedures. Lavelle was later jailed for lying to Congress. In 1984, weary of agency harassment, Sanjour went on loan to the Congressional Office of Technology Assessment (OTA), where he wrote a report critical of EPA hazardous waste regulations. The report appeared in OTA's 1985 study, *Superfund Strategy*.

When Sanjour returned to the EPA, he had been removed from his position as head of the hazardous waste implementation branch and reassigned as a policy analyst. In this capacity he wrote regulations for government procurement of recycled materials, including lubricating oil, retread tires, and insulating materials. Sanjour received an outstanding performance award for these achievements. In 1989 Sanjour and Kaufman garnered national press attention for their criticism of plans to clean up Boston Harbor, which they charged did not address adequately the problem of contaminated sludge. In 1995 Sanjour was assigned to assist the Superfund ombudsman, investigating citizen complaints against regional EPA offices in their implementation of the Superfund program. He eventually became frustrated in the position by the lack of cooperation from the agency and was reassigned to a position as policy analyst for the Technology Innovation Office at the EPA. In this position, which he held from 1997 until his retirement in 2001, his duties included developing nationwide programs for public-private partnerships to promote new technologies for hazardous waste cleanup.

Since his retirement, Sanjour has written about environmental and whistleblower protection, and has served on the boards of the North Carolina Waste Awareness and Reduction Network, and the National Whistleblower Center. He is also a fellow of the Environmental Research Foundation. Sanjour was given the Sentinel Award by the Association of Certified Fraud Examiners in 2007.

**BIBLIOGRAPHY**
"Collected Papers of William Sanjour," pwp.lincs.net/sanjour/; Sanjour, William, "In Name Only," *Sierra*, 1992; Tye, Larry, "US Judge Lashes out at EPA Pair," *Boston Globe*, 1989.

## Sargent, Charles Sprague
(April 24, 1841–March 22, 1927)
Dendrologist

Dendrologist Charles Sprague Sargent was the country's foremost expert on trees during the late 1800s, the author of a 14-volume illustrated encyclopedia of the trees growing in North America (*The Silva of North America*, 1891–1902). Sargent made the first official surveys of the nation's forests and became an influential advocate of the establishment of state and national forest preserves.

# SARGENT, CHARLES SPRAGUE

Charles Sprague Sargent (Library of Congress, Prints & Photographs Division, LC-USZ62-103958)

Charles Sprague Sargent was born into a wealthy Boston family on April 24, 1841. His father was a merchant who traded goods from the East Indies. Sargent was sent to private preparatory schools and then to Harvard University, where he studied under the eminent botanist ASA GRAY. Upon graduation from Harvard in 1862, Sargent enlisted in the Union Army, rising to the rank of major during the Civil War. When the war ended, he traveled to Europe, where he spent three years studying horticulture. He returned to Harvard in 1872, where he was appointed director of Harvard's Botanic Garden, which Gray had developed. In 1873 Sargent became director of the university's new Arnold Arboretum, a 260-acre estate in Jamaica Plain, Massachusetts, a recent bequest to Harvard. Sargent worked with landscape architect FREDERICK LAW OLMSTED SR. to design the plantings throughout the property's meadows, rolling hills, and gentle valleys. Over the course of his 54 years as director of Arnold Arboretum, Sargent oversaw its transformation into the nation's most important study center for dendrology, the study of trees and shrubs. In addition to the groves of hemlocks, cedars of Lebanon, and rare oaks, Sargent assembled a well-stocked herbarium and a grand botanical library on the property. Students traveled from the world afar to study at Sargent's Arnold Arboretum.

In 1880, Sargent was asked to coordinate a survey of the nation's forest resources for the tenth census. He worked with a large team of field botanists and then prepared his *Report on the Forests of North America* for publication in 1884. At the same time he engaged in a collection project for the American Museum of Natural History in New York City. He assembled specimens of American trees, and his wife, Mary Allen Robeson, made more than 400 watercolor paintings of flowers and fruits for a large exhibit. This work led to his appointment to the Northern Pacific Transcontinental Survey, which traveled westward in 1882 and 1883 to survey the wild lands of the West. Impressed by the botanical value of the lands he passed through, Sargent began to lobby for the preservation of certain tracts, particularly the area that later became Glacier National Park in northern Montana. Following that, in 1884 and 1885, Sargent was named chairman of the New York State Commission on Forestry, which successfully recommended the preservation of the Adirondack and Catskill forests. During the 1890s, the weekly *Garden and Forest* magazine that Sargent edited sounded a steady call for the systematic preservation of the valuable forests of the United States.

Sargent and the young GIFFORD PINCHOT, who was at the dawn of his career in forestry, acted together to lobby the federal government for a national forest policy. After garnering endorsements from such influential institutions as the New York Board of Trade and New York Chamber of Commerce, the National Academy of Sciences appropriated $25,000 to pay for a survey and a study of the forests of the United States. A six-man commission, headed by Sargent with Pinchot serving as secretary, set out for a two-year survey of the forests of the West, from Montana to Arizona. The forested areas the group was visiting were obviously in trouble: unregulated lumber cutting and livestock grazing were seriously degrading fragile forests. But the committee was split on what type of policy to recommend. Sargent and committee adviser JOHN MUIR believed their task was to recommend which areas of forest were most in need of preservation; Pinchot and committee member Arnold Hague of the U.S. Geological Survey surveyed the forests with an eye to which ones could be exploited for timber. Sargent and Muir were in favor of immediate instatement of army patrols to protect the forests. Pinchot favored control of the forests by trained forest managers, who would supervise limited cutting and grazing. The report that the committee drew up leaned toward the Sargent-Muir position, but Pinchot signed it anyway. It recommended the establishment of 13 forest preserves to protect an area totaling 21.4 million acres. Pres. Grover Cleveland approved the creation of these new preserves during his last days in office, but soon after he left office, Congress—swayed by the western logging and livestock lobbies—voted to undo 11 of these 13 reserves and to allow managed use of the remaining two. Pinchot soon became director of the country's new Division of Forestry and implemented a forest management policy that preservation-oriented Sargent and Muir bitterly disagreed with.

The rest of Sargent's career was dedicated to travel and collection of specimens, further study of dendrology, and development of the Arnold Arboretum. He received a medal of honor for his services to horticulture from the Garden Club of America in 1920, and the American Genetics Association presented him with the Frank N. Meyer Horticultural Medal in 1923 for his work in plant introduction. Sargent died on March 22, 1927, in Brookline, Massachusetts.

### BIBLIOGRAPHY

Fox, Stephen, *The American Conservation Movement: John Muir and His Legacy*, 1981; Nash, Roderick, *Wilderness and the American Mind*, rev. ed., 1973; "Our History" The Arnold Arboretum of Harvard University—arboretum.harvard.edu/aboutus/history.html Rehder, Alfred, "Charles Sprague Sargent," *Journal of the Arnold Arboretum*, 1927; Sutton, S.B., *Charles Sprauge Sargent and the Arnold Arboretum*, 1970.

## Sawhill, John

(June 12, 1936–May 18, 2000)
President of The Nature Conservancy

John Sawhill began his environmental career in 1974 when he was named director of the Federal Energy Office, or "energy czar," for the White House. In 1990, he became president of The Nature Conservancy (TNC), one of the largest conservation organizations active in the United States today. During his tenure at TNC, which ended with his death in 2000, TNC was able to protect more than seven million acres of land in the U.S.

John Crittenden Sawhill, the oldest of four children, was born to James Mumford Sawhill and Mary Munroe Gipe Sawhill on June 12, 1936, in Cleveland, Ohio. Soon after his birth his family moved to Baltimore, where Sawhill attended private schools. He went to college at Princeton, where he studied in the Woodrow Wilson School of Public and International Affairs. During this time, Sawhill was active in many extracurricular activities. He wrestled, played intramural hockey, and was a member of the prestigious Colonial dining club. In

1958, Sawhill married Isabel Van Devanter, with whom he had one child, James Winslow Sawhill. He graduated in 1959 with a B.A. degree and spent the next two years working in the underwriting and research departments of the investment brokerage firm of Merrill, Lynch, Pierce, Fenner, and Smith.

In 1960, Sawhill enrolled in New York University's Graduate School of Business Administration, earning a Ph.D. in economics, finance, and statistics by 1963. During his time there, he was employed as assistant to the dean and instructor in 1960 and 1961 and later as assistant dean and assistant professor. He also worked as senior consulting economist for the House Committee on Banking and Currency of the U.S. Congress. From 1963 to 1965 Sawhill was director of credit research and planning for the Commercial Credit Company in Baltimore, and from 1965 to 1968 he was a senior associate for McKinsey and Company in Washington. In 1968, he returned to the Commercial Credit Company, where he advanced to senior vice president in the following year.

In April 1973, Sawhill gave up this $100,000 a year job and accepted a $38,000 per year position as one of the four associate directors of the Office of Management and Budget for the Nixon administration. In this capacity Sawhill was responsible for programs relating to energy, science, and natural resources. During the fall of 1973, energy became an increased concern in the United States when the Arab oil-producing nations imposed a trade embargo on the West. The newly created Federal Energy Office (FEO), headed by John A. Love, failed to relieve the pressure of the intensifying fuel shortage crisis, and in early December Richard Nixon announced the resignation of Love. Nixon then signed an executive order that officially established the FEO within the White House and named Sawhill as the deputy director, subordinate only to William E. Simon, the newly named administrator. The FEO's most important task was preventing fuel shortages, through price regulation of domestic crude oil and a mandatory allocation program.

In April 1974, Simon was named Treasury Secretary, and Sawhill was chosen to replace him as FEO chief, the so-called energy czar. This post took on additional significance in May when Nixon signed a bill converting the FEO into the Federal Energy Administration. This bill turned the FEO into a temporary independent executive agency and gave it authority to impose conservation measures, collect data from industry, and otherwise support the administration's efforts to reduce U.S. reliance on foreign energy sources. Sawhill remained in this post until the beginning of 1975, pushing the development of domestic energy supplies and encouraging energy conservation. And even after the embargo ended in March 1974, Sawhill's agency continued to support conservation by offering energy-saving advice to consumers, encouraging the production of fuel-efficient automobiles, and asking big businesses to cut down on energy use. In late 1974, having frustrated the administration of Gerald Ford through his continued advocacy of mandatory conservation (a position not shared by Ford or the newly appointed head of the Energy Resources Council, Rogers C. Morton), Sawhill was forced to resign.

Sawhill became the 12th president of New York University on April 12, 1975, serving until 1979, when he briefly returned to public service. He was appointed secretary of the Department of Energy until 1980, when he returned to the private sector as chairman of the U.S. Synthetic Fuels Corporation. He stayed in this position for one year, joining the board of directors of McKinsey and Co. in Washington in 1980, where he remained for the next ten years. In 1990 Sawhill became president of The Nature Conservancy. At this time, The Nature Conservancy was feeling the effects of the rapid growth that had occurred throughout 1980s and was, in many ways, outgrowing its own infrastructure. When Sawhill arrived, many basic organizational systems had been unable to keep up with the growth: the financial system was unable to produce reports on time, and the marketing system was not able to provide accurate up-to-date information on members. Sawhill brought new leadership and organization to The Nature Conservancy, correcting these problems and encouraging a shift in conservation strategy away from simple land acquisition and toward the science-based, compatible economic development strategies being utilized today. During Sawhill's 10 years as president, The Nature Conservancy membership doubled, its revenues from land sales increased fivefold, and the size of the staff tripled.

The Nature Conservancy, founded in 1951, has been referred to as "the titan of the green groups." The Conservancy has nearly a billion dollars in assets and is constantly in the process of obtaining cash donations from individual members and corporate sponsors such as Arco, DuPont, British Petroleum, and many others. Known as "nature's real estate agent," it is a nonpolitical organization, focusing on the purchase of private lands for the purpose of conserving habitats and wildlife.

As president of The Nature Conservancy, Sawhill's main focus shifted from energy conservation to habitat conservation. In a talk given at Harvard University in February 1998, he spoke about what he saw as the most pressing of the environmental issues humans face; the extinction of species. He said that a normal extinction rate is about one or two species per year, while today, largely because of human activities, we face the extinction of up to one species per hour. This rate is similar to that of the massive extinction event at the end of the Cretaceous that led to the end of the dinosaurs.

According to Sawhill, the most significant culprit leading to these extinctions is the fragmentation of natural habitats due to development. In his talk, he outlined the tactics advocated by The Nature Conservancy for dealing with this problem. The first step is to identify successful, environmentally responsible economic strategies. An example of this type of strategy can be found in The Nature Conservancy's attempts to work with Malaysian companies in identifying ecologically compatible forest management practices that generate profits and meet the needs of local people. The next step in preventing extinction is to build strong public-private partnerships, a practice that combines private and corporate funds to purchase private land in the public's interest. This type of cooperation can lead to "acceptable conservation strategies to seemingly intractable problems." Finally, and most important, people need to develop a strong conservation ethic. From Sawhill's perspective, only when people understand and embrace the importance of conservation will the problem of extinction be effectively and meaningfully challenged.

Sawhill died due to complications related to diabetes on May 18, 2000 in Richmond, Virginia.

**BIBLIOGRAPHY**

Howard, Alice, and Joan Magretta, "Surviving Success: An Interview with The Nature Conservancy's John Sawhill," *Harvard Business Review*, 1995; Levy, Claudia, "Environmentalist John Sawhill, 63, Dies," *Washington Post*, 2000; Moritz, Charles, ed., *Current Biography Yearbook*, 1979; Sawhill, John C., The "Business" of Conservation" *Geotimes*, 1997; Sawhill, John C. and Richard Cotton, *Energy Conservation: Successes and Failures*, 1986.

## Schlickeisen, Rodger

(January 24, 1941– )
President of Defenders of Wildlife

Rodger Schlickeisen has been the president and chief executive officer (CEO) of Defenders of Wildlife since 1991. Defenders of Wildlife is a national organization dedicated to the protection of native plant and animal species and their natural habitats. Through advocacy, education, litigation, and research, the group strives to conserve species, habitat, and international biodiversity. Its efforts include helping to return wolves and bears to their natural habitats, creating and maintaining wildlife refuges, conserving wild birds and marine life, and promoting wildlife education and appreciation through their quarterly publication, *Defenders* magazine.

Born to parents Oscar Schlickeisen and Alice Rennemo on January 24, 1941, Rodger Schlickeisen grew up in Seattle, Washington, and southern Oregon, spending much of his childhood exploring the Cascade Mountains. In 1963 he earned a B.A. in economics from the University of Washington. He went on to the Harvard Business School, earning an M.B.A. in 1965, and to George Washington University, where he received his doctorate in business administration in 1978.

Schlickeisen began his professional life with a string of government jobs. From 1966 to 1968 he was a captain in the United States Army. From 1968 to 1970 he served as a finance loan officer for Latin America with the United States Export-Import bank. From 1970 until 1974 Schlickeisen volunteered with the Virginia chapter of Common Cause, where he helped to put in place a number of open government reforms, making government meetings and decisions more freely accessible to the voting public. In 1974 Schlickeisen joined the U.S. Senate Committee on the Budget, working with that group until 1979. In 1979 Schlickeisen became the associate director for economics and government in the Office of Management and Budget for the Carter administration, serving in that office until 1981.

Schlickeisen's environmental career was launched when he joined Craver, Mathews, Smith & Company as its CEO in 1982. The Washington, D.C., and California firm consults with a number of national environmental and other organizations on such issues as fundraising and organizational development. Schlickeisen directed operations at Craver, Mathews, Smith & Company until 1987. During this time the company consulted for various congressional campaigns as well as organizations including Greenpeace, the Sierra Club, and the Natural Resources Defense Council, improving their fundraising through direct mail marketing techniques.

In 1987 Schlickeisen became the chief of staff for Sen. Max Baucus, a Democrat from Montana and one of the only pro-environment senators from the northern Rockies states. Baucus is a ranking member of the Senate Environment and Public Works Committee. Schlickeisen worked with Baucus until 1991, helping him to win reelection to a third term in the Senate.

Defenders of Wildlife hired Schlickeisen as president and CEO in 1991. Since joining Defenders of Wildlife, Schlickeisen has increased membership in the organization from 62,000 to more than 500,000. He is a staunch supporter of the Endangered Species Act (ESA), claiming that it is the "single most effective tool for keeping our lands biologically healthy for future generations." Defenders of Wildlife continues to help enforce the ESA and is a member of the Endangered Species Coalition, which is housed in the Defenders of Wildlife's offices. Defenders has been a champion of the efforts to return wolves, the top natural predator, to the lower 48 states, Canada and Mexico. Schlickeisen believes that the wolf represents "the very embodiment of wild nature" to Americans. For this reason he sees the success of the reintroduction efforts as pivotal to other similar conservation endeavors. Throughout North America, Defenders seeks to protect and restore many other species, and their habitat, as well, including grizzlies, black-footed ferrets, prairie dogs, jaguars, pygmy owls and more.

In addition to serving as president of Defenders of Wildlife, Schlickeisen heads Defenders of Wildlife Action Fund, which works to elect pro-conservation candidates to Congress and the White House.

Schlickeisen serves on the board of the League of Conservation Voters and its Education Fund. He was the founding chair of the Partnership Project, which builds unity among environmental organizations. He sits on the advisory committees of the Earth Communications Organization and the Environmental Media Association. He resides in Alexandria, Virginia, with his wife, Susan, and their son, Derek.

**BIBLIOGRAPHY**
"Defenders of Wildlife," www.defenders.org; "Defenders of Wildlife Action Fund," www.defendersactionfund.org; Rembert, Tracey C., "Rodger Schlickeisen: Defending America's Wilder Ways," *E Magazine*, 1998; Schlickeisen, Rodger, "After 25 Years, Still Protecting Endangered Species," *Christian Science Monitor*, 1998; Schlickeisen, Rodger, "Connection with Wolves," *Defenders*, 1994/1995.

## Schneider, Stephen
(February 11, 1945– )
Climatologist

Climatologist Stephen Schneider was one of the first prominent U.S. scientists to warn of the impending dangers of global warming in the late 1970s and has continued to lead the field in the 40 years since then. Throughout his career, Schneider has attempted to encourage long-term, scientifically grounded policy decisions, by means of sharing his findings with the public and with policy makers through books, magazine articles, and television and radio interviews. He believes in the strength of interdisciplinary research and has collaborated on research teams and government committees with experts and scientists from a variety of disciplines.

Stephen Henry Schneider was born in New York City on February 11, 1945, to Samuel and Doris (Swarte) Schneider. He loved science, having built a five-foot-long telescope before he grew that tall, and used it with wide-eyed excitement to see the craters of the moon, the rings of Saturn, or the phases of Venus. By high school that enthusiasm turned to the drag racing track, where he and his brother won trophies (Schneider, not yet 16, was the mechanic; his older brother Peter was the driver).

Schneider entered Columbia University in 1962, where he studied mechanical engineering and received his B.S. in 1966. He continued his studies at Columbia, earning an M.S. in 1967 and a Ph.D. in mechanical engineering and plasma physics in 1971. Schneider was working in plasma physics as a graduate student in 1970 at Columbia University when the first Earth Day came along. He was shocked to learn that pollution could affect the global climate and even more surprised to discover that very little research had been done on the subject. As a result, he changed his field of research and became a postdoctoral fellow in 1971 at the Goddard Institute for Space Studies (GISS) of the National Aeronautics and Space Administration (NASA) in New York City as a National Research Council research associate, working on the role of greenhouse gases and suspended particulate material on climate. He remained at GISS until 1972, when he was awarded a postdoctoral fellowship at the National Center for Atmospheric Research (NCAR), which facilitated his move to Boulder, Colorado, for the yearlong fellowship. He remained with NCAR until 1996, cofounding its Climate Project and working in various capacities on climate issues.

In 1975, Schneider founded the journal, *Climatic Change*, an interdisciplinary, international journal devoted to the description, causes, and implications of climatic change. He continues to serve as its editor. As a research scientist, Schneider has done pioneering modeling work in the fields of atmospheric science and global climatology and in particular has explored the relationship of biological systems to global climate change. He is known for coupling models of the atmosphere to models of other climate subsystems such as oceans, ice, or biosphere, as well as to social systems (via economic models, and so on). He has initiated new research and policy directions in environmental issues, in part by crossing disciplinary boundaries and combining disciplinary research contributions, original interdisciplinary syntheses, popular publications, legislative testimony, media appearances, television documentary productions, and the organization of scientific and public policy meetings and seminars.

With support from numerous federal and private foundation grants, Schneider has conducted research on the earth's climate, exploring such issues as the climatic effects of nuclear war, climatic impacts on society, the ecological implications of climate change, and the application of climate modeling to policy making. Of particular interest to Schneider is the greenhouse effect, the atmospheric process whereby carbon dioxide and water vapor in the earth's atmosphere trap solar radiation, creating temperatures capable of sustaining life as we know it on the surface of the planet. These "greenhouse gases" are necessary for sustaining life on earth. However, the greater the amount of greenhouse gases there is in the atmosphere, the more solar radiation gets trapped. Thus, when we emit unnatural amounts of carbon dioxide into the atmosphere, we are creating a situation where more heat will be trapped and the surface temperature of earth will rise. As early as the mid 1970s, Schneider was issuing warnings about the global warming dangers brought about by the massive amounts of carbon dioxide humans were pumping into the atmosphere through the burning of fossil fuels. Nearly 25 years later, and after a decade of slowly rising temperatures, the question among scientists of whether or not global warming will take place is largely moot. Nowadays it is more a question of how much the climate will change and what type of impact these rising temperatures will actually have. It is believed that they will lead to a rise in sea level, to more variable and extreme weather, to changes in local precipitation patterns, and to the expansion of deserts into grazing and agricultural lands. Schneider's suggestions for dealing with global warming include the reduction of emissions, the elimination of the use of chlorofluorocarbons, the halting of deforestation, as well as the implementation of reforestation efforts.

While at NCAR in Boulder, Schneider also examined the theory of nuclear winter, a theory that attempts to explain the possible climatic and atmospheric ramifications of a nuclear war. He is also interested in advancing public understanding of science and in improving formal environmental education in primary and secondary schools. Schneider firmly believes in the public airing of scientific issues in language understood by the majority of people (including and especially lawmakers). This belief has made Schneider unpopular with some of his colleagues, but he has made a continuous practice of "going public" with his scientific findings. Ultimately, he believes, science can only provide probabilities, and it is up to the citizens to decide how much risk to take.

Schneider is the author of *The Genesis Strategy: Climate and Global Survival* (1976), *The Co-Evolution of Climate and Life* (1984), *Global Warming: Are We Entering the Greenhouse Century?* (1989), *Laboratory Earth: The Planetary Gamble We Can't Afford to Lose* (1997) and *Wildlife Responses to Climate Change: North American Case Studies* (2002). He has authored papers for the Working Group of the Intergovernmental Panel on Climate Change (IPCC), a United Nations-affiliated advisory group of experts on climate change, which collectively shared the 2007 Nobel Peace Prize with AL GORE. And he has edited several other important books, including the *Encyclopedia of Climate and Weather* (1996). He has authored or coauthored more than 450 scientific papers, proceedings, legislative testimonies, edited books, and book chapters as well as some 140 book reviews, editorials, and published newspaper and magazine interviews. He is a frequent contributor to commercial and non-commercial print and broadcast media on climate and environmental issues: *Nova*, *Planet Earth*, *Nightline*, *Today Show*, *Tonight Show*, *Dateline*, and programs on the Discovery Channel and British, Canadian, and Australian Broadcasting Corporations, among many others.

Schneider has received many awards for his scientific achievements. In 1979, he was selected as one of 35 Top Americans Under 35 by *U.S. Magazine*; in 1991, he was awarded the American Association for the Advancement of Science/Westinghouse Award for Public Understanding of Science and Technology; in 1992 he received a MacArthur Fellowship; and in 2002 Schneider was elected to the National Academy of Sciences. He is a frequent witness at congressional and parliamentary hearings. He has been a member of the Defense Science Board Task Force on Atmospheric Obscuration and was a consultant to the White House in the Carter, Nixon, Reagan, Bush, and Clinton administrations. Today, Schneider continues his research into global change and teaches courses on climate and environmental policy at Stanford University in California.

Since 1992, Schneider has lived in California. He has two grown children, Rebecca and Adam, from a previous marriage, and is married to Terry Root, Senior Fellow at the Woods Institute of the Environment at Stanford University.

**BIBLIOGRAPHY**

Athanasiou, Tom, "Greenhouse Blues," *Socialist Review*, 1991; Johnson, Dan, "Earth's Changing Climate," *The Futurist*, 1997; McDaniel, Carl, *Wisdom for a livable planet: the visionary work of Terri Swearingen, Dave Foreman, Wes Jackson, Helena Norberg-Hodge, Werner Fornos, Herman Daly, Stephen Schneider, and David Orr*, 2005; Schneider, Stephen H., *Global Warming: Are We Entering the Greenhouse Century?*, 1989; Schneider, Stephen H., "The Greenhouse Effect: Science and Policy," *Science*, 1989, "Stephen H. Schneider, Climatologist," stephenschneider.stanford.edu.

## Schultes, Richard Evans

(January 12, 1915– April 10, 2001)
Ethnobotanist

Widely considered the father of ethnobotany and the last of the great explorers, Richard Evans Schultes was deeply influential in forwarding both conservation and a respect for indigenous cultures and knowledge in his work and research. The foremost botanist of the Amazon of the twentieth century, Schultes's career significantly advanced conceptions of the plant world in both academic and public spheres.

Richard Evans Schultes was born January 12, 1915, in Boston, Massachusetts. Though he would often describe himself as a fourth- or fifth-generation Bostonian, he was also the grandson of German immigrants on his father's side. Schultes was quite ill as a child and was advised by his family doctor to stay close to home instead of commuting by trolley through the damp and congested tunnel that connected East Boston, where he lived, to the mainland to attend Boston Latin, the most prestigious public school in the city and the most appropriate for a student of Schultes's caliber. So he attended East Boston High School, where he excelled in all disciplines, especially Greek, Latin, chemistry, and foreign languages. In his spare time he read, raised rabbits, worked in the family garden, and ran errands, working for a nickel a day, which he put toward future college expenses. He applied only to Harvard, did well on his entrance exams, and became the first member of his family to attend university. His plan was to become a doctor. Rather than staying in residence at Harvard, Schultes saved money by commuting from home.

At the end of his first year, Schultes received financial support in the form of the Cudworth Scholarship, a small award given by the Unitarian Church of East Boston. The scholarship was endowed to help Harvard students of good moral standing who hailed either from East Boston or Lowell. Looking for work during his second year to supplement his scholarship, Schultes took a job at the Botanical Museum, filing cards and stacking books in the Economic Botany Library. There, he fell under the influence of economic botany professor Oakes Ames, the museum's director and a millionaire many times over.

Intrigued by the material he was organizing, Schultes decided to enroll in Ames's biology course—"Plants and Human Affairs"—in the spring. As part of the course requirements, Schultes had to prepare a report on a monograph entitled "Mescal: The Divine Plant and Its Psychological Effects," by the German psychiatrist, Heinrich Klüver. Published in 1928, this monograph was the only study in English that described the pharmacological effects of peyote. Inspired by Klüver's descriptions of peyote's uses and effects, Schultes asked Ames whether he might write about peyote for his undergraduate thesis. Ames agreed on one condition: that research of the literature would not be sufficient; Schultes would have to travel west to Oklahoma and see the plant in use. Ames told Schultes that little was known about peyote, and a history of the plant's use would be a valuable study. He even promised his eager pupil some grant money; Schultes discovered some years later that the money had come directly from Ames's own pocket. So began a long and distinguished career of field study into the cultural and scientific mysteries of plants with psychoactive powers. Schultes completed his A.B., *cum laude*, in 1937 and immediately went to work on an A.M., completing his Ph.D. in biology in 1941.

Torn between accepting a one-year research fellowship in South America and staying in the United States in case the war in Europe should spread, Schultes was persuaded by Ames, who believed that biologists should work in the field as well as the laboratory, to opt for the research fellowship. Shultes went to Bogotá, Colombia. From Bogotá, he took buses as far as the roads would go, before transferring himself and his equipment to horses to cross the Andes. Across the Andes, he changed to dugout canoe to paddle down uncharted tributaries of the Amazon River. The area that Schultes had chosen to study remains today one of the wildest and least-explored areas on earth. His only guide was the diary of his boyhood hero Richard Spruce, an English botanist who had explored the same area some 90 years earlier. For a botanist who grew up in New England where there are 1,900 species of plants, the Amazon jungle with an estimated 80,000 plant species was overwhelming.

Despite the remote location of his study site, Schultes learned of the Japanese attack on Pearl Harbor on a trader's radio within a few weeks of the event. He decided to return to Bogotá, to the American embassy, to enlist in the U.S. military. The trip took a month and a half. Embassy officials decided that Schultes could be of most use by continuing his botanical studies. The Japanese had captured all the rubber plantations in Southeast Asia, and the Allies were in desperate need of a new source of natural rubber for the war effort. Accordingly, in early 1942, Schultes was hired as a field agent for a government entity known as the Rubber Development Corporation. His task was to locate rubber trees in Amazonia and to teach local natives how to extract the latex.

When the war ended, the Colombian government and the U.S. Department of Agriculture asked Schultes to stay on and help develop a living nursery of rubber trees. He gladly accepted, as it would also allow him to continue his research of the medicinal and poisonous plants used in the Amazon jungle. Over the next 13 years, Schultes returned to New England only for occasional two-month Christmas breaks, where he could see his family, skate, and ski.

The relationship Schultes established with the indigenous people with whom he lived and from whom he learned is among the most impressive aspects of his career. Desiring to learn from them rather than teach them, Schultes gained virtually full acceptance among many tribes. Though he acknowledged proficiency in understanding only two Amazonian languages, he apparently managed to communicate with little difficulty with tribal peoples who spoke other tongues.

Schultes's one-year fellowship turned into a 13-year sojourn and might have lasted even longer, had not someone in Harvard's administrative offices discovered that an honorary research fellow named Schultes had been on a leave of absence since 1941. Schultes returned to Harvard in 1954. Between annual trips back to the northwest Amazon, he taught economic botany, the oldest science course at Harvard and the one that had captivated him when he was a student. He was eventually appointed director of the Botanical Museum and during his life received countless awards, most notably the highest honor offered by the Republic of Colombia, the Cross of Boyaca, in 1983 and, the following year, the World Wildlife Fund's Gold Medal and the Tyler Prize for environmental achievement. In 1986, in recognition of his contributions to conservation in that country, the government of Colombia named a 2.2-million-acre protected tract "Sector Schultes."

Schultes married Dorothy Crawford McNeil, an operatic soprano, in 1959. Together they had three children. Portraying himself as conservative and almost Victorian, Schultes nevertheless was concerned about the need for conservation in the Amazon in the 1940s before the emergence of the general recognition that the region was in danger. Chewing coca leaves and sampling potent hallucinogens and various witch doctors' brews also seems out of character for such a straitlaced Bostonian, who always took tins of baked beans into the jungle along with his botanical supplies.

By the time he retired in 1985 to suburban Massachusetts, Schultes had identified three previously unidentified genera and more than 120 species of Amazonian plants. In addition, a large species of Amazonian cockroach was named for him. Over the course of his long career, Schultes collected 24,000 species, hundreds of which were previously unknown to science. Schultes's scholarship and contributions of specimens to the Botanical Museum at Harvard have significantly increased scientists' understanding of the plant world. Furthermore, his recognition of the importance of conserving ethnobotanical lore superceded the awareness of most biologists of any conservation problems in tropical areas.

Schultes died on April 10, 2001.

### BIBLIOGRAPHY

Clark, Tim, "Old Man Amazon," *Yankee*, 1986; Davis, Wade, *One River: Explorations and Discoveries in the Amazon Rain Forest*, 1996; Davis, Wade, *The Serpent and the Rainbow*, 1985; Kahn, E. J., Jr., "Jungle Botanist," *New Yorker*, 1992; Kandell, Jonathon, "Richard E. Schultes, 86, Dies; Trailblazing Authority on Hallucinogenic Plants, *New York Times*, 2001; Krieg, Margaret B., *Green Medicine*, 1964; Schultes, Richard Evans, and Robert F. Raffauf, *Vine of the Soul: Medicine Men, Their Plants and Rituals in the Columbian Amazonia*, 2004; Schultes, Richard Evans, and Siri Von Reis, *Ethnobotany: Evolution of a Discipline*, 1995.

## Schurz, Carl

(March 2, 1829–May 14, 1906)
Secretary of the Interior

Journalist, senator, abolitionist, and revolutionary, Carl Schurz was a visionary in several fields, including forestry. As secretary of the interior for the administration of Pres. Rutherford B. Hayes, Schurz proposed conservationist policies that were far ahead of his time and that would be adopted 30 years later.

Carl Schurz was born on March 2, 1829, near the town of Liblar, Germany. He was the oldest of three children. His mother, Marianne, was the daughter of a tenant farmer, and his father, Christian, was a schoolteacher turned small businessman. Schurz attended local schools until his father was thrown into debtors' prison. After completing his studies on his own, Schurz entered the University of Bonn in 1847, with a view toward studying history and entering the professorate. While at the university, Schurz met Prof. Gottfried Kinkel. Kinkel was a leader in the German revolutions of 1848 and 1849, and Schurz got caught up in the movement, becoming a staff aide to Kinkel during the last battles of 1849. Schurz fled the country in late 1849 but returned in 1850 to rescue Kinkel, who had been sentenced to life in prison. After months of planning, Schurz bribed a guard, lowered Kinkel out of the window of the Spandau prison, and fled to France to begin a life of permanent exile.

After being forced to leave France because of his political views, Schurz stayed for a time in England before emigrating to the United States in 1852. In 1856 Schurz bought a farm in Wisconsin. He became a passionate abolitionist and one of the great orators of his day, which attracted the attention of Wisconsin Republicans. He was nominated but never elected as lieutenant governor and served as chairman of the Wisconsin delegation to the Republican convention of 1860, which nomi-

Carl Schurz (Library of Congress, Prints & Photographs Division, LC-DIG-cwpbh-04020)

nated Abraham Lincoln. During the Civil War Schurz served as a brigadier-general for the Union Army, where his German ancestry made him the scapegoat for several defeats. After the war Schurz began a career in journalism, eventually accepting the editorship of the German-language paper *Westliche Post* in St. Louis, Missouri. Schurz continued to be active in Republican politics and was elected to the U.S. Senate from Missouri in 1868. He grew disillusioned with the corruption and imperialism of the Republican administration of Ulysses S. Grant and led a revolt that resulted in the formation of the Liberal Republican Party. The reformers nominated Horace Greeley, but the revolt was unsuccessful, and President Grant was reelected in 1872.

In 1876 Schurz supported the presidential candidacy of Republican Rutherford B. Hayes and was rewarded with the post of secretary of the interior. Schurz was the first German-born citizen to hold a seat in the cabinet. One of Schurz's drives was to eliminate the corruption that political patronage had wrought upon the executive branch. He advocated, somewhat successfully, for civil service reform throughout the Department of the Interior. This principle led to real reform in the treatment of Native Americans, whose treaties had often been negotiated and administered by agents whose first priority was their own pocketbooks. Schurz held hearings to expose unscrupulous agents and calmed the hysteria that had arisen after Custer's defeat at the Battle of the Little Bighorn. Schurz also managed to halt a move in Congress to transfer Indian affairs to the War Department, which almost certainly would have resulted in even bloodier resolution of Indian conflicts.

Schurz brought to his post a German sensibility regarding forest conservation. Germany had long been interested in managing its forests and had developed early principles of reforestation. Schurz saw that the U.S. government's management of natural resources, just as in Indian affairs, was dominated by greed and corruption. Lumber companies stole timber from public lands, and Schurz intervened to try to pass legislation halting the practice. Schurz put forth the first policy for public conservation, though Congress failed to enact the reforms he suggested until the administration of Pres. THEODORE ROOSEVELT set aside the first national forests in the early 1900s, 30 years later. As secretary, Schurz did successfully institute the U.S. Geological Survey, which conducted geological research and made land use policy recommendations.

After leaving the cabinet, Schurz settled in New York City, where he continued to press for civil and conservation reform in writing. He wrote for and edited a number of journals, including the *New York Evening Post*, *The Nation*, and *Harper's Weekly*. Carl Schurz died on May 14, 1906, of pneumonia. He was buried in Sleepy Hollow Cemetery in Tarrytown, New York.

**BIBLIOGRAPHY**
Camp, Helen, "Carl Schurz," *American Reformers*, 1985; "Carl Schurz," rs6.loc.gov/ammem/today/oct29.html; Fuess, Claude Moore, *Carl Schurz: Reformer (1829-1906)*, 1963; Schafer, Joseph, *Carl Schurz,*

*Militant Liberal*, 1930; Terzian, James P., *Defender of Human Rights: Carl Schurz*, 1965; Trefousse, Hans, *Carl Schurz*, 1998.

## Schwarzenegger, Arnold

(July 30, 1947—)
Governor of California

The 38th Governor of California, Republican Arnold Schwarzenegger was sworn in on November 17, 2003, following a special recall election on October 7, only a year into former Democratic Governor Joseph Graham "Gray" Davis's second term in office. Schwarzenegger was re-elected in November 2006. Schwarzenegger has said he wants to be the greenest governor in California history. During his first year in office, legislation was approved for creating the Sierra Nevada Conservancy, putting 25 million acres under conservation management in a region of northern California producing 65 percent of the state's water supply and half of all its timber. In September of 2006 Schwarzenegger signed the ambitious Global Warming Solutions Act. He also has undertaken joint environmental initiatives, such as the West Coast Governors' Agreement on Ocean Health, with neighboring states. Before holding public office, Schwarzenegger had a notable career in film. He played iconic roles such as the robot in *The Terminator* (1984, and its sequels in 1991 and 2003), with one-liners such as "I'll be back" and "Hasta la vista, baby." Schwarzenegger is also a successful businessman, with investments in real estate and restaurants.

Arnold Alois Schwarzenegger was born July 30, 1947, in a small village outside of Graz, Austria, and grew up in a home without a telephone or refrigerator until he was fourteen years old. He became naturalized as a U.S. citizen in 1983. He initially came to America in 1968 with the intent of becoming a movie star and marrying a member of the Kennedy family. He succeeded on both counts. He has been nominated for or won Golden Globe awards (1976, 1994), many of his films have done spectacularly well at the box office, and in 1986 he married award-winning television journalist and author Maria Owings Shriver, niece of President John F. Kennedy. They have four children, Katherine, Christina, Patrick, and Christopher.

From an early age Schwarzenegger was keen on physical fitness. He won the title of Mr. Universe five times. Schwarzenegger became famous with *Conan the Barbarian* (1982) and has starred in many action roles, often playing villains such as Mr. Freeze in *Batman & Robin* (1997). He has also starred in popular comedies, such as *Twins* (1988) and *Kindergarten Cop* (1990). In 1990 Schwarzenegger was named chairman of President Bush's President's Council on Physical Fitness. In 1993 he published with Charles Gaines the three-volume *Arnold's Fitness for Kids*. For years Schwarzenegger and his wife have been involved in causes related to the welfare of children, including launching the Inner City Games Foundation, and backing the After School Education and Safety Act of 2002 (California Proposition 49).

Schwarzenegger's commitment to the environment came a bit later on in life. His wife's cousin ROBERT F. KENNEDY, JR., the environmental lawyer, author of *Crimes Against Nature* (2004), and founder of the Waterkeeper

Alliance, introduced TERRY TAMMINEN to Schwarzenegger. Tamminen was involved in the creation of several Waterkeeper programs in California affiliated with Kennedy's organization, and is an expert on climate change policy. Schwarzenegger credits Tamminen with his commitment to a green future. Tamminen helped with Schwarzenegger's gubernatorial campaign and became his first Secretary of California's Environmental Protection Agency. In 2004 he was named Cabinet Secretary, the Chief Policy Advisor to the Governor. Tamminen now heads the New America Foundation's Climate Policy Program, working tirelessly with other U.S. states and cities to create a de facto national climate change policy in the absence of one from Washington, D.C.

Assembly Bill 32, the Global Warming Solutions Act by Assembly Speaker Fabian Nuñez (D-Los Angeles), was signed by Schwarzenegger at the end of September 2006. It is the first-in-the-world comprehensive program of regulatory and market mechanisms to achieve significant, quantifiable, cost-effective reductions of greenhouse gases. It seeks to reduce carbon emissions to 1990 levels by the year 2020, and to reduce emissions 80 percent below 1990 levels by 2050. Mandatory reporting rules are to be adopted by January 2009 for significant sources of greenhouse gases. Mandatory caps on emissions are to begin in 2012.

This legislation has been hailed by dignitaries from across the globe. It is very meaningful because California is the world's seventh largest economy and twelfth largest emitter of carbon. Two other important pieces of legislation implemented during Schwarzenegger's tenure are California's tailpipe emission standards, which would require new vehicles to cut global warming emissions by 30 percent by model year 2016, and the Low-Carbon Fuel Standard, which seeks to achieve a 10 percent reduction in the carbon intensity of transportation fuels in California by 2020.

In December of 2005 the California Air Resources Board requested a waiver of federal pre-emption of the state's tougher-than-federal greenhouse gas vehicle emission limits under the Clean Air Act. California's standards require not just higher fuel efficiency, but the direct regulation of four greenhouse gases which contribute to global warming. After two years of inaction, in December 2007 the EPA denied California's waiver request for the first time ever, after having granted the state more than 40 waiver requests in the past. On January 2, 2008, Schwarzenegger announced that the state of California was filing suit against the U.S. EPA to overturn its decision. Holding a large stake in the suit are thirteen states that have adopted California's standards, as well as nine other states that are on their way to adopting these standards. Together with California, they represent more than 100 million persons in the U.S.

With a new administration in the White House in less than a year, California's waiver request could be granted immediately by the new EPA Administrator, perhaps ahead of a ruling on the matter by the courts. Governor Schwarzenegger will continue to hold office until 2010 and he is expected to remain as committed as ever to his green agenda, which includes supporting an even larger growth in the green collar sector in these economically challenging times for his state and the nation.

**BIBLIOGRAPHY**

"Arnold Schwarzenegger," *Biography Resource Center*, 2008; Hayes, Christopher, "True Colors," *Outside Magazine*, April 2007; "50 People Who Could Save the Planet," *The Guardian*, January 5, 2008; Office of the Governor—State of California, gov.ca.gov; www.terrytamminen.com.

## Chief Sealth (Seattle)
(mid-1780s–June 7, 1866)
Chief of the Suquamish and Duwamish, Orator

Chief of the Suquamish and Duwamish, two tribes in Puget Sound, Sealth is best known as a powerful orator and a friend of White settlers, who named a small settlement after him. Although Sealth's gift of oratory and friendliness toward Whites are well documented, the authenticity of a famous speech attributed to him, often presented as representative of Indian views of the environment, is open to question.

Sealth was born on what is today known as Bainbridge Island sometime during the mid-1780s. He was the son of Schweabe, chief of the Suquamish, and Scholitza, a Duwamish woman. Sealth was a boy when he encountered his first White men, George Vancouver and the crew of the *Discovery*, who anchored off Bainbridge Island in May 1792. Young Sealth was awed by the White men's technology and later in life often spoke of the favorable impression Vancouver made on him.

When Sealth came of age, he chose a bride from his mother's tribe. His first wife, who was known as La Daila, bore him one child, Kick-is-mo-lo, whom Whites later called Princess Angeline. La Daila died shortly after giving birth, greatly grieving Sealth, who took at least one other wife from his mother's tribe.

When Sealth was in his early twenties, he responded to a call for help from the Duwamish, who were threatened by a large group of warriors from a hostile inland tribe. Sealth developed a unique defensive strategy that resulted in the rapid defeat of the invaders, a feat for which he was elected chief. After his rise to the chieftainship, Sealth became known as a peacemaker and never again participated in armed combat. He converted to Catholicism in the late 1830s after the arrival of "blackrobes" from Quebec and remained a follower of the faith for the rest of his life.

The first White American settlers came to the area presently occupied by the city of Seattle in 1851, three years after Britain had relinquished its claim to the area below the 49th parallel. The settlers named their small settlement after the chief, modifying his Indian name to the present-day spelling Seattle. The chief was upset over the tribute, however, since his people's custom prohibited the use of a deceased person's name. Though the chief was still very much alive, he was worried that after he died, his name would be spoken by thousands of people everyday.

In January 1855, Sealth participated in the Point Elliott Council, signing the resultant treaty with the United States on behalf of the Duwamish and Suquamish. His recorded comments were conciliatory and hopeful, and he pledged his support to the Whites. The years immediately after the treaty council saw many skirmishes between Whites and Indians, including a famous if not particularly successful attack on the city of Seattle led by Owhi of the Yakamas, Quilquilton of the Upper Puyallups, and Leschi of the Nisquallis and Lower Puyallups. Sealth took no part in any of the conflicts and, keeping with his reputation as a man of peace and friend of the Whites, he has been credited with warning the White settlers of more than one impending attack. Sealth maintained friendly relations with local Whites for the remainder of his life, though he did not refrain from expressing his displeasure with the Whites' less than forthright implementation of the promises made during the 1855 Point Elliott Council. He died on June 7, 1866, and was buried at Suquamish, across Puget Sound from the city of Seattle.

In 1887, Henry Smith, a Seattle doctor and occasional newspaper columnist, wrote what would become one of the most famous documents in American Indian history. Smith claimed that the piece was based on a speech Sealth made at a reception welcoming Isaac Stevens, Indian agent and first governor of

Washington Territory, to the region. Smith, who claimed to have witnessed the event, did not assert that the speech was recorded verbatim but rather that it was but a "fragment of his speech," one that lacked "all the charm lent by the grace and earnestness of the sable old orator." Smith's version of the speech, which is not documented anywhere else, is not the environmentalist tract that contemporary renditions have made it out to be. Instead, it is a dirge to the indigenous inhabitants of Puget Sound, who the author of the speech was convinced were headed toward extinction, and an admonition to the Whites that the spirits of the dead Indians would forever stay with the land. "At night, when the streets of your cities and villages shall be silent and you think them deserted, they will throng with the returning hosts that once filled and still love this beautiful land. The white man will never be alone."

Since the 1960s, non-Indians have embellished and manipulated the text so as to make it more amenable to a national, non-Indian audience concerned about environmental degradation. The particularities of place are often removed, reinforcing the notion of a generalized Indian free from a specific tribal affiliation, and anachronisms have been added—the shooting of buffalo from trains, for example. Although the line does not appear in Smith's version, "How can we buy or sell the sky?" has even become a bumper-sticker slogan.

Although some scholars, such as anthropologist Crisca Bierwert and Lutshoodseed elder Vi Hilbert, argue that the core of the speech is Sealth's, others, such as historian Albert Furtwangler and archivist Jerry Clark, argue that the version as recorded by Smith is too far removed from its source to be a useful account of Sealth's views of White settlement and the environment. Literature scholar Denise Low asserts that contemporary versions of the speech, based loosely on Smith's rendition, are more representative of a dominant culture that has created a "white man's Indian" of Sealth, a stereotyped "noble savage" who has been used as a pawn to advance a political agenda. Whatever the case may be, the authenticity of every version of the famous speech by Chief Seattle is open to question.

## BIBLIOGRAPHY

Bierwert, Crisca, "Remembering Chief Seattle: Reversing Cultural Studies of a Vanishing Native American," *American Indian Quarterly*, 1998; Clark, Jerry L. "Thus Spoke Chief Seattle: The Story of an Undocumented Speech," *Prologue*, 1985; Furtwangler, Albert, *Answering Chief Seattle*, 1997; Hilbert, Vi, "When Chief Seattle Spoke," *A Time of Gathering: Native Heritage in Washington State*, Robin K. Wright, ed., 1991; "HistoryLink Essay: Chief Seattle's Speech," www.historylink.org/ESSAYS/OUTPUT.CFM?FILE_ID=1427; Kaiser, Rudolf, "Chief Seattle's Speech(es): American Origins and European Reception," *Recovering the Word: Essays in Native American Literature*, Brian Swann and Arnold Krupat, eds., 1987; Low, Denise, "Contemporary Reinvention of Chief Seattle: Variant Texts of Chief Seattle's 1854 Speech," *American Indian Quarterly*, 1995; Metcalfe, James Vernon, "Chief Seattle," *The Catholic Northwest Progress*, 1964.

## Seeger, Pete
(May 3, 1919– )
Singer, Songwriter

A major force in the movement to revive the American folk song, troubador Pete Seeger has composed songs and sung about social justice and the environment since 1940. From his home overlooking the Hudson River, Seeger coordinated the creation of *Clearwater*, a replica of an eighteenth-century Hudson River sloop that has become both a tool and a symbol of the restoration of Seeger's beloved river.

Peter Seeger was born in New York City on May 3, 1919, to Charles and Constance Seeger, a musicologist and violin teacher respectively, both of whom taught at the Juilliard Institute. After forcing his two older brothers to play the violin, the Seegers decided not to impose music lessons on young Pete, yet he always had access to the family's collection of musical instruments and showed an early curiosity in whistles, the squeezebox, marimbas, and the like. At the age of eight he learned to play the ukelele, then at 13 switched to the tenor banjo, and when he traveled to a North Carolina folk music festival with his father in 1936 and discovered the five-string banjo, he immediately fell in love with that instrument. Seeger entered Harvard College with the class of 1940 but dropped out in 1938 to join a troupe of puppeteers, which toured New York State and performed at meetings for a large strike of dairy farmers. He wrote his first songs for the strike, pulling tunes from old folk songs and making up new strike-inspired lyrics for them.

In 1940 Seeger began working for folklorist Alan Lomax at the Library of Congress Archives of Folk Song. At a benefit concert for migrant workers that year, he met WOODY GUTHRIE, who became his inspiration and mentor. They formed the Almanac Singers, together with Lee Hays and Millard Lampell, and performed songs that melded folk traditions with progressive politics, in support of unions, migrant workers, and other social causes. The group disbanded at the outset of World War II. Seeger served in the United States Army during the war. During a period of leave in 1942 he married Toshi Ohta, to whom he gives much credit for the success of all of his later endeavors.

When the war ended, Seeger and Lee Hays, Ronnie Gilbert, and Fred Hellerman founded the Weavers, whose songs decried injustice yet persisted in their constructive optimism. Hayes and Seeger collaborated on many songs, including the classic "If I Had a Hammer." The song's inspirational power was recognized immediately by the editors of the folk-song publication *Sing Out*, who printed it on the cover of the magazine's first issue. The Weavers were very popular until Seeger's Federal Bureau of Investigation file was leaked to the press, and it was revealed that he and other members of the Weavers were being investigated for their leftist political leanings. The Weavers' concerts began to be canceled unexpectedly at the last minute, and eventually the group fell apart. Seeger was subpoenaed by Joseph McCarthy's House Un-American Activities Committee and testified in 1956 about his own involvement in radical political organizations, including the Communist Party (he had been a member for about eight years during the 1940s). He refused to give the committee the names of his friends and associates who were also involved, and for this he was indicted for contempt of Congress and sentenced to ten years in prison. He never had to serve time, however, as his case was eventually dismissed on a technicality. Because he was blacklisted during the McCarthy area, Seeger was able to obtain bookings only at college campuses and small-town school auditoriums, scraping together a living for his family. One of the favorite songs of his small audiences was a rearrangement of an old gospel tune that he had learned from union organizer Zilphia Horton, "We Shall Overcome." Highlander school song leader Guy Carawan taught it to civil rights protesters in 1960, and it became the veritable anthem of those doing civil disobedience through the South during the 1960s.

The folk music revival blossomed during the 1960s with such singers as Bob Dylan and Phil Ochs incorporating the words and melodies that Lomax, Guthrie, and Seeger had rediscovered. Some of the songs that Seeger wrote or recorded became better known in their recordings by folk singers Joan Baez, Peter, Paul and Mary, and others; Seeger was never offended or hurt by that, since he himself had done the same with old folk songs or gospel songs.

During the 1960s, Seeger found a new interest—still firmly rooted in social justice—in the environment. He read and was spurred into action by RACHEL CARSON's *Silent Spring* when it was serialized in the *New Yorker*, in 1963. "Up till then," he told Steve Curwood on the public radio program *Living on Earth*, "I'd thought the main job to do is to help the meek inherit the Earth... But I realized if we didn't do something soon, what the meek would inherit would be a pretty poisonous place to live." Seeger began an all-out campaign to educate himself, reading books by PAUL EHRLICH and BARRY COMMONER. He recorded his first environmental-themed album in 1965, *God Bless the Grass*, titled after a song by Malvina Reynolds.

Seeger also started paying more attention to what was happening close to his home. He and Toshi had built a log cabin on a few forested acres overlooking the Hudson River in 1949, and by the mid-1960s, the river was widely acknowledged to be a contaminated mess. In addition to the raw sewage and industrial waste flowing into the river, environmentalists were greatly concerned by a proposal to build a pump storage power plant at perhaps the most famous Hudson River landmark, Storm King Mountain. Local environmental groups were engaged in a massive lawsuit against the Federal Power Commission to stop its construction. Seeger soon dreamed up his own creative response to the Hudson's sorry state. After learning from a friend that the main form of transportation in the Hudson River Valley during the eighteenth century had been sloops—graceful, sleek sailboats of at least 70 feet in length—he came up with an idea that he felt had the power to both symbolize and enable the movement for a cleaner environment. Seeger recounted to Curwood, "I wrote a letter to my friend: wouldn't it be great to build a replica of one of these? Probably cost $100,000. Nobody we know has that money, but if we got 1,000 people together we could all chip in. Maybe we could hire a skilled captain to see it's run safely and the rest of us could volunteer." Seeger and a group of Hudson River neighbors and friends did just that; 3,000 people formed a nonprofit corporation called the Hudson River Sloop Restoration, Inc., and raised funds to build a boat. Seeger held a series of "sloop concerts" that raised about $60,000 for the project. The *Clearwater*, a 106-foot wooden sailing ship, was finally completed in 1969. It has been used as a classroom, laboratory, and stage, sailing from community to community to take nearly 13,000 schoolchildren and adults on educational sailing trips each year. The boat's motto is "Clearwater's cargo is people. Her work is making them care." The organization, now called Clearwater, with more than 15,000 members, works with other environmental organizations up and down the river to fight for the cleanup of polychlorinated biphenyl (PCB) contamination, improved water quality, better public access to the river's shores, and more effective local water conservation. Clearwater organizes dozens of festivals each year, from the Great Hudson River Revival, which attracts some 20,000 people, to smaller town shad, strawberry, corn, and pumpkin harvest festivals. At all of these, the sloop serves as a waterborne stage for performers, and guests are invited on board for short river rides.

Seeger has composed numerous songs about the *Clearwater* and the Hudson, including "My Dirty Stream":

> Sailing up my dirty stream
> Still I love it and I'll keep the dream
> That some day, though maybe not this year
> My Hudson River will once again run clear.

Another song is "Sailing Down My Golden River":

> Sailing down this golden river,
> Sun and water all my own
> Yet I was never alone.
> Sun and water, old life-givers
> Wherever I do chance to roam.
> And I am not far from home.

Pete and Toshi Seeger continue to live in their cabin overlooking the Hudson and to serve Clearwater as active members.

**BIBLIOGRAPHY**

"Hudson River Sloop Clearwater," www.clearwater.org/; Dunaway, David King, *How Can I Keep from Singing*, 1981; Hajdu, David, "Pete Seeger's Last War," *Mother Jones*, 2004; Hope, Jack, "A Man, A Boat, a River, a Dream," *Audubon*, 1971; Seeger, Pete, *The Incompleat Folksinger*, 1972; Seeger, Pete, *Where Have All the Flowers Gone: A Musical Autobiography*, 1996; Wilkinson, Alec, "The Protest Singer," *The New Yorker*, 2006.

## Selikoff, Irving
(January 15, 1915–May 20, 1992)
Physician, Asbestos Researcher

A pioneer in environmental and occupational medicine, Irving Selikoff conducted the first studies to demonstrate the damaging effects of asbestos exposure. Selikoff's research resulted in a ban on most asbestos products in the 1980s and successful compensation claims by thousands of workers who had contracted cancer and asbestosis on the job. He was the founding director of the first hospital division in the United States devoted to environmental and occupational medicine; it was at New York's Mount Sinai Medical Center. Selikoff was the author of numerous books and articles in this field, including 1988's *Living in a Chemical World*.

Irving J. Selikoff was born in Brooklyn, New York, on January 15, 1915, to Abraham and Tilli (Katz) Selikoff. He attended Columbia University, graduating with a B.S. in 1935. He received his medical training at Anderson's College of Medicine in Scotland and the University of Melbourne, Australia. He went abroad to study probably because of anti-Semitic prejudice at medical schools in the U.S., and then switched medical schools midstream because of the outbreak of World War II. Selikoff completed an internship in internal medicine at Newark, New Jersey's Beth Israel Hospital in 1944 and his residency at Sea View Hospital in New York in 1947. He joined the staff of Barnert Hospital in Paterson, New Jersey, in 1947. There, in collaboration with Dr. Edward Robitzek, he conducted successful clinical trials of a powerful new drug, isoniazid, for the treatment of tuberculosis. In 1955 they were awarded the Albert Lasker Award in Medicine from the American Public Health Association for this work.

In his work at the chest clinic in Paterson, Selikoff began treating 17 patients who worked at a local asbestos plant, Union Asbestos and Rubber Company (UNARCO). All 17 had unusual illnesses, and within the first seven years, 6 of the men were dead. Eventually, 13 of Selikoff's patients died of cancer or asbestosis, and Selikoff began what he called "shoe-leather epidemiology." He first tried to get personnel files from UNARCO, and when the company refused to cooperate, Selikoff used other means, including union records and Federal Bureau of Investigation files, to track down 877 of the 933 men who had worked at the plant during World War II. Their lung cancer rates were seven times higher than normal, their stomach and colon cancer rates twice as high. In 1964 Selikoff published the results of his research in the *Journal of the American Medical Association* as "Asbestos Exposure and Neoplasia." This study was one of the first to establish the link between cancer and asbestos. In 1983 the article was voted one of 50 landmark essays published in the journal's first 100 years.

In 1966 Selikoff founded the Division of Environmental and Occupational Medicine at Mount Sinai, where he and his colleagues continued to document asbestos damage and the effects of other environmental substances. They completed studies of carpenters, firefighters, painters, plumbers, roofers, and textile workers. The research helped convince the Occupational Safety and Health Administration to impose standards protecting workers against exposure. It also convinced the Environmental Protection Agency (EPA) in 1989 to ban most uses of asbestos. Not content to merely study the effects of asbestos, Selikoff began an active campaign to educate Congress and the public about its dangers. Selikoff was a public health advocate, testifying before Congress, addressing unions and public health groups, and writing on the topic in a wide variety of venues, including the op-ed page of the *New York Times*. He served as a consultant to a number of government agencies, including the World Health Organization. His research convinced him that 95 percent of cancers have environmental causes, and his work helped generate public awareness of the dangers of chemicals in the environment. Selikoff earned particular respect from unions, with which he worked closely; he was named an honorary member of the International Association of Heat and Frost Insulators and Asbestos Workers.

Selikoff also played an important role in establishing the legitimacy of environmental and occupational medicine. In addition to founding the division at Mt. Sinai, Selikoff founded and played an active editorial role in two important journals, the *American Journal of Industrial Medicine* and *Environmental Research*. In 1982 he co-founded the Collegium Ramazzini, a group of scientists and public health advocates organized "to advance the study of occupational and environmental health issues around the world." The Collegium defines its purpose as serving "as a bridge between the world of scientific discovery and those social and political centers which must act on these discoveries to conserve life and prevent disease." The Collegium conducts research and political advocacy, in part to counter the efforts of industry to limit regulation of environmental hazards. In 1988, Dr. Ellen Silbergeld, a toxicologist employed by the Environmental Defense Fund, said of Selikoff, "He is one of the great historical figures in medicine and public health. His major contribution has been to move occupational medicine out of a second-class position in the field of medicine and in the opinion of the public."

Selikoff worked at Mt. Sinai until his retirement in 1985. He died of cancer in Ridgewood, New Jersey, on May 20, 1992. In 1997 the Collegium Ramazzini conducted a symposium in Selikoff's honor, published by the New York Academy of Sciences as *Preventive Strategies for Living in a Chemical World*.

**BIBLIOGRAPHY**

Bartrip, P.W.J., "Irving John Selikoff and the Strange Case of the Missing Medical Degrees," *Journal of the History of Medicine and Allied Sciences*, 2003; "Collegium Ramazzini," www.collegiumramazzini.org; Goodman, Billy, "Health Science Pioneer," *Environmental*

*Defense Fund Newsletter*, 1988; Hooper, Joseph, "The Asbestos Mess," *New York Times*, 1990; Washburn, Lindy, "Irving J. Selikoff," *Bergen Record*, 1992.

# Seo, Danny

(April 22, 1977– )
Entrepreneur, Green Style Trendsetter

Danny Seo founded the youth environmental organization Earth 2000 at the age of 12 in 1989. Within six years there were 25,000 members of Earth 2000, and the group had become internationally famous for its success in protecting undeveloped land from real estate developers, inspiring a massive British boycott of Faroe Island seafood, and passing a law in the Pennsylvania state legislature that gave students the right to refuse to dissect animals in secondary school biology classes. At the age of 18, he retired from his position as chief executive officer (CEO) of Earth 2000, and since then he has dedicated his time to fundraising, writing, and promoting sustainable and vegetarian lifestyles. He has written several books on achieving a green life with style, edits several magazines and features on the topic, and appears frequently television to promote simple and green—yet stylish—living.

Danny J. Seo says that being born on Earth Day, April 22, 1977, was just the first of a series of "accidents" that led him down the path to his environmental commitment and the fame that followed. During Seo's 12th year, in 1988–1989, the revival of Earth Day was receiving a lot of press. At the same time, newspaper headlines about environmental catastrophe—more pessimistic every day—were terrifying him. Seo threw a small birthday party that year and asked his friends not to bring him gifts—for his realization that material goods did not lead to happiness was another key event in his life that year—but instead to join Earth 2000, a youth environmental organization that he had just decided to establish.

Earth 2000's first project was to raise money through recycling cans to sponsor an animal at the local Philadelphia zoo. The animal was a prairie dog, which escaped from the zoo soon after Earth 2000 sent in the money. The group's next project was to fight a housing development in Seo's neighborhood: developers wanted to raze a 66-acre forest with a pond and build new homes. Seo recalls that this project was another turning point for him because he learned how to be an effective ecosoldier. Seo recruited top environmental lawyers, who agreed to work pro bono for him. Seo learned to appeal to the public's affection for children. He says that everyone, even the real estate developers, thought he was "adorable," until it became evident that he could win. The officials at his private prep school, proud at first to have such an ecohero in the student body, disbanded his organization once Seo began to be served subpoenas during gym class. The clincher in this fight was triggered by another "accident." Seo was hiking through the forest in question, tripped over an unidentified, partially buried piece of rubble, dug it up, and discovered a colonial-era bottle. The forest was an archaeological site! Through some savvy media work, Seo and his group convinced the public that no one would want to ruin an archaeological site by building houses on it. The developers abandoned their plans.

Seo's next fight was against the pilot whale hunters of the Faroe Islands, a territory of

Denmark. In March 1993, Earth 2000 organized a demonstration at the Danish embassy in Washington, D.C. Advance press coverage was extensive; Earth 2000 had learned how important media attention was to the success of its events. The Danes alerted the State Department, which arranged for extensive vigilance of the demonstration. News of Earth 2000's demonstration—13 kids and their inflatable dolphin accompanied by seven State Department agents—caused hilarious uproar in Great Britain, which buys 98 percent of Faroe Island seafood exports. A major boycott was organized in Great Britain; the boycott is still in existence because Faroe Island fishermen have not ceased hunting whales. This experience reiterated for Seo a lesson he had learned with the housing project fight: that if he allowed the media to exploit him, his adorableness, and his youth, his projects would enjoy overwhelming success. This was free advertising, reaching many more people and touching them much more deeply than traditional advertising. Over a span of ten years, Seo collected more than 500 newspaper and magazine articles about himself and his projects.

Earth 2000's various projects took a toll on Seo's academic life. Seo, by his own admission, was a terrible student. He graduated from Governor Mifflin High School in Shillington, Pennsylvania, 129th out of a class of 130. He saw the irony of the situation: at the same time that he was working with Pennsylvania state legislators to write, lobby for, and pass the right-not-to-dissect bill, he was earning an F in his civics class. Seo's later degrees have been issued by the school of life; he has not attended university nor does he have any plans to do so. In 1995, Seo stepped down as CEO of Earth 2000 and began writing books. His first two were directed towards young people: *Generation React* (1997) and *Heaven on Earth* (1999), which lists ten steps to assured success and instructs activists in pain-free fundraising. Both books express his certainty that young people are capable of tremendous success if they really believe in what they are doing.

Around the turn of the century, Seo found his niche as a green and simple lifestyle trendsetter. His book *Conscious Style* came out in 2001, followed by the first two books in Seo's Simply Green series: *Simply Green Parties* and *Simply Green Giving*, both published in 2006. He wrote a calendar for 2008 entitled *Do Just One Thing*, with one small action per day to conserve resources.

Seo writes a column called "Fresh Thinking" in *Country Home* magazine, and served as guest editor with LAURIE DAVID on a special green issue of *Elle* magazine. He makes appearances on the CBS *Early Show* to offer green style tips, and created and hosted the cable TV show "Simply Green with Danny Seo." *People* magazine called him one of the "50 Most Beautiful People in the World."

**BIBLIOGRAPHY**

Czape, Chandra, "The Most Powerful People in Their Twenties," *Swing Magazine*, 1998; "Danny Seo," www.dannyseo.com; Seo, Danny, "Activism 101," (speech at University of Colorado–Boulder), 1998.

## Sessions, George

(June 10, 1938– )
Ecophilosopher

A leading proponent of deep ecology in the United States, George Sessions is a popular spokesperson for the long-range deep ecology movement, which he sees as the forwarding of the western environmental ethic first set out by ALDO LEOPOLD. His studies of and writings about deep ecology have helped the movement to gain ground by clarifying much of this ecophilosophy's foundation and positing methods for its pragmatic implementation.

George Sessions was born June 10, 1938, in Stockton, California, and was raised in Fresno. He attended Fresno State University, completing a B.A. in philosophy in 1960. After three years in the United States Air Force, Sessions started his graduate studies in philosophy at the University of Chicago in 1964. He completed his M.A. in 1968, specializing in the philosophy of science.

As a youth, Sessions enjoyed outdoor recreation—especially rock climbing—and worked as a garbage collector in Yosemite National Park. He joined the Sierra Club when he was 15 and became influenced by the writings of JOHN MUIR and DAVID BROWER. It was not until 1968, however, after the completion of his studies, that Sessions's interest in ecology began to develop. Sessions started teaching at Humboldt State University and shared an office with sociologist BILL DEVALL. Both were influenced by the growing popularity and impetus of ecology, which culminated with Earth Day in 1970. Together, Sessions and Devall sought some kind of ecophilosophy that would push toward an overriding environmental ethic. In 1973, Arne Naess published his now-famous short paper, "The Shallow and the Deep, Long-Range Ecology Movement," in *Inquiry*. Like Devall, Sessions knew that this work—and the long-range deep ecology movement in general—provided the philosophical framework within which to develop his own analyses of the environmental movement and its progress in North America toward a biocentric environmental ethic. Naess distinguished between the anthropocentric environmental concern of the shallow ecology and the spiritual, biocentric perspective of the deep ecology.

Sessions left Humboldt State University in the fall of 1969 to teach philosophy at Sierra College, in Rocklin, California, where he would remain for the duration of his career. He and Devall remained in contact, and between 1978 and 1981 they further developed the distinction between shallow (or reform) ecology and deep ecology and used it as a basis for classifying and describing the various ecophilosophical positions. In 1984, Sessions worked with Naess to draft a more neutral deep ecological platform designed to appeal to a broader audience, from different philosophical and religious backgrounds. Sessions and Naess raised eight widely quoted points that were central to the long-range deep ecology movement:

1. The well-being and flourishing of human and nonhuman life on earth have a value in themselves. These values are independent of the usefulness of the nonhuman world for human purposes.
2. The richness and diversity of all life forms contribute to the realization of the previously mentioned values and are also values in themselves.
3. Humans have no right to reduce this richness and diversity except to satisfy vital needs.
4. The flourishing of human life and cultures is compatible with a substantial decrease of the human population. The flourishing of nonhuman life requires such a decrease.

5. Present human interference with the nonhuman world is excessive, and the situation is rapidly worsening.
6. Policies affecting basic economic, technological, and ideological structures must therefore be changed. The resulting state of affairs will be deeply different from the present.
7. The ideological change is mainly that of appreciating life quality (dwelling in situations of inherent value) rather than adhering to an increasingly higher standard of living. There will be a profound difference between big and great.
8. Those who subscribe to the foregoing points have an obligation directly or indirectly to try to implement the necessary changes.

Sessions collaborated with Devall on *Deep Ecology: Living as if Nature Mattered* (1985), a widely read primer on this ecophilosophy, or ecosophy. More recently, Sessions wrote *Deep Ecology for the Twenty-First Century* (1995), arguing in it that "the crucial paradigm shift the Deep Ecology movement envisions as necessary to protect the planet from ecological destruction involves the move from an anthropocentric to a spiritual/ecocentric value orientation... Humanity must drastically scale down its industrial activities on Earth, change its consumption lifestyles, stabilize and then reduce the size of the human population by humane means, and protect and restore wild ecosystems and the remaining wildlife on the planet." Although critics of deep ecology still question the relative validity or feasibility of a nonanthropocentric biocentrism, Sessions has continually defended such a perspective on the grounds that while it may seem to lack any distinct precedent in the history of Western civilization, such a paradigm shift toward an environmental ethic is crucial if we are to salvage what is left of this fragile planet.

Sessions has written extensively and remains active since his retirement from Sierra College in 1998. He has acted as an editorial adviser to *Wild Earth*, the journal associated with the Wildlands Project, and has conducted several interviews for the *New Dimensions* radio show and other interest groups on deep ecology and bioregionalism. He lives in the Sierra foothills, east of Sacramento.

**BIBLIOGRAPHY**
Devall, Bill, and George Sessions, *Deep Ecology: Living as if Nature Mattered*, 1985; Sessions, George, "The Deep Ecology Movement: A Review," *Environmental Review*, 1987; Sessions, George, ed., *Deep Ecology for the Twenty-First Century*, 1995.

## Seton, Ernest Thompson
(August 14, 1860–October 23, 1946)
Writer, Illustrator, Lecturer

Ernest Thompson Seton (also known as Ernest Seton-Thompson and Ernest Evan Thompson) was one of North America's most effective publicists of nature and wild animals during his more than 50-year career as a writer, illustrator, and lecturer. He published scientific guides featuring his own pen-and-ink drawings of birds and animals, including the four-volume *Lives of Game Animals* (1925–1928), but was best known for his prolific animal stories, of which *Wild Animals I Have Known* (1898) was the most famous. Critics—most notably naturalist JOHN BURROUGHS—held that these stories, usually starring an animal of great intelligence and loyalty that lives a good life but dies valiantly at the end, did not portray animals realistically. Nonetheless, Seton's stories, for all the fiction they contained, inspired many young readers of the early 1900s to pursue careers as naturalists and conservationists.

Ernest Evan Thompson was born in South Shields, Durham County, England, on August 14, 1860, the eighth of the ten surviving sons of Alice Snowden and Joseph Logan Thompson. He changed his last name later in life to honor his father's side of the family, the Setons. A member of this side of the family had been forced to change his name to Thompson to escape retribution after being on the losing side of the Stuart Rebellion of 1745. The Thompson family moved to a farm in Lindsay, Ontario, in 1866, after Joseph Thompson's shipping business went bankrupt. Young Ernest fell in love with nature and life on the frontier while living on the farm. He was particularly moved one day when he watched a tiny kingbird act with enough bravery to drive off an eagle. His first literary work, written when he was 16 years old and published when he was 19, would be about this animal, the poem "The King Bird: A Barnyard Legend."

Although the family sold the farm and moved to Toronto in 1870, Ernest returned periodically during his teenage years, to recover from bouts of ill health. He studied birds by shooting and dissecting them, and he developed a key to identifying hawks and owls that would later lead to *A Key to the Birds of Canada*, published in 1895. Seton divided his time during the 1870s and 1880s between studying art in London, New York, and Toronto and exploring the wilds of Manitoba, to refine his sketching skills and knowledge of natural history. He was invited to join the American Ornithologists Union in 1884 and began writing for its publication, *The Auk*. His *The Birds of Manitoba* came out in 1891, and he was contracted by ornithologist FRANK CHAPMAN to illustrate two of his bird books, *Handbook of Birds of Eastern North America* (1895) and *Bird Life* (1897).

Seton studied painting at Julian's Academy in Paris from 1890 to 1892 and was fascinated by news articles about a hunter who was killed in the Pyrenees by wolves, after the hunter had killed several members of the wolf pack. Seton painted a huge canvas of this scene, showing the hunter's clothes scattered on the ground, and wolves gnawing a human skull. Because of its gruesome realism, *The Triumph of the Wolves* was not shown at exhibits he submitted it to in Paris or Toronto, and although the jury of the Chicago World's Fair in 1893 voted not to show it because it would present a bad image of Canada, the painting was controversial enough that the organizers of the fair agreed to exhibit it.

Later that year, Seton was hired for a five-month stint killing wolves on a New Mexico cattle ranch. His experience yielded "Lobo, the King of Currumpaw," published in *Scribner's Magazine* in 1894. The story was about Lobo, a male wolf of extraordinary size, strength, and intelligence, who died courageously in one of Seton's traps. This was followed by *Wild Animals I Have Known* (1898), an immediate best-seller that is still in print more than 100 years later.

In 1896 Seton married Grace Gallatin, a writer and activist for women's rights, who accompanied him on some of the many expeditions he made during the first few years of their marriage and helped him edit and design his books. Seton's popularity grew, and he became a well-known lecturer, earning around $12,000 per year for his presentations. In 1903, naturalist and writer John Burroughs, who believed that writings about natural history should be as scientifically accurate as possible, attacked Seton in an *Atlantic* article entitled "Real and Sham Natural History." Burroughs claimed that Seton's stories portrayed animals unrealistically, especially when they were shown to possess the same types of intellectual and reasoning processes as humans. He was especially adamant that it was wrong to pretend that fiction was fact, as he claimed Seton had in his stories. Seton arranged to be seated next to Burroughs at a

Ernest T. Seton (center) with three Blackfeet Indians. (Library of Congress, Prints & Photographs Division, LC-USZ62-107591)

dinner party given by Andrew Carnegie shortly after this critique was published, and Seton reportedly interrogated Burroughs until he found out that Burroughs had no personal experience with wolves. Burroughs accepted an invitation to visit Seton's home, with his thousands of stuffed animal specimens, and Burroughs acknowledged in a 1904 *Atlantic* article that Seton was indeed a knowledgeable naturalist. Yet he did give the caveat in this article that Seton's work was "truly delightful" for those readers "who can separate the fact from the fiction in his animal stories."

In addition to his popular stories, and the highly praised, scientific works *Life Histories of Northern Animals* (1909) and the later four-volume *Lives of Game Animals* (1925–1928), Seton is remembered as the founder of the scouting movement in the United States. He recruited a group of boys who lived near his Greenwich, Connecticut, home to visit his "Indian village," where he led them in athletic competitions and outdoor skills for camping, hunting, and tracking. The organization was called the Woodcraft Indians, and the boys organized themselves into what Seton told them was "Indian society," with an elected chief, medicine man, war chief, and so on. The charter and by-laws of his group were published in *Ladies Home Journal*, and soon similar groups sprouted up throughout the country and abroad. Grace Gallatin Seton founded the Girl Pioneers in 1910, which later changed its name to the Camp Fire Girls. English lieutenant general Sir Robert Baden-Powell adopted Seton's 1906 handbook, *The Birch Bark Roll of the Woodcraft Indians*, but changed the Indian-inspired titles and mission of the organization to military ones. Baden-Powell officially founded the Boy Scouts in 1908, with Seton—despite his misgivings about Baden-Powell's appropriation of the group and its new militaristic model—heading the committee that organized the Boy Scouts of America. Seton wrote *Boy Scouts of America Handbook* in

1910, which has sold more copies than any other book except the Bible. Seton's Woodcraft Indians had emphasized activities based on nature, but on the eve of World War I, the military-oriented leaders were pushing the Boy Scouts of America away from that orientation, and Seton resigned in protest in 1915.

Seton and his wife slowly drifted apart, and Seton became involved with his secretary, Julia M. Buttree Moss, an expert on mysticsm and Indians and author of several books herself. In 1930, Seton sold his home in Connecticut and moved to New Mexico, where the Seton Castle was built on 2,500 acres near Santa Fe, to house Seton's vast collection of books and artwork. Seton divorced Gallatin and married Moss in 1935. Seton and Moss enjoyed a productive literary and intellectual partnership and adopted a daughter, Beulah, in 1938. Seton died at home on October 23, 1946, of pancreatic cancer.

**BIBLIOGRAPHY**

Anderson, H. Allen, *The Chief: Ernest Thompson Seton and the Changing West*, 1986; "Blue Sky—the Ernest Thompson Seton Pages," www.etsetoninstitute.org; Keller, Betty, *Black Wolf: The Life of Ernest Thompson Seton*, 1984; Morris, Brian, *Ernest Thompson Seton, Founder of the Woodcraft Movement 1860-1946: Apostle of Indian Wisdom and Pioneer Ecologist*, 2006; Seton, Ernest Thompson, *Trail of an Artist-Naturalist, The Autobiography of Ernest Thompson Seton*, 1940; Wadland, John Henry, *Ernest Thompson Seton: Man and Nature and the Progressive Era, 1880–1915*, 1978.

## Shabecoff, Philip

(March 5, 1934– )
Journalist

Philip Shabecoff has documented the growing environmental movement in the United States since the 1970s. As chief environmental reporter for the *New York Times*, Shabecoff was the first in his field; he made the environment a topic worthy of regular media attention. When taken off the environmental beat in 1991, he left the *Times* to write *A Fierce Green Fire*, his acclaimed overview of environmentalism in American history. He was founder and publisher of the daily news service *Greenwire* until 1999. Recently, Shabecoff has delved more deeply into environmental history and has produced two more volumes on the topic, *A New Name for Peace* (1996) and *Earth Rising* (2000).

Philip Shabecoff was born on March 5, 1934, in the Bronx, New York City. He received his bachelor's degree in journalism from Hunter College in 1955, then continued his studies to earn a master's degree from the University of Chicago in 1957. After a two-year stint in the United States Army, Shabecoff was hired by the *New York Times* in 1959 and soon proved his mettle as a reporter. As foreign correspondent for the paper in the mid-1960s, he reported from Europe and Asia. When he returned to the United States, he satisfied his lifelong love of nature by acquiring property in an unspoiled section of the Berkshire Hills of Massachusetts. With his wife, Alice, and their two children, he built a summer home, clearing much of the heavily wooded site by axe. Their "remote" farmstead was quickly surrounded by development, which chagrined Shabecoff and increased his interest in environmental issues.

In 1970, Shabecoff was transferred to the *Times*'s bureau in Washington, D.C., where he saw firsthand that the environment had become a matter of national concern. Although his first requests to write about environmental subjects were turned down, by 1977 he was able to convince editors to let him cover such issues part-time. The job soon filled all his hours. When the struggle for environmental action came to the forefront during the Reagan administration, Shabecoff was there, on the scene.

As witness to a major social movement, Shabecoff documented the changing national zeitgeist. Americans had begun accepting responsibility for protecting and preserving the natural world, and they wanted to be informed about progress and setbacks. Reporting on industrial pollution and waste of resources, Shabecoff often fought federal agencies and corporations for access to data. For his efforts, he won the James Madison Award of the American Library Association (ALA) in 1990. The ALA credited him with "leadership in expanding freedom of information and the public's right to know."

Shabecoff's balanced, reasoned pieces about environmental efforts and legislation were never radical. Nevertheless, in 1991, Washington bureau chief Howell Raines told Shabecoff that the newspaper wanted to move him to the Internal Revenue Service beat, suggesting he was too "pro-environment" and had ignored the "economic costs" of environmental protection. Shabecoff felt betrayed and was unwilling to take the new assignment. He left the *Times* to become founder and publisher of *Greenwire*, the electronically distributed environmental news daily.

Within two years he had also produced a book that blazed through environmental circles. Published in 1993, *A Fierce Green Fire* was among the first and best overviews of the green movement in the United States. It traced the history of environmentalism, from HENRY DAVID THOREAU to RACHEL CARSON to 1970s activists. Shabecoff's position in Washington had granted him access to governmental officials and environmental leaders, and these contacts informed his work. In the mid-1990s, the book and his past record won him the Sierra Club's David Brower Award, given annually to environmental journalists.

Shabecoff continued to follow environmental issues. His contacts with policy makers expanded, and he kept tapes of his many interviews. In spring 1997 he donated all his taped archives to the environmental journalism program at Michigan State University, sharing his many years' experience at the *New York Times* and *Greenwire* with students and others in his field. He was also among the initial group of journalists who founded the Society of Environmental Journalists.

In 1992, the secretary-general of the United Nations Conference on Environment and Development asked him to cover the Earth Summit in Rio de Janeiro. He was granted full access to diplomatic sessions on acid rain, ozone depletion, and more. The conference helped him formulate theories on the interconnected economy and environment. His 1999 volume, *A New Name for Peace*, explores these ideas. Moving from ancient Babylonian times until the present, Shabecoff outlines the efforts of international organizations, nations, and environmental groups to deal with the economic and ecological ramifications of overconsumption. He argues that poverty, hunger, and disease are environmental issues, since the world will not reform its economic systems until these are conquered.

As a freelancer based in Becket and Newton, Massachusetts, Shabecoff has continued to explore environmental issues and policy. His latest work has taken a global approach. *Earth Rising* (2000) examines issues and problems confronting today's environmentalists. It notes that future activists will have to take on broader roles, protecting the earth by reforming education, taming the global economy, and working for political reform, especially in regard to corporate campaign finance.

Shabecoff has served on several environment-related boards, including the Commission on Environmental Cooperation/NAFTA, the Dow Chemical Company Environmental Advisory Council, the Rachel Carson Council, and the Urban Tree Commission in the city of Newton, Massachusetts.

BIBLIOGRAPHY

Shabecoff, Philip, *Earth Rising: American Environmentalism in the 21st Century*, 2000; Shabecoff, Philip, *A Fierce Green Fire*, 1993; Shabecoff, Philip, *A New Name for Peace*, 1999.

## Shapiro, Andrew L.

(May 7, 1968—)
Journalist, Lecturer, Attorney, Founder and CEO of GreenOrder

Consultant, journalist, lecturer, and attorney, Andrew L. Shapiro is the founder and CEO of GreenOrder, a New York City-based management consulting firm specializing in strategies to combine the goals of environmental sustainability and business profitability. Since its founding in 2000, GreenOrder has helped to make environmental practices an integral part of business as usual for some of the world's largest enterprises, such as General Electric and General Motors. Given that fifty-one of the world's largest economies are corporations, not countries, making big business go green is very significant. He was named one of "50 entrepreneurs who are changing the way we live today" by *Inc.* magazine in 2006, and one of two dozen "Enviro All-Stars" by *Outside* magazine in 2007. A 2006 *New York Times* profile of him was titled, "A Dollars-and-Cents Man with a Green Philosophy."

Andrew Lamport Shapiro was born on May 7, 1968, in New York City to Ellen and Daniel S. Shapiro. His father is a founding partner of law firm Schulte Roth & Zabel, and his mother has worked in design and the arts. Although he is a native New Yorker and considers himself an urbanite first and foremost, he attributes his appreciation for nature to summers spent at Camp Keewaydin in Salisbury, Vermont, which emphasized environmental education and responsibility, as well as regular trips to Aspen, Colorado, where he met his wife Nina Bauer Shapiro. They have two young children.

Shapiro graduated in 1990 from Brown University, where he was elected to Phi Beta Kappa. In 1992, he published *We're Number One! Where America Stands—and Falls—in the New World Order*, which details America's less than stellar social, economic, and environmental indicators compared with other industrialized countries. He graduated from Yale Law School in 1995, where he held editorial posts at two law journals. He was admitted to the New York State Bar in 1996, clerked for Judge Pierre N. Leval of the U.S. Second Circuit Court of Appeals, and he argued a voting rights case in court addressing the effects of felon disenfranchisement laws.

In 1999, he published *The Control Revolution: How the Internet Is Putting Individuals in Charge and Changing the World We Know*, which considers how the Internet has revolutionized politics, culture, and business. The Internet provides more personal control over the acquisition and creation of information, but poses challenges to public values such as truth, community, and democracy. The book also addresses issues of privacy, security, and reliability vis-à-vis the Internet. It was an Amazon bestseller and identified by *Industry*

Andrew Shapiro (Photograph courtesy of Melanie Rose)

*Standard* magazine as one of 1999s "Ten Books that Matter." Shapiro's two books have been published in five languages. He has also written for many publications, such as *The New York Times*, *Wired*, and *The Nation*, where he was a contributing editor for nearly a decade. He has also appeared on National Public Radio, the Public Broadcasting Service, and Cable News Network. Shapiro has also lectured at the Aspen Institute, where he continues to lead seminars, at Columbia and Yale law schools, and has been a research fellow at Harvard and New York universities.

Following what might be termed his chronicles of the digital revolution, Shapiro has played an active role in the green revolution mandated by accelerated climate change and other ecological crises. "There's a connection between the way the Internet has transformed institutions and the way companies now must transform themselves in response to the challenges of sustainability," he says.

Shapiro cofounded GreenOrder with his brother Peter, who from 1996 to 2001 owned the Wetlands Preserve, a popular rock club in downtown New York that was an early proponent of green business practices. One of the Shapiro brothers' motivations for starting GreenOrder was to help businesses of all sizes go green while staying in the black. Peter Shapiro, an entertainment producer, also is the cofounder of the Green Apple Festival, a series of Earth Day events that, with GreenOrder's help, will be held in eight U.S. cities in 2008.

Shapiro has said he may not be an environmentalist in the traditional sense. Rather, in a 2006 interview he stated, "What I am passionate about is an idea: how to convince businesses that being leaders in environmental performance will also make them leaders in business performance." Whether a traditional environmentalist or not, Shapiro's and GreenOrder's services have resulted in huge benefits to the earth. Some of his top clients are companies whose environmental and/or social records have been criticized in the past by activists, yet they are converting their businesses in tangible ways. DuPont has instituted a Sustainable Growth Initiative focusing on energy-efficient products, among other things. BP, one of the world's largest oil companies, has invested billions of dollars in alternative energy technologies including solar power and biofuels research. Other GreenOrder clients have included Citi, General Motors, Office Depot, Pfizer, Polo Ralph Lauren, and the World Trade Center redevelopment. GreenOrder helped to make 7 WTC the first LEED-certified office building in New York.

No company has been linked with GreenOrder as much as GE, whose CEO Jeffrey Immelt is fond of the motto "Green is green." Founded by Thomas Edison 125 years ago, and now a giant conglomerate operating in 100 countries with half of its customers abroad, GE is the leading manufacturer in the world of power plants, jet engines, locomotives, and medical equipment. While GE once contaminated about 85 Superfund sites, including most notoriously the yet-to-be-dredged PCBs on the bed of the Hudson River, its giant wind turbines now power the largest offshore wind energy farm in the world in the Irish Sea. Since 2004, GreenOrder has played a key role in developing and implementing GE's Ecomagination initiative, which includes commitments to invest in and commercialize innovative products and services to help customers meet today's biggest environmental challenges. Since its launch in 2005, Ecomagination has grown to include more than 60 cutting-edge products (and growing), from locomotives to washing machines, all offering both outstanding environmental performance and financial returns. According to Lorraine Bolsinger, GE's Corporate Vice President of Ecomagination, "GreenOrder has been a trusted partner to GE in almost every aspect of ecomagination: from its conception as a growth strategy, to the creation of a scorecard process to qualify offerings and quantify benefits, to making the initiative a source of innovation and value for our businesses, customers, and partners. The firm's mix of strategic insight, analytical rigor, domain expertise, and creativity is uniquely valuable."

**BIBLIOGRAPHY**
Gregor, Alison, "A Dollars-and-Cents Man With a Green Philosophy," *New York Times*, 2006; Little, Amanda Griscom, "G.E.'s Green Gamble," *Vanity Fair*, 2006; www.greenorder.com; ge.ecomagination.com.

## Shuey, Chris
(January 13, 1955– )
Environmental Health Specialist with the Southwest Research and Information Center

Chris Shuey started his career as a journalist but found himself frustrated by the limits of a reporter's power. He turned instead to environmental activism, becoming an advocate for communities harmed by the environmental and health impacts of uranium mining and oil exploration. He has spent much of his time working with and for Navajo communities in the Four Corners states, battling mining companies that have left groundwater polluted, land permanently contaminated, and people dying of cancer. Since 1981, Shuey has been a member of the senior professional staff of the Southwest Research and Information Center (SRIC) in Albuquerque, New Mexico. As an environmental health specialist at the multicultural research and education organization, Shuey directs the Uranium Impact Assessment Program, which offers technical and organizational assistance on uranium mining contamination and public health concerns to the communities most impacted by this problem, in northwestern New Mexico.

Christopher Lincoln Shuey was born in Springfield, Ohio, on January 13, 1955. He is one of five sons born to farmers Lin and Ruth Ann, who continue to live in Ohio. Growing up and working on the family farm, Shuey developed an appreciation of the land at an early age. Much of this came from his father, who was an early practitioner of soil conservation techniques, using crop rotation and contour cropping to prevent soil erosion and protect water quality. Shuey cites two events that shaped him as a teenager and led him to question government decisions in the 1960s. The first was the Vietnam War; the second, the government's condemnation of half the family farm's acreage in a river bottom for a dam project. Although questions were raised about the necessity of the dam and just compensation for landowners, the Shuey family lost its case in court.

Shuey attended Ohio University from 1973 to 1974, with a major in journalism. He transferred to Arizona State University (ASU) in 1974 and continued there until 1981. While pursuing his education at ASU, he worked as a staff writer for the *Daily Progress* in Scottsdale and freelanced for the Time/Life Inc. magazine chain. While Arizona was, and continues to be, a very conservative state, the publisher of the *Daily Progress*, Jonathan Marshall, was a mainstream liberal Democrat. Shuey believes that because of this the paper was much more willing to cover all sides of an issue, which he saw as a valuable lesson. He wrote about water and environmental and Native American issues; he also covered the police department and the courts. Several of his articles on the Fort McDowell Yavapai Apache tribe's opposition to the Orme Dam and the Central Arizona project won statewide journalism awards. While at the paper, he covered early uranium miner issues and developed a strong interest in the health problems of the miners.

Shuey was enjoying success with his writing but said he became "disillusioned by the institutional constraints of traditional journalism." While covering public debates on the Palo Verde nuclear power plant in Arizona in the mid-1970s, Shuey realized that the views of thoughtful, intelligent people opposed to the plant were systematically censored by the mainstream Phoenix press. At the same time, he said, he felt that the small "liberal" paper he worked for was not being taken seriously. "If that were the case from a journalistic perspective, why not just be an advocate? Journalism did not provide an outlet to be an advocate," he said.

He left the paper in 1978 and became involved with the antinuclear movement, working with like-minded individuals to start Arizonans For a Better Environment in 1979. The project had difficulty in raising funds and was given up after a year. Shuey became acquainted with staffers of the Southwest Research and Information Center in 1978 while tracking down information about the high lung cancer rate among uranium miners in the Four Corners area of Arizona and New Mexico. SRIC is a nonprofit, progressive public education and scientific organization founded in 1971, whose mission is "to promote the health of people and communities, protect natural resources, promote citizen participation, and ensure environmental and social justice now and for future generations."

Shuey started working at SRIC in 1981 after it had raised some money to publish a magazine on mining impacts. When Shuey was offered the job as editor of *Mine Talk*, he packed up his car and made the move to Albuquerque. Funding soon ran out for *Mine Talk*, but SRIC's work with communities impacted by mining continued, and Shuey became a key member of SRIC's team, delivering technical services to communities that requested them. He sees his role with SRIC as a "poor people's consultant" and aims to help people understand the technical aspects of pollution and the science behind the data. That way, he hopes to help people use the law to make changes in their communities. "We want to be able to not just conduct research and give out information, but to take the next step to help people build their own expertise and skills, so it's community people advocating for themselves," said Shuey. Shuey helped launch the Eastern Navajo Diné Against Uranium Mining (ENDAUM); the group fights to keep future uranium mines from opening on Navajo land. In 2005, the president of the Navajo Nation, Joe Shirley, Jr., signed a tribal law to ban uranium mining and milling on Navajo land, but this has not prevented private mining companies from attempting to initiate new projects.

Once in Albuquerque, Shuey finished his undergraduate studies at the University of New Mexico (UNM), earning a B.A. in university studies in 1990. He complete a masters degree in public health with a concentration in environmental epidemiology from UNM in 2002. His thesis work examined the effects of chronic ingestion of uranium in drinking water, and the development of kidney disease as a result. He is a co-Principal Investigator in the federally funded Navajo Uranium Assessment and Kidney Health Project, a community-based cross-sectional study of the role of environmental exposures in the high rates of chronic kidney disease in the Eastern Navajo Agency. SRIC is a partner in the study with the Eastern Navajo Health Board and the University of New Mexico's Community Environmental Health Program. Shuey wants to help communities within mining and mineral development areas to do their own environmental monitoring. Toward that end, he assisted Churchrock Chapter of the Navajo Nation in conducting an extensive environmental assessment of radiation levels and heavy metals in residential areas near abandoned uranium mines. The assessment led to the USEPA initiating a Superfund enforcement action to reclaim one of the largest abandoned mines on the Navajo Nation near Churchrock, and conducting an emergency removal of contaminated soils around six Navajo homes in 2007. He is also interested in the challenges of measuring and modeling health risks from multiple contaminant sources in areas that produce oil and natural gas.

Much of the uranium mining takes place on Indian lands, and as a result, Shuey has developed a keen interest in Native American history and culture, particularly that of the Navajo. He has studied the language and culture of the *Diné*, and has spent considerable time in Navajo communities to better his proficiency in both the written and spoken language of the *Diné*, "the People."

Shuey has written numerous papers and reports on issues relating to uranium mining and other resource development as it occurs on Navajo Nation land. In one 1979 article, "The Widows of Red Rock," published in the *Saturday Magazine* of the Scottsdale *Daily Progress*, he examined a Navajo community torn apart by uranium mining. By the late 1970s, dozens of Navajo miners had died of lung cancer, leaving families destitute and women to pick up the slack. Years later, Shuey contributed to an SRIC report, "Uranium Mining in Navajo Ground Water: The Risks Outweigh the Benefits," that pointed out deficiencies in the U.S. Nuclear Regulatory Commission's Draft Environmental Impact Statement on the Crownpoint Uranium Solution Mining Project. The deficiencies identified in the report eventually became the core set of issues that ENDAUM used in its legal challenge of new uranium mining.

Groundwater issues on a state and local level continue to occupy much of Shuey's time. He served on the New Mexico Governor's Ground-water Quality Advisory Committee from 1988 to 1989. On a local level, he served on the Ground Water Protection Advisory Committee for the Albuquerque City Council and Bernalillo County Commission from 1988 to 1994. That work resulted in a Groundwater Protection Policy and Action Plan in 1994 and that policy is now integrated into the area's overall water resources management plan. In addition, he has served on U.S. Environmental Protection Agency–sponsored technical teams that evaluated oil and gas regulatory programs in oil- and gas-producing states in the 1980s and 1990s.

In 1995, Shuey was awarded the Karl Souder Award by the New Mexico Environmental Law Center. Named for a former state hydrologist, the award honors those who have had significant roles in advocacy and in the protection of groundwater in New Mexico. In 2006, Shuey and his colleagues at SRIC received the Nuclear Free Future Award, sponsored by International Physicians for the Prevention of Nuclear War and Seventh Generation Fund. Shuey and his wife, Laura, live in Albuquerque with their sons, Bryant and Conor.

**BIBLIOGRAPHY**

Malcewska-Toth B, O. Myers, C. Shuey, and J. L. Lewis, "Recommendations for a Uranium Health-based Ground Water Standard," Report to New Mexico Environment Department, Ground Water Bureau (Santa Fe, NM). prepared by the University of New Mexico Community Environmental Health Program, May 2003; Shuey, Chris, "Policy and Regulatory Implications of Coal-bed Methane Development in the San Juan Basin, New Mexico and Colorado," *Proceedings of the First International Symposium on Oil and Gas Exploration and Production Waste Management Practices*, New Orleans, Louisiana, sponsored by the U.S. Environmental Protection Agency, 1990; Shuey, Christopher, "The Widows of Red Rock," *Daily Progress*, 1979; Shuey C, J. deLemos J and C. George, "Uranium mining and community exposures on the Navajo Nation," presentation at American Public Health Association Annual Meeting, Washington, DC, November 7, 2007; Shuey, Christopher, and W. P. Robinson, "Characterization of Ground Water Quality Near a Uranium Mill Tailings Facility and Comparison to New Mexico Standards," *Proceedings of a Symposium on Water Quality and Pollution in New Mexico*, New Mexico Bureau of Mines and Mineral Resources Hydrologic Report 7, 1984; Shuey, Christopher, Paul Robinson, and Lynda Taylor, "The Costs of Uranium: Who's Paying with Lives, Lands and Dollars?," *The Workbook*, 1985; "Southwest Research and Information Center," www.sric.org.

## Silkwood, Karen
(February 19, 1946–November 13, 1974)
Anti-Nuclear Activist

Karen Silkwood was a nuclear-plant worker and Oil, Chemical, and Atomic Workers International Union (OCAW) activist in life, but she is remembered for her brave, self-sacrificial efforts to expose the plutonium safety violations and dangerous work practices of the Kerr-McGee Nuclear Corporation in Cimarron, Oklahoma.

Karen Gay Silkwood was born in Longview, Texas, on February 19, 1946, and grew up the very lively and outspoken child of house painter Bill Silkwood and bank loan officer Merle Biggs. She was raised in the town of Nederland, Texas, where she played sports and the flute and was an honor student at the local high school. She graduated in 1964 and earned a scholarship to study medical technology at Lamar College in nearby Beaumont. Silkwood married Bill Meadows one year later, at the age of 19, and together they had three children. The couple divorced in 1972, and Silkwood gave custody of the children to her ex-husband.

In August of that year, Silkwood began work at the Kerr-McGee Nuclear Corporation. She took an analyst position in the metallurgy laboratory, where she ran quality-control tests on plutonium pellets manufactured at the plant. Shortly after beginning work at Kerr-Mcgee, Silkwood became an active member of the OCAW and participated in a two-month strike against the company that ended in January 1973. Her involvement in the strike gave her the opportunity to learn about the plant's work hazards. Coworkers taught her about the dangers of working with plutonium and of the company's poor handling of incidents in which workers and town residents risked contamination from the plant. Her outspoken mistrust of the company and increased involvement in the OCAW earned her a position—the first ever to be held by a woman—on the union's negotiating committee.

While serving on the committee, Silkwood began collecting evidence of the company's cover-ups. Beginning in 1974, she gathered documentation of careless plutonium handling, defective plutonium rod production, and safety violations that went unreported to the Atomic Energy Commission (AEC). She was increasingly harassed as her accumulation of information and public speeches on health and safety continued, and she was put in physical danger when her apartment was contaminated with radioactive materials. Silkwood endured threats, jeers, and insults from antagonistic coworkers and company management on a daily basis and was afraid for her safety during most of the fall of 1974, but she felt driven to see the work to completion. On the night of November 13, 1974, very afraid but only 40 minutes away from her meeting with boyfriend Drew Stephens and a reporter from the *New York Times*, her white Honda Civic ran off of the road into a ditch. She died instantly. The side of Silkwood's car had new dents, indicating that she had been run off the road, but local and federal investigators concluded that Silkwood had been driving while on antidepressants and had caused her own death.

Silkwood's family and friends were devastated and outraged and sued the Kerr-McGee Nuclear Corporation for negligence, noncompliance with AEC regulations, civil rights violations, and interference in union activities. On May 18, 1979, Silkwood's work was finally rewarded. The jury in the case found Kerr-McGee guilty of negligence in its plants and noncompliance with federal safety regulations. Silkwood's death was not considered during the case, but her sacrifice fueled the country's antinuclear and occupational safety and health movements and accelerated the passage of state "whistle-blower" laws that protect workers who speak out against their employers.

**BIBLIOGRAPHY**

Jackson, Kenneth T., Karen E. Markoe, and Arnold Markoe, eds., *Dictionary of American Biography*, 1994; Kohn, Howard, *Who Killed Karen Silkwood?* 1981; Rashke, Richard L. *The Killing of Karen Silkwood: the Story Behind the Kerr-McGee Plutonium Case, 1981*; *Silkwood*, 1983 (motion picture); "The Silkwood Mystery," *Time*, 1975.

## Sive, David

(September 22, 1922– )
Professor of Environmental Law, Environmental Litigator, Cofounder of the Natural Resources Defense Council

Known in legal circles as the "father of environmental law," David Sive has distinguished himself as an outstanding environmental litigator, scholar, and advocate. For 30 years, he has argued in the courts in defense of the environment, lectured in classrooms to future and current lawyers about its importance and how to best defend it, published numerous articles on environmental law, and provided leadership to several significant environmental organizations.

The middle of three children, David Sive was born to Abraham and Rebecca Sive on September 22, 1922, in Brooklyn, New York. Raised in an urban setting, the young Sive had very little exposure to the great outdoors, and the idea of hiking and camping was completely foreign to him. His fondness for snow, however, led him to begin exploring the Adirondack and Catskill Mountains of New York State as a teenager, and it was there, at the age of 15, that he began to discover for himself the wonders and beauty of nature. Sive also enjoyed the classic nature writers, and the combination of reading HENRY DAVID THOREAU, RALPH WALDO EMERSON, WALT WHITMAN, and JOHN MUIR and climbing mountains instilled in the young Sive a deep commitment to nature and its preservation.

After high school, Sive attended Brooklyn College, graduating in 1943 with a bachelor's degree in political science. That same year he enlisted in the United States Army and joined the European troops in World War II, serving in combat in Europe for ten months as part of the Ninth Infantry Division. He was twice wounded before being discharged in 1945; he received both the Purple Heart and the Oak Leaf Cluster military honors. After discharge, Sive, like many of his generation, was able to take advantage of a tuition benefit program for disabled veterans. Sive enrolled at Columbia Law School at the age of 23, and upon graduation three years later he passed the New York bar exam and moved to the New York suburbs with his wife, Mary Robinson.

Sive entered law practice as an associate of Levien, Singer & Neuburger, later moving to Seligson, Morris & Neuburger as an associate and then a partner. During his early years as litigator, Sive focused on commercial litigation. In 1961, he founded Sive, Paget & Riesel, specializing in commercial litigation and transactions.

Sive had been an attorney for about 12 years when the environmental movement began to take shape, and he soon began applying his legal skills to protecting the environment. During the early years of the development of environmental law, Sive was involved in several significant landmark cases, including the founding case of environmental law, the *Scenic Hudson Preservation Conference v. Federal Power Commission* (1965, 1971). At issue was whether the natural beauty of Storm King Mountain and the surrounding area was important enough to preserve from becoming a site for a pump storage power plant. Sive's initial involvement in the case was as a board member of the Scenic Hudson Organization, but by the time the case made its way through the courts, he was on board as counsel. Ultimately, Sive and the other attorneys representing the organization were successful in obtaining a mediated settlement that protected the mountain and the river. Sive has been fighting legal battles to protect the environment ever since.

Sive was lead counsel on several groundbreaking cases that followed the Scenic Hudson case, including *Citizens Committee for the Hudson Valley v. Volpe* (1970), *Concerned About Trident v. Schlesinger* (1975), and *Mohonk Trust v. Board of Assessors of Town of Gardiner* (1979). *Hudson Valley v. Volpe* was the first major environmental lawsuit that permanently prevented a major construction project; in this case, construction was halted on the Hudson River Expressway. *Trident v. Schlesinger* attempted to stop the construction of the Trident Nuclear Submarine Base on the Hood Canal in Washington. Although the injunction was refused, the case established the principle that projects involving the navy, army, and air force are subject to the environmental review and assessment process of the National Environmental Policy Act. The Town of Gardiner case established tax exempt status for nature trusts and preserves in New York State, and similar tax exemption laws have been adopted in many states based on this case.

In the 1970s, Sive also began writing and lecturing about environmental law, contributing significantly to its development as a separate body of legal study and practice. His extensive list of publications includes articles on subjects ranging from examining expert witnesses and legal instruments to protect the environment, to the role of litigation in environmental policy, the use of scientists as expert witnesses, and ethical issues in environmental litigation. His articles have appeared in major law journals such as the *Columbia Law Review*, *Michigan Law Journal*, *Iowa Law Journal*, *National Law Journal*, the *New York Law Journal*, and *Environmental Law Commentary*. For nearly three decades he has guided the organization and development of environmental continuing legal education courses for the American Law Institute–American Bar Association, and his visiting professorships include the law schools at Columbia University, New York University, Cornell University, and the University of Wisconsin. In 1994, he received a Fulbright Scholar Award and traveled to Australia to lecture on environmental law, and in 1995, he joined the faculty of Pace Law School as a professor of environmental law.

Sive has served in leadership roles in numerous environmental organizations throughout his career. In 1971, he helped found the Natural Resources Defense Council, and for more than two decades he served on that organization's executive and legal committees. He chaired the Atlantic Chapter of the Sierra Club from 1965 to 1969, the Friends of the Earth Foundation from 1986 to 1992, and the Environmental Law Institute from 1972 to 1982. He has been a board member of numerous other organizations, including New York Lawyers for the Public Interest, Sierra Club, Association for the Protection of the Adirondacks, National Research Council, and Adirondack Council.

In large degree due to Sive's work, the environment is now one of the two or three most important areas of public law, and environmental law has expanded to become a part of the curriculum, or a distinct area of study, at numerous law schools throughout the United States. Sive and his peers have established a large body of environmental law, and a strong foundation of laws and regulations is in place. The work of future environmental lawyers, Sive believes, will be to utilize this foundation to extend protection to greater areas of land and to more populations threatened by development, contamination, and the like.

Sive has been honored with numerous awards throughout his career from organizations such as the New York State Bar Association (Outstanding Volunteer Service to the Community Which Has Reflected Honor on the Legal Profession, 1977), the American Law Institute–American Bar Association (Award of Merit for Contributions to Continuing Legal Education in the Field of Environmental Law, 1983), and the Environmental Law Institute (Award in Recognition of Outstanding Contributions to the Improvement of Environmental Law and Policy, 1984). His papers are collected in the David Sive Manuscript Collection, at Pace law School's Library.

Sive has five children and six grandchildren. He hikes and climbs mountains from his homes in Montclair, New Jersey, and Margaretville, New York. He is professor emeritus at Pace University and continues as a member of his law firm, which for the years 2006, 2007 and 2008 has been ranked the Number One Environmental Law Firm in New York by the Chambers and Partners guide.

**BIBLIOGRAPHY**

"Sive Patet & Riesel," www.sprlaw.com; "Pace Law School—Sive Archive," www.pace.edu/page.cfm?doc_id29829; Sive, David, and Frank Friedman, *A Practical Guide to Environmental Law*, 1987.

## Smith, Rocky
(April 30, 1950– )
Public Lands and Forest Policy Analyst, Activist

Rocky Smith, an expert on environmentally sound forest planning and land use, analyzes management plans and project proposals for public lands for several Colorado environmental organizations, including Colorado Wild, Inc. His dedication to the cause, attention to detail, and speaking skills made him an effective member of the team that defeated the controversial Two Forks dam project near Denver, Colorado.

Born on April 30, 1950, in Oak Park, Illinois, Rocky Smith grew up spending as much time as possible outside. With his school buddies, Smith rode his bicycle to parks and undeveloped lots, fished in a neighborhood fishing hole, and vacationed with his family at lakes and forest preserves near Chicago and in Wisconsin and Minnesota. At the University of Wisconsin–Madison, Smith initially studied meteorology, but he switched and graduated with a B.A. in communication and public address in 1972.

After moving to Colorado in 1975 and experiencing a tremendous awe at the beauty of the Rocky Mountains, Smith spent all the time he could hiking, mountain climbing, and cross-country skiing. A July, 1979 Colorado Mountain Club (CMC) trip to the Weminuche Wilderness Area in the San Juan National Forest catalyzed his latent environmentalism. His group shared a meadow camp with a 43-person group from the Chicago Mountaineering Club. The excessive size of that group, the destruction wrought by their pack horses, and—to top it off—the sauna that they had packed in seemed wholly inappropriate for a wilderness area. Smith wrote an article about this encounter in the CMC magazine *Trail and Timberline* in late 1979. The CMC's conservation director called Smith and asked him to write a letter to the San Juan National Forest administration about the problem. The Forest Service response was to invite Smith to participate in a Land and Resource Management Planning Process, which was to determine what management emphases would be given to various areas of that national forest. He did take part in analyzing that and all the other initial plans for Colorado's national forests, and within a couple of years he participated in the design of similar plans for all of Colorado's national forests. In the process Smith became known as the state expert on national forest planning. In the second round of national forest planning for Colorado, Smith led the design of citizen management alternatives for three national forests.

Until 1983, Smith did this as a volunteer. To earn a living, he worked at a factory, where he made packing crates, did metal work, and later did carpentry and other labor for house remodeling. In 1983, he began earning a $100 per month stipend from the CMC, which soon rose to $400. As his reputation grew, he was asked to analyze individual timber sales and was invited to speak at conferences.

When the Two Forks dam controversy erupted in Colorado in the mid-1980s, Smith studied the project and the alternatives to it and concluded that it should not be built. In 1985, the Colorado Open Space Council (now the Colorado Environmental Coalition) hired him part-time to begin organizing against Two Forks. The dam project would have created a very large reservoir near Deckers, Colorado, to supply water to the Denver area. Environmentalists claimed that it would have violated the Endangered Species Act, since a decrease in water flow in the South Platte River would have threatened three rare birds that inhabit the Platte in central Nebraska: the whooping crane, the piping plover, and the interior least tern. Smith became an effective publicist, convincing anglers, boaters, fiscal conservatives, environmentalists, and hikers that Two Forks was a bad idea and that the environmentalists' alternative for water delivery was much better. He spoke to groups frequently for three years and rallied dam opponents to attend public hearings and to write letters. Smith's efforts paid off; in 1990 Environmental Protection Agency administrator WILLIAM K. REILLY rejected the dam and adopted the alternative plan.

During most of the 1990s, Smith worked for the Colorado Environmental Coalition (CEC), responding to forest management plans, as well as individual timber sales and other projects. Smith traveled throughout Colorado's public land system for his work; he also developed a network of locals familiar with public land sites. He and environmentalist Roz McClellan of the Southern Rockies Ecosystem Project developed a new way of communicating environmentalist objectives to the U.S. Forest Service: "citizens' management alternatives." Instead of merely reacting to a land and resource management plan, they would mobilize local environmentalists to write their own alternative for such a plan, always with the goal of maintaining the biological diversity of the area in question. This effort has paid off, as U.S. Forest Service management plans now include the goal of biodiversity maintenance in their plans.

Smith left CEC in 1998. He currently works as the ForestWatch Campaign Director for Colorado Wild, a group he helped found in 1998, whose mission is to conserve the integrity of Colorado forests and to maintain and enhance wildlife and their habitat therein. He is well recognized as the Colorado environmental community's expert on national forest planning and management, silviculture, and many aspects of forest ecology. Smith resides in Denver, Colorado.

**BIBLIOGRAPHY**

"Colorado Wild," www.coloradowild.org; Garner, Joe, "Coalition Battles Ski Resort; Foes Organize to Appeal Forest Service Approval of Lake Catamount Area Planned near Steamboat," *Rocky Mountain News*, 1991; Hood, Andrew, "Vail Expansion Fight Isn't Over," *Denver Post*, 1997; Roberts, Chris, "Salvage Logging Impact Debated," *Boulder Daily Camera*, 1995.

## Sneed, Cathrine

(1955– )
Founder of the Horticulture Project and the Garden Project of San Francisco

Recognizing the power of tending a garden to transform both individual and community, Cathrine Sneed founded the Horticulture Project, an innovative program in San Francisco's county jail that puts prisoners to work growing organic vegetables and provides them with the gratification of productive work and a therapeutic appreciation for their environment. She later created a similar post-release program called the Garden Project that provides work experience in planting trees, gardening, and community cleanup and has become one of the most successful community-based crime prevention programs in the country. Besides giving recently released inmates an opportunity to restructure their lives, the Garden Project promotes organic farming and sells its fresh produce to restaurants in the area and at the local farmer's market. Sneed's motivation comes from her belief that it is not possible to restore the earth unless the people are restored first; in a state like California, where more money is spent on prisons than on schools, she has gone to the heart of matter, providing job training, employment, and environmental appreciation to people in need.

Cathrine Sneed was born in 1955 and grew up in urban Newark, New Jersey. The first of fourteen children, she dropped out of high school and moved to California. With two children herself and few job prospects, Sneed soon wound up on welfare. But out of concern for her children's future, she sought a new direction: She passed her high school equivalency test, enrolled in college, and began working in the San Francisco County Jail No. 3 counseling women prisoners, many of whom were drug users or prostitutes. Then in 1982, when she was only 27, she contracted an untreatable kidney disease and nearly lost her life. A friend brought her a copy of John Steinbeck's *The Grapes of Wrath* while she was in the hospital, which gave her an appreciation for the healing power of working the soil. When, against all odds, she recovered from her illness, she remembered the book and wanted to share her new love of the land with her clients in the jail.

Although she had no tools or money to start with, she convinced the sheriff to let her dig a garden plot out of the brambles on some idle acres adjoining the jail. In the meantime she went to a horticultural school in England and took a six-month course at the University of California. Even though they had to pull up blackberry brambles with no tools other than their hands, the prisoners who volunteered to help her create the garden responded enthusiastically, and before long there was a waiting list of prisoners who wanted to join the program. Sneed sought donations from local businesses for the purchase of tools, seeds, and watering equipment, and the Horticulture Project was soon producing organic radishes, lettuce, leeks, and strawberries for the jail kitchen, for local soup kitchens, and for pantries of organizations that assisted people with acquired immunodeficiency syndrome (AIDS). Today more than 100 prisoners at a time learn the rudiments of gardening, gaining a sense of pride and self-discipline and a chance to participate in healthy physical labor and the experience of nurturing and long-term planning. In addition, before discovering how good fresh produce tasted, many of the prisoners had lived on junk food, and Sneed has come to believe that a poor diet contributes to many drug users' cravings for drugs.

Along the way, Sneed realized that the Horticulture Project was not enough to keep prisoners from returning to crime or drug abuse once they were released from the jail. In 1990, sponsored by the San Francisco Sheriff's Department and with donations from local businesses, Sneed launched a postrelease bridge program called the Garden Project. It offers structure and support to former offenders through on-the-job training in gardening and tree care, counseling, and assistance in continuing education. Former inmates are given the opportunity to gain work experience and earn a living wage; they are able to live in two nearby drug-free homes and also to bring their children to work at the garden with them. They are required to work at least 16 hours a week and to earn a high school diploma if they do not already have one. Reliable work in the Garden Project often leads to jobs elsewhere through another of Sneed's projects—the Green Teams, which contract with businesses and the city to plant trees and gardens and to provide community cleanups. Besides providing a source of fresh, locally grown organic produce for area restaurants, the project has been successful at crime prevention and environmental awareness. The recidivism rate for those who have worked at the Garden Project is less than half that of the average postrelease population. The original Garden Project has now expanded to a second site, near the jail.

In 1993 Sneed came up with the idea of selling the organic Garden Project produce at a local farmer's market, held on Saturday mornings. Now, in addition to selling to local restaurants, the project sells to the public, giving employees an opportunity to interact directly with clients and to see a different side of city life than they see in their normal daily lives.

Sneed received the U.S. M.F.K. Fisher Award in 1996, and in 1997, she received the Harry Chapin Self-Reliance Award; the work of the Garden Project has also received numerous awards and has been featured in national and international publications. The U.S. Department of Agriculture found the program so successful that it distributed a report describing it all across the country.

Sneed has now set up a project called Tree Corps that has planted over 2,000 trees along streets in San Francisco, many of which were treeless. She continues her work with the Garden Project, helping former prisoners restore their lives, their communities, and their families. She lives in San Francisco.

**BIBLIOGRAPHY**

Clavin, Tom, "As I Watch Them in the Garden, I Think, This Is Where It Begins, Pride and Respect," *Family Circle*, 1994; "The Garden Project," www.gardenproject.org; Klug, Elizabeth, "Cultivating New Lives for Inmates," *Corrections Today*, 2001; Sneed, Cathrine, "The Garden Project," *Whole Earth*, 1998.

## Snyder, Gary
(May 8, 1930– )
Poet, Writer, Translator

The writings of poet Gary Snyder incorporate his knowledge and studies of Amerindian folklore, comparative mythology, Eastern religions, and natural history to articulate ecological ways of living on earth. As a young man he participated in the San Francisco poetry renaissance and later was a leader of the West Coast beat generation writers. A poet, scholar, citizen, and naturalist with a reverence for all things autochthonic, Snyder helped popularize notions of "stewardship," "reinhabitation," "bioregion," and "watershed" in literary and public policy circles and was an early protagonist in the back-to-the-land movement of the late 1960s and early 1970s. Since the first Earth Day in 1970, he has been active in the international environmental movement and in the environmental issues that have come up for the Yuba River watershed of Nevada County, northern California. Among his more than 30 books are *Mountains and Rivers without End* (1970), *Earth House Hold* (1969), the Pulitzer Prize-winning *Turtle Island* (1975), *The Practice of the Wild* (1990), and *The Gary Snyder Reader* (1999).

Gary Snyder was born on May 8, 1930, in San Francisco, California, to Harold Snyder and Lois Wilkey. His family moved from San Francisco when Gary was a few months old, and he spent the remainder of his childhood on a small farm north of Seattle. During World War II, the family moved to Portland, Oregon. His parents maintained a readerly household, and young Snyder was studious. As a teen, Snyder worked at a camp in Spirit Lake, Washington, and mingled with Northwest lumberjacks, Wobblies (members of the Industrial Workers of the World), and Indians, and he developed an interest in Amerindian folklore and myths. He attended Reed College on scholarship, graduating with a B.A. in anthropology in 1951. At Reed, he met two other young poets, Lew Welch and Philip Whalen, who, with Snyder, would become popular "beat" Buddhist poets of the mid-1950s San Francisco literary scene.

Snyder married Alison Gass as a senior in college in 1951, but by 1952 they had divorced, and he decided, in some sense, to marry himself to a contemplative life, seeking wisdom and serenity from nature and from his growing knowledge of Eastern religious practices. As a fire lookout and trail crew member in Washington State and Yosemite National Park, he read and meditated, and by the age of 24, Snyder had become the bohemian independent scholar and outdoorsman later mythologized by novelist Jack Kerouac as Japhy Ryder in *The Dharma Bums* (1958).

Snyder continued his formal studies in oriental languages at the University of California at Berkeley (UCB), during which time he participated in the circles of the San Francisco poetry renaissance and redefined his poetics under the influence of Kenneth Rexroth, Robert Duncan, and others of the Bay area cultural world. He was also part of a new generation of American poets that included Jack Kerouac, Allen Ginsberg, Michael McClure, and Lawrence Ferlinghetti, who inspired young people to question authority and traditional notions of progress in the United States. Snyder's aesthetic is rooted in what he called, in *A Controversy of Poets* (1965), "the most archaic values on earth. They go back to the late Paleolithic: the fertility of the soil, the magic of animals, the power-vision in solitude, the terrifying initiation and rebirth; the love and ecstasy of the dance, the common work of the tribe. I try to hold both history and wilderness in mind, that my poems may approach the true measure of things and stand against the unbalance and ignorance of our times."

Without completing the master's program at UCB, Snyder shipped out for Japan in 1956 on a scholarship from the First Zen Institute of America. He stayed for nearly 12 years of part-time monastic life, practicing zazen, translating classic Chinese and Japanese poetry, and writing much of the poetry that would appear in his books, *Riprap and Cold Mountain Poems* (1965) and *Mountains and Rivers without End* (1970). Masa Uehara gave birth to Snyder's and her son, Kai, in 1968, and they moved to northern California to take up residence in the Sierra Nevada foothills in 1970. He built a house in the ponderosa pine and black oak woods where he would ripen as a wilderness philosopher, poet, academic, and activist.

Snyder would redefine political boundaries by bioregion or watershed. He trained to be the poet/shaman who writes songs that heal and he has written prayers, hymns, and spells, making traditional native literary forms contemporary and American. He practices "singing a mountain range," literally using the peaks and valleys as a musical scale to create topographical notes. In discussing his poems about animals, he talks about getting inside the minds of animals through the shamanic practice of mimicry. His "Smokey the Bear Sutra" was widely published in the alternative press in the United States and Canada and was later included in *A Place in Space: Ethics, Aesthetics, and Watersheds* (1995).

> Smokey the Bear
> A handsome smokey-colored brown bear standing on his hind legs, showing that he is aroused and watchful.
> Bearing in his right paw the Shovel that digs to the truth beneath appearances; cuts the roots of useless attachments, and flings damp sand on the fires of greed and war;
> His left paw in the mudra of Comradly Display—indicating that all creatures have the full right to live to their limits and that of deer, rabbits, chipmunks, snakes, dandelions, and lizards all grow in the realm of the Dharma....

Snyder is best known for the creativity of his expressions and the solutions he proposes. In 1972 Snyder joined STEWART BRAND, Joan McIntyre, and Project Jonah to lobby the United Nations Environmental Conference in Stockholm, Sweden, on behalf of whales. His report to the UN, "Mother Earth: Her Whales," appeared in the *New York Times* on July 13,

1972, as a poetic diatribe against policies of the power hungry in Brazil, Japan, China, and North America.

Snyder has always sought to apply his craft as a writer to a larger mission, "the real work," to be a worthy spokesman for the wild, as he attested in a 1973 interview: "My political position is to be a spokesman for wild nature. I take that as a primary constituency. And for the people who live in dependence on that, the people for whom the loss of that would mean the loss of their livelihood, which is Paiute Indians, Maidu Indians, Eskimos, Bushmen, the aborigines of New Guinea, the tribesmen of Tibet, to some extent the Kurds, people all over the world for whom that's their livelihood."

In his Pulitzer Prize-winning book *Turtle Island* (1975), Snyder compiles a range of work from snapshot-like images from nature in poems such as "The Night Herons," "Straight Creek–Great Burn," and "The Real Work," to his brief expository essays explaining his ecological views. The writing is embedded with his knowledge of folklore, archaeology, botany, and an ear tuned to the American idiom.

Apart from the Pulitzer Prize in 1975 for *Turtle Island*, and his 2004 *Danger on Peaks: Poems* nomination for a National Book Critics Circle Award, Snyder is the recipient of the Bollingen Poetry Prize, a Guggenheim Fellowship, an American Academy of Arts and Letters Award, the Robert Kirsch Lifetime Achievement Award from the *Los Angeles Times*, and the John Hay Award for Nature Writing. In 1998, he became the first literary figure in the United States to receive the prestigious Buddhism Transmission Award by the Japan-based Bukkyo Dendo Kyokai Foundation. Snyder is a member of the American Academy of Arts and Letters. Since 1985 he has taught at the University of California at Davis, where he was instrumental in founding the Nature and Culture program, an undergraduate academic major program for students of society and the environment. He gives public readings of his work when he can get away from his chores on the land he stewards with his wife since 1991, Carole Koda, in the Yuba River watershed of Nevada County, California.

**BIBLIOGRAPHY**

Faas, Ekbert, ed., *Towards a New American Poetics: Essays & Interviews*, 1978; Schuler, Robert, *Journeys Toward the Original Mind: The Long Poems of Gary Snyder*, 1994; Snyder, Gary, *The Gary Snyder Reader: Prose, Poetry and Translations 1952–1998*, 1999; Snyder, Gary, *Myths and Texts*, 1978; Snyder, Gary, *The Practice of the Wild*, 1990; Snyder, Gary, *Real Work: Interviews and Talks*, 1980; "UCD English: Gary Snyder," www.english.ucdavis.edu/faculty/snyder/snyder.htm.

## Soleri, Paolo

(June 21, 1919– )
Architect

A visionary architect who seeks to develop ecologically sound cities, Paolo Soleri is the author of the philosophy of "arcology," which unites architecture and ecology. Soleri is building a city in the Arizona desert, Arcosanti, which he hopes will embody the principles of arcology. Arcosanti is designed to make maximum use of sun,

Arcosanti, as it looked in July 1980. (AP Images/Suzanne Vlamis)

wind, and other renewable resources and bans cars and urban sprawl in favor of compact, vertical use of space.

Paolo Soleri was born on June 21, 1919, in Turin, Italy. He was awarded his Ph.D. in architecture from Torino Politecnico in 1946, with the highest honors. He emigrated to the United States in 1947. He studied with Frank Lloyd Wright in Taliesen, Arizona, from 1947 to 1949. During this time he captured international recognition for a bridge design, displayed at the Museum of Modern Art in New York and published in Elizabeth Kassler's *The Architecture of Bridges* (1949). In 1950 he returned to Italy to study ceramics and was commissioned to design the Solimene ceramics factory in Vietri-sul-Mare, Italy. He completed the commission in 1955 and returned to the United States, settling in Scottsdale, Arizona.

In 1956 Soleri and his wife, Corolyn, began the Cosanti Foundation to serve as a teaching compound in Scottsdale. Soleri had been influenced by the ideas of Frank Lloyd Wright, but where Wright's designs emphasize horizontal lines, Soleri's are vertical. The 1950s were a period of suburban sprawl; the booming economy promised a house with a two-car garage for every middle class family in the United States. As part of the greater Phoenix area, Scottsdale provided an example of sprawl, right on Soleri's doorstep. He began to see that urban design was tending to the needs of the automobile over human needs. In Phoenix, for example, more than 50 percent of the horizontal space was dedicated to moving and storing vehicles. Although Soleri believed that in principle cities were fundamental to human civilization and evolution, he saw that in the United States of the 1950s, they had become the source of spiritual alienation and ecological harm due to pollution, natural resource depletion, and a shrinking amount of land available for farming.

Soleri developed the concept of arcology in hopes that architecture and urban planning could work in harmony with, rather than against, the grain of ecology. Arcology is based in part on the idea that as organisms evolve, they tend toward increasing complexity, and Soleri argues that complexity should be tied to miniaturization. Large systems tend to dissipate energy, where small systems concentrate and conserve. As human society gets more complex, it should also, in a sense, get smaller. Urban sprawl works against this principle, spreading out rather than condensing, using resources in inefficient, wasteful ways. Soleri began to envision cities growing up rather than out, using vertical organization to contain the increasing complexity of human civilization.

In 1969 Soleri published *Arcology: The City in the Image of Man*, in which he laid out the principles of his urban designs. Soleri envisions cities without cars, where walking would be the principal mode of transportation. People would live close together, in integrated, vertical communities. Cities would have farms and gardens, in order to be as self-supporting as possible, and would rely on renewable sources of energy. Soleri's arcology was a response to the many problems of urban civilization, a recognition that these problems could not be solved without radical redesign of urban landscapes. In 1970, the Corcoran Gallery of Art in Washington, D.C., staged the widely attended exhibit "The Architectural Visions of Paolo Soleri," which eventually made a successful tour of the country. Soleri's designs were startling and spellbinding. They reenvisioned human civilization on a massive scale, and Soleri was described as both prophet and megalomaniac.

The exhibit coincided with the initiation of work on Arcosanti, Soleri's model city at Cordes Junction in central Arizona, on 4,060 acres along the Agua Fria River. The city was designed to house 7,000 people, using only 25 acres of the 4,060-acre site for actual buildings. Once it is completed, Arcosanti will use only 2 percent of the average landmass covered by conventional towns of comparable size. The city is being constructed of modular forms, made of concrete, which Soleri calls the most flexible kind of masonry. Designs use passive solar principles and aim to conserve space and energy.

Building Arcosanti has been a slow process, in part because of limited funding. Arcosanti has been funded in large part by sale of ceramic and bronze wind-bells, designed and cast by Soleri, drawing on his experience with ceramics in Italy. Labor has been largely donated, often by architecture interns who pay a stipend to work on Arcosanti as part of their course of study. The city does have a restaurant, a bakery, a greenhouse, and several performance spaces and is a popular site for visiting tourists. The only residents of Arcosanti today are builders, who stay for several weeks at a time. Estimates for completion costs and dates vary wildly. Soleri continues to develop Arcosanti and divides his time between the city and his compound in Scottsdale.

**BIBLIOGRAPHY**
"Arcosanti," www.arcosanti.org; Blumenthal, Ralph, "Futuristic Visions in the Desert," *New York Times*, 1987; Howells, Robert, "The Anti-burb," *Smithsonian*, 2004; Sheppard, Harrison, "In Arizona, Architect's City of Dreams Remains a Mirage," *Boston Globe*, 1998; Soleri, Paolo, "The Frugal City: Interview with Paolo Soleri," *New Perspectives Quqrterly*, 2000; Wall, Donald, *Visionary Cities*, 1971.

## Solomon, Susan

(1956—)
Senior Scientist at the National Oceanic and Atmospheric Administration

National Oceanic and Atmospheric Administration researcher Dr. Susan Solomon showed why there is an Antarctic "ozone hole" in 1986, and her work subsequently led an international effort to ban chemicals that deplete Earth's ozone layer. As a result of the ban, the hole is expected to begin healing in 2010 and completely heal by about 2060. This achievement is cited among the most important global environmental turnaround in history. Her work on behalf of the planet did not stop there. In 2007, Susan Solomon was one of the lead scientists of the Nobel Peace Prize winning Intergovernmental Panel on Climate Change that provided undeniable evidence of global warming and enhanced confidence in humanity's dominant role in causing it.

Susan Solomon was born in1956 in Chicago, Illinois. Her early penchant for oxygen experiments was first publicly recognized while in high school when she placed third in the international science fair and began life-long research into oxygen and atmospheric chemistry. She earned an undergraduate degree in chemistry from the Illinois Institute of Technology. In 1977, at 21 years old, she began studying and working at the National Center for Atmospheric Research in Boulder, Colorado. By the age of 25, she had a doctorate from the University of California at Berkeley (1981) specializing in atmospheric chemistry. Upon completing her doctoral thesis she took a job with NOAA Aeronomy Laboratory in Boulder, where she has worked throughout her career.

At NOAA Solomon was afforded the opportunity to expand the frontiers of her own curiosity, and along with it, new frontiers in studying our stratosphere, particularly one vital form of oxygen known as ozone. In the band that stretches from about ten to twenty miles (15-30 kilometers) above Earth's surface, high concentrations of ozone serve to filter ultraviolet radiation from the sun. The discovery of a tear in the ozone layer in the 1980s, and with reports showing that ozone depletion could cause skin cancer, cataracts, and weakened immune systems in humans, fueled Solomon's research into the causes of the depletion of the ozone layer. Known suspects included the trio of chlorine, fluorine, and carbon atoms, which, when compounded, are known as chlorofluorocarbons (CFCs), used widely at the time in aerosol sprays, air conditioners, and refrigerators needing coolants. CFCs in the stratosphere break apart in ultraviolet sunlight, releasing their chlorine atoms, which, in turn, roam free to break up many tens of thousands of ozone molecules, depleting Earth's protective filter, or ozone shield.

Much of Solomon's work with CFCs at NOAA built upon earlier ozone depletion research by Dr. F. Sherwood Rowland, and her fellow classmate at UC Berkeley, Dr. Mario Molina. Her computer models of the composition of our atmosphere led a hunch that the damage was concentrated in the cold lower

Susan Solomon at her office in Boulder, Colorado. (Photograph courtesy of the National Oceanic and Atmospheric Administration, U.S. Department of Commerce)

stratosphere of the Antarctic due to clouds common there during spring and winter.

In August 1987, as spring in Antarctica approached, Solomon was chosen to lead the first National Ozone Expedition to the Antarctic. The expedition showed her hypothesis to be correct. The ice crystals in the clouds above Antarctica transformed the chlorine molecules from the CFCs into a virulent consumer of our ozone.

Following Solomon's work, twenty-four nations sent representatives to Montreal in 1987 and signed the Montreal Protocol on Substances that Deplete the Ozone Layer and its amendment to ban CFCs. Her research into the cause and effect of global warming proved no less earth-saving. She was elected one of two co-chairs of the Science Working Group I of the Intergovernmental Panel on Climate Change in 2002. The work of this Solomon-led team resulted in demonstrating beyond the shadow of reasonable doubt that the world is warming, and that the increases are very likely dominated by human activities.

Making this formal declaration required culling research from thousands of scientists, more than six hundred reviewers, and at least thirty-thousand comments. Imagine eleven chapters with 10-15 opinionated authors. Imagine 113 governments looking over your shoulder. Solomon's inherent trust in participating nations to do the right thing on this issue relied on dozens of formal governmental administrative reviews as well. The twenty-two page Summary for Policy Makers spawned new respect for the limits to the carrying capacity of the planet.

As one of the lead scientists and authors of the Intergovernmental Panel on Climate Change Report, Solomon hopes that the this work goes beyond a Nobel Peace Prize, and culminates in a better global understanding of the issues the world faces. She shared the 2007 Nobel Peace Prize with AL GORE and hundreds of scientists who worked on the Intergovernmental Panel. She has garnered other laurels as well, including the National Medal of Science awarded by then-President Bill Clinton. Dr. Solomon continues to serve as a de facto ambassador of science. She currently works at NOAA and at the University of Colorado at Boulder where she lives with her husband, Barry Sidwell.

BIBLIOGRAPHY:

Morell, Virginia, "Ahead in the Clouds," *Smithsonian Magazine,* February 2007; Glanz, James. "How Susan Solomon's Research Changed Our View of Earth," ]*R&D Magazine,* 1994, 34(9), 46; White, Pamela, "Behold the Power of Science: An Interview with Susan Solomon," *Boulder Weekly,* December 27, 2007; celebrating200years.noaa.gov/historymakers/solomon/welcome.html.

## Soulé, Michael

(May 28, 1936– )
Evolutionary Biologist, Conservation Biologist, Founder of the Society for Conservation Biology, Cofounder of the Wildlands Project

Founder of the Society for Conservation Biology and the Wildlands Project and hailed as the "Father of Conservation Biology," Michael Soulé is one of the preeminent conservation biologists in North America. Through his research, work, and writing, Soulé strives to make conservation biology and the restoration of ecosystems accessible to a broader audience. His work with the Wildlands Project has been based in "rew-

Michael Soulé (Photograph courtesy of Michael Soulé and the *Denver Post*)

ilding" North America. Specific goals include the reintroduction of extirpated species; the design of connecting corridors (especially through areas with significant human obstacles); overcoming fragmentation and achieving habitat connectivity, wildlife population viability, and restoring top-down, predator-driven interactions and ecologically effective populations.

Michael Ellman Soulé was born Michael Leon Herzoff, the son of Herman and Berenice (Ellman) Herzoff on May 28, 1936, in San Diego, California. His father died when he was two, and his mother married Alan Soulé, who adopted young Michael. Although neither of his parents was an environmentalist, naturalist, or outdoors recreation enthusiast, Soulé developed a passion for nature at a young age. Growing up in San Diego, close to the desert, the mountains, and the sea, Soulé developed a keen interest in wildlife, particularly butterflies, marine invertebrates, and lizards. His parents supported his interest, to the extent that his mother, who was afraid of snakes, even allowed him to keep them in the house.

Soulé's transition from naturalist to conservationist occurred gradually as he witnessed the increasing urban sprawl in San Diego. Graduating from high school in 1954, Soulé started studying at the University of California at Berkeley, then moved to the University of California at Santa Barbara, and then finally to California State University in San Diego, where he received his B.A. in zoology in 1959. He did his graduate work in population biology and evolution at Stanford University under PAUL EHRLICH, earning an M.A. in 1962 and his Ph.D. in 1964.

Soulé spent the next two years in Malawi as a lecturer in zoology at the University of Malawi in Limbe, before returning to the United States and joining the Department of Biology at the University of California at San Diego (UCSD) in 1967. With his family, he left UCSD in 1979 as a full professor to become the director of the Kuroda Institute for the Study of Buddhism and Human Values in Los Angeles. Soulé's temporary hiatus from academia was to pursue his interest in Buddhism. While at the Zen Center of Los Angeles, he finished two books, among other scientific activities. Soulé also directed the Zen Center's medical clinic for a year or so and even directed the Zen Center for a period of time. He returned to academia as a visiting and adjunct professor at the University of Michigan in the School of Natural Resources in 1984. Soulé founded the Society for Conservation Biology in 1985 and served as its president from 1985 to 1989, at which point he left the University of Michigan to become chair and professor of environmental studies at the University of California at Santa Cruz (UCSC). Soulé became professor emeritus there in 1996.

In 1991, he helped to found the Wildlands Project, serving as its president from 1996 to 1998, currently chairing its board, and working for it as a scientific advisor as well. The Wildlands Project, a nonprofit organization, is led by a group of conservation biologists and citizen conservationists from across the continent devoted to developing a North American conservation strategy, beginning with "Mega-Linkages," which are the continental-scale pathways or corridors for wildlife movement, that link major natural places and allow many species to adapt to climate change. The land in these pathways is usually a combination of public and private, and the Wildlands Project promotes voluntary actions by private landholders to protect biodiversity, and on public lands, changes in land use policies. Wildlands emphasizes science and boldness of vision. Its current emphasis is the implementation of Wildlands Network Designs in the Spine of the Continent region—an initiative that will link habitat from Alaska to Mexico. The Wildlands Project supports this campaign through funding, networking, and offering technical expertise.

Soulé has published more than 150 journal and symposium articles, editorials, commentaries, book reviews, forewords, and open letters. In addition, he has published nine books on biology, conservation biology, and the social context for contemporary conservation. His main research interests have revolved around three related themes: the application of island biogeography theory to conservation, the salience of ecological effectiveness of keystone species, and conservation genetics. The island biogeography model, designed by entomologist E. O. WILSON with mathematician Robert MacArthur, is used to explain species-area relationships and to predict the number and percentage of species that would become extinct if habitats were isolated. Originally used for islands, this model has since been adapted to explore national parks and nature reserves that are surrounded by damaged habitat. These reserves can be considered habitat islands, surrounded by unsuitable habitat. The Wildlands Project's Megalinkages effort responds to this phenomenon. With respect to keystone species, Soulé contends that extinction of large carnivores results in rapid habitat degradation and species loss from "release" of smaller carnivores and large herbivores. Soulé's work in conservation genetics has focused on the need to maintain genetic diversity, which in turn reduces the risk of species extinction.

Soulé consults on conservation internationally, is a popular keynote speaker in academic and nonacademic settings, and has served on boards of directors for several conservation groups, including the Rewilding Institute, Island Conservation, Round River Conservation Studies, the Marine Conservation Biology Institute, The Wilderness Society (Australia), and the Southern Rockies Ecosystem Project. Soulé currently resides in western Colorado, where he continues to work with conservation organization, consults on the protection of wild places, and writes about biological diversity, human nature, and compassion for all forms of life.

**BIBLIOGRAPHY**

Frankel, O. H., and Michael E. Soulé, *Conservation and Evolution*, 1981; "Rewilding Institute," www.rewilding.org; Soulé, Michael E., "Conservation Biology in Context: An Interview with Michael Soulé," *Environmental Policy and Biodiversity*, R. E. Grumbine, ed., 1994; Soulé, Michael E., ed., *Conservation Biology: The Science of Scarcity and Diversity*, 1986; "Wildlands Project," www.twp.org.

## Speth, James Gustave

(March 4, 1942– )
Cofounder of the Natural Resources Defense Council, Founder of the World Resources Institute, Dean of the Yale School of Forestry and Environmental Sciences

Cofounder of the Natural Resources Defense Council (NRDC) in 1970 and founder of the World Resources Institute (WRI) in 1982, James Gustave Speth led President Carter's Council on Environmental Quality (CEQ) and the United Nations Development Program. Currently he is the Carl W. Knoblock Jr. dean and the Sara Shallenberger Brown Professor In the Practice of Environmental Policy at of The Yale School of Forestry and Environmental Studies. Speth has been a strong proponent of sustainable development; he believes that the best way to address the world's severe environmental problems is by integrating environmental, economic, and developmental concerns.

James Gustave ("Gus") Speth was born on March 4, 1942, in Orangeburg, South Carolina. As a youth he spent much time fishing and hunting. He attended Yale College, where he studied political science, graduating *summa cum laude* in 1964. A Rhodes Scholar, Speth studied economics at Oxford for two years, earning an M.Litt. in 1966. He returned to Yale Law School, graduating with a J.D. in 1969, and then clerked one year for U.S. Supreme Court Justice Hugo Black. Thinking about the roles of the American Civil Liberties Union (ACLU) and the National Association for the Advancement of Colored People (NAACP) legal fund, he realized that the environment needed its own legal defense fund, and he recruited classmates and faculty at Yale to cofound with him the Natural Resources Defense Council in 1970. He worked as senior attorney for NRDC for seven years, leading its programs in energy and water.

Pres. JIMMY CARTER recruited Speth in 1977 for the CEQ, which he chaired in 1979 and 1980. He helped produce the influential *Global 2000 Report*, whose forecast of spiraling population growth, environmental degrada-

Gus Speth (Photograph by Julie Brown)

tion, and worsening poverty has largely proven true. From 1980 to 1982, Speth taught environmental and constitutional law at Georgetown University. In 1982, Speth founded the World Resources Institute, with the goal of bringing to the attention of world leaders the problems of natural resource destruction, pollution, and degradation of the world's ecosystems. The center seeks to provide irrefutable scientific information and policy analysis to these leaders and help them include solutions to environmental problems in their political agendas. Ambitious in scope, WRI has achieved broad recognition and success; during its first two decades it expanded to work with partner institutions in more than 50 countries and influence the governments of many more countries. A biennial report, *World Resources*, provides information on the state of natural resources and the environment in every country in the world. Speth served as WRI's president until 1992, when he left to become senior adviser to Pres. Clinton's transition team, heading the team on natural resources, energy, and the environment.

In 1993, Speth was tapped to serve as administrator of the United Nations Development Program (UNDP), the UN agency founded in 1970 to provide technical assistance to developing countries. As with the approach of the World Resources Institute, Speth integrated environmental concerns into UNDP poverty-alleviation projects. One example of the sustainable development projects that Speth's administration promoted was the Songhai Center in Benin, where local people raised domesticated fowl for slaughter and sale, using waste products to grow fruits and vegetables and for aquaculture. Not only is such a project environmentally friendly and an efficient use of resources, he wrote in *Foreign Affairs*, it is "an integrated, sustainable facility that trains people and produces income." Upon his departure from the UNDP, United Nations Secretary-General Kofi Annan thanked him for his work to "reform, reshape, and revitalize" an agency that had been plagued by inefficiency. Annan said that Speth had advanced "a vision of development that is both sustainable and centered on the real-life experience of human beings."

In 1999, Speth was recruited to become dean of the Yale School of Forestry and Environmental Studies, founded in 1900 with a grant from the family of GIFFORD PINCHOT as the nation's first institution to teach the principles of forest management and conservation. Speth's expertise in sustainable development was seen as an important qualification for the job, as Yale's leaders recognized that students need to understand the international, economic, and developmental context in order to design effective environmental solutions. The four books that Speth has published since taking his post at Yale have focused on these issues: *Worlds Apart* (2003), in which leading thinkers contributed essays that discuss the effect of globalization on the world environment; *Red Sky at Morning* (2004), a call-to-action prescribing specific changes to achieve sustainability; *Global Environmental Governance* (2006) co-edited with Peter Haas, a primer on international environmental law and policy; and most recently, *The Bridge at the Edge of the World: Capitalism, the Environment and Crossing from Crisis to Sustainability* (2008), which provides an agenda for American environmentalism.

At a celebration for the Environmental Law Institute (ELI) lifetime achievement award he was given in 1999, Speth summed up the 30-year evolution of his thinking: "In 1969, we created a separate environmental sector; today we must make every economic sector an environmental sector. Every agency must be an environmental protection agency. The pollutant-by-pollutant, problem-by-problem approach must be replaced by a holistic approach that sees the challenge of sustaining the biosphere in all its complexity and richness and responds accordingly."

In addition to the ELI award, Speth has received numerous others, including the National Wildlife Federation's Resource Defense Award in 1975, the Keystone Center's National Leadership Award in 1991, the Blue Planet Prize in 2002, and the Global Environmental Award from the International Association for Impact Assessment in 2005. He is an honorary trustee of the NRDC and has served on the board of directors of numerous environmental organizations, including WRI, the U.S. Committee for UNDP, the Environmental Law Institute, and the Woods Hole Research Center.

Speth resides in New Haven, Connecticut, with his wife, Cameron. They have three children.

### BIBLIOGRAPHY

Fellman, Bruce, "The Forest and the Trees," *Yale Alumni Magazine*, 1999; Speth, James Gustave, "The Plight of the Poor," *Foreign Affairs*, 1999; "United Nations Development Program," www.undp.org/; "World Resources Institute," www.wri.org/; "James Gustave Speth—Yale School of Forestry and Environmental Studies," www.environment.yale.edu/people/240-James-Gustave-Speth/cv/parent:faculty/.

## Standing Bear, Chief Luther
(1868–February 20, 1939)
Chief of the Lakota Sioux, Writer

Luther Standing Bear was the chief of the Lakota Sioux from 1905 until his death in 1939. During his leadership of the Lakota people he worked ceaselessly to improve conditions on the reservation and restore a sense of pride to his people. He wrote four books, all about Indian life and the connection of that life to the natural world. He was an educator of his people and strove to enlighten the White man about the way of the Lakota.

Luther Standing Bear was born Ota K'te (Many Kill) on the Pine Ridge Reservation in South Dakota in 1868. His father was Chief Standing Bear the first of the One Horse band, and his mother was Pretty Face of the Swift Bear band. Standing Bear was reared in a traditional Sioux manner and trained from a young age to be a Sioux warrior, although by the time he reached fighting age the Lakota no longer engaged in physical warfare. In 1879 Standing Bear was sent to Pennsylvania and became a member of the first class to attend the Carlisle Indian School. Much of what he wrote about in his autobiographical books was influenced by his experiences at Carlisle, where Indian children were forced to cut their hair, wear the White man's clothes, and give up their customs, religion, families, and language.

Standing Bear spent five years at Carlisle, then returned to Pine Ridge and resumed living in the Lakota way. He was shocked to see

Chief Luther Standing Bear (Library of Congress, Prints & Photographs Divison, LC-USZ62-56421)

students returning from the East who had lost all knowledge of their native language and customs. For a short time Standing Bear became a teacher at the reservation school. Soon, however, all Lakota teachers were replaced by outsiders, White people who had no knowledge of or interest in anything Lakota.

In 1898 Standing Bear joined Buffalo Bill's Wild West show, traveling as far as England to perform before the king. The following year he was badly injured in a train wreck that killed members of the troupe. His experience with the show led him to California, where he joined a lecture circuit and became a member of the Indian Actor's Association in Hollywood. He also appeared in a few movies, although he opposed the way Native people were portrayed in these films.

Although he lived in California for some years, Standing Bear remained a leader of his people. He was continually appalled by the degradation on the reservation. He was angered and saddened by seeing his people, once strong and self-sufficient, belittled to the point of extreme poverty and helplessness. He became a champion of the Lakota in approaching the government for improved conditions and in striving to display to the White man that the Sioux were not ignorant savages as they were so often portrayed.

In 1928 Standing Bear published *My People the Sioux*, his first book about Sioux life. In this book he attempted to explain his people to a world tainted by an image told only from the White point of view. *My Indian Boyhood* followed in 1930 and painted a picture of what it was to grow up as a Lakota. Here Standing Bear describes childhood in a traditional Lakota setting. The boys learned through various games to become hunters and warriors. They also learned to care for and respect all members of the tribe and to appreciate and learn from all things in nature. Standing Bear often compared the Lakota ways to those of the White man, especially in the understanding of and love for nature: "The Indian tried to fit in with Nature and to understand, not to conquer and to rule. We were rewarded by learning much the white man will never know."

In 1933 Standing Bear wrote to Pres. FRANKLIN D. ROOSEVELT to lobby for a bill that would make Indian history, religion, art, philosophy, and culture a part of all public school curricula. His letter remains unanswered by the U.S. government. The same year, Standing Bear's third book, *Land of the Spotted Eagle*, was published. This was another general description of Lakota life and values, but Standing Bear openly criticized government policy as it applied to the education and overall treatment of the Lakota people. Standing Bear strongly believed that Lakota children should have Lakota teachers and should be taught not only the White man's ways and history but their own as well.

Standing Bear claimed that "the white man has come to be the symbol of extinction for all things natural to this continent" and lamented that, by the White man, his people were "thrust... from [their] age-old mode of living into one that was foreign to [them] in every respect; religious, tribal, and social... placed in the impossible position of trying to remake or remould himself into a European." *Land of the Spotted Eagle* was the first book in which he so openly criticized the U.S. "Indian policy."

Standing Bear's fourth book, *Stories of the Sioux*, was published in 1934. This was a summary of many traditional Sioux legends and stories.

Standing Bear died on February 20, 1939.

### BIBLIOGRAPHY

Anderson, Mark S., "The Works of Luther Standing Bear," *Journal of the West*, 2007; "Standing Bear, Luther, *Land of the Spotted Eagle*, 1933; Standing Bear, Luther, *My Indian Boyhood*, 1930; Standing Bear, Luther, *My People the Sioux*, 1928; Standing Bear, Luther, *Stories of the Sioux*, 1934; Warrior, Robert, "A Room of One's Own at the ASA: An Indigenous Provocation," *American Quarterly*, 2003.

## Steel, William

(September 7, 1854–October 21, 1934)
Commissioner of Crater Lake National Park, First President of the Mazamas

Progressive conservationist William Steel, the first president of the Mazamas, a mountaineering and conservation organization based in Portland, Oregon, is popularly known as the "father of Crater Lake." Steel fought for 17 years to obtain national park designation for Crater Lake, Oregon's only national park. He spent the last 20 years of his life as superintendent and commissioner of the park, actively promoting the area and working to facilitate public access. He was also a participant in the campaign that led to the establishment of the Cascade Forest Reserve and was well known in the Northwest as a publicist of outdoor recreation and nature appreciation.

William Gladstone Steel was born on September 7, 1854, in Stafford, Ohio. His father, William, was a Scottish immigrant; his mother, Elizabeth, a native of Virginia. The Steel family moved to Kansas in 1868, and it was there that Steel first read about Crater Lake. He determined to see the spectacular lake in the wilds of far-off Oregon for himself. His family moved to Portland, Oregon, four years later, where they joined two of Steel's brothers, who had become successful financiers. Steel graduated from high school in Portland and began a three-year apprenticeship as a pattern maker for Smith Brothers Iron Works.

During this period, Steel acquired two interests that he would maintain for the rest of his life, writing and mountaineering. In 1879 he established the *Albany (Ore.) Herald*, but after a couple of years as a newspaper publisher, Steel returned to Portland, where he began work as a substitute letter carrier. He worked for the post office for 14 years, twice filling the post of superintendent of letter carriers. In 1883, he organized the first letter carrier's association in the United States.

In his spare time, Steel went mountaineering, climbing most of the peaks of the Cascades, including Mt. Hood, which he climbed more than 30 times in his life. He first visited Crater Lake in 1885. At that time very few people had heard of it—it was seven years after his arrival in Oregon before Steel met someone who had actually been there. The moment he saw the lake, Steel determined to have it protected as a national park so that all could enjoy its beauty. The next year he succeeded in obtaining an executive order from Pres. Grover Cleveland that withdrew land in the vicinity of the lake from public entry, but it would be 17 years before Steel's efforts to gain national park status for Crater Lake reached full fruition.

Two years after visiting Crater Lake, Steel organized the Oregon Alpine Club to attract attention to the Northwest's mountain scenery. In 1889, he published a collection of pamphlets in a promotional book, *The Mountains of Oregon*, with descriptions of the club's activities. Financial difficulties limited the organization's success, however, and in July 1894 Steel helped formed the Mazamas, a mountaineering club that is still active today. The club was named after Mount Mazama, the dormant volcano in whose crater Crater Lake has formed. It was Steel's idea to make the ascent of a glacier-clad peak a membership requirement that he felt would make the Mazamas a more successful organization than the moribund Oregon Alpine Club. He was elected the organization's first president.

With the support of the Mazamas, Steel continued in his efforts to make Crater Lake a national park. During the 1880s and 1890s, Steel engaged in and supported scientific study of the lake. He also successfully fended off repeated attempts to establish a state park there, believing the state could not provide the necessary maintenance and protection. He was particularly concerned about the impact of sheep and other livestock. Whether or not to allow livestock grazing was a key issue in another campaign Steel participated in, the establishment of the Cascade Forest Reserve. Created in 1893, this 300-mile-long reserve, which included Crater Lake, stretched from the Columbia River to the California border.

In 1895, Steel traveled to Washington, D.C., where he helped foil an attempt to rescind the executive order that established the Cascade Reserve. He also lobbied senators and representatives in an attempt to convince them that Crater Lake deserved national park status. "I was about as popular with them as the plague," he related in a column 18 years later. "When they asked me what my motive was and I said 'My love for Oregon and my desire to be of benefit to future generations is my only motive,' they would look at me, shake their heads and instruct their doorkeepers not to admit me again as I was a crank." His persistence finally paid off, however, when he convinced Secretary of the Interior Ethan A. Hitchcock to lend his support to the plan. U.S. Forestry Division chief GIFFORD PINCHOT also enthusiastically endorsed national park status for the lake, which he considered one of the great natural wonders of the continent. Pres. THEODORE ROOSEVELT signed the bill making Crater Lake a national park on May 22, 1902.

Steel's efforts to protect and promote Crater Lake did not end in 1902, however. He spent the rest of his life lobbying for funds to develop the park. He believed that everyone should have a chance to enjoy the area, not just the privileged few. He became the park's first concessionaire in 1907, providing transportation for tourists, a tent camp at Annie Springs, and boat tours of the lake, in which he had planted the first trout. A couple of years later he provided funds for the construction of Crater Lake Lodge. In 1913, Steel replaced W. F. Arant as superintendent of the park. Three years later, after the establishment of the National Park Service and the first federal appropriations to the park, Steel was promoted to commissioner of the park. Soon after his promotion, he began a campaign to raise $700,000 to establish a highway to Crater Lake. Although it would be several years before the highway was built, the first road encircling the rim of the lake was completed in 1918. The road-building efforts at Crater Lake were linked to the See America First campaign, spearheaded by STEPHEN MATHER, first supervisor of the National Park Service.

In 1921, Steel rejoined the Mazamas after a 15-year estrangement sparked by a dispute about his role in the organization and the nomination of Pres. Roosevelt as an honorary member. Steel also continued his publicity efforts in the 1920s, publishing an occasional pamphlet series and working for a time as editor of the Grants Pass *Courier*. In 1929, he moved to Medford, where he worked to expand and develop Oregon's state park system. He made his last visit to Crater Lake in the summer of 1932. Lydia, his wife of more than 30 years, died shortly thereafter, and Steel, too, fell ill.

Steel passed away on October 21, 1934, after two years of failing health. His pall bearers were rangers from Crater Lake National Park, and he was interred in Medford's Siskiyou Memorial Park wearing his Park Service uniform. He was survived by his daughter, Jean.

**BIBLIOGRAPHY**

LaPlant, Don, *Resolutions: William Gladstone Steel and Crater Lake National Park*, 2000; Lockley, Fred, "In Earlier Days," *Oregon Journal*, 1913; Mark, Stephen R., "Seventeen Years to Success: John Muir, William Gladstone Steel, and the Creation of Yosemite and Crater Lake National Parks," *Mazama*, 1990; "Mazama's Main Menu," //www.mazamas.org/mainmenu.htm; Steel, W. G., *The Mountains of Oregon*, 1889; Weiselberg, E. "He All but Made the Mountains: William Gladstone Steel, Mountain Climbing, and the Establishment of Crater Lake National Park, *Oregon Historical Quarterly*, 2002; "William G. Steel, Father of Crater, Called by Death," *Medford Mail Tribune*, 1934.

## Stegner, Wallace
(February 18, 1909–April 12, 1993)
Writer, Historian

A prolific and successful author, Wallace Stegner won nearly every major award given a writer, except the Nobel Prize, and penned works spanning everything from fiction to biography and history. He is remembered as an eloquent voice for the early environmental movement as it gained public recognition and momentum through such contentious issues as the attempted damming of Dinosaur National Monument. He was a consistent and vehement supporter of federal wilderness preservation and management.

Wallace Stegner was born February 18, 1909, on a farm near Lake Mills, Iowa. He was the second son of George and Hilda Paulson Stegner. He spent his early days with his mother and brother, Cecil, following along on his father's epic traipse through the West in search of what Stegner would later term "The Big Rock Candy Mountain, where something could be had for nothing, where life is effortless." For Stegner this journey included Iowa, Washington, and the Canadian province of Saskatchewan, effectively ending in 1921 in Salt Lake City, Utah, where he completed his high school education in 1925 and enrolled in the University of Utah, obtaining a B.A. degree in English in 1930. For George, this journey would not end until the summer of 1940, when he killed himself in a hotel room in Salt Lake City.

Stegner continued his education at the University of Iowa, completing his master's thesis in 1932. It comprised a series of three short stories, two of which were later published. He then went to the University of California, Berkeley, to begin his doctorate work but found the program unsatisfactory. He moved back to Iowa, finishing his graduate work by the summer of 1935. During this time he met Mary Stuart Page, whom he married in 1934. Together they had a son, Page, born in 1937.

He wrote his first novel in 1936 after reading an advertisement for a novel-writing contest sponsored by the Little, Brown Publishing Company in Boston. The prize was for $2,500. At this time Stegner was an instructor at the University of Utah, making only $1,700 a year. He wrote *Remembering Laughter*, submitted it, and won. Thus began a writing career that would lead to 34 books and many essays and articles.

Stegner was an influential author/historian/biographer, who was often decades ahead of the general thinking. *One Nation*, published in 1945, is a collection of essays and photographs originally produced for *Look* magazine. It confronts the race problems faced by the United States, which was in the process of fighting World War II with a racially segregated army and was busy interning Japanese Americans by the thousands. Stegner describes the "wall" splitting the United States. On one side are the white Protestant gentiles, and on the other are those who, because of race, religion, or color, are not considered full U.S. citizens.

Stegner was unique as a writer from, and grounded in, the American West. This region had a profound effect on the way he thought and wrote about the natural environment. The vast, wide-open spaces left an indelible impression on him, defining him as a person and as an artist. He later spoke of the immense distances, of the roads and telephone lines that disappear on the horizon, of a massive circle of observation with him always at the focal point. He saw wilderness preservation as a necessity because to him wilderness was nothing less than "the challenge against which our character as a people was formed."

Stegner is mainly remembered as a voice for a sensible western land ethic. He was a staunch supporter of federal management of public lands, stating that "without the federal bureaus, the west would be a wasteland." And though he thought of himself primarily as an author, he also wore the hat of sometime activist. In 1954 DAVID BROWER of the Sierra Club enlisted his help in the campaign to prevent the damming of the confluence of the Green and Yampa Rivers at Echo Park in Dinosaur National Monument on the Colorado-Utah border. This proposed Bureau of Reclamation project would have flooded a spectacular area of the monument with 500 feet of water. Stegner edited and contributed to a book entitled *This Is Dinosaur: Echo Park Country and Its Magic Rivers*, which was presented to members of Congress in an attempt to keep the project from going forward. The campaign was successful, and Dinosaur was not submerged. The victory was only partial, however, for the compromise that was reached with the environmentalist lobby allowed for a dam to be built farther downstream on the Colorado River, flooding Glen Canyon, a part of the Colorado that was nearly inaccessible and familiar to only a few people. Stegner was one of these few, having traveled this stretch of the river in preparation for his biography on JOHN WESLEY POWELL: *Beyond the Hundredth Meridian: John Wesley Powell and the Second Opening of the American West*.

Stegner's views on wilderness preservation are best expressed in a letter he wrote in 1960 to David E. Pesonen, consultant to the Outdoor Recreation Resources Review Commission, which was in the process of reviewing for Congress the need for wilderness legislation. In this letter Stegner stresses the necessity for preserving wilderness, stating that its worth cannot be measured only by its usefulness. He concludes by saying: "We simply need that wild country available to us, even if we never do more than drive to the edge and look in. For it can be a means of reassuring ourselves of our sanity as creatures, as a part of the geography of hope."

Stegner's son Page, a retired Professor of English at University of California-Santa Cruz, has recently published a collection of his father's letters, with letters from his early years in the 1930s all the way up to the 1980s, in which he expressed worries about President Ronald Reagan's environmental policies.

Wallace Stegner died April 12, 1993, of injuries sustained in a car accident in Santa Fe, New Mexico.

## BIBLIOGRAPHY

Benson, Jackson, *Wallace Stegner, His Life and Work*, 1996; Colberg, Nancy, *Wallace Stegner, A Descriptive Bibliography*, 1990; Fratkin, Philip, *Wallace Stegner and the American West*, 2008; Rankin, Charles E., ed., *Wallace Stegner: Man and Writer*, 1996; Simpson, Richard H., *Dictionary of Literary Biography: American Novelists 1910–1945*, Vol. 9, 1981; Stegner, Page, *The Selected Letters of Wallace Stegner*, 2007.

## Steingraber, Sandra

(August 27, 1959– )
Ecologist, Poet

Sandra Steingraber is an ecologist and poet who holds degrees in both biology and creative writing. She has conducted field studies in Costa Rica, Africa, and the United States and has published a volume of poetry. Her first book, *Living Downstream: An Ecologist Looks at Cancer and the Environment* (1997), was highly acclaimed for its eloquent presentation of cancer as a human rights issue, linking the alarming worldwide patterns of cancer incidence to the use of agricultural chemicals and other toxins. A cancer survivor herself, she brings a personal perspective to her crusade to expose agricultural and industrial recklessness and its effect on human health.

Sandra Kathryn Steingraber was born on August 27, 1959, in Champaign, Illinois, and was adopted by Wilbur and Kathyrn Steingraber, both teachers. She grew up with a younger sister in the town of Pekin, Illinois, surrounded by farmland. When she was 15 years old, her mother was diagnosed with metastatic breast cancer. Although her mother survived it, the experience had a profound impact on Steingraber and provoked her interest in biology. In 1979, when she was a biology student at Illinois Wesleyan University, she was diagnosed with bladder cancer. Having grown up in a county with 15 hazardous waste sites and several carcinogen-emitting industries, she became interested in whether the toxins she was exposed to as a child could have contributed to her contracting cancer.

Steingraber finished her B.A. in biology and graduated from Illinois Wesleyan University in 1981 and then received her M.A. in creative writing from Illinois State University in 1982. In the same year she married, and a few years later she accepted a fellowship to study ghost crabs in Costa Rica. In 1989, by the age of 29, she had earned her Ph.D. in biology from the University of Michigan. Upon finishing her graduate studies she was still concerned with the connections between human health and the environment, and she decided that someday she would become a scientist within the activist community. She started teaching at Columbia College in Chicago in 1990 and stayed for three years. Then in 1993 a Bunting Fellowship allowed her to start writing full-time, and she completed a book of poetry called *Post-Diagnosis* in 1995. Her next book brought her instant acclaim and provided crucial information that was, until then, not easily available. Called *Living Downstream: An Ecologist Looks at Cancer and the Environment* (1997), it brought together information gathered under new right-to-know laws on toxic releases and newly released cancer registry data. From this and other lines of evidence, she concluded that environmental influences are more crucial than heredity in causing cancer. Her own experience provides an example of this. She and several other members of her family, including her mother, an aunt, and many uncles, all contracted cancer—leading one to suppose that it simply runs in the family. Yet she was adopted and shares no genetic history with any family members. She also used the example of immigrants coming to this country with little or no history of cancer, who gradually assimilated until their cancer rates equal those of their new host country. Clearly, environment plays a large role.

Sandra Steingraber (Photograph by Frank DiMeo/Cornell University Photography)

In *Living Downstream*, Steingraber frequently referred to RACHEL CARSON, who died of breast cancer herself shortly after her influential book *Silent Spring* was published. In *Silent Spring*, Carson called for a systematic evaluation of the contribution of toxic chemicals to increased human cancers. Over 30 years later, Steingraber—whom *Sierra* magazine called "Rachel's Daughter in 1999—is repeating this call and emphasizes that Carson's warning has not been heeded. She cites the fact that between 45,000 and 100,000 chemicals are now in common use, and only 1.5 to 3 percent of them have been tested for carcinogenicity. While there are regulations in effect that require the evaluation of old, untested pesticides, the tests themselves will not be completed until 2010. Until then the pesticides can still be sold and used. In a country where more than 750 million tons of toxic chemical wastes have been discarded since the late 1950s and where detectable pesticide residues are found in 35 percent of the food consumed, Steingraber insists that uncertainty should not be an excuse to do nothing. She advocates a human rights approach, one that shows respect for life on the planet by not allowing untested chemicals free access to the environment.

Steingraber's second book was *Having Faith: An Ecologist's Journey to Motherhood* (2001), in which she chronicles her own pregnancy and describes all the toxic contamination her child was exposed to in-utero and as a nursing infant. She calls amniotic fluid a "glowing liquid jewel" and breast milk "magical holy water kind of formula" with antibodies and nutrients impossible to replicate. Yet because we have breathed in and eaten so many toxic chemicals from our polluted environment, these life-giving substances are replete with toxins. Breast milk, in fact, contains more dioxin, more polychlorinated biphenyls (PCBs), and more dichlordiphenyltrichlor (DDT) than any food allowed on the market. This, she believes is intolerable. But her goal is not to scare women into not having babies, rather she seeks to inform her readers and inspire them to act to stop the poisoning.

Her most recent work is about the falling age of puberty in girls. She has written a report about this phenomenon, the first comprehensive literature review of the timing of puberty, available from the Breast Cancer Fund (www.breastcancerfund.org).

Steingraber is a passionate and popular speaker and has given talks on environmental health issues at Harvard University, Yale University, Cornell University, Woods Hole Oceanographic Institute, the First World Conference on Breast Cancer, and many other venues. She is a scholar in residence at Ithaca College, and she writes for such publications as *Orion, Mother Earth News, New Scientist* and *Ms*.

Steingraber's efforts have earned her rewards and recognition. *Ms. Magazine* named her a woman of the year for 1997, in 1998 she won the Altman Award for the inspiring and poetic use of science to elucidate the causes of cancer, and in 2001 she received the biennial Rachel Carson Leadership Award from Chatham College. She resides in upstate New York and with her husband Jeff de Castro has two children, Faith and Elijah.

**BIBLIOGRAPHY**

Gross, Liza, "Rachel's Daughter," *Sierra Magazine*, 1999; Lindsey, Karen, "Sandra Steingraber," *Ms. Magazine*, 1998; "Sandra Steingraber's Website," www.steingraber.com; Steingraber, Sandra, *Having Faith: An Ecologist's Journey to Motherhood*, 2001; Steingraber, Sandra, *Living Downstream: An Ecologist Looks at Cancer and the Environment*, 1997.

## Stone, Christopher
(October 2, 1937- )
Legal Scholar

Author of the 1972 classic *Should Trees Have Standing?*, Christopher Stone has helped shape the terms of how the law addresses environmental issues. In that work Stone argued that natural objects—rivers, oceans, forests, and the environment itself—should be granted legal standing as "persons" with rights, specifically the right to bring suit if threatened with harm. Though this argument has never been fully accepted in the courts, Stone's work has helped expand the grounds on which environmental issues can be fought in the courts, by weakening the necessity for plaintiffs to suffer immediate personal harm in order to have standing to sue. In this and other writing, Stone has influenced the development of environmental ethics.

Christopher Stone was born on October 2, 1937, in New York City. Stone is the son of the independent journalist I. F. Stone and inherited from his father an interest in philosophy and progressive politics. He graduated from Harvard University in 1959 with an A.B. in philosophy and from Yale University with an LL.B. in 1962. After serving as a fellow in law and economics at the University of Chicago from 1962 to 1963, Stone was hired by the School of Law at the University of Southern California in Los Angeles. He was granted tenure in 1966. In 1969 the U.S. Forest Service granted Walt Disney Enterprises the right to build a resort complex in Mineral King Valley, located in the Sierra Nevada. The Sierra Club went to court to block the development and won a temporary restraining order. That initial success was overturned, however, when the court ruled that the club did not have legal standing to bring the suit. The Sierra Club would not be directly injured by the resort's destruction of Mineral King Valley, the court ruled, and therefore could not pursue its claim. Stone intervened to challenge this narrow view of standing. What if, Stone argued, the valley itself was seen to have standing, and the Sierra Club to serve as its guardian? Stone rushed his ideas into print through the *University of Southern California Law Review*, in hopes of influencing the Sierra Club case, then pending before the U.S. Supreme Court. Though the Sierra Club lost the case, "Should Trees Have Standing?" was cited favorably in the dissenting opinion of Supreme Court Justice WILLIAM O. DOUGLAS; through his advocacy, it was picked up by other lawyers and the media. Stone's argument began to influence the debate over environmental rights, particularly the question of whether the issues could be more effectively argued from a human or nonanthropocentric viewpoint.

Stone made the case for an environment-centered approach in three main parts, the first demonstrating that conceiving of the environment as having legal rights could be no more "unthinkable" than rights for women or children had been at other points in Western history. In the second part, Stone addressed the "legal-operational aspects" of his argument and demonstrated that while natural objects currently had no legal rights per se, there were legal precedents and structures in place that could be usefully and reasonably reinterpreted so as to confer such rights on the environment. Finally, Stone addressed the "psychic and socio-psychic aspects" of his argument, specifically the need to re-imagine the relationship between humankind and nature less as "man over nature" than with a view of humanity as part of the interconnected, organic whole of nature. In the years following its publication, Stone's argument began to be used in actual cases. Complaints were filed in the name of several nonhumans, including a polluted river in southern Connecticut, Death Valley Monument in southern

California, and the endangered palilla bird in Hawaii. These cases, however, involved joint plaintiffs, wherein the nonhuman complainant was linked with a human individual or group, so the principle of full legal rights for natural objects remains unestablished. Stone's ideas are in circulation, but not fully in practice.

Since the publication of *Should Trees Have Standing?* in book form in 1972, Stone has contributed two further volumes to the discussion of environmental ethics. 1987's *Earth and Other Ethics* follows up on Stone's earlier work in an extended meditation on the limitations of what he terms "moral monism." Stone argues that conventional ethics tends to put forth a single principle—for example, the greatest good for the greatest number—as the key to all ethical dilemmas. Stone argues that this framework inherently privileges human over nonhuman actors and therefore should be replaced with a pluralist approach, recognizing differences among situations, actors, and acts. Stone suggests that this approach can give greater weight to the standing and rights of natural objects. *The Gnat Is Older than the Man: Global Environment and the Human Agenda* (1993) is less philosophically and more practically oriented. In particular Stone addresses finding solutions to pressing issues of global environmental degradation, with a particular emphasis on the need for international treaties. Treaties, he argues, offer greater hope for constructive environmental action than the courts, which are slow to respond to immediate danger. Stone argues for the importance of what he calls the Global Commons, the skies and the oceans, the places where human and natural interests transcend national sovereignties.

*The Gnat Is Older than the Man* was influenced by Stone's work as a researcher and consultant to governmental and nongovernmental agencies, including the American Bar Association, the National Science Foundation, and the Department of Energy. He is the J. Thomas McCarthy Trustee Chair In Law at the University of Southern California and lives in Los Angeles.

**BIBLIOGRAPHY**

Staff Editors, "Developing an Environmental Ethos," *Tennessee Law Review*, 1988; Wenham, Brian, "Towards a Treaty of Life for the Global Commons," *Financial Times of London*, 1993; Westing, Arthur, "Should Trees Have Standing?" *Environment*, 1997.

## Stone-Manning, Tracy

(September 18, 1965—)
Executive Director of Clark Fork Coalition, Founder of Headwater News

Tracy Stone-Manning founded Headwater News (1998) as an online news service for the Rocky Mountain area, but truly launched her environmentalist career as Executive Director of the Clark Fork Coalition (CFC) where she and her staff ran a successful campaign to close down the Milltown Dam and restore the Clark Fork River and the largest EPA superfund site in America.

The youngest of five children, and the only girl, Tracy Stone was born September 18, 1965, in Springfield, Virginia. When she was five years old, her conservative, Catholic, Navy family moved to Washington, D.C., where she spent the rest of her childhood.

Tracy Stone-Manning (Photograph courtesy of Clark Fork Coalition)

When she was eighteen, one of her brothers took her camping and she slept outdoors for the first time. Tracy says this experience literally changed her life, bringing out a strong interest in nature and the environment. After she acquired a B.A. in Radio and Television from the University of Maryland, an increased interest in environmentalism led her to think about a degree in science, to use her communication skills to translate what scientists were finding.

She spent a year at the University of Exeter in Devon, England. There she gained a new perspective on American conservation versus a European ethic. Stone said she realized America has so many wild places, whereas in England, which she walked across, she never had to carry a tent because she could always get to the next town. On returning stateside, she received an internship with the National Wildlife Foundation in D.C., in the public affairs office. But Stone wanted to be more engaged in action than in talking about it. She applied to the University of Montana's environmental studies program, which was the only environmental studies program with an advocacy component. While visiting Montana she suddenly felt at home. Back in Washington, D.C., to care about the environment was considered "quaint." In Montana the environment was the residents' bread and butter.

After receiving an M.S. in Environmental Studies, she worked as a consultant and freelance writer and married Richard Manning, an environmental writer. In short order, she became the director of the Five Valley Land Trust, launched a campaign to use public funds to buy a mountain on the edge of Missoula, and began community work for various nonprofits, including Defenders of Wildlife, the organization Ecotrust, based in Oregon, where she ran the program for a year and a half but always craned for Montana.

In 1998, she launched Headwater News, an online clip service for the Rocky Mountain region. At this time she also joined the board of the Clark Fork Coalition (CFC). In 1999 Stone-Manning became the Executive Director determined to implement what she had learned at Ecotrust and move the organization from mere advocacy work to community building. Stone-Manning and her staff set out to practice conservation in a different way than it had been approached before, in order to take away the stereotype that conservationists were elitists who don't care about people. Instead, they sought to portray the environment as the life and the future of the community. Stone-Manning said the staff at CFC tried very hard to make the work they did accessible, understandable, and vital to a much larger constituency.

The primary mission of the CFC is to preserve and restore the upper Clark Fork River, running from Butte, Montana, to Sandpoint, Idaho.

Butte was once considered the "richest hill on earth" with its enormous copper deposit, and was mined for over a century. Before environmental regulation, the Butte copper mine piled up their tailings next to the Clark Fork River. With flooding, all those tailings rushed 140 miles downstream to the Milltown Dam. Six million cubic yards of mineral sediments, iron, manganese, copper and arsenic built up behind the dam.

In 1983 the full 140 miles of the Clark Fork River south of Butte was listed as an EPA Superfund site which included a reservoir of drinking water at the Milltown Dam. When the Clark Fork Coalition was founded in 1985, its first act was to add the entire upper river listed to the Superfund site.

In 1996, an enormous ice jam on the Blackfoot River threatened the Milltown Dam. Terrified dam owners dumped the reservoir, with hopes of grinding the ice jam to a halt. But large chunks of ice coming down the Clark Fork River kicked up over the dam, resulting in an enormous fish kill, between 50 percent to 85 percent of fish in some species. Only then did Montanans learn that the dam was holding back toxic waters which could spill over and kill the fish population.

When Stone-Manning took on the position of Executive Director of the CFC in 1999, she recognized that the dam only generated 1.3 megawatts of electricity, and left fish endangered and potable water problems. Her proposed solution, considered crazy at first, was to take out the dam. By 2003, 10,000 Montana citizens had gotten behind the idea and Republican Governor Judy Mart called for the removal of the dam and the cleanup of the reservoir.

Stone-Manning attributes the success of this campaign to the residents of Montana seeing this issue as a community and health issue, instead of an isolated environmental issue. She said that once people realized their drinking water and their fish population were at risk, they got over the idea of taking a dam out as being anti-progress. The Coalition's work resulted in toxic sediments being dug out and a major cleanup of the Clark Fork River.

In early 2007, Stone-Manning left her position as Executive Director of the CFC when newly elected Senator Jon Tester asked her to run his Missoula field office where she now advises on natural resources, especially forest health issues.

"After years of pushing from the outside, now I'm seeing how it runs from the inside," said Stone-Manning of her new position.

Tracy Stone-Manning lives with her husband Richard in Missoula, Montana, while remaining indirectly active in her hometown of Washington, D.C.

## BIBLIOGRAPHY

Personal interview, 1/24/08; www.clarkfork.org; www.westernwateralliance.org; www.fvlt.org; www.headwatersnews.org; www.semesterinthewest.org/pivot/entry.php?id=63&w=journal#body; www.missoulanews.com/News/News.

## Subra, Wilma

(August 14, 1943– )
Analytical Chemist, Citizen Advocate

Chemist and MacArthur Foundation award winner Wilma Subra has helped innumerable communities in her native Louisiana and 20 other states to study the health risks posed by local environmental contamination. She also helps them work toward cleaning up the damage.

Wilma Subra was born in Morgan City, Louisiana, on August 14, 1943, the eldest of six sisters. She was raised with a strong Samaritan ethic: her family helped whoever needed a hand—relatives, friends, neighbors. She became interested in chemistry as a child working for her father, who owned a lab that ground oyster shell into fine powder that could be used in paint, makeup, pharmaceuticals, even as a filler for tires.

Subra attended the University of Southwestern Louisiana in Lafayette, earning a B.S. in 1965 and an M.S. 1966, both in microbiology and chemistry. She taught mathematics to junior high school students for one year and then in 1967 began working for the Gulf South Research Institute, a research laboratory that contracted with government agencies and private companies to do cancer and viral studies, pharmaceutical testing, environmental evaluations, environmental impact statements, and other similar work. One memorable contract was from the Environmental Protection Agency (EPA) to visit Love Canal in 1980 for a quick response project, a rapid evaluation of the community's health problems. During this and other similar evaluations, Subra found herself in the uncomfortable position of knowing more about the residents' health problems through blood analyses and air sampling results than the residents knew themselves, yet her employer prohibited her from informing them of what she knew.

Subra found it more satisfying to be able to communicate openly with people subject to environmental contamination and offer her

Wilma Subra (Photograph courtesy of Wilma Subra)

assistance, and began doing this in the mid-1970s. She and her colleagues at Gulf South were often approached by private citizens living in the area who were concerned about environmental contamination near their homes. Subra did chemical analyses of soil, air, and water at the laboratory, and evenings would hold meetings with these citizens to explain the results. If they were interested, Subra would instruct them on how to learn more, accompanying them to state regulatory agencies to find out which local industries had permits to pollute, which were discharging waste into the air or waterways, and which ones were exceeding the limits of their permits.

Subra has worked in this capacity with 400 grassroots citizens groups in many areas of Louisiana. She has helped communities around Lake Charles succeed in having commercial hazardous waste facilities cleaned up, preventing new ones from opening, tightening permit regulations for industry, and relocating people living on top of contaminated groundwater plumes. She worked with the citizens of Calcasieu Parish to demand an end to the contamination of the Calcasieu estuary. Her tests of contaminated soil served as evidence to convince the EPA to establish three new Superfund sites in the heavily contaminated Vermilion Parish. The Houma Indians asked her to help monitor pollution in their community at Grand Bois, where land farming of commercial oilfield wastes (packing these toxic wastes into the soil) was poisoning land and air. She worked with residents of her native Morgan City to prevent the reopening of the Marine Shale Processors plant, the largest hazardous waste incinerator in the United States, after it had been shut down by the government for exceeding its emissions limits. For families living in Norco, Louisiana, next to a chemical company that emitted chemicals that were causing respiratory problems and cancer, she was able to negotiate a relocation plan, through which 300 households were paid above-market prices for their homes and all of their relocation costs to new locations they were free to choose.

In addition to her technical skills, Subra is effective because of her ability to clearly explain science to laypeople, and because she has a soft-spoken manner which allows her to speak truth without alienating opponents to her causes. She is committed to providing information, experience, and support to the communities she helps, but she does not lead their fights, as she feels the community will "own" their struggle if they lead it themselves.

Subra has served on transition teams for environmental issues for two Louisiana governors, Buddy Roemer, elected in 1987, and Edwin Edwards, elected in 1991. The transition teams toured the state to meet with local citizens to learn about their environmental problems, wrote a report, then toured the state again to present the report. She serves on various Louisiana state government committees that work with regulatory agencies and on several EPA committees as welladvocating for grassroots citizens groups. Subra estimates that one-third of her time is spent volunteering for the EPA, and that does not include the time she spends meeting with citizen groups to learn what they want from the EPA.

Subra's work is not limited to Louisiana. She has worked in more than 20 states since 1987 with the National Citizens Network on Oilfield Waste, reviewing deficiencies in state regulations for oilfield waste treatment and offering technical assistance to citizens groups living near oilfield waste–processing plants.

Subra has owned a chemical laboratory and environmental consulting firm, Subra Company, Inc., since 1981 that analyzes lots of suspected toxic substances—as well as hot sauce from the nearby tabasco factory. She does receive some technical assistance grants for evaluating site investigation data at Superfund sites. But Subra spends most of her work weeks—20 hours a day, seven days a week—offering volunteer assistance to victims of environmental contamination.

Subra received a 1999 MacArthur Foundation "genius" grant of $370,000, which she uses to fund even more work for environmental causes. Other awards she has received include the 1989 Woman of Achievement award from Connections, a Lafayette, Louisiana, organization; and the Louisiana Wildlife Federation Governor's Conservation Achievement Award, the top environmental award in the state, also in 1989. Both were given to her in recognition for her work with citizens' groups on environmental issues, as well as work on Governor Roemer's transition team and her participation in various state committees. In 1999 she was recognized by the Coalition to Restore Coastal Louisiana for her work with coastal communities on environmental issues. And in 2004 she was one of three finalists for the Volvo for Life Environmental Award.

Subra has been married since 1965 to Clint Subra, a medical technician whose work includes bloodwork analysis when necessary for people who live near toxic contamination sites. Together they have three grown children, who grew up accompanying Subra to meetings and on trips throughout the United States as Subra collected data for new projects.

**BIBLIOGRAPHY**

Cohen, Sharon, "Genial Grandmother is 'Top Gun' in Environmental Activism," *Common Dreams.org*, 2001, www.commondreams.org/headlines01/1020-03.htm; Dunne, Mike, "La. Activists, Scientists Making a Difference," *Baton Rouge Advocate*, 1999; Schultz, Bruce, "La. Environmentalist Wilma Subra Receives MacArthur Grant," *Baton Rouge Advocate*, 1999; Schwab, Jim, *Deeper Shades of Green*, 1994; "Volvo for Life Awards: Wilma Subra," www.volvoforlifeawards.com/cgi-bin/iowa/english/heros/hero2004/4305.html.

## Suckling, Kierán
(October 11, 1964– )
Cofounder of Center for Biological Diversity

Kierán Suckling founded and heads the Tucson-based Center for Biological Diversity, a nonprofit environmental organization that successfully uses the court system to fight for habitat and wildlife protection. Due to Suckling's effective leadership, and an ever-growing need for the type of work the Center does, the Center for Biological Diversity has grown from a very small operation relying on pro-bono opportunities working only in New Mexico, to having, currently 15 prominent environmental lawyers and eight scientists who work full time, exclusively on its nationwide campaigns. Ninety three percent of their lawsuits result in victories for saving habitat and species.

Kierán Francis Suckling was born on October 11, 1964, in Winchester, Massachusetts, to an Irish mother and English father. He moved frequently as a child, because his father worked for an engineering company that built large industrial plants throughout the world. A self described "moderate achiever and fairly constant discipline problem" in high school, Suckling was nonetheless hungry for knowledge—especially in the fields of linguistics and philosophy—and devoured a collection of philosophy books that he inherited from an uncle's Jesuit seminary. Suckling became involved in nuclear disarmament and Central American justice issues during his high school years. He studied at Salve Regina College in Rhode Island and Worcester Polytechnical Institute in Massachusetts, where he set up a chapter of Student Pugwash, an organization founded by Albert Einstein that explores the social implications of technology and works against the arms race. He transferred to the philosophy program at the College of the Holy Cross in Worcester, Massachusetts, graduating *magna cum laude* in 1987, with a B.A. in philosophy, and winning the school's McCarthy Award in philosophical research.

Upon graduation, Suckling set off to explore the West. After hiking the canyons and mountain country of western North America, he enrolled in the State University of New York (SUNY) at Stony Brook's graduate program in philosophy, focusing on Greek philosophy, phenomenology, deconstruction, and language extinction. Because he was convinced that there was a relationship between extinction of languages and of species, Suckling surveyed endangered spotted owls and northern goshawks for the U.S. Forest Service (USFS) in Arizona and New Mexico. He became so dismayed by the evidence that these birds were in danger of extinction that he vowed to save them. Suckling and his survey partner, biologist Peter Galvin, joined with emergency room doctor Robin Silver in 1990 to brainstorm the Southwest Center for Biological Diversity, an organization dedicated to saving endangered species and habitats. Suckling completed his coursework at SUNY, passed his history of philosophy exam with honors in 1991, and returned in 1991 to direct the Southwest Center (now called the Center for Biological Diversity; CBD).

The CBD quickly became one of the region's most active and best known environmental groups. It first sought to protect habitat and wildlife of New Mexico, then expanded to protect the wild Southwest, and now works nationwide, fighting ranchers, loggers, the government agencies that enable them, and any other agency that destroys or develops wildlands. Eschewing the current trend of working with all parties concerned with the land, in order to arrive at consensus or a compromise, the CBD is adamant about environmental preservation. Cofounder Galvin, who currently works as CBD conservation director and litigation coordinator, explained the CBD's position to *Outside Magazine:* "The developers and the extractors have eaten nine pieces of a ten-piece pie... and they want to negotiate about the tenth piece. I'm happy to stick my fork in their hand."

During the CBD's early years, Suckling and Galvin were tutored in environmental litigation by Biodiversity Legal Foundation director JASPER CARLTON. Funded by memberships foundation support, the CBD works by filing lawsuits to prevent environmentally destructive development projects. They monitor the activities of the U.S. Forest Service and the U.S. Fish and Wildlife Service (USFWS), filing Freedom of Information requests to obtain the information they need. In one of its early cases, in 1995, at a time when the Republican-dominated U.S. Congress had placed a year-long moratorium on new endangered species listings and a salvage logging rider had lifted all timber-cutting regulations in national forests, the CBD convinced a judge to halt all logging in the Southwest until its effects on the threatened Mexican spotted owl could be investigated. The injunction on cutting in national forests was lifted when the USFS agreed 16 months later to abide by the USFWS Mexican spotted owl recovery plan.

The CBD has also tried to reform the USFS. Suckling told reporter Michael Kiefer of the *Phoenix New Times*, "We've got an economic system designed to make money by destroying nature, whether it's timber sales or grazing allotments. A lot of groups like ours that traditionally did not deal with economics, are starting to look at ways to both expose and to take advantage of the economic system. Because the way it's set up now, they're just giving away trees and giving away grass to the ranchers and the loggers." The CBD collaborated with environmental groups in the Northwest on pushing for "unlogging" permits: leases on national forest lands through which the purchaser would pay for the right to *not* log the forests, but in February of 1997 USFS employees rejected the idea without consulting their supervisors at the U.S. Department of Agriculture. The rejection was rescinded, and the issue is still under review.

The CBD counts among its many successes the salvation of the San Pedro River, a 130-mile-long tributary of the Gila River on whose banks half of all the 800 bird species known in North America have been sighted. *Birding* magazine has called it the world's best birding area, and the Nature Conservancy has declared it one of the world's eight "Last Great Places." In addition to birds, the San Pedro harbors the second-highest concentration of mammalian species in the world, behind Costa Rica's montane rain forests. It is so biologically rich that it has been declared one of only two National Riparian Conservation Areas in the country. The San Pedro was in danger of hydrological collapse because of its proximity to the United States Army's Fort Huachuca and the nearby town where Fort Huachuca employees live, Sierra Vista, both of which pump water from the aquifer below the San Pedro. Filing suits on behalf of many endangered species that inhabit the San Pedro, the CBD persevered through five years of litigation until Fort Huachuca agreed in 1999 to reduce its water use and support reductions throughout the river basin.

For their feisty and successful approach to conservation and their persistence, Suckling and Galvin won recognition as "Deep Ecologists of the Year" from the Oregon-based Fund for Wild Nature in 1996, and in 1997 the *Arizona Business Journal* highlighted Suckling as one of the eight people most likely to shape Arizona's future. CBD's unique brand of activism has been featured in the *New Yorker*, *Wall Street Journal*, *Washington Post*, *San Francisco Chronicle*, *High Country News*, *Backpacker*, *Outside*, and many other magazines and newspapers. Suckling resides in Tucson, Arizona.

**BIBLIOGRAPHY**

Aleshire, Peter, "A Bare-knuckled Trio Goes after the Forest Service," *High Country News*, 1998; "Center for Biological Diversity," www.biologicaldiversity.org/; Kiefer, Michael, "Cow Punchers: Ranching Takes a Blow in the Courts, an Uppercut to the Bottom Line and a Jab in the Marketplace," *Phoenix New Times*, 1997; Kiefer, Michael, "Owl See You in Court," *Phoenix New Times*, 1996; Skow, John, "Scorching the Earth to Save It," *Outside Magazine*, 1999.

## Susanka, Sarah
(1957—)
Architect, Author

Sarah Susanka is a charismatic residential architect, author, and social commentator. Her observations about home design in the United States have helped to draw attention to the fact that the focus on square footage often inhibits sustainable building practices and meaningful lives. Her mission is to move American home design and the American way of life away from the super-size mentality to an appreciation of quality over quantity. Her Not So Big titles—*The Not So Big House* (1998), *Creating The Not So Big House* (2000), *Not So Big Solutions for Your Home* (2002), *Home by Design* (2004), *Inside the Not So Big House* (2005), *Outside the Not So Big House* (2006), and *The Not So Big Life* (2007)—have sold well over one million copies. As a public speaker she inspires thousands of Americans to live better, not bigger.

Born in Kent, England, in 1957 to an industrial designer and a ballet teacher, Sarah Susanka relocated with her family to Los Angeles, California, in 1971. At fourteen, Susanka (then Sarah Hills) began attending a high school that had three times the number of people in it than the village she had come from. The contrasts between the world she'd come from and the world she had moved to informed her enormously, and over the years she grew to observe more subtle contrasts in the ways we engage our lives, and the spaces we inhabit. At sixteen, she announced to her parents that she intended to become a writer, a passion she'd been pursuing informally throughout her childhood. But her father sagely advised that she wait until she had some marketable skills under her belt, and had something developed in a field she could write about. So Susanka turned her focus instead to the study of architecture, graduating from the University of Oregon in 1978 with a bachelor's degree in Architecture, and later

Sarah Susanka (Photograph by Cheryl Muhr)

acquiring a master's degree in Architecture from the University of Minnesota in 1983.

As an architect and active member of the American Institute of Architects, Susanka became well known in the Minneapolis area. The same year that she received her master's degree, she founded a residential architectural practice with partner Dale Mulfinger, that later became known as Mulfinger, Susanka, Mahady & Partners, Inc., and which was selected to design the 1999 Life Dream House.

The firm grew largely through serving clients of average means who were interested in smaller, better-designed houses. Susanka had intuited early on that McMansions, trophy homes, and "starter castles" would before long become unappealing to home buyers. In fact, she realized, most people were building such houses not for their own comfort, and not for what features fit their own lives, but for the resale market. They were in effect building their houses for the imagined needs of the next buyers rather than for themselves.

Susanka recognized that those imagined needs were the residue of a bygone lifestyle but not appropriate for today. The blueprint being used for the typical American home was a century out of date, and was in dire need of an update. It was this insight that inspired her passionate first book, *The Not So Big House* (1998), a book that has had a dramatic impact on shifting the perception of what constitutes a well-designed home.

*The Not So Big House* makes design recommendations (for example, eliminate formal rooms while refining informal rooms) and showcases "not so big houses." Susanka writes: "Tailoring is a basic ingredient of the Not So Big House. If you just make a house smaller, but still generic, it won't have any more appeal than its larger cousins. What makes the Not So Big concept work is that superfluous square footage is traded for less tangible but more meaningful aspects of design that are about beauty, self-expression, and the enhancement of life."

The popularity of the book confirmed to architects and builders around the country that there was an enormous market for smaller, better designed homes.

At the same time she began publishing her understandings, she also started to recognize the parallel between the interior designs of our homes and the interior designs of our lives. By remodeling a home, she discovered, she could help individuals move toward more sustainable lives, giving them a means to something even more valuable than the pursuit of happiness—the pursuit of meaningfulness itself.

After leaving her firm in 1999 to pursue her new vocation as writer and public speaker, Susanka began to adhere ever more closely to her Not So Big philosophy not only in *where* she lived, but in *how* she lived. In 2007 *The Not So Big Life: Making Room for What Really Matters* was published, giving the tools to implement shifts in the designs of our lives, just as *The Not So Big House* had done nine years earlier with respect to the designs of our homes. Where her previous books were about space, this one was about time. As Susanka puts it, "It's the same basic message, but translated from the third dimension—space, to the fourth dimension—time."

Her ability to articulate the concept of a lifestyle based on "living smaller, more consciously, and more sustainably" has made Susanka a sought-after public speaker and cultural visionary. She has appeared on the Oprah Winfrey Show and Charlie Rose and was the 2007 recipient of the ANNE MORROW LINDBERGH Award. Sarah Susanka lives in North Carolina with her husband.

**BIBLIOGRAPHY**

Sarah Susanka's Bridges to the Future speech, Denver University, January 15, 2007, www.du.edu/bridges/events/video.html; Susanka, Sarah, "Big Ideas Behind Not So Big Houses," *Architecture Week*, July 26, 2000; Susanka, Sarah, *The Not So Big House*, 1998; www.notsobig.com; www.susanka.com.

## Swearingen, Terri
(November 24, 1956- )
Grassroots Toxics Activist

During the 1990s, registered nurse and dental technician Terri Swearingen became a powerful opponent of a toxic waste incinerator that was built in her hometown of East Liverpool, Ohio. Even after she exposed the dangers of toxic emissions being released only a few blocks away from an elementary school, revealed the corruption and disregard for the law that led to the permits being granted by the Environmental Protection Agency (EPA), and led thousands of local residents to protest the siting, the incinerator was built and is in operation today. Although Swearingen and the others fighting the Waste Technologies Industries (WTI) incinerator did not succeed in stopping its construction, they are credited for forcing the EPA in 1993 to set national standards for siting hazardous waste management facilities.

Teresa Joyce Swearingen was born in East Liverpool, Ohio, on November 24, 1956, one of five siblings whose family has a long history in the Ohio River Valley. Her father worked in a steelmill, and her mother worked in an elementary school cafeteria. Swearingen studied nursing at the Ohio Valley Hospital School of Nursing, graduating first in her class in 1978. Also a trained dental technician, she worked in the dental office of her husband, Lee Swearingen. She was actively involved in various committees at her church, where she also taught Sunday School. In her free time, she enjoyed making stained glass windows and other crafts.

All of that changed one day in 1982, when a patient of her husband told her about plans to construct one of the world's largest hazardous waste incinerators in a poor minority neighborhood in East Liverpool. The burner, permitted to release 4.7 tons of lead and 1.28 tons of mercury annually, was to be built 400 yards from a 400-student elementary school and 320 feet from the nearest home. From her medical training, Swearingen knew that lead exposure was dangerous, especially to children during critical periods of growth and development. Mercury exposure can cause irreversible nerve damage and many other serious problems, particularly for children. Swearingen was especially shaken by this news because she was pregnant with her first and only child, Jaime.

Swearingen began talking to friends and neighbors about the proposed incinerator, writing to elected officials and to local newspapers. She continued to have faith that the EPA would never permit such a dangerous project. But in 1989, Waste Technologies Industries began preparing for construction. It was then that Swearingen realized that the project was indeed moving forward and that if she did not get more involved, she could not expect anyone else to either. So she jumped to action.

Swearingen began a process of self-education, starting with the book, *Rush to Burn: Solving America's Garbage Crisis*, a 1988 publication compiling articles by reporters from *Newsday*. She tracked down everyone cited in the book: citizen activists, politicians, and experts. They referred her in turn to more articles and studies, and she called everyone who authored or was cited in those as well. Soon Swearingen was well connected with many other grassroots toxics activists and very well versed about the hazards of incineration. She and other local activists hosted town meetings and conducted public information sessions to spread the word about the incinerator. In 1990 she cofounded the Tri-State Environmental Council (TSEC) to coordinate the activities of those in Ohio, Pennsylvania, and West Virginia who opposed the incinerator.

When, in January 1991, the EPA held a public hearing about a modification to their permit for the incinerator, Swearingen invited nationally known experts to testify about its dangers. They included dioxin expert PAUL CONNETT, EPA whistleblower HUGH KAUFMAN, and several others. Since each member of the public was allowed five minutes to speak, local attendees would stand up every five minutes to take the microphone and cede their time to the expert currently testifying. Upset that the meeting had effectively been seized by the incinerator's opposition, EPA officials changed the rules for testimony mid-meeting—after most of the anti-incinerator experts had testified but before the WTI expert even arrived. Swearingen and her colleagues realized that in spite of their success at getting accurate information communicated during the hearing, it was basically a sham. The EPA was ready to rubber-stamp the modified WTI plant design. Later hearings and meetings with the EPA showed the activists that EPA officials were unable to dispute damning evidence presented by activists and experts yet still refused to recall the permit. TSEC began to pursue other tactics to express their opinion.

During the early 1990s, Swearingen and others organized dozens of rallies and protest marches, attended by thousands of local residents, most of whom had never before been involved in protests. Their tactics were creative. An early action, dubbed "Hands Across the River," was a march by 1,000 people from Pennsylvania, Ohio, and West Virginia through all three states, culminating on the Jennings Randolph bridge over the Ohio River, to express tri-state opposition to the incinerator. On one of their frequent trips to Ohio governor George Voinovich's mansion, protesters erected "For Sale" signs on his lawn because they believed he had sold out to toxic polluters.

The group was very disappointed in the Clinton-Gore team, which had made WTI a campaign issue and had made WTI the very first environmental issue they addressed after their election. Once in office, however, they failed to keep their promise not to allow WTI to operate. This was especially ironic because AL GORE's book *Earth in the Balance* specifically criticized incineration. In late 1993 the group "recalled" Gore's environmental treatise and deposited hundreds of copies with a guard at the White House gate. During other protests, Swearingen and others were arrested for illegal trespassing onto the incinerator site and in Washington—including once inside the Clinton White House—to protest the lack of action taken by federal authorities.

Although TSEC was ultimately unsuccessful in stopping the WTI incinerator in East

Liverpool, their efforts did halt other commercial incinerators from being built around the country. Ohio enacted a moratorium on the construction of new hazardous waste incinerators. The protesters motivated Congress to conduct its first-ever hearing to look at the ways the EPA bent the rules to help the industries they are supposed to regulate. They forced an overhaul of federal combustion regulations, including the development of more stringent emission limits for toxic heavy metals and the first-time emission limit for dioxin under the Resource Conservation and Recovery Act (RCRA; the Federal hazardous waste law). The day after a mass arrest of 54 protesters, including Swearingen along with members of other citizens' groups and Greenpeace, who had chained themselves to a mock incinerator complete with a belching smoke stack outside the White House gates, the EPA announced a new policy governing hazardous waste incineration and declared an 18-month freeze on new incinerator construction. The May 18, 1993, announcement gave satisfaction to the group, but Swearingen, barred from attending the press conference, could not help noticing the irony of EPA administrator CAROL BROWNER's top priority for the new combustion and waste management strategy: "increased public participation."

Swearingen is now world famous for her leadership of the struggle against toxic incinerators and their siting in poor and minority neighborhoods where people are less likely to protest. She and her fellow activists have been credited as the driving force behind the EPA's action to implement first-time national siting standards for hazardous waste management facilities.

Swearingen has received many awards and much recognition for her work. Her story was told in the 2005 book *Wisdom for a Livable Planet*, and many other studies of environmental justice struggles as well. She received the 1999 William E. Gibson Achievement Award presented during the 211th General Assembly of the Presbyterian Church (USA) by Presbyterians for Restoring Creation and a 1999 Women at Their Best Award Winner from Cover Girl and *Glamour* magazine. She was the recipient of the 1997 Goldman Environmental Prize for North America and the 1997 National Peace Award from Clergy and Laity Concerned. She was named one of six "Ecowarriors" by *marie claire* magazine in 1997, was a TOYA (Ten Outstanding Young Americans) Award nominee in 1995, and was named the Ohioan of the Year in 1994. Also in 1994, *Time* magazine named Swearingen, along with John F. Kennedy, Jr., Oprah Winfrey, and Bill Gates, as one of the 50 most promising leaders in America. In 1993 she was inducted into the Citizens Clearinghouse for Hazardous Waste Grassroots Honor Roll and Hall of Fame. In the same year, she received the Joe A. Calloway Award for Civic Courage administered by the Shafeek Nader Trust for the Community Interest.

Currently, Swearingen continues to serve the environmental justice movement by working with other organizations involved in environmental justice struggles, including the American Environmental Health Studies Project.

**BIBLIOGRAPHY**
Brown, T. C., "A Slow Burn," *Cleveland Plain Dealer Sunday Magazine*, 1998; Gorisek, Sue, and Ellen Stein Burbach, "Ohioan of the Year: The Housewife That Roared," *Ohio Week Magazine*, 1994; McDaniel, Carl, *Wisdom for a livable planet: the visionary work of Terri Swearingen, Dave Foreman, Wes Jackson, Helena Norberg-Hodge, Werner Fornos, Herman Daly, Stephen Schneider, and David Orr*, 2005; Rembert, Tracey C., "Terri Swearingen: The Long War with WTI," *E Magazine*, 1997; Schneider, Keith, "For Crusader against Waste Incinerator, a Bittersweet Victory," *New York Times*, 1993; Schwab, Jim, *Deeper Shades of Green*, 1994; "Terri Swearingen, Goldman Prize," www.goldmanprize.org/node/166.

# American Environmental Leaders

From Colonial Times to the Present

## Tall, JoAnn
(1953– )
Environmental Activist and Organizer, Cofounder of Native Resource Coalition, Cofounder of Indigenous Environmental Network

JoAnn Tall, Oglala Lakota, is an environmental activist whose work has focused on environmental justice issues at her native Pine Ridge Reservation in South Dakota. Since the 1980s, she has led grassroots struggles to protect Pine Ridge and other reservations from such environmental threats as nuclear testing and toxic waste dumping. Tall is an active member of the American Indian Movement (AIM), she helped to create the Native Resource Coalition and the Indigenous Environmental Network, and has served on the board of directors of the Seventh Generation Fund.

Joann Tall is an Oglala Lakota (Sioux), born in 1953 on the Pine Ridge Reservation in South Dakota. Her introduction to activism came in 1973 when she participated in the American Indian Movement's occupation of the village of Wounded Knee on the reservation. Wounded Knee was the site of an 1890 massacre in which more than 200 unarmed Native American men, women, and children were slaughtered by the U.S. Seventh Cavalry (the same regiment Gen. George Custer had led into Little Big Horn in 1876). The cavalry also succeeded in killing 25 of their own soldiers in crossfire. Despite this heavy casualty toll in the face of an unarmed and fleeing enemy, the regiment received 20 Congressional Medals of Honor. In his book, *In the Spirit of Crazy Horse*, PETER MATTHIESSEN writes, "After Wounded Knee, the soldiers were replaced by bureaucrats, including 'educators' whose official task was to break down the cultural independence of the people." The Lakota were forbidden to participate in traditional spiritual ceremonies, were not allowed to wear Indian dress, and were discouraged from speaking their own language. Their children were taken and relocated to government boarding schools. This type of oppression characterized the U.S. government's relationship to the Lakota over the course of the next century.

AIM was founded in the late 1960s with the idea that Native Americans needed to find ways to solve their own problems, rather than continuing to rely on the destructive supervision of the U.S. government. On February 28, 1973, a group of several hundred AIM members and supporters took over the historically significant community of Wounded Knee to protest the U.S. government's treatment of Native Americans on the Pine Ridge Reservation. AIM issued a public statement demanding an investigation of the corrupt Bureau of Indian Affairs (BIA) and a hearing on the Fort Laramie Treaty of 1868 (this treaty granted the Lakota "absolute and undisturbed use of the Great Sioux Reservation" and has been ignored and broken by the United States ever since). Tall participated in the 71-day sit-in at Wounded Knee, during which the community was surrounded by U.S. marshals, Federal Bureau of Investigation agents, and tribal police, who exchanged gunshots with the occupiers, killing two of them. After the protesters had held out for more than two months, the U.S. government agreed to AIM's demands on the condition that Wounded Knee be vacated. Once AIM had left Wounded Knee, hearings on the Fort Laramie Treaty never took place, nor was an investigation into the BIA ever undertaken.

Tall's environmental activism spans more than 20 years and is grounded in her people's reverence for, and respect of, the natural world. She has a spiritual connection with "Grandmother Earth" that is outside of the experience of many Americans. Her motives for protecting the earth are not so much a desire to "conserve" or "preserve," as they are a moral imperative. Her belief system simply requires her to respect and appreciate the life-sustaining land. Tall has been guided by dreams since she was a young child and is quoted on the "Greening of the Future" website as saying, "One [dream] was of going into this forest, when a doe came towards me in tears. I followed her to a clearing. One of her fawns was dying, the other was trying to get up. I looked around their habitat. It was contaminated. I told her 'I will not be able to help you, but I am going to find out who did this and deal with them the best I can.' That dream has followed me over the years in health, land and environmental issues."

In 1987, a defense contractor, Honeywell, announced plans to conduct weapons testing in a Black Hills canyon on the Pine Ridge reservation, sacred to the Lakota. Tall utilized the locally owned and operated Pine Ridge radio station, known as KILI, to inform reservation residents of the threat to their ancient burial ground and ceremonial site. Then, at a public meeting in which Honeywell planned to convince local residents that the testing would be harmless, Tall "tore into the PR guy." A *Ms. Magazine* article reports her demanding, "How dare you try to desecrate our church? That's what the Black Hills mean to us: they're our church... We're going to win this war." Tall then organized a "resistance camp" of more than 150 people at the proposed testing site in the Black Hills. They camped out for three months, until Honeywell abandoned the project.

Tall followed this success by helping to found the Native Resource Coalition (NRC), a group whose first action was to protest plans to build a 5,000-acre landfill and incinerator site on the Pine Ridge Reservation. The NRC found that over a two-year period more than 60 Indian reservations nationwide had been targeted by the waste industry as sites for disposal. This was due to the fact that, having sovereign status, many reservations had much less stringent regulations than the U.S. government about the treatment of toxic waste. Especially attractive to the waste industry were Native American tribes for whom a language barrier prevented their full understanding of what they were agreeing to. These people had no words in their traditional languages for poisons such as polychlorinated biphenyls (PCBs) or dioxins.

In 1991, NRC joined forces with other grassroots groups to organize a conference in the Black Hills, the purpose of which was to educate and inform the many tribal groups that were being subjected to the environmental racism and economic blackmail of the waste disposal industry. Largely thanks to this conference and to Tall's leadership, the native councils rejected proposals for toxic waste disposal sites on the Pine Ridge, Rosebud, and other nearby reservations. It was at this conference that Tall helped to organize the Indigenous Environmental Network, which now consists of more than 50 member organizations, working to educate indigenous people about environmental threats in the United States and in Canada.

Tall is the mother of eight children. She looks to the future with optimism. As she says on the "Greening of the Future" website, "When I look at all of us with our work, our sacrifices, there's hope. You always have to have hope, because we talk about the children, the future generations. My dream tells me there is hope for the future." She continues to live on the Pine Ridge Reservation where, increasingly, she is taking on the role of elder, adviser, and educator. She has served on the board of directors of the Seventh Generation Fund, a foundation and advocacy organization that supports Native Americans through grants, technical training, and issue advocacy. In 1993, she received an environmental hero award from the Goldman Environmental Foundation.

## BIBLIOGRAPHY

Breton, Mary Joy, *Women Pioneers for the Environment*, 1998; "The Greening of the Future," www.motherjones.com/news/feature/1995/03/heroes.sidebar.html; Matthiessen, Peter, *In the Spirit of Crazy Horse*, 1980; Taliman, Valerie, "Saving Native Lands," *Ms. Magazine*, 1994.

## Tamminen, Terry

(March 7, 1952– )
Author, Entrepreneur, Director of New America Foundation's Climate Policy Program

Climate change policy guru, author, entrepreneur, and founder of several environmental watchdog groups, Terry Tamminen travels the world to forge collective governmental and business action to control emissions of greenhouse gases. The former head of California's EPA and advisor to Governor ARNOLD SCHWARZENEGGER, Tamminen is now the Director of the New America Foundation's Climate Policy Program. He is also an expert on swimming pools, sheep ranching, and a theater enthusiast, having published and performed on multiple occasions a one-man, audience interactive play about Shakespeare's life.

Terrance Arthur Tamminen was born in Milwaukee, Wisconsin, on March 7, 1952. His family moved to Los Angeles in 1963, then to Brisbane, Australia. His father Art Arndt served in the Marines during World War II in the Pacific. His mother, Iris Langdon, worked as a medical assistant. His sister, Laurie, was born in 1949. Tamminen came back to the U.S. for college at California State University/Northridge and moved to Florida in 1984, where he worked in real estate. He moved back to California for good in 1990, having subsequent career experiences in Europe, Africa, Latin America, and all over the U.S. His wife, Leslie, worked for the Los Angeles-based environmental organization Heal the Bay and they worked together when he founded the Santa Monica Baykeeper.

Ever since he was a child Tamminen was interested in the undersea world. He was involved in efforts to protect manatees in Florida in the 1980s, and in 1993 he founded the Santa Monica Baykeeper, for which he was Executive Director for six years and a citizen aqua cop extraordinaire. He roved the Los Angeles County shoreline by boat with cameras and water sampling equipment to document pollution. By 1995, his organization had been involved in assisting with 131 environmental legal cases, he had helped co-found four more Waterkeeper programs along the California coast, and he helped to set up the Frank G. Wells Environmental Law Clinic at the School of Law at UC Los Angeles, named after the late president of the Walt Disney Company, who shared Tamminen's passion for preserving the Santa Monica Bay.

In the meantime, Tamminen, who has studied animal husbandry, managed the largest sheep ranch east of the Mississippi, and later was the "poolman to the stars" with his Palisades Malibu Pools business, which included Dustin Hoffman and Barbra Streisand among its clients. Tamminen has published three books on the maintenance of pools, hot tubs, and other home water features. It was through hobnobbing with celebrities that Tamminen, a devout Democrat, first met Maria Shriver, the author, journalist, and wife of Republican Governor Arnold Schwarzenegger. With the additional connection to Shriver's cousin Robert Kennedy, Jr., environmental lawyer and founder of the national network of Waterkeepers Tamminen became involved in Schwarzenegger's campaign the summer before his successful recall election win in November of 2003. Tamminen hashed out an environmental agenda with Schwarzenegger over many lunch meetings, and eventually joined his staff in several capacities, working at the state and international level, before being named Cullman Senior Fellow at the New America Foundation in April 2007.

The Climate Policy Program which Tamminen directs at the New America Foundation seeks to keep global atmospheric concentration of $CO_2$ equivalent gases from surpassing the scientific and widely recognized "climate stabilization" level of 450 parts per million. Going beyond this fundamental tipping point would result in massive environmental and economic displacement worldwide within the next two decades. This program which was launched at the end of March 2007 focuses on designing and implementing a national response to climate change by aggregating the action of state and local governments, in the absence of meaningful progress from the federal government in Washington, DC. The NAF climate agenda's five program areas are in transportation, emissions reductions, comprehensive climate action plans, renewable energy portfolio standards, and standards for energy efficiency. With Tamminen's direct assistance in many instances, as of October 2007, 27 states in the U.S. have or are in the process of completing comprehensive climate plans, most of which involve alliances with neighboring U.S. states, and some with Canadian provinces and Mexican states.

In 2006 Tamminen published *Lives per Gallon: The True Cost of Our Oil Addiction*, which is peppered with literary references very much on point regarding the follies of humanity. He lays out in great detail how America's addiction to oil is costing us billions in what would otherwise be unnecessary costs in public health, and environmental cleanups of our air, water, and landscapes, resulting in enormous setbacks in economic productivity of workers and agricultural yields, and damage to materials and buildings. He also presents the scandalously high taxpayer subsidies to the oil and auto industries, which in some instances involve public funds to secure oil abroad held in the hands of private corporations, a process often resulting in environmental Chernobyls and political Fallujas in places like the Arauca Province of Colombia.

In his book Tamminen familiarizes the reader with the deceptive and monopolistic practices shared by the tobacco and the oil and auto industries, pointing out in addition that toxins from cigarette smoke resemble those of petroleum smoke in every respect except that the latter still contains lead in many parts of the world. Tamminen also lays out a plan for energy independence, and makes a compelling case for how state attorneys general across the U.S. ought to band up and sue the oil and auto industries as 46 of them did when they sued the tobacco companies, winning a $2 trillion settlement in 1998 to be disbursed to litigating states in the next 25 years. He lays out five tort legal theories under which they could sue which have been successful in the past.

Tamminen has been an active participant in the boards of many educational and environmental institutions and has won numerous awards, most recently the California Resource Recovery Association's Rick Best Environmental Advocacy Award.

## BIBLIOGRAPHY

Chronicle Publishing Company, "Aqua-Cop Prowls L.A. Shoreline on Lookout for Polluters," *San Francisco Chronicle*, 1995; Darmiento, Laurence, "State's EPA Head Thinks New Role is Perfect Fit," *San Diego Business Journal*, 2004; Porton, Zipporah, "Political Pool Man," *Pool & Spa News*, 2005; Wingfield, Brian, "Climate Controller: Terry Tamminen," *Forbes.com*; www.terrytamminen.com.

### Q & A with Tamminen

**1. In the course of your involvement with environmentalism, what environmental laws have had an impact on the nation, your region, or you personally?**

The Clean Air Act and the Clean Water Act, both enacted more than 30 years ago, have set the standard for environmental laws, both with effective policy, process, and results. As we consider climate change legislation at the state and federal levels, we look to these successful models for inspiration. It is worth noting that California enacted state versions of these laws ahead of the federal government and, once again, has passed the Global Warming Solutions Act in 2006, ahead of any other state or our federal government.

The most significant elements of these two landmark laws are the ability to measure progress and the citizen enforcement provision. As a result, I have been a plaintiff in numerous air and water cases, eliminating significant amounts of pollution from the environment.

**2. What scientific discoveries have had a major impact on the nation, your region, your field of work, or you personally?**

Perhaps the most profound scientific discoveries are those related to global warming. More than any other environmental challenge, climate change has made us realize that we are literally connected to every other living creature on this planet and that our actions will change the lives of others dramatically. The work of the United Nations' Intergovernmental Panel on Climate Change has also set a new standard for scientific collaboration and investigation. These discoveries led me, as Secretary of the California Environmental Protection Agency, to recommend to Governor Arnold Schwarzenegger the greenhouse gas reduction targets and the action steps to achieve them, which resulted in the passage of our Global Warming Solutions Act in 2006.

**3. What impact have environmental organizations or actions had on the nation, your region, your field of work, or you personally?**

Environmental groups have shown us what's at stake when we pollute or endanger the lives of other species. They've also shown us the path forward to change and become more sustainable. I am especially grateful to the International Waterkeeper Alliance and Robert F. Kennedy Jr. for the tireless work protecting the waterways of the U.S. and beyond. The examples set by Waterkeepers in New York and San Francisco inspired me to create the Santa Monica Baykeeper in 1993 and, by following the model set by these leaders, we were able to significantly improve the quality of our coastal waters, restore the kelp habitat that supports hundreds of marine species, and engage hundreds of ordinary citizens in the protection of our natural resources.

## Tchozewski, D. Chet

(January 25, 1954– )
Activist, Organizer, Executive Director of Global Greengrants Fund

Chet Tchozewski was an important protagonist in the antinuclear movement of the late 1970s and 1980s, organizing mass protests for ten years at the Rocky Flats Nuclear Weapons plant in Colorado until it was closed in 1989. Currently Tchozewski is the founder and executive director of Global Greengrants Fund, which makes small grants to grassroots environmental organizations in developing countries.

Darrell Michael Tchozewski was born on January 25, 1954, in Shelby, Michigan, and grew up with six siblings in nearby Montague, on the banks of Lake Michigan. His father worked at the Hooker Chemical Company chlorine plant, and Tchozewski remembers that at least once a week the whole town reeked of the chemical. No one worried about it then, but after toxic releases decimated the area's fish and local wells were found to be contaminated, both the Hooker plant and a neighboring DuPont Chemical freon factory were shut down and declared Superfund sites. Tchozewski attributes his environmentalism in part to this early influence.

D. Chet Tchozewski (Photograph by Ray Ng, courtesy of Global Greengrants Fund)

Tchozewski was the first in his family to attend college. He started at a community college in Muskegon, continued at Michigan State University, and then in 1974 moved west

Rocky Flats Encirclement-October 15, 1983. (Photograph by Siri Jodha Singh Khalsa, Ph.D.- Boulder, CO)

to Colorado and attended classes at the University of Colorado. When the protests at the Rocky Flats Nuclear Weapons Plant just northwest of Denver began in 1978, Tchozewski joined them. The first protest he attended in April of that year was planned as a 24-hour vigil in which 250 protesters were to symbolically block the railroad tracks used for shipping out the nuclear triggers manufactured at the plant. After one night on the tracks, Tchozewski and a group of 35 others decided to stay there. That marked the birth of the Rocky Flats Truth Force (RFTF), a vanguard grassroots nonviolent direct action group dedicated to closing the Rocky Flats Plant through civil disobedience.

Tchozewski helped set up an office for the RFTF. He worked there full-time and spent the summer of 1978 learning about the nationwide antinuclear movement by traveling to protests at nuclear power plants all over the United States. By the spring of 1979, when the Three Mile Island nuclear reactor in Harrisburg, Pennsylvania, melted down and public opinion turned solidly against nuclear power, the focus for protests shifted to nuclear weapons. Tchozewski worked through the RFTF and later the Rocky Flats Project of the American Friends Service Committee to organize major protests attended by thousands of people, as well as smaller on-going vigils on the tracks. One of the most effective events was a 20,000-person encirclement of the plant in 1983; others involved marches from Boulder, 12 miles away, to the plant; others were combined with huge concerts on the plant's grounds by such antinuclear musicians as Jackson Brown and John Denver.

In 1983, Tchozewski cofounded the Rocky Mountain Peace and Justice Center in Boulder to work on closing Rocky Flats and on other peace, justice, and environmental issues. In the spring of 1986, Tchozewski learned that despite Soviet president Gorbachev's promise not to test Soviet nuclear weapons unless the United States tested its weapons, the Department of Energy (DOE) was testing nuclear weapons underground at its Nevada Test Site near Las Vegas. Greenpeace activists had attempted to prevent an earlier test by sneaking onto the test site and alerting the DOE of their presence; Tchozewski wanted to do the same. So one afternoon, after learning that another test was scheduled for sometime that week, he recruited three friends for the expedition. By 7:30 that evening they were on a plane to Las Vegas. A contact picked them up and drove them to the test site, and at midnight they were hiking toward Ground Zero. The contact alerted the local press and DOE officials, who searched the area by helicopter. Once the DOE believed the protesters were not at Ground Zero, the bomb was detonated. As it turned out, Tchozewski and his companions were still miles away from Ground Zero when the bomb went off, but when they hiked off the site 36 hours later they were greeted by a large group of sympathizers. During the next year or so the Rocky Mountain Peace and Justice Center coordinated activists who took turns making well-publicized forays onto the rugged backcountry of the Test Site to prevent or delay nuclear testing.

Meanwhile, back at Rocky Flats, after 11 years of almost continuous protests, the Environmental Protection Agency (EPA) in 1989 discovered that the contractors who operated Rocky Flats had been engaged in many illegal activities. Through overhead infrared nighttime photos of the plant, the EPA obtained proof that illegal incineration was occurring, and in June 1989 the Justice Department authorized the Federal Bureau of Investigation to raid the plant and shut it down. Since then, the EPA and the Colorado Department of Health and Environment have overseen a cleanup of all of the radioactive waste contaminating the plant site. The Rocky Flats Plant was eventually closed for good in 1994 and the multi-billion dollar clean up was completed about ten years later.

Tchozewski left Colorado in June 1989 for the San Francisco office of Greenpeace, which hired him as its Southwest regional director. He worked for three years supervising 200 employees working in the southwest part of the United States and in Latin America and the Pacific Rim. At this point, during the resurgence of the environmental movement marked by the *Exxon Valdez* oil spill, the growing awareness of global warming and the hole in the ozone layer, and the 20th anniversary of Earth Day, Greenpeace was the largest environmental organization in the world, with a peak membership of three million.

In 1992 Tchozewski and his wife, Susan Carabello, left for a year-long sabbatical trip through Asia. During that year, Tchozewski realized that the environmental issues facing poor countries were even more serious and complicated than those of the United States, but relatively easy to address with consciousness raising and classic community organizing. There were grassroots groups to address the problems, but their lack of funding was crippling. By the time the couple returned to Colorado in 1993, Tchozewski had brainstormed a solution. He would start a foundation that could serve as a conduit for U.S. donations to grassroots groups in developing nations around the world. Global Greengrants Fund was established at the Tides Foundation in 1993, funded by donors whom Tchozewski had met over the years, including some antinuclear protesters from the 1970s who had since made lots of money. Building on the 'resource mobilization' theory of change to demonstrate the high impact of small grants in developing economies, Tchozewski earned the confidence of traditional foundations and philanthropists to raise tens of millions of dollars to irrigate the grassroots.

The Global Greengrants Fund works with a self-organizing global network of volunteer advisors consisting of U.S.-based nonprofit groups that work on international environmental issues (Friends of the Earth, Earth Island Institute, Rainforest Action Network, Pesticide Action Network, the Pacific Environment and Resources Center, and the International Rivers Network) and a vast multi-dimensional global network of local leaders. Because these organizations are in close contact with grassroots environmental groups abroad, they can help determine which groups should receive small donations (less than $5000) that together amount to millions of dollars, five million in 2008. Tchozewski continues to be amazed at how much a small group abroad can do with as little as $750; he believes that grassroots groups are probably the most economical and efficient environmental organizations in existence. Since its founding, Global Greengrants has provided more than 4,000 grants, totaling almost $20 million, in 120 different countries.

The Council on Foundations gave Tchozewski the Robert W. Scrivner Award—given to grant-makers who demonstrate outstanding creativity. Tchozewski lives in Boulder, Colorado, with his wife and their daughter, Tian.

## BIBLIOGRAPHY

"Global Greengrants Fund," www.greengrants.org; Hickman, Jason, "Rocky Flats Protesters Meet Again Twenty Years Later," *Boulder Daily Camera*, 1998; Human, Katy, "Flats Activists Look Back," *Boulder Daily Camera*, 1998; Kelly, Paula J., "A Conversation with Chet Tchozewski," *Foundation News & Commentary*, 2004, www.foundationnews.org/CME/article.cfm?ID=2903; Levitt Ryckman, Lisa, "Crossroads at Rocky Flats, Yearlong 'Occupation' 20 Years Ago This Month Challenged Public Acceptance of Nuclear Facility," *Rocky Mountain News*, 1998.

## Tewa, Debby
(June 16, 1961– )
Solar Electrician

Debby Tewa is a solar electrician who for 11 years directed the Hopi Foundation's NativeSUN project, which brings solar electricity to people living off the grid on the Hopi and neighboring Diné Reservations. Currently she contracts with Sandia National Laboratories Sandia Tribal Energy Program to help people who live on Indian reservations learn about and maintain photovoltaic units on their homes.

Debby Tewa of the Coyote Clan was born on June 16, 1961, in Phoenix, Arizona. She grew up in her grandmother's traditional stucco and sandstone home on the ceremonial plaza of Hotevilla, a village on the Hopi reservation. She describes her childhood as adventurous: solitary hikes around the silent plateau lands of the reservation stimulated her curiosity, imagination, and sense of exploration. She recalls, even as a child, inquisitively examining the gears on her bicycle, demonstrating her love of the mechanical. In 1979, Tewa graduated as valedictorian from Sherman Indian High School, a boarding school run by the Bureau of Indian Affairs in Riverside, California. She attended Northern Arizona University for two years as a liberal arts major. She earned her certificate as an electrician at the Gila River Career Center. Tewa worked at commercial outfits and for government housing authorities in the Phoenix area for several years until 1989, when the Hopi Foundation offered to send her to a photovoltaics workshop put on by Solar Energy International and held in Carbondale, Colorado. She tried working as a solar technician on the Hopi Reservation soon after the training, but sales were too slow. She returned to Phoenix and worked there until 1991, when funding became available for her to work on the Reservation.

One-third of the villages on the Hopi Reservation refuse to connect to the local electric company's grid. They dislike the visual pollution of power lines. They do not want to cede a right-of-way to the power company for installation and repair. They worry that if people cannot pay their bills, the power company may retaliate by claiming Hopi land as collateral. Some residents use propane or generators, but they must haul fuel, maintain the generators, and deal with noise and safety. For this reason, individually owned solar energy systems offer an ideal way to provide electricity without compromising traditional values.

NativeSUN offers low-interest loans to people who want to purchase a solar electricity system for their home. Once the loan (usually between $5,000 and $6,000) is repaid, the owner can enjoy as much free electricity as his or her panels can generate. Tewa had installed about 300 systems by 2000, including some upgrades of previously existing systems.

After 11 years directing NativeSUN, Tewa left to complete a B.S. degree in Applied Indigenous Studies and a minor in Environmental Science. In 2002 she was recruited by Sandra Begay-Campbell, director of the Sandia National Laboratories Sandia Tribal Energy Program, to work with tribes that have received Department of Energy grants for solar energy.

Tewa recognizes that solar energy cannot satisfy all of the requirements of modern life, since the four- to eight-panel systems do not run washers, dryers, or freezers. Some people combine their solar energy with propane or generators. Tewa knows that, for convenience, some of her neighbors would prefer to connect to the power grid. She believes that even if her village signs up with the power company, people will conserve electricity. Dependence on solar energy "teaches you to be conservative, because you're getting your power from batteries," she told WINONA LADUKE, author of *All Our Relations*.

Tewa has lectured throughout the United States about the Hopi Foundation and NativeSUN at conferences and solar demonstrations, colleges and universities, high schools and summer camps. She has appeared on numerous radio shows. She was featured in the Public Broadcasting Service documentary "Honey We Bought the Company." In 1998 and 1999 she traveled to the SUN21 Conference in Switzerland to share the successes of NativeSUN and learn about similar projects in other countries. She has traveled to Ecuador twice, in 1992 and 1994, with the Center for International Indigenous Rights and Development to teach indigenous people in small villages how to build solar ovens as an alternative to gathering the little available firewood. In 1996, NativeSUN received a Renew America award and was a runner up for the Christopher Reeves Environmental Award. Over the years, they have received grants from many organizations, including the Hitachi Foundation, the Joyce Mertz Gilmore Foundation, the Charles Stewart Mott Foundation, and the Lannan Foundation.

Tewa's interests outside solar energy are archaeology and art.

**BIBLIOGRAPHY**

Cole, Nancy, and P. J. Skerrett, "Debby Tewa, Profiles in Activism," *Solar Today*, 1995; LaDuke, Winona, *All Our Relations: Native Struggles for Land and Life*, 1999; LaDuke, Winona, "Debbie Tewa—Building a Future with her Community," *Indigenous Woman*, 1994; LaDuke, Winona, "Solar Self-Reliance" *Mother Earth News*, 2004; Leiva, Miriam, and Richard G. Brown, *Geometry: Explorations and Applications*, 1998; O'Callahan, "Hopi Power: One of Their Own Gives the Gift of Electricity to Her Native American Tribe," *Seedmagazine.com*, 2006; Stone, Laurie,

"Amazon Power: Women and PV," *Home Power*, 1997–1998; Tewa, Debby and Connie Brooks, "NativeSUN: A Model for Sustainable Solar Electric Systems on Indian Lands," 2006, www.eere.energy.gov/tribalenergy/pdfs/nativesun0601.pdf.

## Thompson, Chief Tommy Kuni

(Mid-1850s to early-1860s–April 12, 1959)
Chief of the Wyams, Fishing Rights Advocate

Chief Tommy Kuni Thompson, salmon chief of the great fishery at Celilo Falls and leader of Celilo Village, a small Native fishing community 11 miles east of The Dalles, Oregon, was a tireless defender of both Columbia River salmon and Indian fishing rights during the first half of the twentieth century. His life represents an important chapter in the history of Native peoples' efforts to protect diverse and productive ecosystems across North America. While ultimately unsuccessful in preventing the damming of the Columbia and the destruction of what was perhaps the most productive inland fishery in the world, his integrity as a leader is recognized to this day by Indians and non-Indians alike.

Kuni, which means "full of knowledge" in the Sahaptin language, was born by the banks of Nch'i-Wána, later known as the Columbia River, sometime between the mid-1850s and the early 1860s. He was told that his ancestors had always lived and fished at Wyam, which means "the echo of falling water." His great-uncle was the renowned Chief Stocket-ly, who signed the 1855 Middle Oregon treaty for the Wyams and was killed nine years later while acting as a scout for the United States Army. Kuni's father died when he was still an infant, and his mother died a few years later while on a berry-picking expedition. Before she died, she urged Kuni to listen carefully at the councils so that he might grow up to be a great chief like his uncle Stocket-ly.

His mother's advice came to fruition when, despite his repeated protestations, both the Wyams and the Skinpa, who lived across the river, elected him their chief. Kuni, whose White playmates many years earlier had named Tommy Thompson, was only about 20 years old, the youngest chief in memory.

As a result of the massive migration of Whites into the region during Chief Thompson's youth, Celilo Village had changed dramatically by the time he assumed the chieftainship. What had been a community of 600 to 700 people, and host to thousands more who came from all over the region to trade and visit, had shrunk to fewer than 200. While most of the Indians moved to one of the region's reservations, many of the River People remained by the banks of the Columbia. The Wyams and other river Indians adapted to the new economy the Whites developed, working in the orchards and railroads and selling fish to the canneries that cropped up along the mid-Columbia in the last two decades of the nineteenth century.

Celilo was the center of the Indian contribution to the commercial fishing industry. The miles of rapids, eddies, and narrow channels leading up to the great falls concentrated the migrating salmon, making them easy targets for experienced dipnetters. The fishery at Celilo became especially important during the twentieth century owing to the gradual destruction of traditional fishing sites and salmon runs in such tributary streams as the Yakima, Clearwater, and Umatilla. Chief Thompson struggled to maintain traditional management of the fishery at Celilo, where, by the 1940s, dipnetters scooped more than 2.5 million pounds of salmon out of the river every year. In addition to determining which families had rights to specific fishing places, as salmon chief, Chief Thompson opened and closed the fishery on both an annual and a daily basis. However, as Columbia River salmon runs declined and increasing numbers of both Indians and Whites came to Celilo to fish, traditional management practices became harder to enforce.

In 1934, several dozen Indian leaders from the Warm Springs, Yakama, and Umatilla reservations met to discuss the conflicts over the Columbia River salmon fishery between Whites and Indians and among Indians themselves. Chief Thompson urged the attendees to fish in harmony and to heed fishing traditions as handed down by their ancestors. He lamented the fact that fishermen at Celilo were exhibiting selfish attitudes, claiming priority of rights to productive fishing stations. He declared that he was often troubled to maintain peace and a cooperative spirit among the growing number of Indian fishermen.

The gathered leaders decided to form an intertribal fishery management agency, the first of its kind. They dubbed it the Celilo Fish Commission and elected Chief Thompson as the first chair. Though the members became embroiled in a bitter debate over whether the Nez Perce had rights at Celilo, the commission's primary objective was to promote and protect Indian fishing rights. The tribes' right to fish at off-reservation fishing places like Celilo, a right they reserved in the treaties of 1855, was threatened on two sides. The fish and game agencies of Oregon and Washington saw the Indians as competitors in a zero-sum game and used discriminatory regulations in an attempt to minimize Indian harvest. More alarming, however, were the federal government's plans to dam the Columbia River, which threatened to destroy entirely the River People's most sacred resource, the salmon.

Upon learning of the Army Corps of Engineers' plans to build Bonneville Dam 54 miles downstream from Celilo, Chief Thompson urged U.S. attorney Carl C. Donaugh to protest the dam as a violation of Indian fishing rights. Despite firm tribal opposition, the Corps commenced construction of Bonneville in 1934, using Public Works Administration funds meant to help ameliorate the nation's dire economic situation. In addition to interfering with salmon migration and destroying important main-stem spawning habitat, the dam flooded numerous Indian homes, as well as the Great Cascades, an important Indian fishery.

A few years after the Corps finished Bonneville, the state fishery agencies attempted to close the river above the dam to commercial fishing. Though they claimed it was for conservation purposes, it was clear they were targeting the Indians, who made up the majority of commercial fishermen above Bonneville. Chief Thompson voiced his opposition to Congress and started a petition campaign against Washington governor Mon C. Wallgren's scheme to buy out Indian fishing rights. The chief argued forcefully in a statement to Congress, translated from his native Sahaptin, that tribal fishing rights included the right to sell part of their harvest, since their ancestors had always traded fish. The tribes successfully stopped the states from closing their commercial fishery, but only temporarily. Only the *U.S. v. Oregon* (1969) and *U.S. v. Washington* (1974) decisions would come close to addressing the problem of discriminatory regulation of the salmon fishery, which still occasionally occurs.

The greatest challenge Chief Thompson faced in preserving salmon and Native fishing rights came in the form of the Dalles Dam, a power and navigation project that destroyed the Celilo dipnet fishery in 1957. The tribes of the Nez Perce, Umatilla, Warm Springs, and Yakama reservations, as well as unaffiliated River People such as the Wyams, fought a long and ultimately unsuccessful battle against this dam. Chief Thompson testified numerous times in opposition to the project. He conducted a prayer and song ceremony in a final attempt to save Celilo Falls, reminding Congress that "the Almighty took a long time to make this place." When other Indian leaders finally relented, accepting a $27 million settlement, Chief Thompson adamantly refused to "signature his salmon away." His life was the river, the great falls, and the salmon. He neither knew nor wanted any other.

On March 10, 1957, the Corps of Engineers filled the reservoir of the Dalles Dam, flooding Celilo Falls and old Celilo Village, resulting in the dispersal of more than half the residents. Indians gathered from around the region to mourn the loss of their most important fishery. The elderly chief was confined to a nursing home, however, and did not witness the destruction. He died on April 12, 1959. Flora, his wife of 20 years, was convinced the loss of Celilo killed him. More than a thousand people came from around the region to pay their respects to the great chief. He was survived by his wife and many children, grandchildren, and great-grandchildren. Despite their loss, many of Chief Thompson's people continue to fish for salmon, and Celilo Village, though much reduced, still sits by the side of Nch'i-Wána.

**BIBLIOGRAPHY**

Allen, Cain, "They Called It Progress: Salmon, Indian Fishing Rights, and the Industrialization of the Columbia River," master's thesis, Portland State University, 2000; Barber, Katrine, *After Celilo Falls: The Dalles Dam, Indian Fishing Rights, and Federal Energy Policy on the Mid-Columbia River*, Ph.D. dissertation, Washington State University, 1999; McKeown, Martha, "Celilo Indians: Fishing Their Way of Life," *The Oregonian*, 1946; Ulrich, Roberta, *Empty Nets: Indians, Dams, and the Columbia River*, 2000; Wagenblast, Joan Arrivee, and Jeanne Hillis, *Flora's Song: A Remembrance of Chief Tommy Kuni Thompson of the WyAms*, 1993; "Where Have All the Fishes Gone?" *Wana Chinook Tymoo*, 1992; Woody, Elizabeth, *Seven Hands, Seven Hearts*, 1994.

## Thoreau, Henry David
(July 12, 1817–May 6, 1862)
Writer

Henry David Thoreau wrote *A Week on the Concord and Merrimack Rivers* (1849) and *Walden* (1854). Although these were the only two books he published in his lifetime, they, along with his poetry, essays, and extensive journals, provided a philosophical and aesthetic base for the later movement to preserve wilderness. "In Wildness is the Preservation of the World," he wrote in "Walking," and his lifetime of observations helps support this truth. Yet his best writing reaches beyond "facts" and "common sense": "The verses of Kabir have four different senses; illusion, spirit, intellect, and the esoteric doctrine of the Vedas; but in this part of the world it is considered ground for complaint if a man's writings admit of more than one interpretation," he complains in the Conclusion of *Walden*. "While England endeavors to cure the potato-rot, will not any endeavor to cure the brain-rot, which prevails so much more widely and fatally?" This element in Thoreau—that his writing always has more senses than are immediately apparent—is part of why readers were at first slow to accept him and why his work is still pertinent today and alive to further interpretation.

Henry David Thoreau was born in Concord, Massachusetts, on July 12, 1817. His father, John Thoreau, was an easy-going storekeeper who, with his son's help, had some success in the pencil business. His mother, Cynthia Dunbar Thoreau, often more than supplemented the family's income by taking in boarders. The Thoreaus were a close family with four children: Helen, John, Henry, and Sophia. Henry was sent to Harvard, where he earned a bachelor of arts degree in 1837. Back in Concord, he began to meet with RALPH WALDO EMERSON's circle of transcendentalists. Emerson, almost 15 years older than Thoreau, had been a Unitarian minister and was by that time a well-known writer. Emerson encouraged Thoreau to write and later to publish. The two men became friends for life.

*Transcendentalism* was then used as a loose term for free-thinking alternatives to local notions of spirituality. The term derived from the philosophy of Immanuel Kant and philosophical and aesthetic systems opposed to the "rationalism" of John Locke and other founders of the "scientific method" (with their belief that knowledge comes only through the senses, and so on). Whereas Western orthodox sciences and religions tend to subjugate nature to man, God, or both—claiming "dominion"—transcendentalists generally argue for a unity of nature and spirit and for enlightenment through intelligent communion with the natural world. In this sense the Concord transcendentalists had sympathies in common with Native American spiritualism, but they also freely imported Eastern spiritual traditions, European romanticism, natural philosophy, and anything else that interested them.

In 1839, having tried a few trades (school teaching, pencil making, farm labor), Thoreau took a "fluvial excursion" with his brother, John, that would provide material for *A Week on the Concord and Merrimack Rivers*. When John died of an infection three years later, Thoreau began expanding even more on his journal accounts, turning them into a book that was (among other things) a tribute to his late brother. Publishers eventually refused to finance it, even with Emerson's strong recommendations. Although they were impressed with its "nature writing," most found the heresies of Thoreau's "pantheism" unacceptable. Thoreau paid to have it published in 1849, losing more money than he could afford in exchange for hundreds of unsold copies in the family attic. That and *Walden* would be the only two books Thoreau published during his lifetime, and together they would bring paltry financial returns. Nor was he paid for lyrics and essays published in the transcendentalists' magazine, *The Dial*, though he derived some small fame and profit from lecturing.

Henry David Thoreau (Library of Congress, Prints & Photographs Division, LC-USZ61-361)

By 1841 Thoreau had moved into the Emerson household, serving as a handyman in exchange for room and board. In 1843 he went to New York to make literary contacts and tutor Emerson's brother's children, but he was unhappy with city life and returned to Concord early in 1844.

In July 1845 he moved into a hut he had built himself on some of Emerson's remote land near Walden Pond. He would spend the next two years there, working on *A Week on the Concord and Merrimack Rivers*, writing in his journals, and taking close note of what happened in the pond and in its immediate surroundings.

*Walden*, after eight drafts with many revisions and additions, was published in 1854. In it, Thoreau imparts what he sees as the unity of all life, all spheres of existence, involved in a vast and intricate economy. At the center of *Walden* is the pond: "earth's eye; looking into which the beholder measures the depth of his own nature." Thoreau makes the pond into an eye, a mirror, a window, a lens—mingling visions and insights through the complex optical device of his inner and outer eye(s). Opening a window through the pond's ice, Thoreau reports that "Heaven is under our feet as well as over our heads." Describing a "concord" within a "thrilling discord" of owls on a winter night, he adds: "I also heard the whooping of the ice in the pond, my great bed-fellow in that part of Concord…" letting his reader draw the connection from the owl to Minerva, wisdom, tradition—and back to the immediate "eye" and "I" of Walden Pond in a vision that unites wildness, wisdom, owl, goddess, ice, pond, author, and reader… in an amazed concordance. Through and throughout *Walden*, Thoreau sees the unity of all life, all spheres of existence, involved in a vast intricate economy.

"Economy," the first and longest chapter in *Walden*, begins to develop the intricacy and extent of the term as Thoreau uses it, expanding the root (Gr. *oikos:* house, home) and meaning toward the later term: *ecology*. The argument is fundamentally Confucian: Home economics is the foundation of our treatment of nature (the ecosystem). If men's hearts, homes, villages (in that order) are in order, then the state, and the world, will be in order. True order is not imposed from above; it comes from the hearts of individuals, as plants grow from seeds. This was also a premise of transcendentalism, and originally of democracy, though hierarchies of church, business, and government continually reverse the natural sequence. In Thoreau's unities, arrogant enforcement of power, economic and ecological imbalance—or any exploitation of a natural economy—damages individuals and society as a whole.

By "wildness" Thoreau meant more than "wilderness." His rambles through the woods and studies of nature were a large part of his passion, but humankind too was part of his nature. "Great persons are not soon learned, not even their outlines, but they change like the mountains and the horizon as we ride along," he wrote in his journal in 1842. His friends were required to have open minds. He admired such "wild" contemporaries as WALT WHITMAN, Joe Polis (an Indian guide), and abolitionist John Brown. He verbally assaulted churches, states, and fixed doctrines of any sort. His stance was poetic and transcendental: "If you stand right fronting and face to face with a fact, you will see the sun glimmer on both its surfaces, as if it were a cimeter, and feel its sweet edge dividing you through the heart and marrow," he wrote in *Walden*.

Although Thoreau was not widely known in his lifetime, his writings have become classics, and their influence has been vast. His essay, "On the Duty of Civil Disobedience" (1849), written after one night he spent in jail for not paying the church tax, and other essays on civil resistance became important to Mahatma Gandhi, Martin Luther King, and other subsequent reformers. JOHN MUIR and others of the nineteenth-century preservation movement drew inspiration from what Muir called "the pure soul of Thoreau." Thoreau's works were republished in 1906, leading to appreciation of his ideas for a new generation. They have been and continue to be essential to those who love the environment and aspire to preserve it.

On May 6, 1862, at the age of 44, Henry David Thoreau died of tuberculosis.

**BIBLIOGRAPHY**
Atkinson, Brooks, ed., *The Writings of Ralph Waldo Emerson*, 1940; Bode, Carl, ed., Harding, Walter, *The Days of Henry Thoreau*, 1962; Krutch, Joseph Wood, *Henry David Thoreau*, 1948; Richardson, Robert D., *Henry David Thoreau: A Life of the Mind*, 1986; Robinson, David M., *Natural Life: Thoreau's Worldly Transcendentalism*, 2004; Smith, Harmon, *My Friend, My Friend: the story of Thoreau's relationship with Emerson*, 1999; Thoreau, Henry David, *Walden*, 1854; "Thoreau Society, Established in 1941," www.thoreausociety.org; "The Walden Woods Project," www.walden.org.

## Thorne, Oakleigh, II
(October 12, 1928– )
Ecologist, Educator, Founder of Thorne Ecological Institute

In 1954, Oakleigh Thorne, II founded the nonprofit Thorne Ecological Institute in Boulder, Colorado, a pioneer environmental education organization that offered ecology classes for children and ran corporate ecology seminars. He moved to Boulder to attend the University of Colorado Graduate School and earn his Ph.D. in Biology. The same year, he incorporated Thorne Films, Inc., which eventually produced hundreds of instructional films on ecology, biology, history, elementary science, art, and architecture. Previous to this, while a graduate student at Yale University, he coordinated a successful effort to preserve the Sunken Forest on Fire Island, New York.

Oakleigh Thorne, II was born October 12, 1928, in New York City, the youngest of six children. His family lived at Brookwood, an 80-acre estate on Long Island, with streams, woods, and a lake. His father introduced him to fishing and duck hunting, his uncle started him collecting birds' eggs, and bird artist John Henry Dick encouraged him by giving him ducks and pheasants to raise. When hawks arrived to eat his pigeons, Thorne became interested in raptors. At the age of ten, his father purchased as a gift for him a stuffed Passenger Pigeon, now an extinct species, that he still treasures today.

Oakleigh Thorne, II (Photograph courtesy of Thorne Ecological Institute)

At Millbrook School in upstate New York, renowned for its ornithology and natural history programs, Thorne studied with biology teacher Frank Trevor, who taught him to band birds and make films. After high school he summered for several years at the Valley Ranch near Cody, Wyoming, where he became familiar with western wildlife species and wilderness survival skills that he learned from Roy Glasgow, an old mountain man who was part American Indian. Thorne returned to the Ranch every summer through his college years, developing a strong, spiritual connection to nature. One summer (1949), however, he stayed in Connecticut and worked at the Audubon Center in Greenwich, where he met ROGER TORY PETERSON, RICHARD POUGH, and Charles Mohr, each of whom deepened his understanding of ecology, conservation, and ornithology.

Thorne earned a B.S. in Biology at Yale in 1951 and continued there to study with Paul B. Sears and Albert E. Burke in the Yale Conservation Program, from which he received an M.S. in 1953. He stayed at Yale for an extra year to become musical director of the Yale "Whiffenpoofs," the famous men's *a cappella* singing group founded in 1909. Concurrently with his Master's studies, Thorne worked on his first conservation project: to save the Sunken Forest on Fire Island from development. He obtained $15,000 from the Old Dominion Foundation, with the help of Pough, RACHEL CARSON, and John Oakes (a well-known *New York Times* editorial writer). Thorne eventually raised $45,000, which was passed through the recently-formed Nature Conservancy. This was the Conservancy's first effort to preserve natural areas after receiving its tax exempt status in 1952.

Thorne moved to Boulder, Colorado, in 1954, where that same year he opened Thorne Ecological Research Station and incorporated it and Thorne Films, Inc. His first film was about the Sunken Forest, a unique ecosystem composed mainly of American holly trees behind sand dunes on a barrier island off Long Island. Another early film, "Arctic Wildlife Range," was made together with Bob Krear, who had photographed northeast Alaska on the famous Murie expedition to the Brooks Range. He traded a copy of this film to DAVID BROWER, who used it as he successfully lobbied for the preservation of this area through the Sierra Club.

One of the most effective products of Thorne Films were film loops, which were popular through the 1960s. These were three- to five-minute silent movies in Technicolor cartridges that were as simple to operate as an audiocassette: children of grade-school age could project the film loops against the wall at the back of the room without disturbing the rest of the class. Teachers could use them during their lectures, and there was no language barrier because they were silent. A film loop about a starfish was as interesting to college students as it was to kindergarten children. Thorne saw the "silent moving image" as "a powerful teaching tool"… a lesson he learned from Charlie Chaplin and Stan Brakhage. At its peak, Thorne Films had 40 employees and was selling thousands of film loops each year. It was bringing in $500,000 annually because the U.S. Department of Health, Education, and Welfare (HEW) was paying half the cost of the projectors and films for schools, but after President Nixon vetoed the HEW funding bill in 1971, the company quickly went out of business.

The nonprofit Thorne Ecological Institute survived, however, and grew during the next decades. One of its most successful programs has been the Thorne Natural Science School, which since 1957 has helped to connect children to nature through hands-on field trips. More than 60,000 students have been served by this program alone.

Thorne Ecological Institute was one of the first environmental groups in the world to assist industries and public agencies in applying the Principles of Ecology to environmental problems. Thorne, with Dr. Bettie Willard, who had begun working for the Institute during the early 1960s, helped start the Colorado Open Space Coordinating Council (COSCC), an environmental group that met regularly with the Colorado Association of Commerce and Industry (CACI). By 1967 Thorne and Willard developed Seminars in Environmental Arts and Science (SEAS), whose objective was to teach Ecological Principles to the heads of government and key corporations. These yearly programs were held in Aspen, Colorado, from 1967 to 1984. This was the first attempt to connect ecology with economics. Thorne Ecological Institute also helped Elizabeth Paepcke form the Aspen Center for

Environmental Studies (ACES). Charles Luce of ConEdison came to a SEAS meeting and went back to New York City and had "Conserve Energy" painted on all of the company's trucks. General Cassidy of the Army Corps of Engineers attended a seminar, returned to Omaha, hired an ecologist, and set up the National Environmental Advisory Board for the Corps. Stan Dempsey of American Metals Climax (AMAX) came to SEAS and later requested help from the Institute before developing the Henderson molybdenum mine in central Colorado. A group of ecologists and engineers met for two years in the late 1960s to figure out how to reduce the environmental impact of the mine. Their "Experiment in Ecology," as it was called, resulted in the first environmental impact statement nationally, produced before such statements were required by the passage of the National Environmental Policy Act (NEPA) in 1969.

In 1969 Thorne bought the Valley Ranch near Cody, Wyoming. More than 3,000 people visited the Ranch and learned from him both Ecological Principles and wilderness philosophy. Over the years, however, it was never able to attract enough paying guests, and the property was lost through foreclosure in 1987. Dr. Thorne then moved back to Boulder.

Thorne Ecological Institute currently focuses on environmental education for children. After two years of negotiations, the Institute worked out a unique partnership with the City of Boulder Open Space and Mountain Parks Department and the Boulder Valley School District to preserve the Sombrero Marsh near Boulder and create an ecological instruction program there. It also operates a center outside of Denver (in Littleton) at Waterton Canyon. Thorne himself continues to teach bird banding to teenagers through the Institute and Ecological Principles to college students through the University of Colorado's Alumni Mentoring program. In addition, he taught nature photography at New Vista High School for 13 years, and is mentor to several undergraduate singing groups at the University. He strongly believes that providing environmental education opportunities to young people will help save the Earth and better the odds for survival of the human species.

In addition to its work in environmental education, Thorne Ecological Institute helped to cofound local chapters of the Audubon Society, The Nature Conservancy, and the Sierra Club. In fact, Thorne became the first official Colorado representative for The Nature Conservancy when he moved west in 1954. He also collaborated with Boulder environmental activists to form People's League for Action Now (PLAN)–Boulder County, a citizen's planning group that helped pass the innovative Open Space Sales Tax in 1967. The tax, which has now been emulated by many other communities nationwide, is set up to preserve unique open space sites and prevent urban sprawl.

Thorne continues to live in Boulder, Colorado, and his four children, Jonathan, Sarah, David, and Schuyler, live in Colorado and Wyoming. His oldest daughter, Susan, died in 1993 from mental illness. He spends half of each workday at Thorne Ecological Institute and has absolutely no plans to retire.

## Bibliography

Human, Katy, "Thorne Ecological Institute to Celebrate 45th Anniversary," *Daily Camera*, 1999; Roberts, Chris, "Instituting Knowledge of Nature," *Daily Camera*, 1996; Shindelman, Rachael, "Swallow Tale: Bird in the Hand Proves Students' Worth," *Daily Camera*, 1998; Shindelman, Rachael, "Thorne's Birds Educate," *Boulder Planet*, 1999; Smith, Sue-Marie, "Oakleigh Thorne, People Making a Difference," *Daily Camera*, 1998; Thorne, Oakleigh, "Sombrero Marsh—A Shallow Wetland," *Boulder County Kids*, 2000; "Thorne Ecological Institute," www.thorne-eco.org.

## Thorpe, Grace

(December 10, 1921–April 1, 2008)
Antinuclear Activist, Cofounder of National Environmental Council of Native Americans

Grace Thorpe, Oklahoma Sauk and Fox, convinced her tribe in 1993 to reject a proposal from the Department of Energy (DOE) to store radioactive waste on tribal lands. She and others went on to found the National Environmental Council of Native Americans (NECONA), which helps other tribes keep radioactive waste off their land. With support from NECONA, more than 75 Indian nations in Alaska, Canada, and the lower 48 states have declared their lands "nuclear-free."

Grace Frances Thorpe, Oklahoma Sauk and Fox, was born in Yale, Oklahoma, on December 10, 1921. Her father, Jim Thorpe, was a 1912 Olympic decathlon and pentathlon champion, star football and baseball player, and first president of the organization that became the National Football League. She attended Indian boarding schools in Kansas and Oklahoma and joined the Women's Army Corps during World War II. She was stationed in New Guinea when the first atomic bomb was dropped on Hiroshima in August 1945. Thorpe and her fellow soldiers were delighted to hear that the bomb had ended the war, but once she moved to Japan afterwards she was shocked by the horror of atomic war and felt guilty for her country's actions. Thorpe remained in Japan during the postwar occupation, working for Gen. Douglas MacArthur as a personnel interviewer. In 1946 she married Fred Seely, a paratrooper she had met in New Guinea. They had two children before divorcing, and she returned to the United States in 1950 with the children.

Thorpe became involved with the Indian rights movement of the 1960s, acting as public relations liaison for the occupation of Alcatraz in 1969 and the takeover of the Fort Lawton, Washington, surplus military base in 1970. She worked with the Pit River Indians of California to defend their land against Pa-

Grace Thorpe (AP Images/Jean Yaeger)

cific Gas and Electric and helped to found the Deganawidah-Quetzalcoatl University in Davis, California, in 1970. During the 1960s and 1970s, Thorpe organized economic development conferences for the National Congress on American Indians and served as legislative aide to the U.S. Senate Subcommittee on Indian Affairs; member of American Indian Policy Review Board of the U.S. House of Representatives; and director of the Return Surplus Lands to the Indians Project. She was named an urban fellow at the Massachusetts Institute of Technology in 1972. In 1974 she obtained a paralegal certificate from Antioch School of Law and in 1976 earned a B.A. in history from the University of Tennessee at Knoxville.

Thorpe retired in 1976 to Oklahoma, where she took up the artistic pursuits of painting and ceramics and served the Sauk and Fox people as a tribal court judge and a member of the Health Commission. In 1992, her retirement abruptly ended when she learned that the Sauk and Fox tribal council had accepted a $100,000 Department of Energy grant to study the feasibility of establishing a storage site for nuclear waste on tribal land. The DOE sought temporary storage for high-level radioactive waste from nuclear power plants in a "monitored retrievable storage" (MRS) system and offered research funds to any community willing to consider setting up such a site. DOE negotiators knew that the money would be enticing to impoverished tribal councils and also targeted Indian reservations because their sovereign status allowed state environmental laws to be bypassed.

After researching the problem and becoming convinced that transportation and storage of spent nuclear fuel rods was potentially disastrous, Thorpe sprang into action. She was outraged that her tribe had accepted the money, and she gathered enough signatures to request a special meeting of the tribe. Seventy-five tribal members attended the special meeting in February 1993, and 70 of them—all but the five tribal council members present—voted to return the uncashed check to the DOE.

After this victory, the Indigenous Environmental Network invited Thorpe to be the keynote speaker at its Third Annual Gathering in 1993. Soon she realized that many other Native antinuclear activists were in the same predicament: with the DOE on one side trying to convince tribes to consider housing the waste and the tribal councils, on the other side, tempted to accept the huge sums of money being offered. In 1993, Thorpe cofounded the National Environmental Council of Native Americans, whose goals are to educate Indians about the health dangers of radioactivity and the transportation of nuclear waste by rail and road, develop networks of Indian and non-Indian environmental groups to counteract the efforts of the nuclear industry, and encourage the creation of nuclear-free zones on Indian land across the country. Thorpe has served as president of NECONA since its founding.

Thorpe's speeches explain what environmental racism is and appeal to Native Americans to resist it. Thorpe, whose Indian name, No-ten-oh-quah, translates as "Woman with the Power of the Wind that Blows Up before a Storm," told the National Congress of American Indians at its December 1993 conference:

> It is wrong to say that it is natural that we, as Native Americans, should accept radioactive waste on our lands, as the U.S. Department of Energy has said. It is a perversion of our beliefs and an insult to our intelligence to say that we are "natural stewards" of these wastes. The real intent of the U.S. government and the nuclear industry is to place this extremely hazardous garbage on Indian lands so they can go and generate more of it. They are poisoning the earth for short term financial profit. They try to flatter us about our ability as "earth stewards." They tell us, when our non-Indian neighbors object to living near substances poisonous for thousands of years, that this is an issue of "sovereignty." It is not! It is an issue of the earth's preservation and our survival.

Thanks to grassroots activists and NECONA coordination, 75 tribes have declared themselves "nuclear free," and all but three of the 17 tribal councils that had accepted DOE grants to study MRS feasibility have rejected it. MRS study grants were discontinued in 1993, after Thorpe appealed personally to Sen. Jeff Bingaman from New Mexico. However, the federal government is still pursuing a plan to move nuclear waste to a permanent underground storage site at Yucca Mountain, located on Western Shoshone lands in Nevada. (The Western Shoshone oppose the plan and argue they have never sold their land to the U.S. government.) Thorpe and other NECONA activists believe that such a storage system is not only dangerous, but also encourages the nuclear industry to continue generating the deadly waste. In the speech cited earlier, Thorpe later asked "What kind of society permits the manufacture of products that cannot be safely disposed of? Shouldn't we have a basic law of the land that prohibits the production of anything we cannot safely dispose?" Her three-part goal for radioactive waste was: "Leave it where it is. Secure it. Stop producing it." She believed that it was important to promote alternative energy sources such as hydroelectricity and solar and wind power.

In addition to her work on nuclear waste issues, Thorpe was a tireless promoter of her father's memory. She successfully pushed to have her father's 1912 Olympic gold medals returned to the family—they had been taken back by the Olympic Committee when it was learned that Thorpe had played minor league baseball in 1909 and 1910—and convinced the U.S. Post Office to issue a Jim Thorpe postage stamp. She worked beginning in 1996 to proclaim her father athlete of the century, a goal that was realized when the American Broadcasting Companies (ABC) voted to bestow this title on him at the 2000 Super Bowl in Atlanta. She also worked with Miss Indian USA, Anna McKibben, Quapaw Oklahoma, to place Thorpe's picture on the Wheaties box.

Thorpe worked with several other organizations in addition to NECONA. She served on the board of directors of the Nuclear Information and Resource Service and on the Greenpeace American Indian Advisory Committee; she was a member of the Alliance for Nuclear Accountability, based in Seattle. She was a delegate to President Clinton's 1995 White House Conference on Aging, was a member of his Aging advisory group, and lobbied on issues of importance to the elderly, veterans, and American Indians. She was awarded the Nuclear-Free Future Resistance Award in Los Alamos, New Mexico, in 1999. Thorpe died of heart failure on April 1, 2008, and is survived by her daughter Dagmar Thorpe Seely and granddaughter Tena Malotte.

### BIBLIOGRAPHY

"NECONA," www.alphacdc.com/necona/; Neill, Michael, "G.F. Thorpe Fights Dumping of Nuclear Waste on Tribal Lands," *People*, 1996; Rogers, Keith, "Thorpe Battles Nuclear Waste," *Las Vegas Review-Journal*, 1996; Thorpe, Grace, "The Jim Thorpe Family History," *Chronicles of Oklahoma*, 1981.

## Tidwell, Michael

(March 19, 1962– )
Writer, Filmmaker, Founder and Director of Chesapeake Climate Action Network

Author of six books, filmmaker, and climate change activist, Tidwell is best known as a natural disaster expert. Drawing on first-hand observation and published research, he compellingly predicted the August 2005 Katrina hurricane disaster in New Orleans in his 2003 book *Bayou Farewell*. He has written countless articles for publications such as *National Geographic Traveler*, *The Washington Post*, and *Grist* on topics ranging from the Mbuti Pygmies of Africa to combating global warming. He is the founder and director of the Chesapeake Climate Action Network, and of the U.S. Climate Emergency Council. Since Katrina, Tidwell has been featured as an expert commentator in major media outlets.

Michael Wayne Tidwell was born on March 19, 1962, in Memphis, Tennessee. He was raised in Marietta, Georgia, and has been a longtime resident of Takoma Park, Maryland, in the Washington, D.C. metro area, where he lives with his son Sasha. As a child he developed a reverence for the beauty and complexities of nature in the woods near his home, and during annual family camping trips in the Great Smoky Mountains and the ocean. He received his first lessons in survival training as a Boy Scout and Eagle Scout.

Tidwell attended the University of Georgia, receiving a B.A. He was a U.S. Peace Corps Volunteer from 1985-87 in what was then Zaire. His first book, *The Ponds of Kalambayi* (1990), is an autobiographical account of that two-year experience. He taught impoverished cotton farmers of a remote tribal kingdom in the central region of the country how to build ponds and raise fish for extra protein and profit.

Tidwell's second book, *In the Shadow of the White House* (1992), deals with poverty, the war on drugs, crack cocaine addiction, and redemption in the nation's capital of Washington, D.C. It stems in part from his years as a drug counselor. *Amazon Stranger* (1996) is about efforts to save the Coffin native people of the Cuyabeno wildlife reserve and the Ecuadorian rainforest from oil companies. *In the Mountains of Heaven* (2000) is a compendium of travel essays.

In 1999 Tidwell traveled to Louisiana's remote Cajun Bayou to write a story for *The Washington Post's* Travel section. He discovered that the biggest story pertaining to the region was not fishing or zydeco, but that Louisiana was the fastest disappearing land mass on Earth. A detailed account of both the causes and solutions associated with land loss is found in his book *Bayou Farewell* (2003), and in his latest book, *The Ravaging Tide* (2006).

Tidwell explains that in every great river system, there are two basic geological processes at work: flooding, whereby sediments create wetland marshes and barrier islands, and land subsidence or sinking, which happens when the soil deposited by flooding eventually shrinks in volume. In an undisturbed river delta, a net gain in land occurs from these two processes. Following the flood of 1927, levees were built in New Orleans by the Army Corps of Engineers that prevented flooding and land building. Moreover, oil companies built thousands of miles of shipping canals which further eroded the wetlands. The result has been the loss over the past 75 years of an ecologically rich area the size of Delaware.

The incremental destruction of the buffer created by coastal wetlands and barrier islands, the sinking of New Orleans itself farther below sea level, as well as the more widely reported failure of its levee system, was what made the disaster following Katrina possible. The political failure to implement a coastal rescue plan known as Coast 2050 made it utterly predictable. Tidwell's concern for the world's coastal cities is that with a rise in sea level caused by global warming, coastal land loss would be staggering everywhere, and storms and hurricanes would find nothing in their path to slow down their high water and winds when they reach land, compounding the problem further.

In *The Ravaging Tide* (2006), Tidwell explains that 2001 was the year he became a committed global warming activist. In January of that year, he read about the prediction by the U.N.'s Intergovernmental Panel on Climate Change (IPCC) that Earth's atmosphere would warm between 3 and 10 degrees Fahrenheit by 2100. That same year the IPCC predicted a rise in sea level between one and three feet in the same time period as a result of this atmospheric warming.

According to the EPA, a rise of just two feet in sea level will eliminate up to 43 percent of coastal wetlands worldwide. A rise of three feet would completely wipe out the Chesapeake's 28,000-acre Blackwater National Wildlife Refuge. Acutely aware of this, in 2001 Tidwell decided to turn his home into a model of ecological sustainability. He achieved this inexpensively through conservation, by installing solar panels, and by using a corn stove to keep his house warm, a first in his region, reducing his greenhouse gas emissions from home heating by 85 percent. After much effort by Tidwell and others, in November 2002 a corn granary was installed on Takoma Park property which provides organic kernels for sixty families in a co-op to heat their homes.

Tidwell took his commitment to fight global warming further by founding and directing the Chesapeake Climate Action Network. Launched in 2002, it is the first grassroots, nonprofit organization dedicated exclusively to fighting global warming in Maryland, Virginia, and Washington, D.C. The organization conducts public education through teach-ins, films, and the weekly *Earthbeat* radio program hosted by Tidwell. It is engaged in legislative activities on issues such as establishing renewable portfolio standards and clean cars.

Tidwell claims that traveling to New Orleans ten weeks after Hurricane Katrina in the fall of 2005 was the most harrowing experience of his life. Moreover, since December of 2005, JAMES HANSEN, the director of NASA's Goddard Institute for Space Studies, has been warning that we may be reaching a "tipping point" toward catastrophic sea-level rise due to the melting of the Greenland ice sheet. Unless greenhouse gas emissions are stabilized by 2015 and then promptly cut, human beings won't be able to control the melting and disintegration of this ice sheet, thus possibly leading to sea-level rise of up to 23 feet by 2100.

Because of what Tidwell witnessed in New Orleans, and given the even more pressing nature of the global warming time-crunch disclosed by Hansen and other scientists, in 2006 Tidwell founded and is the director of the U.S. Climate Emergency Council, which engages in direct action, and public education. Its first campaign focused on the suppression of science information at the National Oceanic and Atmospheric Administration.

Tidwell remains optimistic that the U.S. and all the nations of Earth will be able to save the planet from accelerated global warming and the ravages of climate change. There are historical examples of success amid impending ecological devastation, such as the pre-industrial forestation plans that saved Japan 300 years ago (as detailed by Conrad Totman, cited in *The Ravaging Tide*). Also, there are many large-scale instances of modern-day conservation, such as the 11 percent drop in aggregate electricity use in the state of California over five months in 2001 during the Enron rate-gouging scandal. Additionally, retrofitting existing coal plants with cogeneration, and otherwise switching to wind, solar, biomass, geothermal, and wave energy sources also hold enormous promise.

Tidwell's frequent travel writings for *The Washington Post* have earned him four Lowell Thomas awards, the highest prize in travel journalism. He is a former grantee of the National Endowment for the Arts. In 2003 Tidwell received the Audubon Naturalist Society's prestigious Conservation Award.

## BIBLIOGRAPHY

Tidwell, Mike, *The Ponds of Kalambayi: An African Sojourn*, 1990; *In the Shadow of the White House: Drugs, Death, and Redemption in the Streets of the Nation's Capital*, 1992; *Amazon Stranger: A Rainforest Chief Battles Big Oil*, 1996; *In the Mountains of Heaven: Tales of Adventure on Six Continents*, 2000; *Bayou Farewell: the Rich Life and Tragic Death of Louisiana's Cajun Coast*, 2003; *The Ravaging Tide: How Future Katrinas Will be More Frequent, More Ferocious, and More Fatal to America's Cities* 2006; *Strange Weather, Future Katrinas, and the Coming Death of America's Costal Cities*, 2007.

## Tokar, Brian

(April 9, 1955– )
Writer, Educator, Cofounder of Vermont Greens

Author of *Earth for Sale: Reclaiming Ecology in the Age of Corporate Greenwash* (1997), Brian Tokar has been writing and agitating for environmental change since the 1970s. Active in the antinuclear movement, the early years of the Green Party, and campaigns against genetically altered food, Tokar brings to his writing the experience of a grassroots activist. His first book, *The Green Alternative* (1987; revised 1992), is a comprehensive examination of Green politics in the United States, while *Earth for Sale* looks at the corporate sellout of the environmental movement by mainstream, national groups. As teacher, journalist, organic gardener, and activist, Tokar works to develop green alternatives to market-dominated, consumer culture.

Brian Tokar was born on April 9, 1955, in Brooklyn, New York. He grew up in New York City and attended Stuyvesant High School in Manhattan during the most turbulent years of the 1960s. As a student at the Massachusetts Institute of Technology (MIT) during the early 1970s, he became more deeply involved in the anti–Vietnam War movement, community organizing, the early food co-op movement, and antinuclear activism. He graduated from MIT in 1976 with a B.S. in biology and physics and earned an M.A. in biophysics from Harvard in 1981, specializing in the neurophysiology of the visual system. Tokar then moved to Vermont and became active in local progressive politics, including a founding role in the Vermont Greens and neighborhood organizing in Burlington's old North End. He began teaching at the Institute for Social Ecology in Plainfield, Vermont, in 1983. The institute had been co-founded in 1974 by MURRAY BOOKCHIN and Daniel Chodorkoff; it brings together a community of scholars and activists from various fields, including anthropology, ecology, feminism, agriculture, education, architecture, social theory, and biology. The influence of this community is clearly visible in *The Green Alternative*, in which Tokar stresses the diverse roots of Green politics. With the European Green movement as a jumping-off point, Tokar uses examples from a wide variety of groups and actions across the United States to illustrate the underlying principles of the Greens. He emphasizes the central role played by feminism in the Greens and suggests that Green politics involve not only ecological justice but also a commitment to social and economic justice, as well as peace and nonviolence. The Greens are not united by a single issue, or even a single name, but rather by a vision of a more just and ecologically balanced society. In Tokar's characterization, "The Green movement is working to evolve a broad vision for a transformed society that can thrive in harmony with the rest of nature and that fosters harmony, equality and freedom among its citizens." *The Green Alternative* was one of the first books in the United States to look specifically at the broad agenda of both the European and U.S. Green movements and helped shape the direction of grassroots politics in the late 1980s and early 1990s.

*Earth for Sale* looks at evolutionary patterns in environmental politics in the 1990s and comes to the conclusion that the major national environmental groups are no longer able to effectively advocate for ecological justice. Tokar identifies three major trends that have led to what he and others have called the "greenwashing" of American culture, that is, the way in which the political and corporate United States pay lip service to environmental ideals without making any real progress toward changing ecologically destructive practices. Tokar argues first that mainstream environmental groups such as the Sierra Club and Environmental Defense have traded environmental convictions for a seat at the table of Washington political power. These groups have been co-opted by party politics and corporate-funded foundations, so that often their own funding depends on the financial success of antienvironment corporations such as oil companies and timber interests. Second, Tokar outlines the emergence of "corporate environmentalism," wherein corporations conduct public relations campaigns, touting sponsorship of Earth Day events or other superficial environmental commitments, as cover for their underlying assaults on the environment. Corporate environmentalism was on display at the Earth Summit in Rio de Janeiro in 1992, when groups like the Business Council for Sustainable Development used its power behind the scenes to quiet discussion of the role played by transnational corporations in worldwide environmental degradation. Third, Tokar critiques "green consumerism," the tendency to reduce environmental problems to the level of consumer choice. Green consumerism is based on the myth that individuals can solve environmental problems by choosing "natural" and recycled products while still maintaining consumerist lifestyles. Tokar argues that the emphasis on green products masks the underlying economic structures that have driven the world to the brink of ecological collapse.

As an antidote to the "selling of the earth" in the name of market forces, Tokar offers a hopeful assessment of grassroots environmental activism. While mainstream environmental groups have grown closer to corporate interests, grassroots activists have given their energy to a broad variety of local initiatives, including campaigns for environmental justice and radical, effective forest-protection projects. This kind of activism, Tokar argues, has the potential to offer a thorough critique of corporate culture and to develop a strong, competing system of ethics in which human needs and the integrity of natural ecosystems take precedence over market profit. Grassroots activists can reclaim ecology from corporate greenwash, and Tokar continues to be committed to this work through his writing and political activism.

For many years, Tokar has dedicated himself to challenging the genetic engineering of food. He organized Biodevastation 2000, a March 2000 gathering of activists opposed to genetic engineering, which took place in Boston, and led to annual events countering the biotechnology industry's international conventions. In 1998 he wrote an exposé of Monsanto's aggressive history of biotechnology promotion and corporate irresponsibility, and this article won a 1999 Project Censored award. He has edited two books about the topic in recent years, *Redesigning Life?* (2001), and *Gene Traders* (2004), both international collections of essays by scholars and activists concerned about the negative effects of genetic manipulation and other biotechnologies.

Tokar writes regularly for *Z Magazine*, *Synthesis/Regeneration*, *Toward Freedom*, and other national and international publications. His most recent writings focus on the politics of global warming and the emergence of a global climate justice movement.

Tokar currently directs the Institute for Social Ecology, teaches at the University of Vermont and Prescott College, and lectures internationally on environmental issues and movements. He lives in East Montpelier, Vermont.

**BIBLIOGRAPHY**

"Biodevastation to Biojustice," www.biodev.org; "The Institute for Social Ecology," www.social-ecology.org; "Native Forest Network," www.nativeforest.org; Tokar, Brian, "Monsanto: A Checkered History," *The Ecologist*, 1998; Tokar, Brian, "The Real Scoop on Biofuels," *Synthesis/Regeneration*, 2007, www.greens.org/s-r/42/42-03.html; "Z Magazine," www.zmag.org; "Z-Space—Brian Tokar," www.zcommunications.org/zspace/briantokar.

## Tompkins, Douglas
(1943– )
Environmental Philanthropist

Land conservation philanthropist and former businessman, Douglas Tompkins, his wife Kristine McDivitt Tompkins, and their associates have amassed what was described in 2006 as the largest privately run land conservation project in the world. It includes eleven wilderness parks covering almost two million acres of temperate rainforest, wetlands, grasslands, and coastal areas in Chile and Argentina. Throughout the years since Tompkins began buying land in 1988, much of the holdings have been or will be donated to the governments of Chile and Argentina, or to foundations or non-governmental organizations based in those countries. Tompkins also started the Foundation for Deep Ecology, based on the tenets of the Norwegian philosopher and mountaineer Arne Naess.

Douglas Tompkins was born in 1943 in Millbrook, New York, a summer resort for Manhattan's well-to-do. His father was an antique dealer and his mother an interior designer, teaching Tompkins his first lessons in business and artistic creativity. He visited Chile for the first time in 1961 and fell in love with the land. He moved to California around that time after dropping out of boarding school in Connecticut, hoping to make it onto the 1964 U.S. Olympic ski team. He failed to do so, but became an expert outdoorsman in the Sierra Nevada and leading others to enjoy trekking, having founded the California Mountain Guide Service in 1963.

In 1966 he founded the mountaineering apparel company North Face, and sold it in 1968. Soon thereafter he met and married his first wife Susie Russell, with whom he would found in 1970 the hugely successful clothing company Esprit de Corps. They had two daughters, Summer and Quincey. In the late 1980s Tompkins read GEORGE SESSIONS AND BILL DEVALL'S *Deep Ecology: Living as if Nature Mattered*. This led him to reorient his life according to the deep ecology eight-point platform, which seeks to restore nature's standing as partner, rather than a commodity, to humans. It emphasizes a reverence for humans along with the rest of nature, opposing both anthropocentrism and misanthropy. Deep ecology is critical, in Tompkins's words, of the "techno-industrial juggernaut" of capitalist market fundamentalism and a blind trust in science and technology, which is not compatible with sustaining life on Earth.

Because of the substantial wealth he made as a capitalist, he was able to start buying land in Patagonia, initially in Chile's Lake District, for modest sums compared to California land prices. In 1990 he sold his share of Esprit for around $150 million, and went on to found his Deep Ecology Foundation, which initially gave grants to NGOs and now focuses on its in-house publishing program of books with a large, photographic format, showcasing environmental destruction caused by unsustainable practices so as to galvanize people to action. Tompkins and his first wife divorced around the time he sold his share of Esprit, and he purchased and moved into what would become a homestead community in Chile's Reñihué Fjord, in the province of Palena, where he now lives most of the year with his second wife Kristine, whom he married in 1993. She is the former CEO of Patagonia Inc., the company she helped start with Yvon Chouinard, Tompkins's fellow adventurer, conservationist, and passionate lover of the natural beauty of the American continent's southern cone.

In the 1990s Tompkins, his wife Kristine and Esprit's former CFO, Debra Ryker, set up the Conservation Land Trust and Conservación Patagónica to continue acquiring land in Chile and Argentina. All of it is intended for natural conservation in perpetuity. Tompkins's personal stamp has been left most prominently at Parque Pumalín (named after the pumas that roam there), Chile's seventh largest national park, about the size of California's Yosemite National Park. In 2005 it was declared a "Sanctuary for Nature," a special designation from the Chilean state protecting it from industrial activity. The park is 98 percent natural lands, with a network of hiking trails, hot springs, and seven small plots that double as organic farms and ranger posts, creating employment opportunities inside and outside the park for ecotourism and agricultural businesses. Tompkins designed all the operations and buildings of the park to the minutest details.

The park is also collaborating with the University of Chile in projects such as the "Alerce 3000," which seeks to restore the alerce, also known as the Patagonian cypress or false larch (*Fitzroya cupressoides*), to its natural habitat by producing new saplings and planting them in formerly logged areas. The alerce is the most spectacular tree in the region, with dimensions similar to the redwoods, and on occasion living more than 4,000 years, a longevity second only to the bristlecone pine (*Pinus longaeva*).

As Tompkins himself has admitted, conservation projects of the scale on which he has embarked for almost two decades always elicit some resistance, particularly when one is a foreigner. In Chile and Argentina there have been conflicts with peasants, and with politicians and others concerned about the sovereignty of their countries, both because of the immensity of the holdings and because of the strict prohibition on industrial activity of any kind on the land, thus preventing traditional generation of jobs and wealth.

However, many in the southern cone increasingly appreciate the enormity of the gift of wild nature that he has bequeathed them. Even his longtime nemesis, the archconservative Senator Antonio Horvath, who led an unsuccessful legal battle against Tompkins, has joined him in opposing the Endesa and Hydro-Quebec dam construction proposals in the Aisén District. Chilean president Michelle Bachelet herself has expressed a preference for run-of-river projects, which have less environmental impact than dams.

In the midst of the current planetary biological emergency caused by human pollution, misuse, and abuse of the earth, Tompkins's conservation efforts have been crucial. In the context of global warming alone, he is not just preserving but increasing carbon sinks, and he is not just preserving indigenous flora and fauna, but in many instances reintroducing them in places where they were in danger of disappearing.

**BIBLIOGRAPHY**

Tompkins, Douglas, "Wildlands Philanthropy," *Resurgence*, November–December 1998; Langwiesche, William, "Eden: A Gated Community… After Making a Fortune as Founder of North Face and Esprit, Douglas Tompkins Embraces the Principles of Deep Ecology," *The Atlantic Monthly*, June 1999; Rohter, Larry, "An American in Chile Finds Conservation a Hard Slog," *The New York Times*, Aug. 7, 2005; Collier, Robert, "Saving the Last Frontier/Douglas and Kristine Tompkins Fight to Save the Wilds of Chile and Argentina Despite Local Opposition," *San Francisco Chronicle*, Sept. 10, 2006; Reel, Monte, "Argentine Land Fight Divides Environmentalists, Rights Advocates," *The Washington Post*, Sep. 24, 2006.

## Toor, Will

(October 21, 1961– )
Activist, Mayor, County Commissioner

Elected mayor of Boulder, Colorado in 1998 and County Commissioner in 2004, Will Toor is a long-time peace and environmental activist. During the 1980s Toor helped organize a long series of actions against the Rocky Flats nuclear weapons plant and worked at Eco-Cycle, one of the most successful recycling centers in the United States. Toor has also been an advocate for affordable and cooperative housing projects. As a city council member, mayor, and currently County Commissioner, Will Toor has lobbied for alternative transportation, open space and wildlife protection, and managed growth policies.

Will Toor was born in Pittsburgh, Pennsylvania, on October 21, 1961, the son of two college professors. Early in life he exhibited phenomenal ability in math and science and started attending college seminars at age 11. He graduated from Carnegie Mellon University in Pittsburgh in 1979 with a B.S. in physics. In 1980 Toor was hitchhiking across the country when the car in which he was riding broke down in Boulder. He liked the college town and decided to stay. During his early years in Boulder, Toor was active in the campaign against nuclear weapons production at nearby Rocky Flats, a campaign that involved many of the region's progressive activists. Rocky Flats was finally shut down as a weapons facility in 1989. He also ran an outreach campaign for a successful municipal initiative against U.S. policies in El Salvador and Nicaragua. From 1982 to 1985 Toor worked at Eco-Cycle, a pioneering community nonprofit recycling center. As operations supervisor, Toor helped develop curbside recycling services that were run with a shoestring budget, volunteer labor, and aging school buses. Eco-cycle has grown into a model agency that now runs the city's multimillion-dollar recycling center.

In 1985, Toor enrolled at the University of Chicago to resume his work in physics. He completed an M.S. in 1987 and his Ph.D. in 1992, conducting his dissertation research on electro-rheological fluids, which have important applications in robotics. While in Chicago, Toor was involved in a variety of environmental groups, including the Student Environmental Action Coalition, the 1990 CATALYST conference, a national convention of student environmental activists, and the University of Chicago Environmental Concerns Organization, of which he was a founding member. From 1989 to 1991 he directed the University of Chicago recycling program.

In 1992 he returned to Boulder as director of the Environmental Center at the University of Colorado. The program promotes recycling, alternative transportation, and energy conservation and develops student environmental leadership. Toor co-authored *Transportation and Sustainable Campus Communities* (with Spence Havlick, 2004), which discusses such aspects of the transportation issue as public transit, parking, coordination of efforts, etc. Toor remained director of the Environmental Center until 2005; Under Toor's leadership, the Center was recognized by the U.S. Department of Energy for its role in initiating the largest university green power program in the country.

In 1997 Toor ran for Boulder's city council, on a platform of a healthy environment, economic opportunity, fiscal responsibility, prevention of urban sprawl, and reduction of traffic pollution and congestion. He won election with the highest vote total among the candidates. In 1998 the city council elected Toor to the post of mayor.

Boulder, along with much of the rest of the Front Range region of Colorado, is facing unprecedented urban growth. Boulder has been in the forefront in the preservation of open space in the area, and Toor has been a strong advocate for keeping land free from development. He has played a major role in the purchase of strategic open space parcels to prevent large-scale development of open lands in adjacent counties. Growth has put pressure on housing and transportation, two of the most volatile issues in Boulder. The city of Boulder is facing an explosion in housing costs. Many poor and middle-income citizens have been forced out of the city, unable to find affordable housing. Toor has voted consistently to fund low-cost housing programs and has been an outspoken advocate for laws to support cohousing and other alternative housing arrangements, in part because he has often lived in cooperative living situations. Until 1996 the city had a law that barred more than three unrelated persons from sharing living quarters, and Toor was instrumental in overturning that rule. Toor has also been a strong advocate for alternative transportation, calling for free bus passes for all the city's residents. Toor is an outspoken critic of plans to develop more highways and expand lanes on the region's already-existing major arteries, arguing that the money could be more wisely spent on railways, high-speed bus lanes, and other alternative transportation projects. In the spring of 2000 Toor went to Brazil to study the transportation system in Curitiba, which is known as Brazil's "green" city in part because of its model bus system.

Toor was elected as County Commissioner in 2004, and has remained committed to environmental issues at this level. He led the County in its adoption of two resolutions on Sustainability and Zero Waste, and currently is designing programs and policies to reduce energy waste and transition to sources of renewable energy. He chairs the Regional Transit Committee for the county, which strives to improve transportation—including public transit—throughout the county. Toor and his fellow commissioners recently resolved a years-long debate about permissible size of new houses within the unincorporated areas of the county: as a response to the infusion of "monster homes" mushrooming throughout rural areas of the county, a new home must either measure less than 6000 square feet, or purchase "development credits" from smaller houses or vacant lots. The decision also includes new rules about "compatibility" between new houses and existing neighborhoods or townships.

Toor is an adjunct professor in the University of Colorado College of Architecture and Planning and lives in Boulder with his wife, Mariella Colvin, and their children, Nikolaus and Theresa.

**BIBLIOGRAPHY**

"Commissioner Will Toor," www.bouldercounty.org/bocc/board/toor.htm; "CU Environmental Center," ecenter.colorado.edu; Dizon, Kristin, "From Activist to Mayor," *Boulder Daily Camera*, 1998; Snider, Laura, "Boulder County approves limits on house sizes, *Boulder Daily Camera*, 2008; Toor, Will, "A Boulder Vision," *Boulder Daily Camera*, 2000.

## Turner, Frederick Jackson
(November 14, 1861–March 14, 1932)
Historian

Considered by many to be the father of the history of the American West, Frederick Jackson Turner articulated ideas that have dominated the way twentieth-century historians have interpreted American history. One of his many important contributions was to emphasize the significance of the frontier to the identity of the United States. In his view, the presence of an ever-receding frontier, where land and resources were free and abundant, was a major influence on this country's national character. This thesis offered a theoretical base to the environmental consciousness emerging during his lifetime.

Frederick Jackson Turner was born on November 14, 1861, in Portage, Wisconsin, to Andrew Jackson Turner, a newspaper editor and lover of the outdoors, and Mary Hanford, a former schoolteacher. He completed undergraduate work in the ancient classical course at the University of Wisconsin at Madison in 1884 and master's work in history, also at the University of Wisconsin, in 1888. He was awarded a Ph.D. in history from Johns Hopkins University in 1891. Turner's dissertation, on the Wisconsin Indian trade, was an elaboration of the master's thesis he completed at Wisconsin. By 1889, the year he married Caroline Mae Sherwood, Turner's influential 35-year career as an academic was underway. He and his wife had three children, only one of whom survived past childhood.

Turner's ideas about American history, and specifically his frontier thesis published in *The Significance of the Frontier in American History* (1893), became the prominent interpretation of the history of the United States for more than 50 years. In his thesis Turner argued that the social and political uniqueness of the United States derives from the settlement and development of the American frontier. According to Turner, "The existence of an area of free land, its continuous recession, and the advance of American settlement westward, explain American development." Thus, Turner claimed, American development did not merely advance along a single line; it evolved as a return to primitive conditions on a continually advancing frontier line and a new development of that area. In other words, social development in the United States, unlike the development of European countries, began over and over again on the frontier as settlers moved westward, always attracted to the free land and abundant resources just out of their reach. Turner asserted that this process shaped the American character by promoting self-reliance, individualism, mobility, materialism, resourcefulness, originality, and optimism in its citizens. These same qualities, while essential for forming a strong economy and young democracy, could also lead, Turner noted, to the exploitation and depletion of natural resources. But never again, Turner predicted a dozen or so pages into *The Significance of the Frontier in American History*, would such gifts of free land offer themselves. Although the frontier offered new opportunities to citizens, they came at a price. The problem of the United States, once the frontier was gone, would be how to save and wisely use the remaining resources.

In *The Significance of the Frontier in American History* Turner also introduced sectionalism, a concept specifying that residents of geographic regions (for instance, New England, the South, the West) develop different identities, desires, and political interests. In essence, Turner's sectionalism, which became an emergent field in the study of history, foreshadowed the importance today's environmentalists place on the stability fostered by citizens caring for their own local communities. Turner believed that such a geographic identity would provide "a highly organized provincial life to serve as a check upon mob psychology on a national scale, and to furnish that variety which is essential to vital growth and originality."

As an academic, Turner was always torn between his own scholarly work and his teaching duties. He taught at the University of Wisconsin, Madison, where he was named head of the history program, from 1899 until 1910. In 1910 he accepted an appointment as a distinguished chair of history at Harvard University, a decision that Turner half regretted since it led to an increased teaching load and since he felt that his ideas about western history and sectionalism were better received by students at Wisconsin than by students at Harvard. At both Wisconsin and Harvard, Turner was a popular and well-loved teacher; he was especially well regarded by graduate students, many of whom became prominent historians themselves. Thanks in part to Turner's efforts and talents, Wisconsin and Harvard housed two of the great history departments of the twentieth century.

Turner was always plagued by not having written a major book, an accomplishment generally expected of someone of his stature. His essays, which appeared in some of the nation's most influential and scholarly journals and which were revisions of lectures Turner had already delivered, were collected by Turner and others throughout his career and after his death. *The Frontier in American History*, first published in 1920, is perhaps his most important collection. *The Significance of Sections in American History* (1932) was posthumously awarded the Pulitzer Prize in 1933.

Although Turner's frontier thesis remains an important explanation of American development even to this day, criticism of Turner's ideas began to appear in the 1930s. Recent critics have been especially hard on Turner, noting, for example, his easy rejection of Europe's influence on the early development of the United States and his dismissal of the emergence of urbanization in this country. Such attention, albeit negative, only highlights Turner's position as one of the most influential American thinkers of the twentieth century.

After retiring from academics in 1924 due to poor health, Turner worked as a senior research associate at the Huntington Library in San Marino, California, until his death on March 14, 1932.

**BIBLIOGRAPHY**

Billington, Ray A., *Frederick Jackson Turner: Historian, Scholar, Teacher*, 1973; Bogue, Allan, *Frederick Jackson Turner: Strange Roads Going Down*, 1998; Farragher, John Mack, ed., *Rereading Frederick Jackson Turner: The Significance of the Frontier in American History and Other Essays*, 1998; Jacobs, Wilbur R., *On Turner's Trail: 100 Years of Western Writing*, 1994; Limerick, Patricia Nelson, Clyde A. Milner II, and Charles E. Rankin, eds., *Trails toward a New Western History*, 1991.

## Turner, Ted

(November 19, 1938– )
Media Magnate, Philanthropist

Ted Turner created the Turner Broadcasting System cable channel (TBS) in 1976 and Cable News Network (CNN) in 1980; he has long been interested in utilizing mass media to bring about positive social change and environmental awareness.

His cable channels have led the way in environmental programming, airing such popular shows as *Earthwatch* and environmentally focused documentaries. Turner is the largest private landowner in the United States, and takes personal responsibility for protecting and restoring more than one million acres of land in the United States and South America. He also founded the Turner Family Foundation, which gives $25 million every year to nonprofit environmental organizations.

Robert Edward (Ted) Turner III, the first child of Ed and Florence (Rooney) Turner, was born on November 19, 1938, in Cincinnati, Ohio. Florence Turner came from a family of Cincinnati grocers, and Ed Turner was a salesman for a billboard advertising company. By 1939, he had created his own billboard advertising company, the Turner Advertising Company. Ted Turner spent the first six years of his life in Cincinnati with his family. He was a handful as a young boy, amusing himself with activities such as spreading mud all over the neighbor's freshly washed sheets as they hung on the line drying. In 1944, Turner's father volunteered for the United States Navy and was assigned to a station on the Gulf Coast. Turner's parents decided to leave him at a boarding school in Cincinnati, but they took his younger sister along with them. This early abandonment had a significant negative impact on young Ted. Turner attended two separate military academies, having generally negative experiences until his last couple of years at the McCallie School in Chattanooga, Tennessee. There he came into his own, helping to organize a sailing club (he would eventually become a world-class sailor, winning the Americas Cup in 1977), joining the Debate Club, and winning a state debating contest.

After graduating from the McCallie School in 1956, Turner wanted to attend the U.S. Naval Academy; however, his father steered him to Brown University in Providence, Rhode Island. Turner was suspended for a semester because of the part he played in a ruckus at the neighboring women's college, Wheaton. He spent six months in the Coast Guard, then returned to Brown, but he was expelled for good halfway through his junior year after being caught with a woman in his dorm room, a violation of Brown's rules of the time.

Turner moved to Florida, and after fulfilling his obligation to the Coast Guard—he still owed them a tour of duty—he began working as a junior salesman for his father's advertising company in 1960. Three years later, in 1963, Turner's father committed suicide. He left his son in charge of a large but ailing billboard advertising company, which Ted was able to revitalize over the next decade. In 1970, Turner bought two television stations, one in Atlanta, Georgia, the other in Charlotte, North Carolina. Once these stations began turning a profit, he purchased two Atlanta professional sports teams, the Braves (baseball) and the Hawks (basketball), ensuring that he would be able to air their games on his stations. In 1972, he turned his attention to cable television. He invested in the equipment necessary for broadening cable broadcast ranges with satellites, and in 1976, he began broadcasting his original Atlanta television station around the United States, thus launching the cable channel TBS. This channel would air many environmentally focused programs, including the popular *Earthwatch* series, which began in the early 1990s. In 1980, Turner created CNN, which became a vastly successful 24-hour news network. To these he added Turner Network Television (TNT) in 1988, and in 1994, Turner Classic Movies (TCM). In 1996, Turner merged his media holdings with Time-Warner, a move that made Time-Warner the largest media company in the world. His current position involves overseeing the cable operations of Time-Warner.

1985 was an important year for Turner. Prior to that year, many people believed that he was on a path similar to the one that had led his father to suicide. He talked about suicide himself, and according to a 1992 *Time* article, he "was doing his best to imitate his father." In 1985, Turner sought help from an Atlanta psychologist who helped him to move out from beneath his father's shadow. The doctor also began prescribing the drug lithium, which according to those nearest to Turner, brought about miraculous changes in his behavior. Strengthened by his newfound sense of permanence and purpose, Turner apparently began looking outside of himself for ways to make a difference in the world.

In 1985, he founded the Better World Society, whose mission was one of "Harnessing the Power of Television to Make a Better World" and whose logo was a heart-shaped earth. It utilized information from such sources as the Worldwatch Institute to develop television programming that dealt with environmental and social global crisis. The society produced over 30 documentaries before folding in 1991. Turner also created *Captain Planet*, a cartoon show featuring an ecologically minded hero and five multiracial Planeteers who battle against overpopulation, global warming, the depletion of endangered species, and other such environmental evils.

In a 1988 speech to the Hollywood Radio and Television Society, Turner presented a list of ten "voluntary initiatives" designed to replace the "obsolete" Ten Commandments. Included on the list are "I promise to have love and respect for the planet earth and the living things thereon, especially my fellow species—humankind," "I promise to have no more than two children, or no more than my country suggests," and "I pledge to use as little non-renewable resources as possible." In 1991, Turner created the Turner Family Foundation, which gives about $10 million per year to organizations involved in advocacy, organizing, public education, and hands-on conservation work in the areas of habitat conservation, sustainable living, and restoration of communities damaged by non-sustainable practices. "Then," Turner told *Audubon* in 1999, "we stay out of their way." The foundation gives to about 300 organizations annually.

Turner is the largest private American landowner. He owns two million acres of land, with 20 properties in 10 states. None of this land, Turner has pledged, will ever be developed, and 14 of his properties host active conservation projects. Turner is committed to restoring his property to its natural state. He has rid it of domestic livestock, such as cattle and sheep, replacing them with native species, such as bighorn sheep and bison in his western holdings. He has also helped reintroduce native predators. "All we are doing," he told the *Audubon* reporter, "is allowing the ecosystem to be as natural as possible. We are trying to replace as many missing pieces to the environment as we can… we're trying to save the natural world." To help with this endeavor he has a large staff of ranchers, scientists, and academics who experiment with restoration and wildlife management strategies and have published, so far, more than 50 scientific papers.

Turner is also a humanist. He staged the first Goodwill Games in Moscow in 1986 in an effort to ease Cold War tensions. The games have taken place at an interval of every four years since then. The most recent were held in New York City in 1998. In 1997, Turner pledged one billion dollars to the United Nations, an organization he believes must play a critical role in the rapidly developing global society. Turner has received many awards for his efforts, including being named Man of the Year by *Time* in 1992. Turner is married to actress Jane Fonda and has five children from two previous marriages: Laura Lee, Robert Edward, IV, Beauregard, Rhett, and Jennie.

## BIBLIOGRAPHY

Auletta, Ken, *Media Man: Ted Turner's Improbable Empire*, 2004; Bibb, Porter, *It Ain't as Easy as It Looks*, 1993; Golberg, Robert, and Gerald Jay Golberg, *Citizen Turner*, 1995; Lanham, Julie, "The Greening of Ted Turner," *The Humanist*, 1989; Painton, Priscilla, "The Taming of Ted Turner," *Time*, 1992; "Turner Foundation," www.turnerfoundation.org; Webster, Donovan, "Welcome to Turner Country," *Audubon*, 1999; West, Krista, "The Billionaire Conservationist," *Scientific American*, 2002.

# American Environmental Leaders

From Colonial Times to the Present

## Udall, Morris

(June 15, 1922–December 12, 1998)
U.S. Representative from Arizona

During his 30 years in the House of Representatives, Morris Udall, the younger brother of Pres. John F. Kennedy's secretary of the interior, STEWART UDALL, became known as an environmentalist and a reformer. Morris Udall was the catalyst of several bills for the protection or restoration of the nation's natural resources, including bills concerned with land use planning and strip-mining. His concern for Native Americans and love of the environment resulted in numerous pieces of legislation moving through Congress. His greatest environmental achievement might be considered his efforts to pass the Alaskan Wilderness bills. A contender for the Democratic nomination for president in 1976, Udall preached environmental responsibility and awareness that natural resources had a finite capacity and must, therefore, be used more sparingly and thoughtfully.

Morris King Udall was born on June 15, 1922, in St. Johns, Arizona, to Levi Stewart, a chief justice of the Arizona Supreme Court, and Louise (Lee) Udall. Udall attended public schools in St. Johns. When he was seven, he lost his right eye in an accident, but this loss did not prevent him from becoming cocaptain of his high school basketball team, quarterback for the football team, student body president, and valedictorian; nor from playing professional basketball with the Denver Nuggets and serving in the U.S. Army Air Force during World War II. In 1949, after graduating with an LL.B. with distinction from the University of Arizona, he was admitted to the bar of Arizona and entered into a partnership with his brother in Tucson, which lasted until Stewart Udall became secretary of the interior in 1961.

"Mo" Udall was elected to the U.S. House of Representatives in 1961, in a special election to replace his brother's vacant position. Like the majority of first-time representatives to Congress, he struggled to adapt to the complex protocols of the House during his first term. During his next term in office, he organized a workshop for incoming congressmen. Out of this experience came Udall's book, *The Job of the Congressman*, which is still generally regarded as an essential primer for freshman congressmen.

Udall was one of the most productive members of Congress in the latter part of the twentieth century and quickly established a reputation as an environmentalist and a reformer. His work for political reform resulted in the Campaign Finance Law of 1974 that established a campaign spending limit as well as the public funding of presidential elections. But his environmental influence had an even more lasting legacy. Among his chief accomplishments was the Alaska Lands Act of 1980, which effectively doubled the size of the national park system and tripled the size of the national wilderness system. Other significant legislation includes the Central Arizona Water Project (though he would later publicly regret his support for it), the Strip Mining Reclamation Act, the Nuclear Waste Management Policy Act, the Arizona Wilderness Act, the Indian Gaming Act, the Arizona Desert Wilderness Act, and the Tongass Timber Reform Act.

In 1974, Udall was approached by several colleagues who persuaded him to run for the Democratic presidential nomination in 1976. Although initially he was not taken seriously, being a relatively unknown figure from a small state, Udall became a serious contender as his campaign progressed. Throughout 1974 and 1975, Udall appeared at several Democratic fundraising events around the country, lending support to fellow Democrats in their campaign efforts as well as making himself better known among the party leadership. During his campaign he was often compared to both Abraham Lincoln, because of his

Rep. Morris Udall (D-AZ), Aug. 4, 1967, after a six-day trip down the Colorado River. (AP Images)

height (he was six feet five inches tall), and Will Rogers, for his story-telling abilities. By the end of 1975, Udall was considered one of only a few candidates who had a legitimate chance at winning the nomination. With the support of many moderate and liberal Democrats, he fared well in the 1976 primaries.

Udall's environmental advocacy was also a significant part of his presidential campaign. His platform concentrated on what he called "the three E's": energy, environment, and economy. On environmental issues Udall insisted upon careful and planned use of natural resources. During his campaign he warned that "we have come to the end of an era: the era of cheap, abundant land, oil, timber, minerals, food, and water. The age of unlimited growth is over." With respect to the other two "E's," Udall's energy platform advocated the breaking up of big oil companies into smaller, more competitive companies and supported programs to develop other energy sources. To strengthen the nation's economy, Udall proposed a government-guaranteed full employment program, a cut in the defense budget, and the federalization of the welfare system. He also supported the Equal Rights Amendment and a national health insurance plan. Such policies earned Udall the respect of many politicians and media people who considered him the only candidate to pledge to be an activist president.

In spite of his strong results in the early primaries, Udall never actually won a primary. He finished second so many times that he jokingly called himself "ol' second-place Mo." After losing the Ohio primary in 1976, Udall withdrew from the race. While he was widely recognized as the second-place candidate, Udall knew he would not win the Democratic nomination. He also contended that a presidential campaign "tests your marriage, your sanity, your digestion, your sense of humor, and just about everything else." Further amusing anecdotes can be found in his autobiography, *Too Funny to be President*. Udall returned to the House and was named chairman of the House Committee on Interior and Insular Affairs (now Committee on Resources) in 1977; he held that position until 1991.

Udall's interest in the environment was not restricted to land use policy. He also enjoyed outdoor recreation; throughout his life, Udall was an avid hiker and mountain climber. In 1979, Udall was diagnosed with Parkinson's disease, a neurological disorder impairing movement and speech. Udall was hospitalized for the first four months of 1991, before stepping down in May 1991. He was reluctant to resign his seat in the House until he had served a full 30 years. He died on December 12, 1998, leaving six children, one stepson, and his third wife, Norma Gilbert Udall.

**BIBLIOGRAPHY**

Berry, James, "This Fella from Arizona," *Audubon Magazine*, 1981; Carson, Donald W. and James W. Johnson, *Mo: The Life & Times of Morris K. Udall*, 2001; Cook, James, "The Enigma of Mo Udall," *Arizona Republic*, 1971; Udall, Morris K., "A National Park for the Sonoran Desert," *Audubon Magazine*, 1966; Udall, Morris K., "Standing Room Only on Spaceship Earth," *Reader's Digest*, 1969.

## Udall, Stewart

(January 31, 1920– )
Secretary of the Interior, U.S. Representative from Arizona

Nominated by Pres. John F. Kennedy as U.S. secretary of the interior in 1961, Stewart Udall served as secretary until 1969. At his post he was a staunch supporter of both conservation and the development of the nation's natural resources and authored many influential books and articles about conservation issues.

Stewart Lee Udall was born January 31, 1920, in St. Johns, Arizona, the son of Levi Stewart, a lawyer and state justice, and Louise (Lee) Udall. Udall's grandfather was David King Udall, a Mormon missionary who founded the town of St. Johns in 1880. Levi Stewart Udall was chief justice of the Supreme Court of Arizona, and Udall followed in his father's footsteps by pursuing a career in law. Udall attended Eastern Arizona Junior College and graduated LL.B. in 1948 at the University of Arizona.

Udall's education was interrupted by service with the U.S. Army Air Forces in Italy during World War II, where he served as a gunner in a B-24. After completing his college education when he returned home from the war, Udall was admitted to the Arizona bar in 1948. He practiced law in Tucson with his brother MORRIS UDALL for six years before running and being elected as a Democrat to the U.S. House of Representatives from the 2d Congressional District of Arizona in 1954. Udall took his seat in the 84th Congress in January 1955 and was reelected to the next three Congresses.

Early in his political career, Udall demonstrated a concern for conservation issues when, in 1955, he fought for the repurchase and return to the Coconino and Sitgreaves National Forests of 100,000 acres that had been detached from them by a court order. Recognizing the dangers and severity of water shortage in the arid Southwest, Udall voted for a plan to develop the Colorado River Basin. In 1960, Udall fought for a bill to control

Secretary of Interior Stewart Udall, left, points to a map during a ceremony on Oct. 2, 1968, at the White House. President Lyndon Johnson signed four bills to conserve natural resources, create several national parks, trails and the National System of Wild and Scenic Rivers. (AP Images/Charles Tasnadi)

water pollution and introduced another bill to provide federal aid to states for water desalinization plants.

After his appointment by President Kennedy as secretary of the Department of the Interior, Udall took charge of administering a staff of roughly 50,000 employees and an annual budget in excess of $800 million. Udall sought to advance a traditional conservation agenda—efficient resource management, public recreation, and expansion of the national parks—when the conservation movement was in a period of transformation. The Kennedy administration (and the subsequent Johnson administration) was subject to pressure from the emerging environmental movement that lobbied forcefully for wilderness preservation and environmental protection. Udall was not always sensitive to these rising concerns, but the Department of the Interior under Udall was more responsive than the previous Eisenhower administration had been.

As secretary of the interior, Udall was responsible for the custody of 750 million acres of federally owned lands; conservation and development of natural resources, mineral, animal, and vegetable; management of certain hydroelectric power systems; geological and topographical mapping of the nation; reclamation of arid lands through irrigation; and the administration of the nation's national parks. It was in these last two capacities that Udall was perhaps at his most prominent and controversial. In certain respects, cast in the same mould as GIFFORD PINCHOT, Udall was a utilitarian; he felt that nature should be used to human advantage. Nevertheless, he saw the national parks as a prime example of how nature was valuable if left alone. Udall argued that the national parks generated more income than their lumber ever could.

With respect to aridity and irrigation, however, Udall provoked considerable controversy and protest from conservation groups, most notably DAVID BROWER and the Sierra Club. In 1963, Udall made public the Bureau of Reclamation's billion-dollar Pacific Southwest Water Plan. In an effort to resolve the long-standing water shortage problems of the American Southwest, reclamationists proposed diverting water from the Pacific Northwest through a series of tunnels, ducts, and canals to the arid lower Colorado River basin. The scope of this ambitious plan was unprecedented. Dams would be built at Bridge and Marble Canyons in the Grand Canyon to finance the project and to generate hydroelectric power to pump water into central Arizona. The project would, however, affect 40 miles of the Grand Canyon National Monument and 13 miles of Grand Canyon National Park. That state and federal governments could destroy such a valuable cultural and ecological icon inflamed preservationists. Brower led an effective campaign against the proposed Pacific Southwest Water Plan. On February 1, 1967, Udall announced that the Johnson administration had changed its mind about the Grand Canyon dams. Later that year, Udall and his family visited the Grand Canyon; after a raft trip through the canyon, Udall conceded that he had erred in making an "armchair" decision about the dams.

Leaving his position as secretary of the interior in 1969, Udall spent a year as an adjunct professor of environmental humanism at Yale University and returned to writing, which he had started with his important and topical *The Quiet Crisis*, published in 1963. Several books on environmental issues would follow, including *The National Parks* in 1966, *America's Natural Treasures: National Nature Monuments and Treasures* in 1971, and *The Energy Balloon* in 1974. While each book is poignant and well written, none matched the reception or popularity of *The Quiet Crisis*, in part an environmental history lesson, which effectively argued for contemporary expansion of the concept of conservation in the United States. *The Quiet Crisis* is equally pertinent and accessible today as it was almost 40 years ago.

Udall married Ermalee Webb on August 1, 1947. Together they had six children: Thomas, Scott, Lynn, Lori, Denis, and James. Not one to appreciate or work for the protection of the outdoors only from behind a desk, Udall has enjoyed hiking, hunting, fishing, swimming, horseback riding, and camping much of his life.

**BIBLIOGRAPHY**

Nas, Roderick, *Wilderness and the American Mind*, 3d ed., 1982; Smith, Thomas G., "John Kennedy, Stewart Udall, and New Frontier Conservation," *Pacific Historical Review*, 1995; Udall, Stewart Lee, "Human Values and Hometown Snapshots: Early Days in St. Johns," *American West*, 1982; Udall, Stewart Lee, and Jack Loeffler, "Stewart Udall: Sonoran Desert National Park," *Journal of the Southwest*, 1997.

# V

# American Environmental Leaders

From Colonial Times to the Present

## Vogt, William

(May 15, 1902–July 11, 1968)
Writer, Ornithologist, Ecologist

Author of the 1948 classic *Road to Survival*, William Vogt was a writer, administrator, and ornithologist. As a fellow member of the New York birding community, he encouraged ROGER TORY PETERSON to create *A Field Guide to the Birds* and convinced Houghton Mifflin to publish it. He studied the guano birds of Peru and served as chief of the conservation section for the Pan American Union, forerunner of the Organization of the American States. *Road to Survival* was an influential treatise on the damaging effects of overpopulation, and following its publication Vogt served as national director of the Planned Parenthood Federation of America. As researcher, population expert, and naturalist, Vogt is seen today as a pioneer ecologist.

William Vogt was born on May 15, 1902, in Mineola, Long Island, New York. He contracted polio as a child and was left with a noticeable, somewhat limiting limp. He attended St. Stephens (now Bard) College in Annandale-on-Hudson, New York, where he edited the college literary magazine and graduated with a B.A. in journalism in 1925. While working as a journalist in New York City, Vogt got involved in the Linnaean Society of New York and joined the Bronx County Bird Club (BCBC), where he met Roger Tory Peterson. Peterson later traced the birth of his famous field guide to a suggestion made by Vogt during one of the BCBC's annual Christmas bird counts. In 1932 Vogt went to the office of Robert Moses, New York City's director of parks, to lodge a complaint, and Moses was so impressed with Vogt that he appointed him curator of the Tobay wildlife sanctuary at Jones Beach. Vogt served in this position from 1932 to 1935, during which time his small home at the sanctuary became a stopping point for many of the century's famous ornithologists.

In 1935 Vogt moved back into New York City, where he edited *Bird Lore* (later *Audubon*) and began to serve as a lecturer and field naturalist for the National Association of Audubon Societies. While editor of *Bird Lore*, Vogt instituted breeding bird surveys that continue to be one of the most important sources of avian population counts. In 1939 Vogt was ousted from his positions with the Audubon Society, after a dispute with Audubon president John H. Baker. Through fellow naturalist Robert Cushman Murphy, Vogt landed a post as consulting ornithologist to the Peruvian Guano Administration Company, and from 1939 to 1942 he lived and studied on Peru's guano islands. What Vogt found was a bird population unique in the world. Millions of birds lived along a narrow band of cold water along the Peruvian coast, producing enough guano to serve as one of Peru's major industries. The Guano Administration Company shoveled the guano into bags and barged it to the mainland, where it served as rich fertilizer for Peruvian and international agriculture. Vogt was called in because every seven years millions of birds died as a result of the El Niño warming in the Pacific Ocean. As the waterways around the islands warmed, the fish migrated away, and bird populations plummeted. Vogt's research documented the complex relations between species and their environment, with attention to concepts such as niche and competitive exclusion that mark the study as sensitive to ecological ideas far ahead of its time.

Vogt's work in Peru also contributed to *Road to Survival* in important ways. Watching the devastation among the island birds, Vogt began meditating on human overpopulation. If birds could be so dependent on their environment, and so rapidly depopulated, what was to prevent a similar disaster among human beings? In 1948 Vogt published his thoughts, to widespread acclaim and alarm. The book looks at the relationship between the carrying capacity of land area; the "biotic potential," the ability of the land to produce food, shelter, and clothing; and "environmental resistance," the limitations that any environment places on biotic potential. Vogt hoped to awaken the world's populace to growing food shortages as land reached its carrying capacity, in hopes of avoiding worldwide disaster. In the book's conclusion, Vogt implicates all human beings in the coming ecological crisis, but the bulk of the work concerns overpopulation in the Third World. Modern-day critics see this as a limitation in the work, in that it scapegoats the weakest members of the world's populace while largely letting wealthier countries and corporations off the hook. Critics have found the book both racist in some of its assumptions and pioneering in its look at the global ecological whole.

After finishing his work in Peru, Vogt worked for the Pan American Union from 1943 to 1950, directing conservation and research efforts in a number of Latin American countries. From 1951 to 1961 he directed Planned Parenthood. In 1960 he published *People!*, a follow-up to *Road to Survival;* the new book updated issues of population explosion and resource degradation. From 1964 to 1967 he served as secretary for the Conservation Foundation. He planned to use his retirement to return to Latin America but was prevented from doing this by a stroke. On July 11, 1968, suffering from depression and limited mobility, William Vogt took his own life.

**BIBLIOGRAPHY**

Duffy, David Cameron, "William Vogt: A Pilgrim on the Road to Survival," *American Birds*, 1989; Hammond, Richard, "William Vogt," *Biographical Dictionary of American and Canadian Naturalists and Environmentalists*, 1997; Peterson, Roger Tory, "William Vogt: A Man Ahead of His Time," *American Birds*, 1989; Stewart, Doug, Lisa Drew, and Mark Wexler, "How Conservation Grew from a Whisper to a Roar," *National Wildlife*, 1999.

# American Environmental Leaders

From Colonial Times to the Present

## Walter, Martin

(January 26, 1945– )
Mathematics Professor

Martin Walter is a University of Colorado at Boulder mathematics professor who developed an environmental math class that teaches the mathematical fluency needed to analyze environmental problems and the critical thinking skills necessary for identifying the faulty assumptions that have led to public misperceptions about environmental conditions and dangers. He believes that there are immense numbers of environmental problems that can benefit from a mathematical perspective.

Martin Edward Walter was born on January 26, 1945, in Lone Pine, California, to Clare and Karl Walter. He spent his early childhood on the eastern edge of Los Angeles, until his father learned that a freeway would be built in the family's backyard, at which time they moved to San Jacinto, at the edge of the Soboba Indian Reservation. Walter spent his free time wandering the remnants of the native chaparral ecosystem, and the family spent vacations visiting national parks. He obtained his B.S. in mathematics at the University of Redlands in Redlands, California, in 1966 and then went on to the University of California at Irvine, where he earned his M.S. in 1968 and his Ph.D. in 1971, both in mathematics. He worked as a research associate at Queen's University in Kingston, Ontario, from 1971 to 1973 and then moved to the University of Colorado, as an assistant professor from 1973 to 1977, an associate professor from 1977 to 1984, and a full professor since 1984, chairing the department from 1996 to 2000. During the early 1980s, he became involved with an ad hoc group of conservationists fighting to preserve wilderness from logging in the lush Bowen Gulch area of Colorado, which borders Rocky Mountain National Park to the west and is home to the state's oldest and largest stand of Engelmann spruce trees. After almost a decade of massive letter-writing

Martin Walter (Photograph by Joy Wu)

and public education campaigns, civil disobedience on site to prevent Louisiana Pacific from cutting trees, and a boycott of that company, Walter and his fellow activists convinced Congressman David Skaggs to obtain federal protection from logging for Bowen Gulch. The so-called Bowen Gulch Rescue Effort changed its name in 1990 to Ancient Forest Rescue and has engaged since then in a number of campaigns to prevent timber sales throughout the state. Walter has devoted much of his free time to this work.

In 1992, after spending many years teaching the basic algebra/trigonometry class to his students and realizing that the material did not inspire great interest or engagement, Walter designed a new class, "Mathematics for the Environment." This class, which he has taught every semester since the fall of 1992, teaches the language of math—mathese, as Walter calls it—through the study of social and environmental problems. Walter originally used a textbook entitled *Consider a Spherical Cow: A Course in Environmental Problem Solving*, written by University of California, Berkeley, professor John Harte (1988). However because most of the students in Walter's classes were not math majors, but rather environmental studies majors focusing on policy instead of science, they needed a text that presented complex mathematical concepts more gradually. So by 1997, Walter had written his own text for the course.

Walter's *Reader* provides a basic structure for the class. The first chapter provides a review of math and science, defining math as the search for and study of patterns and providing 100 pages of examples of how mathematical concepts can facilitate our understanding of the world. Its exercises are based both on pure math and on real-life topics, such as the kinship system of the Warlpiri aboriginal people of Australia, depletion of ocean fisheries, and the annual growth rate of brain cancer. The second chapter, "Media Literacy, Communication: Information, Honesty and Truth," is based on the ideas of media critics Ben Bagdikian and Noam Chomsky. Recounting stories that have been largely censored by the mainstream media (but have been published in such alternative media sources as Pacifica Radio News, *The Nation*, *Covert Action Quarterly*, and *Extra*) this chapter focuses on the importance of the views and facts that could widen Americans' thinking space models, correct common fallacies, and expose hidden assumptions. The third chapter deals with counting, statistics, and probability in environmental contexts, and the fourth, "Connections and Changes," works with population modeling, economics, food and health, and how human activities have altered the earth's ecosystems. An updated electronic copy of the text, *Mathematics for the Environment*, is available on-line at www.colorado.edu/math/earthmath.

The class is designed to give a social and environmental context to show how math can be used as a tool to reveal a bigger picture. It emphasizes the importance of assumptions and how the most complete information possible can help one develop more accurate assumptions. Students learn that conclusions are almost always determined by the assumptions that one makes at the outset, and they are trained to spot when math is being misused or where arguments are fraudulent. Walter's class quickly became so popular that two sections, of at least 30 students each, are now taught each semester.

Walter has also supervised projects by math majors that are based on environmental problems: One M.S. thesis modeled the goshawk population on the Kaibab plateau near the Grand Canyon; another student's independent study used math to explore the patterns of what Walter calls "weatherquakes"—storms and other weather phenomena causing extreme destruction, happening increasingly on a global scale. In addition to Walter's focus on environmental modeling, his mathematical specialties are noncommutative harmonic analysis and self-organizing systems.

Walter has been a visiting professor in Trondheim, Norway, and Leuven, Belgium, and was an Alfred B. Sloan Fellow at the University of California, Berkeley, and the University of Pennsylvania in 1977 and 1978, respectively. He referees for a number of mathematical journals. In addition to attending conferences and giving talks on his mathematical specialties, Walter is well known locally for his environmental activism on campus and beyond. He received the Conservationist of the Year award from the Rocky Mountain Chapter of the Sierra Club in 1990 and was chosen as a CU Favorite Professor by alumni in 1996. Walter lives with his wife, Joy, in Boulder, Colorado.

### BIBLIOGRAPHY

Boyd, David, "Teaching Math through Environment: Professor Reaches Out with Relevant Subject Matter," *Boulder Daily Camera*, 1995; "Marty Walter," math.Colorado.EDU/lists/children/faculty/walter/.

## Warburton, Barbara
(September 10, 1915–September 30, 1996)
Educator

Barbara Warburton taught three generations of secondary and college-level biology students in Brownsville, Texas; founded a biological station in the northeastern Mexican state of Tamaulipas; and fought for the conservation of a cloud forest there that has since become the nucleus of the United Nations Man in the Biosphere El Cielo reserve.

Barbara Ellen Taylor was born on September 10, 1915, in Tomah, Wisconsin. Her father, who worked for the John Deere farm equipment company, died in 1922 when she was seven years old. Her mother, left a widow with no one to help support the family, took a job as a teacher at schools on Indian reservations. Barbara and her sister and brother accompanied their mother to Carson City, Nevada, for one such job, but when she was hired to work on the Navajo reservation in New Mexico, the children were not permitted to accompany her. So they were sent to live with an uncle in southern Texas and visited their mother during the summers. Despite the economic hardship the family faced, Mrs. Taylor insisted that her daughters study. She felt that an education was the only thing that could not be lost or taken away in hard times. Barbara was sent to a high school run by Catholic nuns and then received a scholarship to Baylor Women's College. Her brother worked on ships off Galveston in order to support his sister; Barbara later helped her brother, too, by working as a teacher so he could attend college.

Warburton graduated from Baylor in 1941 with a B.A. in biology. She married Joe Warburton shortly after graduating and moved to La Feria, Texas, with him. In 1943, Warburton commenced what would be a career of more than 50 years teaching biology at Brownsville High School and Junior College, which later became Texas Southmost College and now shares a campus with the University of Texas at Brownsville. During the mid-1950s, Warburton earned a M.S. in biology at the University of Texas at Austin.

In the early 1960s, Warburton read an article in the National Biology Teachers Association magazine about how junior college biology students should be required to do fieldwork just as senior college students were. Knowing that some of her students were embarrassed to be attending a junior college, but fully aware that their education could be as solid as or even more so than that offered by a senior college, Warburton decided to fortify her curriculum with a field laboratory. She asked the college president for funds to build cabins in the nearby Sierra Madre Oriental of the northeastern Mexican state of Tamaulipas, 280 miles south of Brownsville. With the $2,500 from a private bequest left by a retired entomologist, Warburton and a group of enthusiastic students built three cabins themselves.

Once the facilities were set up, Warburton offered all of her students—not just the biology majors—the opportunity to take field trips to Rancho El Cielo. She would lead four-day trips during the spring and fall semesters and longer trips during the summers. Many undergraduates became so enamored with the beauty and diversity of the seven forest zones criss-crossed by rivers and surrounded by arid ecosystems that they changed their major to biology while there. The Mexican neighbors of the reserve were also impressed by its ecological value and worked to have it declared a biosphere reserve, earning it a higher degree of protection by Tamaulipas state authorities even than Mexican national parks. The Gorgas Science Foundation, which had been founded in 1947 by students at Southmost College, collaborates with Tamaulipas authorities and other educational institutions of the region to support the field station at Rancho del Cielo.

Warburton retired from teaching in 1978 but remained keenly interested in the Rancho del Cielo program. She volunteered her time in the Gorgas Science Foundation until her death. Her legacy manifests in hundreds of her students. In a videotaped interview produced by the University of Texas at Brownsville/Texas Southmost College, she and her former students recall how she instilled them with pride in their bilingualism and biculturalism and in the incredibly rich ecology that characterized their binational bioregion. She also encouraged a diligent work ethic, telling her students that the taxpayers were subsidizing their education and that they had to prove that their education was worthwhile. Many former students have pursued the sciences and are now professional scientists at work in the southeast region of Texas that she taught them to appreciate and value.

Warburton died in Brownsville on September 30, 1996, of complications following a heart attack. Her husband died two weeks later. They are survived by one son, Geoff.

**BIBLIOGRAPHY**
Medrano, Manuel, *Barbara Warburton*, 1998 (video-recording available through University of Texas–Brownsville/Texas Southmost College media services); Moreno, Jenalia, "Longtime Professor Warburton Dies at 81," *Brownsville Herald*, 1996; "University of Texas at Brownsville and Texas Southmost College Biological Sciences," www.utb.edu/biology/.

## Waring, George
(July 4, 1833–October 29, 1898)
Sanitation Engineer

George Waring used science and technology to clean up filthy, disease-infested cities of the 1800s. His economic city sewerage systems were the best early models, and as commissioner of New York City's Department of Sanitation from 1895 to 1898, he reduced that city's death rate by 6,000 a year.

George Edwin Waring was born on July 4, 1833, in Poundridge, New York, to George Edwin and Sarah Burger Waring. His father manufactured iron tools and stoves in Stamford, Connecticut, where Waring spent most of his childhood. After graduating from a private high school in Poughkeepsie, New York, in 1849, Waring tried selling hardware for a year and then managed a grist mill for two years. In 1853, he began studying methods of scientific agriculture with the well-known agricultural scientist, James Mapes. Within a year, Waring had learned enough that Mapes encouraged him to tour New England, giving lectures to farmers' clubs on scientific agriculture. Waring continued to do this during the winters of 1853, 1854, and 1855, and at the age of 21 he published his first book, *The Elements of Agriculture.*

Waring became manager of the Chappaqua, New York, farm of abolitionist publisher Horace Greeley in 1855 and then managed the Staten Island farm of FREDERICK LAW OLMSTED SR. in 1857. That same year, Olmsted and Calvert Vaux, designers of New York City's Central Park, enlisted Waring to design the park's drainage system. Waring was the first to break ground when the landscaping began in 1859. He worked full-time on the project until the Civil War broke out. In 1861 he was commissioned major of the Garibaldi Guards, and he served until 1865.

Upon his return from the war, Waring became involved in unsuccessful oil and coal businesses and then in 1867 became manager of the Ogden Farm near Newport, Rhode Island, keeping that position for ten years. During his time there, he continued to pursue his interest in drainage and sanitation. He wrote *Earth Closets* in 1868, which described how human waste could be biodegraded and inoffensively integrated into family garden plots. In 1871 he was contracted to design the sewerage of Ogdensburg, New York, and in 1874 that of Saratoga Springs, New York. In 1877, as his fame in the sanitation field was growing, Waring abandoned farming as a profession to devote himself full-time to sanitation engineering.

As a member of the National Board of Health, Waring was invited to visit Memphis, Tennessee, one of the least sanitary cities in the United States, if not the world. A yellow fever epidemic that hit during two successive years in the late 1870s killed more than 5,000 of the city's 40,000 residents and led more than 20,000 others to flee. Waring found that the city's cisterns and wells for drinking water were almost all contaminated by the city's 6,000 cesspools and outhouses. Because the city was seriously in debt, the solution needed to be as economical as possible. Waring was hired to design a sewerage system. It had several features that were unique at the time: the pipes were narrower than most; they handled household sewage only—no roof or yard runoff was allowed to drain into the system; there were no manholes; and the pipes were well ventilated and flushed out every 24 hours by automatic flush tanks. Notes on the Memphis design were published in French, Dutch, Spanish, and German, and many more city sewerage systems were built following the Memphis model. Waring built two more sewerage systems in his life: one for Buffalo, New York, and another for Santiago, Cuba. He worked during the remainder of his life on perfection of sewage processing, strongly maintaining his faith that naturally occurring bacteria were the best agents for its decomposition. He told the graduating class of 1896 at Yale Medical School that chemical disinfection was "a clog in the wheel of nature's beneficent processes."

Waring is perhaps best remembered for his three years as commissioner of the Department of Sanitation of the City of New York. He took that position in 1895, appointed by reformist mayor William Strong, who had ousted the corrupt Boss Tweed and his Tammany Hall. Up until that time, New York's garbage collectors were hired by party bosses as a favor for their political support and spent most of their time on the job drinking in bars. New York was a filthy, plague-ridden city. Waring's early moves included cutting the pay of the garbage collectors to rid the force of those in there purely for political reasons and requiring the men to wear white uniforms that they purchased themselves. The uniforms gave the corps a military spirit and sense of dignity and might have discouraged the men from frequenting bars while on the clock.

Waring's tight organization and scientific methods worked. Immigrant children were recruited to join the effort, winning prizes and parties for their contributions. During Waring's time in office, 2,500 children joined 44 leagues. The garbage collectors, dubbed "White Angels" by New Yorkers, proudly performed their duties, and New York under Waring transformed into a much cleaner, healthier place. Six thousand fewer people died every year in New York each year Waring was in office. In addition to effective, efficient garbage collection, Waring's force also recycled and sold reusable elements of the solid waste stream. This reduced the amount of refuse to be dumped and raised money for the Department of Sanitation's work. Waring did not approve of dumping trash into the ocean and instead initiated incineration in New York.

Waring traveled widely and wrote prolifically. His many books and articles for the *Nation* magazine were on matters of sanitation as well as about his travels in Europe. In 1898 he traveled to Havana, Cuba, on a U.S. government mission. He was to report how yellow fever could be eradicated from the city of Havana. Waring contracted yellow fever on this visit and died in New York City on October 29, 1898. He left his third wife, Louise Yates, whom he had married earlier that year.

### BIBLIOGRAPHY
FitzSimmons, Neal, "Pollution Fighter: George Waring," *Civil Engineering*, 1971; "George Waring: Giving Sanitation Status," *Civil Engineering*, 1976; Gottlieb, Robert, *Forcing the Spring*, 1993.

## Warshall, Peter
(December 6, 1943– )
Editor of *Whole Earth*, Environmental Consultant

Peter Warshall was the editor of *Whole Earth*, a publication dedicated to fostering social change and environmental restoration through the introduction of diverse new ideas, tools, and practices. In addition to his research and writings for the magazine, he works with a variety of communities on conservation, including indigenous people and ranchers in Arizona and Mexico and corporations seeking to reduce their impact on the environment. He is currently the project director of the Dreaming New Mexico Initiative, a project to re-design the energy system of New Mexico, as well as its food system, to accommodate more local farms and local and healthier foods. Both projects will help reduce the impact of climate change. Although Warshall harbors a concern for the environment as a whole, he has focused on watersheds, wastewater, and wildlife and is dedicated to encouraging and implementing practices that favor biodiversity and sustainability.

Peter Jack Warshall was born December 6, 1943, to parents Hymen and Beulah Warshall in El Paso, Texas. He spent his earliest childhood years in El Paso, moving with his family to Brooklyn, New York, as a young boy. He graduated from Stuyvesant High School in New York in 1960. Warshall then went on to Harvard University, from which he graduated with a B.A. in biology in 1965. From 1965 to 1967, he studied cultural anthropology, with an emphasis on Native American history and mythology, at École Pratique des Hautes Études in Paris, France. In 1968 he returned to Harvard to study biological anthropology, receiving his doctorate in 1971.

From 1972 to 1980 Warshall worked for the Bolinas (California) Public Utilities District, where he developed projects to improve the area's watershed management and water flow conservation. In this capacity, he designed a zero-discharge sewage treatment plant and constructed wetlands. He also initiated the protection of the Bolinas Lagoon, habitat to many shorebirds. During this time period, Warshall served on the governor's Emergency Task Force during the California drought in 1976, creating the first citizen's pamphlet on gray water systems and their reuse.

In 1975, Warshall began writing for *Co-Evolution Quarterly*, a magazine first published in 1974 that encouraged environmental consciousness by introducing concepts such as whole system thinking and voluntary simplicity to its readers. The magazine changed its name to the *Whole Earth Review* in 1985, then *Whole Earth* in 1997 when Warshall became editor. Warshall first wrote about land use and over the years has written on questions of watersheds and water resources, natural history, anthropology, and sustainability. He edited the environmental portions of the *Whole Earth Catalog* for 20 years.

Warshall worked with the Office of Arid Lands in Arizona from 1982 to 1990, developing the first water hyacinth treatment plant in the state and initiating work on home-monitored use of water. In 1986 he became a research scientist for a proposed astronomical observatory site in the Sky Island region of Arizona and New Mexico. The University of Arizona, along with the Vatican, wanted to build 17 astronomical telescopes on Mount Graham, one of the "island" mountains surrounded by desert. Warshall was hired to provide the environmental impact study. During his time on Mount Graham, however, he encountered many rare species endemic to that small area. Perhaps the most notable of these was the Mount Graham red squirrel, formerly thought to be extinct. Warshall knew that developing the proposed telescopes would devastate the entire delicate ecosystem on Mount Graham. His *Whole Earth* articles during this time period mirrored his renewed dedication to wildlife and biodiversity conservation. In the Spring 1986 issue Warshall wrote about preserving wild lands such as Mount Graham through "wildlands philanthropy." He followed up with an article in the Summer 1986 issue on the Gulf of Mexico's diverse ecology and the connection of that ecology with the different cultures living in that bioregion.

Warshall united with the San Carlos Apaches and other environmental groups to fight for the preservation of Mount Graham. This quest led him to both the U.S. Congress and the Vatican and resulted in a decrease in the proposed number of telescopes to be built on Mount Graham. Warshall has also helped the Tohono O'odham people defend their land and water rights. He has worked in Ethiopia hunger camps for the United Nations High Commission for Refugees. Warshall has joined forces with the U.S. Agency for International Development to achieve biodiversity and better use of natural resources in ten other African countries.

Warshall has acted as a consultant to numerous large corporations, including General Mills, Volvo, Trans Hygga, Scandinavian Airlines System (SAS), and Clorox, helping them to reform their environmental practices. He has performed his consulting work through his own small firm, Peter Warshall and Associates, as well as through the Global Business Network, an international collage of innovators, strategists, scientists, and organizations working toward improved global awareness of environment, business, and government. Warshall often lectures at biodiversity and sustainability conferences, and his articles can be found in *San Francisco Chronicle*, *Orion*, *Animal Kingdom*, and *River Voices*. He serves on the board of the Northern Jaguar Project and the Sky Island Alliance, and is a fellow of the World Innovation Foundation. Warshall resides in Tucson, Arizona, and Sausalito, California.

**BIBLIOGRAPHY**

"Bioneers Home Page," www.bioneers.org/warshall.html; "Ecotech," www.ecotech.org/ecotech3/warshall.htm; "Global Business Network: Peter Warshall," www.gbn.com/PersonBioDisplayServlet.srv?pi=22075.

# Watson, Paul

(December 2, 1950– )
Master Mariner, Wildlife Conservationist, Author, Founder of Sea Shepherd

Paul Watson is best known for his direct actions at sea in the defense of seals, dolphins, whales, and other marine wildlife. From the late 1960s, Watson actively campaigned to prevent nuclear testing, to disrupt Canadian seal hunts, and to damage or sink vessels engaged in illegal whaling activities. His bold and daring actions at sea have made him both an admired and controversial figure. The author of six books, Watson was one of the original founders of Greenpeace. In 1977, he founded the Sea Shepherd Conservation Society where he continues to serve as its leader.

The eldest of six children, Paul Watson was born December 2, 1950 in Toronto to Anthony Joseph Watson and Annamarie Larsen. He grew up in the fishing village of St. Andrews, New Brunswick, where at age eight he joined the "Kindness Club," an organization dedicated to environmental education and the humane treatment of animals. At age sixteen, he rode the rails west to Vancouver where he studied communications and linguistics at Simon Fraser University. Watson's career as a mariner began in 1968 when he joined the Canadian Coast Guard. A year later he signed on as a merchant seaman aboard the Norwegian bulk carrier *Bris*, bound for Asia and Africa.

In October 1969, Watson became involved in a Sierra Club campaign to protest U.S. nuclear testing at Amchitka Island in the Aleutian Islands. He was part of a small group called the Don't Make a Wave Committee that planned to sail two ships into the test site. Although the nuclear test was eventually conducted under Amchitka Island, the campaign generated publicity and garnered national attention. In 1972, the Don't Make a Wave Committee took the name of its two ships and became the Greenpeace Foundation. Watson was one of its founding members and directors.

In 1973, Watson worked as a volunteer medic for the American Indian Movement during the occupation of Wounded Knee, South Dakota. While he was there, Watson was given the name Grey Wolf Clear Water by medicine men of the Oglala Sioux, based on a vision he had during a sweat lodge ceremony in which he witnessed a buffalo being shot with arrows that resembled harpoons. The vision crystallized for Watson what would become his lifelong mission: to defend and protect animals of the world, especially whales and other marine wildlife.

In 1975, Greenpeace conducted its first campaign to oppose illegal whaling, confronting the Soviet whaling fleet in the Pacific Ocean. During the encounter, Watson drove his small inflatable boat between a Russian harpoon vessel and a pod of sperm whales. At one point, Watson watched as a harpooned whale carefully avoided hitting his boat. "That dying whale looked right at me and chose not to harm me," Watson said. The confrontation with the Soviet ship was captured on film and later shown on national television in the United States.

That same year, Watson helped to organize and lead the first Greenpeace campaign to protect harp seals in Newfoundland. Watson again put his life on the line when he and another Greenpeace member stopped a large sealing ship by standing on the ice in its path. In 1977, Watson led a second campaign to oppose the seal hunt in which he nearly lost his life at the hands of angry sealers. Upon his return from Newfoundland, Watson was notified by the directors of Greenpeace that he would not be permitted to lead another seal campaign. Watson found himself at odds with Greenpeace over the question of tactics as well as organizational structure, and in 1977 he resigned from Greenpeace.

Based on his belief that direct action campaigns were crucial to the enforcement of laws protecting marine wildlife on the high seas, Watson founded the Sea Shepherd Conservation Society in 1977. A non-profit organization registered in the United States., Sea Shepherd is dedicated to research, conservation, and the defense of marine wildlife. Sea Shepherd is best known for its direct actions at sea, including the sinking or sabotaging of vessels that operate in violation of international maritime law. Since 1979, Sea Shepherd claims to have sunk nine whaling ships. There have been few reports of injuries and no reports of deaths during Sea Shepherd actions. Watson adheres to a principle of "aggressive non-violence"—a direct-action approach that allows for the destruction of property, but not violence against life.

As an activist, Watson has engaged in more than 200 voyages aimed at preventing illegal whaling, disrupting the Canadian commercial seal hunt, confiscating illegal long-lines, stopping dolphin kills in Japan, and, more recently, putting an end to poaching and shark-finning in the Galapagos. For his efforts, he has been threatened, beaten, arrested, imprisoned, and tried for commission of crimes on the high seas. Through it all, Watson has never been convicted of a crime. Sea Shepherd activities are guided by the United Nations Charter for Nature, which authorizes the enforcement of international conservation law by, among other entities, individuals and non-governmental organizations. "We would welcome an enforcement agency," Watson has said about laws and regulations protecting marine wildlife, "but nobody is there and law exists, so therefore the law must be enforced. And that's what Sea Shepherd is. We are a policing body."

Watson has authored six books, including his first, *Sea Shepherd: My Fight for Whale and Seals* (1982), and his latest, *Seal Wars: Twenty-Five Years on the Front Lines with the Harp Seals* (2002). In addition to Greenpeace and Sea Shepherd, Watson has worked with a number of organizations including Defenders of Wildlife, the Fund for Animals, and the Sierra Club, where he served on the board of directors from 2003 to 2006. He has lectured at universities and events throughout the world. In 2000, *Time* magazine named him one of the environmental heroes of the 20th century.

Watson is a U.S. resident and has lived in the United States for more than twenty years. His application for U.S. citizenship has been approved, and he is currently awaiting the official ceremony to mark his citizenship. He has one child from a previous marriage, Lilliolani Paula Lum Watson, born in 1980.

## Bibliography

Watson, Paul, *Sea Shepherd: My Fight for Whales and Seals*, 1982; Morris, David B., *Earth Warrior: Overboard with Paul Watson and the Sea Shepherd Conservation Society.*, 1995; Scarce, Rik, *Eco-Warriors: Understanding the Radical Environmental Movement*, 1990; Ecott, Tim, "Paul Watson: 'There's No Rest on Planetary Duty," *Daily Telegraph*, www.telegraph.co.uk; Official Website for Sea Shepherd: www.seashepherd.org/crew-watson.html; "Transcription of 1 hour interview with Captain Paul Watson of Sea Shepherd," typingisnotactivism.wordpress.com/2007/02/25.

## Waxman, Henry
(September 12, 1939– )
U.S. Representative from California

Henry Waxman has long been recognized as a champion of liberal causes and as an effective and passionate advocate for stronger government regulations in health and environmental issues. He was one of the primary authors of the landmark 1990 Clean Air Act and sponsored 1986 and 1996 amendments to the Safe Drinking Water Act. He has introduced climate change and ozone protection legislation. Waxman has fought on behalf of the elderly and poor and championed improvements in Medicare and Medicaid. He has fought hard for research on acquired immunodeficiency syndrome (AIDS) and battled the big tobacco companies. Waxman was first elected to Congress in 1974 for California's 29th District, which includes the western portion of Los Angeles, including the coastal city of Santa Monica and affluent Beverly Hills.

Henry Arnold Waxman was born on September 12, 1939, in Los Angeles to Lou and Ester Waxman, who raised both Henry and his sister, Miriam, above the family grocery store in Watts. Both parents were staunch Democrats and very interested in the political scene. Waxman remembers not being poor at that time but certainly not wealthy either. He recalls his father talking about the Depression and the importance of the New Deal in giving all people an opportunity for achieving affluence in society. Waxman may have been even more influenced by his grandparents, immigrants from Russia who fled czarist persecution in 1905. "My grandparents would tell me about how the anti-Semites would come into town and destroy property, beat people up, threaten their lives, and they just felt they could no longer stay," he said. His grandparents eventually settled in the Boyle Heights section of Los Angeles. Waxman continues to honor his faith by going to temple, keeping kosher, and not working Saturdays.

As a teenager, Waxman attended Fremont High School, where he not only did well but made his first bid into politics by winning several student body posts. By 1961, Waxman enrolled at the University of California at Los Angeles (UCLA) as a political science major. He graduated with a B.A. in 1964. The civil rights movement fueled his already strong interest in politics and led Waxman to join the California Young Democrats. He was eventually elected statewide president of the organization, becoming more savvy in politics and meeting key friends who would later hold office and play a role in his political success.

In 1968, the 29-year-old Waxman graduated from UCLA Law School, and after a brief stint in law, he took the plunge into the political arena that same year. He ran for the state assembly against a veteran who seemed to be losing support among voters in his southwestern coastal district. Despite spending only $30,000 on the campaign and running as an outsider, Waxman won with 64 percent of the vote. In the state assembly, Waxman distinguished himself as an expert on health care issues and a leading advocate for the elderly. He served as chairman of the assembly Health Committee and on the Committee on Elections and Reapportionment and the Select Committee on Medical Malpractice during his three terms in the assembly.

In 1974, court-ordered reapportionment created a U.S. House of Representatives district seat in West Los Angeles, the very area where Waxman had lived since college. Because of the large concentration of elderly and Jewish voters as well as immigrants and gays, Waxman knew he had a good chance of winning. It was during the height of the Watergate era that Waxman and many other Democrats were swept into Congress. Immediately, he sought a place on the Interstate and Foreign Commerce Committee (now

Henry Waxman (D-CA), second from right, at the international conference on global warming in Kyoto, Japan, December 6, 1997. (AP Images/Katsumi Kasahara)

called Energy and Commerce) because health was an issue addressed by that committee. After just four years he challenged and beat out a senior colleague for the chairmanship of the Health and Environment Subcommittee. He held the chairmanship for 16 years, until the Republican sweep of Congress of 1994 stripped him of the title.

With health and the environment hot topics at the end of the 1970s, Waxman was the right person at the right time to bring about major policy changes. He became a major player in important amendments to legislation protecting the nation's air and water. Throughout the 1980s, he worked on strengthening amendments to the Clean Air Act of 1970. Although Waxman was one of the primary authors of the amendments to the act, he actually held up weaker versions of it for a decade until provisions addressing acid rain and emission controls were strengthened. The acid control programs required major reductions in sulfur dioxide emissions from electric power plants. The hazardous emissions control program replaced what had been an ineffective section of the Clean Air Act with a list of 190 toxic chemicals along with instructions for the Environmental Protection Agency on how to control them. He was able to block a key vote on a weaker version of the bill in the early 1980s by presenting 600 amendments wheeled into the committee room in a shopping cart. The motor vehicle emission standards enacted in 1990 have reduced allowable emissions from new cars by 75 percent.

In other environmental legislation, Waxman also sponsored the 1986 and 1996 Safe Drinking Water Act amendments, the 1996 Food Quality Act that regulates pesticides, the Radon Abatement Act, and the Lead Contamination Control Act. In more recent years he has continued to take the lead on environmental issues by pursuing legislation to address global warming. In 1999 Waxman released the first report in the country to analyze the levels of hazardous air using current monitoring standards. The study was done in Los Angeles and showed that its residents may be exposed to hazardous air pollutants at levels far higher than the goals of the Clean Air Act.

Waxman has been the ranking Democrat on the House Oversight and Government Reform Committee since 1997, and in 2006 when the Democrats won the majority in the House, he became committee chair. He immediately went to work, opening investigations on the Iraq war and the Bush administration's dependence on no-bid contracts to carry it out. The *Post* characterized Waxman as "the Bush Administration's worst nightmare," who has no qualms about probing its role in such environmental debacles as its censorship of global warming reports by government scientists, housing the Hurricane Katrina homeless in trailers that emit formaldehyde, the Environmental Protection Agency's lax enforcement of clean water legislation, and many more major scandals.

Climate change has been the major focus of his efforts to introduce environmental legislation in recent years, with his introduction of several climate change bills.

Waxman and his wife, Janet, maintain residences in Bethesda, Maryland, and Los Angeles, California. They have two children and four grandchildren.

### BIBLIOGRAPHY

Getlin, Josh, "What Makes Henry Tick," *Los Angeles Times*, 1990; Kosterlitz, Julie, "Watch Out for Waxman," *National Journal*, 1989; Meyerson, Harold, "The Liberal Lion in Winter," *Los Angeles Times Magazine*, 1994; "U.S. Rep. Henry Waxman," www.house.gov/waxman; Waxman, Henry, "False Alarms on Clean Air," *Washington Post*, 1997; Weisman, Jonathan, "White House Feels Waxman's Oversight Gaze, *Washington Post*, 2007.

## Werbach, Adam

(January 15, 1973– )
President of the Sierra Club, Television Producer

As the youngest-ever president of the Sierra Club, Adam Werbach led the club for two years, from 1996 to 1998, rejuvenating the membership by attracting a younger crowd, focusing on environmental justice issues, and shifting the club's activities from its former focus on lobbying to more outreach and grassroots organizing. After stepping down, Werbach founded Act Now Productions, through which he produced the Cable TV environmental newsmagazine *The Thin Green Line*, and which currently offers consulting, outreach, and marketing services to companies wishing to increase their sustainability and appeal to a green market.

Adam Werbach was born on January 15, 1973, in Tarzana, California, a suburb of Los Angeles. Although both his parents worked in Los Angeles proper, they chose to raise their two sons on a rustic two-acre ranch. Avid members of the Sierra Club, the Werbachs spent their vacations camping and hiking in national parks. Werbach's first activist episode came at the age of eight, when he recruited 200 of his classmates to sign a petition to dump President Reagan's antienvironmentalist interior secretary, James Watt. As a high school student, he spent one semester at the Mountain School in Vershire, Vermont, a branch of the Milton Academy. His time there was mostly dedicated to environmental education and work on the school's 300-acre organic farm. After living in pristine rural Vermont, he recounts in his 1997 book *Act Now, Apologize Later*, he was shocked by the level of environmental degradation in southern California, especially the choking air pollution that made asthma a virtual epidemic. He immediately got involved in California's Big Green campaign for a broad-based 1990 environmental referendum that would have tightened clean air bills, increased open space and forest preservation, and required greater fuel economy. Werbach's contribution was to organize high school students to campaign for the referendum. The extraction industries outspent Big Green supporters ten to one, however, and Big Green was defeated.

Undaunted by Big Green's defeat, Werbach and the teenagers he had worked with decided to continue to work together as a student group. They persuaded the Sierra Club to fund a summer camp for teenagers that would provide environmental education and rally participants for environmental activism.

Werbach entered Brown University in 1991, where his activism continued and expanded. By this time, he had obtained official endorsement of the Sierra Student Coalition, which grew to 30,000 members and registered thousands of new student voters. They lent critical support to the 1992 California Desert Protection Act, via "dorm storm," in which dormitory residents throughout the country's colleges and universities called their congresspeople to demand their support for the act. The Sierra Student Coalition's creative methods also included selling black snow cones at concerts and fairs to dramatize the effects of drilling for oil in the Arctic National Wildlife Refuge.

After graduating from Brown in 1995 with degrees in political science and media, Werbach returned to California. A member of the national board of the Sierra Club since 1994, Werbach was elected president of the club in 1996 and reelected in 1997, with endorsements from such Sierra Club luminaries as DAVE FOREMAN and DAVID BROWER. Werbach's mission as president was to focus more effort on grassroots organizing, especially around issues of environmental justice, and to attract more young members by spreading the message through such popular media vehicles as MTV and the Internet. He was president in 1998 when the club members voted against a controversial and well-publicized proposal for the club to take a stance against immigration to the United States as a response to overpopulation pressure in this country. Instead, the club vowed to continue work on global population stabilization. During Werbach's term, the Sierra Club also asked President Clinton to cease logging in national forests, a position the club had never advocated previously. He helped lower the average age of U.S. voters by a decade (from 47 to 37 years). He also helped pass the strongest clean air standards in national history. Werbach has gained much attention, both supportive and incredulous, for his proposal to drain Lake Powell by demolishing the Glen Canyon Dam. The dam was built in 1963 after Sierra Club president David Brower agreed that the Sierra Club would accept that dam in return for the federal government's not damming the Green and Yampa Rivers at Echo Park in Dinosaur National Monument. Brower had never seen Glen Canyon, but later when he did have a chance to tour the magnificent site before it was submerged, he realized his mistake. Brower has regretted that compromise ever since. Werbach's proposal to drain Lake Powell has garnered the official support of the Sierra Club, which works with the Glen Canyon Institute to further the dam's demolition.

Werbach founded and heads Act Now Productions, whose first project was to produce *The Thin Green Line*, a newsmagazine that profiled environmental activists and their struggles. for monthly broadcast on the Outdoor Life Network cable channel. Werbach described his interest in the medium of television to Jennifer Hattam of *Sierra*, "TV is signal-rich, but content-poor, while the environmental movement is content-rich, but signal-poor. Our goal is to take the great stories that need to be told to a medium that needs substance." As Act Now evolved, it began to offer services to businesses wishing to become more sustainable, and share this commitment with potential clients through consulting, outreach, and creative services. One of its largest contracts was with Wal-Mart and Sam's Club, for which it developed the Personal Sustainability Project, through which it offered training in sustainable lifestyles to employees, with the goal of improving employee health and promoting community engagement. Act Now has many other corporate clients as well, including Proctor & Gamble, Kaiser Permanente, and organizations like Amnesty International, the National Wildlife Foundation, and CARE. In 2008, Act Now joined Saatchi & Saatchi marketing firm creating a new company, Saatchi & Saatchi S, in which Werbach will bring sustainability to the firm's clients.

Werbach remains involved with the environmental organizations as well. He gave a dramatic speech to his colleagues in the environmental movement in December, 2004, when hope among environmentalists was at a low point, following the reelection of the indiscutabley anti-environmental George W. Bush administration. Werbach declared environmentalism dead, because it relies on win or lose fights and spews gloom, and prescribed a different approach: infusing all progressive political movements with a commitment to sustainability, and insisting on a message of hope. Werbach referred to the focus of linguist and political strategist George Lakoff, who holds that the way in which a discussion is "framed" will determine whether the public will accept it. Werbach's speech was widely distributed and discussed on-line.

Werbach was appointed to the board of Greenpeace in 2006. He resides in San Francisco with his wife Lyn and their daughter, Mila.

**BIBLIOGRAPHY**

"Act Now," www.actnowproductions.com; "Babe in the Woods," *People Magazine*, 1996; Chetwynd, Josh, "'Splatter-casting' the Sierra Club's Message," *U.S. News & World Report*, 1997; Hattam, Jennifer, "Werbach Walks 'Thin Green Line,'" *Sierra*, 1999; King, Patricia, "A Sprout for Sierra," *Newsweek*, 1996; McManus, Reed, "Pitchman for the Planet," *Sierra*, 1996; "November 3rd," www.3nov.com; Werbach, Adam, *Act Now, Apologize Later*, 1997; Wilke, Anne W., "Adam Werbach: The Youngest Sierra Club President Is Aiming for the Grassroots—MTV," *E Magazine*, 1997.

## Whealy, Diane, and Kent Whealy
(January 1, 1950– ; April 27, 1946– )
Cofounders of Seed Savers Exchange

Kent and Diane Whealy work to conserve the genetic diversity of garden crops through Seed Savers Exchange (SSE), a private nonprofit organization they founded in 1975. The Whealys have long recognized the need to conserve food crop diversity because of its importance to sustainable agriculture, human nutrition, cultural richness, and evolution—and doing so is becoming ever more critical as biotechnology and profit-based agriculture threaten to intensify genetic erosion. The thousands of members of Seed Savers Exchange are dedicated to systematically collecting, maintaining, and distributing seeds from nonhybrid vegetables, fruits, and grains, thereby saving them from extinction. Seed Savers Exchange operates a 170-acre farm to maintain its collection of endangered food crops and currently preserves more than 18,000 rare heirloom (traditional) varieties there.

Diane Ott Whealy was born in New Hampton, Iowa, on January 1, 1950, and raised in the small town of Festina, Iowa. She attended Winona State University in Winona, Minnesota, but never graduated. Kent Whealy was born in Sioux Falls, South Dakota, on April 27, 1946, and grew up in Wellington, Kansas. He studied at the University of Kansas and received his bachelor's degree in journalism in 1969. In 1971, shortly after their wedding, the Whealys started building a house in the woods of Missouri. Before they finished, however, Diane's grandfather, Baptist John Ott, became ill. Knowing that Grandpa Ott did not want to leave his family farm near St. Lucas, Iowa, they moved to nearby Decorah, Iowa, to care for him. That summer when they started their first garden, Grandpa Ott gave them tips and, more important, seeds from two plants that his parents had brought from Bavaria in the 1870s; one was a large, pink tomato and the other an exquisite deep purple morning glory.

The Whealys learned a lot from Grandpa Ott, and when he died the next winter they wanted to preserve the legacy he had left them. They began seeking out other gardeners using heirloom varieties—varieties that have been passed down through generations—and became more and more aware of the extensive genetic riches of isolated rural gardens. The diversity of these heirloom varieties vastly outnumbers the entire selection offered by the garden seed industry in North America, yet they had never before been systematically collected or preserved. The Whealys also realized that few gardeners comprehended the scope of their garden heritage and how much was in danger of being lost. Each variety has a unique genetic makeup that manifests differences in plant size, taste, drought or disease resistance, adaptability, and other traits. This diversity is the raw material for evolution, which is a prerequisite for survival. The varieties of food plants now in existence represent all of the breeding material that will ever be available for crops of the future; and in order to deal with diseases and pests, as much genetic diversity as possible is needed. When a strain becomes extinct, particular genetic characteristics are lost forever. What made the situation even more urgent was that many of the living heirlooms they found were being maintained by elderly gardeners—and as rural economic conditions deteriorated, younger generations were forced into more urban settings, leaving no one to replant these unique seeds.

In 1975 the Whealys took action and founded Seed Savers Exchange (SSE). By writing to editors of rural newspapers and gardening magazines, they continued to search for gardeners using seeds that had been passed down through generations. At the end of its first year SSE had six members who traded seeds by mail. The next year, Kent Whealy took a job in a print shop to make ends meet, while SSE grew to 29 members. In order to keep track of what seeds were available to other members, and who had them, the Whealys put together a newsletter; this was the start of the SSE yearbook, which has since grown to 500 pages listing 11,500 varieties of seeds. Starting in 1981, SSE also began compiling and publishing an inventory of all non-hybrid seeds available from seed company catalogs and over the years found an alarming rate of genetic erosion. Hundreds of varieties were dropped from catalogs each year, so SSE began to buy up samples of any variety offered only by a single source, establishing a mechanism for saving threatened varieties before they were lost.

By 1981, Kent Whealy was able to quit his printing job, and he and Diane Whealy began working for SSE full-time, although at the time their operation was not grossing more than $3,000 a year. But it continued to expand, and in 1986 SSE purchased Heritage Farm, a 170-acre tract with limestone bluffs and burr oak woods that now houses their headquarters, their Historic Orchard, and their Preservation Gardens. They have spent the past 13 years developing Heritage Farm into an extensive professional facility. Twenty-three acres of certified organic gardens are open to the public from April to December, and thousands of people visit each year.

In the Historic Orchard, the most diverse public orchard in the United States, 700 varieties of 19th-century apples and 200 kinds of grapes are now maintained and displayed. These orchards are a hedge against the genetic erosion that has been exhausting apple crops—at the turn of the twentieth century there were 7,000 varieties in North America, but fewer than 1,000 of those remain and are steadily dying out. On another part of the farm, the Whealys keep a herd of extremely rare Ancient White Park cattle, a 2,000-year-old breed from the British Isles.

Currently Heritage Farm preserves a vast, ever-increasing collection of seeds that recently exceeded 24,000 varieties of tomatoes, lettuce, watermelons, and beans, among others. The seeds are kept in cold storage vaults, and each year up to 2,000 endangered varieties are planted in the organic Preservation Gardens to multiply seeds, which are then processed and heat-sealed into foil packets and stored in seed vaults. Any remaining seeds are then available to SSE's thousands of members. Distributing and planting heirloom seeds as widely as possible helps ensure their survival, and the Whealys' mission is to get these heirlooms into as many gardens as possible across North America. SSE publishes *Seed to Seed*, a guide to help other gardeners seed save, with instructions for saving seeds from 160 types of vegetables, and what they need for healthy growth, pollination, care and harvest.

In 1989 Diane founded the Flower and Herb Exchange (FHE), a separate organization patterned after SSE. Many of the thousands of varieties of heirloom flowers and herbs offered through FHE have never been available through seed catalogs, having always been passed down from generation to generation within families.

In recognition of their work, Kent and Diane Whealy received honorary doctorates from Luther College in 1991. Kent Whealy was also awarded a MacArthur Fellowship in 1990 for his efforts to conserve genetic resources. With part of the award money, he expanded the scope of the search for heirloom seeds to other countries. In 1992 he started developing Seed Savers International, a network of plant collectors rescuing food crops in foreign countries. Many Eastern European countries have an extremely rich variety of traditional food crops, with seeds still being produced by gardeners and farmers. But Western agricultural technology and seeds are currently encroaching on even the remotest areas, threatening these fragile genetic resources. Seed Savers International has hosted several trips to Eastern Europe and the former Soviet Union to gather seeds, an effort that brought more than 4,000 seed varieties from 30 countries to Heritage Farm.

SSE and Heritage Farm have served as a model for dozens of similar organizations in the United States and overseas. The Whealys' efforts to raise national awareness of heirloom varieties and the dangers of genetic erosion are clearly paying off, with new varieties of fruits, vegetables and flowers beginning to be mainstreamed, showing up in seed company catalogs.

## BIBLIOGRAPHY

Eddison, Sydney, "Saving Seeds for Future Generations," *Organic Gardening*, 1999; Fowler, Cary, and Pat Mooney, *Shattering: Food, Politics, and the Loss of Genetic Diversity*, 1990; Geeslin, Ned, "Kent Whealy's Seedy Operation Provides Garden Variety Veggies from Centuries Past," *People Weekly*, 1987; "Seed Savers," www.seedsavers.org; Sullivan, Dan, "The Stories Seeds Tell," *Organic Gardening*, 2003.

## White, Gilbert F.

(November 26, 1911–October 5, 2006)
Geographer, Natural Hazards Specialist

Geographer Gilbert White devoted his career to understanding—and helping change—how people deal with natural hazards, especially flooding. Starting as a young man during Pres. FRANKLIN D. ROOSEVELT's New Deal administration and continuing throughout his 70-year career, White proposed creative responses to flooding that were much less environmentally harmful than previous approaches. White also made major contributions to other twentieth-century challenges, including water management, water pollution, the environmental effects of dams and reservoirs, desertification, nuclear war, nuclear waste disposal, and global climate change. In all of his efforts, White was a leader in coordinating interdisciplinary work and steering it to influence public policy decisions.

Gilbert Fowler White was born on November 26, 1911, in Chicago to Mary (Guthrie) and Arthur White. Neither of them had attended college, yet both felt it would be of value to their children, so they settled close to the University of Chicago so that their children would be able to attend the university and its Lab School. White spent summers from the time he was ten years old at a ranch of which his family was a part owner, on the Upper Tongue River in Wyoming. It was at the ranch that White first became aware of the environmental consequences of land use; in his biographical essay for *Geographical Voices* (2000), he recalled community debates that asked "When and how was the forest land over-grazed? When was there inadequate drainage leading to soil degradation? What systems of land use made for prosperity or poverty in the local community?"

White graduated from the University of Chicago with an S.B. in 1932 and an M.S. in 1934, both in geography. While at the university he was especially influenced by his professor Harlan Barrows, who had described geography as human ecology in 1923 and who urged White to take classes in plant ecology and urban ecology. As a Quaker, White had already decided by this time to guide his professional life according to the same constructive, nonviolent principles that he wanted to follow in his personal life. He was attracted to geography for its potential to help people live better, in greater harmony with the earth's natural processes.

In 1934 White left Chicago at the invitation of Barrows to work with the New Deal administration on natural resource management issues. Working on reports for the Mississippi Valley Committee, the National Resources Planning Board, and the National Resources Committee, White focused on flood and drought mitigation, searching for a systematic way to analyze social costs and benefits of different uses of the land, especially land vulnerable to floods and droughts. Far ahead of his time, White proposed that federal financing of flood-control dams in California be contingent on state regulation of human occupation of floodplains. His work resulted in his Ph.D. dissertation, "Human Adjustment to Floods," which suggested that single structural solutions, such as dams, levees, and seawalls, be supplemented with multiple solutions adapted to local and geographic context. White continued to expand on these recommendations throughout his career, suggesting such damage-reducing measures as better forecasting and warning, evacuation planning, flood-proofing of buildings, land use planning and floodplain zoning, and flood insurance. He has insisted throughout his career that intensive human occupation of floodplains only invites disaster and that better land use planning could help prevent flood catastrophes while making better use of the natural resources of the floodplain.

White worked nights to complete his dissertation with the help of his fiancée, Anne Underwood, while working during the day from 1940 to 1942 for the executive office of Pres. Franklin D. Roosevelt, handling all legislative matters that pertained to land and water issues. White was granted his Ph.D. from the University of Chicago in 1942. When the United States entered World War II after the bombing of Pearl Harbor, White, who was a pacifist conscientious objector, decided to leave government service so as not to be contributing to the war effort. He traveled to France in 1942 to work with a Quaker refugee relief effort until 1943, when he and 133 other Americans were detained by the Germans. They were held for 13 months in Baden-Baden, during which time White and the other detainees formed their own informal academy. White taught geography to the children, studied German and Russian, and gave a seminar on contemporary geographic theories. When he returned to the United States, he married Anne Underwood, with whom he would enjoy a long marriage and partnership.

Working through the Quaker-run American Friends Service Committee during the war and immediately afterwards, White helped with relief efforts in India, China, and Germany, before being offered in 1946 the presidency of Haverford College in Haverford, Pennsylvania, a position he would hold until 1955. At Haverford, a Quaker college, he increased the endowment, doubled the faculty, and decreased the size of the student body so that everyone could know each other. He taught one course per year in natural resources conservation and continued to serve on government commissions, including the Hoover Commission Task Force on Natural Resources, the United Nations Committee on Integrated River Development, and the new United Nations Educational, Scientific, and Cultural Organization (UNESCO) Advisory Committee on Arid Zone Research. He enjoyed the small college atmosphere but decided to leave the field of administration after Margaret Mead, an anthropology professor at the nearby University of Pennsylvania, warned him that by continuing to climb the administrative ladder, he would never have time to further his research. White realized that she was right and accepted a position as chairman of the Geography Department of the University of Chicago in 1955.

White remained at Chicago for 14 years, supervising the doctoral dissertations of students on groundbreaking topics, ranging from floodplain management problems to waste disposal. Although he continued to participate in high-level commissions dealing with international water planning and won awards for his teaching at Chicago, one of his most satisfying experiences during this period was to study the household use of water in East Africa with his wife, Anne, and medical researcher David Bradley. During this 1966 research project, they studied how more than 700 households in 34 different locations decided how much water to draw from the local water source and how it would be used. They measured the costs to the families in time, calories, and money; the health implications; and the way in which the family determined which source of water to use. This was the first study of its type and was eminently useful to water resource managers. More than 30 years later, an international team studied water use at the same sites to see how conditions and practices had changed.

After 14 years on the faculty at Chicago, the Whites moved to Boulder, Colorado, where he taught geography and headed the Institute for Behavioral Science (IBS) for the University of Colorado. Through the IBS, White and other geographers dealing with natural hazards collaborated with people from other fields, broadening both the scope and the potential audience of their work. White joined with a colleague in recommending the establishment of the Natural Hazards Research Applications and Information Center at the IBS; he served as its first director from 1976 to 1984 and then again from 1992 to 1994.

While working with the Scientific Committee on Problems of the Environment (SCOPE) during the 1970s to evaluate the problems of man-made lakes, White became concerned about the consequences of these and other global changes caused by humans. In 1979, he joined with Mostafa Tolba, director of the United Nations Environmental Programme, in issuing a statement about the dangers facing global life support systems. He was a member of an advisory group on greenhouse gases from 1986 to 1990.

White's complete list of committee memberships and affiliations is too numerous to be mentioned here, but those that stand out include his chairing of the American Friends Service Committee from 1963 to 1969, the Advisory Panel on Reducing Earthquake Losses for the Office of Technology Assessment in 1994, and the Committee on Sustainable Water Supplies for the Middle East of the National Research Council in 1996, through which he helped obtain a consensus on water management issues from Israeli, Palestinian, and Jordanian water experts. Additional work of environmental importance was through his work with the Lower Mekong Coordinating Committee in 1969, the SCOPE Steering Committee on the Environmental Consequences of Nuclear War from 1983 to 1988, and the Aral Sea Basin Diagnostic Panel in 1993. White received numerous honorary degrees and awards for his efforts, including the United Nations Sasakawa International Environmental Prize (1985), the Tyler Prize for Environmental Achievement (1987), the Volvo Environmental Prize (1995), the National Academy of Science Public Service Medal (2000), and the 2000 Millennium Award from the International Water Resources Association.

White died on October 5, 2006, at his home in Boulder, Colorado.

## BIBLIOGRAPHY

Hinshaw, Robert E., *Living with Nature's Extremes: The Life of Gilbert Fowler White*, 2006; Platt, Rutherford H., Tim O'Riordan, and Gilbert F. White, "Classics in Human Geography Revisited: White G.F. 1945: *Human adjustment to floods*," *Progress in Human Geography*, 1997; White, Gilbert, F., "Geographer's Autobiographical Essay," *Geographical Voices*, ed. Peter Gould and Forrest Pitts, 2000; White, Gilbert, F., *Human Adjustment to Floods*, University of Chicago Research Paper 29, 1942; White, Gilbert, F., David J. Bradley, and Anne U. White, *Drawers of Water: Domestic Water Use in East Africa*, 1972.

## White, Lynn, Jr.
(April 29, 1907–March 30, 1987)
Medievalist

Author of the 1967 essay "The Historical Roots of Our Ecological Crisis," Lynn White Jr.'s ideas have profoundly shaped the debate about the relation between religion and the environment. White traced the roots of Western attitudes about nature to the medieval period, particularly the way medieval Christian thought was based on a belief in humankind's "dominion" over nature. White was both praised and attacked for this article, which was seen as anti-Christian by some theologians and laypersons and as asking fundamentally necessary questions by others. By providing a rigorous examination of science, technology, and theology in medieval Europe, White reshaped twentieth-century ideas about ecology.

Lynn Townsend White Jr. was born on April 29, 1907, in San Francisco. White's father was a clergyman, and White followed in his footsteps to Stanford University, earning a B.A. in 1928, and to Union Theological Seminary for an M.A. in 1929. He went on to Harvard University to earn a second M.A. in 1930 and a Ph.D. in 1934. His first academic job was as an instructor in history at Princeton University from 1933 to 1937. He was hired at Stanford University in 1937, where he earned tenure and stayed until 1943, at which time he was hired as president of Mills College in California. In 1958 he became a professor of history at the University of California at Los Angeles (UCLA), where he remained until the end of his career.

When he resumed his teaching career at UCLA, White began his work on medieval technology, which resulted in the publication in 1962 of *Medieval Technology and Social Change*. This work challenges two basic assumptions about medieval history. First, White argues against the belief that the Middle Ages were the "dark" ages, devoid of science and culture. White shows that a number of fundamental technological changes began in the medieval period, including the development of improved plow technology, widespread use of wind and water power, and major advances in machine design. Second, White argues that medieval Europe was much more interactive with the far and near East than had previously been thought. Studies that place greatest importance on the Renaissance period in the development of present-day ideas, White argues, underestimate the cultural and economic exchanges between medieval Europe, Asia, and Africa. White makes a strong case for taking seriously the Middle Ages, rather than relegating them to a footnote between Rome and the Renaissance.

In 1967 White followed up on these ideas with "The Historical Roots of Our Ecological Crisis," published first as an article in *Science*. Here White made an even stronger case for viewing the medieval period as the source of modern ideas about science and technology. The Middle Ages, for White, provided the "psychic foundations" of the spirit of modern technology. White locates this spirit in a number of trends within medieval culture. One of these was the church's assault on paganism, with its animistic view of nature; this assault ensured that reverence toward the natural world would assume an air of blasphemy. Another important element of medieval thought was its emphasis on the dichotomy between spirit and matter; matter comes to be seen as inert, devoid of soul, and hence available for use without ethical qualm. Third, the medieval church emphasized those elements of the Genesis story that give humankind dominion over nature, characterizing the earth as created solely for human use. Finally, White argues that medieval monasticism prepared Western culture to embrace technological development with great energy. European monks in this period celebrated labor as integral to worship, a tenet of faith seen in White's readings of medieval manuscripts and cathedrals. Cathedrals celebrate mechanical clocks and organs, two of the most complex machines operating in pre-modern Europe. White argues that this reflects and helps to create an attitude that sanctioned technology as virtuous and reverent. These trends added up to a tendency to exploit and abuse nature, he believes, and if we are to come to terms with present-day ecological crisis, we need to re-envision a less anthropocentric view of the natural world. White closes with an examination of the ideas of St. Francis of Assisi, in whom White finds a way to recover a respect for nature within a Christian framework. St. Francis proposed equality among all creatures, including humankind, and White urges a return to a radical Franciscan ecology.

"The Historical Roots of Our Ecological Crisis" evoked a storm of controversy. Many theologians took up White's call for a new Christian ecological theology, while some Christians expressed outrage at what they saw as White's anti-Christian bigotry. Today the perspective that there is something inherently negative in Christian beliefs about the environment is called the Lynn White Thesis, and it is still generating articles and books. White continued to develop his own views in this area, many of which are collected in two volumes, *Dynamo and Virgin Reconsidered* (1971) and *Medieval Religion and Technology* (1978). In 1964 White founded UCLA's Center for Medieval and Renaissance Studies, which he directed until 1970. White retired from UCLA in 1974 and continued to write, speak, and teach as an emeritus member of the faculty until shortly before his death. Lynn White Jr. suffered a heart attack at his home and died on March 30, 1987.

**BIBLIOGRAPHY**
Bennett, John, "On Responding to Lynn White: Ecology and Christianity," *Ohio Journal of Religious Studies*, 1977; Ruether, Rosemary, "Biblical Vision of the Ecological Crisis," *Christian Century*, 1978; Whitney, Elspeth, "Lynn White, Ecotheology, and History," *Environmental Ethics*, 1993; Wolkomir, Michelle, Michael Futreal, Eric Woodrum, and Thomas Hoban, "Substantive Belief and Environmentalism," *Social Science Quarterly*, 1997.

## Whitman, Walt
(May 31, 1819–March 26, 1892)
Poet

Walt Whitman is the grandfather of American poetry. What Dante is for Italy, Shakespeare to England, Walt Whitman is to the United States. The Good Gray Poet is best known for his *Leaves of Grass* (1855). The most quoted book of American poetry, *Leaves of Grass* is a declaration of personal independence and the interdependence of all things. Poet Walt Whitman believed that the wild places in the United States were demonstrative of the national character, and he promoted the American landscape as the primary agent of Americanness. Environmentalists, naturalists, and general readers alike have been nourished by the enormous optimism of *Leaves of Grass*, and Whitman's pioneering spirit led many to take to the open road and explore this country's wilderness.

Walter Whitman was born at West Hills, Long Island, New York, on May 31, 1819, to Walter Whitman Sr. and Louisa Van Velsor Whitman. The second of eight children, Whitman came from long-established native stock, landowners, farmers, builders, and horse breeders. Falling on hard times, the Whitmans moved from West Hills in 1823 to Brooklyn, where Walter Sr. worked as a carpenter. During a Fourth of July parade through the streets of Brooklyn in 1825, Revolutionary War hero General Lafayette stooped down to kiss six-year-old Walt, who was watching the procession.

He was educated by his attentive parents and in public schools until he was 11. He showed an early knack for journalism; by the age of 12, he was already writing what he called "sentimental bits" for the *Long Island Patriot* (edited by Samuel E. Clements), and during his teens he published a couple of pieces in the *New York Mirror*. At 20, Whitman had saved enough money from teaching in country schools to purchase a press and type, and he briefly published the weekly *The Long Islander* of Huntington. Whitman did almost all the work, including deliveries throughout Long Island on horseback. Recognizing it as an unsustainable venture, he found work at *The Aurora*, *The Tattler*, and, later, a good position editing *The Brooklyn Eagle*. He took an interest in Democratic Party politics, wrote an early account of a base-

Walt Whitman (Library of Congress, Prints & Photographs Division, LC-USZ62-79938)

ball game in Brooklyn, and also covered a series of lectures by New England transcendentalist RALPH WALDO EMERSON. In 1848, Whitman was relieved of his editorship, as his political positions were contrary to those of the publisher, and he took the opportunity to travel for the remainder of the year. With his brother Jeff, Whitman went to New Orleans for a brief stint at a newspaper and traveled by boat to St. Louis, LaSalle, Chicago, Milwaukee, and Buffalo before returning to New York for more freelance journalism.

The constraints of editorial and newspaper reporting clearly could not contain Whitman's poetic voice. In his early thirties he declared: "I will also be a master after my own kind, making the poems of emotions, as they pass or stay, the poems of freedom, and the exposé of personality—singing in high tones democracy and the New World of it through These States." Whitman set out to write the poetry of America in the American language. He rejected conventional literary themes, rhyme, and formalism, anything that reflected the old world poetic traditions and social orders in favor of something new and bold, which he felt embodied the American landscape. The time between 1850 and 1855 was an incubation period for Whitman the poet. He read a lot and took long walks on the beach before penning the first versions of *Leaves of Grass*, which made its print debut on July 6, 1855, selling for two dollars. He would continue to revise and expand the work in subsequent editions his entire life.

The original edition did not include titles for the poems, but once they were added in the 1860 edition, Americans would know the best of them: "Song of Myself," "The Sleepers," "I Sing the Body Electric." Although the book's principal focus is the self, it also includes Whitman's vision of the United States in all its wild, bucolic, and industrious glory. From "Song of Myself," verse 31:

> I believe a leaf of grass is no less than the
>     journeywork of stars,
> And the pismire is equally perfect, and a
>     grain of sand, and the egg of the wren
> And the tree-toad is a chef-d'ouevre for
>     the highest,
> And the running blackberry would adorn
>     the parlors of heaven,
> And the narrowest hinge in my hand puts
>     to scorn all machinery,
> And the cow crunching with depressed head
>     surpasses any statue,
> And a mouse is a miracle enough to stagger
>     sextillions of infidels,
> And I could come every afternoon of my
>     life to look at the farmer's girl boiling her
>     iron tea-kettle and baking shortcake.

Whitman's glorification of nature and the human spirit satisfied Ralph Waldo Emerson's criteria for what an American poet ought to bring to the national culture, and he said so in a 1856 letter to the poet. Whitman also gave a copy to HENRY DAVID THOREAU, and his response was also laudatory, but not without reservations about the more sensual passages in the work. Thoreau wrote in a letter to Harrison Blake that he thought Whitman "has spoken more truth than any American or modern that I know. I have found his poem exhilarating, encouraging.... Though rude and sometimes ineffectual, it is a great primitive poem—an alarm or trumpet-note ringing through the American camp." Whitman consulted naturalist and nature writer JOHN BURROUGHS on the hermit thrush, the symbolic bird in his elegy to Abraham Lincoln, "When Lilacs Last in the Dooryard Bloom'd" (*Drumtaps*), and generally drew as much information from naturalists and other nature writers as he could. In kind, Whitman's raw exuberance and love for life found in his "Song of the Open Road," "Song of the Broad Axe," or "Song of the Rolling Earth" had a profound influence on Burroughs and JOHN MUIR and more recent generations of naturalists and nature writers. Many took Whitman's lead, who, upon seeing "the white-topped mountains point up in the distance," flung out his fancies toward them.

During the Civil War years, Whitman worked in Union army hospitals, a friend and comrade of the sick and wounded. He received a clerkship in the Department of the Interior from President Lincoln, but was later removed by Secretary Harland on account of the unorthodox character of poetical writings found in his desk. *Drumtaps* (1865) recounted the war years and included his elegy to Abraham Lincoln, whose assassination affected the poet greatly. Whitman worked at the attorney general's office until 1873, when, owing to a paralytic shock, he retired to his brother's home in Camden, New Jersey. The sudden death of his mother, a few months later, led to a relapse and partial paralysis. It was after this stroke that Whitman sought peace in the wild. Weak from illness and still depressed from the experience of the Civil War, Whitman retreated to the woods and creeks where he found solitude from "the whole cast-iron civilized life." His later writings, *Democratic Vistas* (1871) and *Specimen Days* (1882), were more reflective. Whitman's vision for the United States was being corrupted by ambition and urban industrialism. The pastoral idyll—a reflection of the Jeffersonian farmer and the source, Whitman believed, of American identity—was rapidly disappearing. Whitman also intimated in his poetry that the American was becoming overcivilized. "Without enough wilderness America will change," he asserted. "Democracy, with its myriad personalities and increasing sophistication, must be fibred and vitalized by regular contact with outdoor growths—animals, trees, sun warmth and free skies—or it will dwindle and pale."

The ecstatic spirit of *Leaves of Grass* that earned Whitman his national and international renown eventually evolved to a somewhat melancholic but empathetic view. Whitman died on March 26, 1892, in Camden, New Jersey, where he is buried. Although Walt Whitman was never awarded literary prizes and accolades during his lifetime, there are schools, bridges, and parks all over the United States bearing his name.

**BIBLIOGRAPHY**

Allen, Gay Wilson, *The Solitary Singer: A Critical Biography of Walt Whitman*, 1967; Canby, Henry S., *Walt Whitman, An American: A Study in Biography*, 1943; Kaplan, Justin, *Walt Whitman: A Life*, 1982; Whitman, Walt, *The Collected Writings of Walt Whitman*, ed. Gay Wilson Allen and Sculley Bradley, 1963; Woodress, James, *Critical Essays on Walt Whitman*, 1983.

## Willcox, Louisa
(May 9, 1955– )
Wildlife Advocate

Louisa Willcox's assertiveness and resolve have helped to make her one of the most highly effective and recognized environmental leaders in the Rocky Mountain West. She has held leadership positions in several conservation organizations in the region, beginning with her ten-year directorship of the Greater Yellowstone Coalition (GYC)—during which time she fought to protect the unique ecosystem of the area surrounding Yellowstone National Park. She also became closely involved in the restoration of the grizzly bear, a threatened species that is integral to a healthy balance in Rocky Mountain ecological systems. To this end, she served as director of Wild Forever, a grizzly bear recovery project based in Bozeman, Montana, then as project coordinator for the Bozeman-based Sierra Club Grizzly Bear Ecosystems Project, and currently is a senior wildlife advocate for the Natural Resources Defense Council.

Louisa Willcox was born on May 9, 1955, and raised in a Quaker family in Newton Square, Pennsylvania. Her father, John, was a mechanical engineer who died when she was 12, leaving her mother, Joyce, to raise Louisa and her two siblings alone. During her teenage years, Willcox spent summers working on ranches in Wyoming and Montana and fell in love with the West. After graduating from high school in Pennsylvania, she returned to Wyoming and became an expedition leader for the National Outdoor Leadership School (NOLS), teaching mountaineering, kayaking, skiing, and desert hiking. For the next nine years, in between attending Williams College in Massachusetts, Willcox continued conducting NOLS expeditions. In 1980 she finished her bachelor's degree at Williams, majoring in English with a concentration in environmental studies and graduating *magna cum laude*. She then attended the School of Forestry at Yale University, earning a master's degree in forestry in 1984, with an emphasis on natural resource policy and ecosystem dynamics. From 1984 to 1986, she was field studies director of the Teton Science School in Jackson, Wyoming, organizing, planning, and instructing all residential field ecology programs.

In 1986 Willcox was named program director for the Greater Yellowstone Coalition, an alliance of environmental groups founded in 1983 to conserve and protect the greater Yellowstone ecosystem, an area of about 18 million square miles centered around Yellowstone and Grand Teton National Parks. Willcox, with her knowledge of the region's ecology and her political savvy, was uniquely suited to the position. Her aggressive style also served her well as she coordinated the advocacy efforts of the group's 140 member organizations, lobbied agencies and public officials involved in Yellowstone conservation issues, and did fundraising and public speaking.

As part of her work for the GYC, Willcox fought a 1990 request by Crown Butte Mines Inc., the U.S. subsidiary of a giant Canadian conglomerate, Noranda Inc., to mine for gold on Henderson Mountain in Montana. The proposed site was near Yellowstone National Park, and Willcox believed pollution from the mine would harm Yellowstone's intricate ecosystem. Though Crown Butte officials insisted their mine would be environmentally safe, their plan included dumping five million cubic tons of toxic residue into a mile-wide pit located only two miles from Yellowstone's northern boundary. Willcox went into high gear to fight the mine, speaking at informal gatherings of Wyoming and Montana residents and making sure government officials reviewed the GYC's scientific studies of the region's aquatic ecology, including the potential for mine runoff to leach into groundwater.

Well aware that politics would also influence the decision, Willcox rounded up 12 Montana residents who opposed the mine and flew with them to lobby Montana congressman Pat Williams in Washington, D.C. The issue had not been resolved by the time Willcox left GYC, but eventually an agreement was reached among the Clinton administration, Crown Butte Mines, Inc., and GYC for a buy-out of the proposed mining project.

Willcox and the GYC also battled the Church Universal and Triumphant (CUT), a controversial New Age–oriented religious group headquartered near the north entrance of Yellowstone Park. The church planned a series of developments up and down the 50-mile-long Paradise Valley in Montana, close to the Wyoming border, and wanted to tap a hot spring for a swimming pool and to heat an office building. Fearing that the drilling could potentially damage the area's elaborate underground geothermal structure, the GYC loudly opposed the development, and thanks in part to its efforts, the U.S. Senate placed a moratorium on all drilling in geothermal areas until proper studies could be carried out. In 1994 the moratorium was lifted after the U.S. Geological Survey concluded that the plans would not affect geothermal features in the park; GYC along with three other local environmental groups then filed suit to try to block development on the 33,000 acres of church land, citing environmental concerns. Several years later, after running into financial troubles, CUT agreed to relinquish its geothermal water rights and to sell, trade, or place conservation easements on 7,850 acres of land on the north edge of Yellowstone, opening up public access and protecting valuable wildlife habitat.

Willcox left GYC in 1995 to become director of Wild Forever, a newly formed collaborative grizzly bear project based in Bozeman, Montana, that includes the Sierra Club, the National Audubon Society, Earthjustice Legal Defense Fund, and the Greater Yellowstone Coalition. Listed as threatened under the Endangered Species Act, grizzlies have been eliminated from 99 percent of their original range over the past 120 years. They once numbered as many as 100,000 and ranged throughout the mountains and plains of the West, but they have been reduced to about 1,000 bears, most of them in Yellowstone and Glacier National Parks and Montana's Bob Marshall Wilderness. Wild Forever develops and coordinates grassroots efforts to establish a strong grizzly bear recovery program that guarantees adequate habitat protection—which entails setting aside large roadless areas and recreating corridors to link isolated bear populations. In addition, Willcox and Wild Forever stood up to the U.S. Fish and Wildlife Service to challenge its 1993 Grizzly Bear Recovery Plan, a proposal to de-list the Yellowstone population of grizzly bears from its threatened species status and remove existing protections.

In 1998 the Wild Forever effort folded into the Bozeman-based Sierra Club Grizzly Bear Ecosystems Project, a coalition of about 60 regional, local, and national conservation groups working to restore and recover grizzly bears in the lower 48 states. Willcox was the project coordinator for the new group until 2002, helping coordinate the advocacy and communication efforts of the groups and working closely with members of the press.

Currently she is senior wildlife advocate for the Natural Resources Defense Council (NRDC). From her headquarters in Livingston, Montana, she monitors decisions affecting the health of grizzlies, wolves, and other endangered species and their habitat. To achieve long-term and lasting recovery of grizzlies and wolves, Willcox is promoting the conservation of large connected ecosystems in the Northern Rockies and adjacent lands in Canada, according to the principles of conservation biology. Recognizing that excessive human-caused mortality remains a significant obstacle to recovery of wolves and bears, she is also working on new efforts to improve human-carnivore co-existence practices.

As with most conservation efforts, the work is never done. In 2007 the federal government de-listed grizzlies under the Endangered Species Act, which meant that protections were weakened outside of national parks and designated "recovery zones." NRDC and 10 other conservation organizations are challenging the decision in court. In the meantime, climate change is damaging food sources and habitat, adding a new challenge to the fight for survival.

In addition to her work with the NRDC, Willcox is president of Grizzly People, a grassroots organization dedicated to preserving bears and their habitat, and to raising the level of affection and concern that humans feel for grizzlies, so that it is on par with how people feel about dolphins and whales.

Willcox lives in Livingston, Montana with her husband, Douglas Honnold, a lawyer with Earthjustice, who collaborates with Willcox's efforts to preserve wilderness and endangered species.

**BIBLIOGRAPHY**
"Grizzly People," www.grizzlypeople.com; "NOLS—Profile: Louisa Willcox," www.nols.edu/about/profiles/alumni/louisa_willcox.shtml; Reed, Susan, "Dig They Mustn't: A Yellowstone Guardian Opposes a Gold Mine," *People Weekly*, 1993; "Switchboard, from NRDC, Louisa Willcox's Blog," www.switchboard.nrdc.org/blogs/lwillcox; Willcox, Louisa, "The Last Grizzlies of the American West: The Long Hard Road to Recovery," *Endangered Species Update*, 1997; Willcox, Louisa, "Bear With Us: An Alternative Path to Grizzly Recovery in the Lower 48 States," NRDC, 2004, www.nrdc.org/wildlife/animals/grizzlyrecovery/contents.asp; Willcox, Louisa, "The Yellowstone Experience: The Use of Science, with Humility, in Public Policy," *BioScience*, 1995.

## Wille, Chris

(February 23, 1947– )
Chief of the Rainforest Alliance's Sustainable Agriculture Network

Working with Central and South American conservation organizations, conservation broker Chris Wille has convinced the tropical fruit-growing industry that it pays to use environmentally friendly cultivation methods that work with nature rather than against it and to treat workers well so that they may lead healthy and dignified lives. Wille and his partners in the Rainforest Alliance have designed guidelines for responsible agroproduction, and award growers who follow these guidelines with the ECO-O.K. The ECO-O.K. Program was so successful that Wille was able to develop the Sustainable Agriculture Network, a coalition of Latin American conservation groups interested in the same area, that have developed best management practices and standards for environmentally and socially responsible cultivation. Wille's work is especially effective and unique because he works with an industry commonly cited for environmental damage with the specific goal of helping growers become more humanitarian and less damaging to the environment.

Chris Wille was born in Porterville, California, on February 23, 1947. He credits his dedication to the environment to a very intense early interest in butterflies. He received a B.S. in wildlife science from Oregon State University and an M.S. in English from Oklahoma State University. Wille was primed for his work in ecocertification by nearly 20 years of service to various conservation entities, in-

Chris Wille (Photograph by David Dudenhoefer, Rainforest Alliance)

cluding the National Audubon Society, the National Wildlife Federation, the Guam Department of Fisheries and Wildlife, and the Oklahoma Department of Wildlife Conservation. In each of these jobs, Wille specialized in disseminating information on conservation: editing publications, producing television and radio programs, and developing environmental education curricula.

Wille and his wife, DIANE JUKOFSKY, were two of the founding members of the Rainforest Alliance, an international conservation organization whose mission is to "develop and promote economically viable and socially desirable alternatives to the destruction of this endangered, biologically diverse natural resource." The Rainforest Alliance grew out of the world's first major rain forest conference ("Tropical Forests, Interdependence, and Responsibility," held in 1988 in New York City). At a time when most rain forest activists were boycotting rain forest wood products, the Rainforest Alliance united environmentalists, scientists, government officials, and industry representatives to design practical yet environmentally stringent guidelines for loggers.

The result was a program called Smartwood that stimulated genuine change in the logging industry by certifying operators that meet certain standards.

Observing the success of Smartwood and the destruction wrought by banana companies in Costa Rica, Wille and Jukofsky organized multidisciplinary teams to study the problems associated with fruit farming and to recommend solutions. After nearly two years of work, the conservationists, scientists, community leaders, and banana industry representatives had found a middle ground, and standards were written for socially and environmentally responsible banana production. Specially trained teams of agronomists and biologists began inspecting farms, using the standards as guidelines. The banana industry was reluctant at first, and only small, independent farmers opened their farms to the inspectors. But eventually, Chiquita Brands—the industry leader—joined the Better Banana Program and enrolled farms throughout the region. Now, the banana industry is changing rapidly, controlling and reducing use of agrochemicals, improving conditions for workers, reforesting, protecting rivers, managing wastes, recycling, and seeking better relations with local communities. The program prohibits further deforestation for banana farms.

Meanwhile, Wille was brainstorming with a group of biologists in Guatemala called the Interamerican Foundation for Tropical Research (Fundación Interamericana de Investigación Tropical or FIIT). These naturalists had been studying wildlife populations in coffee farms, one of the few crops that can be grown in harmony with the rain forest. Unfortunately, many coffee farmers throughout the Americas are bulldozing their beautiful old forested farms and replacing them with new, high-tech, "factory farms" that leave no place for wildlife. Wille brought FIIT and the Rainforest Alliance together to create another certification program, ECO-O.K., which certifies ecofriendly coffee farms that meet strict standards for wildlife habitat and worker welfare.

Wille guided another group of biologists, the Conservation and Development Corporation (Corporación de Conservación y Desarrollo or CCD) in Ecuador, in using the ECO-O.K. model to create standards for forest-friendly cocoa production. In Brazil, another affiliate group, Instituto de Manejo e Certificacão Florestal e Agrícola (IMAFLORA), directed a two-year, consensus-building effort among sugarcane farmers, workers, and environmentalists to negotiate standards for low-impact sugar production.

In 1998, these groups banded together as the Sustainable Agriculture Network. Although the specific requirements for certification vary from crop to crop and from country to country, they are always based on nine common principles and the three pillars of sustainable agriculture: community well-being, environmental protection, and economic vitality. The standards guide farmers in using nature as an ally on the farm and serving as stewards of soils, waters, wildlife, and other natural assets. On certified farms, the people involved in cultivation and harvest enjoy a safe, dignified, and economically just life, and farmers work in concert with local conservationists to promote a healthy habitat for native wildlife on the farm and in neighboring parks and refuges.

Farmers are interested both for reasons of conscience and profit; they know that many consumers prefer certified products and will pay more for them. Since the program originated in 1990, it has certified more than 100 banana plantations and five coffee farms in Ecuador and Colombia and throughout Central America. With support from the World Bank, El Salvador's leading conservation group, SalvaNATURA, is using the ECO-O.K. standards to evaluate farms in that country and plans to certify 200 farms in two years. The Rainforest Alliance certification programs in 1995 received the coveted Peter F. Drucker Award for Nonprofit Innovation.

**BIBLIOGRAPHY**
"Rainforest Alliance," www.rainforest-alliance.org; Rainforest Alliance, *Rainforest Alliance, Celebrating Ten Years*, 1997.

## Williams, Terry Tempest
(September 8, 1955– )
Writer, Naturalist

Terry Tempest Williams is a celebrated and accomplished writer of natural history, whose books expand on her observations as a naturalist and remind readers to pay attention to the natural world. A native of Utah, she brings to her writing a profound appreciation for the land in which she grew up—and through her example she presents a means for people to locate their own connection to nature. She also conveys a unique perspective on one of the tragic consequences of disregarding the environment—while growing up in Utah, she and her family were exposed to radioactive fallout from nuclear testing, and nine female members of her family eventually contracted cancer. After her mother died from cancer, Williams grew even more active in the environmental movement in her state and has fought for protection of Utah's wild areas.

Terry Tempest was born on September 8, 1955, in Salt Lake City, Utah, and grew up within sight of the Great Salt Lake. Her parents, Diane Dixon and John Henry Tempest

III, raised Terry and her three younger brothers in the Mormon faith, which Terry later described as bestowing her with a strong spiritual appreciation of the land. At the age of five, her grandmother gave her a field guide to western birds, and one of her favorite activities was accompanying her grandmother on bird-watching expeditions to Bear River National Wildlife Refuge. When she was ten her grandmother decided she was old enough to join the Audubon Society on a birding outing to the wetlands surrounding Great Salt Lake. In 1971, when Tempest was 15, the family had a scare when her mother was diagnosed with breast cancer. After a mastectomy she completely recovered (though 12 years later the cancer would reappear in her ovaries).

After high school Tempest attended the University of Utah, where she studied English. She worked part-time in a bookstore in Salt Lake City and was pleasantly surprised one day when a customer approached the register, his arms filled with her favorite nature books. The customer, Brooke Williams, asked her for a date, and six months later, in June 1975, they were married. In 1978, she received her bachelor's degree in English.

Williams's first book, coauthored with Ted Major, was a work for children entitled *The Secret Language of Snow* (1984). It examines over a dozen different types of snow and explains how snow interacts with the environment. The book won a Children's Science Book Award from the New York Academy of Sciences. Also in 1984 she received a master's degree in environmental education from the University of Utah. After graduating, Williams taught Navajo children at the Navajo Reservation in Montezuma Creek, Utah. She found that the children taught her more about environmental education than she had known beforehand, and the experience led to her next book, *Pieces of White Shell: A Journey to Navajoland* (1984). Inspired by the children's' stories and by Navajo legends and rituals, Williams used her gift as a storyteller to describe aspects of Navajo culture that exemplify a sense of respect for the earth. The next year she published *Between Cattails* (1985), a free-verse children's book about the lives of herons, muskrats, grebes, ducks, and other marsh life.

In 1991, with the publication of *Refuge: An Unnatural History of Family and Place*, Williams began to gain significant recognition. In the book, she tells the story of her mother's poignant second battle with cancer, this time ovarian, which claimed her life in 1987. Interwoven with this family history, Williams describes how rising water levels in the Great Salt Lake during this period threatened the fragile wetlands surrounding the lake, important habitat for birds and other marsh species. After her mother's death Williams learned that her family had been exposed to radioactive fallout when the United States performed above-ground nuclear testing at Yucca Flats, Nevada. These tests continued from 1951 to 1962, exposing many people in the region to radiation. She attributes the cancer of her mother, six aunts, and her grandmother to their living downwind of nuclear test sites and describes her anger and frustration at the governmental deceit surrounding the radioactive contamination with which her family and many others in the region grew up. By paralleling the story of her mother's death with descriptions of changes in the Great Salt Lake wetland ecosystems, Williams captures the significance of change in the environment and shows that people can change as a result of their environment too. She also reveals how she drew comfort and even a greater understanding of death from the landscape during the difficult time of her mother's illness, illustrating the importance of the natural world in people's lives.

Three years after *Refuge* came out, Williams published a collection of essays called *An Unspoken Hunger: Stories from the Field* (1994). Though the essays are connected by their central theme of women as intermediaries between human actions and the earth, they cover a wide range of subject matter—from nuclear protesting to life on the African Serengeti. She also focuses on the importance of family and reminds readers of the fragility of life on the planet.

Having become increasingly active in environmental causes since the death of her mother, in the summer of 1995 Williams helped lead a fight against the Utah Public Lands Management Act, a congressional proposal to open 22 million acres of southern Utah's buttes and canyons to commercial development—including mining, logging, oil-drilling, and dam building. She spoke out in opposition to the act before a Senate subcommittee hearing. In addition, she and fellow Utah writer Stephen Trimble persuaded 18 prominent western writers to contribute to a book of essays in defense of Utah's wilderness. These essays were combined into a limited-edition book called *Testimony: Writers in Defense of the Wilderness*, which was handed out to every senator and representative. It became a landmark document in the environmental movement and may have played a role in the eventual defeat of the Utah Public Lands Management Act.

Williams' first two books of the 21st century are composed of essays, poems, meditations, prayers, and dream journal entries. *Leap* (2000) centers around the Hieronymus Bosh tryptich *Paradise, Hell,* and the *Garden of Earthly Delights*, which had always fascinated Williams. *Red* (2001) is about the redrock desert of southern Utah—and the many people of multiple civilations that have lived in and loved it. Infusing all of Williams' writings is a reminder of the importance of preserving natural places, which can only be accomplished through them commitment and engagement of people who love them. Williams' *The Open Space of Democracy* (2003) proposes a model for active democracy that is based on the ethics and politics of place, spirit, and citizen responsibility.

Williams, who has had two biopsies for breast cancer and surgery for a tumor between her ribs diagnosed as borderline malignant, continues to write about the great beauty of the western landscape—and also its misuse. Her connection with her homeland is so great that it pains her to go on trips to make public appearances. She has been the naturalist at the Utah Museum of Natural History and is currently a visiting professor of English at the University of Utah. Williams has received many awards and recognition for her work, including a Guggenheim Fellowship, a Lannan Literary Fellowship, the "Spirit of the West" award from the Mountain-Plains Booksellers Association, and the Lila Wallace-*Reader's Digest* Writer's Award in 2000.

Williams and her husband, an environmental consultant, live in Emigration Canyon, near Salt Lake City, Utah.

**BIBLIOGRAPHY**

Ball, Jena, "The Power of Storytelling," *Mother Earth News*, 2007; Kupfer, David, "Terry Tempest Williams," *The Progressive*, 2005; Lassila, Kathrin Day, "Testimony: Writers of the West Speak on Behalf of Utah Wilderness," *The Amicus Journal*, 1997; Reed, Susan, "Friend of the Earth," *People Weekly*, 1996; Tredinnick, Mark, *The Land's Wild Music: encounters with Barry Lopez, Peter Matthiessen, Terry Tempest Williams, and James Galvin*, 2005; Williams, Terry Tempest, Leap, 2000; Williams, Terry Tempest, *The Open Space of Democracy*, 2004; Williams, Terry Tempest, Pieces of White Shell: A Journey to Navajoland, 1983; Williams, Terry Tempest, *Red*, 2001; Williams, Terry Tempest, *Refuge: An Unnatural History of Family and Place*, 1991; Williams, Terry Tempest, An Unspoken Hunger, 1994.

## Wilson, Diane
(1948– )
Environmental Activist, Founding Member of CODEPINK

Diane Wilson is a fourth-generation commercial shrimper and the mother of five children who became an environmental activist after learning about industrial contamination in her home county of Calhoun, Texas. She also co-founded the women's peace organization, CODEPINK, prior to the U.S. invasion of Iraq in 2003.

Born in 1948, Diane Wilson was born and raised in Seadrift, Texas, a fishing village along the Gulf Coast. Her family has lived and fished in the area for more than 100 years and she carried on the family tradition, working as a commercial fisherwoman aboard her boat, the *SeaBee*.

In 1989, Wilson learned that Formosa Plastics Corporation, the U.S. affiliate of Taiwan-based Formosa Plastics Group, was planning an expansion of its facility at Point Comfort, Texas. After learning more about the chemicals being released and their effects on the bay, nearby communities and fish populations, Wilson called a public meeting. That meeting launched her foray into the world of activism. Recalling that meeting during a 2008 interview, she says she had no intentions of becoming an activist; nor did she consider herself an "environmentalist." She says, "I thought, 'I'm just a fisherwoman and I'm doing what I believe is right.' I didn't have a plan. I just took care of what I had to take care [of] at that moment."

With a high school education, and a self-professed lack of a "natural speaking ability" or leadership skills, Wilson says she didn't feel she had the expertise to be an activist. "In the back of my mind, I was kinda waiting for the right person that was just going to walk up and I was going to say, 'Oh, this is the person that's going to take it over and they're going to be the perfect one.'" Three or four years passed, she says, before she realized she was actually the perfect person to fight Formosa.

"I had a passion for the bay, and that was the key: having a passion."

In her 2005 biography, *An Unreasonable Woman*, Wilson writes about her battle against Formosa. In addition to describing her battles against the company (and the local, state and federal agencies Wilson found lax in their environmental enforcement duties), Wilson describes life along the Texas Gulf Coast, where fish populations are dwindling, fishermen are disappearing, worker safety is compromised and rural economies are rushing to embrace polluting industries in the name of "economic development." Toward the end of the book, she describes the power one person can have:

> There is nothing like the roundabout way an enemy's eye can send fresh inspiration when you need it most. I sit at the dragon's threshold without any men, yet I know that when the final Coast Guard cutter sails off, I won't. I won't leave. I will howl and the rain and the wind will howl in matching octaves above my own and nobody will hear, but we will make a stand. It doesn't take a continent. It doesn't even take a country. Sometimes all it takes is just one unreasonable woman and nature in alliance.

She also contributed a chapter to the 2005 book, *Stop the Next War Now: Effective Responses to Violence and Terrorism*, and in it, writes about how her environmental and anti-war activism are connected:

> My environmental activism flowed into the peace movement, and that flowed into CODEPINK. Just like the ecosystem where I shrimp, it's all connected. The corporations like Formosa and Dupont and Dow are destroying the Texas bays and killing small communities like my town, and the federal government is bombing a whole country to control its oil. It's the same destructive mentality at work.

Today, Wilson still lives in Seadrift, Texas. "It's like the trenches down here," she says.

"It's like hand-to-hand combat." In addition to continuing her fight to keep Formosa and other chemical companies along the Gulf from destroying her beloved bay, she has also turned her sights toward two proposed coal-fired power plants, a liquid natural gas terminal and a nuclear power plant. Having been arrested 19 times due to her activism, Wilson has also learned firsthand of the unjust conditions in county jails across the nation and is involved with the Texas Jail Project. She is also completing a second book, titled *Holy Rollers*, about her upbringing within the Pentecostal Church.

### BIBLIOGRAPHY

Benjamin, Medea and Jodie Evans, *Stop the Next War Now: Effective Responses to Violence and Terrorism*, 2005; Wilson, Diane, *An Unreasonable Woman: A True Story of Shrimpers, Politicos, Polluters and the Fight for Seadrift, Texas*, 2005; Wilson, Kelpie, "An Unreasonable Woman: An Interview with Diane Wilson," truthout.org, March 28, 2006, www.truthout.org/cgi-bin/artman/exec/view.cgi/58/18695.

## Wilson, Edward O.
(June 10, 1929– )
Entomologist

Harvard University entomologist Edward O. Wilson can be credited with inserting "biodiversity" into the public vernacular and has been instrumental in raising the alarm about the accelerated loss of planetary biodiversity during the 1980s and 1990s. During his long and productive career, he has advanced the study of his specialty, social insects (especially ants); pioneered new fields of biology, such as population biology, island biogeography, and sociobiology; and written prolifically for both specialists and the general public. His eloquence has made him the most popular American spokesperson for the preservation of biodiversity.

Edward Osborne Wilson was born in Birmingham, Alabama, on June 10, 1929, the only child of Inez and Edward O. Wilson. Growing up as a lonely, solitary boy in the Deep South of the 1930s, Wilson immersed himself in the fantastic ecology of the Gulf Coast. From the age of seven, the year his parents divorced, he was allowed to wander alone through the beaches, marshes, and mangroves of the area, observing wildlife and collecting specimens. According to Wilson's autobiography *The Naturalist* (1994), this freedom came with certain risks. He suffered four serious accidents: one while fishing that blinded his right

Edward O. Wilson (AP Images)

eye, another in which he slashed himself to the bone with a machete, and two more involving venomous snakes.

Wilson's childhood interest in Gulf Coast wildlife became focused during his adolescence. His choice to specialize in ants—slow, silent insects—was a result of two disabilities: a congenital hearing defect and his partial blindness. As a Boy Scout and a student in a military high school, Wilson adopted a work ethic that has allowed him tremendous productivity in his professional life. While still in high school he performed a survey of the ants of Alabama, which he continued at the University of Alabama. His professors at Alabama treated him as a colleague and gave him space in their laboratories. Wilson graduated from Alabama in 1949 with a B.S. and earned an M.S. there in 1950. He gained admission to Harvard University in 1951, earned his Ph.D. in 1955, and immediately joined the faculty as assistant professor of biology. He has moved through the ranks and since 1976 has been the Frank B. Baird Jr. Professor of Science, as well as the entomology curator at Harvard's Museum of Comparative Zoology.

Wilson performed the first inventories of ants through most of the South Pacific, and during these explorations of tropical islands, he began to suspect that the chaotic display of life in the tropics concealed what was actually an orderly distribution of species. This suspicion led him to found a new field of science with mathematician and ecologist Robert MacArthur in 1962. "Island biogeography" relates the number of species on an island to its area and its distance from the mainland. This theory has been applied more recently to a different type of "island," shrinking islands of natural habitat in seas of deforested pastures or suburban residential expansion. Wilson's and MacArthur's work was expanded by tropical ecologist THOMAS LOVEJOY in his forest fragment project in Brazil, which studies species composition in forest patches of different sizes and distances from one another within heavily deforested Amazonian cattle ranches. The results from Wilson's and Mac-Arthur's work and from Lovejoy's on-going experiment give conservationists more accurate data about minimum sizes for potential wildlife reserves and about how species numbers will decrease if reserves are deforested.

At the same time he was charting ant populations and articulating island biogeography, Wilson made the landmark discovery that ants are able to communicate with pheromones, chemicals they secrete to influence others. Wilson's work with social insects led him to extrapolate and develop a field called sociobiology, which studies the biological basis of animal behavior. Scientists largely praised the book, but Wilson fell under widespread attack for the chapters of *Sociobiology* (1975) that suggested that human behavior was also controlled in part by our struggle for the survival of our genes. Critics felt that such an assertion denied the effect of environment on our behavior and could be used to promote racism. Wilson was hurt by what he felt was a misunderstanding of his proposal and retreated from sociobiology. In the years since he wrote the book, however, sociobiology has become a bona fide field of study.

*Biophilia* (1984) represented a new turn in Wilson's career. It was a more personal book than his previous works and explored why humans are drawn to other forms of life. "We learn to distinguish life from the inanimate and move toward it like moths to a porchlight," he claimed. The book attracted attention from a variety of fields, and a later volume (*The Biophilia Hypothesis*, 1993), edited by Wilson and social ecologist STEPHEN KELLERT, includes essays from 15 writers of different professions about how biophilia fits into their fields.

From the beginning of his career, Wilson was aware of habitat destruction and the danger it posed to the forms of life he adored and depended upon professionally. His shy personality and the embarrassment he suffered after *Sociobiology* prevented him from becoming a public advocate of environmental conservation until 1979. In that year, British ecologist Norman Myers published data that suggested that deforestation was claiming global forests at the rate of approximately 1 percent per year and that they were taking with them one-quarter of 1 percent of the world's species each year. Myers predicted that this rate would grow, owing to population increases and deep poverty in most tropical countries. Wilson's conscience pushed him to action, and he joined an informal alliance of biologists (including Myers, Jared Diamond, PAUL EHRLICH, THOMAS EISNER, DANIEL JANZEN, and Thomas Lovejoy) committed to conservation. Soon, Wilson became the science adviser to the World Wildlife Fund–U.S., joined its board of directors, and began to publish papers and give talks on the biological diversity crisis.

In 1986, the National Academy of Sciences (NAS) and the Smithsonian sponsored an international conference on biodiversity, and Wilson edited the proceedings, a collection of 56 essays entitled *Biodiversity* that became one of the best-selling books ever published by the National Academy Press. (With his characteristic generosity and respect for his colleagues, Wilson reminds his readers in *The Naturalist* that he should not be credited for inventing the term *biodiversity*, because it was proposed first by NAS administrator Walter Rosen.)

In recent years, Wilson has advocated frequently and with increasing urgency for a deeper appreciation for biodiversity and a stronger international effort to conserve it, with *The Future of Life* (2003) and *The Creation: An Appeal to Save Life* (2006).

Wilson has been honored with two Pulitzer Prizes (for *On Human Nature*, 1979, and *The Ants*, 1990, which he cowrote with Bert Hölldobler and which was the first strictly scientific book ever to win the prize) and numerous awards, including the National Medal of Science (1977), the Royal Swedish Academy of Science's Crafoord Prize (1990, shared with Paul Ehrlich), the WWF Gold Medal in 1990, and in 1993 the Japanese International Prize for Biology.

Wilson has been married to Renee Kelley since 1955, and together they have one daughter, Catherine, born in 1963. He resides near Boston, Massachusetts.

## BIBLIOGRAPHY

Christen, Kris, "Why Biodiversity Matters," *Environmental Science and Technology*, 2000; Diamond, Jared, "Portrait of the Biologist as a Young Man," *New York Review of Books*, 1995; McKibben, Bill, "More Than a Naturalist," *Audubon*, 1996; Wilson, E. O., *The Diversity of Life*, 1992; Wilson, E. O., *In Search of Nature*, 1996; Wright, Robert, "E.O. Wilson," *Smithsonian*, 2005; Wade, Nicholas, "Taking a Cue from Ants on Evolution of Humans," *New York Times*, 2008

## Winter, Paul

(August 31, 1939– )
Musician, Composer

Saxophonist Paul Winter, who pioneered "earth music," the genre that incorporates the sounds of wildlife such as humpback whales, wolves, and bird song into musical meditations, became famous by fusing his two passions: music and preserving wildlife. Over the course of his career, which has so far yielded 32 albums, he has visited 35 countries, both to perform and to record wildlife sounds for his music. He continually works to promote music as an expression that can reconnect people with nature. He has

Paul Winter (AP Images/Nancy Palmieri)

donated the royalties from some of his albums to conservation organizations that protect wilderness and wildlife species and has given benefit concerts for a variety of environmental groups. Independent and innovative, Winter established his own record label, Living Music Records, which produces his work and reflects his respect for the musical traditions and natural environments of the earth.

Paul Theodore Winter was born on August 31, 1939, in Altoona, Pennsylvania, the son of Paul Theodore and Beulah (Harnish) Winter. He grew up in a family bound together by music. His grandfather, at 17, had been the youngest bandleader in the Civil War and had later owned the local music store. His father helped run the store and worked as a piano tuner. Winter dove into music lessons young, playing drums at age five, piano at six, and clarinet at eight, but he chafed under the academic rigidity of the classical music he was forced to practice. Even so, music had gotten under his skin, and by the time he was 12 he had picked up on jazz and latched on to the saxophone. He played in the local symphony and at 17 toured with the Ringling Brothers Circus Band.

He attended Northwestern University, where he again shied away from structured musical training and majored in English composition, obtaining his B.A. in 1961. That year he assembled some college student musicians and formed the Paul Winter Sextet, which went on to win first prize in an intercollegiate jazz competition and was signed by Columbia Records. The following year the group recorded its first album, *The Paul Winter Sextet*, and then toured 23 countries in Latin America, a liberating experience that added new influences to Winter's musical style. At about that time, Winter reached a turning point: He had been accepted for admission to the University of Virginia Law School but decided against a career as an attorney in favor of a career in music. Between 1962 and 1965, he and his group toured Latin America twice more, performed at jazz festivals and on television shows, and cut seven albums for Columbia Records. Sales of the group's recordings in the mid-1960s did not meet the expectations of executives at Columbia Records, however, and the Paul Winter Sextet lost its contract and disbanded.

In 1967 Winter formed the Paul Winter Consort, an ensemble that fused together a broad range of musical elements such as rock, classical, jazz, folk, and Brazilian sounds. He lived and worked out of a stone cottage in rural Connecticut, recording three albums with the Paul Winter Consort for A&M Records in the next few years. One of these, *Road* (1971), was so well loved by astronauts on Apollo 15 that they left a cassette of it on the moon and named two lunar craters after two of its songs. Meanwhile, Winter had begun pursuing another avenue, one that he later described as having opened the doors of nature to him and that eventually led to the creation of his distinctive "earth music." It had begun in 1968 when he first heard a recording of the sounds of humpback whales and had been amazed by their musical intelligence and shocked to learn that they were being hunted nearly to extinction. Over the next several years, Winter sailed the shores of such places as El Salvador, Scotland's Inner Hebrides, Newfoundland, and British Columbia, seeking whales and other sea mammals and playing his saxophone to them. To his delight, off Baja California, he found he could call whales to his raft with his music.

Appreciating and understanding wildlife became a new passion for Winter, who also developed a lifelong admiration for timber wolves at around this time. In 1973 he visited Minnesota to see the last wild population of timber wolves in the lower 48 states. Two years later at a wildlife research center in the Sierra Nevada of California, he played his saxophone to captive wolves and heard their howling response as a kind of celebration. Expanding on these ideas, Winter began creating musical compositions that incorporated the actual voices of animals and sounds of nature, pioneering a genre of New Age music that would become abundantly popular. In 1977 the first of these albums, *Common Ground*, appeared, including whale songs, wolf howls, and the cry of an African fish eagle on various music tracks. Winter shared royalties from the album with environmental groups that supported whales, wolves, and eagles. His next release, *Callings* (1980), included the sounds of 13 different sea mammals.

Winter grew tired of working with big-label record companies, feeling that they did not know how to define his music and tended to just ignore it, so in 1980 he created his own label, Living Music Records. Also that year, Winter was named artist in residence at the Cathedral of St. John the Divine in New York City. While there he wrote an ecumenical mass for life on earth, *Missa Gaia/Earth Mass* (1982), which the Paul Winter Consort recorded partly at the cathedral and partly at the Grand Canyon. Beginning in the summer of 1984, Winter embarked on a series of visits to the wilderness areas of the Soviet Union, especially attracted to Lake Baikal, the world's deepest and largest freshwater lake—home to 1,200 species of wildlife found nowhere else on earth. Over the next ten years he collaborated with various Russian artists to produce a series of albums, hoping to spread through the universal language of music the message that love and respect for the earth can be a common ground for peace. In 1985 an album celebrating the Grand Canyon was released. Titled *Canyon*, it was recorded by the Paul Winter Consort during four rafting expeditions down the 279-mile length of the Colorado River, using the side canyons and natural amphitheaters as a "studio of the earth." *Canyon* was nominated for a Grammy in 1987 and made it to fourth place on *Billboard*'s jazz chart. This was followed by *Whales Alive* (1987), which used melodies "composed" by the whales themselves. Winter donated royalties from *Whales Alive* to the World Wildlife Fund.

By this point, Winter had achieved international recognition and had defined a whole new style of music that many describe as New Age, a label to which he objects. He prefers "earth music" or "living music," to remind himself that the purpose of his music is to honor the earth and its tapestry of life. Over the years, in addition to recording 32 albums (four of which have won Grammy Awards), he has performed benefit concerts for the Sierra Club, the Wilderness Society, Greenpeace, the ceremonial environmental observances of the United Nations, and the 1992 Earth Summit in Rio de Janeiro, Brazil. At the 1985 United Nations General Assembly on World Environment Day, Winter was given a World Environment Day Award in recognition of his work in promoting environmental causes; he has also received the Humane Society of the United States' Joseph Wood Krutch Medal for service to animals (1982), the Peace Abbey's Courage of Conscience Award (1991), and the Promise to the Earth Award from the National Arbor Day Foundation (1996). He lives with his wife, Chez Liley, whom he married in 1991, and daughter, Keetu, on a 77-acre farm near Litchfield, Connecticut.

**BIBLIOGRAPHY**

Jerome, Jim, "Paul Winter; From Canyon to Cathedral, His Soaring Sax Calls Out to Seekers of a New Age," *People Weekly*, 1986; "Paul Winter's World of Living Music," www.livingmusic.com; Sullivan, Karin Horgan, "Ode to the Wilderness: Paul Winter Honors Animals with His Music," *Vegetarian Times*, 1995; Verna, Paul, "Winter Takes His Studio Outside," *Billboard*, 1997.

## Wolf, Hazel

(March 10, 1898–January 19, 2000)
Environmental Activist, Secretary of Seattle Audubon Society

A sharply intelligent and witty charmer, known for her tendency to defy rules, Hazel Wolf was one of the Pacific Northwest's most admired activists for environmentalism and social reform. As secretary of the Seattle chapter of the National Audubon Society, she helped found more than 20 chapters in Washington State and pressured the society and other environmental organizations to broaden their focus to include more ethnic and low-income members. She cofounded the Community Coalition for Environmental Justice, a social and environmental organization committed to improving the quality of life in low-income, inner-city neighborhoods. Although her environmental activism did not start until she was in her sixties, she more than made up for lost time through her fervent involvement: She organized and attended protests and rallies, recruited other supporters, lobbied officeholders, and built coalitions. For all this she was recognized with more than a dozen conservation awards.

Hazel Anna Cummings Anderson was born March 10, 1898, in Victoria, British Columbia, to a U.S. mother and a British seaman father who died when she was ten. She grew up in poverty and learned to be a fighter at an early age. When warned by her mother to be obedient or face the "boogey man," who her mother said was out on the porch waiting for her, Hazel eventually grew exasperated and one night threw open the front door to confront him, only to find that he did not exist. She also balked at having to do the dishes unless her brother had to do them too. As she got older, she dreamed of becoming a doctor, even though it was virtually unheard of for a woman in that era. She married early, but divorced soon after, and moved to the United States in 1923 with her daughter Nydia. (A later marriage to Herbert Wolf also ended in divorce.) Settling in Seattle, Washington, she took odd jobs and struggled to make ends meet as a single mother. During the Depression she relied on welfare and lived in a Catholic boardinghouse in downtown Seattle, all the while following politics closely. Ever the reformer and activist, Wolf was fired from a job at the Works Progress Administration for trying to organize a union. She joined the Communist Party for a period because they crusaded for a system of unemployment assistance and other social programs.

In 1949 Wolf took a job as a legal secretary for noted Seattle civil-rights attorney John Caughlan, and she helped him promote civil rights and social reform. Meanwhile, her continuing activism had caught the attention of immigration officers and the Federal Bureau of Investigation, who threatened her with deportation to Canada. In addition, her former ties to the Communist Party caused her trouble during the McCarthy era, and in 1955, 13 years after she had left the party, she was arrested and charged with "attempting to overthrow the government by force of violence." She spent half a day in jail working on a jigsaw puzzle before friends bailed her out. Eventually her employer helped to get the charges dropped, and her case, which had reached the Supreme Court, was dismissed. Finally, in 1970 she became a U.S. citizen.

At the age of 62, shortly before she retired from her secretarial job, Wolf humored a friend by joining the National Audubon Society and participating in a bird-watching field trip. She became enchanted watching a brown creeper, a small, inconspicuous bird that works its way meticulously up tree trunks in search of insects, and felt protective of it. Soon after, she became secretary of the Audubon Society's Seattle chapter, a position she held for 37 years—during which time she helped organize more chapters than anyone in the national organization's history—23 of the 26 chapters in Washington State and one in her birthplace, Victoria, British Columbia. She recruited members wherever she went, prompting a friend to comment that there probably is not a person who has sat next to her on an airplane who has not joined Audubon.

Wolf, whose personal philosophy was "everything connects," went beyond her work for the Audubon Society to become a skilled coalition builder among other groups. In 1979 she organized a conference of American Indian tribes from the Pacific Northwest together with environmental organizations, forming associations that have lasted many years. The purpose of the meeting was to strategize ways to protect the Columbia River from further dam building and to protest a proposal for an expanded irrigation project. The government eventually dropped the expansion plans, and Wolf later spoke of the conference as the most valuable and interesting thing she ever did. She also joined the Federation of Western Outdoors Clubs, serving as president from 1978 to 1980 and serving as editor of their environmental newsletter, *Outdoors West*, until she died. During the 1980s she made several trips to Nicaragua to study the Sandinistas' environmental record and endeared herself to the Nicaraguan people, who came to consider her their special saint.

With her infectious spark and wit, Wolf became a much-loved public speaker on environmental issues and lectured at many conferences, conventions, and schools. When asked by children if she had a boyfriend, Wolf would reply no, but she was searching for one who could cook. While attending environmental conferences all around the country, she often succeeded in confiscating the microphone during a plenary session to campaign for a particular cause. Possessed of seemingly endless energy, whenever Wolf was not doing Audubon Society work or editing for *Outdoor West*, she was testifying at hearings, lobbying officials, participating in rallies and protests, and urging others to get involved and to register to vote. She also pressured Seattle Audubon and other environmental organizations to reach beyond their largely White, middle- or upper-class membership. In 1993 she cofounded the first environmental justice group in the Seattle area, the Community Coalition for Environmental Justice (CCEJ), a multiethnic nonprofit organization that deals with social, economic, and environmental health issues, such as industrial pollution, that disproportionately affect people of color, women, children, and low-income people.

Wolf received numerous conservation awards over the years, including the Washington State Department of Game's Award for her work in wildlife protection (1978), the State of Washington Environmental Excellence Award (1978), the National Audubon Society's Conservationist of the Year Award (1978), and the Association of Biologists and

Ecologists of Nicaragua's Award for nature conservation (1988). On March 10, 1996, on her 98th birthday, the governor of Washington issued a proclamation declaring her birthday Hazel Wolf Day. She received the Audubon Medal for Excellence in Environmental Achievement in 1997, and in June of that year Seattle University granted her, at 99, an honorary doctorate in humanities, upon which she asked to be called "Doc." For her 100th birthday, King County honored her by renaming the 166-acre Saddle Swamp on the Sammamish River the Hazel Wolf Wetlands. Also in honor of her 100th birthday, the Audubon Society created a Kids for the Environment fund to foster environmental appreciation among young people. By January 2000 Wolf had accomplished the goal of having her life span touch three centuries. She asked friends to help plan her memorial service to make it into a fund raiser for Kids for the Environment, and she requested that if anyone showed up at the service who was not registered to vote, that they be registered on the spot. On January 19, 2000, she died in Port Angeles, Washington. She is survived by her daughter, five grandchildren, five great-grandchildren, and four great-great-grandchildren.

**BIBLIOGRAPHY**

Breton, Mary Joy, *Women Pioneers for the Environment*, 1998; Broom, Jack, "Honoring Hazel Wolf: Seattle Environmentalist Turns 100," *Seattle Times*, 1998; "Hazel Wolf's Web Site," members.tripod.com/~HazelWolf/; Robin, Joshua, "Environmentalist Hazel Wolf Dies at 101," *Seattle Times*, 2000.

## Wolke, Howie
(June 17, 1952– )
Wildlands Conservationist, Cofounder of Earth First!, Wilderness Guide

In 1980, wildlands conservationist Howie Wolke, along with DAVE FOREMAN and three other environmental activists founded the radical environmental activist group, Earth First!, a group that has become well known for its dramatic and extreme methods of defending the ecological integrity of the earth. Wolke left Earth First! in 1990 and since 1994, through his nonprofit Big Wild Advocates, has been working to assure the proper management of existing wilderness areas under the 1964 Wilderness Act and the designation of new Wilderness Areas through the proposed Northern Rockies Ecosystem Protection Act, which he co-wrote. He has worked particularly to build public support for the Roadless Area Initiative of the U.S. Forest Service (USFS), which has the potential to protect up to 50 million acres of Forest Service land as roadless wilderness. Wolke and his wife Marilyn Olsen also work as outfitters and guides for wilderness trips through their Paradise Valley, Montana-based company, Big Wild Adventures.

The older of Arthur and Beverly Wolke's two children, Howie Wolke was born on June 17, 1952, in Brooklyn, New York. When Wolke was six years old, his family moved from New York to Nashville, Tennessee. Wolke claims that he was born with the "Neanderthal gene," a recessive trait that crops up in some individuals, making them fanatical lovers of the wild. This gene first manifested itself in Wolke when he was a child in Tennessee. He explored and enjoyed the woods, lakes, streams, and animals and decided that he wanted to be a forest ranger when he grew up. After two more moves with his family (to Pennsylvania and New Jersey), Wolke enrolled in college at the University of New Hampshire Forestry School, where he learned what foresters actually do and decided that he did not want to be one after all. He changed his field of study and graduated in 1974 with a B.S. in environmental conservation and wildlife ecology.

After graduation, Wolke worked until he had saved up enough money to head west. He loaded his car with all of his belongings and drove to Wyoming, where he lived, mostly in Jackson, from 1975 to 1986. When he first arrived, he volunteered with the Sierra Club and the Wilderness Society and soon became the Wyoming representative for Friends of the Earth. He supported his activism by working as a ranch hand and a bouncer at the Cowboy Bar in Jackson. During this time, Wolke catalogued roadless areas and advocated for the protection of large tracts of wilderness through the USFS's second national review of unprotected roadless lands (the Roadless Area Review Evaluation [RARE] II process). Through RARE II, the USFS was seeking public participation in determining how many acres of these roadless areas should be preserved as such. Ultimately, the USFS recommended the protection of only 15 million acres out of the 62 million under consideration (Wolke felt that a total of 80 million roadless acres should have been considered, but the USFS excluded 18 million of them). In his first book, *Wilderness on the Rocks*, Wolke writes, "RARE II was the grandiose defeat for the modern wilderness movement."

This defeat led directly to the formation of Earth First!, formed in 1980 by the disgruntled Wolke along with Dave Foreman, Mike Roselle, Bart Koehler, and Susan Morgan. Earth First! evolved out of the idea that a system of multi-million-acre wildland reserves should be developed in every major eco-region of the United States. This was a controversial proposition in 1980 but has since become more mainstream, as conservation biologists today assert that this is just the type of program that needs to be implemented if we are to maintain an acceptable level of biological diversity. Earth First! also advocated dam removal, an idea so unthinkable in 1980 that it was literally dismissed outright. Twenty years later, however, in 2000, the U.S government was holding hearings to consider the removal of dams on the Snake River.

Earth First! was originally intended to act as the strategic arm of the wildland conservation movement. This meant that while Earth First!'s official position on the use of sabotage and other forms of civil disobedience was to "neither condemn nor advocate it," some individual members of the organization did employ such tactics as desurveying roads, tree-sitting, and tree-spiking (hammering nails into trees to ruin saw blades—a tactic later abandoned by most direction action activists after a sawmill worker was injured by a spike in the trunk he was hewing). In 1985 Wolke was caught pulling survey stakes out of the ground in the Grayback Ridge Roadless Area in Wyoming, in an attempt to prevent the Forest Service from bulldozing a new logging road and an oil field. He received a sentence of six months in jail, during which time he wrote a draft of *Wilderness on The Rocks* (1991), an extended critique of the U.S. land management bureaucracies.

Since 1986 Wolke has lived in Montana with his wife, Marilyn Olsen, and together they work on wilderness protection issues in the Yellowstone/Northern Rockies region. For several years, Wolke served as president of Wilderness Watch, which works to see that existing wilderness areas are properly managed and stay wild under the 1964 Wilderness Act. Wolke's co-wrote with Dave Foreman a catalog of these 385 Wilderness Areas in the lower 48 states, *The Big Outside* (1992).

Wolke and Olsen, through their wilderness advocacy organization Big Wild Advocates, still provide support for these efforts, and they also work to designate new Wilderness Areas. While still president of Wilderness Watch, Wolke initiated a campaign to have the Gallatin Range of the Yellowstone Ecosystem designated as a Wilderness Area. They are pushing for the proposed Northern Rockies Ecosystem Protection Act, always emphasizing and building public support for the Roadless Area Initiative, a USFS administrative action that, like RARE II, has the potential to provide a significant degree of protection for 50 million acres of USFS roadless areas.

Wolke, Olsen, and Olsen's son Josh currently live in Paradise Valley, north of Yellowstone National Park. In addition to Big Wild Advocates, they run an outfitting and guiding business, Big Wild Adventures.

### BIBLIOGRAPHY

"Big Wild Adventures," www.bigwildadventures.org "Big Wild Advocates," www.bigwildadvocates.org; Foreman, Dave, and Howie Wolke, *The Big Outside*, 1992; Kane, Joe, "Mother Nature's Army," *Esquire*, 1987; Kane, Joe, "One Man's Wilderness," *Sierra*, 2000; Wolke, Howie, *Wilderness on the Rocks*, 1991.

## Woodwell, George
(October 23, 1928– )
Ecologist, Founder of the Woods Hole Research Center

George Woodwell, a life scientist with broad interests in global environmental issues, has studied terrestrial and marine ecosystems for many years, concentrating on how pesticides, nutrients, radioactive isotopes, and organic compounds are cycled through the environment. And despite criticism from some colleagues for abandoning scientific discretion, Woodwell has always been very vocal about the impact that humans are having on the global ecosystem. His research and testimony were instrumental in a case that ultimately led to the ban on dichlordiphenyltrichlor (DDT) in the United States in 1972, and he has never hesitated to spread the message about the effects of global warming and the need for rational policy responses. He founded and directs the Woods Hole Research Center and has been active in the founding of several environmental organizations, including Environmental Defense, the National Resources Defense Council, and the World Resources Institute.

George Masters Woodwell was born on October 23, 1928, in Cambridge, Massachusetts, the son of Philip and Virginia (Sellers) Woodwell. He grew up in Cambridge, spending summers in rural Maine, and came to love the changing landscape, the diversity, the water, and the history of the New England coast. He received a bachelor's degree in zoology from Dartmouth College, graduating with distinction in 1950. After three years of service in the United States Navy, he returned to school, this time to Duke University, where he earned a master's degree in 1956, and then a Ph.D. in botany in 1958. He began teaching in 1957 at the University of Maine at Orono, first as assistant professor, later as associate professor of botany. In 1961 he started working at the Brookhaven National Laboratory in Upton, New York, as an assistant scientist, eventually becoming senior scientist and building a program of basic ecological research.

Woodwell's scope of research has always been broad. He studies the planet's biosphere as a whole and addresses questions of how the global environment functions as a single system and what impact human activities have on it. In the 1960s, he became one of the first scientists to study the ecological effects of chronic exposure to ionizing radiation. He also published pioneering investigations on the circulation and effects of chemical toxins in different ecosystems and closely studied forests and estuaries in North America. In the 1950s, he had studied the negative impact of DDT, which was being sprayed on forests in Maine to battle spruce budworm, and was consulted by RACHEL CARSON during her research for *Silent Spring*. He studied DDT again in the late 1960s, this time in Michigan, where it was contaminating groundwater and harming wildlife. Not content to merely publish his findings and move on, Woodwell became one of the first to take legal action against the producers of DDT, and thanks in part to his urging and in part to the lobbying efforts of the Environmental Defense Fund (which used Woodwell's research to back them up), the Environmental Protection Agency banned the pesticide in 1972.

In 1975 he founded and became the first director of the Ecosystems Center at the Marine Biological Laboratory in Woods Hole, Massachusetts, while also working as assistant director for education there. For ten years, Woodwell continued his studies of the earth's carbon, nitrogen, and sulfur cycles from the Ecosystems Center, before branching out and founding and becoming director of the Woods Hole Research Center in 1985. He founded the center to pursue a broader range of scientific studies and to explore the public policy implications of that research. The Woods Hole Research Center has come to be well known for its ecological research and studies of global climate change.

By approaching his work with a constant awareness of its ramifications, Woodwell set a new standard for science. In the traditional model of good science, scientists conduct high-quality research and then publish it for the benefit of colleagues. But Woodwell insists that another step is now necessary. Since they study the processes that support life and the impact of human activities, ecologists have a responsibility to inform the general public of the implications of their work. Woodwell has publicly articulated his own findings on a wide range of subjects. For example, he frequently speaks out about the controlling influence of global forests on climate and urges an immediate halt to deforestation around the world in order to counteract the impoverishing effect it has on biodiversity and the escalating effect it has on global warming. He advocates an international protocol that would regulate deforestation and implement a program to increase forested areas worldwide in order to store more carbon. In recent years, Woodwell's public testimony and policy recommendations regarding his studies of global climate change have placed him at the forefront of the issue, and he is often consulted by other scientists, the U.S. Congress, and foreign governments. Throughout his years of research, Woodwell has achieved distinction in elucidating biotic interactions associated with the warming of the earth. And he has proven his commitment to increasing the influence of scholarship on public policy, showing that scientists can take part in and even lead public policy debates.

In addition to the research and advocacy work he conducts from Woods Hole Research Center, where he currently is senior scientist and director emeritus, Woodwell has been active in many other organizations. From 1981 to 1984 he served as chairperson of the World Wildlife Fund, he has served as vice president (1976–1977) and president (1977–1978) of the Ecological Society of America, and he has been on the board of trustees at the Sea Education Association (1980–1985). From 1982 to 1983, he was chairperson of the Conference on Long Term Biological Consequences of Nuclear War. Since 1969 he has been a lecturer at the School of Forestry at Yale University and has published over 300 major papers and books in ecology.

He has also been instrumental in the founding of several environmental organizations, including the Environmental Defense Fund (1967), the National Resources Defense Council (1970), and the World Resources Institute (1982). He is a member of the National Academy of Sciences and a fellow of the American Academy of Arts and Sciences. He has been recognized with the Green World Award from the New York Botanical Garden (1975), the Distinguished Service Award from the American Institute of Biological Sciences (1982), the Silver Bowl Award from the Connecticut River Watershed Council (1984), the Hutchinson Medal from Garden Clubs of America (1993), the Heinz Environment Award (1996), and the Volvo Environment Prize (2001) plus numerous honorary doctorates.

He is married to Katharine, who for many years was the administrator of Wood's Hole. They have four children. He lives in Woods Hole, Massachusetts.

**BIBLIOGRAPHY**
Woodwell, George M., "Ecological Science and the Human Predicament," *Science*, 1998; Woodwell, George, ed., *Biotic Feedback in the Global Climatic System: Will the Warming Feed the Wakening?* 1993; Woodwell, George, ed., *The Earth in Transition: Patterns and Processes of Biotic Impoverishment*, 1991; Woodwell, George, ed., *Forests in a Full World*, 2001; "Woods Hole Research Center," www.whrc.org.

## Worster, Donald
(November 14, 1941– )
Environmental Historian

One of the leading scholars and teachers of environmental history, Donald Worster is a catalyst of this rapidly growing discipline that examines the relationships between nature and culture over time. One of Worster's particular emphases has been to give nature agency in environmental history. Too often, nature has played a subsidiary role in environmental history rather than that of a leading character. Such a model is flawed if we are to properly appreciate the human place in the natural environment. Worster's work in the environmental history of the American West has sought to correct that flaw and push for more enlightened perspectives of the natural world.

Donald Eugene Worster was born November 14, 1941, in Needles, California, to Bonnie Pauline (Ball) and Winfred Delbert Worster, a railroad worker. He completed his B.A. at the University of Kansas in 1963 and earned an M.A. the following year, both degrees in English and communications. During the summer of 1965, he studied American history at Harvard University, before going to Yale for American studies. He received an M.Phil. in 1970 and was awarded his doctorate in 1971.

Worster started his teaching career at Brandeis University in 1971. He spent three years there before moving to the University of Hawai'i at Manoa, where he spent nine years in American studies before returning to Brandeis University to become the Meyerhoff Professor of American Environmental Studies in 1984. Worster left Brandeis University in 1989 to become Hall Distinguished Professor of American History at the University of Kansas.

In 1979, Worster produced *Dust Bowl: The Southern Plains in the 1930s*. More than two decades after its publication, *Dust Bowl* is still regarded as the definitive work on the history of the ecological disaster that wrought havoc during the Depression. Worster argues that capitalist economic culture—which led to ecologically unsound farming practices in the interest of short-term financial gain—played as significant a role in the formation of the massive dust storms as did drought and high winds. The following year this book won the Bancroft Prize for the best book in American history.

In 1981, Worster was awarded a Guggenheim fellowship and became the president of the American Society for Environmental History for two years. He spent the summer of 1984 as a Humanities Research Centre Fellow at the Australian National University in Canberra and was elected to the Society of American Historians in 1988. In 1995, he was awarded the Balfour Jeffrey Achievement Award for research in the humanities and social sciences from the University of Kansas and received a Distinguished Achievement Award from the Society for Conservation Biology in 1997.

Worster has also published eight other books and collections of essays, some of which have been translated into five languages. Two of Worster's books, *Rivers of Empire: Water, Aridity, and the Growth of the American West* (1986) and *The Wealth of Nature: Environmental History and the Ecological Imagination* (1993), have been nominated for the Pulitzer Prize. His work is constantly seeking to push the boundaries of environmental history. In *The Wealth of Nature*, Worster presents a dozen essays on topics that range from a review of the religious traditions of American environmentalism, to a brief history of the U.S. Soil Conservation Service, to promoting the idea of a Darwinian approach to history with an emphasis on chaos theory and its impact on ecology. Worster's central theme in the book is the contention that crucial aspects of a society's past, present, and future can be best explained by an examination of the manner in which it organizes itself and reorganizes nature in order to extract from the land those resources necessary for survival. Environmental history, he argues, gains its power from a three-level analysis. The first of its three layers is the character of the natural environment in the time and place under study. Such a discussion requires that environmental historians explore other fields of academic study such as ecology, physics, archaeology, genetics, and so on. The next level is the environmental historian's exploration of the role of technology and the modes of production of a society. Worster defends this near-Marxian concept by arguing that recent history is all about capitalism and its expansion to be the globally dominant form of social organization. He describes modes of production as cultural mechanisms that determine how the available technologies are employed to relate to the landscape by a particular people at a particular time and in a particular place. But before going so far as to grant technology an autonomous moral existence, Worster emphasizes the importance of the third level of analysis, which he identifies as the importance of culture and the specific manner in which a whole human society has perceived and valued nature. Combined, Worster argues, these three levels make environmental history a valuable and distinct field that bridges the divide between the social and the natural sciences. This book has been translated into four languages.

Worster's latest book are *A River Running West: The Life of John Wesley Powell* (2001), an important contribution to scholarship on this explorer and the federal response to his policy suggestions, and *A Passion for Nature: The Life of John Muir* (2008), a biography of the influential California naturalist and founder of the Sierra Club.

Worster still teaches environmental and western American history at the University of Kansas, as the Joyce and Elizabeth Hall Professor of U.S. History. Outside of his academic work, Worster is a member of the Board of Directors of the Land Institute in Salina, Kansas, and has served on the boards of the Kansas Land Trust and the Thoreau Society.

Worster is married to Beverley Marshall Worster. They have two children.

BIBLIOGRAPHY

"Donald E. Worster," www.history.ku.edu/faculty/worster; Worster, Donald, *Nature's Economy:*

*The Roots of Ecology*, 1977; Worster, Donald, *A Passion for Nature: The Life of John Muir*, 2008; Worster, Donald, *A River Running West: The Life of John Wesley Powell*, 2002; Worster, Donald, "Transformations of the Earth: Toward an Agroecological Perspective on History," *Journal of American History*, 1990; Worster, Donald, *Under Western Skies: Nature and History in the American West*, 1992.

# American Environmental Leaders

From Colonial Times to the Present

Y

## Yard, Robert Sterling

(February 1, 1861–May 17, 1945)
Editor, Founder of National Parks Association, Cofounder and Secretary of the Wilderness Society

Editor and publicist Robert Sterling Yard produced much of the early promotional material about the U.S. National Park Service, lifting this country's national parks from relative obscurity to worldwide fame. He worked as chief educational secretary for the National Park Service under director STEPHEN MATHER from 1915 to 1918 and then founded the National Parks Association (NPA), a nonprofit organization that raises private funds for the national parks. Yard was one of the seven original founders of the Wilderness Society in 1935 and served as its president and permanent secretary until his death in 1945.

Born on February 1, 1861, in Haverstraw, New York, Robert Sterling Yard graduated in 1883 from Princeton University. For the first 30 years of his professional life he lived and worked in the publishing world, mostly in New York City, in such capacities as head of foreign cables and correspondence at the W. R. Grace and Co. shipping firm, reporter at the New York *Sun*, Sunday editor at the New York *Herald*, book advertising manager at Charles Scribner's Sons, and editor in chief at the influential *Century Magazine*.

It was not until Yard was 53 years old that he entered the field for which he is principally remembered, that of wilderness preservation. He was invited to Washington, D.C., in 1915 to assist his former colleague and best friend from the *Sun*, Stephen Mather, who had just become assistant secretary of the interior in charge of national parks. Yard's job paid only $30 per month, but millionaire Mather supplemented his salary so that he was earning about $5,000 per year. Throughout the rest of Mather's life, while Yard was working for the government and later for the nonprofit National Parks Association, Mather continued to bankroll Yard's work.

The more than 1,000 articles that Yard wrote, edited, or inspired with his press releases during his four years with the national parks helped convince Congress to pass the National Park Service Act, the law that created the National Park Service to manage all U.S. national parks. Yard's articles also raised public awareness of the parks and critical public support for them. His promotional articles could be tailored to any segment of society. He convinced the automotive industry that supporting national parks would help their business. (It did. Automobiles were just becoming more affordable to the middle class, and families were using them to drive cross-country to visit such wonders as Mesa Verde and Glacier National Parks.) Railroad companies, which built special spurs to Yellowstone, Zion, Bryce, Grand Canyon, and Mount Rainier National Parks, among others, financed widely distributed picture books about the parks. Yard distributed almost 350,000 feet of movies free to schools.

Despite his productivity and success, Mather had to dismiss Yard in 1918, because a new law prohibited private payment to government employees. With Mather's financial backing, Yard went on to found the National Parks Association, whose mission, according to its charter, was "to defend the National Parks and National Monuments fearlessly against the assaults of private interests and aggressive commercialism." The NPA applied vital pressure at key moments in history. In 1919, shortly after its founding, Yard and the NPA lobbied Congress to kill the Falls-Bechler bill, which would have allowed dams to be built within national parks. Yard continued as executive secretary of the NPA until 1933, when he stepped down because the organization lacked the funds to pay him. At that time he was named editor of publications, a post he kept until he was succeeded by DEVEREUX BUTCHER in 1942.

In 1935, Yard's friend ROBERT MARSHALL, the director of forestry at the Bureau of Indian Affairs, invited him to cofound the Wilderness Society (TWS) along with himself and six others (BENTON MACKAYE, Harvey Broome, Harold Anderson, Bernard Frank, ALDO LEOPOLD, and Ernest Oberholtzer). Marshall was a staunch defender of wilderness, opposing the same private assaults on public wild lands as Yard and the NPA. Marshall paid Yard's salary, personally contributed at least 80 percent of TWS's operating budget, and controlled TWS membership so that its work could be focused on wildlands preservation, unhampered by internal debate. For 30 years, TWS pushed for legislation that would declare certain wilderness areas inviolable by roads, vehicles, buildings, or any other artificial development. Its work finally bore fruit with the 1964 passage of the Wilderness Act, which signed nine million acres into untouchable wilderness and gave Congress the possibility of declaring other areas untouchable too. In the years since, 64 million more acres of wilderness have been set aside through the Wilderness Act.

TWS founder Marshall died suddenly in 1939, leaving Yard to run the TWS office from his Washington, D.C., apartment. Yard served as TWS's executive secretary, its president, and editor of its quarterly magazine *Living Wilderness* until his death on May 17, 1945, at the age of 84. Yard was survived by his wife, Mary, and one daughter, Margaret.

### BIBLIOGRAPHY

Albright, Horace M., "The National Park Service: Horace Albright Remembers the Origins," *National Parks*, 1985; Fox, Stephen, *John Muir and His Legacy: The American Conservation Movement*, 1981; Glover, James M., *A Wilderness Original: The Life of Bob Marshall*, 1986; Shankland, Robert, *Steve Mather of the National Parks*, 1970; "The Wilderness Society," www.wilderness.org/; Yard, Robert Sterling, *The Book of the National Parks*, 1919.

# American Environmental Leaders

From Colonial Times to the Present

## Zahniser, Howard

(February 25, 1906–May 5, 1964)
Executive Secretary and Executive Director of The Wilderness Society, Editor

As executive secretary and executive director of the Wilderness Society (TWS) from September 1945 to May 1964, Howard Zahniser led two major conservationist battles: the first to prevent a dam from being built in Dinosaur National Monument and the second to convince Congress to pass a wilderness bill that established the National Wilderness Preservation System. Both accomplishments required cooperation among many conservation and civic organizations that previously had not collaborated. Zahniser is remembered for his skill and diplomacy in building coalitions and developing local leadership for national conservation struggles.

Howard Clinton Zahniser was born on February 25, 1906, in Franklin, Pennsylvania, and grew up in Tionesta, Pennsylvania. His father was an energetic Free Methodist minister and, later, district elder whose diary records 227 pastoral calls in the first quarter of the year he died of heart trouble. His mother was descended from colonist Mary Jemison, who was captured by the Seneca tribe and chose to live with them even after Indian-White relations normalized. An early lover of the Allegheny landscape and its birds, Zahniser joined a Junior Audubon Society as a fifth grader. In college he concentrated on English literature and journalism, editing the student newspaper; he graduated with a B.A. in 1928 from Greenville College in Illinois. His first jobs were as reporter and editor for newspapers in Pittsburgh and Greenville and as English teacher for the Greenville High School. In 1930 he went to work for the U.S. Department of Commerce's Division of Publications as editorial assistant. In 1931 he transferred to the U.S. Department of Agriculture's Bureau of Biological Survey, which later became the Department of the Interior's U.S. Fish and Wildlife Service. There he was mentored in an ecological view of the world by naturalists Edward Preble and OLAUS J. MURIE and by J. NORWOOD "DING" DARLING, Ira N. Gabrielson, and ALDO LEOPOLD and worked briefly with RACHEL CARSON. Zahniser wrote, edited, and produced broadcasts on topics of wildlife research, management, and conservation. In 1942 he became principal research writer for the Department of Agriculture's Bureau of Plant Industry, Soils, and Agricultural Engineering and directed publicity for the World War II Victory Gardens campaign. Beginning in 1935, Zahniser moonlighted as books editor for *Nature Magazine* and contributed entries on conservation and wilderness preservation to the *Encyclopaedia Britannica* yearbook series.

Zahniser was a charter member of the Wilderness Society, which had been founded in 1935. In 1945, when TWS executive secretary ROBERT STERLING YARD died, Zahniser was recruited as its new executive secretary and editor of its journal, *Living Wilderness*. He had started to question continued government service because of the U.S. use of atomic bombs. Zahniser created a news section for *Living Wilderness* that became a national clearinghouse for conservation and related civic issues. This work was key to his later coalition building. Zahniser first emerged into public view in the struggle to oppose the Echo Park dam proposed inside Dinosaur National Monument in the 1950s. He was instrumental in building and coordinating this first national coalition for a conservation cause and coleading the six-year struggle with DAVID BROWER, then head of the Sierra Club, who produced WALLACE STEGNER's illustrated book *This Is Dinosaur* and a film. Zahniser, based in Washington, D.C., testified, lobbied, and marshaled grassroots support. In 1956, the Colorado River Storage Project Act provided that "no dam or reservoir constructed under the authorization of the Act shall be within any National Park or Monument." Zahniser negotiated the historic final settlement on behalf of conservationists. It established the principle of the inviolability of National Park System lands, threatened since Hetch Hetchy Valley in Yosemite National Park was dammed earlier that century.

Beginning in 1946 and through the Dinosaur years, Zahniser brainstormed about a national program for preserving wilderness. He urged the idea at the biennial national wilderness conferences that TWS cosponsored with the Sierra Club and also at the 1955 National Citizens Planning Conference on Parks and Open Spaces for the American People. The Sierra Club in 1955 resolved to support federal protection of wilderness. Upon the Dinosaur victory, Zahniser drafted a wilderness bill, and he and Brower determined to turn the Echo Park coalition toward pursuing it. Zahniser circulated the four-page document to friends and allies in conservation and civic groups and convinced Sen. Hubert H. Humphrey and Rep. John P. Saylor to introduce the legislation in Congress.

In the eight-year battle for the Wilderness Act, Zahniser and the Wilderness Society worked closely with David Brower and the Sierra Club and with many national and regional conservationist organizations and civic, garden, and women's clubs. No legislation in history had generated so many letters to Congress. Despite overwhelming grassroots support, industry groups vehemently opposed the wilderness bill. Timber, oil, grazing, and mining interests and proponents of motorized access to wild lands lobbied against the legislation, saying it would "lock up" such areas for lesser numbers of hikers and campers. Zahniser patiently countered opposition with ecological, spiritual, and philosophical viewpoints derived from the conservation tradition of GEORGE PERKINS MARSH, HENRY DAVID THOREAU, and JOHN MUIR and his intimate knowledge of the writings of the Book of Job, Dante Alighieri, and William Blake. Zahniser agreed with Wilderness Society cofounder ROBERT MARSHALL that wilderness offered social, mental, and spiritual health. He also believed that wilderness can help humans sense themselves as interdependent members of the whole community of life on earth. Zahniser articulated these ideas in his articles for *Nature*, *National Parks*, *American Forests*, *Living Wilderness*, and the *Britannica* yearbooks.

Zahniser devoted himself to assuring passage of a wilderness bill. He took his family—his wife, Alice Bernita Hayden, and their four children—on numerous backpack and canoe trips during these years to see areas proposed for wilderness preservation. Zahniser testified at every public hearing for the bill, in Washington, D.C., and in several western states. In his travels he made his own share of "pastoral calls" on congressmen, newspaper editors, other conservationists, and civic leaders. He wore suits his son Ed called "fabric filing cabinets," whose tailor-made oversized pockets held quantities of wilderness leaflets and usually a book by Thoreau, Dante, or Blake. Under Zahniser's leadership, TWS membership grew from 2,000 to 27,000.

During the final stretch toward passage of the Wilderness Act, Zahniser died of a heart attack at the age of 58 years, on May 5, 1964, at the family's home in Hyattsville, Maryland.

The fight for passage of the act and for wilderness preservation generally was carried on by Zahniser's long-time TWS associate Michael Nadel and by STEWART BRANDBORG, Zahniser's successor as executive director of TWS. The legislation was passed in August 1964 and signed by Pres. Lyndon B. Johnson on September 3, 1964. At 9 million acres, the initial National Wilderness Preservation System was far less than the 60 million acres Zahniser originally proposed. However, the Wilderness Act provided a mechanism that has, in the years since 1964, enabled wilderness preservationists to secure the preservation of the system's present 104 million acres.

### BIBLIOGRAPHY

Fox, Stephen, *The American Conservation Movement: John Muir and His Legacy*, 1981; Harvey, Mark, *Wilderness Forever: Howard Zahniser and the Path to the Wilderness Act*, 2005; "Howard Clinton Zahniser, 1906–1964," *Living Wilderness*, 1964; Nash, Roderick, *Wilderness and the American Mind*, rev. ed., 1973; Scott, Douglas, "The Visionary Role of Howard Zahniser," *Sierra*, 1984; Zahniser, Ed, "Howard Zahniser, Father of the Wilderness Act," *National Parks*, 1984.

## Zwick, David
(1942– )
Environmental Campaign Organizer, Founder of Clean Water Action

David Zwick is a water quality advocate and environmental lobbyist. As one of RALPH NADER's Raiders in the late 1960s, he produced a shocking report on water pollution in the United States that spawned The Clean Water Act of 1972. He founded Clean Water Action with the mission of guaranteeing that the law is applied. Zwick and Clean Water Action promote legislation and enforcement at the state, federal, and local level to protect and clean up our watershed, wetlands, rivers, lakes and seas.

David Zwick was born in Rochester, New York on May 1, 1942 to Ruth Clemons Zwick and Frederick Daniel Zwick. He attended the United States Coast Guard Academy where he received a B.S. in 1963. Later he obtained his J.D. from Harvard Law School and an M.P.P. from Harvard's Kennedy School of Government.

While a graduate student at Harvard in 1969, his ideals ran high. Zwick joined public interest law advocate, Ralph Nader, with Center for Study of Responsive Law in Washington, D.C. to investigate the state of our water. They toured some of the country's most polluted sites – including the Cuyahoga River which spontaneously combusted due to the high levels of toxins in it, and Lake Erie which had been declared biologically dead. After Nader and Zwick released *Water Wasteland: The Ralph Nader Report on Water Pollution* (Grossman, 1971), the public outcry and ensuing lobbying effort, spearheaded by Zwick, led to Congressional passage of the Clean Water Act. It became law over President Richard Nixon's veto in 1972. While the Clean Water Act was being debated, David Zwick succeeded in composing several key sections, including upholding citizens' right to sue when the government is not enforcing the Clean Water Act, and mandating watershed cleanup plans. The law sets water quality standards and regulates all discharges of contaminants. Senator EDMUND MUSKIE, a sponsor and author of the act, cites Zwick and Water Wasteland as a primary source and inspiration for this central piece of environmental law in the United States.

After the publication of *Water Wasteland*, David Zwick founded the Fisherman's Clean Water Action Project, which later became Clean Water Action, one of the rare environmental lobbying organizations in Washington that maintains a widespread grassroots effort across the country. It canvasses door-to-door, in addition to knocking on the doors of elected representatives in state legislatures and the U.S. Congress. The organization helped enact the 1974 Safe Drinking Water Act and oversee Environmental Protection Agency's Superfund toxics cleanup activity. Whenever and wherever the laws were not being enforced, Zwick and Clean Water Action apply pressure, at times leveling law suits to defend water quality standards. A Virginia law suit resulted in a 1975 Supreme Court decision that released billions of tax dollars for sewage treatment, as required by the Clean Water Act. In Texas, Zwick prevented then-Governor George W. Bush from lowering water quality standards to accommodate paper manufacturers.

President George Bush's Administration's non-compliance with the Clean Water Act and Safe Drinking Water Act has redoubled Clean Water Action's efforts. It was revealed that the Environmental Protection Agency under President Bush failed to pursue 304 potential violations over an eighteen-month period, from July 2006 to December 2007. Jurisdictional uncertainty brought on by anti-Clean Water Act court decisions of 2003 and 2007 left U.S. drinking water and recreational waters vulnerable to polluters again. Clean Water Action and Zwick mobilized a public awareness campaign and began preparing new legislation, The Clean Water Authority Restoration Act. By 2008, Clean Water Action's membership swelled to 1.2 million members, with over 30 field offices around the country.

David Zwick stepped down as head of Clean Water Action in 2007 but continues to work with organizations around the country. His mission is to inspire and prepare a new generation of public interest activists and advocates. He remains vigilant in his demand that our water is safe to fish in, swim in, and drink.

**BIBLIOGRAPHY**

Zwick, David, and Ralph Nader, *Water Wasteland: The Ralph Nader Report on Water Pollution*, 1971; Green, Mark, *Selling Out: How Big Corporate Money Buys Elections, Rams Through Legislation, and Betrays Our Democracy*, 2002; Green, Mark, James Fallows, and David Zwick, *Who Runs Congress*, 972; www.cleanwateraction.org.

# Key Documents

## American Environmental Leaders

From Colonial Times to the Present

# AMERICAN ENVIRONMENTAL LEADERS KEY DOCUMENTS

## TABLE OF CONTENTS

| | | |
|---|---|---|
| 12th-13th century | The Constitution of the Iroquois Nations: The Great Binding Law | 903 |
| 1791 | Travels through North & South Carolina, Georgia, East & West Florida, the Cherokee Country, the Extensive Territories of the Muscogulges, or Creek Confederacy, and the Country of the Choctaws<br>From the Travel Journal of William Bartram | 904 |
| 1844 | *Nature*<br>From *Essays* by Ralph Waldo Emerson | 905 |
| 1854 | *Walden*, excerpt<br>By Henry David Thoreau | 907 |
| 1857 | Letter from Charles Darwin to Asa Gray, excerpt | 910 |
| 1864 | *Man and Nature*, excerpt<br>By G. Perkins Marsh | 913 |
| 1877 | Speech by Sitting Bull, excerpt | 914 |
| 1948 | *Our Plundered Planet*, excerpt<br>By Fairfield Osborn | 915 |
| 1961 | The Wilderness Letter / Wilderness Letter Introduction<br>By Wallace Stegner | 919 |
| 1968 | MIT Faculty Statement<br>Union of Concerned Scientists | 925 |
| 1969 | Arithmetic, Population and Energy<br>By Albert Bartlett | 926 |
| 1972 (2004) | *Limits to Growth*, excerpt<br>By Donella H. Meadows, Jorgen Randers and Dennis Meadows | 941 |
| 1991 | Seventeen Principles of Environmental Justice, preamble | 946 |
| 1992 | World Scientists Warning to Humanity | 948 |
| 1992 | Kyoto Protocol, summary | 952 |
| 1995 | Presentation to the United Nations<br>By Carol Jabobs, Cayuga Bear Clan Mother | 954 |

## Key Documents

| | | |
|---|---|---|
| 2000 | **Myth of Chief Seattle** By William S. Abruzzi | 956 |
| 2000 | **Hannover Principles: Design for Sustainability** | 961 |
| 2003 | **Climatology of 1980-2003/07 Extreme Weather and Climate Events** National Climatic Weather Center | 963 |
| 2004 | **An Evangelical Call to Civic Responsibility, excerpt** | 979 |
| 2007 | **The "Six Sins of Greenwashing"** By TerraChoice Environmental Marketing | 980 |
| 2007 | **Steps Toward Ecological Sustainability, Equity, Sufficiency and Peace** From Manifesto on Global Economics | 995 |
| 2008 | **Global Warming 20 Years Later: Tipping Points Near** By James Hansen | 998 |

# KEY DOCUMENTS

## Introduction to Key Documents

To present a complete bibliography of works that moved great American environmental leaders would be marvelous yet probably impossible. No compilation of texts, or list of texts, could ever adequately represent the myriad currents running through American environmental thought and action. Editors ultimately have to choose, and choose sparingly, from an enormous canon of literature spanning many genre.

The following selection of 23 key documents are historical touchstones that have inspired heroic protective acts and lifetimes of dedication of many of the individuals profiled in this second edition. They were chosen from letters, speeches, essays, government documents and declarations. These documents move chronologically, from pre-Colonial times to 2008.

We begin with two brief passages from the Iroquois. The roots of America's most enduring policy document, the U.S. Constitution, run through The Constitution of the Iroquois Nations: The Great Binding Law. Before the founding of the United States, the Iroquois council of six nations began their meetings with this convocation: "In every deliberation we must consider the impact on the seventh generation… even if it requires having skin as thick as the bark of a pine. " [from the Mohawk] Thomas Jefferson, James Madison, and other members of the U.S. Continental Congress were aware of the Iroquois Constitution. Passages are said to have provided perspective for parts of the U.S. Constitution.

An American lineage of nature writers developed in the mid-19th century. To represent these, we chose excerpts from Ralph Waldo Emerson's "Nature" and Henry David Thoreau's "Walden," since they served as seeds for this genre for over 150 years. Their introduction to seeing natural facts as spiritual facts continues into 20th century American literature, as exhibited in works by many of the writers profiled in this reference work, e.g. Gary Snyder, *Turtle Island* (1974); Edward Abbey, *The Monkey Wrench Gang* (1975); Barry Lopez, *Arctic Dreams* (1986); Terry Tempest Williams, *Refuge* (1991); Barbara Kingsolver, *The Poisonwood Bible* (1998).

One hidden driver of environmentalism in America has been the power of its epistolary. As examples, we chose two early, very potent letters, the first from Charles Darwin to Asa Gray (1857), and the second is "The Wilderness Letter" from Thoreauvian American writer, Wallace Stegner, to the Wildland Research Center at the University of California at Berkeley (1960).

The many famous speeches that publicly address environmental concerns include Dr. Benjamin Spock's at the University of California at Riverside, Earth Day, 1970, and Senator Edmund Muskie's speech in Philadelphia upon the passage of the Clean Air Act of 1970. We've included two other examples to reprint here: an excerpt from Albert Bartlett's "Arithmetic, Population and Energy" speech in 1969; and the words of Iroquois leader, Carol Jacobs, Cayuga Bear Clan Mother, to the United Nations in 1995, famously declaring (in part), "The forces that are injuring our Mother the Earth are not waiting to create subcommittees, to set dates for meetings, to set budgets."

Poor and ethnic minorities have been likened to canaries in coal mines, often the first-exposed to toxic contamination, and can be vital first-responders to American environmental degradation. While environmental justice appeals and principles are difficult to synthesize or synopsize, The Principles of Environmental Justice, signed at the First National People of Color Environmental Leadership Summit, made specific public policy proposals, including full compensation and

# KEY DOCUMENTS

health care for victims of environmental crimes that are still being committed today. They serve as a record of the ultimate goals of the environmental justice movement, and are reprinted here.

While naturalists revere the innocence and beauty of nature, environmentalists worry about its well-being. Their unheeded warnings and admonishments over centuries still spur actions today to preserve and protect the environment. We've included excerpts of the following three examples: Fairfield Osborn's *Our Plundered Planet* (1948); World Scientists Warning to Humanity (1992); and "Tipping Points Near" by Dr. James E. Hansen, Director of the National Aeronautics and Space Administration's Goddard Institute for Space Studies.

Prescriptions for what can be done for the environment range in their prevailing sense of immediacy, and American senses of practicality. When the timing is right, the impact of articles and editorials can be remarkable. A prime example is Irving Selikoff's landmark essay for the *Journal of the American Medical Association*, "Asbestos Exposure and Neoplasia," and his subsequent Op Ed piece in the *New York Times*, led to the banning of asbestos in the United States, and elsewhere. Our example is the 1968 MIT Faculty Statement that spawned the Union of Concerned Scientists.

Like the selection of environmental leaders in this reference work, the Key Documents have been drawn from local, regional, national, and international sources. Their recommendations for what can be done are more powerful when there is a strong consensus. The Kyoto Protocol, a summary of which is reprinted on the following pages, is a prime example.

We also cite another growing consensus in American environmentalism: Rampant consumerism is an enemy to our ecology. We cannot continue to consume and produce such massive quantities of dangerous materials or dominate larger and larger swaths of the landscape. The "Six Sins of Greenwashing™": A Study of Environmental Claims in North American Consumer Markets is included here in an attempt to inoculate readers to industry's justifications for increased consumption and old methods of measuring economic growth.

We end this section with a selection from the forward thinking Manifesto on Global Economic Transitions, September 2007, titled Steps Toward Ecological Sustainability, Equity, and Peace by Jerry Mander.

Our hope is that these Key Documents will give the reader a sense of the marvel, urgency, and hope felt at the time they were created. We hope, too, that they are the inspiration for further research.

*Anne Becher and Joseph Richey*

# THE CONSTITUTION OF THE IROQUOIS NATIONS: THE GREAT BINDING LAW

Whenever the Confederate Lords shall assemble for the purpose of holding a council, the Onondaga Lords shall open it by expressing their gratitude to their cousin Lords and greeting them, and they shall make an address and offer thanks to the earth where men dwell, to the streams of water, the pools, the springs and the lakes, to the maize and the fruits, to the medicinal herbs and trees, to the forest trees for their usefulness, to the animals that serve as food and give their pelts for clothing, to the great winds and the lesser winds, to the Thunderers, to the Sun, the mighty warrior, to the moon, to the messengers of the Creator who reveal his wishes and to the Great Creator who dwells in the heavens above, who gives all the things useful to men, and who is the source and the ruler of health and life.

Then shall the Onondaga Lords declare the council open. The council shall not sit after darkness has set in.

...

The Lords of the Confederacy of the Five Nations shall be mentors of the people for all time. The thickness of their skin shall be seven spans—which is to say that they shall be proof against anger, offensive actions and criticism. Their hearts shall be full of peace and good will and their minds filled with a yearning for the welfare of the people of the Confederacy. With endless patience they shall carry out their duty and their firmness shall be tempered with a tenderness for their people. Neither anger nor fury shall find lodgement in their minds and all their words and actions shall be marked by calm deliberation.

---

Courtesy of the National Public Telecomputing Network (NPTN). The *Constitution of the Iroquois Nations* can be found in its entirety at www.indigenouspeople.net/iroqcon.htm. Prepared by Gerald Murphy, The Cleveland Free-Net-aa300.

## TRAVELS THROUGH NORTH & SOUTH CAROLINA, GEORGIA, EAST & WEST FLORIDA, THE CHEROKEE COUNTRY, THE EXTENSIVE TERRITORIES OF THE MUSCOGULGES, OR CREEK CONFEDERACY, AND THE COUNTRY OF THE CHOCTAWS

*By William Bartram*

### Introduction

"The attention of a traveler should be particularly turned in the first place, to the various works of Nature, to mark the distinctions of the climates he may explore, and to offer such useful observations on the different productions as may occur. Men and manners undoubtably hold the first rank—whatever may contribute to our existence is also of equal importance whether it be found in the animal and vegetable kingdom; neither are the various articles, which tend to promote the happiness and convenience of mankind to be disregarded."

Philadelphia: Printed by James & Johnson, 1791. Used with Permission of "Documenting the American South," The University of North Carolina at Chapel Hill Libraries.

# NATURE

## *From* Essays: Second Series (1844)

*By Ralph Waldo Emerson*

To go into solitude, a man needs to retire as much from his chamber as from society. I am not solitary whilst I read and write, though nobody is with me. But if a man would be alone, let him look at the stars. The rays that come from those heavenly worlds, will separate between him and what he touches. One might think the atmosphere was made transparent with this design, to give man, in the heavenly bodies, the perpetual presence of the sublime. Seen in the streets of cities, how great they are! If the stars should appear one night in a thousand years, how would men believe and adore; and preserve for many generations the remembrance of the city of God which had been shown! But every night come out these envoys of beauty, and light the universe with their admonishing smile.

The stars awaken a certain reverence, because though always present, they are inaccessible; but all natural objects make a kindred impression, when the mind is open to their influence. Nature never wears a mean appearance. Neither does the wisest man extort her secret, and lose his curiosity by finding out all her perfection. Nature never became a toy to a wise spirit. The flowers, the animals, the mountains, reflected the wisdom of his best hour, as much as they had delighted the simplicity of his childhood.

When we speak of nature in this manner, we have a distinct but most poetical sense in the mind. We mean the integrity of impression made by manifold natural objects. It is this which distinguishes the stick of timber of the wood-cutter, from the tree of the poet. The charming landscape which I saw this morning, is indubitably made up of some twenty or thirty farms. Miller owns this field, Locke that, and Manning the woodland beyond. But none of them owns the landscape. There is a property in the horizon which no man has but he whose eye can integrate all the parts, that is, the poet. This is the best part of these men's farms, yet to this their warranty-deeds give no title.

To speak truly, few adult persons can see nature. Most persons do not see the sun. At least they have a very superficial seeing. The sun illuminates only the eye of the man, but shines into the eye and the heart of the child. The lover of nature is he whose inward and outward senses are still truly adjusted to each other; who has retained the spirit of infancy even into the era of manhood. His intercourse with heaven and earth, becomes part of his daily food. In the presence of nature, a wild delight runs through the man, in spite of real sorrows. Nature says,–he is my creature, and *maugre* all his impertinent griefs, he shall be glad with me. Not the sun or the summer alone, but every hour and season yields its tribute of delight; for every hour and change corresponds to and authorizes a different state of the mind, from breathless noon to grimmest midnight. Nature is a setting that fits equally well a comic or a mourning piece. In good health, the air is a cordial of incredible virtue. Crossing a bare common, in snow puddles, at twilight, under a clouded sky, without having in my thoughts any occurrence of special good fortune, I have enjoyed a perfect exhilaration. I am glad to the brink of fear. In the woods too, a man casts off his years, as the snake his slough, and at what period soever of life, is always a child. In the woods, is

---

Source: www.emersoncentral.com/ Jone Johnson Lewis. Reprinted with permission.

perpetual youth. Within these plantations of God, a decorum and sanctity reign, a perennial festival is dressed, and the guest sees not how he should tire of them in a thousand years. In the woods, we return to reason and faith. There I feel that nothing can befall me in life,–no disgrace, no calamity, (leaving me my eyes,) which nature cannot repair. Standing on the bare ground,–my head bathed by the blithe air, and uplifted into infinite space,–all mean egotism vanishes. I become a transparent eye-ball; I am nothing; I see all; the currents of the Universal Being circulate through me; I am part or particle of God. The name of the nearest friend sounds then foreign and accidental: to be brothers, to be acquaintances,–master or servant, is then a trifle and a disturbance. I am the lover of uncontained and immortal beauty. In the wilderness, I find something more dear and connate than in streets or villages. In the tranquil landscape, and especially in the distant line of the horizon, man beholds somewhat as beautiful as his own nature.

The greatest delight which the fields and woods minister, is the suggestion of an occult relation between man and the vegetable. I am not alone and unacknowledged. They nod to me, and I to them. The waving of the boughs in the storm, is new to me and old. It takes me by surprise, and yet is not unknown. Its effect is like that of a higher thought or a better emotion coming over me, when I deemed I was thinking justly or doing right.

# WALDEN (or LIFE IN THE WOODS)

## Excerpt

*by Henry David Thoreau*

The shore is irregular enough not to be monotonous. I have in my mind's eye the western, indented with deep bays, the bolder northern, and the beautifully scalloped southern shore, where successive capes overlap each other and suggest unexplored coves between. The forest has never so good a setting, nor is so distinctly beautiful, as when seen from the middle of a small lake amid hills which rise from the water's edge; for the water in which it is reflected not only makes the best foreground in such a case, but, with its winding shore, the most natural and agreeable boundary to it. There is no rawness nor imperfection in its edge there, as where the axe has cleared a part, or a cultivated field abuts on it. The trees have ample room to expand on the water side, and each sends forth its most vigorous branch in that direction. There Nature has woven a natural selvage, and the eye rises by just gradations from the low shrubs of the shore to the highest trees. There are few traces of man's hand to be seen. The water laves the shore as it did a thousand years ago.

A lake is the landscape's most beautiful and expressive feature. It is earth's eye; looking into which the beholder measures the depth of his own nature. The fluviatile trees next the shore are the slender eyelashes which fringe it, and the wooded hills and cliffs around are its overhanging brows.

Standing on the smooth sandy beach at the east end of the pond, in a calm September afternoon, when a slight haze makes the opposite shore-line indistinct, I have seen whence came the expression, "the glassy surface of a lake." When you invert your head, it looks like a thread of finest gossamer stretched across the valley, and gleaming against the distant pine woods, separating one stratum of the atmosphere from another. You would think that you could walk dry under it to the opposite hills, and that the swallows which skim over might perch on it. Indeed, they sometimes dive below this line, as it were by mistake, and are undeceived. As you look over the pond westward you are obliged to employ both your hands to defend your eyes against the reflected as well as the true sun, for they are equally bright; and if, between the two, you survey its surface critically, it is literally as smooth as glass, except where the skater insects, at equal intervals scattered over its whole extent, by their motions in the sun produce the finest imaginable sparkle on it, or, perchance, a duck plumes itself, or, as I have said, a swallow skims so low as to touch it. It may be that in the distance a fish describes an arc of three or four feet in the air, and there is one bright flash where it emerges, and another where it strikes the water; sometimes the whole silvery arc is revealed; or here and there, perhaps, is a thistle-down floating on its surface, which the fishes dart at and so dimple it again. It is like molten glass cooled but not congealed, and the few motes in it are pure and beautiful like the imperfections in glass. You may often detect a yet smoother and darker water, separated from the rest as if by an invisible cobweb, boom of the water nymphs, resting on it. From a hilltop you can see a fish leap in almost any part; for not a pickerel or shiner picks an insect from this smooth surface but it manifestly disturbs the equilibrium of the whole lake. It is wonderful with what elaborateness this simple fact is advertised—this pis-

---

*Walden*, Boston and New York: Houghton Mifflin, 1919, pp. 206–211.

cine murder will out—and from my distant perch I distinguish the circling undulations when they are half a dozen rods in diameter. You can even detect a water-bug (Gyrinus) ceaselessly progressing over the smooth surface a quarter of a mile off; for they furrow the water slightly, making a conspicuous ripple bounded by two diverging lines, but the skaters glide over it without rippling it perceptibly. When the surface is considerably agitated there are no skaters nor water-bugs on it, but apparently, in calm days, they leave their havens and adventurously glide forth from the shore by short impulses till they completely cover it. It is a soothing employment, on one of those fine days in the fall when all the warmth of the sun is fully appreciated, to sit on a stump on such a height as this, overlooking the pond, and study the dimpling circles which are incessantly inscribed on its otherwise invisible surface amid the reflected skies and trees. Over this great expanse there is no disturbance but it is thus at once gently smoothed away and assuaged, as, when a vase of water is jarred, the trembling circles seek the shore and all is smooth again. Not a fish can leap or an insect fall on the pond but it is thus reported in circling dimples, in lines of beauty, as it were the constant welling up of its fountain, the gentle pulsing of its life, the heaving of its breast. The thrills of joy and thrills of pain are undistinguishable. How peaceful the phenomena of the lake! Again the works of man shine as in the spring. Ay, every leaf and twig and stone and cobweb sparkles now at mid-afternoon as when covered with dew in a spring morning. Every motion of an oar or an insect produces a flash of light; and if an oar falls, how sweet the echo!

In such a day, in September or October, Walden is a perfect forest mirror, set round with stones as precious to my eye as if fewer or rarer. Nothing so fair, so pure, and at the same time so large, as a lake, perchance, lies on the surface of the earth. Sky water. It needs no fence. Nations come and go without defiling it. It is a mirror which no stone can crack, whose quicksilver will never wear off, whose gilding Nature continually repairs; no storms, no dust, can dim its surface ever fresh;—a mirror in which all impurity presented to it sinks, swept and dusted by the sun's hazy brush—this the light dust-cloth—which retains no breath that is breathed on it, but sends its own to float as clouds high above its surface, and be reflected in its bosom still.

A field of water betrays the spirit that is in the air. It is continually receiving new life and motion from above. It is intermediate in its nature between land and sky. On land only the grass and trees wave, but the water itself is rippled by the wind. I see where the breeze dashes across it by the streaks or flakes of light. It is remarkable that we can look down on its surface. We shall, perhaps, look down thus on the surface of air at length, and mark where a still subtler spirit sweeps over it.

The skaters and water-bugs finally disappear in the latter part of October, when the severe frosts have come; and then and in November, usually, in a calm day, there is absolutely nothing to ripple the surface. One November afternoon, in the calm at the end of a rain-storm of several days' duration, when the sky was still completely overcast and the air was full of mist, I observed that the pond was remarkably smooth, so that it was difficult to distinguish its surface; though it no longer reflected the bright tints of October, but the sombre November colors of the surrounding hills. Though I passed over it as gently as possible, the slight undulations produced by my boat extended almost as far as I could see, and gave a ribbed appearance to the reflections. But, as I was looking over the surface, I saw here and there at a distance a faint glimmer, as if some skater insects which had escaped the frosts might be collected there, or, perchance, the surface, being so smooth, betrayed where a spring welled up from the bottom. Paddling gently to one of these places, I was surprised to find myself surrounded by myriads of small perch, about five inches long, of a rich bronze color in the green water, sporting there, and constantly rising to the surface and dimpling it, sometimes leaving bubbles on it. In such transparent and seemingly bottomless water, reflecting the clouds, I seemed to be floating through the air as in a balloon, and their swimming impressed me as a kind of flight or hovering, as if they were a compact flock of birds passing just beneath my level on the right or left, their fins, like sails, set all around them. There were many such schools in the pond, apparently improving the short season before winter would draw an icy shutter over their broad skylight, sometimes giving to the surface an appearance as if a slight breeze struck it, or a few rain-drops fell there.

# LETTER TO ASA GRAY, September 5th, 1857

*by Charles Darwin*

My dear Gray—

I forget the exact words which I used in my former letter, but I daresay I said that I thought you would utterly despise me, when I told you what views I had arrived at, which I did because I thought I was bound as an honest man to do so....

I did not feel in the least sure that when you knew whither I was tending, that you might not think me so wild & foolish in my views (God knows arrived at slowly enough, & I hope conscientiously) that you would think me worth no more notice or assistance. To give one example, the last time I saw my dear old friend Falconer, he attacked me most vigorously, but quite kindly, & told me "you will do more harm than any ten naturalists will do good"— "I can see that you have already *corrupted* & half-spoiled Hooker"(!!). Now when I see such strong feeling in my oldest friends, you need not wonder that I always expect my views to be received with contempt. But enough & too much of this.—...

As you seem interested in subject, & as it is an *immense* advantage to me to write to you & to hear *ever so briefly*, what you think, I will enclose (copied so as to save you trouble in reading) the briefest abstract of my notions on the *means* by which nature makes her species. Why I think that species have really changed depends on general facts in the affinities, embryology, rudimentary organs, geological history & geographical distribution of organic beings. In regard to my abstract you must take immensely on trust; each paragraph occupying one or two chapters in my Book. You will, perhaps, think it paltry in me, when I ask you not to mention my doctrine; the reason is, if anyone, like the Author of the Vestiges, were to hear of them, he might easily work them in, & then I shd'have to quote from a work perhaps despised by naturalists & this would greatly injure any chance of my views being received by those alone whose opinion I value.—...

My dear Dr. Gray

Believe me with much sincerity

Your's truly

C. Darwin...

### Enclosure

I. It is wonderful what the principle of Selection by Man, that is the picking out of individuals with any desired quality, and breeding from them, and again picking out, can do. Even Breeders have been astonished at their own results. They can act on differences inappreciable to an uneducated eye. Selection has been *methodically* followed in *Europe* for only the last half century. But it has occasionally, and even in some degree methodically, been followed in the most ancient times. There must have been, also, a kind of unconscious selection from the most ancient times,—namely in the preservation of the individual animals

---

Charles Darwin, letter to Asa Gray, September 5th, 1857; Reprinted in Frederick Burkhardt, ed., *Charles Darwin's Letters: A Selection 1825–1859*, New York: Cambridge University Press, 1996, pp. 177–179.

© Cambridge University Press, 1996. Reprinted with the permission of Cambridge University Press.

(without any thought of their offspring) most useful to each race of man in his particular circumstances. The "rogueing," as nurserymen call the destroying of varieties, which depart from their type, is a kind of selection. I am convinced that intentional and occasional selection has been the main agent in making our domestic races. But, however, this may be, its great power of modification has been indisputably shown in late times. Selection acts only by the accumulation of slight or greater variations, caused by external conditions, or by the mere fact that in generation the child is not absolutely similar to its parent. Man by this power of accumulating variations adapts living beings to his wants,— he *may be said* to make the wool of one sheep good for carpets and another for cloth, &c.—

II. Now suppose there were a being, who did not judge by mere external appearance, but who could study the whole internal organization—who was never capricious,—and should go on selecting for one end during millions of generations, who will say what he might not effect! In nature we have some *slight* variations, occasionally in all parts: and I think it can be shown that a change in the conditions of existence is the main cause of the child not exactly resembling its parents; and in nature geology shows us what changes have taken place, and are taking place. We have almost unlimited time: no one but a practical geologist can fully appreciate this: think of the Glacial period, during the whole of which the same species of shells at least have existed; there must have been during this period millions on millions of generations.

III. I think it can be shown that there is such an unerring power at work, or *Natural Selection* (the title of my Book), which selects exclusively for the good of each organic being. The elder De Candolle, W. Herbert, and Lyell have written strongly on the struggle for life; but even they have not written strongly enough. Reflect that every being (even the Elephant) breeds at such a rate, that in a few years, or at most a few centuries or thousands of years, the surface of the earth would not hold the progeny of any one species. I have found it hard constantly to bear in mind that the increase of every single species is checked during some part of its life, or during some shortly recurrent generation. Only a few of those annually born can live to propagate their kind. What a trifling difference must often determine which shall survive, and which perish—

IV Now take the case of a country undergoing some change; this will tend to cause some of its inhabitants to vary slightly; not what I believe most beings vary at all times enough for selection to act on. Some of its inhabitants will be exterminated, and the remainder will be exposed to the mutual action of a different set of inhabitants, which I believe to be more important to the life of each being than mere climate. Considering the infinitely various ways, beings have to obtain food by struggling with other beings, to escape danger at various times of life, to have their eggs or seeds disseminated, &c. &c., I cannot doubt that during millions of generations individuals of a species will be born with some slight variation profitable to some part of its economy; such will have a better chance of surviving, propagating, which again will be slowly increased by the accumulative action of Natural Selection; and the variety thus formed will either coexist with, or more commonly, will exterminate its parent form. An organic being like the woodpecker or misletoe may thus come to be adapted to a score of contingencies: natural selection, accumulating those slight variations in all parts of its structure which are in any way useful to it, during any part of its life.

V. Multiform difficulties will occur to everyone on this theory. Most can I think be satisfactorily answered.— "Natura non facit saltum" answers some of the most obvious.— The slowness of the change, and only a very few undergoing change at any one time answers others. The extreme imperfection of our geological records answers others.—

VI. One other principle, which may be called the principle of divergence plays, I believe, an important part in the origin of species. The same spot will support more life if occupied by very diverse forms: we see this in the many generic forms in a square yard of turf (I have counted 20 species belonging to 18 genera),—or in the plants and insects, on any little uniform islet, belonging almost to as many genera and families as species.— We can understand this with the higher, animals whose habits we understand. We know that it has been experimentally shown that a plot of land will yield a greater weight, if cropped with several species of grasses than with 2 or 3 species. Now every single organic being, by propagating so rapidly, may be said to be striving its utmost to increase in numbers. So it will be with the offspring of any species after it has broken into varieties, or sub-species or true species. And it follows, I think, from the foregoing facts, that the varying offspring of each species will try (only few will succeed) to seize on as many and as diverse places in the economy of nature, as possible. Each new variety or species, when formed will generally take the place of and so exterminate its less well-fitted parent. This, I believe, to be the origin of the classification or arrangement of all organic beings at all times. These always *seem* to branch and sub-branch like a tree from a common trunk; the flourishing twigs destroying the less vigorous,—the dead and lost branches rudely representing extinct genera and families.

This sketch is *most* imperfect; but in so short a space I cannot make it better. Your imagination must fill up many wide blanks.— Without some reflexion it will appear all rubbish; perhaps it will appear so after reflexion.—

C. D.

This little abstract touches only on the accumulative power of natural selection, which I look at as by far the most important element in the production of new forms. The laws governing the incipient or primordial variation (unimportant except as to groundwork for selection to act on, in which respect it is all important) I shall discuss under several heads, but I can come, as you may well believe, only to very partial & imperfect conclusions.—

# MAN AND NATURE (or PHYSICAL GEOGRAPHY AS MODIFIED BY HUMAN ACTION)

## Excerpt

*By G. Perkins Marsh*

The object of the present volume is: to indicate the character and approximately, the extent of the changes produced by human action and the physical conditions of the globe we inhabit; to point out the dangers of imprudence and the necessity of caution in all operations which, on a large scale, interfere with the spontaneous arrangements of the organic and inorganic world; to suggest the possibility and the importance of the restoration of disturbed harmonies and the material improvement of waste and exhausted regions; and incidentally, to illustrate the doctrine that man is, in both kind and degree, a power of a higher order than any of the other forms of animated life, which like him, are nourished at the table of bounteous nature.

Purely untutored humanity, it is true interferes comparatively little with the arrangements of nature, and the destructive agency of man becomes more and more energetic and unsparing as he advances in civilization, until the impoverishment, with which his exhaustion of the natural resources of the soil is threatening to him, at last awakened him to the necessity of preserving what is left, if not of restoring what has been wantonly wasted. The wandering savage grows no cultivated vegetable, fells no forest, and extirpates no useful plant, no noxious weed. If his skill in the chase enables him to entrap numbers of the animals on which he feeds, he compensates this loss by destroying also the lion, the tiger, the wolf, the otter, the seal, and the eagle, thus would otherwise become the booty of beasts and birds of prey. But with stationary life, or rather with the pastoral state, man at once commences an almost indiscriminate warfare upon all the forms of animal and vegetable existence around him, and as he advances in civilization, he gradually eradicates or transforms every spontaneous product of the soil he occupies....

*Man and Nature*, New York: Charles Scribner, 1864.

## SITTING BULL 1877

### *Excerpt*

"They claim this Mother Earth of ours for their own and fence their neighbors away from them. They degrade the landscape with their buildings and their waste. They compel the natural earth to produce excessively and when it fails, they force it to take medicine to produce more. This is evil."

Sitting Bull speech at the Powder River Council, 1877.

# "THE NEW WORLD"

## Excerpt from Our Plundered Planet

*By Fairfield Osborn*

And now come to the United States, the country of the great illusion, the country that "can feed the world." What has happened there during its turbulent and inconceivable period of development and what is happening there today?

The story of our nation in the last century as regards the use of forests, grasslands, wildlife and water sources is the most violent and the most destructive of any written in the long history of civilization. The velocity of events is unparalleled and we today are still so near to it that it is almost impossible to realize what has happened, or, far more important, what is still happening. Actually it is the story of human energy unthinking and uncontrolled. No wonder there is this new concept of man as a large-scale geological force, mentioned on an earlier page.

In the attempt to gain at least some perspective let us review a little. Our people came to a country of unique natural advantages, of varying yet favorable climates, where the earth's resources were apparently limitless. Incredible energy marked the effort of a young nation to hack new homes for freedom-loving people out of the vast wilderness of forests that extended interminably to the grassland areas of the Midwest. Inevitably the quickest methods were used in putting the land to cultivation, not the desirable methods. Great areas of forest were completely denuded by ax or fire, without thought of the relationship of forests to water sources, or to the soil itself. Constantly there was the rising pressure for cultivable land caused by the rapid inpouring of new settlers. By about 1830 most of the better land east of the Mississippi was occupied. In that year there were approximately 13,000,000 people in this country, or less than one tenth of the present population. In the meanwhile the land in the South, long occupied and part of the original colonies, was being devoted more and more expansively to cotton, highly profitable as export to the looms in England, and tobacco, for which there was a growing world market. These are known as clean-tilled crops, meaning that the earth is left completely care except for the plantings and is a type of land use most susceptible to loss of topsoil by erosion. Today a large proportion, in many areas from one third to one half, of the land originally put to productive use for the growing of cotton and tobacco has become wasteland and has had to be abandoned. It is not unusual for Southerners to blame the Civil War and its aftereffects for their impoverishment. There are other reasons.

There is no particular point in tracing the westward surge of settlers over the great grass plains that lay beyond the Mississippi and on to the vast forested slopes bordering the Pacific. Everyone knows the story. It is significant, however, that the movement, dramatic as any incident in human history, was symbolized by the phrases "subjugating the land" and "conquering the continent." It was a positive conquest in terms of human fortitude and energy. It was a destructive conquest, and still continues to be one, in terms of human understanding that nature is an ally and not an enemy.

*Our Plundered Planet*, Fairfield Osborn, Boston: Little, Brown & Company, 1948, pp. 175–185. Reprinted with permission.

Incidentally, it is not generally realized that the prairies, the long-grass country, and the plains, the short-grass country, occupy nearly 40 per cent of the land surface of the United States. Here today are the greatest corn and grain producing regions in the world—as well as the great natural ranges for cattle and other livestock. Here limitless areas of natural grassland have been plowed for crop production. The possibilities of a continued and relentless process of land deterioration are involved. Proper land use can prevent these, but are we prepared and organized to apply the available knowledges regarding the correct utilization and long-term protection of productive soils? One is reminded of the farmer who was not doing right by his land and was urged to go to a meeting on methods of soil conservation. "There's no use my going to that meeting about farming batter," he said. "I don't farm as good as I know how to now." The final test of our nation, a crisis yet to be met, is whether the national attitude will be similar to that of the farmer, or will we have the foresight and intelligence to act before we are met with the disaster that is steadily drawing nearer?

A detailed presentation of what has happened area by area would fill many volumes. A large amount of precise information has been gathered together by various governmental services, by other conservation agencies, and by a handful of individuals whose perception has led them to give attention to an unfolding drama that is as yet visible to so few.

The submission of the following general facts may serve to throw light on what has happened to our land since those bright days when we began to "conquer the continent."

The land area of the United States amounts to approximately one billion nine hundred million acres. In its original or natural state about 40 percent was primitive forest, nearly an equal amount was grass or range lands, the remainder being natural desert or extremely mountainous.

Today the primeval or virgin forest has been so reduced that it covers less than 7 per cent of our entire land area. If to this there are added other forested areas consisting of stands of seconds- or even third-growth forests, many of which are poor in condition, and if scattered farm woodlands are also included, it is found that the forested areas now aggregate only slightly more than 20 per cent of the total land area of our country. If urban lands, desert and wastelands, and mountaintop areas, are subtracted there is left somewhat over one billion acres which can be roughly divided into three categories: farm croplands, farm pasture lands and range-grazing lands.

The situation as to our remaining forests is becoming increasingly serious. Some idea of recent and present trends can be gained from the information contained in the last annual report of the Forest Service of the Federal Government, wherein it is stated that the estimated total stand of saw timber in the country in 1909 was 2826 billion board feet and that the estimate for the year 1945 totaled only 1601 billion board feet, indicating that in 36 years the nation's "woodpile" has been reduced by 44 per cent. The report goes on to state that the drop in volume of standing timber since 1909 has been much greater than these figures indicate. Many kinds of trees which were considered of no value in 1909 are now being used and are included in the 1945 estimate. It is significantly pointed out that more than half of the present total saw-timber resource is in what is left of our virgin forests and that 96 per cent of the virgin timber is in the Western states. This latter statement is of particular interest in the light of a new and serious kind of threat that will be commented on in a moment.

While the drain on our forests for fuel wood, pulpwood, and manufacturing uses, together with losses resulting from fires, wind and ice storms, damage by insects and tree diseases, is almost being met by each year's growth, the bulk of our forestry industry depends on saw timber. For this purpose the annual drain on the nation's forests approximates 54 billion board feet, while the annual growth is only approximately 35 billion board feet. In other words, the annual loss exceeds growth by more than 50 per cent. It does not take much mathematics to prove that our country cannot go on this way much, longer. We are repeating the errors that, as we have seen, have undermined so many other countries in earlier periods of history.

At this very moment a new body blow is being struck at our forests. This is a triple-threat blow, because a blow at forest reserves is one of synchronized impact upon water sources and fertile soils—as deadly ultimately as any, delayed-action bomb. Highly organized minority groups are now engaged in determined attempts to wrest away the public lands of the Western states, and turn these regions to their own uses. Within the boundaries of these public domains lie the extensive grazing lands that help support the cattle industry of the West. These lands are open to use by individual cattle owners at small, in fact, nominal cost. Within these boundaries, too, lie almost all our last great forest reserves. These public lands, in which every American owns a share, lie principally in eleven Western states, namely: Arizona, California, Colorado, Idaho, Montana, Nevada, New Mexico, Oregon, Utah, Washington, Wyoming.

The public lands came into existence in the earliest days of our nation. They were created as a solution to a vexatious question that arose in the deliberations of the thirteen original states at the time the Union was formed. The small seaboard states insisted that provision be made in the Articles of Confederation to prevent the land-rich states on the Appalachian frontier from expanding their boundaries indefinitely to the west and thus dominating the government. All of the original states at that time agreed to give up their claims to the Western lands and ceded them to the Federal Government. As settlement progressed westward, it was planned that these vast tracts would be formed into new states with the same rights as enjoyed by the original states. In 1787 the Constitution that was evolved upon this basic understanding became a fundamental of American law. Since that year the United States has; been enlarged by a series of acquisitions under treaties with other powers, such as the Louisiana Purchase, the Florida Purchase and the Admission of Texas. That is another story. In all thirty-five states have been carved from the public domain, each of them receiving a gift of land, often of many millions of acres, and' yet, as each new state was created, there were retained in the name of the Federal Government, for the benefit of all of the people of the nation, these areas of public lands. During the nineteenth century land appeared to be limitless and few people were at all concerned about how it was used, although even as early as 1836 bills began to appear in Congress to provide some protecting regulations for the lands owned by the government. The proportion of Federal lands remaining as public domain varies in each state, ranging from under 100,000 acres in Iowa to 87 per cent in Nevada. This disparity in the ratio of Federal lands to state and private holdings is one of the reasons for the present controversy. It should not be thought of as a major reason, however. The powerful attacks now being made by small minority groups upon the public lands of the West have one primary motivation and one consuming objective—to exploit the grazing lands and these last forest reserves for every dollar of profit that can be wrung from them. As we have seen in other countries the profit motive, if carried to the extreme, has one certain result—the ultimate death of the land.

The eleven Western states which contain the largest proportion of Federal lands have become known as the "public land states." In practically all of them either the cattle business or lumbering is the major industry. Use of the public lands by cattle owners has always been permitted and, in turn, permits for controlled cutting in the national forests are regularly granted. These rights have frequently been gained at extremely low cost. The fees paid today by cattle-grazing permittees are to all intents and purposes merely nominal ones. Overgrazing in the public lands reached such an alarming point a number of years ago that legislation known as the Taylor Grazing Act was passed in 1934 to control the abuses. For a while this legislation did some good, but as far as beneficial results today are concerned, this act, which was designed to "prevent overgrazing and soil deterioration," might almost as well never have been enacted into law. Powerful minority groups of cattlemen now dominate its administration, their representatives comprising the personnel of the advisory boards that were established in each of the cattle-industry states. In effect these boards are not advisory at all but over the years have acquired sufficient power to greatly influence the regulations, as to both the number of cattle that can graze in a region and the fees for grazing rights to be paid by cattle owners, half of which go to the counties in which the land is situated, mainly for the benefit of rural schools, and the other half to the Federal Government.

The maneuvers of the powerful minority groups of livestock men, skillfully supported by their representatives in Congress, have a definite bearing on the preservation of the remaining reserves of forests in the Western states. Having taken over virtual control of the Federal Grazing Service they now are attempting similarly to control the Forest Service, and, from their point of view, with good reason. The national forests in the Western states contain approximately 135,000,000 acres of land, of which some 80,000,000 acres are now being grazed by cattle or sheep. So far the Forest Service's control of the number of animals permitted to graze in a region has been reasonably effective, although actually there has already been considerable overgrazing in some of the national forests.

But the livestock owners are not satisfied and want more privileges. The game is almost too easy, the methods of getting what they want almost too simple. The Grazing Service was emasculated by Congress's reducing its field service budget to one third of what was needed to provide proper supervision of the ranges. There's generally more than one way of accomplishing an end! Overgrazing in forested areas is ultimately as damaging to forests, because of soil erosion, as slash cutting for the sawmill. As to the latter, let no American think that certain self-seeking groups in the lumber industry are not out to hack what they can from the public domain. They will pay for the right to cut but they can never pay enough because there are not enough forests left. Heretofore our national parks have been held inviolate but even now one of them, the Olympic in the state of Washington, is threatened by legislation pending in Congress that would turn over to exploitation a tract of some 56,000 acres of virgin timber. Wilderness heritages going to the buzzsaw!

# "THE WILDERNESS LETTER"

*By Wallace Stegner*

December 3, 1960                                                                                                           Los Altos, Calif.

David E. Pesonen
Wildland Research Center
Agricultural Experiment Station
243 Mulford Hall?
University of California
Berkeley 4, Calif.

Dear Mr. Pesonen:

I believe that you are working on the wilderness portion of the Outdoor Recreation Resources Review Commission's report. If I may, I should like to urge some arguments for wilderness preservation that involve recreation, as it is ordinarily conceived, hardly at all. Hunting, fishing, hiking, mountain-climbing, camping, photography, and the enjoyment of natural scenery will all, surely, figure in your report. So will the wilderness as a genetic reserve, a scientific yardstick by which we may measure the world in its natural balance against the world in its man-made imbalance. What I want to speak for is not so much the wilderness uses, valuable as those are, but the wilderness idea, which is a resource in itself. Being an intangible and spiritual resource, it will seem mystical to the practical minded—but then anything that cannot be moved by a bulldozer is likely to seem mystical to them.

I want to speak for the wilderness idea as something that has helped form our character and that has certainly shaped our history as a people. It has no more to do with recreation than churches have to do with recreation, or than the strenuousness and optimism and expansiveness of what the historians call the "American Dream" have to do with recreation. Nevertheless, since it is only in this recreation survey that the values of wilderness are being compiled, I hope you will permit me to insert this idea between the leaves, as it were, of the recreation report.

Something will have gone out of us as a people if we ever let the remaining wilderness be destroyed; if we permit the last virgin forests to be turned into comic books and plastic cigarette cases; if we drive the few remaining members of the wild species into zoos or to extinction; if we pollute the last clear air and dirty the last clean streams and push our paved roads through the last of the silence, so that never again will Americans be free in their own country from the noise, the exhausts, the stinks of human and automotive waste. And so that never again can we have the chance to see ourselves single, separate, vertical and individual in the world, part of the environment of trees and rocks and soil, brother to the other animals, part of the natural world and competent to belong in it. Without any remaining wilderness we are committed wholly, without chance for even momentary reflection and rest, to a headlong drive into our technological termite-life, the Brave New World of a completely man-controlled environment. We need wilderness preserved—as much of it as is still left, and as many kinds—because it was the challenge against which our character as a people was formed. The reminder and the reassurance that it is still there is good for our spiritual health even if we never once in ten years set foot in it. It is good for us when we are young, because of the incomparable sanity it can bring briefly, as vacation and

---

www.wilderness.org/OurIssues/Wilderness/wildernessletter.cfm.

rest, into our insane lives. It is important to us when we are old simply because it is there—important, that is, simply as an idea.

We are a wild species, as Darwin pointed out. Nobody ever tamed or domesticated or scientifically bred us. But for at least three millennia we have been engaged in a cumulative and ambitious race to modify and gain control of our environment, and in the process we have come close to domesticating ourselves. Not many people are likely, any more, to look upon what we call "progress" as an unmixed blessing. Just as surely as it has brought us increased comfort and more material goods, it has brought us spiritual losses, and it threatens now to become the Frankenstein that will destroy us. One means of sanity is to retain a hold on the natural world, to remain, insofar as we can, good animals. Americans still have that chance, more than many peoples; for while we were demonstrating ourselves the most efficient and ruthless environment-busters in history, and slashing and burning and cutting our way through a wilderness continent, the wilderness was working on us. It remains in us as surely as Indian names remain on the land. If the abstract dream of human liberty and human dignity became, in America, something more than an abstract dream, mark it down at least partially to the fact that we were in subdued ways subdued by what we conquered.

The Connecticut Yankee, sending likely candidates from King Arthur's unjust kingdom to his Man Factory for rehabilitation, was over-optimistic, as he later admitted. These things cannot be forced, they have to grow. To make such a man, such a democrat, such a believer in human individual dignity, as Mark Twain himself, the frontier was necessary, Hannibal and the Mississippi and Virginia City, and reaching out from those the wilderness; the wilderness as opportunity and idea, the thing that has helped to make an American different from and, until we forget it in the roar of our industrial cities, more fortunate than other men. For an American, insofar as he is new and different at all, is a civilized man who has renewed himself in the wild. The American experience has been the confrontation by old peoples and cultures of a world as new as if it had just risen from the sea. That gave us our hope and our excitement, and the hope and excitement can be passed on to newer Americans, Americans who never saw any phase of the frontier. But only so long as we keep the remainder of our wild as a reserve and a promise—a sort of wilderness bank.

As a novelist, I may perhaps be forgiven for taking literature as a reflection, indirect but profoundly true, of our national consciousness. And our literature, as perhaps you are aware, is sick, embittered, losing its mind, losing its faith. Our novelists are the declared enemies of their society. There has hardly been a serious or important novel in this century that did not repudiate in part or in whole American technological culture for its commercialism, its vulgarity, and the way in which it has dirtied a clean continent and a clean dream. I do not expect that the preservation of our remaining wilderness is going to cure this condition. But the mere example that we can as a nation apply some other criteria than commercial and exploitative considerations would be heartening to many Americans, novelists or otherwise. We need to demonstrate our acceptance of the natural world, including ourselves; we need the spiritual refreshment that being natural can produce. And one of the best places for us to get that is in the wilderness where the fun houses, the bulldozers, and the pavement of our civilization are shut out.

Sherwood Anderson, in a letter to Waldo Frank in the 1920s, said it better than I can. "Is it not likely that when the country was new and men were often alone in the fields and the forest they got a sense of bigness outside themselves that has now in some way been lost.... Mystery whispered in the grass, played in the branches of trees overhead, was caught up and blown across the American line in clouds of dust at evening on the prairies.... I am old enough to remember tales that strengthen my belief in a deep semi-religious influence that was formerly at work among our people. The flavor of it hangs over the best work of Mark Twain.... I can remember old fellows in my home town speaking feelingly of an evening spent on the big empty plains. It had taken the shrillness out of them. They had learned the trick of quiet...."

We could learn it too, even yet; even our children and grandchildren could learn it. But only if we save, for just such absolutely non-recreational, impractical, and mystical uses as this, all the wild that still remains to us.

It seems to me significant that the distinct downturn in our literature from hope to bitterness took place almost at the precise time when the frontier officially came to an end, in 1890, and when the American way of life had begun to turn strongly urban and industrial. The more urban it has become, and the more frantic with technological change, the sicker and more embittered our literature, and I believe our people, have become. For myself, I grew up on the empty plains of Saskatchewan and Montana and in the mountains of Utah, and I put a very high valuation on what those places gave me. And if I had not been able to periodically to renew myself in the mountains and deserts of western America I would be very nearly bughouse. Even when I can't get to the back country, the thought of the colored deserts of southern Utah, or the reassurance that there are still stretches of prairies where the world can be instantaneously perceived as disk and bowl, and where the little but intensely important human being is exposed to the five directions of the thirty-six winds, is a positive consolation. The idea alone can sustain me. But as the wilderness areas are progressively exploited or "improve", as the jeeps and bulldozers of uranium prospectors scar up the deserts and the roads are cut into the alpine timberlands, and as the remnants of the unspoiled and natural world are progressively eroded, every such loss is a little death in me. In us.

I am not moved by the argument that those wilderness areas which have already been exposed to grazing or mining are already deflowered, and so might as well be "harvested". For mining I cannot say much good except that its operations are generally short-lived. The extractable wealth is taken and the shafts, the tailings, and the ruins left, and in a dry country such as the American West the wounds men make in the earth do not quickly heal. Still, they are only wounds; they aren't absolutely mortal. Better a wounded wilderness than none at all. And as for grazing, if it is strictly controlled so that it does not destroy the ground cover, damage the ecology, or compete with the wildlife it is in itself nothing that need conflict with the wilderness feeling or the validity of the wilderness experience. I have known enough range cattle to recognize them as wild animals; and the people who herd them have, in the wilderness context, the dignity of rareness; they belong on the frontier, moreover, and have a look of rightness. The invasion they make on the virgin country is a sort of invasion that is as old as Neolithic man, and they can, in moderation, even emphasize a man's feeling of belonging to the natural world. Under surveillance, they can belong; under control, they need not deface or mar. I do not believe that in wilderness areas where grazing has never been permitted, it should be permitted; but I do not believe either that an otherwise untouched wilderness should be eliminated from the preservation plan because of limited existing uses such as grazing which are in consonance with the frontier condition and image.

Let me say something on the subject of the kinds of wilderness worth preserving. Most of those areas contemplated are in the national forests and in high mountain country. For all the usual recreational purposes, the alpine and the forest wildernesses are obviously the most important, both as genetic banks and as beauty spots. But for the spiritual renewal, the recognition of identity, the birth of awe, other kinds will serve every bit as well. Perhaps, because they are less friendly to life, more abstractly nonhuman, they will serve even better. On our Saskatchewan prairie, the nearest neighbor was four miles away, and at night we saw only two lights on all the dark rounding earth. The earth was full of animals—field mice, ground squirrels, weasels, ferrets, badgers, coyotes, burrowing owls, snakes. I knew them as my little brothers, as fellow creatures, and I have never been able to look upon animals in any other way since. The sky in that country came clear down to the ground on every side, and it was full of great weathers, and clouds, and winds, and hawks. I hope I learned something from looking a long way, from looking up, from being much alone. A prairie like that, one big enough to carry the eye clear to the sinking, rounding horizon, can be as lonely and grand and simple in its forms as the sea. It is as good a place as any for the wilderness experience to happen; the vanishing prairie is as worth preserving for the wilderness idea as the alpine forest.

So are great reaches of our western deserts, scarred somewhat by prospectors but otherwise open, beautiful, waiting, close to whatever God you want to see in them. Just as a sample, let me suggest the Robbers' Roost country in Wayne County, Utah, near the Capitol Reef National Monument. In that desert climate the dozer and jeep tracks will not soon melt back into the earth, but the country has a way of making the scars insignificant. It is a lovely and terrible wilderness, such as wilderness as Christ and the prophets went out into; harshly and beautifully colored, broken and worn until its bones are exposed, its great sky without a smudge of taint from Technocracy, and in hidden corners and pockets under its cliffs the sudden poetry of springs. Save a piece of country like that intact, and it does not matter in the slightest that only a few people every year will go into it. That is precisely its value. Roads would be a desecration, crowds would ruin it. But those who haven't the strength or youth to go into it and live can simply sit and look. They can look two hundred miles, clear into Colorado: and looking down over the cliffs and canyons of the San Rafael Swell and the Robbers' Roost they can also look as deeply into themselves as anywhere I know. And if they can't even get to the places on the Aquarius Plateau where the present roads will carry them, they can simply contemplate the idea, take pleasure in the fact that such a timeless and uncontrolled part of earth is still there.

These are some of the things wilderness can do for us. That is the reason we need to put into effect, for its preservation, some other principle that the principles of exploitation or "usefulness" or even recreation. We simply need that wild country available to us, even if we never do more than drive to its edge and look in. For it can be a means of reassuring ourselves of our sanity as creatures, a part of the geography of hope.

Very sincerely yours,

Wallace Stegner

Portions of Wallace Stegner's "Wilderness Letter," have been widely quoted. Wilderness scholars may be interested in the full text, which is sometimes hard to find. We've provided it here, along with an introduction to the letter written by Stegner for *The Living Wilderness* magazine in December 1980.

# THE GEOGRAPHY OF HOPE

## Introduction to Wilderness Letter

*By Wallace Stegner*

When I wrote my "wilderness letter" to David Pesonen 20 years ago, I had probably been prompted to do so by David Brower. He was usually the cattleprod that woke me from other preoccupations and from my workaholism and directed my attention to something important. In this case what he woke me to was close to my heart. I had been lucky enough to grow up next to wilderness, or quasi-wilderness, of several kinds, and I was prepared to argue for the preservation of wilderness not simply as a scientific reserve, or a land-bank, or a playground, but as a spiritual resource, a leftover from our frontier origins that could reassure us of our identity as a nation and a people. The Wilderness Bill, already debated for years and the subject of hundreds of official pages, had not yet passed. The ORRRC report, with its inventory of what remained of our outdoors and its promise of reorganization of the bureaus managing it, seemed a good place to put in a word.

By luck or accident or the mysterious focusing by which ideas whose time has come reach many minds at the same time, my letter struck a chord. Before it had time to appear in the ORRRC report, Secretary of the Interior Stewart Udall had picked it up and used it as the basis of a speech before a wilderness conference in San Francisco, and the Sierra Club had published it as a document of that conference. It was published in the *Washington Post* and the ORRRC report, and I included it in my collection of essays, *The Sound of Mountain Water.* Before long, some friend of mine saw it posted on the wall in a Kenya game park. From there, someone in South Africa or Rhodesia carried it home and had an artist named C. B. Cunningham surround it with drawings of African animals and birds, and turned it into a poster which the Natal Park Board, a Rhodesian kindness-to-animals organization and perhaps other groups have distributed all over south and east Africa. A quotation from it captions a Canadian poster, with a magnificent George Calef photograph of caribou crossing river ice; and I have heard of, but not seen, a similar Australian poster issued with the same intent. The Sierra Club borrowed its last four words, "the geography of hope," as the title for Eliot Porter's book of photographs of Baja California. Altogether, this letter, the labor of an afternoon, has gone farther around the world than other writings on which I have spent years.

I take this as evidence not of special literary worth, but of an earnest, world-wide belief in the idea it expresses. There are millions of people on every continent who feel the need of what Sherwood Anderson called "a sense of bigness outside ourselves"; we all need something to take the shrillness out of us.

Returning to the letter after 20 years, I find that my opinions have not changed. They have actually been sharpened by an increased urgency. We are 20 years closer to showdown. Though the Wilderness Bill in which we all placed our hopes was passed, and though many millions of acres have been permanently protected—the magnificent Salmon River wilderness only a few weeks ago—preservation has not moved as fast as it should have, and the Forest Service, in particular, has shown by its reluctance and foot-dragging that it often puts resource use above preservation. Its proposed wilderness areas have consistently been minimal, and RARE II was a travesty.

Nevertheless, something saved. And something still to fight for. And also, since the BLM Organic Act, another plus-minus development. It is now possible that out of the deserts and dry grasslands managed by the BLM there may be primitive areas set aside as wilderness, as I suggested in my letter to Pesonen and as some of us proposed to Secretary Udall as early as 1961. Unhappily, the Organic Act was contemporary with the energy crisis and the growing awareness that the undeveloped country in the Rocky Mountains states is one of the greatest energy mines on earth. That discovery, at a time of national anxiety about energy sources, has brought forward individuals, corporations, and conglomerates all eager to serve their country by strip mining the BLM wasteland, or drilling it for oil and gas. Economic temptation begets politicians willing to serve special economic interests, and they in turn bring on a new wave of states'-rights agitation, this time nicknamed the Sagebrush Rebellion. Its purpose, as in the 1940s when Bernard DeVoto headed the resistance to it, (it was then called Landgrab) is to force the transfer of public lands from federal control the control of the states, which will know how to make their resources available to those who will know what to do with them. After that they can be returned to the public for expensive rehabilitation.

The Sagebrush Rebellion is the worst enemy not only of long-range management of the public lands, but of wilderness. If its counterpart in the 1940s had won, we would have no wilderness areas at all, and deteriorated national forests. If it wins in the 1980s we will have only such wilderness as is already formally set aside. Federal bureaus are imperfect human institutions, and have sins to answer for, and are not above being influenced by powerful interests. Nevertheless they represent the public interest, by and large, and not corporate interests anxious to exploit public resources at the public's expense.

In my letter to David Pesonen 20 years ago I spoke with some feeling about the deserts of southern Utah–Capitol Reef, the San Rafael Swell, the Escalante Desert, the Aquarius Plateau. That whole area has been under threat for nearly a decade, and though the Kaiparowits Complex was defeated and the Intermountain Power Project forced to relocate northward into the Sevier Desert near Lynndyl, the Union Pacific and 13 other companies are still pushing to mine the coal in the Kaiparowits Plateau, surrounded by national parks; and a group of utilities wants to open a big strip mine at Alton, four miles from Bryce, and a 500-megawatt power plant in Warner Valley, 17 miles from Zion, and a 2,000-megawatt plant north of Las Vegas, and two slurry pipeline to serve them. The old forest road over the Aquarius is being paved in from both ends, the equally beautiful trail over the Hightop from Salina to Fish Lake is being widened and improved. Our numbers and our energy demands inexorably press upon this country as beautiful as any on earth, country of an Old Testament harshness and serenity.

It is in danger of being made—of helping to make itself—into a sacrifice area. Its air is already less clear, its distances less sharp. its water table, if these mines and plants and pipelines are created, will sink out of sight, its springs will dry up, its streams will shrink and go intermittent. But there will be more blazing illumination along the Las Vegas Strip, and the little Mormon towns of Wayne and Garfield and Kane Counties will acquire some interesting modern problems.

What impresses me after 20 years is how far the spoiling of that superb country has already gone, and how few are the local supporters of the federal agencies which are the only protection against it. They would do well to consider how long the best thing in their lives has been preserved for them by federal management, and how much they will locally lose if the if the Sagebrush Rebellion wins. Furthermore, the land that the Sagebrush Rebellion wants transferred, the chickenhouse that it wants to put under the guard of the foxes, belongs as much to me, or to a grocer in Des Moines, or a taxi driver in Newark, as to anyone else. And I am not willing to see it wrecked just to increase corporate profits and light Las Vegas.

# 1968 MIT FACULTY STATEMENT OF UNION OF CONCERNED SCIENTISTS

## Founding Document

Below is the text of the Faculty Statement written at the Massachusetts Institute of Technology in December 1968. This document was originally signed by 50 senior faculty members, including the heads of the biology, chemistry, and physics departments, and was later circulated to the entire faculty for endorsement. Faculty and student actions on the concerns that prompted this statement resulted in the founding of the Union of Concerned Scientists in early 1969.

> Misuse of scientific and technical knowledge presents a major threat to the existence of mankind. Through its actions in Vietnam our government has shaken our confidence in its ability to make wise and humane decisions. There is also disquieting evidence of an intention to enlarge further our immense destructive capability.
>
> The response of the scientific community to these developments has been hopelessly fragmented. There is a small group that helps to conceive these policies, and a handful of eminent men who have tried but largely failed to stem the tide from within the government. The concerned majority has been on the sidelines and ineffective. We feel that it is no longer possible to remain uninvolved.
>
> We therefore call on scientists and engineers at MIT, and throughout the country, to unite for concerted action and leadership: Action against dangers already unleashed and leadership toward a more responsible exploitation of scientific knowledge.
>
> With these ends in mind we propose:
>
> 1. To initiate a critical and continuing examination of governmental policy in areas where science and technology are of actual or potential significance.
>
> 2. To devise means for turning research applications away from the present emphasis on military technology toward the solution of pressing environmental and social problems.
>
> 3. To convey to our students the hope that they will devote themselves to bringing the benefits of science and technology to mankind and to ask them to scrutinize the issues raised here before participating in the construction of destructive weapons systems.
>
> 4. To express our determined opposition to ill-advised and hazardous projects such as the ABM system, the enlargement of our nuclear arsenal, and the development of chemical and biological weapons.
>
> 5. To explore the feasibility of organizing scientists and engineers so that their desire for a more humane and civilized world can be translated into effective political action.
>
> As a first step toward reaching these objectives, we ask our colleagues—faculty and students—to stop their research activity at MIT on March 4 and join us for a day devoted to examination of the present situation and its alternatives. On that day, we propose to engage in intensive public discussion and planning for future actions along the lines suggested above.
>
> If you share our profound apprehension, and are seeking a mode of expression which is at once practical and symbolic, join us on March 4.

Reprinted with permission of the Union of Concerned Scientists.

# ARITHMETIC, POPULATION AND ENERGY

*By Dr. Albert Bartlett;*
*Edited by Denis Morel*

Thank you very much, Hugh.

It's a great pleasure to be here, and to have a chance just to share with you some very simple ideas about the problems we're facing. Some of these problems are local, some are national, some are global.

They're all tied together. They're tied together by arithmetic, and the arithmetic isn't very difficult. What I hope to do is, I hope to be able to convince you that the greatest shortcoming of the human race is our inability to understand the exponential function.

Well, you say, what's the exponential function?

This is a mathematical function that you'd write down if you're going to describe the size of anything that was growing steadily. If you had something growing 5% per year, you'd write the exponential function to show how large that growing quantity was, year after year. And so we're talking about a situation where the time that's required for the growing quantity to increase by a fixed fraction is a constant: 5% per year, the 5% is a fixed fraction, the "per year" is a fixed length of time. So that's what we want to talk about: its just ordinary steady growth.

Well, if it takes a fixed length of time to grow 5%, it follows it takes a longer fixed length of time to grow 100%. That longer time's called the doubling time and we need to know how you calculate the doubling time. It's easy.

You just take the number 70, divide it by the percent growth per unit time and that gives you the doubling time. So our example of 5% per year, you divide the 5 into 70, you find that growing quantity will double in size every 14 years.

Well, you might ask, where did the 70 come from? The answer is that it's approximately 100 multiplied by the natural logarithm of two. If you wanted the time to triple, you'd use the natural logarithm of three. So it's all very logical. But you don't have to remember where it came from, just remember 70.

I wish we could get every person to make this mental calculation every time we see a percent growth rate of anything in a news story. For example, if you saw a story that said things had been growing 7% per year for several recent years, you wouldn't bat an eyelash. But when you see a headline that says crime has doubled in a decade, you say "My heavens, what's happening?"

OK, what is happening? 7% growth per year: divide the seven into 70, the doubling time is ten years. But notice, if you want to write a headline to get people's attention, you'd never write "Crime Growing 7% Per Year," nobody would know what it means. Now, do you know what 7% means?

Let's take an example, another example from Colorado. The cost of an all-day lift ticket to ski at Vail has been growing about 7% per year ever since Vail first opened in 1963. At that time you

---

Source: http://globalpublicmedia.com/transcripts/645. Reprinted with permission.

paid $5 for an all-day lift ticket. What's the doubling time for 7% growth? Ten years. So what was the cost ten years later in 1973? (showing slides of rapidly increasing prices) Ten years later in 1983? Ten years later in 1993? What was it last year in 2003, and what do we have to look forward to? (shows "2003: $80; 2013: $160; 2023: $320; audience laughter)

This is what 7% means. Most people don't have a clue. And how is Vail doing? They're pretty much on schedule.

So let's look at a generic graph of something that's growing steadily. After one doubling time, the growing quantity is up to twice its initial size. Two doubling times, it's up to four times its initial size. Then it goes to 8, 16, 32, 64, 128, 256, 512, in ten doubling times it's a thousand times larger than when it started. You can see if you try to make a graph of that on ordinary graph paper, the graph's gonna go right through the ceiling.

Now let me give you an example to show the enormous numbers you can get with just a modest number of doublings.

Legend has it that the game of chess was invented by a mathematician who worked for a king. The king was very pleased. He said, "I want to reward you." The mathematician said "My needs are modest. Please take my new chess board and on the first square, place one grain of wheat. On the next square, double the one to make two. On the next square, double the two to make four. Just keep doubling till you've doubled for every square, that will be an adequate payment." We can guess the king thought, "This foolish man. I was ready to give him a real reward; all he asked for was just a few grains of wheat."

But let's see what is involved in this. We know there are eight grains on the fourth square. I can get this number, eight, by multiplying three twos together. It's 2x2x2, it's one 2 less than the number of the square. Now that continues in each case. So on the last square, I'd find the number of grains by multiplying 63 twos together.

Now let's look at the way the totals build up. When we add one grain on the first square, the total on the board is one. We add two grains, that makes a total of three. We put on four grains, now the total is seven. Seven is a grain less than eight, it's a grain less than three twos multiplied together. Fifteen is a grain less than four twos multiplied together. That continues in each case, so when we're done, the total number of grains will be one grain less than the number I get multiplying 64 twos together. My question is, how much wheat is that?

You know, would that be a nice pile here in the room? Would it fill the building? Would it cover the county to a depth of two meters? How much wheat are we talking about?

The answer is, it's roughly 400 times the 1990 worldwide harvest of wheat. That could be more wheat than humans have harvested in the entire history of the earth. You say, "How did you get such a big number?" and the answer is, it was simple. We just started with one grain, but we let the number grow steadily till it had doubled a mere 63 times.

Now there's something else that's very important: the growth in any doubling time is greater than the total of all the preceding growth. For example, when I put eight grains on the 4th square, the eight is larger than the total of seven that were already there. I put 32 grains on the 6th square. The 32 is larger than the total of 31 that were already there. Every time the growing quantity doubles, it takes more than all you'd used in all the proceeding growth.

Well, let's translate that into the energy crisis. Here's an ad from the year 1975. It asks the question "Could America run out of electricity?" America depends on electricity. Our need for electricity actually doubles every 10 or 12 years. That's an accurate reflection of a very long history of steady growth of the electric industry in this country, growth at a rate of around 7% per year, which gives you doubling every 10 years.

Now, with all that history of growth, they just expected the growth would go on, forever. Fortunately it stopped, not because anyone understood arithmetic, it stopped for other reasons. Well, let's ask "What if?" Suppose the growth had continued? Then we would see here the thing we just saw with the chess board. In the ten years following the appearance of this ad, in that decade, the amount of electrical energy we would have consumed in this country would have been greater than the total of all of the electrical energy we had ever consumed in the entire proceeding history of the steady growth of that industry in this country.

Now, did you realise that anything as completely acceptable as 7% growth per year could give such an incredible consequence? That in just ten years you'd use more than the total of all that had been used in all the proceeding growth?

Well, that's exactly what President Carter was referring to in his speech on energy. One of his statements was this: he said, "In each of those decades (1950s and 1960s) more oil was consumed than in all of mankind's previous history." By itself that's a stunning statement.

Now you can understand it. The president was telling us the simple consequence of the arithmetic of 7% growth each year in world oil consumption, and that was the historic figure up until the 1970s.

There's another beautiful consequence of this arithmetic. If you take 70 years as a period of time—and note that that's roughly one human lifetime—then any percent growth continued steadily for 70 years gives you an overall increase by a factor that's very easy to calculate. For example, 4% per year for 70 years, you find the factor by multiplying four twos together, it's a factor of 16.

A few years ago, one of the newspapers of my hometown of Boulder, Colorado, quizzed the nine members of the Boulder City Council and asked them, "What rate of growth of Boulder's population do you think it would be good to have in the coming years?" Well, the nine members of the Boulder City council gave answers ranging from a low of 1% per year. Now, that happens to match the present rate of growth of the population of the United States. We are not at zero population growth. Right now, the number of Americans increases every year by over three million people. No member of the council said Boulder should grow less rapidly than the United States is growing.

Now, the highest answer any council member gave was 5% per year. You know, I felt compelled, I had to write him a letter and say, "Did you know that 5% per year for just 70 … " I can remember when 70 years used to seem like an awful long time, it just doesn't seem so long now. (audience laughter). Well, that means Boulder's population would increase by a factor of 32. That is, where today we have one overloaded sewer treatment plant, in 70 years, we'd need 32 overloaded sewer treatment plants.

Now did you realise that anything as completely all-American as 5% growth per year could give such an incredible consequence in such a modest period of time? Our city council people have zero understanding of this very simple arithmetic.

Well, a few years ago, I had a class of non-science students. We were interested in problems of science and society. We spent a lot of time learning to use semi-logarithmic graph paper. It's printed in such a way that these equal intervals on the vertical scale each represent an increase by a factor of 10. So you go from one thousand to ten thousand to a hundred thousand, and the reason you use this special paper is that on this paper, a straight line represents steady growth.

Now, we worked a lot of examples. I said to the students, "Let's talk about inflation, let's talk about 7% per year." It wasn't this high when we did this, it's been higher since then, fortunately it's lower now. And I said to the students, as I can say to you, you have roughly sixty years life expectancy ahead of you. Let's see what some common things will cost if we have 60 years of 7% annual inflation.

The students found that a 55-cent gallon of gasoline will cost $35.20; $2.50 for a movie will be $160; the $15 sack of groceries my mother used to buy for a dollar and a quarter, that will be $960; a $100 suit of clothes, $6,400; a $4000 automobile will cost a quarter of a million dollars; and a $45,000 home will cost nearly 3 million dollars.

Well, I gave the students these data (shows overhead). These came from a Blue Cross, Blue Shield ad. The ad appeared in *Newsweek* magazine and the ad gave these figures to show the cost escalation of gall bladder surgery in the years since 1950, when that surgery cost $361. I said, "Make a semi logarithmic plot, let's see what's happening." The students found that the first four points lined up on a straight line whose slope indicated inflation of about 6% per year, but the fourth, fifth, and sixth were on a steeper line, almost 10% inflation per year. Well, then I said to the students, "Run that steeper line on out to the year 2000, let's get an idea of what gall bladder surgery might cost," and this was, 2000 was four years ago—the answer is $25,000. The lesson there is awfully clear: if you're thinking about gall bladder surgery, do it now. (audience laughter)

In the summer of 1986, the news reports indicated that the world population had reached the number of five billion people growing at the rate of 1.7% per year. Well, your reaction to 1.7% might be to say "Well, that's so small, nothing bad could ever happen at 1.7% per year." So you calculate the doubling time, you find it's only 41 years. Now, that was back in 1986; more recently in 1999, we read that the world population had grown from five billion to six billion . The good news is that the growth rate had dropped from 1.7% to 1.3% per year. The bad news is that in spite of the drop in the growth rate, the world population today is increasing by about 75 million additional people every year.

Now, if this current modest 1.3% per year could continue, the world population would grow to a density of one person per square meter on the dry land surface of the earth in just 780 years, and the mass of people would equal the mass of the earth in just 2400 years. Well, we can smile at those, we know they couldn't happen. This one make for a cute cartoon; the caption says, "Excuse me sir, but I am prepared to make you a rather attractive offer for your square."

There's a very profound lesson in that cartoon. The lesson is that zero population growth is going to happen. Now, we can debate whether we like zero population growth or don't like it, it's going to happen. Whether we debate it or not, whether we like it or not, it's absolutely certain. People could never live at that density on the dry land surface of the earth. Therefore, today's high birth rates will drop; today's low death rates will rise till they have exactly the same numerical value. That will certainly be in a time short compared to 780 years. So maybe you're wondering then, what options are available if we wanted to address the problem.

In the left hand column, I've listed some of those things that we should encourage if we want to raise the rate of growth of population and in so doing, make the problem worse. Just look at the list. Everything in the list is as sacred as motherhood. There's immigration, medicine, public health, sanitation. These are all devoted to the humane goals of lowering the death rate and that's very important to me, if it's my death they're lowering. But then I've got to realise that anything that just lowers the death rate makes the population problem worse.

There's peace, law and order; scientific agriculture has lowered the death rate due to famine—that just makes the population problem worse. It's widely reported that the 55 mph speed limit saved thousands of lives—that just makes the population problem worse. Clean air makes it worse.

Now, in this column are some of the things we should encourage if we want to lower the rate of growth of population and in so doing, help solve the population problem. Well, there's abstention, contraception, abortion, small families, stop immigration, disease, war, murder, famine, accidents. Now, smoking clearly raises the death rate; well, that helps solve the problem.

Remember our conclusion from the cartoon of one person per square meter; we concluded that zero population growth is going to happen. Let's state that conclusion in other terms and say it's obvious nature is going to choose from the right hand list and we don't have to do anything—except be prepared to live with whatever nature chooses from that right hand list. Or we can exercise the one option that's open to us, and that option is to choose first from the right hand list. We gotta find something here we can go out and campaign for. Anyone here for promoting disease? (audience laughter)

We now have the capability of incredible war; would you like more murder, more famine, more accidents? Well, here we can see the human dilemma—everything we regard as good makes the population problem worse, everything we regard as bad helps solve the problem. There is a dilemma if ever there was one.

The one remaining question is education: does it go in the left hand column or the right hand column? I'd have to say thus far in this country it's been in the left hand column—it's done very little to reduce ignorance of the problem.

So where do we start? Well, let's start in Boulder, Colorado. Here's my home town. There's the 1950 census figure, 1960, 1970—in that period of twenty years, the average growth rate of Boulder's population was 6% per year. With big efforts, we've been able to slow the growth somewhat. There's the 2000 census figure. I'd like to ask people: let's start with that 2000 figure, go another 70 years—one human life time—and ask: what rate of growth would we need in Boulder's population in the next 70 years so that at the end of 70 years, the population of Boulder would equal today's population of your choice of major American cities?

Boulder in 70 years could be as big as Boston is today if we just grew 2.58% per year. Now, if we thought Detroit was a better model, we'll have to shoot for 31?4% per year. Remember the historic figure on the preceding slide, 6% per year? If that could continue for one lifetime, the population of Boulder would be larger than the population of Los Angeles. Well, I'll just tell you, you couldn't put the population of Los Angles in the Boulder valley. Therefore it's obvious, Boulder's population growth is going to stop and the only question is, will we be able to stop it while there is still some open space, or will we wait until it's wall-to-wall people and we're all choking to death?

Now, every once in a while somebody says to me, "But you know, a bigger city might be a better city," and I have to say, "Wait a minute, we've done that experiment!" We don't need to wonder what will be the effect of growth on Boulder because Boulder tomorrow can be seen in Los Angeles today. And for the price of an airplane ticket, we can step 70 years into the future and see exactly what it's like. What is it like? There's an interesting headline from Los Angeles. ("...carcinogens in air...") Maybe that has something to do with this headline from Los Angeles. ("Smog kills 1,600 annually...")

So how are we doing in Colorado? Well, we're the growth capital of the USA and proud of it. The Rocky Mountain News tells us to expect another million people in the Front Range in the next 20 years, and what are the consequences of all this? ("Denver's traffic...3rd worst in US...") These are totally predictable, there are no surprises here, we know exactly what happens when you crowd more people into an area.

Well, as you can imagine, growth control is very controversial, and I treasure the letter from which these quotations are taken. Now, this letter was written to me by a leading citizen of our community. He's a leading proponent of "controlled growth." "Controlled growth" just means "growth." This man writes, "I take no exception to your arguments regarding exponential growth." "I don't believe the exponential argument is valid at the local level."

So you see, arithmetic doesn't hold in Boulder. (audience laughs) I have to admit, that man has a degree from the University of Colorado. It's not a degree in mathematics, in science, or in engineering. All right, let's look now at what happens when we have this kind of steady growth in a finite environment.

Bacteria grow by doubling. One bacterium divides to become two, the two divide to become 4, the 4 become 8, 16 and so on. Suppose we had bacteria that doubled in number this way every minute. Suppose we put one of these bacteria into an empty bottle at 11:00 in the morning, and then observe that the bottle is full at 12:00 noon. There's our case of just ordinary steady growth: it has a doubling time of one minute, it's in the finite environment of one bottle.

I want to ask you three questions. Number one: at what time was the bottle half full? Well, would you believe 11:59, one minute before 12:00? Because they double in number every minute.

And the second question: if you were an average bacterium in that bottle, at what time would you first realise you were running of space? Well, let's just look at the last minutes in the bottle. At 12:00 noon, it's full; one minute before, it's half full; 2 minutes before, it's a quarter full; then an 1?8th; then a 1?16th. Let me ask you, at 5 minutes before 12:00, when the bottle is only 3% full and is 97% open space just yearning for development, how many of you would realise there's a problem?

Now, in the ongoing controversy over growth in Boulder, someone wrote to the newspaper some years ago and said "Look, there's no problem with population growth in Boulder, because," the writer said, "we have fifteen times as much open space as we've already used." So let me ask you, what time was it in Boulder when the open space was fifteen times the amount of space we'd already used? The answer is, it was four minutes before 12:00 in Boulder Valley. Well, suppose that at 2 minutes before 12:00, some of the bacteria realise they're running out of space, so they launch a great search for new bottles. They search offshore on the outer continental shelf and in the overthrust belt and in the Arctic, and they find three new bottles. Now that's an incredible discovery, that's three times the total amount of resource they ever knew about before. They now have four bottles, before their discovery, there was only one. Now surely this will give them a sustainable society, won't it?

You know what the third question is: how long can the growth continue as a result of this magnificent discovery? Well, look at the score: at 12:00 noon, one bottle is filled, there are three to go;

12:01, two bottles are filled, there are two to go; and at 12:02, all four are filled and that's the end of the line.

Now, you don't need any more arithmetic than this to evaluate the absolutely contradictory statements that we've all heard and read from experts who tell us in one breath we can go on increasing our rates of consumption of fossil fuels, in the next breath they say "Don't worry, we will always be able to make the discoveries of new resources that we need to meet the requirements of that growth."

Well, a few years ago in Washington, our energy secretary observed that in the energy crisis, "we have a classic case of exponential growth against a finite source." So let's look now at some of these finite sources. We turn to the work of the late Dr. M. King Hubbert. He's plotted here a semi-logarithmic graph of world oil production. You can see the lines have been approximately straight for about 100 years, clear up here to 1970, average growth rate very close to 7% per year. So it's logical to ask, well, how much longer could that 7% growth continue? That's answered by the numbers in this table (shows slide). The numbers in the top line tell us that in the year 1973, world oil production was 20 billion barrels; the total production in all of history, 300 billion; the remaining reserves, 1700 billion.

Now, those are data. The rest of this table is just calculated out assuming the historic 7% growth continued in the years following 1973 exactly as it had been for the proceeding 100 years.

Now, in fact the growth stopped; it stopped because OPEC raised their oil prices. So we're asking here, what if? Suppose we just decided to stay on that 7% growth curve? Let's go back to 1981. By 1981 on the 7% curve, the total usage in all of history would add up to 500 billion barrels; the remaining reserves, 1500 billion. At that point, the remaining reserves are three times the total of everything we'd used in all of history. That's an enormous reserve, but what time is it when the remaining reserve is three times the total of all you've used in all of history? The answer is, it's two minutes before 12:00.

We know for 7% growth, the doubling time is 10 years. We go from 1981 to 1991. By 1991 on the 7% curve, the total usage in all of history would add up to 1000 billion barrels; there would be 1000 billion left. At that point, the remaining oil would be equal in quantity to the total of everything we'd used in the entire history of the oil industry on this earth, 130 years of oil consumption. You'd say, "That's an enormous reserve." But what time is it when the remaining reserve is equal to all you've used in all of history? And the answer is, it's one minute before 12:00. So we go one more decade to the turn of the century—that's like right now—that's when 7% would finish using up the oil reserves of the earth.

So let's look at this in a very nice graphical way. Suppose the area of this tiny rectangle represents all the oil we used on this earth before 1940; then in the decade of the 40s, we used this much (uncovering part of chart): that's equal to all that had been used in all of history. In the decade of the 50s, we used this much (uncovering more of chart) : that's equal to all that had been used in all of history. In the decade of the 60s, we used this much (uncovering more of chart): again that's equal to the total of all the proceeding usage. Here we see graphically what President Carter told us. Now, if that 7% growth had continued through the 70s. 80s, and 90s, there's what we'd need (uncovering rest of chart) . But that's all the oil there is.

Now, there's a widely held belief that if you throw enough money at holes in the ground, oil is sure to come up. Well, there will be discoveries in new oil; there may be major discoveries. But look: we would have to discover this much new oil if we would have that 7% growth continue ten more years. Ask yourself: what do you think is the chance that oil discovered after the close of our meeting today will be in an amount equal to the total of all we've known about in all of history? And then realise if all that new oil could be found, that would be sufficient to let the historic 7% growth continue ten more years.

Well, it's interesting to see what the experts say. Here's from an interview in *Time* magazine, an interview with one of the most widely quoted oil experts in all of Texas. They asked him, "But haven't many of our bigger fields been drilled nearly dry?" And he responds, saying "There's still as much oil to be found in the US as has ever been produced." Now, lets assume he's right. What time is it? And the answer: one minute before 12:00. I've read several things this guy's written; I don't think he has any understanding of this very simple arithmetic.

Well, in the energy crisis about thirty years ago, we saw ads such as this (shows slide). This is from the American Electric Power Company. It's a bit reassuring, sort of saying, now, don't worry too much, because "we're sitting on half of the world's known supply of coal, enough for over 500 years." Well, where did that "500 year" figure come from? It may have had its origin in this report to the committee on Interior and Insular Affairs of the United States Senate, because in that report we find this sentence: "At current levels of output and recovery, these American coal reserves can be expected to last more than 500 years."

There is one of the most dangerous statements in the literature. It's dangerous because it's true. It isn't the truth that makes it dangerous, the danger lies in the fact that people take the sentence apart: they just say coal will last 500 years. They forget the caveat with which the sentence started. Now, what were those opening words? "At current levels." What does that mean? That means if—and only if—we maintain zero growth of coal production.

So let's look at a few numbers. We go to the *Annual Energy Review*, published by the Department of Energy. They give this (pointing) as the coal demonstrated reserve base in the United States. It has a footnote that says "about half the demonstrated reserve base… is estimated to be recoverable." You cannot recover —get out of the ground and use—100% of the coal that's there. So this number then, is ½ of this number (pointing). We'll come back to those in just a moment. The report also tells us that in 1971, we were mining coal at this rate, twenty years later at this rate (pointing). Put those numbers together, the average growth rate of coal production in that twenty years: 2.86% per year. And so we have to ask, well, how long would a resource last if you have steady growth in the rate of consumption until the last bit of it is used?

I'll show you the equation here for the expiration time. I'll tell you it takes first year college calculus to derive that equation, so it can't be very difficult. You know, I have a feeling there must be dozens of people in this country who've had first year college calculus, but let me suggest, I think that equation is probably the best-kept scientific secret of the century!

Now, let me show you why. If you use that equation to calculate the life expectancy of the reserve base, or of the 1?2 they think is recoverable, for different steady rates of growth, you find if the growth rate is zero, the small estimate would go about 240 years and the large one would go close to 500 years. So that report to the Congress was correct. But look what we get if we plug in steady growth. Back in the 1960s, it was our national goal to achieve growth of coal production up around 8% per year. If you could achieve that and continue it, coal would last between 37 and 46 years. President Carter cut that goal roughly in half, hoping to reach 4% per year. If that could continue, coal would last between 59 and 75 years. Here's that 2.86%, the average for the recent period of twenty years. If that could continue, coal would last between 72 and 94 years. That's within the life expectancy of children born today.

The only way you are going to get anywhere near this widely quoted 500 year figure, is to be able to do simultaneously two highly improbable things: number one, you've got to figure out how to use 100% of the coal that is in the ground; number two, you've got to figure out how to have 500 years of zero growth of coal production. Look at those figures: those are facts.

Back in the 1970s, there was great national concern about energy. But these concerns disappeared in the 80s. Now, the concerns about energy in the 70s prompted experts, journalists, and scientists to assure the American people that there was no reason to be concerned. So let's go back now and look at some of those assurances from the 70s so we can see what to expect now that the energy crisis is returning.

Here is the director of the energy division of the Oakridge National Laboratories telling us how expensive it is to import oil, telling us we must have big increases (and) rapid growth in our use of coal. Under these conditions, he estimates, America's coal reserves are so huge they can last "a minimum of 300 years, probably a maximum of 1000 years." You've just seen the facts, now you see what an expert tells us, and what can you conclude?

There was a three-hour television special on CBS on energy. The reporter said, "By the lowest estimate, we have enough (coal) for 200 years, by the highest, enough for more than 1000 years." You've just seen the facts, now you can see what a journalist tells us after careful study, and what can you conclude?

In the *Journal of Chemical Education*, on the page for high school chemistry teachers in an article by the scientific staff of the journal, they tell us our proven coal reserves are "enormous" and they give a figure: "these could satisfy present US energy needs for nearly 1000 years." Well, let's do long division. You take the coal they say is there, divide by what was then the current rate of consumption, you get 180 years. Now they didn't say "current rate of consumption," they said "present US energy needs." Coal today supplies about 1?5, about 20% of the energy we use in this country, so if you'd like to calculate how long this quantity of coal could satisfy present US energy needs, you have to multiply this denominator by five. When you do that you get 36 years. They said nearly 1000 years.

*Newsweek* magazine, in a cover story on energy, said that at present rates of consumption, we have enough coal for 666.5 years—the point 5 means they think it'll run out in July instead of January. (audience laughter) If you round that off, and say roughly 600 years, that's close enough to 500 to lie within the uncertainty of our knowledge of the size of the resource. So with that observation, that's a reasonable statement; but what this lead into was a story about how we have to have major rapid growth in coal consumption. Well, it's obvious isn't it? If you have the growth that they're writing about, it won't last as long as they said it would last with zero growth. They never mentioned this. I wrote them a long letter, told them I thought it was a serious misrepresentation to give the readers the feeling we can have all this growth that they were writing about and still have coal around for 600 years. I got back a nice form letter; it had nothing to do with what I'd tried to explain to them.

I gave this talk at a high school in Omaha, and after the talk, the high school physics teacher came to me, and he had a booklet. He said, "Have you seen this?" and I hadn't seen it; he said, "Look at this: 'We've got coal coming out of our ears.'" As reported by Forbes magazine (that's a prominent business magazine), the United States has 437 billion tons of coal reserves. That's a good number; this is equivalent to a lot of BTUs or it's "enough energy to keep 100 million large generating plants going for the next 800 years or so…" And the teacher said to me, "How can that be true? That's one large electric generating plant for every two people in the United States!" I said, "Of course it can't be true, it's absolute nonsense. Let's do long division to see how crazy it is." So you take the coal they say is there, divide by what was then the current rate of consumption, you find you couldn't keep that up for 800 years and we hardly at that time had 500 large electric plants—they said it would be good for a 100 million such plants.

*Time* magazine tells us that "beneath the pit heads of Appalachia and the Ohio Valley, and under the sprawling strip mines of the west, lie coal seams rich enough to meet the country's power needs for centuries, no matter how much energy consumption may grow." So I give you a very fundamental observation: don't believe any prediction of the life expectancy of a non-renewable resource until you have confirmed the prediction by repeating the calculation. As a corollary, we have to note that the more optimistic the prediction, the greater is the probability that it's based on faulty arithmetic or on no arithmetic at all.

Again from *Time* magazine: "Energy industries agree that to achieve some form of energy self-sufficiency, the US must mine all the coal that it can." Now think about that for just a moment. Let me paraphrase it: the more rapidly we consume our resources, the more self-sufficient we'll be. Isn't that what it says?

David Brower called this the policy of "strength through exhaustion." Here's an example of strength through exhaustion: here is William Simon, energy advisor to the president of the United States. Simon says, "We should be trying to get as many holes drilled as possible to get the proven oil reserves." The more rapidly we can get the last of that oil up out of the ground and finish using it, the better off we'll be.

So let's look at Dr Hubbert's graph for the lower 48 states in oil production, again it's semi-logarithmic. Here we have a straight line section of steady growth, but for quite a while now, production has fallen below the growth curve, while our demand continued on up this growth curve until the 1970s. It's obvious the difference between the two curves has to be made up with imports. And it was in early 1995 that we read that the year 1994 was the first year in our nation's history in which we had to import more oil than we were able to get out of our own ground.

Well, maybe you're wondering, does it make any sense to imagine that we can have steady growth in the rate of consumption of a resource till the last bit of it was used, then the rate of consumption would plunge abruptly to zero? I say no, that doesn't make sense. Okay, you say, why bother us with the calculation of this expiration time? My answer is this: every segment of our society, our business leaders, government leaders, political leaders, at the local level, state level, national level—every one aspires to maintain a society in which all measures of material consumption continue to grow steadily, year after year after year, world without end.

Since that's so central to every thing we do, we ought to know where it would lead. On the other hand, we should recognise there's a better model and again we turn to the work of the late Dr Hubbert. He's plotted the rate of consumption of resources that have already expired; he finds yes, there is an early period of steady growth in the rate of consumption. But then the rate goes through a maximum and comes back down in a nice symmetric bell-shaped curve. Now, when he did this, some years ago, and fitted it to the oil production in the US, he found at that time we were right there (pointing). We were at the peak; we were halfway through the resource. That's exactly what that Texas expert said that I quoted a minute ago.

Now, let's see what it means. It means that from now on, domestic oil production can only go downhill, and it's downhill all the rest of the way, and it doesn't matter what they say inside the beltway in Washington DC.

Now, it means we can work hard and put some bumps on the downhill side of the curve; you'll see there are bumps on the uphill side. The debate is heating up over drilling in the Arctic Wildlife Refuge. I've seen the estimate that they might find 3.2 billion barrels of oil up there. 3.2 billion is the area of that little tiny square (pointing); that's less than one year's consumption in the United States. So let's look at the curve in this way: the area under the total curve, that represents the total resource in the United States. It's been divided into three parts: here is the oil we've taken from the ground (pointing): we've used it, it's gone. This vertical shaded band, that's the oil we've drilled into: we've found it, we're pumping it today. Shaded in green on the right is the undiscovered oil. We have very good ways now of estimating how much oil remains undiscovered. This is the oil we've got to find if we're going to make it down the curve on schedule.

Now every once in a while somebody says to me, "But you know, a hundred years ago, somebody did a calculation and predicted the US would be out of oil in 25 years." The calculation must've been wrong; therefore, of course, all calculations are wrong. Let's understand what they did. One hundred years ago, this band of discovered oil was over in here somewhere (points to beginning of curve). All they did was to take the discovered oil, divide it by how rapidly it was being used, and came up with 25 years. They had no idea then how much oil was undiscovered. Well, it's obvious; you've got to make a new calculation every time you make a new discovery. We're not asking today how long will the discovered oil last, we're asking about the discovered and the undiscovered—we're now talking about the rest of the oil. And what does the US Geological Survey tell us?

Back in 1984, they said the estimated US supply from undiscovered resources and demonstrated reserves was 36 years at present rates of production, or 19 years in the absence of imports. Five years later in 1989, that 36 years is down to 32 years, the 19 years is down to 16 years. So the numbers are holding together as we march down the right-hand side of the Hubbert curve.

Well, every once in awhile we run into somebody who says we shouldn't worry about the problem, we can solve it. In this case, we can solve it by growing corn, distilling it into ethanol, and run all the vehicles in the US on ethanol. Lets just look what he says, he says today ethanol production displaces over 43½ million barrels of imported oil annually. That sounds pretty good doesn't it, until you think. First question you've got to ask: 43½ million barrels, what fraction is that of US vehicle consumption in a year? The answer is, it's 1%.

You would have to multiply corn production devoted to ethanol by a factor of 100 just to make the numbers look right. There isn't that much total agricultural land in the United States. There's a bigger problem. It takes diesel fuel to plough the ground to plant the corn, to make the fertiliser to make the corn grow, to tend the corn, to harvest the corn. It takes more energy to distil it. You finally get a gallon of ethanol, you will be lucky if there's as much energy in the gallon as it took to produce it. In general, it's a loser. But this guy (Paul Harvey) says not to worry, we can solve it that way.

Well, back in 1956, Dr Hubbert addressed a convention of petroleum geologists and engineers. He told them that his calculations led him to believe that "the peak of US oil and gas production could be expected to occur between 1966 and 1971." No one took him seriously. So let's see what's happened. The data here is from the Department of Energy. Here is steady growth (pointing). Here is 1956, when Dr Hubbert did his analysis. He said at that time that peak would occur between 1966–1971. There's the peak, 1970. It was followed by a very rapid decline. Then the Alaskan pipeline started delivering oil, and it was a partial recovery. That production has now peaked and everything's going downhill in unison in the right hand side of the curve. And when I go to my home computer to figure out the parameters of the curve that's the best fit to the data, from that fit it looks to me as though we have consumed ¾ of the recoverable oil that was ever in our ground in the United States and we are now coasting downhill on the last 25% of that once enormous resource. So we have to ask about world oil.

Dr Hubbert in 1974 predicted that the peak of world oil would occur around 1995, so lets see what's happened. Here we have the data from the Department of Energy. A long period of steady growth, there's quite a big drop there (pointing), and then there was a speedy recovery; then an enormous drop and a very slow recovery. Those drops are each due to a price hike from OPEC. Well, it's clear we're not yet over the peak, so when I now go to fit the curve, I need one more bit of information before I can do the fit. I have to go to the geology literature and ask the literature, "What do you think is the total amount of oil we will ever find on this earth?" The consensus figure in the literature is 2000 billion barrels. Now, that's quite uncertain, plus or minus maybe 40 or 50%. If I plug that in and do the fit, the peak is this year (2004). If I assume there is 50% more than the consensus figure, the peak moves back to 2019. If I assume there's twice as much as the consensus figure, the peak moves back to 2030.

So no matter how you cut it, in your life expectancy, you are going to see the peak of world oil production. And you've got to ask yourself, what is life going to be like when we have a declining world production of petroleum, and we have a growing world population, and we have a growing world per capita demand for oil. Think about it.

In the March 1998 issue of *Scientific American*, there was a major article by two real petroleum geologists. They said this peak would occur before 2010, so we're all in the same ball park. Now, that article in *Scientific American* triggered a lot of discussion. Here is an article in *Fortune* magazine, November 1999, talking about "Oil Forever," and in that article, we see a criticism of the geologists' analysis, and this is from an emeritus professor of economics at MIT. And he said, "This analysis (by the geologists) is a piece of foolishness, the world will never run out of oil, not in 10,000 years." So let's look at what's been happening.

Here we have two graphs, on one scale, we have here in the graphs, that's the annual discoveries of oil each year (pointing); here is the annual production of oil each year. Notice since the 1980s, we've been producing about twice as much as we've been finding. Yet you've seen and read and heard statements from PhD non-scientists saying that we have greater resources of petroleum now than ever before in history. What in the world are they smoking? (audience laughter)

Now, here is another look at world oil production, but this is per capita. This is litres per person each day. There is two litres (pointing). A litre is about a quart, and so two litres is about ½ gallon. The upper curve assumes there was no growth in the world population since 1920, that it stayed fixed at 1.8 billion. This then is just a copy of that earlier curve. The lower curve uses the actual population of the world, and what you find is that with a growing world population, this curve is pulled down more and more as you go farther to the right. And notice it peaked at about 2.2 litres per person a day in the 1970s. It is now down to about 1.7 litres a person a day, so we can say that on any day any one of us uses more than 1.7 litres of petroleum directly or indirectly, we're using more than our share. Now, just think about what that means.

Well, we do have to ask about new discoveries. Here is a discussion from about eleven years ago about the largest discovery of oil in the Gulf of Mexico in the past twenty years, an estimated 700 million barrels of oil. That's a lot of oil, but a lot compared to what? At that time, we were consuming 16.6 million barrels every day in the United States. Divide the 16.6 into 700 and you find that discovery would meet US needs for 42 days.

On the front page of the *Wall Street Journal,* we read about the new Hibernia oil field off the south coast of Newfoundland. Please read this one line in the headline: "Now it will last fifty years." That gives you some kind of a feeling for what amount of oil may be up there. So let's follow up and read from that story in the *Wall Street Journal*: "The Hibernia field, one of the largest oil discoveries in North America in decades, should deliver its first oil by the end of the year. At least 20 more fields may follow, offering well over one billion barrels of high-quality crude, promising a steady flow of oil just a quick tanker-run away from the energy-thirsty East Coast".

So let's do some arithmetic. We take the amount of oil that we think is up there, a billion barrels. Now the US consumption has grown to about 18 million barrels a day; divide the 18 million into the billion and you find that would meet US needs for 56 days.

Now, what was the impression you had from that line in the headline in the *Wall Street Journal*? And as you think about this, think about the definition of modern agriculture: it's "the use of land to convert petroleum into food." And we can see the end of the petroleum.

Dr Hubbert testified before a committee of the Congress. He told them that "the exponential phase of the industrial growth which has dominated human activities during the last couple of centuries is now drawing to a close. Yet during the last two centuries of unbroken industrial growth, we have evolved what amounts to an exponential-growth culture." I would say, it's more than a culture: it's our national religion, because we worship growth. Pick up any newspaper; you'll see headlines such as this: "State forecasts 'robust' growth."

Have you ever heard of a physician diagnosing a cancer in a patient and telling the patient, "You have a robust cancer?" And it isn't just in the United States that we have this terrible addiction (quoting *Wall Street Journal*): "The Japanese are so accustomed to growth that economists in Tokyo usually speak of a recession as any time the growth rate dips below 3% per year."

So, what do we do?

In the words of Winston Churchill, "Sometimes we have to do what is required." First of all, as a nation we've got to get serious about renewable energy. As a a start, we ought to have a big increase in the funding for research in the development and dispersion of renewable energy. We have to educate all of our people to an understanding of the arithmetic and the consequences of growth, especially in terms of populations and in terms of the earth's finite resources. We must educate people to recognise the fact that growth of populations and growth of rates of consumption of resources cannot be sustained. What's the first law of sustainability? You've heard thousands of people talking endlessly about sustainability; did they ever tell you the first law? Here it is: population growth and/or growth in the rates of consumption of resources cannot be sustained. That's simple arithmetic. Yet nobody that I'm encountering will tell you about that when they're talking about sustainability. So I think it's intellectually dishonest to talk about saving the environment, which is sustainability, without stressing the obvious fact that stopping population growth is a necessary condition for saving the environment and for sustainability.

We must educate people to see the need to examine carefully the allegations of the technological optimists who assure us that science and technology will always be able to solve all of our problems of population growth, food, energy, and resources.

Chief amongst these optimists was the late Dr Julian Simon, formerly professor of economics and business administration at the University of Illinois, and later at the University of Maryland. With regard to copper, Simon has written that we will never run out of copper because "copper can be made from other metals." The letters to the editor jumped all over him, told him about chemistry. He just brushed it off: "Don't worry," he said, "if it's ever important, we can make copper out of other metals."

Now, Simon had a book that was published by the Princeton University Press. In that book, he's writing about oil from many sources, including biomass, and he says, "Clearly there is no meaningful limit to this source except for the sun's energy." He goes on to note, "But even if our sun was not so vast as it is, there may well be other suns elsewhere." Well, Simon's right; there are other suns elsewhere, but the question is, would you base public policy on the belief that if we need another sun, we will figure out how to go get it and haul it back into our solar system? (audience laughter)

Now, you cannot laugh: for decades before his death, this man was a trusted policy advisor at the very highest levels in Washington DC.

Bill Moyers interviewed Isaac Asimov. He asked Asimov, "What happens to the idea of the dignity of the human species if this population growth continues?" and Asimov says, "It'll be completely destroyed. I like to use what I call my bathroom metaphor. If two people live in an apartment, and there are two bathrooms, then they both have freedom of the bathroom. You can go to the bathroom anytime you want, stay as long as you want, for whatever you need. And everyone believes in freedom of the bathroom. It should be right there in the constitution. But if you have twenty people in the apartment and two bathrooms, then no matter how much every person believes in freedom of the bathroom, there's no such thing. You have to set up times for each person, you have to bang on the door, 'Aren't you through yet?' and so on." And Asimov concluded with one of the most profound observations I've seen in years. He said, "In the same way, democracy cannot survive overpopulation. Human dignity cannot survive overpopulation. Convenience and decency cannot survive overpopulation. As you put more and more people into the world, the value of life not only declines, it disappears. It doesn't matter if someone dies, the more people there are, the less one individual matters."

And so, central to the things that we must do, is to recognise that population growth is the immediate cause of all our resource and environmental crises.

And in the last one hour, the world population has increased by about 10,000 people and the population of the United States has increased by about 280 people. So to be successful with this experiment of human life on earth, we have to understand the laws of nature as we encounter them in the study of science and mathematics. We should remember the words of Aldous Huxley, that "facts do not cease to exist because they're ignored". We should remember the words of Eric Sevareid; he observed that "the chief source of problems is solutions." This is what we encounter every day: solutions to problems just make the problems worse. We should remember the message of this cartoon: "Thinking is very upsetting, it tells us things we'd rather not know." We should remember the words of Galileo; he said, "I do not feel obliged to believe that the same god who has endowed us with sense, reason, and intellect has intended us to forgo their use." If there is one message, it is this: we cannot let other people do our thinking for us.

Now, except for those petroleum graphs, the things I've told you are not predictions of the future, I'm only reporting facts, and the results of some very simple arithmetic. But I do so with confidence that these facts, this arithmetic and more importantly, our level of understanding of them, will play a major role in shaping our future. Now, don't take what I've said blindly or uncritically, because of the rhetoric, or for any other reason. Please, you check the facts. Please check my arithmetic. If you find errors, please let me know. If you don't find errors, then I hope you'll take this very, very seriously.

Now, you are important people because you can think. If there's anything that is in short supply in the world today, it's people who are willing to think. So here's a challenge. Can you think of any problem, on any scale, from microscopic to global, whose long term solution is in any demonstratable way, aided, assisted, or advanced by having larger populations in our local levels, state levels, national level, or global level? Can you think of anything that can get better if we crowd more people into our cities, our towns, into our state, our nation, or on this earth?

And I'll close with these words from the late Reverend Martin Luther King Jr. He said, "Unlike the plagues of the dark ages, or contemporary diseases which we do not yet understand, the modern plague of overpopulation is solvable with means we have discovered and with resources we possess. What is lacking is not sufficient knowledge of the solution, but universal consciousness of the gravity of the problem and the education of the billions who are its victims."

So I hope I've made a reasonable case for my opening statement, that I think the greatest shortcoming of the human race is our inability to understand this very simple arithmetic.

Thank you very, very much.

# LIMITS TO GROWTH: THE 30-YEAR UPDATE

*By Donella Meadows, Jorgen Randers, Dennis Meadows*

## Excerpt

### Overshoot

> The future is no longer ... what it might have been if humans had known how to use their brains and their opportunities more effectively. But the future can still become what we reasonably and realistically want.
>
> —Aurelio Peccei, 1981

To overshoot means to go too far, to go beyond limits accidentally—without intention. People experience overshoots every day. When you rise too quickly from a chair, you may momentarily lose your balance. If you turn on the hot-water faucet too far in the shower, you may be scalded. On an icy road your car might slide past a stop sign. At a party you may drink much more alcohol than your body can safely metabolize; in the morning you will have a ferocious headache. Construction companies periodically build more condominiums than are demanded, forcing them to sell units below cost and confront the possibility of bankruptcy. Too many fishing boats are often constructed. Then fishing fleets grow so large that they catch far more than the sustainable harvest. This depletes the fish population and forces ships to remain in harbor. Chemical companies have produced more chlorinated chemicals than the upper atmosphere can safely assimilate. Now the ozone layer will be dangerously depleted for decades until stratospheric chlorine levels decline.

The three causes of overshoot are always the same, at any scale from personal to planetary. First, there is growth, acceleration, rapid change. Second, there is some form of limit or barrier, beyond which the moving system may not safely go. Third, there is a delay or mistake in the perceptions and the responses that strive to keep the system within its limits. These three are necessary and sufficient to produce an overshoot.

Overshoot is common, and it exists in almost infinite forms. The change may be physical—growth in the use of petroleum. It may be organizational—an increase in the number of people supervised. It may be psychological—continuously rising goals for personal consumption. Or it may be manifest in financial, biological, political, or other forms.

The limits are similarly diverse—they may be imposed by a fixed amount of space; by limited time; by constraints inherent in physical, biological, political, psychological, or other features of a system.

The delays, too, arise in many ways. They may result from inattention, faulty data, delayed information, slow reflexes, a cumbersome or quarreling bureaucracy, a false theory about how the system responds, or from momentum that prevents the system from being stopped quickly despite the best efforts to halt it. For example, delays may result when a driver does not realize

---

Reprinted from *Limits to Growth: The Thirty Year Update* copyright © 2004 by Donella Meadows, Dennis Meadows, Jorgen Randers, Eric Tapley. With permission from Chelsea Green Publishing Co., White River Junction, Vermont.

how much his car's braking traction has been reduced by ice on the road; the contractor uses current prices to make decisions about construction activity that will affect the market two or three years in the future; the fishing fleet owners base their decisions on data about recent catch, not information about the future rate of fish reproduction; chemicals require years to migrate from where they are used to a point in the ecosystem where they cause severe damage.

Most instances of overshoot cause little harm. Being past many kinds of limits does not expose anyone to serious damage. Most types of overshoot occur frequently enough that when they are potentially dangerous, people learn to avoid them or to minimize their consequences. For example, you test the water temperature with your hand before stepping into the shower stall. Sometimes there is damage, but it is quickly corrected: Most people try to sleep extra long in the morning after a late night drinking in the bar.

Occasionally, however, there arises the potential for catastrophic overshoot. Growth in the globe's population and material economy confronts humanity with this possibility. It is the focus of this book.

Throughout this text we will grapple with the difficulties of understanding and describing the causes and consequences of a population and economy that have grown past the support capacities of the earth. The issues involved are complex. The relevant data are often poor in quality and incomplete. The available science has not yet produced consensus among researchers, much less among politicians. Nonetheless, we need a term that refers to the relation between humanity's demands on the planet and the globe's capacity to provide. For this purpose we will use the phrase *ecological footprint*.

The term was popularized by a study Mathis Wackernagel and his colleagues conducted for the Earth Council in 1997. Wackernagel calculated the amount of land that would be required to provide the natural resources consumed by the population of various nations and to absorb their wastes.[1] Wackernagel's term and mathematical approach were later adopted by the World Wide Fund for Nature (WWF), which provides data on the ecological footprint of more than 150 nations in its *Living Planet Report*.[2] According to these data, since the late 1980s the earth's peoples have been using more of the planet's resource production each year than could be regenerated in that year. In other words, the ecological footprint of global society has overshot the earth's capacity to provide. There is much information to support this conclusion...

The potential consequences of this overshoot are profoundly dangerous. The situation is unique; it confronts humanity with a variety of issues never before experienced by our species on a global scale. We lack the perspectives, the cultural norms, the habits, and the institutions required to cope. And the damage will, in many cases, take centuries or millennia to correct.

But the consequences need not be catastrophic. Overshoot can lead to two different outcomes. One is a crash of some kind. Another is a deliberate turnaround, a correction, a careful easing down. We explore these two possibilities as they apply to human society and the planet that supports it. We believe that a correction is possible and that it could lead to a desirable, sustainable, sufficient future for all the world's peoples. We also believe that if a profound correction is not made soon, a crash of some sort is certain. And it will occur within the lifetimes of many who are alive today.

These are enormous claims. How did we arrive at them? Over the past 30 years we have worked with many colleagues to understand the long-term causes and consequences of growth in human population and in its ecological footprint. We have approached these issues in four ways—in effect using four different lenses to focus on data in different ways, just as the lenses of a microscope and a telescope give different perspectives. Three of these viewing devices are widely used and easy to describe: (1) standard scientific and economic theories about the global system; (2) data on the world's resources and environment; and (3) a computer model to help us integrate that information and project its implications. Much of this book expands on those three lenses. It describes how we used them and what they allowed us to see.

Our fourth device is our "worldview," an internally consistent set of beliefs, attitudes, and values—a paradigm, a fundamental way of looking at reality. Everybody has a worldview; it influences where they look and what they see. It functions as a filter; it admits information consistent with their (often subconscious) expectations about the nature of the world; it leads them to disregard information that challenges or disconfirms those expectations. When people look out through a filter, such as a pane of colored glass, they usually see *through* it, rather than seeing it—and so, too, with worldviews. A worldview doesn't need to be described to people who already share it, and it is difficult to describe to people who don't. But it is crucial to remember that every book, every computer model, every public statement is shaped at least as much by the worldview of its authors as by any "objective" data or analysis.

We cannot avoid being influenced by our own worldview. But we can do our best to describe its essential features to our readers. Our worldview was formed by the Western industrial societies in which we grew up, by our scientific and economic training, and by lessons from traveling and working in many parts of the world. But the most important part of our worldview, the part that is least commonly shared, is our systems perspective.

Like any viewpoint-for example, the top of any hill—a systems perspective lets people see some things they would never have noticed from any other vantage point, and it may block the view of other things. Our training concentrated on dynamic systems—on sets of interconnected material and immaterial elements that change over time. Our training taught us to see the world as a set of unfolding behavior patterns, such as growth, decline, oscillation, overshoot. It has taught us to focus not so much on single pieces of a system as on connections. We see the many elements of demography, economy, and the environment as *one planetary system*, with innumerable interactions. We see stocks and flows and feedbacks and thresholds in the interconnections, all of which influence the way the system will behave in the future and influence the actions we might take to change its behavior.

## *The Next Revolution: Sustainability*

It is as impossible now for anyone to describe the world that could evolve from a sustainability revolution as it would have been for the farmers of 6000 BC to foresee the corn and soybean fields of modern Iowa, or for an English coal miner of AD 1800 to imagine an automated Toyota assembly line. Like the other great revolutions, the coming sustainability revolution will also change the face of the land and the foundations of human identities, institutions, and cultures. Like the previous revolutions, it will take centuries to unfold fully—though it is already under way.

Of course no one knows how to bring about such a revolution. There is not a checklist: "To accomplish a global paradigm shift, follow these 20 steps." Like the great revolutions that came before, this one can't be planned or dictated. It won't follow a list of fiats from government or a proclamation from computer modelers. The sustainability revolution will be organic. It will arise from the visions, insights, experiments, and actions of billions of people. The burden of making it happen is not on the shoulders of anyone person or group. No one will get the credit, but everyone can contribute.

Our systems training and our own work in the world have affirmed for us two properties of complex systems germane to the sort of profound revolution we are discussing here.

First, information is the key to transformation. That does not necessarily mean *more* information, better statistics, bigger databases, or the World Wide Web, though all of these may play a part. It means *relevant, compelling, select, powerful, timely, accurate* information flowing in new ways to new recipients, carrying new content, suggesting new rules and goals (rules and goals that are themselves information). When its information flows are changed, any system will behave differently. The policy of *glasnost*, for example—the simple opening of information channels that had long been closed in the Soviet Union—guaranteed the rapid transformation of Eastern Europe beyond anyone's expectations. The old system had been held in place by tight control of information. Letting go of that control triggered total system restructuring (turbulent and unpredictable, but inevitable).

Second, systems strongly resist changes in their information flows, especially in their rules and goals. It is not surprising that those who benefit from the current system actively oppose such revision. Entrenched political, economic, and religious cliques can constrain almost entirely the attempts of an individual or small group to operate by different rules or to attain goals different from those sanctioned by the system. Innovators can be ignored, marginalized, ridiculed, denied promotions or resources or public voices. They can be literally or figuratively snuffed out.

Only innovators, however—by perceiving the need for new information, rules, and goals, communicating about them, and trying them out—can make the changes that transform systems. This important point is expressed clearly in a quote that is widely attributed to Margaret Mead, "Never deny the power of a small group of committed individuals to change the world. Indeed that is the only thing that ever has."

We have learned the hard way that it is difficult to live a life of material moderation within a system that expects, exhorts, and rewards consumption. But one can move a long way in the direction of moderation. It is not easy to use energy efficiently in an economy that produces energy-inefficient products. But one can search out, or if necessary invent, more efficient ways of doing things, and in the process make those ways more accessible to others.

Above all, it is difficult to put forth new information in a system that is structured to hear only old information. Just try, sometime, to question in public the value of more growth, or even to make a distinction between growth and development, and you will see what we mean. It takes courage and clarity to challenge an established system. But it can be done.

In our own search for ways to encourage the peaceful restructuring of a system that naturally resists its own transformation, we have tried many tools. The obvious ones are displayed through this book—rational analysis, data gathering, systems thinking, computer modeling, and the clearest words we can find. Those are tools that anyone trained in science and economics would automatically grasp. Like recycling, they are useful, necessary, and they are not enough.

We don't know what will be enough. But we would like to conclude by mentioning five other tools we have found *helpful*. We introduced and discussed this list for the first time in our 1992 book. Our experience since then has affirmed that these five tools are not optional; they are essential characteristics for any society that hopes to survive over the long term. We present them here again in our concluding chapter "not as *the* ways to work toward sustain ability, but as *some* ways."

"We are a bit hesitant to discuss them," we said in 1992, "because we are not experts in their use and because they require the use of words that do not come easily from the mouths or word processors of scientists. They are considered too 'unscientific' to be taken seriously in the cynical public arena."

What are the tools we approached so cautiously?

They are: visioning, networking, truth-telling, learning, and loving.

It seems like a feeble list, given the enormity of the changes required. But each of these exists within a web of positive loops. Thus their persistent and consistent application initially by a relatively small group of people would have the potential to produce enormous change—even to challenge the present system, perhaps helping to produce a revolution.

"The transition to a sustainable society might be helped," we said in 1992, "by the simple use of words like these more often, with sincerity and without apology, in the information streams of the world." But we used them with apology ourselves, knowing how most people would receive them.

Many of us feel uneasy about relying on such "soft" tools when the future of our civilization is at stake, particularly since we do not know how to summon them up, in ourselves or in others. So we dismiss them and turn the conversation to recycling or emission trading or wildlife preserves or some other necessary but insufficient part of the sustainability revolution—but at least a part we know how to handle.

## End Notes

[1] M. Wackernagel et al., "Ecological Footprints of Nations: How Much Nature Do They Use? How Much Nature Do They Have?" (Xalapa, Mexico: Centro de Estudios para la Sustentabilidad [Center for Sustainability Studies], March 10, 1997). See also Mathis Wackernagel et al., "Tracking the Ecological Overshoot of the Human Economy," *Proceedings of the Academy of Science* 99, no. 14 (Washington, DC, 2002): 9266–9271. Also available at www.pnas.org/cgi/doi/10.1073/pnas.142033699.

[2] World Wide Fund for Nature, *Living Planet Report 2002* (Gland, Switzerland: WWF, 2002).

# PRINCIPLES OF ENVIRONMENTAL JUSTICE

## *Preamble*

WE THE PEOPLE OF COLOR, gathered together at this multinational People of Color Environmental Leadership Summit, to begin to build a national and international movement of all peoples of color to fight the destruction and taking of our lands and communities, do hereby re-establish our spiritual interdependence to the sacredness of our Mother Earth; to respect and celebrate each of our cultures, languages and beliefs about the natural world and our roles in healing ourselves; to insure environmental justice; to promote economic alternatives which would contribute to the development of environmentally safe livelihoods; and, to secure our political, economic and cultural liberation that has been denied for over 500 years of colonization and oppression, resulting in the poisoning of our communities and land and the genocide of our peoples, do affirm and adopt these Principles of Environmental Justice:

1. Environmental justice affirms the sacredness of Mother Earth, ecological unity and the interdependence of all species, and the right to be free from ecological destruction.

2. Environmental justice demands that public policy be based on mutual respect and justice for all peoples, free from any form of discrimination or bias.

3. Environmental justice mandates the right to ethical, balanced and responsible uses of land and renewable resources in the interest of a sustainable planet for humans and other living things.

4. Environmental justice calls for universal protection from nuclear testing, extraction, production and disposal of toxic/hazardous wastes and poisons and nuclear testing that threaten the fundamental right to clean air, land, water, and food.

5. Environmental justice affirms the fundamental right to political, economic, cultural and environmental self-determination of all peoples.

6. Environmental justice demands the cessation of the production of all toxins, hazardous wastes, and radioactive materials, and that all past and current producers be held strictly accountable to the people for detoxification and the containment at the point of production.

7. Environmental justice demands the right to participate as equal partners at every level of decision-making including needs assessment, planning, implementation, enforcement and evaluation.

8. Environmental justice affirms the right of all workers to a safe and healthy work environment, without being forced to choose between an unsafe livelihood and unemployment. It also affirms the right of those who work at home to be free from environmental hazards.

9. Environmental justice protects the right of victims of environmental injustice to receive full compensation and reparations for damages as well as quality health care.

10. Environmental justice considers governmental acts of environmental injustice a violation of international law, the Universal Declaration On Human Rights, and the United Nations Convention on Genocide.

11. Environmental justice must recognize a special legal and natural relationship of Native Peoples to the U.S. government through treaties, agreements, compacts, and covenants affirming sovereignty and self-determination.

12. Environmental justice affirms the need for urban and rural ecological policies to clean up and rebuild our cities and rural areas in balance with nature, honoring the cultural integrity of all our communities, and providing fair access for all to the full range of resources.

13. Environmental justice calls for the strict enforcement of principles of informed consent, and a halt to the testing of experimental reproductive and medical procedures and vaccinations on people of color.

14. Environmental justice opposes the destructive operations of multi-national corporations.

15. Environmental justice opposes military occupation, repression and exploitation of lands, peoples and cultures, and other life forms.

16. Environmental justice calls for the education of present and future generations which emphasizes social and environmental issues, based on our experience and an appreciation of our diverse cultural perspectives.

17. Environmental justice requires that we, as individuals, make personal and consumer choices to consume as little of Mother Earth's resources and to produce as little waste as possible; and make the conscious decision to challenge and reprioritize our lifestyles to insure the health of the natural world for present and future generations.

Adopted today, October 27, 1991, in Washington, D.C. by delegates to the First National People of Color Environmental Leadership Summit.

# WORLD SCIENTISTS' WARNING TO HUMANITY (1992)

*Some 1,700 of the world's leading scientists, including the majority of Nobel laureates in the sciences, issued this appeal in November 1992. The World Scientists' Warning to Humanity was written and spearheaded by the late Henry Kendall, former chair of UCS's board of directors.*

## INTRODUCTION

Human beings and the natural world are on a collision course. Human activities inflict harsh and often irreversible damage on the environment and on critical resources. If not checked, many of our current practices put at serious risk the future that we wish for human society and the plant and animal kingdoms, and may so alter the living world that it will be unable to sustain life in the manner that we know. Fundamental changes are urgent if we are to avoid the collision our present course will bring about.

## THE ENVIRONMENT

The environment is suffering critical stress:

### The Atmosphere

Stratospheric ozone depletion threatens us with enhanced ultraviolet radiation at the earth's surface, which can be damaging or lethal to many life forms. Air pollution near ground level, and acid precipitation, are already causing widespread injury to humans, forests, and crops.

### Water Resources

Heedless exploitation of depletable ground water supplies endangers food production and other essential human systems. Heavy demands on the world's surface waters have resulted in serious shortages in some 80 countries, containing 40 percent of the world's population. Pollution of rivers, lakes, and ground water further limits the supply.

### Oceans

Destructive pressure on the oceans is severe, particularly in the coastal regions which produce most of the world's food fish. The total marine catch is now at or above the estimated maximum sustainable yield. Some fisheries have already shown signs of collapse. Rivers carrying heavy burdens of eroded soil into the seas also carry industrial, municipal, agricultural, and livestock waste—some of it toxic.

### Soil

Loss of soil productivity, which is causing extensive land abandonment, is a widespread by-product of current practices in agriculture and animal husbandry. Since 1945, 11 percent of the earth's vegetated surface has been degraded—an area larger than India and China combined—and per capita food production in many parts of the world is decreasing.

### Forests

Tropical rain forests, as well as tropical and temperate dry forests, are being destroyed rapidly. At present rates, some critical forest types will be gone in a few years, and most of the tropical

---

Reprinted with permission Union of Concerned Scientists.

rain forest will be gone before the end of the next century. With them will go large numbers of plant and animal species.

### Living Species

The irreversible loss of species, which by 2100 may reach one-third of all species now living, is especially serious. We are losing the potential they hold for providing medicinal and other benefits, and the contribution that genetic diversity of life forms gives to the robustness of the world's biological systems and to the astonishing beauty of the earth itself. Much of this damage is irreversible on a scale of centuries, or permanent. Other processes appear to pose additional threats. Increasing levels of gases in the atmosphere from human activities, including carbon dioxide released from fossil fuel burning and from deforestation, may alter climate on a global scale. Predictions of global warming are still uncertain—with projected effects ranging from tolerable to very severe—but the potential risks are very great.

Our massive tampering with the world's interdependent web of life—coupled with the environmental damage inflicted by deforestation, species loss, and climate change—could trigger widespread adverse effects, including unpredictable collapses of critical biological systems whose interactions and dynamics we only imperfectly understand.

Uncertainty over the extent of these effects cannot excuse complacency or delay in facing the threats.

## POPULATION

The earth is finite. Its ability to absorb wastes and destructive effluent is finite. Its ability to provide food and energy is finite. Its ability to provide for growing numbers of people is finite. And we are fast approaching many of the earth's limits. Current economic practices which damage the environment, in both developed and underdeveloped nations, cannot be continued without the risk that vital global systems will be damaged beyond repair.

Pressures resulting from unrestrained population growth put demands on the natural world that can overwhelm any efforts to achieve a sustainable future. If we are to halt the destruction of our environment, we must accept limits to that growth. A World Bank estimate indicates that world population will not stabilize at less than 12.4 billion, while the United Nations concludes that the eventual total could reach 14 billion, a near tripling of today's 5.4 billion. But, even at this moment, one person in five lives in absolute poverty without enough to eat, and one in ten suffers serious malnutrition.

No more than one or a few decades remain before the chance to avert the threats we now confront will be lost and the prospects for humanity immeasurably diminished.

## WARNING

We the undersigned, senior members of the world's scientific community, hereby warn all humanity of what lies ahead. A great change in our stewardship of the earth and the life on it is required, if vast human misery is to be avoided and our global home on this planet is not to be irretrievably mutilated.

## WHAT WE MUST DO

Five inextricably linked areas must be addressed simultaneously:

**We must bring environmentally damaging activities under control to restore and protect the integrity of the earth's systems we depend on.**
We must, for example, move away from fossil fuels to more benign, inexhaustible energy sources to cut greenhouse gas emissions and the pollution of our air and water. Priority must be given to the development of energy sources matched to Third World needs—small-scale and relatively easy to implement.

We must halt deforestation, injury to and loss of agricultural land, and the loss of terrestrial and marine plant and animal species.

**We must manage resources crucial to human welfare more effectively.**
We must give high priority to efficient use of energy, water, and other materials, including expansion of conservation and recycling.

**We must stabilize population.**
This will be possible only if all nations recognize that it requires improved social and economic conditions, and the adoption of effective, voluntary family planning.

**We must reduce and eventually eliminate poverty.** (xp **We must ensure sexual equality, and guarantee women control over their own reproductive decisions.**

## *DEVELOPED NATIONS MUST ACT NOW*

The developed nations are the largest polluters in the world today. They must greatly reduce their overconsumption, if we are to reduce pressures on resources and the global environment. The developed nations have the obligation to provide aid and support to developing nations, because only the developed nations have the financial resources and the technical skills for these tasks.

Acting on this recognition is not altruism, but enlightened self-interest: whether industrialized or not, we all have but one lifeboat. No nation can escape from injury when global biological systems are damaged. No nation can escape from conflicts over increasingly scarce resources. In addition, environmental and economic instabilities will cause mass migrations with incalculable consequences for developed and undeveloped nations alike.

Developing nations must realize that environmental damage is one of the gravest threats they face, and that attempts to blunt it will be overwhelmed if their populations go unchecked. The greatest peril is to become trapped in spirals of environmental decline, poverty, and unrest, leading to social, economic, and environmental collapse.

Success in this global endeavor will require a great reduction in violence and war. Resources now devoted to the preparation and conduct of war—amounting to over $1 trillion annually—will be badly needed in the new tasks and should be diverted to the new challenges.

A new ethic is required—a new attitude towards discharging our responsibility for caring for ourselves and for the earth. We must recognize the earth's limited capacity to provide for us. We must recognize its fragility. We must no longer allow it to be ravaged. This ethic must motivate a great movement, convincing reluctant leaders and reluctant governments and reluctant peoples themselves to effect the needed changes.

The scientists issuing this warning hope that our message will reach and affect people everywhere. We need the help of many.

- We require the help of the world community of scientists—natural, social, economic, and political.
- We require the help of the world's business and industrial leaders.
- We require the help of the world's religious leaders.
- We require the help of the world's peoples.

**We call on all to join us in this task.**

# KYOTO PROTOCOL

## Summary

The Kyoto Protocol is an international agreement linked to the United Nations Framework Convention on Climate Change. The major feature of the Kyoto Protocol is that it sets binding targets for 37 industrialized countries and the European community for reducing greenhouse gas (GHG) emissions .These amount to an average of five per cent against 1990 levels over the five-year period 2008–2012.

The major distinction between the Protocol and the Convention is that while the Convention **encouraged** industrialised countries to stabilize GHG emissions, the Protocol **commits** them to do so.

Recognizing that developed countries are principally responsible for the current high levels of GHG emissions in the atmosphere as a result of more than 150 years of industrial activity, the Protocol places a heavier burden on developed nations under the principle of "common but differentiated responsibilities."

The Kyoto Protocol was adopted in Kyoto, Japan, on 11 December 1997 and entered into force on 16 February 2005. 180 nations have ratified the treaty to date. The detailed rules for the implementation of the Protocol were adopted at COP 7 in Marrakesh in 2001, and are called the "Marrakesh Accords."

## The Kyoto mechanisms

Under the Treaty, countries must meet their targets primarily through national measures. However, the Kyoto Protocol offers them an additional means of meeting their targets by way of three market-based mechanisms.

The Kyoto mechanisms are:

- *Emissions trading*—known as "the carbon market"
- the *clean development mechanism (CDM)*
- *joint implementation (JI)*.

The mechanisms help stimulate green investment and help Parties meet their emission targets in a cost-effective way.

## Monitoring emission targets

Under the Protocol, countries'actual emissions have to be monitored and precise records have to be kept of the trades carried out.

*Registry systems* track and record transactions by Parties under the mechanisms. The UN Climate Change Secretariat, based in Bonn, Germany, keeps an *international transaction log* to verify that transactions are consistent with the rules of the Protocol.

*Reporting* is done by Parties by way of submitting annual emission inventories and national reports under the Protocol at regular intervals.

---

Source: http://unfcc.int/kyoto_protocol/items/2830.php. United Nations Framework Convention on Climate Change.

A *compliance* system ensures that Parties are meeting their commitments and helps them to meet their commitments if they have problems doing so.

## Adaptation

The Kyoto Protocol, like the Convention, is also designed to assist countries in adapting to the adverse effects of climate change. It facilitates the development and deployment of techniques that can help increase resilience to the impacts of climate change.

The *Adaptation Fund* was established to finance adaptation projects and programmes in developing countries that are Parties to the Kyoto Protocol. The Fund is financed mainly with a share of proceeds from CDM project activities.

## The road ahead

The Kyoto Protocol is generally seen as an important first step towards a truly global emission reduction regime that will stabilize GHG emissions, and provides the essential architecture for any future international agreement on climate change.

By the end of the first commitment period of the Kyoto Protocol in 2012, a new international framework needs to have been negotiated and ratified that can deliver the stringent emission reductions the *Intergovernmental Panel on Climate Change (IPCC)* has clearly indicated are needed.

# PRESENTATION TO THE UNITED NATIONS JULY 18, 1995

*by Carol Jacobs, Cayuga Bear Clan Mother*

Mr. Ambassador, Chief Shenandoah, Distinguished Guests, Chiefs, Clanmothers, panel: It is my duty to help bring to and end the Haudenosaunee presentation. Chief Harvey Longboat of the Cayuga Bear Clan will be doing the actual closing.

You have heard how we began our meeting today, bringing our minds together in thanks for every part of the natural world. You have heard how we are grateful that each part of the world continues to fulfill the responsibilities that have been set for it by our Creator. It is how we begin every meeting, and how we end every meeting, and how we will end this day.

Most of our ceremonies are about giving thanks, at the right time and in the right way. They are what was given to us, what makes us who we are. They enable me to speak to you about life itself.

We draw no line between what is political and what is spiritual. Our leaders are also our spiritual leaders. Maintaining our ceremonies is an important part of the work of the chiefs and clan mothers. This is right: there is nothing more important than preserving life, recording life, and that is what the ceremonies do.

We are told that when this land was being created, our Creator was challenged to a bet by his brother. The subject of their game was: would there be life? And in one throw, supported by all the living forces of the natural world, our Creator won this bet. He won it all for us. He won it for all of us. We commemorate this each year in part of our Midwinter ceremonies.

This is not just a quaint legend. It is a reminder that, as scientists now agree, life on earth is the result of chance, as well as of intent. Life on earth is a fragile matter. That magnificent gamble could have gone the other way: life could just as easily not have been at all.

That is a reason for constantly giving thanks. We know very well how close life still is to not being. The reminders are all around us.

Among us, it is women who are responsible for fostering life. In our traditions, it is women who carry the seeds, both of our own future generations and of the plant life. It is women who plant and tend the gardens, and women who bear and raise the children. It is my right and duty, as a woman and a mother and a grandmother, to speak to you about these things, to bring our minds together on them.

In our ceremonies and dances, we move counter-clockwise. That is, in this part of the world, earth-wise. In our dances, the women's feet never leave the ground, never leave Mother Earth. This is intentional: we constantly remind ourselves of our connection to the earth, for it is from the earth that life comes.

Our prophecies tell us that life on earth is in danger of coming to an end. Our instructions tell us that we are to maintain our ceremonies, however few of us there are, and to maintain the spirit of those ceremonies, and the care of the natural world.

---

Published in *Akwesasne Notes New Series*, Fall—October/November/December—1995, Volume 1 #3 & 4, pp. 116–117. and reproduced here with permission by *Indian Time* Newspaper.

In making any law, our chiefs must always consider three things: the effect of their decision on peace; the effect on the natural world; and the effect on seven generations in the future. We believe that all lawmakers should be required to think this way, that all constitutions should contain these rules.

We call the future generations "the coming faces". We are told that we can see the faces of our children to come in the rain that is falling, and that we must tread lightly on the earth, for we are walking on the faces of our children yet to come. That attitude, too, we want to have you learn and share.

To us, it does not matter whether it can be scientifically proved that life as we know it is in danger. If the possibility exists, we must live every day as if it were true—for we cannot afford, any of us, to ignore that possibility. We must learn to live with that shadow, and always to strive toward the light.

We are not a numerous people today. We believe that people who are close to the earth do not allow their numbers to become greater than the land can bear.

We are not an industrialized people today. We do not carry economic power. Our people and lands are like a scattering of islands within a sea of our neighbours, the richest nations in the world.

And yet I tell you that we are a powerful people. We are the carriers of knowledge and ideas that the world needs today. We know how to live with this land: we have done so for thousands of years and have not suffered many of the changes of the Industrial Revolution, though we are being buffeted by the waves of its collapse.

Our families are beyond the small, isolated nuclear families that are so convenient to big industry and big government and so damaging to communities.

Our clans and names give people identity, not facelessness.

Our governments still follow natural law.

Our governments also face challenges—physical, political, legal and moral. We recognize that those challenges come from within our communities as well as from the peoples around us.

We know that we, as communities and as a people, are facing an environmental crisis. We know that we do not have the resources to be able to resolve that crisis by ourselves. That is why we are here, seeking partners.

But we also know that all the world faces the same crisis; that every people and every living thing shares the same challenges. And we are here to offer our partnership, our knowledge and our ideas.

It is time to move beyond "calls to action" and well-meaning agendas. The forces that are injuring our Mother the Earth are not waiting to create subcommittees, to set dates for meetings, to set budgets.

Today we have met, we have taken one another's hands, and we have begun to make commitments. As we leave, the words of thanksgiving will echo in our ears, reminding us that not only our own future generations, but every living thing, relies on us to fulfill our responsibilities as they fulfill theirs.

**We need no greater challenge than that.**

# THE MYTH OF CHIEF SEATTLE

*By William S. Abruzzi*

As the world faces increasing environmental challenges, people have sought wisdom and inspiration from a variety of sources. One of those sources is the speech which Chief Seattle delivered nearly 150 years ago. Seattle was a Suquamish Indian from the American northwest who delivered a speech in 1854 to Isaac Williams, the Territorial Governor of Washington, as Williams negotiated with him for the sale of land that was to become the city of Seattle (named in the chiefs honor). The speech has been revered by many people for the inspirational message it provides and for the respect for the environment it displays. Below is a short excerpt of that speech as it appeared in vice-president Al Gore's book, *Earth in Balance: Ecology and the Human Spirit:*

> How can you buy or sell the sky? The land? The idea is strange to us. If we do not own the freshness of the air and the sparkle of the water, how can you buy them? Every part of this earth is sacred to my people. Every shining pine needle, every sandy shore, every mist in the dark woods, every meadow, every humming insect. All are holy in the memory and experience of my people.... If we sell you our land, remember that the air is precious to us, that the air shares its spirit with all the life it supports. The wind that gave our grandfather his first breath also received his last sigh. The wind also gives our children the spirit of life. So if we sell you our land, you must keep it apart and sacred, a place where man can go to taste the wind that is sweetened by the meadow flowers. Will you teach your children what we have taught our children? That the earth is our mother? What befalls the earth befalls all the sons of the earth.
>
> This we know: the earth does not belong to man, man belongs to the earth. All things are connected like the blood that unites us all. Man did not weave the web of life, he is merely a strand in it. Whatever he does to the web, he does to himself. One thing we know: Our God is also your God. The earth is precious to Him and to harm the earth is to heap contempt on its Creator. (Gore 1992, 159)

The above quote was taken from the larger 1200-word speech generally attributed to Chief Seattle. This speech has become popular not only because it illustrates for many Seattle's poetic appreciation of nature and his deeply spiritual understanding of the interconnectedness of all living things, but also because it epitomizes the ancient wisdom that is widely believed to be contained within Native American cultures generally — a wisdom that many view as lost in the highly technical and materially oriented urban industrial societies of the late 20th century.

For these reasons, Chief Seattle's Speech has been duplicated and disseminated throughout Europe and the U.S. It has been used by the United Society for the Propagation of the Gospel in London and by the Woman's Day World of Prayer (Kaiser 1987, 498). Portions of the speech have been published in such diverse publications as *Passages* (Northwest Airlines in-flight magazine), *Environmental Action*, Sierra Club editorials, Canada's "Green Plan" and NASA's "Mission to Planet Earth" (see Kaiser 1987, 498–500; Adams 1994, 52). Joseph Campbell even included the chief's speech in his book, *The Power of Myth*, with Bill Moyers (1988) and later read from the

---

William S. Abruzzi (abruzzi@hal.muhlberg.edu) is an Associate Professor of Sociology and Anthropology in the Department of Sociology and Anthropology, Muhlenberg College, Allentown, PA 18104 USA.

Reprinted with permission from William S. Abruzzi and *Human Ecology Review*, Vol. 7, No. 1, 2000.

speech in his video series, *Transformation of Myth through Time*. In addition, not only have excerpts from the chiefs speech appeared on T-shirts, buttons and other items, but they have even found their way into scholarly works on American Indians (c.f.,Thornton 1987, 225) and on the environment (c.f., Collard 1989 and Dobson 1995). There is, however, a fundamental problem with this rather uncritical dissemination of Chief Seattle's speech; the words attributed to Chief Seattle were never spoken by him, nor could they have been.

## *Critical Considerations*

A critical evaluation of the full 1200-word modern text of Chief Seattle's speech reveals its inauthenticity. Just prior to the section of the speech that is quoted in Gores book, Seattle states, "I have seen a thousand rotting buffaloes on the prairie left by the white man who shot them from a passing train," (Kaiser 1987, 527). Seattle could not have made such a statement. To begin with, a single person could not have witnessed one individual shoot anywhere near one thousand buffalo from a passing train, given the speed of a train combined with the time that would have been needed to reload and fire a rifle used in 1854 (Not even Amtrak moves that slowly!). There also were no buffalo at the Puget Sound where Seattle lived. Seattle lived over a thousand miles from the Great Plains, and there is no evidence that he ever traveled to the plains. Finally, the transcontinental railroad was not completed until 1869, and the Euro-American bison slaughter did not begin until the 1870s. Seattle gave his speech in 1854, a full 15 years before the railroad was completed and nearly 20 years before whites began to slaughter the remaining buffalo in large numbers. He, therefore, could not possibly have commented on it in his speech. Finally, Seattle died in 1866 (Kaiser 1987, 502), making it quite difficult—to say the least! — for him to have witnessed an event that occurred a full decade after his death. The modern version of Seattle's speech also contains the quote, "What is there to life if a man cannot hear the lovely cry of a whippoorwill?" (Kaiser 1987, 527). Since the whippoorwill is also not native to the Northwest, Seattle could not likely have known of its existence either. Similarly, the modern text of Seattle's speech contains a reference by Seattle to the white man's urban pollution. However, since his speech was made as part of the negotiations for the initial purchase by whites of Suquamish and Duamish land, Seattle could not have commented on developments that were to follow by many years the very land transfer he was negotiating. The reality is that the current version of Chief Seattle's speech represents but the latest rendition of an evolving work of fiction. The original text of Seattle's speech was written by Dr. Henry A. Smith and published in the *Seattle Sunday Star* on October 29, 1887 (Kaiser 1987, 503). Smith claimed that the text he published was a direct copy of a speech given by Seattle in 1854 during treaty negotiations with Isaac Williams. However, there are several problems associated with the Smith's version of the speech that raise serious doubts about its authenticity. First of all, Smith's text was published a full 33 years after Seattle gave his original speech. This time lapse alone raises serious questions regarding its accuracy and reliability. In addition, Seattle spoke no English. His speech was given in Lushotseed, his native tongue, and was then translated into Chinook Jargon, a regional trading language containing a mixture of French, English and local Indian words. As a trading language, Chinook Jargon contained a limited vocabulary and has been described as "barely suitable for bartering" (Adams 1994, 53). It is highly unlikely, therefore, that Chinook Jargon could express many of the conceptual images contained in Smith's version of Seattle's speech, including such statements as "Yonder sky that had wept tears of compassion upon our fathers for centuries untold ..." (see Kaiser 1987, 503). Finally, the scene set by Smith in his account of Seattle's speech was described in too melodramatical a form to represent an objective historical account. For example, Smith wrote that "Chief Seattle arose with all the dignity of a senator who carries the responsibility of a great nation on his shoulders" (*ibid.*). Indeed, Kaiser, who has done perhaps the most exhaustive review of the history of Chief Seattle's speech, has shown that substantial differences exist between the original Smith text and two short treaty speeches attributed to Seattle in the National Archives. He concludes that "the selection of the material and the formulation of the — (Smith) — text is (*sic*) possibly as much Dr. Smith's as Seattle's" (*ibid.* 506).

The original Smith text has over time been supplanted by increasingly modified versions of the Seattle speech (c.f. Bagley 1931; Rich 1932; Arrowsmith 1969). The most radical revision of Seattle's speech was created in 1971 by Ted Perry, a Texas scriptwriter. Perry composed a radically altered and enlarged version of the previously evolving Seattle speech to accompany a program on ecology produced by the Southern Baptist Radio and Television Commission. Perry's script departed sharply from all previous versions of Seattle's speech (see Kaiser 1987) and soon generated its own offspring (see Abruzzi 1999), including: (1) a version of the speech distributed at the 1974 Spokane Expo; (2) an anonymous booklet titled *The Decidedly Unforked Message of Chief Seattle*; (3) an anonymous 1991 revision of the 1974 Spokane text titled "This Earth is Precious" and (4) a poetic adaptation of the original Perry script published in the *Midwest Quarterly* in 1992 under the title, "Chief Seattle Reflects on the Future of America, 1855" (see Low 1995, 410).

Perry's script also provided the text for a children's book titled *Brother Eagle, Sister Sky* produced in 1991 by Susan Jeffers. Jeffer's took credit only for the illustrations which she produced in the book, attributing the text itself to Seattle. Ironically, Jeffer's book, which sold over 250,000 copies, ranked fifth on the *New York Times* bestsellers list for *nonfiction* in 1992 (Bordewich 1996, 132). That same year, The Nature Company advertised a small book in its Christmas Catalogue titled *Chief Seattle's 1854 Speech* (see Low 1995, 407).

Needless to say, all modern versions of Chief Seattle's speech are inauthentic. Indeed, given the fictional nature of Perry's 1971 script and the fact that all modern versions of Seattle's speech derive from his original text, the latter are all, by definition, themselves works of fiction.

## Would the Real Chief Seattle Please Stand Up

Through time and repeated textual revision, Chief Seattle has been completely removed from the nineteenth century social and political context within which he lived. He has, instead, been fashioned and refashioned into successive, politically correct versions of the white man's Indian.

Inasmuch as Seattle presented his speech during treaty negotiations with Isaac Williams, the significance of the speech must be understood within that context. Seattle's speech was made as part of an argument for the right of the Suquamish and Duamish peoples to continue to visit their traditional burial grounds following the sale of that land to white settlers. This specific land was sacred to Seattle and his people because his ancestors were buried there, not because land as an abstract concept was sacred to all Indians. The very fact that Seattle was chosen by the U.S.

Government to represent his people in treaty negotiations raises critical questions. Who was Seattle and why was he and not someone else chosen by the Americans to negotiate for the local population? The Northwest native peoples were organized into a variety of clans and possessed no centralized leadership or political structure. As in other situations where colonial governments encountered land occupied by tribal societies, the United States Government needed friendly leaders to serve as representatives for the various indigenous peoples of this region. Chief Seattle was one of the local leaders chosen for that purpose. Seattle was likely selected because he demonstrated allegiance rather than opposition to whites. He had, in fact, converted to Roman Catholicism around 1830 (Kaiser 1987, 503) and was favorably disposed towards white settlement. Seattle never fought a war against the Americans and even sided with them during one Indian uprising (Adams 1994, 52–53). He was, significantly, the first Indian to sign the 1855 treaty. Seattle was not, however, simply a pawn of the U.S. Government. He needed whites to protect and advance his own economic and political interests. Seattle was commercially allied with a Dr. David Maynard in the curing and packing of salmon (Adams 1994, 53) and needed whites to help him in his conflict with other native leaders for control over the fishing rights that were essential to his newly developing commercial venture. In one of the original treaty speeches preserved in the National Archives, Seattle refers to the U.S. Army as a "bristling wall of strength" which will assure that "ancient enemies will no longer frighten his people" (*ibid.*). He was, thus, likely using whites to protect and advance his own interests, just as they were using him to advance theirs.

## *Discussion*

Chief Seattle has emerged as one of the premiere icons of Native American values for many whites seeking an alternate ecological perspective. Unfortunately, however, the Chief Seattle known to most people is mostly fictional, a fabrication by whites for whites. This creation of a false Indian stereotype is hardly new. Throughout American history, whites have fabricated Indians into images that served their own interests. During the nineteenth century, when the Euro-American population of the United States competed for land with Native Americans, Indians were popularly viewed as savages who needed to be tamed, settled and civilized. Later, defeated and placed on reservations, Indians were viewed nationally as children in need of white supervision. More recently, with the growth of large environmental and countercultural new age movements, a new Indian image has emerged. Native Americans have become the repositories of a traditional wisdom to those challenging institutionalized beliefs and practices in contemporary industrial societies. However, this latter-day Indian stereotype represents yet another white fiction serving the interests of those who believe in it. Significantly, each new incarnation of Seattle's speech, beginning with the original Smith text and ending with the latest adaptation of Ted Perry's script, has been created entirely by non-Indians. Not one native peoples has translated Seattle's speech into their own indigenous language (Low 1995, 416).

This brief essay has been offered as a cautionary tale. One goal of human ecology is to understand and explain historical and contemporary human environmental relations objectively and on the basis of solid empirical research. It is only through such research that viable and sustainable development programs can be proposed. Inasmuch as an extensive body of ecological research exists which demonstrates that Native American populations have responded to environmental circumstances in the same manner as have other human populations, environmentalists and human ecologists need to adopt a more critical approach to the study of indigenous peoples ecology than has been demonstrated by those who have uncritically accepted and promoted the Chief Seattle myth.

## *References*

Abruzzi, W. 1999. The real Chief Seattle was not a spiritual ecologist. *Skeptical Inquirer* 23(2), 44–48.

Adams, R. 1994. Chief Seattle and the Puget Sound buffalo wallow. *Borealis* 15, 50–54.

Arrowsmith, W. 1969. Speech of Chief Seattle, January 9th, 1855. *Arion* 8, 461–464.

Bagley, C.B. 1931. Chief Seattle and Angeline. *Washington Historical Quarterly* 22, 243–275.

Bordewich, F.M. 1996. *Killing the White Man's Indian: Reinventing Native Americans at the End of the Twentieth Century*. New York: Doubleday.

Collard, A. with J. Contrucci. 1989. *Rape of the Wild: Man's Violence against Animals and the Earth.* Indianapolis: Indiana University Press.

Dobson, A. 1995. *Green Political Thought: An Introduction, Second Edition.* New York: Routledge.

Gore, A. 1992. *Earth in Balance: Ecology and the Human Spirit.* New York: Houghton Mifflin.

*Human Ecology Forum, 74 Human Ecology Review, Vol. 7, No. 1, 2000*

Jeffers, S. 1991. *Brother Eagle, Sister Sky: A Message from Chief Seattle.* Dial Books: New York.

Kaiser, R. 1987. Chief Seattles speech(es): American origins and European reception. In B. Swann and A. Krupat (eds.), *Recovering the Word: Essays on Native American Literature*, 497–536. Berkeley, CA: University of California Press.

Low, D. 1995. Contemporary reinvention of Chief Seattle: Variant texts of Chief Seattles 1854 speech. *American Indian Quarterly* 19, 407–421.

Porterfield, A. 1990. American Indian spirituality as a countercultural movement. In Christopher Vecsey (ed.), *Religion in Native North America*, 152–164. Moscow: University of Idaho Press.

Rich, J. 1932. *Seattle's Unanswered Challenge.* Fairfield, Washington: Ye Galleon Press.

Thornton, H. 1987. *American Indian Holocaust and Survival: A Population History Since 1492.* Norman: University of Oklahoma Press.

# THE HANNOVER PRINCIPLES: DESIGN FOR SUSTAINABILITY

## Prepared for EXPO 2000, The World's Fair, Hannover, Germany

1. **Insist on rights of humanity and nature to co-exist** in a healthy, supportive, diverse and sustainable condition.

2. **Recognize interdependence.** The elements of human design interact with and depend upon the natural world, with broad and diverse implications at every scale. Expand design considerations to recognizing even distant effects.

3. **Respect relationships between spirit and matter.** Consider all aspects of human settlement including community, dwelling, industry and trade in terms of existing and evolving connections between spiritual and material consciousness.

4. **Accept responsibility for the consequences of design** decisions upon human well-being, the viability of natural systems and their right to co-exist.

5. **Create safe objects of long-term value.** Do not burden future generations with requirements for maintenance or vigilant administration of potential danger due to the careless creation of products, processes or standards.

6. **Eliminate the concept of waste.** Evaluate and optimize the full life-cycle of products and processes, to approach the state of natural systems, in which there is no waste.

7. **Rely on natural energy flows.** Human designs should, like the living world, derive their creative forces from perpetual solar income. Incorporate this energy efficiently and safely for responsible use.

8. **Understand the limitations of design.** No human creation lasts forever and design does not solve all problems. Those who create and plan should practice humility in the face of nature. Treat nature as a model and mentor, not as an inconvenience to be evaded or controlled.

9. **Seek constant improvement by the sharing of knowledge.** Encourage direct and open communication between colleagues, patrons, manufacturers and users to link long term sustainable considerations with ethical responsibility, and re-establish the integral relationship between natural processes and human activity.

The Hannover Principles should be seen as a living document committed to the transformation and growth in the understanding of our interdependence with nature, so that they may adapt as our knowledge of the world evolves.

### GUIDELINES

The Hannover Principles are a set of maxims that encourage the design professions to take sustainability into consideration. They are descriptive of a way of thinking, not prescriptions or requirements. The guidelines below demonstrate the City of Hannover's intention to apply these principles as elements of the overall design competitions associated with EXPO 2000. They take

---

Source: www.mcdonough.com/full.htm. William McDonough & Partners, 410 East Water Street, Charlottesville, VA 22902, tel.: 804–979–1111. fax: 804–979–1112.

© 1992 William McDonough Architects. All rights reserved. Reprinted with permission.

the form of a framework, based on the enduring elements of Earth, Air, Fire, Water, and Spirit, in which design decisions may be reviewed and evaluated. The guidelines offer critical instruction on the responsibility of designers.

It is hoped that those who enter the competitions will bring to their task uncommon ability, skill and care, assuring that their creative acts will be able to blend aesthetic concerns with ecological principles and provide a new inspiration for the challenge of design. In this way, design becomes a didactic tool to demonstrate that sustainable thinking can be put into practice in the real world.

# A CLIMATOLOGY OF 1980–2003 EXTREME WEATHER AND CLIMATE EVENTS

*By Tom Ross and Neal Lott*

## 1. INTRODUCTION

The National Climatic Data Center (NCDC) is responsible for monitoring and assessing the Earth's climate. Each month NCDC provides comprehensive analyses of global and U.S. temperature and precipitation to place the current state of the climate into historical perspective. Identification and assessment of extreme weather events is part of this effort. An "Extreme Weather and Climate Events" suite of web pages (Figure 1) highlights these events and provides access to images, descriptions, statistics, and other detailed information for each event via the worldwide web (http://www.ncdc.noaa.gov/extremes.html).

One of our more popular reports in the "Extreme Weather and Climate Events" suite is the "Billion Dollar U.S. Weather Disaster" web page (http://www.ncdc.noaa.gov/ol/reports/billionz.html), which focuses on extreme events that caused more than $1 billion in monetary losses in the United States, and provides links to detailed reports on many of these events. During the 1980–2003 period, there were 58 of these billion-dollar weather disasters in the United States with 46 of these events occurring since 1990. Total costs of the 58 events were nearly $350 billion, using an inflation/wealth index to adjust damage amounts to 2002 dollars. This paper provides a climatology of these disasters and the damage and loss of life they caused.

## 2. U.S. EVENTS, 1980–2003

The U.S. sustained 58 weather-related disasters during the 1980–2003 period in which overall losses reached or exceeded $1 billion dollars at the time of the event. This analysis did not include any events that had unadjusted damages/losses less than $1 billion dollars and then subsequently may have reached $1 billion after applying the GNP inflation/wealth index. Forty-nine of these disasters occurred since 1988 with total unadjusted losses of nearly $220 billion. Seven events occurred in 1998 alone, the most for any year in this summary period, though other years have recorded higher damage totals.

Below is a list of these disasters in chronological order, beginning with the most recent. Two damage figures are given for events prior to 2002. The first figure represents actual dollar costs at the time of the event and is not adjusted for inflation. The value in parenthesis (if given) is the dollar cost normalized to 2002 dollars using a Gross National Product (GNP) inflation/wealth index. The total normalized losses from the 58 events are nearly $350 billion. Figures 2 through 6 provide graphical representations of these statistics.

A wide variety of sources were used to compile these statistics and represent the authors' effort to estimate the total costs for these events in both dollars and lives. These sources include NCDC's Storm Data publication, the National Weather Service, the Federal Emergency Management Agency, other U.S. government agencies, individual state emergency management agencies, regional and state climatologists, and insurance industry estimates. The process of gathering this

---

National Climatic Data Center Technical Report 2003–01. Courtesy of US Department of Commerce NOAA/ NESDIS National Climatic Data Ceter Asheville, NC 28801–5001, December 2003.

information, verifying the data, and keeping it up-to-date is complex. In this report, damage estimates include both insured and uninsured losses. Fatality totals incorporate both direct and indirect deaths (i.e., deaths not directly caused by the event but closely tied to it). Economic costs are included, if available, for widespread, long-lasting droughts (e.g., losses to agriculture plus related industries). Estimates are periodically updated as additional information becomes available.

## 3. CHRONOLOGICAL LISTING OF BILLION DOLLAR EVENTS

### 2003

*Southern California Wildfires*

Late October to early November 2003. Dry weather, high winds, and resulting wildfires in Southern California. More than 743,000 acres of brush and timber burned, over 3700 homes destroyed; at least $2.5 billion damage/costs; 22 deaths.

*Hurricane Isabel*

September 2003. Category 2 hurricane makes landfall in eastern NC, causing considerable storm surge damage along the coasts of NC, VA, and MD, with wind damage and some flooding due to 4–12 inch rains in NC, VA, MD, DE, WV, NJ, NY, and PA; estimate of over $4 billion in damages/costs; at least 47 deaths.

*Severe Storms and Tornadoes*

Early May 2003. Numerous tornadoes over the midwest, MS River valley, OH/TN River valleys, and portions of the southeast, with a modern record one-week total of approximately 400 tornadoes reported; over $3.1 billion in damages/costs; 41 deaths.

*Storms and Hail*

Early April 2003. Severe storms and large hail over the southern plains and lower MS River valley, with TX hardest hit, and much of the monetary losses due to hail; over $1.6 billion in damages/costs; no deaths reported.

### 2002

*Widespread Drought*

Spring through Fall 2002. Moderate to extreme drought over large portions of 30 states, including the western states, the Great Plains, and much of the eastern U.S.; estimate of over $10 billion in damage/costs; no deaths reported.

*Western Fire Season*

Spring through Fall 2002. Major fires over 11 western states from the Rockies to the west coast, due to drought and periodic high winds, with over 7.1 million acres burned; over $2.0 billion in damage/costs; 21 deaths.

### 2001

*Tropical Storm Allison*

June 2001. The persistent remnants of Tropical Storm Allison produce rainfall amounts of 30–40 inches in portions of coastal TX and LA, causing severe flooding especially in the Houston area, then moves slowly northeastward; fatalities and significant damage reported in TX, LA, MS, FL, VA, and PA; estimate of approximately $5.0 (5.1) billion in damage/costs; at least 43 deaths.

*Midwest and Ohio Valley Hail and Tornadoes*

April 2001. Storms, tornadoes, and hail in the states of TX, OK, KS, NE, IA, MO, IL, IN, WI, MI, OH, KY, WV, and PA, over a 6-day period; over $1.9 (1.9) billion in damage/costs, with the most significant losses due to hail; at least 3 deaths.

## 2000

*Drought/Heat Wave*

Spring-Summer 2000. Severe drought and persistent heat over south-central and southeastern states causing significant losses to agriculture and related industries; estimate of over $4.0 (4.2) billion in damage/costs; estimated 140 deaths nationwide.

*Western Fire Season*

Spring-Summer 2000. Severe fire season in western states due to drought and frequent winds, with nearly 7 million acres burned; estimate of over $2.0 (2.1) billion in damage/costs (includes fire suppression); no deaths reported.

## 1999

*Hurricane Floyd*

September 1999. Large, category 2 hurricane makes landfall in eastern NC, causing 10–20 inch rains in 2 days, with severe flooding in NC and some flooding in SC, VA, MD, PA, NY, NJ, DE, RI, CT, MA, NH, and VT; estimate of at least $6.0 (6.5) billion damage/costs; 77 deaths.

*Eastern Drought/Heat Wave*

Summer 1999. Very dry summer and high temperatures, mainly in eastern U.S., with extensive agricultural losses; over $1.0 (1.1) billion damage/costs; estimated 502 deaths.

*Oklahoma-Kansas Tornadoes*

May 1999. Outbreak of F4-F5 tornadoes hit the states of OK and KS, along with TX and TN, Oklahoma City area hardest hit; over $1.6 (1.7) billion damage/costs; 55 deaths.

*Arkansas-Tennessee Tornadoes*

January 1999. Two outbreaks of tornadoes in 6-day period strike AR and TN; approximately $1.3 (1.4) billion damage/costs; 17 deaths.

## 1998

*Texas Flooding*

October-November 1998. Severe flooding in southeast TX from 2 heavy rain events, with 10–20 inch rainfall totals; approximately $1.0 (1.1) billion damage/costs; 31 deaths.

*Hurricane Georges*

September 1998. Category 2 hurricane strikes PR, FL Keys, and Gulf coasts of LA, MS, AL, and FL panhandle, 15–30 inch 2-day rain totals in parts of AL/FL; estimated $5.9 (6.5) billion damage/costs; 16 deaths.

*Hurricane Bonnie*

August 1998. Category 3 hurricane strikes eastern NC and VA, extensive agricultural damage due to winds and flooding, with 10-inch rains in 2 days in some locations; approximately $1.0 (1.1) billion damage/costs; 3 deaths.

*Southern Drought/Heat Wave*

Summer 1998. Severe drought and heat wave from TX/OK eastward to the Carolinas; $6.0-$9.0 (6.6–9.9) billion damage/costs to agriculture and ranching; at least 200 deaths.

*Minnesota Severe Storms/Hail*

May 1998. Very damaging severe thunderstorms with large hail over wide areas of MN; over $1.5 (1.7) billion damage/costs; 1 death.

*Southeast Severe Weather*

Winter-Spring 1998. Tornadoes and flooding related to El Nino in southeastern states; over $1.0 (1.1) billion damage/costs; at least 132 deaths.

*Northeast Ice Storm*

January 1998. Intense ice storm hits ME, NH, VT, and NY, with extensive forestry losses; over $1.4 (1.5) billion damage/costs; 16 deaths.

## 1997

*Northern Plains Flooding*

April-May 1997. Severe flooding in Dakotas and MN due to heavy spring snowmelt; approximately $3.7 (4.1) billion damage/costs; 11 deaths.

*MS and OH River Valleys Flooding & Tornadoes*

March 1997. Tornadoes and severe flooding hit the states of AR, MO, MS, TN, IL, IN, KY, OH, and WV, with over 10 inches of rain in 24 hours in Louisville; estimated $1.0 (1.1) billion damage/costs; 67 deaths.

*West Coast Flooding*

December 1996-January 1997. Torrential rains (10–40 inches in 2 weeks) and snowmelt produce severe flooding over portions of CA, WA, OR, ID, NV, and MT; approximately $3.0 (3.4) billion damage/costs; 36 deaths.

## 1996

*Hurricane Fran*

September 1996. Category 3 hurricane strikes NC and VA, over 10-inch 24-hour rains in some locations and extensive agricultural and other losses; over $5.0 (5.8) billion damage/costs; 37 deaths.

*Southern Plains Severe Drought*

Fall 1995 through Summer 1996. Severe drought in agricultural regions of southern plains–TX and OK most severely affected; approximately $5.0 (6.0) billion damage/costs; no deaths.

*Pacific Northwest Severe Flooding*

February 1996. Very heavy, persistent rains (10–30 inches) and melting snow over OR, WA, ID, and western MT; approximately $1.0 (1.2) billion damage/costs; 9 deaths.

*Blizzard of '96 Followed by Flooding*

January 1996. Very heavy snowstorm (1–4 feet) over Appalachians, Mid-Atlantic, and Northeast; followed by severe flooding in parts of same area due to rain & snowmelt; approximately $3.0 (3.5) billion damage/costs; 187 deaths.

## 1995

*Hurricane Opal*

October 1995. Category 3 hurricane strikes FL panhandle, AL, western GA, eastern TN, and the western Carolinas, causing storm surge, wind, and flooding damage; over $3.0 (3.6) billion damage/costs; 27 deaths.

*Hurricane Marilyn*

September 1995. Category 2 hurricane devastates U.S. Virgin Islands; estimated $2.1 (2.5) billion damage/costs; 13 deaths

*Texas/Oklahoma/Louisiana/Mississippi Severe Weather and Flooding*

May 1995. Torrential rains, hail, and tornadoes across TX–OK and southeast LA–southern MS, with Dallas and New Orleans areas (10–25 inch rains in 5 days) hardest hit; $5.0-$6.0 (6.5–7.1) billion damage/costs; 32 deaths.

*California Flooding*

January-March 1995. Frequent winter storms cause 20–70 inch rainfall and periodic flooding across much of CA; over $3.0 (3.6) billion damage/costs; 27 deaths.

## 1994

*Western Fire Season*

Summer-Fall 1994. Severe fire season in western states due to dry weather; approximately $1.0 (1.2) billion damage/costs; death toll undetermined.

*Texas Flooding*

October 1994. Torrential rain (10–25 inches in 5 days) and thunderstorms cause flooding across much of southeast TX; approximately $1.0 (1.2) billion damage/costs; 19 deaths.

*Tropical Storm Alberto*

July 1994. Remnants of slow-moving Alberto bring torrential 10–25 inch rains in 3 days, widespread flooding and agricultural damage in parts of GA, AL, and panhandle of FL; approximately $1.0 (1.2) billion damage/costs; 32 deaths.

*Southeast Ice Storm*

February 1994. Intense ice storm with extensive damage in portions of TX, OK, AR, LA, MS, AL, TN, GA, SC, NC, and VA; approximately $3.0 (3.7) billion damage/costs; 9 deaths.

## 1993

*California Wildfires*

Fall 1993. Dry weather, high winds and wildfires in Southern CA; approximately $1.0 (1.3) billion damage/costs; 4 deaths.

*Midwest Flooding*

Summer 1993. Severe, widespread flooding in central U.S. due to persistent heavy rains and thunderstorms; approximately $21.0 (26.7) billion damage/costs; 48 deaths.

*Drought/Heat Wave*

Summer 1993. Southeastern U.S.; about $1.0 (1.3) billion damage/costs to agriculture; at least 16 deaths.

*Storm/Blizzard*

March 1993. "Storm of the Century" hits entire eastern seaboard with tornadoes (FL), high winds, and heavy snows (2–4 feet); $3.0-$6.0 (3.8–7.6) billion damage/costs; approximately 270 deaths.

## 1992

*Nor'easter of 1992*

December 1992. Slow-moving storm batters northeast U.S. coast, New England hardest hit; $1.0-$2.0 (1.3–2.6) billion damage/costs; 19 deaths.

*Hurricane Iniki*

September 1992. Category 4 hurricane hits HI island of Kauai; about $1.8 (2.4) billion damage/costs; 7 deaths.

*Hurricane Andrew*

August 1992. Category 5 hurricane hits FL and LA, high winds damage or destroy over 125,000 homes; approximately $27.0 (35.6) billion damage/costs; 61 deaths.

## 1991

*Oakland Firestorm*

October 1991. Oakland, CA, firestorm due to low humidities and high winds; approximately $2.5 (3.5) billion damage/costs; 25 deaths.

*Hurricane Bob*

August 1991. Category 2 hurricane–Mainly coastal NC, Long Island, and New England; $1.5 (2.1) billion damage/costs; 18 deaths.

## 1990

*Texas/Oklahoma/Louisiana/Arkansas Flooding*

May 1990. Torrential rains cause flooding along the Trinity, Red, and Arkansas Rivers in TX, OK, LA, and AR; over $1.0 (1.4) billion damage/costs; 13 deaths.

## 1989

*Hurricane Hugo*

September 1989. Category 4 hurricane devastates SC and NC with ~ 20 foot storm surge and severe wind damage after hitting PR and the U.S. Virgin Islands; over $9.0 (13.9) billion damage/costs (about $7.1 (10.9) billion in Carolinas); 86 deaths (57–U.S. mainland, 29–U.S. Islands).

*Northern Plains Drought*

ummer 1989. Severe summer drought over much of the northern plains with significant losses to agriculture; at least $1.0 (1.5) billion in damage/costs; no deaths reported.

## 1988

*Drought/Heat Wave*

Summer 1988. Drought in central and eastern U.S. with very severe losses to agriculture and related industries; estimated $40.0 (61.6) billion damage/costs; estimated 5,000 to 10,000 deaths (includes heat stress-related).

## 1986

*Southeast Drought/Heat Wave*

Summer 1986. Severe summer drought in parts of the southeastern U.S. with severe losses to agriculture; $1.0-$1.5 (1.8–2.6) billion in damage/costs; estimated 100 deaths.

## 1985

*Hurricane Juan*

October-November 1985. Category 1 hurricane–LA and Southeast U.S.–severe flooding; $1.5 (2.8) billion damage/costs; 63 deaths.

*Hurricane Elena*

August-September 1985. Category 3 hurricane–FL to LA; $1.3 (2.4) billion damage/costs; 4 deaths.

*Florida Freeze*

January 1985. Severe freeze central/northern FL; about $1.2 (2.2) billion damage to citrus industry; no deaths.

## 1983

*Florida Freeze*

December 1983. Severe freeze central/northern FL; about $2.0 (4.0) billion damage to citrus industry; no deaths.

*Western Storms and Flooding*

1982 Early 1983. Storms and flooding related to El Nino, especially in the states of WA, OR, CA, AZ, NV, ID, UT, and MT; approximately $1.1 (2.2) billion in damage/costs; at least 45 deaths.

*Gulf States Storms and Flooding*

1982–Early 1983. Storms and flooding related to El Nino, especially in the states of TX, AR, LA, MS, AL, GA, and FL; approximately $1.1 (2.2) billion in damage/costs; at least 50 deaths.

# KEY DOCUMENTS

*Hurricane Alicia*

August 1983. Category 3 hurricane–TX; $3.0 (5.9) billion damage/costs; 21 deaths.

## 1980

*Drought/Heat Wave*

June-September 1980. Central and eastern U.S.; estimated $20.0 (48.4) billion damage/costs to agriculture and related industries; estimated 10,000 deaths (includes heat stress-related).

## 4. POPULATION CHANGES AND SOCIETAL IMPACTS

The general increase in population since 1900 has placed more people at risk when an extreme weather event occurs. Rapid growth in U.S. coastal population places more people in "harms-way" when hurricanes make landfall. Coastal areas are among the most crowded and developed in the nation. This narrow fringe–comprising less than one-fifth of the contiguous United States land area–accounts for over one-half of the nation's population and housing supply. The population of these areas grew by more than 38 million people between 1960 and 1990. In 1990, over 133 million Americans lived in the 673 coastal counties along the Atlantic and Pacific Oceans, Gulf of Mexico, and Great Lakes, representing about 54 percent of the total U.S. population. Population in the nation's coastal areas increased by 41 percent between 1960 and 1990, slightly faster than the U.S. as a whole. (NOAA Office of Ocean Resources Conservation and Assessment (ORCA), 2003)

For example, the coastal population in Florida increased from approximately one million in 1940, to 4.8 million in 1960, to 12.8 million in 1990 (University of Florida Bureau of Economic & Business Research, 1994). This rate of growth is four times that of the U.S. in general, and is largely due to immigration from other U.S. states. Most of the immigrants prefer to settle close to the shore: seventy-nine percent of Florida's population live within the coastal zone (Culliton et al., 1990). Florida's coastal population increase has not been uniform: the Atlantic coast counties have seen a 175% increase, while the Gulf has experienced a 160% increase (Antonini and Box, 1996). Important demographic changes have accompanied this growth. Large numbers of Florida residents are retired: they are older, generally wealthier, and have more available leisure time than earlier populations. From 1990–2000, Florida's population has grown by 23.5 % or an increase of 3 million persons.

For the years 1980–2003, about 30% of the billion dollar events were either hurricanes or tropical storms. According to Pielke and Landsea (1998), "…all else being equal, each year the United States has at least a 1 in 6 chance of experiencing losses related to hurricanes of at least $10 billion (in normalized 1996 dollars)." Climate patterns can significantly alter these odds (Gray et al., 1997), and each year the stakes rise due to coastal population growth and development. In 1990, Dade and Broward Counties in south Florida were home to more people than lived in all 109 counties along the Gulf and Atlantic coasts from Texas through Virginia in 1930 (Pielke, 1995). Other coastal zones are vulnerable, and hurricanes have come ashore from Texas to Maine. Yet the U.S. population is flocking to the coasts. The 426 coastal counties have just 11 percent of the territory in the continental U.S., but hold 110 million people—45 percent of the population. (In 1940, the population of these counties was 50 million.) Also, insured coastal property values increased by 100% to 300% (depending on location) during the 1980–2003 period.

In the three decades preceding Hurricanes Hugo (1989) and Andrew (1992), few major hurricanes (sustained wind speed greater than 110 miles-per-hour) struck the United States. However, from 1941 through 1950, ten major hurricanes struck the continental United States, seven of which made landfall in Florida. From 1951 through 1960, eight major hurricanes struck the United States, seven along the East Coast. For the next 30 years (1961–1990), the only major hurricane to strike the Florida peninsula was Hurricane Betsy in 1965. Similarly, during this period, no major hurricanes made landfall on the East Coast until the mid-1980s (Ayscue, 1996). However, some studies (Gray et al., 1997) indicate that a return to the more active hurricane seasons typical of the 1940s and 1950s is now occurring.

The combination of more active hurricane seasons, coastal population increases and increasing per capita income along the U.S. East and Gulf coasts provide conditions that may lead to more frequent major disasters. Nationally, the significant increase in the number of homes and businesses built in flood plains over the past fifty years increases the risk and frequency for high-cost flooding events. If these societal trends continue, the costs associated with weather-related disasters will continue to increase, regardless of any factors associated with climate change.

## 5. SUMMARY AND CONCLUSION

In twenty of the past twenty-four years, the U.S. has experienced at least one weather-related billion-dollar disaster. The only years without at least one billion dollar disaster were 1981, 1982, 1984 and 1987. Since 1988, at least one disaster occurred each year, with only one such event in 1988 and 1990, and seven billion-dollar events in 1998. Two of the 1998 disasters were caused by hurricanes. Overall, hurricanes and tropical storms account for 16 of the 58 events and 28% of the monetary losses (normalized to 2002). The ten major droughts/heatwaves which have occurred since 1980 account for the largest percentage (42%) of weather-related monetary losses. Figures 5 and 6 provide additional statistics for the distribution of events by type.

The clearest evidence which explains the increase in losses due to hurricanes, points to changes in society, not in climate fluctuations. In fact, Pielke and Landsea (1998) state, "It is only a matter of time before the nation experiences a $50 billion or greater storm, with multi-billion dollar losses becoming increasingly more frequent. Climate fluctuations that return the Atlantic basin to a period of more frequent storms will enhance the chances that this time occurs sooner, rather than later." Another study suggests, adjustments to historical loss data assembled since the late 1940s shows that most of the upward trends found in financial losses are due to societal shifts leading to ever-growing vulnerability to weather and climate extremes. Geographical locations of the large loss trends establish that population growth and demographic shifts are the major factors behind the increasing losses from weather–climate extremes. (Chagnon et al., 2000)

Although some studies (Chagnon et al., 1999) suggest that trends such as population increases, population shifts into higher risk areas, and increasing wealth have been the key factors in weather related disasters (as opposed to historical trends in the frequency or strength of such events), there is evidence that climate change may affect the frequency of certain extreme weather events. An increase in population and development in flood plains, along with an increase in heavy rain events in the U.S. during the past fifty years (Karl et al., 1996), have gradually increased the economic losses due to flooding. If the climate continues to warm, the increase in heavy rain events is likely to continue. While trends in extratropical cyclones are not clear, there are projections that the incidence of extreme droughts will increase if the climate warms throughout the 21st century (Easterling et al., 2000).

Regardless of these factors and trends, Americans will continue to cope with major economic and human losses due to hurricanes, droughts, and other weather-related disasters. As new events occur and updated statistics become available, NCDC will continue to update its worldwide web system (as shown in Fig 1, accessible via http://www.ncdc.noaa.gov/extremes.html).

## 6. REFERENCES

Antonini, G. A. and Box, P. W. (1996). A regional waterway systems management strategy for southwest Florida. Technical Report TP-83, Florida Sea Grant College Program, University of Florida, Gainesville.

Changnon, Stanley A., R.A.Pielke Jr., D. Changnon, R.T. Sylves and R. Pulwarty., 2000. Human Factors Explain the Increased Losses from Weather and Climate Extremes. *Bulletin of the American Meteorological Society*, Vol. 81, No. 3, March 2000, pp 437–442.

Changnon, Stanley A., K.E. Kunkel, and R.A. Pielke Jr., 1999. Temporal Fluctuations in Weather and Climate Extremes That Cause Economic and Human Health Impacts: A Review, *Bulletin of the American Meteorological Society*, Vol. 80, No. 6, Jun. 1999, pp 1077–1098.

Culliton, T., Warren, M., Goodspeed, T., Remer, D., Blackwell, C., and McDonough, J. (1990). Fifty Years of Population Change Along the Nation's Coasts, 1960–2010. NOAA, Rockville, MD. NOAA Coastal Trends Series.

Easterling, David R., Gerald A. Meehl, Camille Parmesan, Stanley A. Changnon, Thomas R. Karl, and Linda O. Mearns: Climate Extremes: Observations, Modeling, and Impacts, *Science*, Sep 22, 2000: 2068–2074.

Gray, W.M., J.D. Shaeffer, and C.W. Landsea, 1997: Climate Trends Associated with Multidecadal Variability of Atlantic Hurricane Activity. Hurricanes, Climate and Socioeconomic Impacts, H.F. Diaz and R.S. Pulwarty, Eds., Springer, 15–53.

Karl, Thomas R, R.W. Knight, D.R. Easterling, and R.G. Quayle, 1996. Indices of Climate Change for the United States, Bulletin of the American Meteorological Society, Vol. 77, No. 2, Feb. 1996, pp 279–292.

NOAA Office of Ocean Resources Conservation and Assessment, 2003 (ORCA)- Web site, http://spo.nos.noaa.gov/projects/population/population.html.

Pielke, R.A., Jr., 1995: Hurricane Andrew in South Florida: Mesoscale Weather and Societal Responses. National Center for Atmospheric Research, 212 pp.

Pielke, R. A. and C.W. Landsea, 1998: Normalized Hurricane Damages in the United States, 1925-1995, Weather and Forecasting, September 1998, pp. 621–631.

University of Florida Bureau of Economic & Business Research (1994). Florida Statistical Abstracts. University of Florida Press, University of Florida, Gainesville.

# KEY DOCUMENTS

| U.S. Hurricanes | Heavy Precipitation | Temperature Extremes & Drought | U.S. Tornadoes |
|---|---|---|---|
| **Billion $$ Weather Disasters** | | | **Worldwide Weather and Climate Events** |
| **Global Climate Change** | | | **Historical Global Extremes** |
| **El Nino/ La Nina** | | | **Satellite Images** |
| **Climate Monitoring** | **U.S. Local Storm Reports** | **Climatic Data** | **U.S. Radar Composites** |

**Figure 1.** Extreme Weather and Climate Events Web System—www.ncdc.noaa.gov/extremes.html

## KEY DOCUMENTS

**Figure 2.** Billion Dollar U.S. Weather Disaster Map. 1980-2007. Adjusted Costs—www.ncdc.noaa.gov/oa/reports/billionz.html

**KEY DOCUMENTS**

**Billion Dollar U.S. Weather Disasters 1980-2003**
NOAA / NESDIS / NCDC

Figure 3. Bar Chart of Annual Number of U.S. Billion Dollar Weather Disasters, 1980–2003

975

## Key Documents

## Billion Dollar U.S. Weather Disasters 1980-2003

*(Damage Amounts in Billions of Dollars and Costs Normalized to 2002 Dollars Using GNP Inflation / Wealth Index)*

| Year | | | | | |
|---|---|---|---|---|---|
| 1980 | Drought / Heat Wave $48.4  ~10,000 Deaths | | | | |
| 1983 | Hurricane Alicia $5.9  21 Deaths | Florida Freeze $4.0  No Deaths | Gulf Storms / Flooding $2.2  ~50 Deaths | W Storms / Flooding $2.2  ~45 Deaths | |
| 1985 | Florida Freeze $2.2  No Deaths | Hurricane Elena $2.4  4 Deaths | Hurricane Juan $2.8  63 Deaths | | |
| 1986 | Drought / Heat Wave $2.3  ~100 Deaths | | | | |
| 1988 | Drought / Heat Wave $61.6  ~7,500 Deaths | | | | |
| 1989 | Hurricane Hugo $13.9  86 Deaths | N Plains Drought $1.5  No Deaths | | | |
| 1990 | S Plains Flooding $1.4  13 Deaths | | | | |
| 1991 | Hurricane Bob $2.1  18 Deaths | Oakland CA Firestorm $3.5  25 Deaths | | | |
| 1992 | Hurricane Andrew $35.6  61 Deaths | Hurricane Iniki $2.4  7 Deaths | Nor'easter $2.0  19 Deaths | | |
| 1993 | E Storm / Blizzard $5.7  270 Deaths | SE Drought / Heat Wave $1.3  16 Deaths | Midwest Flooding $26.7  48 Deaths | CA Wildfires $1.3  4 Deaths | |
| 1994 | SE Ice Storm $3.7  9 Deaths | Tropical Storm Alberto $1.2  32 Deaths | Texas Flooding $1.2  19 Deaths | W Fire Season $1.2  No Deaths | |
| 1995 | CA Flooding $3.6  27 Deaths | SE / SW Severe Wx $6.8  32 Deaths | Hurricane Marilyn $2.5  13 Deaths | Hurricane Opal $3.6  27 Deaths | |
| 1996 | Blizzard / Flooding $3.5  187 Deaths | Pacific NW Flooding $1.2  9 Deaths | S Plains Drought $6.0  No Deaths | Hurricane Fran $5.8  37 Deaths | W Coast Flooding $3.6  36 Deaths |
| 1997 | Midwest Flood / Tornadoes $1.1  67 Deaths | N Plains Flooding $4.1  11 Deaths | | | |
| 1998 | New England Ice Storm $1.5  16 Deaths | SE Severe Wx $1.1  132 Deaths | MN Severe Storms / Hail $1.7  1 Death | S Drought / Heat Wave $8.3  200 Deaths | Hurricane Bonnie $1.1  3 Deaths |
| | Hurricane Georges $6.5  16 Deaths | Texas Flooding $1.1  31 Deaths | | | |
| 1999 | AR - TN Tornadoes $1.4  17 Deaths | OK - KS Tornadoes $1.7  55 Deaths | E Drought / Heat Wave $1.1  502 Deaths | Hurricane Floyd $6.5  77 Deaths | |
| 2000 | Drought / Heat Wave $4.2  ~140 Deaths | W Fires $2.1  No Deaths | | | |
| 2001 | Tropical Storm Allison $5.1  43 Deaths | Midwest / OH Valley Hail / Tornadoes $1.9  ~3 Deaths | | | |
| 2002 | 30-State Drought $10.0  No Deaths | W Fires $2.0  ~21 Deaths | | | |
| 2003 | Severe Wx / Hail $1.6  No Deaths | Severe Wx / Tornadoes $3.1  41 Deaths | Hurricane Isabel $4.0  47 Deaths | S California Wildfires $2.5  22 Deaths | |

legend: < 5 | 5-20 | 20-30 | 30-40 | > 40  Amounts in Billions of Dollars

Source: National Climatic Data Center, Asheville, NC 28801-5001
www.ncdc.noaa.gov/oa/reports/billionz.html

**Figure 4.** Billion Dollar U.S. Weather Disasters, 1980–2003—Chronological Chart

# Billion Dollar Climate and Weather Disasters
## 1980 - 2003

NOAA's NATIONAL CLIMATIC DATA CENTER
ASHEVILLE, NORTH CAROLINA

**NUMBER OF EVENTS**
- 1 - 3
- 4 - 6
- 7 - 9
- 10 - 12
- 13 - 15
- 16 - 20

| DISASTER TYPE | NUMBER OF EVENTS | PERCENT FREQUENCY | NORMALIZED DAMAGES (Billions of Dollars) | PERCENT DAMAGE |
|---|---|---|---|---|
| Tropical Storms/Hurricanes | 16 | 28.0% | 102 | 29.2% |
| Non-Tropical Floods | 12 | 21.0% | 55 | 15.8% |
| Heatwaves/Droughts | 10 | 17.0% | 144 | 41.2% |
| Severe Weather | 7 | 12.0% | 13 | 3.7% |
| Fires | 6 | 10.0% | 13 | 3.7% |
| Freezes | 2 | 3.5% | 6 | 1.7% |
| Blizzards | 2 | 3.5% | 9 | 2.6% |
| Ice Storms | 2 | 3.5% | 5 | 1.4% |
| Noreaster | 1 | 1.5% | 2 | 0.7% |
| | 58 | | 349 | |

**Figure 5.** Distribution of Events by Type and State, Showing Total Normalized Losses for Each Category

Figure 6. Distribution of Event Frequency by Cumulative Damage Amount, 1980–2003

# FOR THE HEALTH OF THE NATION: AN EVANGELICAL CALL TO CIVIC RESPONSIBILITY, SEPTEMBER 2004

*Excerpt*

## *We labor to protect God's creation*

As we embrace our responsibility to care for God's earth, we reaffirm the important truth that we worship only the Creator and not the creation. God gave the care of his earth and its species to our first parents. That responsibility has passed into our hands. We affirm that God-given dominion is a sacred responsibility to steward the earth and not a license to abuse the creation of which we are a part. We are not the owners of creation, but its stewards, summoned by God to "watch over and care for it" (Gen. 2:15). This implies the principle of sustainability: our uses of the Earth must be designed to conserve and renew the Earth rather than to deplete or destroy it.

The Bible teaches us that God is not only redeeming his people, but is also restoring the whole creation (Rom. 8:18–23). Just as we show our love for the Savior by reaching out to the lost, we believe that we show our love for the Creator by caring for his creation.

Because clean air, pure water, and adequate resources are crucial to public health and civic order, government has an obligation to protect its citizens from the effects of environmental degradation. This involves both the urgent need to relieve human suffering caused by bad environmental practice. Because natural systems are extremely complex, human actions can have unexpected side effects. We must therefore approach our stewardship of creation with humility and caution.

Human beings have responsibility for creation in a variety of ways. We urge Christians to shape their personal lives in creation-friendly ways: practicing effective recycling, conserving resources, and experiencing the joy of contact with nature. We urge government to encourage fuel efficiency, reduce pollution, encourage sustainable use of natural resources, and provide for the proper care of wildlife and their natural habitats.

---

Courtesy of National Association of Evangelicals. Reprinted with permission.

# The "Six Sins of Greenwashing™"

A Study of Environmental Claims in North American Consumer Markets

A 'Green Paper' by
TerraChoice Environmental Marketing Inc.
(November 2007)

terrachoice
environmental marketing

## Table of Contents

Overview ........................................................... 982
Research Methodology .............................................. 983
Defining and Quantifying the Six Sins of Greenwashing .............. 983
      • *Sin of the Hidden Trade-Off* ............................ 983
      • *Sin of No Proof* ........................................ 984
      • *Sin of Vagueness* ....................................... 984
      • *Sin of Irrelevance* ..................................... 985
      • *Sin of Lesser of Two Evils* ............................. 985
      • *Sin of Fibbing* ......................................... 985
Recommendations for Concerned Consumers ........................... 986
Recommendations for Marketers ..................................... 988
Concluding Thoughts ............................................... 989
Appendices ........................................................ 990
Appendix A: Types of Products Reviewed ............................ 990
Appendix B: Eco-Labels ............................................ 991
Appendix C: References ............................................ 994

## The "Six Sins of Greenwashing™"
### A Study of Environmental Claims in North American Consumer Markets

> Green·wash (grēn'wŏsh', -wôsh') – *verb:* the act of misleading consumers regarding the environmental practices of a company or the environmental benefits of a product or service.

## Overview

The recent surge of environmental awareness in North America is unmistakable. It has been documented by many researchers and widely reported in the popular press. The rise in "green" marketing claims has also been well documented. Less studied is the apparent increase in "greenwashing" – false or misleading green marketing claims.

In an effort to describe, understand, and quantify the growth of greenwashing, TerraChoice Environmental Marketing Inc. conducted a survey of six category-leading big box stores. Through these surveys, we identified 1,018 consumer products bearing 1,753 environmental claims. Of the 1,018 products examined, all but one made claims that are demonstrably false or that risk misleading intended audiences.

Based on the survey results, we identified six patterns in the greenwashing, which we now recognize as the "Six Sins of Greenwashing™".

> Of the 1,018 products reviewed, all but **one** committed at least one of the Six Sins of Greenwashing.

These findings suggest that greenwashing is pervasive, the consequences of which are significant:

- Well-intentioned consumers may be misled into purchases that do not deliver on their environmental promise. This means both that the individual consumer has been misled and that the potential environmental benefit of his or her purchase has been squandered.
- Competitive pressure from illegitimate environmental claims takes market share away from products that offer more legitimate benefits, thus slowing the penetration of real environmental innovation in the marketplace.
- Greenwashing may create cynicism and doubt about all environmental claims. Consumers – particularly those who care most about real environmental progress – may give up on marketers and manufacturers, and give up on the hope that their spending might be put to good use. This would eliminate a significant market-based, financial incentive for green product innovation and leave committed environmental advocates with government regulations as the most likely alternative.

### The "Six Sins of Greenwashing™"

1. Sin of the Hidden Trade-Off
2. Sin of No Proof
3. Sin of Vagueness
4. Sin of Irrelevance
5. Sin of Fibbing
6. Sin of Lesser of Two Evils

© 2007. TerraChoice Environmental Marketing Inc. All Rights Reserved.

## The Six Sins Of Greenwashing™

### Research Methodology

In the spring of 2007, TerraChoice sent research teams into six category-leading big box stores with instructions to record every product-based environmental claim they observed. We instructed the teams that, for each environmental claim, they should identify the product, the nature of the claim, any supporting information, and any references offered for further information.

After recording 1,753 environmental claims on 1,018 products (refer to Appendix A), we tested the claims against current best practices in environmental marketing. The sources for these best practices include the International Organization for Standardization (ISO)[1], the U.S Federal Trade Commission[2], U.S Environmental Protection Agency[3], Consumers Union[4], and the Canadian Consumer Affairs Branch[5].

Finally, we studied the resulting list of false or misleading claims for patterns and lessons. We have come to call these patterns the "Six Sins of Greenwashing". Of the 1,018 products that made environmental claims, all but one committed at least one of the Six Sins.

### Defining and Quantifying the Six Sins of Greenwashing

Based on our analysis, we categorized the false or misleading environmental claims into the following "Six Sins of Greenwashing":

☐ <u>Sin of the Hidden Trade-Off</u> – The Sin of the Hidden Trade-off is committed by suggesting a product is "green" based on a single environmental attribute (the recycled content of paper, for example) or an unreasonably narrow set of attributes (recycled content and chlorine free bleaching) without attention to other important, or perhaps more important, environmental issues (such as energy, global warming, water, and forestry impacts of paper). Such claims are not usually false, but are used to paint a "greener" picture of the product than a more complete environmental analysis would support.

Here are some examples from the research:

Examples:

- Paper (including household tissue, paper towel, and copy paper) and lumber products (such as framing products and plywood) that promote their recycled content or sustainable harvesting practices without attention to manufacturing impacts such as air emissions, water emissions, and global warming impacts.
- Household insulation products (such as batt insulation products for home renovation products) that claim indoor air quality benefits without attention to other environmental aspects such as recycled content and manufacturing impacts.

### Sins Committed by Category

- The Sin of Vagueness 11%
- The Sin of Fibbing 1%
- The Sin of No Proof 26%
- The Sin of Lesser of Two Evils 1%
- The Sin of Irrelevance 4%
- The Sin of the Hidden-Trade Off 57%

© 2007. TerraChoice Environmental Marketing Inc. All Rights Reserved.

## The Six Sins Of Greenwashing™

- Office technology (printers, copiers, fax machines) that promote energy efficiency without attention to hazardous material content, indoor air quality, or compatibility with recycled paper or remanufactured toner cartridges.
- Other product claims that committed this sin include ink cartridges, laundry detergents, dish detergent, air fresheners, bathroom cleaners, markers, flooring laminate, bags, multi-purpose cleaners, wood panels, and pesticides.

*The Sin of the Hidden Trade-off was the most frequently committed sin in the study, made by 57% of all environmental claims.*

☐ <u>Sin of No Proof</u> – Any environmental claim that cannot be substantiated by easily accessible supporting information, or by a reliable third-party certification, commits the Sin of No Proof. (For this research, we determined there to be 'no proof' if supporting evidence was not accessible at either the point of purchase or at the product website.)

Among others, our research found these examples of the Sin of No Proof:
- Household lamps and lights that promote their energy efficiency without any supporting evidence or certification.
- Personal care products (such as shampoos and conditioners) that claim not to have been tested on animals, but offer no evidence or certification of this claim.
- Facial tissues and paper towels that claim post-consumer recycled content without providing evidence.

*We found a total of 454 products and approximately 26% of the environmental claims committed the Sin of No Proof; making it the second most frequently committed sin.*

☐ <u>Sin of Vagueness</u> – The Sin of Vagueness is committed by every claim that is so poorly defined or broad that its real meaning is likely to be misunderstood by the intended consumer.

> This mobius loop is intended to mean that the product is made from recycled material. But is it the whole product, or the package? And is it made of 100% recycled material, or less? And is it post-consumer waste, or post-industrial waste? Without a qualifying statement, the symbol is likely to mislead the buyer, committing the Sin of Vagueness.

There are some recurring themes within these vague claims. For example:

- "Chemical-free". In fact, nothing is free of chemicals. Water is a chemical. All plants, animals, and humans are made of chemicals as are all of our products.
- "Non-toxic". Everything is toxic in sufficient dosage. Water, oxygen, and salt are all potentially hazardous.
- "All Natural". Arsenic is natural. So are uranium, mercury, and formaldehyde. All are poisonous.
- "Green", "Environmentally friendly", and "Eco-conscious" (to name just a few) which are utterly meaningless without elaboration.

Some product examples from the research:

- Garden insecticides promoted as "chemical-free".
- "Natural" hair mousse.
- Kitchen (wax) paper that claims "recycled content" but does not quantify it (Would 0.1% qualify?)

© 2007. TerraChoice Environmental Marketing Inc.
All Rights Reserved.

### The Six Sins Of Greenwashing™

- General purpose household cleaners that claim to be "non-toxic" without explanation or third-party substantiation.
  - "100% natural" bathroom cleaners.

*In our research sample, 196 individual products (or 11% of the environmental claims) committed the Sin of Vagueness.*

☐ <u>Sin of Irrelevance</u> – The Sin of Irrelevance is committed by making an environmental claim that may be truthful but is unimportant and unhelpful for consumers seeking environmentally preferable products. It is irrelevant and therefore distracts the consumer from finding a truly greener option.

The most frequent example of an irrelevant claim relates to chlorofluorocarbons (CFCs) – a principal contributor to ozone depletion. Since CFCs have been legally banned for almost 30 years, there are no products that are manufactured with it. Nevertheless, we found many individual products that presented CFC-free claims as an apparently unique environmental advantage. They included:

- CFC-free insecticides,
- CFC-free lubricants,
- CFC-free oven cleaners,
- CFC-free shaving gels,
- CFC-free window cleaners,
- CFC-free disinfectants.

*The Sin of Irrelevance accounted for 78 products and 4% of the environmental claims.*

CFCs have been legally banned for almost 30 years, yet many products still claim CFC-free as if it is a unique competitive advantage.

☐ <u>Sin of Lesser of Two Evils</u> – These are "green" claims that may be true within the product category, but that risk distracting the consumer from the greater environmental impacts of the category as a whole. Examples include:

- Organic cigarettes.
- "Green" insecticides and herbicides.

Obviously, there are some circumstances and consumers that demand these products. Commercial insecticides and herbicides are essential to some agricultural applications. In those circumstances, choosing the greenest option is essential. However, insecticides and pesticides may be unnecessary for many cosmetic applications (such as lawns). Organic tobacco may be a more responsible choice for smokers, but shouldn't most consumers be discouraged from smoking in the first place?

We consider a claim to commit the Sin of Lesser of Two Evils when environmental qualifiers such as "organic" or "green" are placed on products in which the entire product category is of questionable environmental value.

*In this study, 17 products and approximately 1% of environmental claims committed the Sin of Lesser of Two Evils.*

☐ <u>Sin of Fibbing</u> – The Sin of Fibbing is committed by making environmental claims that are simply false.

In our findings, only a few products were found to commit the Sin of Fibbing. Most of these were misuse or misrepresentation of certification by an independent authority. These cases included, for example:

- Several shampoos that claimed to be "certified organic", but for which our research could find no such certification.
- A caulking product that claims to be "Energy Star" registered, but the official Energy Star website suggests this is false.
- A dishwasher detergent that purports to be packaged in "100% recycled paper", and yet the container is plastic.

© 2007. TerraChoice Environmental Marketing Inc.
All Rights Reserved.

## The Six Sins Of Greenwashing™

*10 products (less than 1% of environmental claims) committed the Sin of Fibbing, making it one of the two least fre uentl committed sins*

### Recommendations for Consumers

Governments and standard-setting bodies have attempted to discourage greenwashing. In North America, both the US Federal Trade Commission[6] and the Canadian Consumer Affairs office[7] have issued guidelines for proper use of environmental claims. Under ISO 14024, the International Organization for Standardization establishes guidelines for proper use of environmental information.P[8] But it is our observation that when environmental interest is high, as it is today, greenwashing is nevertheless prolific.

---

**Multi-Attribute Versus Single-Attribute Claims**

When seeking environmentally preferable products, it is important to look at multiple environmental considerations rather than just single environmental issues.

As an analogy, when attempting to identify healthier food choices, it can be useful to look at calorie content. It is more helpful, however, to also examine fat, sugar, and vitamin content.

The most respected environmental claims incorporate multiple environmental considerations throughout every phase of a product's life-cycle, which includes the environmental impacts of the raw materials, manufacturing process, the product itself, and its ultimate disposal.

Single-attribute claims look at only a single environmental issue such as recycled-content or energy-efficiency. While important, single attribute claims can hide important additional environmental considerations.

---

If the good intentions of consumers and the environmental benefits of their choices are not to be squandered, consumers themselves will have to play a role. Here are some suggestions that arise from this study.

1. **Look for Eco-labels.**

Eco-labelling – standardized by ISO 14024 and recognized around the world – arose as an answer to earlier efforts of greenwashing. They remain one of the most useful tools to avoid greenwashing. Look for products that have been certified by a qualified and independent third-party such as EcoLogo$^{CM}$ or Green Seal. Both EcoLogo$^{CM}$ and Green Seal develop standards for environmental leadership in an open, transparent consensus-based process that considers multiple environmental issues throughout a product's lifecycle (from resource extraction to end-of-life). These programs deliver a shortcut to "greener" products through:

- Clear public standards for environmental leadership in each product category;
- Third-party verification that each certified product meets the applicable standards;
- Ongoing surveillance auditing to ensure continued compliance;
- Public listings of certified products.

Additional information on other environmental standards is included in Appendix B.

---

**Example of Multi-Attribute Eco-labels:**

EcoLogo$^{CM}$ — www.ecologo.org

Green Seal — www.greenseal.org

---

© 2007. TerraChoice Environmental Marketing Inc.
All Rights Reserved.

**The Six Sins Of Greenwashing™**

2. Look For Evidence of Any of the "Six Sins" By Asking the Following Questions:

a) Is the "green" claim restricted to just one, or a narrow set of environmental issue(s)? **(The Sin of the Hidden Trade ff.)** If so, you might look for other information that gives a more com lete icture of the environmental im act of the roduct. " kay, this roduct comes from a sustaina ly harvested forest, ut what are the im acts of its milling and trans ortation? Is the manufacturer also trying to reduce those im acts?" *Emphasizing* one environmental issue isn't a problem (indeed, it often makes for better communications). *Hiding* a trade-off between environmental issues is a problem.

b) Does the claim help me find more information and evidence? **(The Sin of No Proof.)** It may not be reasonable to expect a product label or a point-of-purchase brochure to provide detailed scientific explanations of a green claim. It *is* reasonable to expect a product label or brochure to direct you to where you can find further evidence. Good green marketing helps the consumer find the evidence and learn more. Company websites, third-party certifiers, and toll-free phone numbers are easy and effective means of delivering proof.

c) Is the environmental and scientific meaning of the claim specific and self-evident? If not, is the specific meaning given? **(The Sin of Vagueness.)** Products with names like "eco-gadget" and "natur-widget" aren't necessarily making false or misleading claims, but they should cause you to be suspicious. If the marketing claim doesn't explain itself ("here's what we mean by 'eco' …"), the claim is vague and meaningless. Similarly, watch for other popular vague green terms: "non-toxic", "all-natural", "environmentally-friendly", and "earth-friendly." Without adequate explanation, such claims are so vague as to be meaningless.

d) Could all of the other products in this category make the same claim? **(The Sin of Irrelevance.)** The most common example is easy to detect: "CFC-free" is a meaningless claim. It is irrelevant because no products are manufactured with chlorofluorocarbons. Other cases may be harder to detect. Ask yourself if the claim is important and relevant to the product. (If a light bulb claimed water efficiency benefits you should be suspicious.) Comparison-shop (and ask the competitive vendors). If the claim seems illogical and disconnected from the product, it may very well be irrelevant.

e) When I check up on it, is the claim true? **(The Sin of Fibbing.)** This sin can be difficult to detect. The most frequent examples in this study were false uses of third-party certifications. Thankfully, these are easy to confirm. Legitimate third-party certifiers – EcoLogo$^{CM}$, Chlorine Free Products Association (CFPA), Forest Stewardship Council (FSC), Green Guard, Green Seal (for example) – all maintain publicly available lists of certified products. Some even maintain fraud advisories for products that are falsely claiming certification.

f) Is the claim trying to make consumers feel "green" about a product category that is of questionable environmental benefit? **(The Sin of the Lesser of Two Evils.)** Consumers concerned about the adverse effects of tobacco and cigarettes would be better served by quitting smoking than by buying organic cigarettes. Similarly, consumers concerned about the human health and environmental risks of excessive use of lawn chemicals might create a bigger environmental benefit by reducing their use than by looking for greener alternatives.

© 2007. TerraChoice Environmental Marketing Inc.
All Rights Reserved.

## The Six Sins Of Greenwashing™

### Recommendations for Marketers

Green marketing is a vast commercial opportunity, and should be. When it works – when it is scientifically sound and commercially successful – it is an important accelerator toward environmental sustainability. The purpose of this study is not to discourage green marketing, nor to indict particular marketers. Our purpose is to help marketers improve their claims so that:

- Genuinely "greener" products excel;
- Competitive pressure from illegitimate green claims is diminished;
- Consumers do not become jaded and unduly skeptical of green claims; and,
- Marketers employ environmental concerns to establish honest, trustworthy, and long-lasting dialogue with their customers.

Green marketers and consumers are learning about the pitfalls of greenwashing together. This is a shared problem and opportunity.

The Six Sins of Greenwashing does NOT suggest that only perfectly "green" products should be marketed as environmentally preferable. First of all, there is no such thing as a perfectly "green" product. Environmentally preferable products are "greener" not "green", and marketing them as such is entirely fair. Second, environmental progress is necessarily stepwise. Not only should incrementally "greener" innovations and products be encouraged, consumers should and will reward stepwise progress.

Avoiding greenwashing does not require waiting for a perfect product. It does mean that sound science, honesty, and transparency are paramount.

> Green marketers and consumers are learning about the pitfalls of greenwashing together. This is a shared problem and opportunity.

The Six Sins suggest a number of specific guidelines for marketers, outlined below.

1) Avoiding the Sin of the Hidden Trade-Off
   a) **Do** understand all of the environmental impacts of your product across its entire lifecycle.
   b) **Do** emphasize specific messages (particularly when you know your audiences care about those issues) but don't use single issues to distract from other impacts.
   c) **Do** pursue continual improvement of your environmental footprint (across the entire lifecycle), and encourage your customers to join you on that journey.
   d) **Do** draw on multi-attribute eco-labeling standard and certification programs, such as EcoLogo$^{CM}$ and Green Seal for legitimacy of environmental claims.
   e) **Don't** make claims about a single environmental impact or benefit, without knowing how your product performs in terms of its other impacts, and without sharing that information with your customers.

2) Avoiding the Sin of No Proof
   a) **Do** understand and confirm the scientific case behind each green marketing claim.
   b) **Do** provide evidence to anyone that asks, OR rely on third-party certifications such as EcoLogo$^{CM}$ and Green Seal (since those standards are public).

3) Avoiding the Sin of Vagueness
   a) **Do** use language that resonates with your customer, as long as that language is truthful.
   b) **Do** use caution in your use of the recycling/recyclable symbol (the mobius loop). Its use is so widespread and confused that it has become largely meaningless.
   c) **Don't** use vague names and terms (such as environmentally-friendly) without providing precise explanations of your meaning.
   d) **Don't** use the terms "chemical-free" and "all-natural".

© 2007. TerraChoice Environmental Marketing Inc.
All Rights Reserved.

### The Six Sins Of Greenwashing™

4) Avoiding the Sin of Irrelevance
   a) **Don't** claim CFC-free, because it is not a legitimate point of competitive differentiation.
   b) **Don't** claim any environmental benefit that is shared by all or most of your competitors.

5) Avoiding the Sin of the Lesser of Two Evils
   a) **Do** help each customer find the product that is right for them, based on their needs and wants.
   b) **Don't** try to make a customer feel "green" about a choice that is basically harmful or unnecessary.

6) Avoiding the Sin of Fibbing
   a) **Do** tell the truth. Always.
   b) **Always** tell the truth.

The "Six Sins of Greenwashing™"
1. Sin of the Hidden Trade-Off
2. Sin of No Proof
3. Sin of Vagueness
4. Sin of Irrelevance
5. Sin of Fibbing
6. Sin of Lesser of Two Evils

## Concluding Thoughts

Green marketing is a powerful convergence between green buyers and sellers . More and more consumers expect to use their spending as an expression of their environmental commitment. More and more businesses are establishing environmental performance as a point of competitive distinction and social responsibility. When genuine environmental leadership is rewarded in the marketplace (with market share, price premiums, public respect, and increased visibility), it motivates all products to improve. It uses competition and free enterprise to pull the economy toward sustainability.

With that in mind, the purpose of this study is not to discourage green marketing, nor to indict particular marketers. It is not intended to scare consumers away from green claims. Our purpose is to assist marketers and consumers to build a more honest and effective dialogue about the environmental impacts of products.

Although our findings - the Six Sins of Greenwashing – may seem bleak, green marketers and consumers are learning about the pitfalls of greenwashing together. This is a shared problem and opportunity. When green marketing overcomes these challenges, consumers will be better able to trust green claims and genuinely environmentally preferable products will penetrate their markets more rapidly and deeply. This will be great for consumers, great for business, and great for the planet.

We expect to repeat this research annually, and look forward to these positive developments.

**terrachoice**
environmental marketing

This "Green Paper" was prepared by TerraChoice Environmental Marketing. Are you curious about the results? Interested in learning more? Would you like to speak to anyone at TerraChoice? Please visit *www.terrachoice.com/sixsinsofgreenwashing* for more information.

© 2007. TerraChoice Environmental Marketing Inc.
All Rights Reserved.

# APPENDICES

## APPENDIX A — Product Categories In Which Environmental Claims Were Found

- Air Fresheners
- Appliances
- Automotive Cleaner
- Bags
- Bathroom Cleaner
- Body Lotion
- Carpet Cleaner
- Caulking
- Conditioner
- Degreaser
- Deodorant
- Dish Detergent
- Disinfectant Sprays
- Envelopes
- Envelopes
- Fabric Softener
- Facial Tissues
- Floor Cleaner
- Flooring
- Foam Bath
- Furniture Polish
- Gel
- Glass Cleaner
- Green Product Section
- Hairspray
- Hand Lotion
- Hand Soap
- Herbicides
- Ink Cartridges
- Insect/Pesticides
- Insulation
- Laundry Detergent
- Light Bulbs
- Lighting
- Lubricant
- Mousse
- Mouth Wash
- Multi Purpose Cleaner
- Oven Cleaner
- Packaging Materials
- Paint
- Paper
- Portfolios
- Printers/copiers
- Scrub Pads
- Serviettes
- Shampoo
- Shaving Gel
- Shipping Boxes
- Stainless Steel Polish
- Televisions
- Toilet Tissue
- Toothpaste
- Wood (panels)
- Wraps
- Writing Instruments

© 2007. TerraChoice Environmental Marketing Inc.
All Rights Reserved.

## APPENDIX B — Eco-labels

Consumers can avoid greenwashing by seeking products that are certified to meet legitimate environmental standards such as EcoLogo$^{CM}$ or Green Seal. There are, however, a growing number of additional environmental standards and claims being made.

When comparing environmental standards, consumers would be wise to ask the following questions:

### (1) What type of environmental claim is being made?

Is the manufacturer making a claim about a single environmental attribute such as energy efficiency or recycled-content or is the manufacturer making a broader multi-attribute claim that the product meets an environmental leadership standard? While incredibly valuable, single-attribute environmental claims do not address other potentially important human health and environmental issues.

Environmental leadership standards such as EcoLogo$^{CM}$ and Green Seal examine all of the relevant environmental impacts of a product category along with the products currently available in the market when developing a standard. Leadership standards generally are designed so that only the top 20 percent of products in a category can meet it. This allows sufficient competition within the leadership category to help keep prices competitive while still being protective of human health and the environment.

### (2) Is a copy of the environmental standard or testing protocol available for review?

If a manufacturer can not or refuses to provide a copy of the environmental standard or testing protocol, one might suspect that the claim is only a marketing ploy. When they do provide a copy of the standard, review it carefully to determine if it references appropriate national or international environmental and performance standards.

Standard and testing protocols should have a clear and consistent meaning. They should be meaningful and verifiable. Good standards and protocols are designed so that anyone unaffiliated with the standard should be able to read it, interpret it, and know how to evaluate products against it. They should also be designed to ensure consistent evaluation results, meaning that different reviewers would likely reach the same conclusion about whether a product meets the standard or not.

In addition, multi-attribute environmental leadership standards should be based on human health and environmental considerations throughout the lifecycle of the product from raw material extraction, manufacture, use, and ultimate disposal of the product. The lifecycle stages considered and covered by the standard should be explicitly stated.

### (3) How was the environmental standard or testing protocol developed?

It is preferable that standards and testing protocols be developed in an open, public, transparent process similar to the way ANSI, ASTM, ISO 14024 or other public standards are developed. The standard setting organization should make records of the standard development process available for review.

### (4) Who developed the environmental standard or testing protocol?

The most trusted standards are those developed in a consensus-based process by broad stakeholder groups. Standards developed consistently with ISO 14024 protocols will make a list of stakeholder groups available upon request. Consumers should be less trustful of standards developed by an individual manufacturer or trade association because of potentially unmitigated conflicts of interest.

© 2007. TerraChoice Environmental Marketing Inc.
All Rights Reserved.

# Key Documents

(5) What process is used to verify that products actually meet the standard or passed the testing requirements?

There are a variety of procedures to verify that a product meets a standard. Some are more rigorous (and can be more expensive for the manufacturer), but provide a greater degree of assurance. The standard verification procedures range (from most rigorous to least rigorous) as follows:

- Independent third-party certification with on-site audits – An independent organization verifies the products meet the standards based on a review of the product, additional information provided by the manufacturer, and after an onsite visit to verify the accuracy of the information provided by the manufacturer.

- Independent third-party certification – An independent organization verifies the products meet the standard based on a review of the product and additional information provided by the manufacturer.

- Self registration with random audits – Individual companies identify products meeting the environmental standard on their own without any preliminary review, but the standard setting organization or other independent auditors conduct random audits after products are registered to ensure compliance.

- Self registration – Individual companies identify products meeting the environmental standard on their own without any outside review.

It is important to note that a stringent verification process is relatively meaningless if the standard itself is not meaningful.

Widely Accepted Environmental Standards:

*Multi-Attribute Standard Setting and Certification Organizations*

These programs examine multiple environmental issues throughout the entire lifecycle of a product, which includes the environmental impacts associated with the collection of raw materials, the manufacturing process, the impacts of the product during its use, and the impacts when the product is ultimately recycled or disposed of. Before earning certification, an independent third-party auditor must verify that products actually meet the publicly-available standard.

- EcoLogo <www.ecologo.org>

  EcoLogo$^{CM}$ is North America's oldest and most widely known environmental leadership standard. The EcoLogo$^{CM}$ website includes more than 120 environmental standards and almost 7,000 certified products (stock-keeping units or SKUs). Purchasers are using the site to research or develop purchasing specifications and to put together potential bidder lists. EcoLogo$^{CM}$ is the only program in North America to have been accredited by the Global Eco-Labelling Network. It is a Type I eco-label according to ISO, and addresses all of the environmental attributes of the product.

- Chlorine Free Products Association <www.chlorinefreeproducts.org>

  CFPA certifies paper and tissue products meeting its multi-attribute standard.

- Green Seal <www.greenseal.org>

  Green Seal standards provide leadership criteria for the development of many types of products and services. The Green Seal website includes a list of all of the Green Seal-certified products and services with links to the manufacturers and providers.

© 2007. TerraChoice Environmental Marketing Inc. All Rights Reserved.

*Single Attribute Environmental Standard Setting and Certification Organization*

These programs focus on a single environmental issue such as indoor air quality or recycled content. Before earning certification, an independent third-party auditor must verify that products meet the publicly-available standard.

- Forest Stewardship Council <www.fscus.org>

    The Forest Stewardship Council certifies wood products obtained from sustainably harvested forests. It also certifies environmentally preferable papers based on a multi-attribute approach.

- Green-e <www.green-e.org>

    Green-e certifies sources of renewable electricity and renewable energy credits generated from clean energy sources such as wind, solar, or small-scale hydro-electric. It also certifies products that were manufactured in facilities using renewable energy.

- GREENGUARD <www.greenguard.org>

    GREENGUARD focuses exclusively on indoor air quality issues. Its website includes certified products in more than 15 different categories, from paint to baby cribs and mattresses to cleaning systems, flooring, adhesives, wall coverings, HVAC ductwork, window treatments, countertops, tiles, cabinets, and office furnishings. Today, there are over 120 manufacturers participating in the testing program with more than 150,000 products are certified.

*Additional Environmental Standards*

Other programs allow manufacturers to declare their products meet a publicly available standard. They then conduct random audits to maintain the integrity of the environmental declarations. The existence of the public standards also allows others to independently verify the accuracy of the claims.

- Energy Star Program <www.energystar.gov>

    The U.S. Federal Government's Energy Star program establishes energy-efficiency criteria for a wide variety of products in more than 40 product categories. The site lists all of the products meeting the efficiency requirements. It also includes recommended purchasing specifications and online training resources.

- EPEAT <www.epeat.net>

    EPEAT ranks computer desktops, laptops, and monitors into EPEAT Bronze, Silver, or Gold categories based on more than 50 environmental criteria. There are currently more than 600 products from 23 manufacturers on the EPEAT registry.

© 2007. TerraChoice Environmental Marketing Inc.
All Rights Reserved.

# KEY DOCUMENTS

### APPENDIX C — References

[1] http://www.iso.org/iso/iso_catalogue/catalogue_tc/catalogue_detail.htm?csnumber=23145

[2,6] http://www.ftc.gov/be/v970003.shtm

[3] http://www.epa.gov/epp/pubs/claims.htm

[4] http://www.greenerchoices.org/eco-labels/eco-home.cfm

[5,7] http://consumer.ic.gc.ca/epic/site/oca-bc.nsf/en/h_ca02302e.html

© 2007. TerraChoice Environmental Marketing Inc.
All Rights Reserved.

# STEPS TOWARD ECOLOGICAL SUSTAINABILITY, EQUITY, SUFFICIENCY AND PEACE

*Fom Manifesto on Global Economic Transitions, September 2007*

In this document, we have deliberately not offered a fully rationalized single new model for solving the Triple Crisis, that we hope to convey or impose on the world. Our effort seeks to begin processes toward such models, however, and to suggest many of their most obvious ingredients. The following therefore are some of the positions, ideas and steps that we believe will even tually be included in comprehensive sustainable models and practices. We encourage discussion and debate of all of these, and their further amplifications, eventually leading toan international movement that demands fundamental change in the way societies now operate, and how we live, as communities, families and individuals.

Here are the beginnings of a list of steps toward a new economy of sufficiency, equity, sustainability and peace.

1) Rapid withdrawal from all carbon-based energy systems, including adoption by all countries of an "Oil Depletion Protocol", or similar proposals for fixed annual downscalings of oil, coal and gas consumption.

2) Rejection of large-scale so called "alternative" energy systems designed to prolong the industrial growth system. These include nuclear energy, "clean" coal, industrial scale biofuels, and the combustion of hazardous materials and municipal waste, among others.

3) Speedy transition to small-scale, locally orientedand locally owned, ecologically sustainable, renewable energy systems, including wind, solar, small scale hydro and wave, localbiofuels. Equally important is a dramatic increase in the practices of conservation and efficiency—i.e., powering down, together with a corresponding decrease of personal consumption in countries where it has been excessive.

4) Recognition that some nations, because of historic patterns of colonialism, aggression, and resource exploitation have gained disproportionately from control of the planet's resources. All solutions to the current crises must include awareness and an active effort toward reallocation of global resources to restore an equitable balance between and within nations.

5) Rejection of all the primary negative elements and goals of economic globalization, and the highly undemocratic "neoclassical" economic model itself. These negative factors include: hyper economic growth; export-oriented production in agriculture, energy, and manufacturing; deregulation of corporate activity; privatization of the natural commons; privatization of public services; "structural adjustment" of economies toward global trade and away from local needs; emphasis on global markets; destruction of local markets; suppression of protective tariffs and investment controls (meant to protect local resources and businesses). Such features of economic globalization are designed to sustain global corporations, not the environment or viable communities. Any sustainable democratic system will feature values and practices which are virtually the opposite of all those.

http://www.ifg.org/pdf/manifesto.pdf.

Courtesy of International Forum on Globalization. Reprinted with permission.

6) Reorienting the rules of economic activity—trade, investments, standards—to favor economic localization and local political empowerment (subsidiarity) wherever possible. The many global examples of existing sustainable communities should be acknowledged, and local economic well-being should take precedent over global corporate trade and growth. We favor major reforms of current international trade and finance bodies, such as WTO, World Bank and IMF, and export credit agencies, which are now primary actors in supporting the unsustainable global economy of today. Where institutional reform is not achievable, we seek their replacement by new international, national and local institutions and processesthat do not act as surrogates for global corporations, but act in the interests of environmental sustainability, equity among nations and peoples, principles of subsidiarity and democracy; ecological, cultural and biological diversity, within the inherent limits of nature. (See also Cavanagh and Mander, Alternatives to Globalization.)

7) We favor lesslong-distance trade rather than more; moreand deeper regulation of corporate activity; less movement of capital across borders; more emphasis on regional and local self sufficiency, sustainability and control; greater community participation on corporate boards, and increased rules of investment that favor local ownership; graduated, negotiated use of import and export controls as necessary, with corresponding transfers of resources from North to South to offset displacements from reductions in trade; use of trade policy to protect small farmers and small entrepreneurs in all countries, while recognizing the special needs for transitions of farmers and workers in less developed countries; re-empowerment of the concept of the local, regional and national commons; redesign of urban and non-urban living environments to conform to the true realities of a post carbon era; restrictions on all conversion of agricultural lands away from food-growing, and reconversion of many lands that have already been removed from agriculture and their return to local community ownership.

8) Internalization of the full ecological and social costs of corporate production; codification of the "polluter pays" principle.

9) Promotion of an orderly re-ruralization, and revitalization of communities by way of land reform, education and application of eco-agricultural microfarming methods, import/export controls, and emphasis on local democracy; all of these in preparation for the inevitable de-industrialization of agriculture, as cheap energy supply declines.

10) Reintroduction of a modernized version of "import substitution", or regional self reliant models among nations, i.e., where nations seek to satisfy their most fundamental needs such as food, housing, energy, resource production and control, and livelihoods, from local systems and resources rather than being dependent on long distance supply, which routinely leads to dependency, insecurity and exploitation, empowering global players while harming local.

11) Introduction of new standards of measurement regarding the success of societies. Gross Domestic Product (GDP) and Gross National Product (GNP) must be recognized as inadequate and incompatible with societies that now seek basic shifts in values. Emphasis must now become human well-being, environmental sustainability, and the preservation of "natural capital" as primary concerns, rather than exponential growth, corporate profit, or personal wealth accumulation.

12) Within the contexts of global carrying capacity, establishment of global limits on total overall quantity of energy production, and the creation of standards of "sufficiency" equity, sustainability and resource reallocation.

13) Prior rejection, and clear limits upon all technologies assessed as environmentally or socially unsustainable. Application of the "precautionary principle" with respect to all technological development.

14) Recognition that protection and preservation of the natural world—its full biological and genetic diversity, and all of its beings, is a primary goal and necessity of a sane and sustainable system, and that nature has inherent rights to exist on the earth in an undiminished healthy condition, separate from its services to humans.

15) Recognition that personal behavior shares responsibility with systemic conditions for the present problems, and for their solution. Many western industrial peoples have been privileged to enjoy the fruits of the present process, but must now work to change excessive consumption habits, while realizing that such change will actually bring positive benefitsvia greater free time for personal, family, social, recreational and spiritual pursuits.

16) Recognition that many indigenous societies of today, and many countries of the South, have already established societies with priorities and values such as we have listed above, and should be consulted as models and guides for change.

17) The success of all systems and societies should be judged by fulfillment of five fundamental criteria: ecological sustainability; degree of "net energy gain" or loss; degree of social equity, well-being, and "sufficiency" rather than surplus consumption and wealth; democratic decision-making processes; and non-violent conflict resolution.

18) All nations should conform to these principles.

## GLOBAL WARMING TWENTY YEARS LATER: TIPPING POINTS NEAR

*By James Hansen*

My presentation today is exactly 20 years after my 23 June 1988 testimony to Congress, which alerted the public that global warming was underway. There are striking similarities between then and now, but one big difference.

Again a wide gap has developed between what is understood about global warming by the relevant scientific community and what is known by policymakers and the public. Now, as then, frank assessment of scientific data yields conclusions that are shocking to the body politic.

Now, as then, I can assert that these conclusions have a certainty exceeding 99 percent.

The difference is that now we have used up all slack in the schedule for actions needed to defuse the global warming time bomb. The next President and Congress must define a course next year in which the United States exerts leadership commensurate with our responsibility for the present dangerous situation.

Otherwise it will become impractical to constrain atmospheric carbon dioxide, the greenhouse gas produced in burning fossil fuels, to a level that prevents the climate system from passing tipping points that lead to disastrous climate changes that spiral dynamically out of humanity's control.

Changes needed to preserve creation, the planet on which civilization developed, are clear. But the changes have been blocked by special interests, focused on short-term profits, who hold sway in Washington and other capitals.

I argue that a path yielding energy independence and a healthier environment is, barely, still possible. It requires a transformative change of direction in Washington in the next year.

On 23 June 1988 I testified to a hearing, chaired by Senator Tim Wirth of Colorado, that the Earth had entered a long-term warming trend and that human-made greenhouse gases almost surely were responsible. I noted that global warming enhanced both extremes of the water cycle, meaning stronger droughts and forest fires, on the one hand, but also heavier rains and floods.

My testimony two decades ago was greeted with skepticism. But while skepticism is the lifeblood of science, it can confuse the public. As scientists examine a topic from all perspectives, it may appear that nothing is known with confidence. But from such broad openminded study of all data, valid conclusions can be drawn.

My conclusions in 1988 were built on a wide range of inputs from basic physics, planetary studies, observations of on-going changes, and climate models. The evidence was strong enough that I could say it was time to "stop waffling". I was sure that time would bring the scientific community to a similar consensus, as it has.

---

Dr. James E. Hansen, a physicist by training, directs the NASA Goddard Institute for Space Studies, a laboratory of the Goddard Space Flight Center and a unit of the Columbia University Earth Institute. This speech was given by Dr. Hansen, as a private citizen, at the National Press Club on June 23, 2008 and at a Briefing to the House Select Committee on Energy Independence and Global Warming.

www.columbia.edu/~jeh1/2008/TwentyYearsLater_20080623.pdf. Reprinted with permisssion.

While international recognition of global warming was swift, actions have faltered. The U.S. refused to place limits on its emissions, and developing countries such as China and India rapidly increased their emissions.

What is at stake? Warming so far, about two degrees Fahrenheit over land areas, seems almost innocuous, being less than day-to-day weather fluctuations. But more warming is already "in-the-pipeline", delayed only by the great inertia of the world ocean. And climate is nearing dangerous tipping points. Elements of a "perfect storm", a global cataclysm, are assembled.

Climate can reach points such that amplifying feedbacks spur large rapid changes. Arctic sea ice is a current example. Global warming initiated sea ice melt, exposing darker ocean that absorbs more sunlight, melting more ice. As a result, without any additional greenhouse gases, the Arctic soon will be ice-free in the summer.

More ominous tipping points loom. West Antarctic and Greenland ice sheets are vulnerable to even small additional warming. These two-mile-thick behemoths respond slowly at first, but if disintegration gets well underway it will become unstoppable. Debate among scientists is only about how much sea level would rise by a given date. In my opinion, if emissions follow a business-as-usual scenario, sea level rise of at least two meters is likely this century. Hundreds of millions of people would become refugees. No stable shoreline would be reestablished in any time frame that humanity can conceive.

Animal and plant species are already stressed by climate change. Polar and alpine species will be pushed off the planet, if warming continues. Other species attempt to migrate, but as some are extinguished their interdependencies can cause ecosystem collapse. Mass extinctions, of more than half the species on the planet, have occurred several times when the

Earth warmed as much as expected if greenhouse gases continue to increase. Biodiversity recovered, but it required hundreds of thousands of years.

The disturbing conclusion, documented in a paper[1] I have written with several of the world's leading climate experts, is that the safe level of atmospheric carbon dioxide is no more than 350 ppm (parts per million) and it may be less. Carbon dioxide amount is already 385 ppm and rising about 2 ppm per year. Stunning corollary: the oft-stated goal to keep global warming less than two degrees Celsius (3.6 degrees Fahrenheit) is a recipe for global disaster, not salvation.

These conclusions are based on paleoclimate data showing how the Earth responded to past levels of greenhouse gases and on observations showing how the world is responding to today's carbon dioxide amount. The consequences of continued increase of greenhouse gases extend far beyond extermination of species and future sea level rise.

Arid subtropical climate zones are expanding poleward. Already an average expansion of about 250 miles has occurred, affecting the southern United States, the Mediterranean region, Australia and southern Africa. Forest fires and drying-up of lakes will increase further unless carbon dioxide growth is halted and reversed.

Mountain glaciers are the source of fresh water for hundreds of millions of people. These glaciers are receding world-wide, in the Himalayas, Andes and Rocky Mountains. They will disappear, leaving their rivers as trickles in late summer and fall, unless the growth of carbon dioxide is reversed.

---

[1]Target atmospheric CO2: where should humanity aim? J. Hansen, M. Sato, P. Kharecha, D. Beerling, R. Berner, V. Masson-Delmotte, M. Raymo, D.L. Royer, J.C. Zachos, http://arxiv.org/abs/0804.1126 and http://arxiv.org/abs/0804.1135

## KEY DOCUMENTS

Coral reefs, the rainforest of the ocean, are home for one-third of the species in the sea.

Coral reefs are under stress for several reasons, including warming of the ocean, but especially because of ocean acidification, a direct effect of added carbon dioxide. Ocean life dependent on carbonate shells and skeletons is threatened by dissolution as the ocean becomes more acid.

Such phenomena, including the instability of Arctic sea ice and the great ice sheets at today's carbon dioxide amount, show that we have already gone too far. We must draw down atmospheric carbon dioxide to preserve the planet we know. A level of no more than 350 ppm is still feasible, with the help of reforestation and improved agricultural practices, but just barely—time is running out.

Requirements to halt carbon dioxide growth follow from the size of fossil carbon reservoirs. Coal towers over oil and gas. Phase out of coal use except where the carbon is captured and stored below ground is the primary requirement for solving global warming.

Oil is used in vehicles where it is impractical to capture the carbon. But oil is running out. To preserve our planet we must also ensure that the next mobile energy source is not obtained by squeezing oil from coal, tar shale or other fossil fuels.

Fossil fuel reservoirs are finite, which is the main reason that prices are rising. We must move beyond fossil fuels eventually. Solution of the climate problem requires that we move to carbon-free energy promptly.

Special interests have blocked transition to our renewable energy future. Instead of moving heavily into renewable energies, fossil companies choose to spread doubt about global warming, as tobacco companies discredited the smoking-cancer link. Methods are sophisticated, including funding to help shape school textbook discussions of global warming.

CEOs of fossil energy companies know what they are doing and are aware of long-term consequences of continued business as usual. In my opinion, these CEOs should be tried for high crimes against humanity and nature.

Conviction of ExxonMobil and Peabody Coal CEOs will be no consolation, if we pass on a runaway climate to our children. Humanity would be impoverished by ravages of continually shifting shorelines and intensification of regional climate extremes. Loss of countless species would leave a more desolate planet.

If politicians remain at loggerheads, citizens must lead. We must demand a moratorium on new coal-fired power plants. We must block fossil fuel interests who aim to squeeze every last drop of oil from public lands, off-shore, and wilderness areas. Those last drops are no solution. They yield continued exorbitant profits for a short-sighted self-serving industry, but no alleviation of our addiction or long-term energy source. Moving from fossil fuels to clean energy is challenging, yet transformative in ways that will be welcomed. Cheap, subsidized fossil fuels engendered bad habits. We import food from halfway around the world, for example, even with healthier products available from nearby fields. Local produce would be competitive if not for fossil fuel subsidies and the fact that climate change damages and costs, due to fossil fuels, are also borne by the public.

A price on emissions that cause harm is essential. Yes, a carbon tax. Carbon tax with 100 percent dividend[2] is needed to wean us off fossil fuel addiction. Tax and dividend allows the marketplace, not politicians, to make investment decisions.

Carbon tax on coal, oil and gas is simple, applied at the first point of sale or port of entry. The entire tax must be returned to the public, an equal amount to each adult, a half-share for children. This dividend can be deposited monthly in an individual's bank account.

Carbon tax with 100 percent dividend is non-regressive. On the contrary, you can bet that low and middle income people will find ways to limit their carbon tax and come out ahead. Profligate energy users will have to pay for their excesses.

Demand for low-carbon high-efficiency products will spur innovation, making our products more competitive on international markets. Carbon emissions will plummet as energy efficiency and renewable energies grow rapidly. Black soot, mercury and other fossil fuel emissions will decline. A brighter, cleaner future, with energy independence, is possible.

Washington likes to spend our tax money line-by-line. Swarms of high-priced lobbyists in alligator shoes help Congress decide where to spend, and in turn the lobbyists' clients provide "campaign" money.

The public must send a message to Washington. Preserve our planet, creation, for our children and grandchildren, but do not use that as an excuse for more tax-and-spend. Let this be our motto: "One hundred percent dividend or fight!"

The next President must make a national low-loss electric grid an imperative. It will allow dispersed renewable energies to supplant fossil fuels for power generation. Technology exists for direct-current high-voltage buried transmission lines. Trunk lines can be completed in less than a decade and expanded analogous to interstate highways. Government must also change utility regulations so that profits do not depend on selling ever more energy, but instead increase with efficiency. Building code and vehicle efficiency requirements must be improved and put on a path toward carbon neutrality.

The fossil-industry maintains its strangle-hold on Washington via demagoguery, using China and other developing nations as scapegoats to rationalize inaction. In fact, we produced most of the excess carbon in the air today, and it is to our advantage as a nation to move smartly in developing ways to reduce emissions. As with the ozone problem, developing countries can be allowed limited extra time to reduce emissions. They will cooperate: they have much to lose from climate change and much to gain from clean air and reduced dependence on fossil fuels. We must establish fair agreements with other countries. However, our own tax and dividend should start immediately. We have much to gain from it as a nation, and other countries will copy our success. If necessary, import duties on products from uncooperative countries can level the playing field, with the import tax added to the dividend pool.

Democracy works, but sometimes churns slowly. Time is short. The 2008 election is critical for the planet. If Americans turn out to pasture the most brontosaurian congressmen, if Washington adapts to address climate change, our children and grandchildren can still hold great expectations.

---

[2]The proposed "tax and 100% dividend" is based largely on the cap and dividend approach described by Peter Barnes in "Who Owns the Sky: Our Common Assets and the Future of Capitalism", Island Press, Washington, D.C., 2001 (http://www.ppionline.org/ppi_ci.cfm?knlgAreaID=116&subsecID=149&contentID=3867).

# Timeline

## American Environmental Leaders

From Colonial Times to the Present

# TIMELINE OF AMERICAN ENVIRONMENTALISM

**1626** Plymouth Colony regulates the cutting and selling of timber.

**1639** Newport, Rhode Island institutes deer hunting season.

**1681** William Penn orders one acre be left uncut for every five acres of Pennsylvania land cleared.

**1751** Publication of *Observations on the Inhabitants, Climate, Soil, Rivers, Productions, Animals, and Other Matters…From Pennsylvania to Onondago, Oswego and the Lake Ontario in Canada* by botanist John Bartram, a book about his expedition through these regions. Bartram's descriptions of new world flora and fauna were read by natural scientists of the day such as Peter Kalm, Carolus Linnaeus and Benjamin Franklin.

**1791** William Bartam's journal from a four-year expedition, *Travels through North and South Carolina, Georgia, East and West Florida, the Cherokee Country, the Extensive Territories of the Muscogulges, or Creek Confederacy, and the Country of the Choctaws* earns him the title The King's Botanist from King George III. This book became a source for the Romantic literary movement and was enjoyed by Henry David Thoreau. **See Key Documents**.

**1827** *Birds of America* by John James Audubon published in England.

**1836** Asa Gray begins a life-long academic career educating Americans about the botanical world. Both *Elements of Botany*, 1936 and Gray's *Botanical Text-Book*, 1842 are prerequisite texts for biology and botany students for most of the 19th century.

**1848** The US Department of the Interior is established as a Cabinet position to manage and conserve federally owned lands.

**1850** Swamp and Overflowed Lands Act grants the Everglades to the state of Florida on the condition that the US Army Corps of Engineers divert water from the region.

**Late 1850s** Central Park, a squatter's settlement, was re-developed as a recreational area by Frederick Law Olmstead and his associates.

**1862** The 1862 Homestead Act grants 160-acre plots of land to new settlers, encouraging settlement and conversion to farmland of the American plains and the West.

**1863** German painter Albert Bierstadt joins the South Pass Wagon Road Expedition on its search for an overland route from Saint Louis, Missouri's to the Pacific Ocean. He left the group at the Rocky Mountains where he made sketches of the dramatic landscape that he used later to paint 'The Rocky Mountains, Lander's Peak.'

**1864** George Perkins Marsh publishes *Man and Nature*, or *Physical Geography as Modified by Human Action*. **See Key Documents**.

**1868** *Earth Closets* by George Waring, a sanitation engineer, describes sewage treatment and urban waste management.

**1869** John Wesley Powell leads a group of eleven men down 900 miles of the Green and Colorado Rivers and spends three months in the Grand Canyon.

**1871** The Great Chicago Fire leaves 300 Chicagoans dead, 90,000 homeless, and property losses around $200 million.

The creation of the U.S. Fish Commission, later named the U.S. Fish and Fisheries Commission (1881), and then the Bureau of Fisheries (1903).

**1872** The world's first national park, Yellowstone, is established, preserving 2.2 million acres of wilderness.

**1875** The nation's first water purity tests conducted by Ellen Swallow Richards and

1005

# Timeline of American Environmentalism

William Ripley Nichols for the State Board of Health of Massachusetts.

American Forestry Association is founded.

**1879** US Geological Survey is established within the Department of the Interior to study the geological structure and economic resources of the public domain.

**1885** The Department of Agriculture sets up the Division of Economic Ornithology and Mammology, predecessor of the U.S. Biological Survey.

**1891** Forest Reserve Act gives the President the power the set aside National Forests on public lands.

**1892** Sierra Club founded in California by University of California professors Henry Senger and William Armes, who convinced John Muir to serve as its first president.

**1893** The World's Columbian Exposition in Chicago presents ideas for model cities and natural resource management including an influential forestry exhibit by Prussian forester Bernard Fernow and the American Forestry Association, which led to the creation of the US Forest Service.

**1895** American Scenic and Historic Preservation Society founded.

**1896** George Washington Carver begins work at the Tuskegee Institute to remedy soil depletion and pest infestation. He wrote 44 instructional bulletins and educated farmers as he traveled the south in his "moveable school", a wagon equipped with demonstration materials and exhibits.

**1897** The Organic Act of 1897 calls for the proper care, protection and management of new forest reserves, and for an organization to manage them.

**1899** Henry Cowles' *The Ecological Relations of the Vegetation of the Sand Dunes of Lake Michigan* innovates botanical classification methods.

**1900** The Lacey Act makes it crime to transport killed birds across state lines.

Christmas Bird Count proposed by ornithologist Frank Chapman as an alternative to the long-standing Christmas side hunt, in his magazine *Bird Lore*, predecessor to *Audubon Magazine*.

**1900** Society of American Foresters founded.

**1902** The Reclamation and Newlands Acts provides oversight and federal money for the irrigation of arid lands in the West so settlers could use the land to farm.

**1903** Pelican Island in Florida is declared the first federal wildlife refuge.

**1905** National Audubon Society founded and incorporated in New York State, with William Dutcher as its first president.

American Forest Congress initiates an effort to move forest reserves from the Department of Interior to Department of Agriculture, urging the creation of the US Forest Service.

**1908** Grand Canyon is named a National Monument.

President Theodore Roosevelt's National Conservation Commission begins an inventory of natural resources.

**1909** A five-day North American Conservation Conference in Washington, DC defines principles of conservation.

**1911** The Weeks Act allows the federal government to purchase land at headwaters of navigable streams.

**1913** Migratory Bird Act gives responsibility to the Biological Survey to regulate the hunting of migratory waterfowl.

**1915** The Park Bill sets aside 385.5 square miles for Rocky Mountain National Park.

**1916** Ansel Adams' family visits Yosemite National Park for the first time.

The National Park Service Act creates the National Park Service in the Department of the Interior. The parks are under the jurisdiction of the NPS, which facilitates coordination and administration.

# Timeline of American Environmentalism

**1918** Migratory Bird Treaty Act restricts hunting of migratory species

**1919** National Parks Association established.

**1920** Federal Water Power Act gives the federal government the authority to issue hydroelectric power permits.

**1921** George Washington Carver speaks before Congress on the value of growing peanuts and soil conservation.

**1922** Mary Austion publishes the essay 'Science for the Unscientific' which spawned writers Aldo Leopold, Rachel Carson and others.

**1924** Clarke-McNary Act strengthens the federal government's ability to purchase National Forest lands.

**1925** The appearance of the classic textbook by Harvard Medical School Assistant Professor Alice Hamilton, *Industrial Poisons in the United States*, alerts Americans to the dangers of exposure to lead and other toxins.

**1927** Charles Elton's *Animal Ecology* becomes prerequisite in American zoological and ecological academic study.

Charles Lindberg flies *The Spirit of St. Louis* non-stop from New York to Paris in 33 and one half hours.

**1928** McSweeney-McNary Act supports forest research.

**1929** Buchanan Amendment to the Agricultural Appropriations Bill begins to study and control soil erosion.

**Late-1920s to mid-1930s** The Dust Bowl, resulting in part from erosion of farmland due to poor agricultural techniques, ravages the Midwest and forces the evacuation of thousands of farmers.

**1933** As an emergency order, President Franklin D. Roosevelt establishes soil scientist Hugh Hammond Bennett's Soil Erosion Service as a federal agency, to teach farmers erosion control techniques.

President Roosevelt's Secretary of Interior Harold Ickes initiates the Civilian Conservation Corps (CCC), creating jobs for young men in construction, erosion prevention, and reforestation, among other projects.

**1934** Catherine Bauer's *Modern Housing* is published and leads to the passage of U.S. Housing Act of 1937 designed to subsidize affordable housing for average and low-income residents.

First edition of Peterson's *Field Guide to Eastern Birds* is published.

**1935** The Soil Conservation Act expands federal government work in combating soil erosion.

The Wilderness Society founded by a group of eminent conservationists including Robert Marshall, Robert Sterling Yard, Benton MacKaye and Aldo Leopold to help save America's disappearing wilderness.

**1936** President Franklin D. Roosevelt convokes the North American Wildlife Conference in Washington, D.C., resulting in the creation of the General Wildlife Foundation.

**1937** The United States Housing Act of 1937 lays groundwork for future federal housing policy.

Pittman-Robertson Bill establishes the General Wild Life Fund to support state efforts to protect and propagate wildlife.

**1938** The General Wildlife Foundation changes it name to the National Wildlife Federation.

The General Wildlife Fund changes its name to the National Wildlife Fund.

**1940** The Bureau of Fisheries and the Bureau of Biological Survey consolidate to form the Fish and Wildlife Service.

**1944** Soil Conservation Society of America is founded.

**1946** The Bureau of Land Management begins administering the public domain.

**1947** Everglades National Park becomes the largest designated wilderness area east of the Rockies with the strongest mandate to preserve wilderness in legislative history.

# Timeline of American Environmentalism

Defenders of Furbearers (now known as Defenders of Wildlife) founded to protect coyotes and other furry animals from steel-jawed leg hold traps and lethal poisons.

**1948** Smog disaster in Donora, Pennsylvania kills twenty and sickens 6,000.

William Vogt's *Road to Survival* supports the theory that continued population growth eventually depletes non-renewable natural resources.

Federal Water Pollution Control Law enacted.

Fairfield Osborn's *Our Plundered Planet* is published. **See Key Documents**.

**1949** *The Natural History of Mosquitoes* published by Marston Bates becomes an instant classic in entomology and is still read today by parasitologists, malariologists, virologists, epidemiologists, and students of tropical medicine and hygiene.

Aldo Leopold's *A Sand Almanac* and *Sketches Here and There* defines a new ethic toward the land, and a new environmental citizen.

The first Sierra Club Biennial Wilderness Conference is held in California. Attended by about 100 federal and state land managers, and outdoorsmen, its success led to the biennial Wilderness Conferences, which influence conservation policy for decades.

Garrett Hardin's classic textbook, *Biology: Its Human Implication*, is published.

**1951** The Nature Conservancy is founded to purchase and preserve ecologically valuable land and reduce threats to conservation involving climate change, fire, fresh water, forests, invasive species, and marine ecosystems.

**1952** Murray Bookchin publishes *The Problem of Chemicals in Food* under the pseudonym Lewis Herber.

London smog disaster causes over 4,000 deaths increasing concern over environmental air quality in America.

**1954** NCR Corporation and Appleton Paper Company begin dumping PCBs (paper production by-products) into northeastern Wisconsin's Fox River. This will require the largest toxic cleanup in US history.

**1955** The Nature Conservancy makes its first land purchase—the Sunked Forest on Fire Island.

Air Pollution Control Act identifies air pollution as a national problem, announcing the need for research toward improvement. Amendments in 1960 and 1962 extended research and called for the U.S. Surgeon General to determine health effects of various motor vehicle exhaust substances.

**1957** Thirty years after his seminal work *Animal Ecology*, Charles Elton's *The Ecology of the Invasions by Animals and Plants* is published.

**1960** Multi-Use and Sustained-Yield Act declares that the purposes of national forests are recreation, range, timber, watershed, fish, and wildlife. The Secretary of Agriculture administers the renewable national forest surface resources for the 'multiple use and sustained yield' of the services and products obtained from these areas.

**1962** Rachel Carson's *Silent Spring* exposes dangers of synthetic pesticides resulting in U.S. Senate hearings.

**1963** The Clean Air Act is established, creating the Environmental Protection Agency which requires the reduction of air pollutant emissions, and states to develop implementation plans. Under the Act, states and Indian tribes could set stricter standards than federal regulations.

**1964** The Wilderness Act deems 9 million acres as un-exploitable.

**1965** Water Quality Act grows out of the Federal Water Pollution Control Act of 1948, creating water standards and mandates for a water quality assessment program.

In *Scenic Hudson Preservation Conference v. Federal Power*

*Commission*, the court rules that a conservation group has the right to sue to protect the public interest; as a result, Consolidated Edison's plans to build a power plant on Storm King Mountain near the Hudson River are stopped.

**1965** *Earth as a Spaceship* presented at Washington State University by Kenneth Boulding. ***See Key Documents***.

President Lyndon B. Johnson's White House Conference on Natural Beauty explores solutions to unsightly junkyards, utility transmission lines and leads to the passage of the Highway Beautification Act.

**1967** Environmental Defense Fund (now Environmental Defense) founded by a group of Long Island residents working to end the use of the pesticide dichlordiphenyltrichlor (DDT).

**1968** John Muir Institute founded by David Brower and others to promote environmental research and education.

The first *Whole Earth Catalog: Access to Tools and Ideas* outfits the back-to-the-land movement.

*The Population Time Bomb* by Paul Ehrlich projects the ecological impacts of human population growth. ***See Key Documents***.

National System of Wild and Scenic Rivers established as part of the Wild and Scenic Rivers Act.

Thomas Cade and colleagues publish "Peregrines and Pesticides in Alaska" in *Condor* magazine exposing high levels of DDE, DDD and dieldrin in adult peregrines.

MIT Faculty Statement leads to the founding of the Union of Concerned Scientists. ***See Key Documents***.

**1969** National Environmental Policy Act creates the Council on Environmental Quality and requires environmental impact statements for all federal actions.

The Santa Barbara Oil Spill inspired University of California Santa Barbara professor Roderick Nash to pen the "Santa Barbara Declaration of Environmental Rights" and organize the first teach-in about the environment.

Albert Bartlett delivers his famous 'Arithmetic, Population and Energy' speech. ***See Key Documents***.

Ralph Nader founds the Center for Responsive Law to monitor government regulatory agencies.

Friends of the Earth and its partner organization League of Conservation Voters founded by David Brower and others.

**1970** The Occupational Safety and Health Act (OSHA) is established, encouraging safe and healthful working conditions by providing for research, information, education and training to the states.

The first Earth Day is celebrated by 20 million Americans.

Natural Resources Defense Council founded by public interest lawyers, focusing on the creation and enforcement of environmental protection legislation.

Natural Resources Defense Council's first case opposes Storm King's pump storage plant on the Hudson River.

National Environmental Policy Act of 1969 is signed by President Richard Nixon, establishing the federal government's responsibility for maintaining a clean and healthy environment.

Clean Air Act passes and is reenacted in 1977, 1980, 1990.

Environmental Policy Act increases funding for implementing sustainable transportation.

Grape growers meet health and safety demands of the National Farm Workers Association, ending the five-year boycott of grapes and wine initiated by César Chávez.

*High Country News* publishes its first edition dedicated to people, places, trends and ideas that affect the American West.

**1971** Southwest Research and Information Center (SRIC) founded in Albuquerque, New Mexico.

# Timeline of American Environmentalism

Alaska Native Lands Claims Settlement Act.

Frances Moore Lappé's *Diet for a Small Planet* creates a nutritional awakening in America.

Food First is founded in San Francisco, California.

Robert Rodale's *The Basic Book of Organic Gardening* gets Americans back to their gardens.

*Water Wasteland: The Ralph Nader Report on Water Pollution* exposes nationwide abuse of water resources.

**1972** United Nations Conference on the Human Environment in Stockholm, Sweden, resulting in the UN Action Plan for the Human Environment and the Declaration of the United Nations Conference on the Human Environment.

DDT banned by the EPA.

The Clean Water Act establishes a centerpiece of environmental law: citizens' right to sue the government gives polluters a pass. The law sets water quality standards and regulates all discharges of contaminants.

Water Quality Act is amended to require states to develop lists of contaminated water bodies, to set limits on the amount of pollutants coming from point and non-point sources, and to provide funding for sewage treatment.

Marine Mammal Protection Act requires the U.S. Fish and Wildlife Service to list endangered species and implement a plan for recovery of viable populations. Amendments in 1988 and 1994 provide further dolphin protection from commercial fishing.

Sawtooth Recreational Area established and the damming of Idaho's Snake River in Hells Canyon prevented.

Noise Control Act of 1972 establishes Federal noise emissions standards and promotes an environment free from noise that jeopardizes health and welfare.

United States Conference on the Environment in Stockholm, Sweden.

Convention on International Trade in Endangered Species signed.

**1973** Endangered Species Act provides for the protection of endangered or threatened species and the ecosystems in which they range, with amendments in 1977 and 1978 that authorized funding for state cooperation, and required the DOI to monitor the list of endangered and threatened species, and consider the economic impact of protection.

The Deep Ecology movement is born in a seminal essay by Arne Naess from the University of Oslo, "The Shallow and the Deep, Long-Range Ecology Movement."

**1974** Safe Drinking Water Act, amended in 1986 and 1996, requires drinking water standards for all public water systems to follow standards for specified contaminants.

Worldwatch Institute founded by Lester Brown with grant from the Rockefeller Brothers Fund. Worldwatch Institute publishes *Vital Signs* and *State of the World*.

Institute for Social Ecology founded in Plainfield Vermont to create "educational experiences that enhance people's understanding of their relationship to the natural world and each other."

Karen Silkwood documents plutonium abuses of the Kerr-McGee Nuclear Corporation in Cimarron, Oklahoma and is killed in a mysterious car crash.

**1975** Seeds of Change is founded by Diane and Kent Whealy to conserve the genetic diversity of garden crops.

*Train v. NRDC* goes to the Supreme Court to defend the Clean Air Act. The court historically ruled that it is requisite upon the government "to protect the public welfare from any known or anticipated adverse effects associated with the presence of such air pollutant in the ambient air.'

In *National Wildlife Federation v. Coleman*, NWF defends the Endangered Species Act and 40 Mississippi sandhill cranes from the construction of a highway

*Commission*, the court rules that a conservation group has the right to sue to protect the public interest; as a result, Consolidated Edison's plans to build a power plant on Storm King Mountain near the Hudson River are stopped.

**1965** *Earth as a Spaceship* presented at Washington State University by Kenneth Boulding. ***See Key Documents***.

President Lyndon B. Johnson's White House Conference on Natural Beauty explores solutions to unsightly junkyards, utility transmission lines and leads to the passage of the Highway Beautification Act.

**1967** Environmental Defense Fund (now Environmental Defense) founded by a group of Long Island residents working to end the use of the pesticide dichlordiphenyltrichlor (DDT).

**1968** John Muir Institute founded by David Brower and others to promote environmental research and education.

The first *Whole Earth Catalog: Access to Tools and Ideas* outfits the back-to-the-land movement.

*The Population Time Bomb* by Paul Ehrlich projects the ecological impacts of human population growth. ***See Key Documents***.

National System of Wild and Scenic Rivers established as part of the Wild and Scenic Rivers Act.

Thomas Cade and colleagues publish "Peregrines and Pesticides in Alaska" in *Condor* magazine exposing high levels of DDE, DDD and dieldrin in adult peregrines.

MIT Faculty Statement leads to the founding of the Union of Concerned Scientists. ***See Key Documents***.

**1969** National Environmental Policy Act creates the Council on Environmental Quality and requires environmental impact statements for all federal actions.

The Santa Barbara Oil Spill inspired University of California Santa Barbara professor Roderick Nash to pen the "Santa Barbara Declaration of Environmental Rights" and organize the first teach-in about the environment.

Albert Bartlett delivers his famous 'Arithmetic, Population and Energy' speech. ***See Key Documents***.

Ralph Nader founds the Center for Responsive Law to monitor government regulatory agencies.

Friends of the Earth and its partner organization League of Conservation Voters founded by David Brower and others.

**1970** The Occupational Safety and Health Act (OSHA) is established, encouraging safe and healthful working conditions by providing for research, information, education and training to the states.

The first Earth Day is celebrated by 20 million Americans.

Natural Resources Defense Council founded by public interest lawyers, focusing on the creation and enforcement of environmental protection legislation.

Natural Resources Defense Council's first case opposes Storm King's pump storage plant on the Hudson River.

National Environmental Policy Act of 1969 is signed by President Richard Nixon, establishing the federal government's responsibility for maintaining a clean and healthy environment.

Clean Air Act passes and is reenacted in 1977, 1980, 1990.

Environmental Policy Act increases funding for implementing sustainable transportation.

Grape growers meet health and safety demands of the National Farm Workers Association, ending the five-year boycott of grapes and wine initiated by César Chávez.

*High Country News* publishes its first edition dedicated to people, places, trends and ideas that affect the American West.

**1971** Southwest Research and Information Center (SRIC) founded in Albuquerque, New Mexico.

# Timeline of American Environmentalism

Alaska Native Lands Claims Settlement Act.

Frances Moore Lappé's *Diet for a Small Planet* creates a nutritional awakening in America.

Food First is founded in San Francisco, California.

Robert Rodale's *The Basic Book of Organic Gardening* gets Americans back to their gardens.

*Water Wasteland: The Ralph Nader Report on Water Pollution* exposes nationwide abuse of water resources.

**1972** United Nations Conference on the Human Environment in Stockholm, Sweden, resulting in the UN Action Plan for the Human Environment and the Declaration of the United Nations Conference on the Human Environment.

DDT banned by the EPA.

The Clean Water Act establishes a centerpiece of environmental law: citizens' right to sue the government gives polluters a pass. The law sets water quality standards and regulates all discharges of contaminants.

Water Quality Act is amended to require states to develop lists of contaminated water bodies, to set limits on the amount of pollutants coming from point and non-point sources, and to provide funding for sewage treatment.

Marine Mammal Protection Act requires the U.S. Fish and Wildlife Service to list endangered species and implement a plan for recovery of viable populations. Amendments in 1988 and 1994 provide further dolphin protection from commercial fishing.

Sawtooth Recreational Area established and the damming of Idaho's Snake River in Hells Canyon prevented.

Noise Control Act of 1972 establishes Federal noise emissions standards and promotes an environment free from noise that jeopardizes health and welfare.

United States Conference on the Environment in Stockholm, Sweden.

Convention on International Trade in Endangered Species signed.

**1973** Endangered Species Act provides for the protection of endangered or threatened species and the ecosystems in which they range, with amendments in 1977 and 1978 that authorized funding for state cooperation, and required the DOI to monitor the list of endangered and threatened species, and consider the economic impact of protection.

The Deep Ecology movement is born in a seminal essay by Arne Naess from the University of Oslo, "The Shallow and the Deep, Long-Range Ecology Movement."

**1974** Safe Drinking Water Act, amended in 1986 and 1996, requires drinking water standards for all public water systems to follow standards for specified contaminants.

Worldwatch Institute founded by Lester Brown with grant from the Rockefeller Brothers Fund. Worldwatch Institute publishes *Vital Signs* and *State of the World*.

Institute for Social Ecology founded in Plainfield Vermont to create "educational experiences that enhance people's understanding of their relationship to the natural world and each other."

Karen Silkwood documents plutonium abuses of the Kerr-McGee Nuclear Corporation in Cimarron, Oklahoma and is killed in a mysterious car crash.

**1975** Seeds of Change is founded by Diane and Kent Whealy to conserve the genetic diversity of garden crops.

*Train v. NRDC* goes to the Supreme Court to defend the Clean Air Act. The court historically ruled that it is requisite upon the government "to protect the public welfare from any known or anticipated adverse effects associated with the presence of such air pollutant in the ambient air.'

In *National Wildlife Federation v. Coleman*, NWF defends the Endangered Species Act and 40 Mississippi sandhill cranes from the construction of a highway interchange and the destruction of their habitat.

Ed Abbey glorifies monkey-wrenching—sabotaging the machinery of environmental destruction—in his classic, *The Monkey Wrench Gang*.

*Massachusetts v. Milton H. Raphaelson* rules in favor of the Lead Poisoning Prevention Program, whose director ordered Raphaelson to remove or cover lead paint found in two housing units occupied by under age six year old children.

**1976** National Forest Management Act expands the 1974 Act, by requiring an inventory of forest resources, along with identification of land not suited for timber production and cites the importance of protecting soil, watersheds, fish, wildlife, recreation and aesthetic resources.

The Resource Conservation and Recovery Act initiates incentives for recycling and proper waste disposal.

The Toxic Substance Control Act requires the government to assess hazards and monitor all chemicals manufactured in the United States.

Resource Conservation and Recovery Act (Solid Waste Disposal Act) provides for comprehensive regulation of hazardous waste and authorizes environmental agencies to order cleanup of contaminated sites.

**1977** Surface Mining Control and Reclamation Act regulates environmental effects of coal mining in the U.S.

The Clean Water Act set water quality standards for all contaminants in surface waters and strengthens 1972's Water Quality Act.

*Vermont Yankee Nuclear Power Corporation v. NRDC* goes to the Supreme Court

**1978** The Occupational Safety and Health Act renewed with stricter regulating of lead in the workplace.

Toxic waste at Love Canal becomes a federal emergency area.

David Ehrenfeld blames the earth's ecological demise on the philosophy of humanism in *The Arrogance of Humanism*.

**1979** Three Mile Island nuclear power plant accident alerts Pennsylvania of the imminent threat to the environment.

Silvia Earle conducts record-breaking deep sea exploration (1,250 feet) off the coast of the Hawaiian Island of Oahu.

**1980** The World Conservation Strategy is devised by the International Union for the Conservation of Nature and the World Wildlife Fund.

The Federal Bureau of Investigation (FBI) shuts downs Rocky Flats Nuclear Weapons facility for incinerating radioactive waste.

Comprehensive Environmental Response, Compensation, and Liability Act directs federal funds to cleanup hazardous waste dump sites, creates a tax on chemical and petroleum industries and provides federal authority to respond directly to releases or threatened releases of hazardous substances that may endanger public health or the environment.

Earth First! founded by a group of ecoactivists who swear "No Compromise in Defense of Mother Earth" with Dave Foreman as its best-known spokesperson.

Environmental Research Foundation founded by Peter Montague to help people "find the information they need to fight for environmental justice in their own communities."

Alaska Lands Conservation Act protects 100 million acres from industrial exploitation.

**1981** Tom and Kate Chappell roll out Tom's of Maine natural personal-care products.

Fate of the Earth Conference

**1982** In an effort to prevent toxic landfill in his native Warren County, NC, Benjamin Chavis is the first person arrested for defending land from environmentally racist dumping plans.

# Timeline of American Environmentalism

Coastal Barrier Resources Act designates shoreline to be protected from development.

World Resources Institute founded with the goal of drawing world leaders' attention to natural resource destruction and degradation.

Earth Island Institute founded by David Brower to provide institutional support and networking for projects that focus on environmental problems.

Rocky Mountain Institute founded by Amory and Hunter Lovins in Snowmass, Colorado to "foster the efficient and restorative use of resources to make the world secure, just, prosperous, and life-sustaining."

**1983** The National Park Trust is founded to find willing sellers of lands within or near national and state parks or wildlife refuges.

Carl Sagan's article in *Science* magazine explores the effects of nuclear war on global climate.

**1984** Fate of the Earth Conference

World Wildlife Fund (now the World Wide Fund for Nature) initiates the debt-for-nature swap concept.

Silvia Earle breaks her earlier record dive beneath the sea, going 3,280 feet down in a Deep Rover.

**1985** Rainforest Action Network, formed as a working group of the Earth Island Institute, brings to public attention the destruction of rainforests by boycotting Burger King for purchasing beef from cattle grazed on cleared rainforest land in Latin America. The boycott ended when Burger King announced it would no longer buy beef in Latin America.

Society for Conservation Biology founded to promote "the scientific study of the phenomena that affect the maintenance, loss, and restoration of biological diversity."

Greenpeace's Rainbow Warrior sets sails for the South Pacific to prevent nuclear testing, only to be sunk by the French secret service.

**1987** Conservation International founded in Washington D.C. with the goal of empowering worldwide "communities in jungles and deserts to make conservation part of their livelihoods."

Water Quality Act is amended to address sewage, storm water, and other non-point urban pollution.

Samuel LaBudde goes undercover as a cook aboard a Panamanian fishing boat to film the slaughter of dolphins while tuna fishing.

Conservation International saves the Beni Biosphere Reserve in the Bolivian rain forest in the first debt for nature swap.

*Diet for a New America* by John Robbins discusses the abuses in the American meat and dairy industries, inspiring a wave of vegetarianism.

**1988** Dumping Ban Act made it unlawful to dump or transport sewage as sludge and industrial waste into the ocean as of 1992. Until then, dumping had to be negotiated with the state and the EPA.

The first public use of the term global warming by Dr. Thomas E. Hansen speaking before the U.S. Congress.

Alternative Motor Fuels Act amends the Energy Policy and Conservation Act to direct the Secretary of Energy to ensure the maximum practicable number of federal passenger automobiles and light trucks be alcohol powered, dual-energy powered, natural gas powered, or natural gas-dual-energy powered.

Severe drought in the central and eastern US inflicts 5,000–10,000 heat-related deaths and $60 billion in damage.

**1989** Exxon Valdez spills 11 million gallons of oil in Prince William Sound.

First 'Redwood Summer' when militant environmentalists plan direct actions to save the redwood forests.

Residents of "Cancer Alley" march with Gulf Coast Tenants from Baton Rouge to

New Orleans in The Great Louisiana Toxic March.

**1990** The Oil Pollution Act of 1990 mandates polluters to pay for oil cleanups and compensate victims of spills.

First Goldman Prize Award winners are announced, including American Lois Gibbs.

Earth First! and other environmental groups sign a moratorium on tree spiking and other forms of 'ecotage'.

Attempted assassination of environmental heroine Judi Bari in Oakland, California.

Clean Air Act of 1990 requires the EPA to establish National Ambient Air Quality Standards for reducing six of the most prevalent and health-threatening air pollutants.

Alliance to End Childhood Lead Poisoning is founded by Herbert Needleman.

**1991** Endangered Species Project (ESP) launched to investigate illegal wildlife trade.

Biodiversity Legal Foundation founded to defend neglected habitats, and protect endangered species.

First National People of Color Environmental Leadership Summit in Washington D.C. *See Key Documents*.

United Nations Conference on the Environment and Development (UNCED).

*El Pueblo para el Aire y Agua Limpio* v. *County of Kings*. The Center on Race, Poverty & the Environment wins, requiring that an environmental review by all those meaningfully involved requires translation of documents into Spanish.

Biodiversity Legal Foundation founded to defend neglected habitats and protect endangered species.

Wildlands Project founded by Dave Foreman and Reed Noss to advocate for a connected network of wildlands reserves throughout North America.

**1992** United Nations Conference on Environment and Development (Earth Summit) held in Rio de Janeiro, Brazil, with participation by 172 nations. Resulting documents include the Rio Declaration on Environment and Development, the Statement of Forest Principles, the UN Framework Convention on Climate Change, and the UN Convention on Biological Diversity.

Environmental Justice Act is introduced to Congress by Georgia Congressman John Lewis and Tennessee Senator Albert Gore.

The Union of Concerned Scientists' Warning to Humanity. *See Key Documents*.

Surface Transportation Policy Project unites more than 200 environmental organizations

**1994** The Kyoto Protocol sets goals for reducing greenhouse gas emissions. *See Key Documents*.

**1996** Food Quality Protection Act (FQPA) revises pesticide and food safety laws, strengthening safety standards for infants and children and amending the Federal Food, Drug and Cosmetic Act.

Start of United Nations Environmental Program on Human Values of Biodiversity.

**1997** President Clinton issues Executive Order 13045 protecting Children from Environmental Health and Safety Risks.

Turbidity (concentration of sediment) in the drinking water of Milwaukee, Wisconsin causes an outbreak of cryptosporidiosis infecting 403,000, leaving 50–100 dead.

RFK Jr. and the Hudson Riverkeepers negotiate an agreement with Governor George Pataki to protect New York City's drinking water upstream, saving $8 billion dollars in filtration costs.

**1998** Transportation Equity Act of the 21st Century (TEA-21) authorizes federal surface transportation programs for highways, highway safety, and transit, providing jobs and promoting economic growth.

White House Summit on Recycling

# Timeline of American Environmentalism

The U.S. federal government requires federal offices to reduce resource consumption and recycle through President Clinton's Executive Order 13101: "Greening the Government Through Waste Prevention, Recycling and Federal Acquisition."

Indigenous People Council on Biocolonialism founded by Debra Harry to "assist indigenous peoples in the protection of their genetic resources, indigenous knowledge, and cultural and human rights from the negative effects of biotechnology."

Newly elected President George W. Bush announces that the United States is pulling out of the Kyoto Protocol negotiations.

**2005** Hurricane Katrina becomes the most costly natural disaster in US history, killing 1,833 people and causing $125 billion in damage.

**2006** Al Gore's *An Inconvenient Truth* hits the cinemas in an effort to avert catastrophic droughts, floods, plagues and heat waves caused by global climate change.

Widespread drought in the Great Plains and western states causes $6 billion in damages. Wildfires to burn nearly 10 million acres.

**2007** Intergovernmental Panel on Climate Change releases its first report from Working Group I, earning the team a Nobel Prize.

In *Environmental Defense, et al.* v. *Duke Energy Corporation* the U.S. Supreme Court rules in favor of Environmental Defense, et al. successfully protecting key elements of the Clean Air Act.

**2008** The U.S. Government Accountability Office finds political interference from the Bush Administration in scientific decisions concerning the nation's endangered species.

The Natural Resources Defense Council (NRDC), the Center for Biological Diversity and Greenpeace sue the Bush administration to force protection of the polar bear.

A company called GreenCore Air releases an air conditioner than can be powered by a single 170 watt solar panel.

New Orleans in The Great Louisiana Toxic March.

**1990** The Oil Pollution Act of 1990 mandates polluters to pay for oil cleanups and compensate victims of spills.

First Goldman Prize Award winners are announced, including American Lois Gibbs.

Earth First! and other environmental groups sign a moratorium on tree spiking and other forms of 'ecotage'.

Attempted assassination of environmental heroine Judi Bari in Oakland, California.

Clean Air Act of 1990 requires the EPA to establish National Ambient Air Quality Standards for reducing six of the most prevalent and health-threatening air pollutants.

Alliance to End Childhood Lead Poisoning is founded by Herbert Needleman.

**1991** Endangered Species Project (ESP) launched to investigate illegal wildlife trade.

Biodiversity Legal Foundation founded to defend neglected habitats, and protect endangered species.

First National People of Color Environmental Leadership Summit in Washington D.C. *See Key Documents*.

United Nations Conference on the Environment and Development (UNCED).

*El Pueblo para el Aire y Agua Limpio* v. *County of Kings*. The Center on Race, Poverty & the Environment wins, requiring that an environmental review by all those meaningfully involved requires translation of documents into Spanish.

Biodiversity Legal Foundation founded to defend neglected habitats and protect endangered species.

Wildlands Project founded by Dave Foreman and Reed Noss to advocate for a connected network of wildlands reserves throughout North America.

**1992** United Nations Conference on Environment and Development (Earth Summit) held in Rio de Janeiro, Brazil, with participation by 172 nations. Resulting documents include the Rio Declaration on Environment and Development, the Statement of Forest Principles, the UN Framework Convention on Climate Change, and the UN Convention on Biological Diversity.

Environmental Justice Act is introduced to Congress by Georgia Congressman John Lewis and Tennessee Senator Albert Gore.

The Union of Concerned Scientists' Warning to Humanity. *See Key Documents*.

Surface Transportation Policy Project unites more than 200 environmental organizations

**1994** The Kyoto Protocol sets goals for reducing greenhouse gas emissions. *See Key Documents*.

**1996** Food Quality Protection Act (FQPA) revises pesticide and food safety laws, strengthening safety standards for infants and children and amending the Federal Food, Drug and Cosmetic Act.

Start of United Nations Environmental Program on Human Values of Biodiversity.

**1997** President Clinton issues Executive Order 13045 protecting Children from Environmental Health and Safety Risks.

Turbidity (concentration of sediment) in the drinking water of Milwaukee, Wisconsin causes an outbreak of cryptosporidiosis infecting 403,000, leaving 50–100 dead.

RFK Jr. and the Hudson Riverkeepers negotiate an agreement with Governor George Pataki to protect New York City's drinking water upstream, saving $8 billion dollars in filtration costs.

**1998** Transportation Equity Act of the 21st Century (TEA-21) authorizes federal surface transportation programs for highways, highway safety, and transit, providing jobs and promoting economic growth.

White House Summit on Recycling

The U.S. federal government requires federal offices to reduce resource consumption and recycle through President Clinton's Executive Order 13101: "Greening the Government Through Waste Prevention, Recycling and Federal Acquisition."

Indigenous People Council on Biocolonialism founded by Debra Harry to "assist indigenous peoples in the protection of their genetic resources, indigenous knowledge, and cultural and human rights from the negative effects of biotechnology."

Newly elected President George W. Bush announces that the United States is pulling out of the Kyoto Protocol negotiations.

**2005** Hurricane Katrina becomes the most costly natural disaster in US history, killing 1,833 people and causing $125 billion in damage.

**2006** Al Gore's *An Inconvenient Truth* hits the cinemas in an effort to avert catastrophic droughts, floods, plagues and heat waves caused by global climate change.

Widespread drought in the Great Plains and western states causes $6 billion in damages. Wildfires to burn nearly 10 million acres.

**2007** Intergovernmental Panel on Climate Change releases its first report from Working Group I, earning the team a Nobel Prize.

In *Environmental Defense, et al.* v. *Duke Energy Corporation* the U.S. Supreme Court rules in favor of Environmental Defense, et al. successfully protecting key elements of the Clean Air Act.

**2008** The U.S. Government Accountability Office finds political interference from the Bush Administration in scientific decisions concerning the nation's endangered species.

The Natural Resources Defense Council (NRDC), the Center for Biological Diversity and Greenpeace sue the Bush administration to force protection of the polar bear.

A company called GreenCore Air releases an air conditioner than can be powered by a single 170 watt solar panel.

# List of Leaders

## American Environmental Leaders

From Colonial Times to the Present

## List of Leaders by Occupation or Work Focus

### Activists and Organizers
Ansel Adams
Jane Addams
Dana Alston
Adrienne Anderson
Betty Ball and Gary Ball
Judi Bari
Peter Berg
Kevin Bixby
Roberta Blackgoat
Stewart Brandborg
Walt Bresette
Robert Bullard
Majora Carter
Cesar Chávez
Benjamin Chavis
Elizabeth Christy
William Colby
Barry Commoner
Paul and Ellen Connett
Laurie David
Bill Devall
Marjory Stoneman Douglas
Rosalie Edge
Dave Foreman
Lou Gold
Robert Gottlieb
Lois Gibbs
Richard Grossman
Alice Hamilton
Dorothy Webster Harvey
Denis Hayes
Randy Hayes
Julia Butterfly Hill
William Temple Hornaday
Hazel Johnson
Claudia Alta (Lady Bird) Johnson
Van Jones
Jim Jontz
Owen Lammers
Alicia Littletree
Oren Lyons
Mary McDowell
Donella Meadows
Enos Mills
Marion Moses
John Muir
Olaus and Mardy Murie
Steve Packard
Jane Perkins
Cynthia Pryor
Jeremy Rifkin
Jerome C. Ringo
Arturo Sandoval
Karen Silkwood
Rocky Smith
Wilma Subra
Terri Swearingen
JoAnn Tall
Chief Tommy Kuni Thompson
Grace Thorpe
Brian Tokar
William Toor
D. Chet Tzchozewski
Paul Watson
Diane Wilson
Hazel Wolf
David Zwick

### Advertising Executive
Jerry Mander

### Analysts
Gary Ball
Marion Clawson
Donella Meadows
Rocky Smith

### Architects, Landscape Architects, Planners
Carl Anthony
Catherine Baeur
Arthur Carhart
Richard A. Cook
Andrew Jackson Downing
Buckminster Fuller
Robert Gottlieb
Benton MacKaye
Ian McHarg
William McDonough
Lewis Mumford
Frederick Law Olmsted, Jr.
Frederick Law Olmsted, Sr.
Frank Popper
Michael Reynolds
Paolo Soleri
Sarah Susanka

### Artists
John James Audubon
William Bartram
Albert Bierstadt
George Catlin
Thomas Cole
Oren Lyons
Margaret Owings
Roger Tory Peterson
Ernest Thompson Seton

### Attorneys
John Hamilton Adams
Richard Ayres
Michael Bean
Peter Berle
Jasper Carlton
Harry Caudill
Chris Desser
Robert Golten
Ralph Nader
J. William Futrell
Robert F. Kennedy, Jr.
Andrew L. Shapiro
David Sive
Christopher Stone

### Aviators
Anne Morrow and Charles Lindbergh

### Cartoonist
Jay Norwood 'Ding' Darling

### Consultants
Stewart Brand (technology)
Juliet Ellis (transportation)
Benjamin Luce (energy)
Molly Harriss Olson (sustainability)
Marc Reisner (water)
Anne Rolfes (air)
Arthur H. Rosenfeld (energy efficiency)
Peter Warshall (sustainability)

### Editors
Elias Amidon and Elizabeth Roberts
Stewart Brand
Devereux Butcher

## List of Leaders by Occupation or Work Focus

Frank Chapman
Ellen Connett
Mark Dowie
David Ehrenfeld
Charles S. Elton
Robert Underwood Johnson
Betsy Marston
Peter Montague
Peter Warshall
Robert Sterling Yard
Howard Zanheiser

### Educators/Professors
Elias Amidon and Elizabeth Roberts
Adrienne Anderson
Albert Bartlett
Rosalie Bertell
Jack Collom
Paul Connett
Richard Dawson
Robert Golten
Robert Gottlieb
James E. Hansen
Aldo Leopold
Roderick Nash
Eugene Odum
David Orr
David Sive
James Gustave Speth
Oakleigh Thorne, II
Martin Walter
Barbara Warburton

### Elected Officials
*Congresspeople*
John Chafee (Senator, Rhode Island)
John Dingell, Jr. (Representative, Michigan)
Henry Jackson (Senator, Washington)
Jim Jontz (Representative, Indiana)
George Mitchell (Senator, Maine)
Edmund Muskie (Senator, Maine)
Gaylord Nelson (Senator, Wisconsin)
Morris Udall (Representative, Arizona)
Stewart Udall (Representative, Arizona)
Henry Waxman (Representative, California)

*Governors*
Cecil Andrus (Idaho)
Bruce Babbit (Arizona
Jimmy Carter (Georgia)
Gaylord Nelson (Wisconsin)
Russell Peterson (Delaware)
Bill Ritter, Jr. (Colorado)
Arnold Schwarzenegger (California)

*Vice President of the United States*
Albert Gore, Jr.

*Presidents of the United States*
John Quincy Adams
Jimmy Carter
Franklin D. Roosevelt
Theodore Roosevelt

*Mayors*
Michael Bloomberg (New York, New York)
Laura Miller (Dallas, Texas)
Greg Nickels (Seattle, Washington)
William Toor (Boulder, Colorado)

### Entertainers
*Actors*
Ed Begley, Jr.
Leonardo DiCaprio
Woody Harrelson

*Filmmakers/Producers*
Laurie David
Leonardo DiCaprio
Michael Tidwell

*Musicians*
Alicia Littletree
Woody Guthrie
Willie Nelson
Pete Seeger
Paul Winter

*Orators/Lecturers/Storytellers*
Lou Gold
Enos Mills
Chief Sealth (Seattle)
Ernest Thompson Seton

*Radio & Television Personalities*
Peter Berle
Chris and Martin Kratt
Carl Sagan
Adam Werbach

### Electrician
Debby Tewa

### Engineer
George Waring

### Entrepreneurs
Ray Anderson
Kenny Ausubel
Amos Bien
Kate and Tom Chappell
Robin Chase
William Drayton
Rogelio Figueroa
Paul Hawken
Nell Newman
Danny Seo
Terry Tamminen
Ted Turner

### Explorer
John Wesley Powell

### Farmers/Gardeners
Wendell Berry
Elizabeth Christy
Barbara Kingsolver
Helen and Scott Nearing
Robert Rodale
Cathrine Sneed

### Foresters
Mollie Beattie
Jeff DeBonis
Jerry Franklin
Barbara Kingsolver
Robert Marshall
Gifford Pinchot

### Futurists
Buckminster Fuller

## LIST OF LEADERS BY OCCUPATION OR WORK FOCUS

Hazel Henderson
Derrick Jensen

**Health Professionals**
*Nutritionists*
Joan Dye Gussow

*Physicians*
Alice Hamilton
Marion Moses
Herbert Needleman
Irving Selicoff

*Toxicologists*
Eula Bingham

**Historians**
Henry Adams
William Cronon
Bernard Devoto
Samuel P. Hays
George Perkins Marsh
Edmond Meany
Carolyn Merchant
Roderick Nash
Francis Parkman
Wallace Stegner
Frederick Jackson Turner
Lynn White, Jr.
Donald Worster

**Inventors**
George Washington Carver
Buckminster Fuller
George Perkins Marsh

**Leaders of Environmental Organizations & Institutions**
John Hamilton Adams (Natural Resources Defense Council)
Carl Anthony (Urban Habitat)
Kenny Ausubel (Bioneers)
Richard Ayres (Natural Resources Defense Council)
Peter Bahouth (Greenpeace U.S.A.; Turner Foundation)
James Balog (Extreme Ice Survey)
Judi Bari (Earth First!)
Joan Bavaria (Coalition for Environmentally Responsible Economies)
Janine Benyus (Biomimicry Institute)
Peter Berg (Planet Drum Foundation)
Peter Berle (National Audubon Society)
Kevin Bixby (Southwest Environmental Center)
Janine Blaeloch (Western Lands Project)
Barbara Bramble (National Wildlife Federation)
Stewart Brandborg (The Wilderness Society)
David Brower (Sierra Club, Friends of the Earth, League of Conservation Voters, Earth Island Institute)
Janet Brown (Environmental Defense Fund)
Lester Brown (Worldwatch Institute)
Devereux Butcher (National Parks Association)
Jasper Carlton (Biodiversity Legal Foundation)
Marjorie Carr (Florida Defenders of the Environment)
Majora Carter (Sustainable South Bronx)
Aurora Castillo (Mothers of East Los Angeles)
Robin Chase (Zipcar, GoLoco.org, Meadow Networks)
César Chávez (United Farm Workers)
Benjamin Chavis (National Association for the Advancement of Colored People)
Elizabeth Christy (Green Guerillas)
Marion Clawson (Resources for the Future)
William Colby (Sierra Club)
Barry Commoner (Center for the Biology of Natural Systems)
Stuart Conway (Trees, Water & People)
Julian Darley (Post Carbon Institute, Meta Foundation)
Jay Norwood 'Ding' Darling (National Wildlife Foundation)
Jeff DeBonis (Association of Forest Service Employees for Environmental Ethics and Public Employees for Environmental Ethics)
Chris Desser (Muir Investment Trust, Migratory Species Project)
Will Dilg (Izaak Walton League of America)
Hank Dittmar (Surface Transportation Policy Project, Great American Station Foundation)
Richard Donovan (SmartWood)
Louise Dunlap (Environmental Policy Center, Environmental Policy Institute)
WIlliam Drayton (Ashoka)
Alan Durning (Northwest Environmental Watch)
William Dutcher (National Audubon Society)
Juliet Ellis (Urban Habitat)
Dave Foreman (Earth First!)
Dian Fossey (Karisoke Research Center)
Kathryn Fuller (World Wildlife Fund)
J. William Futrell (Environmental Law Institute)
Sherwood M. Gagliano (Coastal Environments, Inc.)
George Bird Grinnell (National Audubon Society, Boone and Crockett Club)
Lois Gibbs (Center for Health, Environment and Justice)
Richard Grossman (Environmentalists for Full Employment, Program on Corporations, Law and Democracy)
Juana Gutierrez (Mothers of East Los Angeles)
Randy Hayes (Rainforest Action Network)

## List of Leaders by Occupation or Work Focus

Jay Hair (National Wildlife Federation)
Woody Harrelson (Oasis Preserve International)
Debra Harry (Indigenous Peoples Council on Biolarionialism)
Tim Hermach (Native Forest Council)
William Temple Hornaday (New York Zoological Society)
Dolores Huerta (United Farm Workers)
Helen Ingram (Udall Center for Studies in Public Policy)
Wes Jackson (The Land Institute)
Michael Jacobson (Center for Science in the Public Interest)
Hazel Johnson (People for Community Recovery)
Diane Jukofsky (Conservation Media Center)
Jim Jontz (American Lands Alliance)
Richard Kamp (Border Ecology Project)
Hal Kane (Pacific Environment and Resources Center)
Daniel Katz (Rainforest Alliance)
Henry Kendall (Union of Concerned Scientists)
Fred Krupp (Environmental Defense)
Winona LaDuke (Indigenous Women's Network)
Owen Lammers (Glen Canyon Action Network)
Francis Lappé (Institute for Food and Development Policy, Center for Living Democracy)
Aldo Leopold (The Wilderness Society)
Amory Lovins and Hunter Lovins (Rocky Mountain Institute)
Benton MacKaye (The Wilderness Society)
Robert Marshall (The Wilderness Society)
Michael McCloskey (Sierra Club)
Donella Meadows (The Sustainability Institute)
Edmond Meany (Washington Mountaineers)
Ilarion (Larry) Merculieff (Alaska Indigenous Peoples' Council for Marine Mammals, International Bering Sea Forum)
Laura Miller (Texas Clean Air Cities Coalition)
Russell Mittermeier (Conservation International)
Peter Montague (Environmental Research Foundation)
Marion Moses (Pesticide Education Center)
Cynthia Moss (Amboseli Elephant Research Project)
John Muir (Sierra Club)
Mardy and Olaus Murie (The Wilderness Society)
Ralph Nader (too numerous to list here)
Carlos Nagel (Friends of Pronatura)
Reed Noss (Society for Conservation Biology)
Sigurd Olson (National Parks Association, The Wilderness Society)
Fairfield Osborn, Jr. (New York Zoological Society, Conservation Foundation)
Margaret Owings (Friends of the Sea Otter)
Paula Palmer (Global Response)
Jane Perkins (Friends of the Earth, American Federation of Labor-Congress of Industrial Organizations)
Russell Peterson (National Audubon Society)
Sandra Postel (Global Water Policy Project)
Richard Pough (The Nature Conservancy)
Paul C. Pritchard (National Parks Trust, National Parks Conservation Association)
Cynthia Pryor (Yellow Dog Watershed Preserve)
Peter Raven (Missouri Botanical Garden)
Henry Red Cloud (Trees, Water & People-Lakota Solar Enterprises)
William Kane Reilly (World Wildlife Foundation, Conservation Foundation)
Celine Rich (Post Carbon Institute, Meta Foundation)
Jeremy Rifkin (Foundation on Economic Trends)
Jerome C. Ringo (Apollo Alliance)
John Robbins (EarthSave International)
Vicki Robin (New Road Map Foundation)
Anne Rolfes (Louisiana Bucket Brigade)
Carl Safina (Living Oceans Program of the National Audubon Society)
Kirkpatrick Sale (E.F. Schumacher Society)
Arturo Sandoval (Center of Southwest Culture, VOCES, Inc.)
John Sawhill (The Nature Conservancy)
Rodger Schlickeisen (Defenders of Wildlife)
Danny Seo (Earth 2000)
Andrew L. Shapiro (GreenOrder)
Christopher Shuey (Southwest Research and Information Center)
David Sive (Natural Resources Defense Council)
Michael Soule (Society for Conservation Biology, Wildlands Project)
James Gustave Speth (Natural Resources Defense Council, World Resources Institute, United Nations Development Program)
William Steel (Mazamas)

## LIST OF LEADERS BY OCCUPATION OR WORK FOCUS

Tracy Stone-Manning (Clark Fork Coalition, Headwater News)
Kieran Suckling (Center for Biological Diversity)
JoAnn Tall (Native Resource Coalition, Indigenous Environmental Network, Seventh Generation Fund)
Terry Tamminen (New America's Foundation-Climate Policy Program)
Oakleigh Thorne, II (Thorne Ecological Institute)
Grace Thorpe (National Environmental Council of Native Americans)
Michael Tidwell (Chesapeake Climate Action Network)
Brian Tokar (Vermont Greens)
D. Chet Tzchozewski (Global Greengrants Fund)
Adam Werbach (Sierra Club)
Paul Watson (Sea Shepherd)
Diane Whealy and Kent Whealy (Seed Savers Exchange)
Louisa Willcox (Greater Yellowstone Coalition, Sierra Club Grizzly Bear Ecosystems Project)
Chris Wille (ECO-OK Certification Program)
Diane Wilson (CODEPINK)
Hazel Wolf (Seattle Audubon Society)
Howie Wolke (Earth First!)
George Woodwell (Woods Hole Research Center)
Howard Zanheiser (The Wilderness Society)
Robert Sterling Yard (National Parks Association, The Wilderness Society)
David Zwick (Clean Water Action)

### Naturalists
Janine Benyus
John Burroughs
Aldo Leopold
Richard Louv
Enos Mills
John Muir
Olaus Murie
Doug Peacock
Terry Tempest Williams

### Philanthropists/Funders
Dana Alston
John D. Rockefeller, Jr.
Laurance Rockefeller
Douglas Tompkins
Ted Turner

### Philosophers
Peter Berg
Thomas Berry
Murray Bookchin
J. Baird Callicott
Bill Devall
Paul Goodman
Stephanie Mills
Lewis Mumford
Scott and Helen Nearing
Bryan Norton
Holmes Rolston, III
Theodore Roszak
George Sessions

### Photographers
Ansel Adams
James Balog
Devereux Butcher
Chris Jordan

### Publishers
Stewart Brand
Ellen and Paul Connett
Ron Mader
Stephanie Mills
Robert Rodale
Mark Dowie

### Recyclers
Pete Grogan
Michael Reynolds

### Scientists
*Life and Physical Scientists*
John James Audubon (ornithologist)
Albert Bartlett (nuclear physicist)
John Bartram and William Bartram (botanists)
Marston Bates (zoologist)
William Beebe (marine biologist, ornithologist)
Hugh Hammond Bennett (soil scientist)
Rosalie Bertell (biochemist)
Tom Cade (ornithologist)
Archie Carr (zoologist)
Marjorie Carr (biologist)
Rachel Carson (biologist)
George Washington Carver (agricultural scientist)
Frank Chapman (ornithologist)
Theo Colborn (zoologist)
Barry Commoner (biologist)
Paul Connett (chemist)
Henry Cowles (botanist, ecologist)
Paul Cox (ethnobotanist)
Frank and John Craighead (wildlife biologists)
Michael Dombeck (fisheries biologist)
René Dubos (microbiologist)
William Dutcher (ornithologist)
Thomas Eisner (entomologist)
Silvia Earle (marine biologist, oceanographer)
David Ehrenfeld (ecologist)
Anne and Paul Ehrlich (biological researcher, population biologist)
Charles S. Elton (ecologist)
Dian Fossey (zoologist)
Sherwood M. Gagliano (geomorphologist)
Henry Allan Gleason (botanist, ecologist, taxonomist)
Stephen Jay Gould (paleontologist)
Asa Gray (botanist)
James E. Hansen (climatologist)
Garrett Hardin (biologist)
Donna House (ethnobotanist)
Wes Jackson (plant geneticist)
Michael Jacobson (microbiologist)
Dan Janzen (tropical ecologist)
Henry Kendall (physicist)
Thomas Lovejoy (tropical ecologist)
Michael E. Mann (climatologist, geophysicist)

## List of Leaders by Occupation or Work Focus

George Perkins Marsh (environmental scientist)
Dennis Martinez (restoration ecologist)
Florence Bailey Merriam (ornithologist)
Russell Mittermeier (zoologist)
Olaus Murie (wildlife ecologist)
Gary Nabhan (ethnobiologist, agricultural and desert ecologist)
Reed Noss (conservation biologist, ecologist)
Eugene Odum (ecologist)
Roger Tory Peterson (ornithologist)
Steve Packard (restoration ecologist)
Mark Plotkin (ethnobotanist)
Ellen Swallow Richards (sanitary chemist)
Peter Raven (botanist)
Arthur H. Rosenfeld (physicist)
Carl Safina (marine ecologist)
Carl Sagan (astronomer)
Charles Sprague Sargent (dendrologist)
Stephen Schneider (climatologist)
Susan Solomon (chemist)
Richard Evans Schultes (ethnobotanist)
Michael Soulé (conservation biologist)
Sandra Steingraber (ecologist)
Wilma Subra (analytical chemist)
Oakleigh Thorne, II (ecologist)
William Vogt (ornithologist, ecologist)
Edward O. Wilson (entomologist)
George Woodwell (ecologist)

### Social Scientists
Kenneth Boulding (economist)
Janet Brown (political scientist)
Lester Brown (economist)
Robert Bullard (sociologist)
Lynton Caldwell (political scientist)
Marion Clawson (agricultural economist)
Herman Daly (economist)
Garrett Hardin (human ecologist)
Hazel Henderson (economist)
Glenn S. Johnson (sociologist)
Stephen Kellert (social ecologist)
Winona LaDuke (economist)
Paula Palmer (sociologist)
Deborah Popper (geographer)
Laura Pulido (sociologist)
Gilbert White (geographer)

### Theologians/Religious Teachers
Thomas Berry
Rosalie Bertell
Richard Cizik
John B. Cobb, Jr.
Oren Lyons
Holmes Rolston, III
Rosemary Radford Ruether

### Government Appointed Officials
Horace Albright (National Park Service Director)
Cecil Andrus (Secretary of the Interior)
Bruce Babbit (Secretary of the Interior)
Mollie Beattie (Director of the U.S. Fish and Wildlife Service)
Hugh Hammond Bennett (Director of the U.S. Soil Conservation Service)
Eula Bingham (Director of the Occupational Safety and Health Administration)
Carol Browner (Administrator of the U.S. Environmental Protection Agency)
Douglas Costle (Administrator of the U.S. Environmental Protection Agency)
Michael Dombeck (Chief of the U.S. Forest Service)
William O. Douglas (Supreme Court Justice)
Newton Drury (National Park Service Director)
Willie Fontenot (Community Liaison Officer in the Louisiana Attorney General's Office)
James E. Hansen (Director of National Aeronautics and Space Administration's Goddard Institute for Space Studies)
Harold Ickes (Secretary of the Interior)
Stephen Mather (National Park Service Director)
George Mitchell (U.S. Attorney)
John Wesley Powell (U.S. Geological Survey Director)
Gifford Pinchot (Founder and First Chief of the U.S. Forest Service)
William K. Reilly (Administrator of the U.S. Environmental Protection Agency)
Carl Schurz (Secretary of the Interior)
Susan Solomon (Senior Chemist at the National Oceanic and Atmospheric Administration)
William Steel (Commissioner of Crater Lake National Park)
Stewart Udall (Secretary of the Interior)

### Whistle-blowers
Adrienne Anderson
Jeff DeBonis
Hugh Kaufman
William Sanjour

### Writers (journalists, poets, nature writers, novelists)
Edward Abbey
Diane Ackerman
Henry Adams
Mary Austin
Marston Bates
William Beebe
Janine Benyus
Wendell Berry
Murray Bookchin
Michael Brown
John Burroughs

# List of Leaders by Occupation or Work Focus

Devereux Butcher
Archie Carr
Rachel Carson
Harry Caudill
Jack Collom
James Fenimore Cooper
Bernard Devoto
Marjory Stoneman Douglas
Mark Dowie
Andrew Jackson Downing
Ralph Waldo Emerson
Rogelio Figueroa
Michael Frome
Theodor Geisel (Dr. Seuss)
Ross Gelbspan
Paul Goodman
Stephen Jay Gould
George Bird Grinnell
James E. Hansen
Dorothy Webster Harvey
Paul Hawken
Edward Hoagland
Derrick Jensen
Diane Jukofsky
Hal Kane
Barbara Kingsolver
Winona LaDuke
Frances Moore Lappé

Aldo Leopold
Anne Morrow and Charles Lindbergh
Barry Lopez
Richard Louv
Benjamin Luce
Ron Mader
Richard Manning
Peter Matthiesen
Bill McKibben
John McPhee
Donella Meadows
Florence Bailey Merriam
Stephanie Mills
John Muir
Gary Nabhan
Helen and Scott Nearing
Nell Newman
Mary Oliver
Sigurd Olson
David Orr
Fairfield Osborn, Jr.
Roger Tory Peterson
Michael Pollan
Marc Reisner
Jeremy Rifkin
John Robbins
Robert Rodale

Theodore Roszak
Carl Safina
Kirkpatrick Sale
Andrew L. Shapiro
Gary Snyder
Luther Standing Bear
Wallace Stegner
Sandra Steingraber
Sarah Susanka
Terry Tamminen
Henry David Thoreau
Michael Tidwell
Brian Tokar
William Vogt
Walt Whitman
Terry Tempest Williams

# Index

## American Environmental Leaders
From Colonial Times to the Present

# Index

Abandoned mines, 752
Abbey, Edward, **3–4**
Abortion, 179, 370
Abraham Path Initiative, 21
Abruzzi, William S., 956–960
Academy Award, 224, 225, 236
Acadia National Park, 688
Acid rain control program, 39, 851
Ackerman, Diane, **4–6**
Acquired immunodeficiency syndrome (AIDS), 759
ACTION, 232
Action Against Dams and for Rivers Water, and Life, 475
Act Now Productions, 853–854
Actors, 71, 119, 557, 780
Adam Joseph Lewis Center for Environmental Studies, 615
Adams, Ansel, **6–8**
Adams, Henry, **8–10**
Adams, John Hamilton, **10–11**
Adams, John Quincy, **12–13**
Adams, Olive Bray, 6
Addams, Jane, **13–15**, 366
Adirondack Mountains, 533
Adirondack Park Act (1971), 79
African Americans, 411, 427, 429. *See also* People of color
African Elephant Conservation Trust, 559
African Wildlife Foundation (1975), 558
After School Education and Safety Act (2002), 732
Agricultural Appropriations Bill, 73
Agricultural Labor Relations Act (1975), 404
Agricultural lands, desertification of, 440
Agricultural Workers Organizing Committee (AWOC), 172
Agriculture, 509, 553
  crop yield on farms of Louisa County, 73
  in developing countries, 476
  mechanization of, 355
  modern, 83
  peanuts, 158
  perennial grains, 417–418
  soil conservation issues, 73
  sustainable, 417
Agua Fria River, 764

AIA Committee on Architecture for Education Honor Award, 527
AIDS (acquired immunodeficiency syndrome), 101, 207, 759, 850
Air pollution, 193
  emissions, 718
  in southern California, 852–853
Airport noise ordinance, 242
Air quality, 387
Alaska Chapter of The Nature Conservancy, 544
Alaska Forum on the Environment, 544
Alaska Indigenous Peoples' Council for Marine Mammals, 544
Alaska Lands Act (1980), 154, 829
Alaska Lands Conservation Act (1980), 28
Alaska National Interest Lands Conservation Act, 570
Alaska Native Lands Claims Settlement Act (1971), 79
Alaska Native Science Commission, 544
Alaska Native Writers, 544
Alaskan peregrines, 135
Alaska Oceans Network, 544
Albert Lasker Award, 738
Albert Schweitzer Prize, 656
Albion Uprising, 483
Albright Group LLC, 125
Albright, Horace, **15–17,** 260, 409, 519, 688
Alcohol Policies Project, 420
"Alerce 3000," 820
*Algeny*, 676
Alice Fay di Castagnola Award, 606
Alicia Patterson Journalism Fellowship, 669
Allee, W. A., 370
Allen, James Van, 367
Alliance for the Wild Rockies, 230
Alliance to End Childhood Lead Poisoning, 587
All My Relations public radio project, 115
Alston, Dana, **17–19**
Altamira dam, 384
Alternative Motor Fuels Act (1988), 265
"Alternative Nobel" Prize, 419. *See also* Right Livelihood Award

Amazon Conservation Team (ACT), 641
Amazon jungle, 729
Amazon rain forest
  logging in, 390
  nonendangered wood species of, 248
Amazon River, 729
Amboseli Elephant Research Project (AERP), 558–559
Amboseli Trust for Elephants (ATE), 559
American Academy of Achievement, 583
American Academy of Arts & Letters Award, 536, 606
American Architecture Award, 527
American Association for the Advancement of Science, 600
American Bison Society, 398
American Book Award, 567
American Conservation Association, Inc., 690
American Council for an Energy Efficient Economy (ACEEE), 702
American Environmental Health Studies Project, 194, 195, 196
American Farmland Trust, 668
American Federation of Labor-Congress of Industrial Organizations (AFL-CIO), 631
American Forest Congress (1905), 638
American Forestry Association, 308
American frontier, thesis on, 823, 824
American Game Association, 346
American Game Protective Association (AGPA), 398
American Horse Slaughter Prevention Act, 591
American Indian Movement (AIM), 795
American Institute of Architects (AIA), 526
American Institute of Planners, 610
American Lands Alliance, 437, 438
American Library Association (ALA), 747
American Museum of Natural History, 268

# Index

American Ornithologists Union (AOU), 268
American Smelting and Refining Company, 27
American Society of Landscape Architects, 609–610
American Wildlife Institute (AWI), 223
America's Farmland Trust, 670
Ames, Oakes, 728
Amidon, Elias, and Elizabeth Roberts, **19–21**
Amme, David, 517
Ancient Forest Protection Act (1991), 438
Ancient Forest Rescue, 841
Anderson, Adrienne, **21–24**
Anderson, Harold, 500
Anderson, Ray, **25–26**
Andrus, Cecil, **27–29**
Andrus Center for Public Policy, 28
*An Evangelical Call to Civic Responsibility*, excerpt, 979
Animal-based foods, health effects of, 682
Animal behavior, 77, 460, 873
Animal rights, 560, 590
Animal tracking technology, 208, 209, 745
Anishinabe culture, 472
Ansel Adams Wilderness, 8
Antarctica, 766
Anthony, Carl, **29–31**
Anti-apartheid movement, 17
Antibiotic drugs, 262
Anti-nuclear activist, 85
Antinuclear movement, 751, 800
Antinuclear unions, 350
Antispearfishing protests, 114
Ants, research work conducted on, 873
Apollo Alliance, 677
Appalachian region (Ky.), 162, 163
Appalachian Trail Club, 499
Appalachian Trail Conference, 655
Appian Way, 237
Aquifer, 786
Architectural Record Award, 526
Architecture and design, 311
Arcology, 764
Arctic National Wildlife Refuge (ANWR), 105
Area de Conservación Guanacaste (ACG) (Costa Rica), 421
Aridity, 833

*Arithmetic, Population and Energy*, 926–940
Arizona Desert Wilderness Act, 895
Arizona Groundwater Management Act (1980), 43
Arizona–Mexico Border Health Foundation, 580
Arizona Wilderness Act, 829
Armstrong Fire-Arms Law (1905), 398
Army Corps of Engineers, 149, 250, 251, 261, 410, 634, 651
Arnold Arboretum (Harvard University), 720, 721
Artists, 9, 37, 58, 89, 188, 401, 566, 876
ASARCO mining company, 24
Asbestos damage, 739
Ashoka, 258
  fellowships, 257
Association of Forest Service Employees for Environmental Ethics (AFSEEE, later FSEEE), 228, 230
Astronomy, 5, 290, 367, 713
Atlanta (Ga.), 427
Atomic Energy Commission (AEC), 754
Audubon Adventures Club, 636
Audubon Award, 636
Audubon Conservation Medal, 634
Audubon, John James, **31–33**, 226
Audubon Medal, 570, 619
Audubon Plumage Bill, 269
Audubon Society, 226, 238, 269
Audubon Society Journalism Award, 509
August, John, 235
Austin, Mary, **33–36**
Australian company Eco Futures Pty Ltd., 611
Ausubel, Kenny, **36–38**
Automated Highway System, 243
Automobiles
  energy efficiency issues, 265, 722
  fuel efficiency standards for, 336
  and park visitation policy, 308
  and urban design, 763
Ayres, Richard, **38–40**

Babbitt, Bruce, **43–44**
Bachman, John, 33
Bacille Capmette-guérin (BCG) vaccine, 263
Back-to-the-land movement, 584, 760
Baden-Powell, Robert, 745

Bad River Ogitchida, 114
Bahouth, Peter, **44–46**
Bailey, Florence Augusta Merriam, **46–48**
Bailey, Vernon, 47
Bainbridge Island, 734
Baker, John, 278
Bald Mountain, 329
Ball, Betty, and Gary Ball, **48–51**
Balog, James D., **51–52**
Banana production, 867
Bari, Judi, **52–54**
Barrows, Harlan, 857
Bartlett, Albert, **55–57,** 926–940
Bartram, John, and William Bartram, **58–60**
Bartram, William, journal excerpt, 904
Bates, Marston, **60–61**
Bauer, Catherine, **61–63**
Bavaria, Joan, **63–64**
Bay Area PoliceWatch, 436
Bay Area Working Group, 287
Bayou Savage National Wildlife Refuge, 297
Beale, Edward, 34
Bean, Michael, **65–67**
Bear Rivers, 379
Bears, grizzly, 144, 208
  in Yellowstone National Park, 209–210
Beattie, Mollie, **67–68**
Beautification projects, 432
Beck, R.W., 347
Beebe, C. William, **69–70**
Beef production, 677, 682
Begley, Ed, Jr., **71–72**
Be-In, 75
Belt, Thomas, 422
Benally, Louise, 96
Ben and Jerry's, 169
Bennett, Hugh Hammond, **73–74**
Benton Box Award, 616
Benyus, Janine, **76–78**
Berg, Peter, **74–76**
Berkeley Free Speech movement, 334
Berkshire Hills, 746
Berle, Peter, **78–80**
Bernard, Mark, 235
Berry, Friar Thomas, **80–82**
Berry, Wendell, **82–84,** 419
Bertell, Rosalie, **84–86**
Best Documentary Feature Diversity Award, 236
Better Banana Program, 867

# INDEX

Better Banana Project, 450
Better World Society, 826
Bien, Amos, **86–88**
Bierstadt, Albert, **89–91**
Big Cypress National Preserve, 415
Big Green campaign (Calif.), 853
Big Wild Advocates, 879, 880
Billings, Frederick, 689
Bingham, Eula, **91–92**
Bio Bio River, 364
Biocentric environmental ethic, 742
Biocultural conservation, 641
Biodegradable products, 526
Biodevastation 2000, 818
Biodiversity, 488, 874
   global warming and, 489
   on indigenous land, 375
   prospecting, 423
   protection of, 400
   strategy for protection of, 248
Biodiversity conservation, 599, 663, 664
   biodiverse regions, 553–554
   and biosphere study, 580, 599
   CI role in, 553
   and cultural diversity, 502, 641, 795
   "debt-for-nature" swaps for, 313
   ecosystem approach to, 144–145
   and Wildlands Project, 768
   *See also* Ecosystems; Tropical rain forests
Biodiversity Legal Foundation (BLF), 143–145
Biofeedback, 49
Biological Dynamics of Forest Fragments Project, 488, 489
Biology field experiments, 488
Biome studies, 305
Biomimicry, 76–77
Biomimicry Institute, 77
Bioneers Award, 616
*Biophilia*, 453, 454, 455
Biophobia, 454
Bioprospecting, 284
Bioregionalism, 75, 76, 715
Biosphere reserve study, 442
Biotechnology
   consequences of, 675–676
   negative effects of, 375
BioWillie, 590
Bird-protection legislation movement, 267
Birds
   banding of, 32
   books on, 33, 46, 47

   breeding biology of, 710
   children's education on, 269
   conservation of, 345
   environmental legislation to protect, 114, 268–269, 277, 346–347
   exhibit of, 166
   goshawks, 650
   guidebooks on, 47, 633, 634, 650, 743
   habitats, 786, 837
   identification and drawing of, 633, 743
   legislative regulations to protect, 32, 166, 398, 403
   and pesticides, 136, 151, 592
   plumage of, 397, 701
   protection of, 650, 651
   sanctuary for, 278
   watching, 633–634
Birregaard, Rob, 488
Bison protection, 398
Bisphenol A, 185
Bixby, Kevin, **93–94**
Blackfoot River, 509, 782
Blackgoat, Roberta, **94–96**
Black Hills, 345, 796
Black, Jack, 224
Black Student Organization, 17
Blaeloch, Janine, **96–98**
Bloomberg, Michael, **98–99**
Blue-Green Working Group, 632
Blue Planet Prize, 283
Blue Revolution, 648
Bob Marshall Wilderness Area, 462, 513
Body Shop, 169
Bohn, Ernest, 62
Boise Cascade Company, 378
Bolinas Lagoon, protection of, 846–847
Bolivia, 672
Bolshevik system, 366
Bonneville Dam, 805
Bookchin, Murray, **100–102**
Boone and Crockett Club, 346, 700
Border Ecology Project (BEP), 445
BOSCOSA Forest Conservation and Management project (Costa Rica), 247
Boston Model Cities program, 644
Boulder Canyon, 35
Boulder (Colorado), 693
Boulder Environmental Activists' Resource (BEAR), 50

Boulder Institute for Nature and the Human Spirit, 19, 20
Boulder Open Space Program, 56
Boulding, Kenneth, **102–104**
Boundary Waters Canoe Area Wilderness, 612, 614
Bourgeois society, 256
Bowen Gulch area of Colorado, 841
Bowen Gulch Rescue Effort (now Ancient Forest Rescue), 841
Bowery Houston Community Farm and Garden (now Liz Christy Bowery-Houston Garden), 177
Boy Scouts, 745
Bradford Williams Medal of American Society of Landscape Architects, 531
Bramble, Barbara, **104–107**
Brandborg, Stewart, **109–112**
Brandis, Detrich, 637
Brand, Stewart, **107–109**
Branford, Victor, 566
Brant, Irving, 167
Braungart, Michael, 200
Brazil, 147, 474, 488, 526
Break the Grip!, 493
Breast cancer, 777
Breeding biology, 710
Bresette, Walt, **113–115**
Bridge Canyon Dam, 259, 261
Broadcast Radio News, 217
Bronx County Bird Club (BCBC), 837
Bronx Environmental Stewardship Training Program, 155. *See also* Sustainable South Bronx (SSBX)
Bronx Zoo, 397, 553, 617
Brooklyn's Prospect Park, 608
Broome, Harvey, 500, 513, 890
Brower, David, **115–117**, 233, 893, 894
Browner, Carol, **124–125**
Brownfields, clean up of, 125
Brown, Janet, **118–119**
Brownlash, 282
Brown, Lester, **119–121**
Brown, Michael, **122–123**
Brown, Susan, 99
Brownsville (Texas), 843, 844
Bryant Park, 199
Bryant, Patrick, 17
"Bubble concept," 203
Bubbly Creek, 529
Buffalo Commons, 643–646
Buffet Finalist Award, 544

# INDEX

Building Economic Alternatives award, 267
Bullard, Robert D., **126–128,** 426
Bullit Foundation, 382, 383
Bureau of Animal Population, 288
Bureau of Indian Affairs (BIA), 513
Bureau of Land Management (BLM), 43, 44
   economic policy analysis, 180
Bureau of Reclamation, 261
Burford, Anne Gorsuch, 451
Burroughs Corporation, 560
Burroughs, John, **129–130,** 743, 863
Burroughs Nature Club, 226
Bush, George H. W., 896
Businesses, 32–33, 124, 168–169, 380
   consulting to, 108
   educational programs for, 315
   and energy efficiency issue, 722
   garbage collection service, 258
   sustainability goal, 491–492
   training courses to tourism, 450
Butcher, Devereux, **131–132**

Cable News Network (CNN), 825
Cade, Thomas, **135–136**
Calcasieu estuary, 784
Calcasieu Parish, 784
Caldwell, Lynton, **137–139,** 416
California Book Award, 642
California Coastal Commission, 232
California Department of Food and Agriculture (CDFA) regulations, 403
California Desert Protection Act (1992), 853
California Housing and Planning Association, 62
California nuclear power plant, 117
California Rural Legal Assistance, 173
California Wilderness Act (1984), 8
Callaway Mills Co., 25
Callicott, J. Baird, **139–141**
Campaign Finance Law (1974), 829
Camp Fire Girls, 745
Camp Perry (Ohio), 235
Caneel Bay Plantation Resort, 690
Captiva Island, 223
Carbon dioxide, 369, 726
Carbon emissions, 324, 733
Carcinogens, 92
Care2, 225
Career Achievement Award, 542
Carhart, Arthur, **141–143**
Caribbean Conservation Corporation (CCC), 146–147

Caribou National Forest, 378
Carleton Natural History Club, 226
Carlton, Jasper, **143–145**
Carnivores, ecological roles of, 599, 768
Carnot Award, 702
Carpets International–Georgia, 25
Carr, Archie, **145–147**
Carr, Marjorie Harris, **148–150**
Car-sharing, 170–171
Carson, Rachel, **150–152**
Carter, Jimmy, **152–154,** 240, 326
Carter, Majora, **155–156**
Cartoonist, 222
Carver, George Washington, **157–158**
Cascade Forest Reserve, 773, 774
Cascade Mountains, 252
Castillo, Aurora, **159–160**
CatalogChoice.org, 450–451
The Catalog of Extinct Experience, 231, 232
Catlin, George, **160–161**
Catskill Mountains, 755
Cattle ranch, 254
Caudill, Harry, **162–163**
Cayuga Bear Clan Mother (Carol Jacobs), 954–955
C. B. Blethen Award, 508, 509
Ceará (Brazil), 215
Cele Peterson Award, 581
Celilo Falls, dipnet fishery in, 805–806
Celilo Fish Commission, 805
Center for Biological Diversity (formerly Southwest Center for Biological Diversity), 785
Center for Conservation Biology (CCB), 283
Center for Environmental Strategy (U. of Surrey), 219
Center for Native Ecosystems, award of, 145
Center for Plant Conservation, 664
Center for Process Studies, 182
Center for Studies of Deserts and Oceans, 580
Center for Study of Responsive Law, 577, 895
Centers for Disease Control, 587
Central Park (New York City), 607
Central Utah Project (CUP), 376
Central Utah Water Conservancy District (CUWCD), 378
Centre for Energy and Climate Solutions (CECS), 702

Centre for the New American Dream, 685
Chafee, John, **164–165**
Chapman, Frank, **166–167**
Chapman, Oscar L., 261
Chappell, Kate, and Tom Chappell, **167–170**
Charles A. and Anne Morrow Lindbergh Foundation, 480, 482
Charles Bannerman Memorial Fellowship, 18
Charles H. Percy Award, 681
Chase, Robin, **170–171**
Chávez, César, **172–174,** 403
Chavis, Benjamin, **174–176**
Chem-Clear Plant Project, 159
Chemical ecology, 284
Chemical prospecting, 285
Chemical toxins, 151, 552, 578, 587, 851
   circulation and effects of, 882
   dioxin and chlorine, 194
   endocrine disruption by, 184–186
   fluoride, 196
   and human cancers, 777–778
   lead, 587
   and worker health and safety, 173, 557, 587
Chemical waste incinerator, 429
Chequamegon National Forest, 244
Chesapeake Climate Action Network, 816
Chesapeake & Ohio Canal, 252
Chevron oil refinery, 287
Cheyenne, 347
Chicago Region Biodiversity Council (Chicago Wilderness Consortium), 624
Chicago River, 529
Children
   bird education program for, 269
   disease in, 557
   environmental education for, 811
   health of, 587
   health problem due to toxic chemicals, 22–23, 173, 198, 587–588, 778
   literature for, 320–322, 336, 455, 462, 641
   nature understanding, articles for, 151–152
   Ojibwe language program for, 472
Children & Nature Network, 487
Chiles, Lawton, 124

# INDEX

Chippewa harvesting rights, 114
Chiquita Brands, 450, 867
Chlorine Chemistry Council (CCC), 147, 185
Chlorofluorocarbons (CFCs), 726, 765
Christian theology and nature, 181–182
Christopher Award, 605
Christy, Elizabeth, **176–177**
Chrysler Award, 672
Church Universal and Triumphant (CUT), 865
Cincinnati (Ohio), 224
Circle of Life Foundation, 394
Citizen Action (CA), 22
Citizens Against Nuclear Trash (CANT), 128
Citizens Clearinghouse on Hazardous Waste (now Center for Health, Environment and Justice [CHEJ]), 325
Citizens Conferences on Dioxin, 195
Citizens for Clean Air (CCA), 388
Citizens Party, The, 193
City Care movement, 314
City Charter Amendment, 55
Civil disobedience, 300, 737
Civilian Conservation Corps (CCC), 16, 260, 409, 697
Civil rights
  legislation, 240
  movement, 379
Civil Rights Act (1964), 426
Cizik, Richard, **178–179**
Clarion Award, 236
Clark Fork River, 780, 781
Clawson, Marion, **179–181**
Clean Air Act (1963, 1970, 1977, 1990), 38, 193, 265, 430, 463, 570, 571, 578, 587, 588, 667, 668, 678, 733, 851
  amendments to, 39
Clean Water Act (1972, 1986, 1987), 165, 551, 678, 895
  violation by Martin Marietta, 23
Clean Water Action, 299, 895, 896
Clean Water Fund, 299
Cleveland, Grover, 773
Climate change, 225, 323, 749. *See also* Global warming
Climate Institute and Friends of China's National Parks, 654
Climate Policy Program, 797–798
Climate Savers Computing Initiative, 681

Climatic impacts, on society, 726
Climatology of 1980-2003 Extreme Weather and Climate Events, 963–978
Clinch River, 335
Clinton, Bill, 43, 258, 611
Coal-fired plants, 368
Coalition for Community Action, 298
Coalition for Environmentally Responsible Economies (CERES), 63, 64
Coal-mining industry, 162
Coastal Barrier Resources Act, 165
Coastal Environments, Inc.(CEI), 320
Coastal habitats, 710
Coastal land loss, 815
Coastal wetlands, 297, 319
Coastal Zone Act, 635–636
Coastal zone management, 314
Coastline protection, 635
Cobb, Clifford W., 216
Cobb, John B., Jr., **181–183**, 216
Cocoa production, 868
Coevolution, 281, 422
Colborn, Theo, **183–186**
Colby, William, **186–188**
Cole, Thomas, **188–190**
Colibrí Ecotourism Award, 502
Collaborative stewardship, 245
Collinson, Peter, 58
Collom, Jack, **190–191**
Colombia, 60, 61, 138, 641, 729
Colorado Citizen Action Network (CCAN), 22
Colorado Environmental Coalition (CEC), 758
Colorado River, 378, 583, 776, 833
Colorado River Storage Project Act (1956), 893–894
Colorado River watersheds, restoration, 474
Columbia Broadcasting System (CBS), 308
Columbia River, 252, 304, 774, 878
  salmon fishery, conflicts over, 805
Commoner, Barry, **192–193**
Common Property. *See* Seventh Generation constitutional amendment
Common Sense Initiative, 125
Communication with Extra-Terrestrial Intelligence (CETI), 713

Communities of color, 436
Community Coalition for Environmental Justice (CCEJ), 877, 878
Community development, 374, 375
  role of agriculture in, 418
Community ecology, 327
Community organizing
  for civil rights, 350
  against CUP, 378
  against hazardous and toxic materials, 22, 159, 175, 298–299, 429, 437, 555, 678
  lettuce boycott, 173
  against the MX land-based missile system, 374
  against Rocky Flats Project, 800–801, 821
  on urban development, 48–49
  against war, 675
Community Service Organization (CSO), 172, 403
Community-supported agricultural groups (CSAs), 461
Community toxics campaigns, 23
Comprehensive Environmental Response Compensation and Liability Act (CERCLA), 152, 165, 203, 240
Congressional Gold Medal, 689, 691
Congressional Renewal of the Abandoned Mine Lands Program, 265
Coniferous forest, 304
Coniferous Forest Biome, 304
Connecticut Fund for the Environment (CFE), 463
"Connecticut Plan," 203
Connett, Ellen, and Paul Connett, **194–196**
Conservation Achievement Award, 225
Conservation and Development Corporation (CCD), 868
*Conservation Biology*, 279
Conservation Community Award, 599
Conservation Foundation, 616
Conservation International (CI), 553
Conservationists, 16, 31, 111, 148–150, 157–158, 160–161, 238–239, 299–301, 520, 522, 546–548, 558–559, 575–577, 597, 612–614, 620, 636, 638, 644–645, 650, 651, 697–699, 701, 773–774, 848–849, 879–881

1031

# INDEX

Conservation Land Trust, 819
Conservation movement, 234
Conservation Planning Institute, The, 600
*Constitution of the Iroquois Nations: The Great Binding Law*, 903
Contaminants, effects of transgeneral exposure to, 185
Convention on International Trade in Endangered Species (CITES), 559, 710
Conway, Stuart, **197–198**
Cook, Richard A., **198–200**
Cooper, James Fenimore, **201–202**
Copper
  deposit, 781
  mines, 114
Corcovado National Park (Costa Rica), 247
Cosanti Foundation, 763
Costa Rica, 86, 88, 147, 247, 383, 421
Costa Rican Natural Reserve Network, 86, 88
Costle, Douglas, **202–204**
Coulee Dam National Recreation Area, 260
Coulter, John Merle, 204
Council on Environmental Quality (CEQ), 105, 416, 636
Country Future Indicators (CFI) index, 388
Covington & Burling, 65
Cowles, Henry, **204–205**
Cow peas, 158
Cox, Paul, **206–208**
Crafoord Prize, 283, 423, 604
Craighead, Frank, and John Craighead, **208–211**
Crater Lake, 773, 774
Creation Care, 178
Crime prevention program, 758
Cronin, John, 458
Cronon, William, **211–212**
Crop
  breeding techniques, 418
  hybrids, 418
  rotation, 58, 74, 750
Cross-Florida Barge Canal, halting construction of, 148, 149
Crown Butte Mines Inc., 864
Crow, Sheryl, 224
Cultural exchanges, 576
Cultural Exchange Service, 579
Cuyahoga River, 895

Dalkon Shield, 253, 254
Dalles Dam (Columbia River), 805
Daly, Herman, **215–217**
Dam projects, 3, 149, 154, 384, 434, 596
  in Boulder Canyon, 35
  Columbia River, 805
  in Dinosaur National Monument, 116, 893
  fight against, 261, 300, 332, 378, 434, 437, 474, 475, 564, 610, 668, 757–758, 782, 805–806, 893–894
  pork-barrel federal, 154
  Teton River, on, 28
  Tuolumne River, on, 187
Danielson, Antje, 170
Darley, Julian and Rich, Celine Fanny, **217–220**
Darley, Raphael Rex, 220
Darling, Jay Norwood "Ding," **220–223**
Darwin, Charles, 344, 910–912
Darwinian evolution, 342
Darwin's theory, 342
Dave Foreman, 599
David, Laurie Ellen (also Laurie Ellen Lennard), **224–225**
Davis, Gray, 232
Dawson, Richard, **226–227**
DDT (dichlordiphenyltrichlor) contamination, 135, 151, 173, 192, 463, 881, 882
Death Valley Monument, 779
DeBonis, Jeff, **228–231**
"Debt for nature" concept, 106
Debt-for-nature swaps, 489
Deep ecology, 93, 101
Deep Ecology Foundation, 819
Deep Ecology movement, 743
Deep Ocean Technologies, 276
Deep-sea exploration, 70
Deering Milliken, 25
Deer Mountain, 270
Defenders of Wildlife, 781
Deforestation, 368
Deloria, Vine, Jr., 399
Democracy, and environment, 477
Denver, 23
Departments of Environmental Quality (DEQ), 658
Departments of Natural Resources (DNR), 658
Desert, 3, 20, 154, 484
Desert Botanical Garden, 576
Desertification, 440

Design Associates Working with Nature (DAWN), 517
Desser, Christina Louise, **231–233**
Devall, Bill, **233–234**
Developing countries, 216
Devoto, Bernard, **234–236**
Diabetes, 472, 576, 683
DiCaprio, Leonardo, **236–237**
Dichlordiphenyltrichlor (DDT), 279, 404, 577, 650
Dietel, William, 120
Diftnet fishing, 470
Diggers, 74–75
Dilg, Will, **238–239**
Dineh Navajo, 94, 399
Dineh resistance movement, 94–96
Dingell, John, Jr., **239–241**, 416
Dinosaur National Monument, 234, 235, 259, 261
Dioxin, 122, 194
Dipnetters, 803–805
Direct action, 3, 45, 53, 233, 384, 482
Director of Public Policy and Advocacy for the Rural Alaska Community Action Program, 544
Discovery Project, 219
Distinguished Investigator Award, 588
Ditmman, Frank, 7
Dittmar, Hank, **241–243**
Dodson, Stanley, 184
Dolphin killings, domestic campaign against, 469, 470
Dombeck, Michael, **244–246**
Dominguez, Joe, 684
Donovan, Richard, **246–249**
Don't Make a Wave Committee, 848
Douglas, Marjory Stoneman, **249–251**
Douglas, William Orville, **251–253**
Dowie, Mark, **253–255**
Downing, Andrew Jackson, **255–257**
Drayton, William, **257–259**
Dreaming New Mexico Initiative, 846
Drought mitigation, 857
Drury, Newton, **259–261**
Du Bois, Paul, 477
Dubos, René, **262–264**
Dunlap & Browder, Inc., 264
Dunlap, Louise, **264–265**
DuPont, 749
Durning, Alan, **265–267**
Dust bowl, 222, 410

Dutcher, William, **267–269**
Dyer, Polly, 253, **270–272**
Dymaxion house (Fuller), 311

Earle, Sylvia, **275–276**
Earth 2000, 740
Earth Action Network, 561
Earth Creatures Company, 462
Earth Day, 72, 231, 232, 382
Earth First!, 53, 54, 234, 299, 483, 879, 880
Earth First! Foundation (now Fund for Wild Nature), 234, 384, 550
Earth Island Institute (EII), 30, 469, 471
    award of, 117
Earth music, 876
Earth Policy Institute, 119, 121
EarthSave International, 682
Earth Ship, designing of, 670–672
Earth Summit (Rio de Janeiro 1992), 18, 106, 447, 526, 818
East African Selous Game Reserve, 522
The East Bay Conversion and Reinvestment Commission, 30
Eastern Navajo Diné Against Uranium Mining (ENDAUM), 751
"The Easy Chair," 234
Eating Green program, 420
Echo Park, 259, 776
Echo Park dam, campaign against construction of, 893–894
Ecocertification, 248
Eco-Cycle, 348, 821
Eco-economy, 119
Ecofeminism, 541–542, 706
Eco Futures Pty Ltd., 612
Ecological legitimacy, 659
Ecological restoration project, 125
Ecology
    Gulf of Mexico, 847
    and human society, 604, 613
    movement, 742
    radical, 541
    regional, 76
    study of, 531
Ecomagination, 750
Economic and industrial development, 379
ECO-O.K. (ecological certification program), 450, 866, 867
Ecosystems
    dry forest, 422
    ecology of tropical, 421
    and impact of dam, 378
    natural, 417
    nonprofit organization to protect, 143
    protection of, 597, 598, 652–654
    restoration of, 509, 518, 600, 625–627, 645, 648–650, 766
    study of, 603, 604
Ecotage, 53
Ecotourism, 717
Ecotrust, 781
Ecuador, 76
Edge, Rosalie, 222, **277–278**
Edited Book Publication Award, 599
Edward J. Cleary Award, 364
Edward T. LaRoe Memorial Award, 599
E. F. Schumacher Society, 715
Ehrenfeld, David, **279–280**
Ehrlich, Anne, and Paul Ehrlich, **281–283**
Eisenhower, Dwight D., 252
Eisner, Thomas, **284–286**
Eldredge, Niles, 342
Eleanor Roosevelt Award, 225
Eliot, Charles, 608
Elk, 378
Ella Baker Center for Human Rights, 436
Ellis, Juliet, **286–287**
Elmore, Billie, 195
El Niño
    storms, 394
    warming, 837
Elton, Charles S., **288–290**
Embargo Act, 32
Emergency Conservation Committee (ECC), 277
Emerson, Ralph Waldo, **290–292**, 807, 905-906
Emily Carr Institute of Art and Design, 219
Emissions controls, 39, 88, 851
Emmy Award, 514
Endangered species, 400, 522, 600
    protection of, 66, 482
Endangered Species Act (ESA, 1973), 68, 240, 596, 597, 724, 757
Endangered Species Project (ESP), 470–471
Endocrine disruption, 184–186
Energy Act (2005), 265
Energy and Commerce Committee (now Commerce Committee), 240
Energy conservation, 311, 491
Energy efficiency, 265, 464
Energy Independence and Security Act (2007), 241
Energy Policy Act (1992, 2005), 265
Energy Policy and Conservation Act, 240
Energy sources, 382
Energy waste, 490, 491
Entomologist, 283
Entropy, 676
Environmental activism, 511–513, 517, 524, 531
    assessment of grassroots, 818
    bioregionalism, 75, 76
    oppression in Wounded Knee, 795
    schools for, 19
    and spiritual activism, 20–21
    SWEC, 93
    tropical deforestation, 488
    "World Alert," 45
Environmental Center (U. of Colorado), 821
Environmental Committee of the Arizona–Mexico/Sonora–Arizona Commissions, 580
Environmental Conservation Committee, 79
Environmental contamination
    causes of, 123
    Quassaic, 458
Environmental Defense Council, 461
Environmental Defense Fund (EDF), 65, 66, 149, 232, 463, 464, 525, 526
    and energy crisis of the 1970s, 118
Environmental degradation, 14, 70, 155, 336
    oil refineries and chemical plants role in, 693–694
    restoration of, 670, 689–690
Environmental education, 581, 583
    children, for, 636
    college students, for, 615
    communities education programs, 626
    land protection, for, 624
    wilderness preservation, for, 614
    women, for, 673
Environmental education program. *See* River of Words Project
Environmental epidemiology, 752
Environmental ethics, 19, 139, 141, 315, 342

Environmental Excellence Award, 544
Environmental history, 884
Environmental Impact Statement (EIS), 138, 416
Environmental issues, books on, 137–138
Environmentalists for Full Employment (EFFE), 349–351
Environmental journalism, 306, 747
Environmental justice, 17–18, 30, 175, 340, 426
*Environmental Justice Curriculum Resource Guidebook*, 427
Environmental Justice Research Center (EJRC), 128
Environmental law, 105, 125. *See also* Environmental protection laws
Environmental Law Institute, 65–66
Environmental Leadership Award, 230
Environmental modeling, 842
Environmental organizations, 350, 364
Environmental philosophy, 139, 695
Environmental policy, 118
Environmental Policy Act (1970), 240
Environmental problem
　copper mines, 114
　loss of biodiversity, 94
　in northern Wisconsin, 114
　population growth, 57
　U.S.-Mexico, 411
Environmental Programs for the Alaska Inter-Tribal Council, 544
Environmental protection, 253, 747
　civil disobedience for, 372
　and economic development, 27
　and native communities, 400
Environmental Protection Agency (EPA), 240, 326, 386, 452, 557, 587, 597, 598, 658, 667, 668, 739
　creation of, 203
　DDT ban by, 136, 173, 882
　fumigant approval, objection to, 196
　illegal incineration at Rocky Flats, 801
　Office of Environmental Equity, 127
　rule-making proceedings under the Clean Air Act, 39

　stove project grant, 198
　toxic waste disposal, 123
　toxic waste programs, 451
Environmental protection laws, 230, 253
Environmental racism, 556
　*Bean v. Southwestern Waste Management*, 126
　coined by, 175
　high-level radioactive waste storage, 813
　and justice, 658, 659
　LULUs in Black communities, 127
　Native American tribes, 796
　toxic dumps construction, 174
　uranium enrichment plant in Black communities, 128
Environmental reforms, 14
Environmental Research Foundation (ERF), 554, 556
Environmental Research Laboratory (U. of Arizona), 20
Environmental restoration project, implications of, 44
Environmental rights, 717
Environmental Science Camp, 226
Environmental Sciences Department (U. of Virginia), 505
Environmental sociology, 426
Environmental Species Act (1975), 331
Environmental Stewardship, 381
Environmental studies program (U. of Colorado-Boulder), 24
"Environment Show" (radio), 80
Erewhon Trading Company, 379
Ernhart, Claire, 587
Erosion, 73, 153, 319, 375
Estes, Richard and Runi, 312
*Esther*, 9
Estrogen disruptors, 185
Estuary, 530
E-Tech International, 446
*E The Environmental Magazine*, 560
Ethnobotany, 206, 626
Eugene, 219
Europe, 217
Euthenics, definition of, 674
Evans, Dan, 271
Everglades (Fla.), 44, 125, 149
Everglades National Park, 44, 249, 250
Exotic animals, 463

Extraterrestrial life, 712, 713
Extreme Ice Survey, 52
*Exxon Valdez*, 63, 364, 561, 801

Fairchild, Nancy Bell, 61
Falealupo rain forest reserve, 206, 207
Family planning, 370
Farley, Joshua, 217
Farm Aid and BioWillie, 590
Farm Bill (1990), 437
Farming practices and crop yield, 73
Farm Placement Service, 172
Farm workers
　pesticide poisonings among, 173
　problems faced by, 172
Faroe Island, 740
Father of Rocky Mountain National Park, 546
Federal Energy Office (FEO), 721, 722
Federal lands
　economic factors related to, 180
　native and old-growth forests on, 391
　policy for, 179
　privatization of, 96
Federal law suit
　for sewage treatment, 896
　against state of Florida, 125
Federal Power Commission, 78
Federation of Western Outdoors Clubs, 878
Figueroa, Rogelio, **295–296**
Financial strategy development, 447
First National People of Color Environmental Summit, 557
Fish and Wildlife Service. *See* United States Department of Fish and Wildlife (USDFW)
Fisherman's Clean Water Action Project (later Clean Water Action), 895–896
Fishing, 516, 521, 544, 560, 583
Five Valley Land Trust, 781
Flood
　damage-reducing measures, 857
　insurance, 857
　land use planning for prevention of, 857
　regulation of, 153
Floodplains, 857
Florida, 44
Florida Defenders of the Environment (FDE), 149
Florida Institute for Conservation Science, 600

# INDEX

Florida Natural Areas Inventory, 598
Flower and Herb Exchange (FHE), 856
Fluoride Action Network (FAN), 196
Flying fox bat, 207
Folksongs, 354
Fontenot, Willie, **296–299**
Food
    additives, 419
    choices, 476
    crop diversity, 854
    packaged, 420
    processing, 352
    safety, 100, 420
Food Quality Act (1996), 851
Food security, community, 340
Ford Foundation Visiting Scholar (U. of Fortaleza), 215
Ford Motor Company, 311
Foreman, Dave, 234, **299–301**
Forest
    conservation, 421
    degradation, 248
    ecology, 758
    policy, 638, 720
    restoration, 423
*Forest and Stream*, 345, 346
Forest management, 228, 391, 518, 723, 758, 770
    and conservation of, 639–641, 700, 701
    scientific methods for, 637–639
Forest preservation, 511, 628, 638
    Sunken Forest, 810
Forestry certification program, 449
Forest Stewardship Council (FSC), 106, 246, 449–450
Formosa Plastics Corporation, 871
Forsman, Eric, 305
Fort Laramie Treaty (1868), 795
Fort Wayne Astronomical Society, 501
Fossey, Dian, **302–304**
Fossil fuels, 216, 323, 368, 369, 418
Foundation for Deep Ecology, 234
Four Corners region (U.S.), 94, 383
Fox, Richard, 197
Fox, Robert F., Jr., 199
Fox, Stephen, 433
Fox Television, 224
France, 217
Francisco, Jefford, 400
Frank, Bernard, 500
Franklin, Jerry, **304–306**
Freedom of information, 747

French-intensive/biodynamic gardening, 380
French nuclear testing, 45
French Prix Mondial del Duca, 567
Fresh water management, 647, 649
Friendly Hills Health Action Group, 22, 23
Friends of Pronatura, 579
Friends of the Earth (FOE), 117, 632
Friends of the Sea Otter, 618, 620
Frome, Michael, **306–309**
"From the Back Country," 129
Front Street project, 199
Fruit farming, problems associated with, 867
Fuel efficiency, 336
Fulbright scholar (U. of Fortaleza), 215
Fulbright senior scholarship, 542
Fuller, Buckminster, **309–312**
Fuller, Kathryn, **312–313**
Funders Working Group on New Technologies, 231, 232
Furbearing animals, 288
Fur Seal Act (1966), 543
Fur seal protection, 398
Futrell, J. William, **314–316**

Gabrielson, Ira N., 893
Gagliano, Sherwood M., **319–320**
Galapagos Islands, 70
Galvin, Peter, 786
Game animals, 682
    conservation of, 345
Game management, 478
Gap Inc., 526
Garbage collection, City of New York, 845–846
Garden Cities, 499
Gardening, 104, 108, 176, 256
Garden Project, 759, 760
Gas drilling, 93, 301
Geddes, Patrick, 565
Geisel, Theodor (Dr. Seuss), **320–322**
Gelbspan, Ross, **323–325**
General Motors (GM), 64, 401, 578
General Wild Life Fund (GWLF, later National Wildlife Federation [NWF]), 223
Genesco Corporation, 144
Genetically modified bacteria, 676
Genetic code, 375
Genetic diversity, of heirloom seeds, 855
Genetic engineering, 375
    protests against, 818

Genetic erosion, 854, 855
Genetic resources, 375
Genetic sequencing, 375
Genuine Progress Indicator (GPI), 448
Geodesic dome design, 311
Geographic information systems (GIS), 531
George Polk award, 515
Geothermal areas, 865
Germany, 217
Get America Working, 259
Gibbs, Lois, 122, **325–327,** 464
Gifford Pinchot National Forest, 304
Gila National Forest, 478
Giraffe Award for Environmental Whistleblowing, 230
Girl Pioneers (later Camp Fire Girls), 745
Glacier National Park, 261, 346
Glacier View Dam, 259, 261
Gleason, Henry Allan, **327–328**
Glen Canyon Dam, 3, 116, 384
    demolishing to drain Lake Powell, 853
    public support for the decommissioning of, 474, 475
Global Biodiversity Hotspots, 553
Global Business Network (GBN), 108, 847
Global economy, 389
Global Forest Policy Project, 106
Global Forum of Spiritual and Parliamentary Leaders, 495
Global Green, 236
Global Greengrants Fund, 799, 801–802
Global Green Millennium Awards, 237
Global Public Media, 217, 219
Global Response, 626
Global warming, 224, 225, 236, 289, 323, 368, 422, 440, 765, 766
    consequences of, 678
    and rise in sea level, 816
Global Warming Solutions Act (2006), 732, 798
*Global Warming Twenty Years Later: Tipping Points Near*, 998–1001
Global Water Policy Project, 647
Gokee, Victoria, 113
Gold Dust Twins, 415
Golden Globe Award, 236
Gold, Lou, **329–330**
Goldman Environmental Award, 470

# INDEX

Gold Medal of the New York Zoological Society, 618
Golten, Robert, **331–332**
Goodall, Jane, 302
Goodman, Paul, **333–335**
Gore, Albert, Jr., 225, **335–337**
Gorgas Science Foundation, 844
Gorillas, 302, 303
Gottlieb, Robert, **338–341**
Gould, Stephen Jay, **341–343**
Governor's Energy Office (GEO), 681
Governor's Writers Award, 267
Grains, perennial, 418
Grand Canyon dams, 833
Grand Staircase–Escalante National Monument, 336
Grand Teton National Park, 583, 689
Grape boycott, 557
Grassroots efforts
　against dam within national park or monument, 893–894
　destructive river development projects, 473
　against environmental racism, 126–127
　to establish grizzly bear recovery program, 865
　funding to, 801
　municipal solid waste incinerator, 195
　against northern Wisconsin's copper mines, 114
　against ozone-destroying CFCs, 464
　for social justice, 17
　sustainable mining, 184
　wilderness preservation, 894
Grawemeyer Award for ideas for improving World Order, 216
Gray, Asa, **343–345**, 910–912
Grazing land, 180
Great American Station Foundation, 243
Great Barrier Reef, researches on, 611
Great Britain, 741
Great Depression, 233
GreaterGood.com, 364
Greater London Area War Risk Study (GLAWARS), 283
Greater Yellowstone Coalition (GYC), 864–865
Great Hudson River Revival, 737
Great Lakes Bioneer of the Year, 550
Great Lakes ecosystem, 184–185

Great Plains ecosystems, 717
Great Plains Restoration Council, 646
Great Salt Lake, 869
Great Smoky Mountain National Park, 307, 409
Green Apple Festival, 749
Green consumerism, 818
Green evangelism, 178
Green Guerillas, 176–177
Greenhouse gas, 367, 506, 534, 726, 733, 797, 859
　reduction of, 733
　role of, 726
"Greening of the Future," 796
Green Jobs Act (2007), 435, 436
Green Leaf Award, 440
Green movement (U.S.), 747
GreenOrder, 748
Green parties, 295
Greenpeace, 44–45, 428, 610, 801, 848
Green revolution, 749
Green Seal, 382
Green Teams, 759
Greenwashing, American culture, 817
GreeNYC, 99
Grey Nuns of the Sacred Heart, 85
Grinnell, George Bird, **345–347**
Grizzly bears, 144, 208, 461, 629, 630
　habitat for, 462
　protection and wilderness conservation, 210
　recovery program, 865
　in Yellowstone National Park, 209–210
Grizzly Gulch, 462
Grizzly People, 866
Grogan, Pete, **347–349**
Grossman, Richard L., **349–351**
Gross National Product (GNP), 216, 387
Groundwater Protection Policy and Action Plan, 752
Group of Ten environmental leaders, 45, 118, 636
"Growthmania" economics, 216
Guano islands, birds in, 837
Guatemala, 60, 197, 198, 248, 442, 867
Guggenheim Fellowship, 630
Gulf Coast of Florida, 223
Gulf Coast wildlife, 872–873
Gulf of Mexico, 250
GulfStream Liberal, 225

Gussow, Joan Dye, **352–354**
Guthrie, Woody, **354–357**, 736
Gutiérrez, Juana Beatriz, **357–359**

Haas, Robert, 474
Habitat
　conservation, 723
　degradation, 768
　restoration, 227
Hague, Arnold, 721
Hair, Jay, **363–365**
Hallwachs, Winnie, 422
Hamilton, Alice, **365–367**
Hands Across the Border, 580
Hannover Principles, 526, 961–962
Hansen, James E., **367–369**, 998–1001
Hardin, Garrett, **370–372**
Hard Rock Mining Law (1872), 378
Harp seals, protection of, 848
Harrelson, Woody (Woody Boyd), **372–374**
Harry, Debra, **374–376**
Hartshorne, Charles, 182
Harvey, Dorothy Webster, **376–379**
Hatfield, Mark, 438
Hawaii, 130, 233, 270, 415, 690, 780
Hawken, Paul, 25–26, **379–381**
Hawkes, Graham, 276
Hawk Mountain, 278
Hawk Mountain Reserve, 132
Hawk Mountain Sanctuary (Pa.), 277, 278
Hawks, 135, 278, 650, 744, 809
Hayes, Denis, **382–383**
Hayes, Randy, **383–385**
Hays, Samuel P., **385–387**
Hayswood Nature Reserve, 387
Hazardous air levels, in Los Angeles, 851
Hazardous emissions control program, 39, 851
Hazardous Substance Response Trust Fund, 551–552
Hazardous waste, 326, 783
　disposal of, 123, 298, 551, 555
　incinerator, 357
　management, 315, 789
　public awareness of, 451
　against the Upjohn Corporation, 463
Hazardous Waste Site Control Division, 452
Headwaters Forest Agreement, 394
Health and safety, 526, 530
　in Packingtown, 529
　pesticides effects on, 556, 557

Health risks
  dioxin, 195
  indoor cooking, 198
  toxic waste disposal, 122–123
Heartwood School (Mass.), 19
Heavy metals, 752, 791
Heineken Prize for Environmental Science, 217
Heinz Award, 588
Heirloom seeds, genetic diversity of, 855
Hemp, 372, 373
Henderson, Hazel, **387–389**
Henderson molybdenum mine, environmental impact of, 811
Heritage Farm, 855, 856
Hermach, Tim, **390–392**
Hetch Hetchy Valley, 186, 187, 434, 547, 894
Hetchy, Hetch, 187
*High Country News*, 514, 515, 524
Highlander Center (Tenn.), 350
Highway Beautification Act (1965), 431
Hill, Julia Butterfly, **392–395**
Historic Orchard, 855
Hitchcock, Ethan, 434
H. J. Andrews Experimental Forest, 304, 305, 306
H. J. Heinz Corporation, 470
Hoagland, Edward, **395–397**
Hoar, George F., 268
Hollywood, 217
Home design and construction, 19
Homestead Act, 653
Honduras stove program, 197–198
Honorary Right Livelihood Award, 217
Hood Canal, 755
Hooker Chemicals and Plastics Corporation, 122
Hooper, Marian, 9
Hoover Commission Task Force on Natural Resources, 858
Hoover Dam, 35, 410
HOPE Worldwide, 200
Hopi Foundation, 802–803
Horace Marden Albright Scenic Preservation Medal, 690
Hornaday, William Temple, 222, **397–399**
Horticulture Project, 759
Houma Indians, 784
House, Donna, **399–402**
Household use of water in East Africa, study of, 858

Housing, 311, 566, 572
  affordable, 29, 30, 552
  legislation, 62
  and transportation, 822
  and urban planning, 61
Housing and Urban Development, Department of (HUD), 61
Houston (Tx.), 215
Hovingh, Peter, 378
Hoxsey project, 37
Huckleberry Land Exchange, 97
Hudson River, 256, 737, 750
Hudson River Expressway, 755
Hudson River Fishermen's Association (HRFA, now Hudson Riverkeeper), 458
Hudson River School of Painting, 189
Hudson River Sloop Restoration, 737
Huerta, Dolores, 172, **402–405**
Hughes, Howard, 236
Hull House, 13, 14, 48, 366, 528
Humane Society International, 470
Human genetic code. *See* Genetic code
Human immunodeficiency virus (HIV), 430
Humanism, 263, 279, 833
Humanist ecology, 342
Humanitas Prize, 225
Human rights, 375, 777
Humboldt National Forest, 378
Humphrey, Robert M., 416
Hunting, 27, 32, 113, 132. *See also* Game animals
Hurricane Katrina, 319
Hybridization, 157
Hydroelectric dam, 364
Hypercar, Inc., 491

Ice crystals, 766
Ickes, Harold, 260, **409–411**
Idaho, 27–28
Idaho Cooperative Wildlife Research Unit (U. of Idaho), 111
Idaho Land Use Planning Act (1975), 28
IDEAS, 49
Ikeda, Daisaku, 389
Illegal whaling, 849
Illinois Environmental Protection Agency (IEPA), 429
Imaflora (Brazil), 248, 868
Immigrants
  foreign-born, 565

  from Italy and Germany, 397
  Mexican, 4
  Norwegian, 415
  pensions for, 403
  Russian-Jewish, 100
Immune systems, 765
INBio (National Biodiversity Institute; Costa Rica), 286, 421, 423
Incinerator, 790
  regulations of, 125
  *See also* Municipal waste incinerator
Index of Sustainable Economic Welfare, 216
India, 281
Indiana, 220
Indiana Dunes, 205
Indian Creek Woods, 387
Indian rights movement, 812
Indicator species, 279, 305
Indigenous Environmental Network, 796, 813
Indigenous peoples, 542
  and cultural preservation, 518
  culture of, 401, 625–626
  ecosystem and tradition conservation, 639–640
  landscape restoration by, 517
  and medicinal plants, 640
  right to self determination, 375
Indigenous People's Restoration Network (IPRN), 517–518
Indigenous Women's Network, 471, 473
Indigo Girls, 473
Individualistic-species model, 328
Industrial cities, social reform in, 14
Industrial food systems, 352
Industrial pollution, 747
Industrial toxins, 365
Industrial Workers of the World, 252
Infectious diseases, 323
Ingram, Helen, **411–412**
Insects
  communication, 284
  ecology, 422
Institut de la Vie Prize, 604
Institute for Behavioral Science (IBS) (U. of Colorado), 858
Institute for Deep Ecology, 20
Institute for Fisheries Resources, 670
Institute for Food and Development Policy (also Food First), 476
Institute for Social Ecology, 102

# Index

Institute for Sustainable Communities (ISC), 204
Institute for the Arts of Democracy (now the Center for Living Democracy), 477
Institutional racism, 29
Intelligence quotients (IQs), 587
Interamerican Foundation for Tropical Research (FIIT), 867
Intercollegiate Social Society, 234–235
Interface, Inc. (now Interface Flooring Systems, Inc.), 25
Interfaith Solidarity Walks, 20
Intergovernmental Panel on Climate Change (IPCC), 335, 505, 727, 799, 815
Intermodal Surface Transportation Efficiency Act (ISTEA), 242
International Bering Sea Forum, 544
International Council for Bird Preservation, 636
International Forum on Globalization (IFG), 504
International free trade, ideology of, 216
International Institute of Concern for Public Health (IICPH), 86
International Prize for Biology, 665
International Rivers Network (IRN), 473–474
International Sonoran Desert Alliance (ISDA), 579, 580
International trade, 312
International Visual Communications Association, 236
Internet, 748
   broadcasting station, 219
Intertribal Bison Cooperative, 646
Invertebrate paleontology, 342
Ionizing radiation, 882
Iowa, 220
Ironwood Forest, 576
Iroquois, 160, 495, 903
Irrigation, 833
   ditch systems, 717
Irrigation Survey Act, 654
Island biogeography, 873
Italy, 217
Izaak Walton League Hall of Fame, 614
Izaak Walton League of America (IWLA), 238

Jackson, Henry (Scoop), **415–417**
Jackson Hole Preserve, 689
Jackson Hole Wildlife Park, 618
Jackson, Wes, **417–419**
Jacobs, Carol, 954–955
Jacobson, Michael, **419–421**
James Beard Award, 642
James Tiptree Jr. award, 704
Janzen, Daniel H., **421–423**
Jean Lafitte National Park, 297
Jensen, Derrick, **424–425**
Jerry Mander & Associates, 503
Joe A. Callaway Award, 556
John Burroughs Medal, 536, 575, 614
John Gardner Leadership Award, 327
John Heinz Environmental Award, 369
John Muir Award, 525, 570
John Muir Institute, 117
John Rieger Service Award, 518
Johnson, Glenn S., **425–428**
Johnson, Hazel, **428–430**
Johnson, Lady Bird (Claudia Alta), **431–432**
Johnson, Louisa Catherine, 12
Johnson, Lyndon B., 370, 431, 570, 894
Johnson, Robert Underwood, **433–435**
John Wesley Powell Award, 536
Joint Public Advisory Committee on Environmental Cooperation (JPAC), 80
Jones, Van, **435–436**
Jontz, Jim, **437–438**
Jordan, Chris, **439–441**
Journalism, 253, 254
Juana de la Cruz, Sor, 5
Jukofsky, Diane, **441–442**
Jules Verne Adventure Film Festival Audience Choice Award, 236

Kaho'olawe Island Reserve Commission, 517
Kamp, Dick, **445–446**
Kane, Hal, **446–448**
Kansas City, 226
Kansas City Wildlands, 227
Kansas Master Teacher Award, 227
Kaplow, David, 517
Karisoke Research Center, 302
Katz, Daniel, **449–451**
Kaufman, Hugh, **451–453**, 719
Kellert, Stephen, **453–455**
Kendall, Henry, **456–457**
Kennebunk Chemical Center, 168
Kennedy, Jackie, 431
Kennedy, Robert F., Jr., 224, **457–460**
Kerr-McGee Nuclear Corporation, 753
Kerry, John, 237
Keystone species, 768
Kidney disease, 752
Kids Against Junk Food, 420
Kids for the Environment fund, 879
Kimbal, Jim, 378
King, Gordon, 235
Kings Canyon (Calif.), 116
Kings Canyon National Park, 277
Kingsolver, Barbara, **460–461**
Kisatchie National Forest woodlands, 314
Klamath–Siskiyou bioregion, 329
Knight Commander of the British Empire, 567
Koehler, Bart, 300
Koford, Carl, 579
Kootenai National Forest, 228
Kratt Brothers' Creature Heroes, 461, 462
Kratt, Chris, and Martin Kratt, **461–463**
*Kratts' Creatures*, 461, 462
Krupp, Fred, **463–465**
Kunin, Medeleine, 68
Kwantlen College (Richmond, British Columbia), 219
Kyoto prize, 423
Kyoto Protocol, 336, 594, 952–953

Labor Housing Conference (LHC), 62
Labor organizing. *See* Union organizing
Labor union movement, 53
LaBudde, Samuel, **469–471**
Lacey Act (1900), 166, 268, 313, 346
Lacey, John F., 268
LaDuke, Winona, **471–473**
Lafayette Park, 256
Lake Chelan National Recreation Area, 271
Lakeside Nature Center, 227
Lake Superior, 113
Lakota Sioux, 771
Lakota Solar Enterprises, 665, 666
Lammers, Owen, **473–475**
Lancer Project, 159
Land and minerals management, 244
Land and Resource Management Planning Process, 757
Land and Water Conservation Fund, 416

# INDEX

Land conservation, 479, 819–820, 826
Land ethic, 245, 479
Landfills, 428
Land management
 agencies, 245
 decision makers, 400
 by private landowners, 66
Land-preservation compromise agreement, 124
Landscape architecture, 607, 608, 609
Land use, 232, 768
 and planning, 643, 644, 645, 646
 policy, 338, 415
Lannan Literary Award, 606
Lannan Prize, 534
La Paz agreement, 445–446
Lappé, Frances Moore, **475–477**
*Large Mammal Restoration*, 599
Latin America
 culture of, 215
 U.S. involvement in resource exploitation in, 119
 *See also* Brazil; Colombia; Costa Rica; Nicaragua; Peru
Lavelle, Rita, 451, 452, 719
Lawrence Berkeley National Laboratory (LBNL), 702
Lead, 193
Leaded gasoline, banning of, 193
Lead Poison Awareness Program, 160
Leadership in Energy and Environment Design (LEED) Platinum certification, 199
League of Conservation Voters, 11, 43, 72, 115, 117, 125, 165, 230, 243, 265
Leatherstocking, 201–202
*Leaves of Grass*, 861, 862, 863
Lee, Charles, 18
Legal rights, 779
Leonardo DiCaprio Foundation, 236
Leopold, Aldo, 223, 233, **478–479**
 pre-*Almanac* literary and philosophical essays, 140
Letter to Asa Gray, 910–912
Lewis and Clark Trail, 223
Lewis Center for Environmental Studies, 527
Liberation theology, 706
Libertarian socialist movement, 100
Liebold, Mathew, 288
Lifeline Program, 286
*Life Magazine*, 578

Lifestyle, 29, 71, 72, 83, 121, 230, 256
Lifetime Achievement Awards, 525
*Limits to Growth*, excerpt, 941–945
Lindbergh, Anne Morrow, and Charles Augustus Lindbergh, **480–482**
Linnaeus, 59
Littletree, Alicia, **482–484**
Livestock, 418, 773
 grazing, 410, 720
 production, 682, 683
Living Music Records, 875
Living Oceans Program, 709
Living Rivers, 473, 475
Lloyd, William Forster, 370
L. L. Winship/PEN New England Award, 605
Locally unwanted land uses (LULUs), 127
Logging. *See* Timber, extraction
Logging industry, 245
Lomax, Alan, 356, 736
London, 217
Long Now Foundation, 108–109
Lopez, Barry, **484–486**
Los Alamos National Laboratory, 493
Los Angeles (Ca.), 338
Lott, Neal, 963–978
Loudon, J.C., 256
Louisiana Bucket Brigade (LABB), 693
Louisiana Environmental Action Network, 296, 299
Louisiana Pacific, 483, 841
Louisiana State University (Baton Rouge), 215, 216
Louv, Richard, **486–487**
Love Canal Homeowners Association (LCHA), 326
Love Canal toxic waste crisis, 79, 122–123
 Superfund legislation, 154
Lovejoy, Thomas, **488–489**
Lovins, Amory, and Hunter Lovins, **490–492**
Luce, Benjamin, **492–494**
Luddites, 714, 715
Ludlow massacre, 687
Lujan, Manuel, 43
Lumber-harvesting, 437
Lumberjacks, 760
Lung cancer, 739
Lyndhurst Prize, 616
Lynn White Thesis, 860
Lyons, Oren, **494–496**

Lyticobodig, research for treatment of, 208

Maathai, Wangari, 237
MacAir, Helen Avis, 235
MacArthur Foundation, 575, 665, 784
MacArthur, Robert, 488
MacKaye, Benton, **499–500**
Macy, Joanna, 20
Mader, Ron, **500–503**
Magna Carta, 416
Magnuson, Warren, 415
Maine Indian Lands Claim settlement (1980), 551
MaintaiNYC, 99
Malthus, Thomas, 56
Mammals, 166, 403, 453, 485, 524, 558, 876
*Man and Nature*, 913
Mander, Jerry, **503–505**
Manifesto on Global Economic Transitions, excerpt, 995–997
Manning, Richard, **507–509**
Mann, Michael E., **505–507**
Mapes, James, 844
Marckwald, Kirk, 232
Marine conservation, 709
Marine ecosystem
 destruction by driftnet fishing, 470
 endangered marine life and, 709
 terrestrial and, 881
Marine fishing, 711
Marine Institute (U. of Georgia), 604
Marine Mammal Fund (MMF), 469
Marine Mammal Protection Act (1972), 240
Marine mammals, 453, 524
Marine wildlife
 laws and regulations governing, 849
 protection of, 848–849
Marjorie Carr Cross-Florida Greenway, 148, 149
Marlboro Man, 594
Marshall, Ray, 91
Marshall, Robert, 409, **512–513**, 890, 894
Marsh-Billings-Rockefeller National Historical Park, 690
Marsh, George Perkins, **510–511**, 913
Marston, Betsy, and Ed Marston, **514–516**
Martínez, Dennis, **516–518**

# INDEX

Martin Litton Environmental Warrior Award, 237
Martin Marietta, 23
Maser, Chris, 305
Massachusetts Institute of Technology (MIT), 537, 650, 673
Mather, Stephen, 15, 16, 260, **519–521,** 889
Matthiessen, Peter, **521–523**
Mattison, Jim, 620
Maya Biosphere Reserve, 248
Mazamas (mountaineering and conservation organization), 773, 774
McCain, John, 225
McClellan, Roz, 758
McCloskey, Michael, **523–525**
McDonald's Corporation, 464
McDonnell, Father Donald, 172
McDonough Braungart Design Chemistry (MBDC), 526
McDonough + Partners project, 526
McDonough, William, **525–527**
McDowell, Mary (Fighting Mary), 14, **528–530**
McGovern, George, 231
McHarg, Ian, **530–532**
McKibben, Bill, 237, **532–534**
McKinsey & Company, 257
McPhee, John, **534–536**
Mead, Margaret, 858
Meadow Networks, 171
Meadows, Dennis, 941–945
Meadows, Donella H., **536–538,** 941–945
Meany, Edmond, **538–540**
Medal of Honor, 618
Medal of the Presidency (Italian Republic), 217
Media, 21, 45, 93, 118, 199, 217. *See also* Television
Medical and pharmaceutical extracts from plants, 640–641
Medicinal plants, 640
Memphis design, 845
Mendel Medal, 697
Mendocino Environmental Center (MEC), 48, 50
Merchant, Carolyn, **540–542**
Merco Joint Venture, 452
Merculieff, Ilarion (Larry), **542–544**
Merriam, Clinton Hart, 47
Merriam, Clinton Levi, 46–47
Meta Foundation, 219
Mexico-U.S. border, 445–446

Michigan, 220
Microbiology, 262
Mid-America Education Hall of Fame, 227
Migratory Bird Act (1913), 347, 398
Migratory Species Project, 231, 232
Miller, Laura, **545–546**
Mills, Enos, **546–548**
Mills, Stephanie, **548–550**
Milltown Dam, 780, 782
Mineral King Valley, 779
Minimum Critical Size of Ecosystems Project (now Biological Dynamics of Forest Fragments Project), 488
Mining
  phosphate, 378
  uranium, 374
Minnesota, 113, 142, 246, 247
Mississippi River Basin Alliance, 296, 299
Missouri Botanical Garden, 664–665
Mitchell, George J., **550–552**
MIT Faculty Statement of Union of Concerned Scientists, 925
Mittermeier, Russell, **553–554**
Mobilization for the Human Family (now Progressive Christians Uniting), 183
Model Cities Act (1966), 570, 571
Mohawk Indians and Canadian government authorities, 495
"Monitored retrievable storage" (MRS) study grants, 813
Montague, Peter, **554–556**
Montana Woodland Caribou Ecology Project, 144
Montreal Protocol, 766
Moore, John Gilmer, 475–476
Moratorium on drilling in geothermal areas, 865
Moretta, John, 159
Morris Run Coal Company, 584
Moses, Marion, **556–558**
Moss, Cynthia, **558–559**
Moss, Doug, **560–562**
Mother Earth, 95–96
Mothers of East Los Angeles (MELA), 159
Mothers of East Los Angeles Water Conservation Program, 358
Motor vehicle emission standards, 851
Motor Vehicle Safety Act, 578
Mountain Grove Center, 518
Mountain lions, 93, 209, 618, 619

Mountaintop mining, 264
Mount Graham, environmental impact of astronomical telescope building in, 847
Mount Mazama, 773
Mount Ranier National Park, 253
Mount Saint Helens, 51
Mount Sinai Medical Center, 738
Muir Investment Trust, 231, 232
Muir, John, 187, 233, **562–565,** 721
Multicultural Motion Picture Association, 236
Mumford, Lewis, 500, **565–567**
Municipal forests, 247
Municipal waste incinerator, 194–195
Murie, Mardy, and Olaus Murie, **568–570**
Museum of Life and the Environment on the Catawba River, 527
Musical instruments, 736
Muskie, Edmund, **570–572,** 895
Mutualism, 422
Myers, John Peterson, 183
Myers, Norman, 873, 874
myspace.com, 225
"The Myth of Chief Seattle," 956–960

Nabhan, Gary, **575–577**
Nader, Ralph, **577–578,** 895
Naess, Arne, 233
Nagel, Carlos, **579–581**
Name, Willard Van, 277
Nash, Roderick, **581–583**
National Academy of Science, 507
National Aeronautics and Space Administration (NASA), 275, 367, 712, 726
National Association for the Advancement of Colored People (NAACP), 174
National Association of Audubon Societies, 269
National Association of Biology Teachers, 227
National Association of Evangelicals (NAE), 178–179, 979
National Audubon Society, 78, 79, 223, 346, 570, 619, 634, 636, 709
  award of, 156
  medal, 620
National Biodiversity Institute (INBio), 421
National Biological Service, 599
National Black United Fund, 17

# INDEX

National Book Award, 531, 567, 605, 704
National Book Critics Circle nomination, 670
National Cancer Institute (NCI), 207
National Center for Atmospheric Research (NCAR), 726
National Clean Air Coalition, 39
National Clearinghouse on Intimidation and Disruption, 483
National Coalition Against Surrogacy, 676
National Conservation Achievement Award, 616
National Conservation Association, 639
National Council of Churches, 225
National Design Award, 527
National Endowment for the Arts grant, 20
National Environmental Council, 813
National Environmental Council of Native Americans (NECONA), 812, 813
National Environmental Justice Advisory Council (NEJAC), 127
National Environmental Policy Act (NEPA) (1969), 78, 79, 111, 137, 138, 315, 378, 386, 415, 416, 755, 811
National Estuary Program, 165
National Farm Workers Association (NFWA), 172, 173, 403
National Forest Commission, 638
National Forest Protection and Restoration Act (NFPRA), 392
National Indicators Program, 448
National Institutes of Health (NIH), 676
National Institutes of Health Primate Ecology, 579
National Landscape Conservation System, 43, 44
National Magazine Award, 254
National Marine Fisheries Service (NMFS), 469
National Medal for Literature, 567
National Medal of Arts, 567
National Medal of Science, 665
National Oceanic and Atmospheric Administration (NOAA), 276, 655
National Outdoor Leadership School (NOLS), 864
National Ozone Expedition, 766
National parks, 16, 501, 519
  automotive industry and railroad companies support to, 889
  conservation of, 610, 689, 697, 699
  exploitation of timber and minerals within, 131
  preservation in, 524
  Tortuguero, 147
  tourist development in, 564
  Yosemite, 8
National Parks Association (NPA; now National Parks and Conservation Association [NPCA]), 131, 260, 612, 614, 655, 889–890
National Park Service Act, 7, 15–16, 520, 889
National Park Service (NPS), 16, 131, 209, 259, 610
National Park System lands, principle of inviolability of, 894
National Park Trust (NPT), 655
National Pesticide Control Act, 588
National Public Service Award, 259
National Riparian Conservation Areas, 786
National Science Foundation's Ethics and Values in Science and Technology Program, 596
National Traffic Act, 578
National Wilderness Preservation System, 416, 894
National Wildflower Research Center, 432
National Wildlife Federation (NWF), 105–106, 111, 220, 223, 331, 363, 589, 616, 677
  awards of, 128, 225, 455
  conservation stamp program, 634
Nation of Islam, 176
Native Alaskans, claims of, 79
Native Americans, 513
  fishing rights, 805
  paintings of, 160
  subjected to environmental racism, 796
  treaty rights and environmental movements, 113
Native Forest Council, 230, 390
Native Forest Protection Act (1989), 391
Native plants, 401, 431, 548
Native Resource Coalition (NRC), 796
Native Seeds/SEARCH, 576
NativeSUN project, 802, 803
Natural Area Council, 650, 651
Natural Capital Institute, 381
Natural history, 341
Natural Lakes Preservation Act, 588
Natural Land Institute, 624
Natural resources
  destruction of, 769
  extraction and commodification of, 375
  sustainable management of, 638
Natural Resources Defense Council (NRDC), 224, 236, 669, 865
  cofounder of, 38
  functionality of, 11
  objective of, 10, 38
Natural rubber, 729
Natural Step (TNS), 610, 612
Natural Systems Agriculture (NSA), 417
*Nature*, 905-906
Nature
  basic human relationship to, 453–454
  conservation programs, 700–701
  dichotomy between culture and, 140
  and human, 642
  preservation of, 627, 628, 636, 697–699
Nature Conservancy, 649, 651, 723, 810
Nature-deficit disorder, 487
Nature writing, 612
Navajo communities, 750, 752
Navajo Natural Heritage Program, 400
Nearing, Helen, and Scott Nearing, **584–586**
Needleman, Herbert, **586–588**
Nelson, Gaylord, **588–589**
Nelson, Willie, **590–591**
Netroots, 225
Nevada Test Site, nuclear weapons testing at, 801
New America Foundation (NAF)
  climate agenda's five program areas of, 798
  objective of, 797
New Deal welfare programs, 223
New Directions Grant Program, 92
New Forestry, 304, 305, 306

# INDEX

Newman, Nell, **591–593**
Newman, Penny, 464
New Road Map Foundation, 684
News of Earth 2000, 741
New York City, 225
    drinking water, protection of source of, 459
    Environmental Defense Fund, 593
New York Zoological Park (also Bronx Zoo), 397
New York Zoological Society (NYZS), 69, 70, 346, 553, 554, 616
Niagara Falls, 122, 325, 326, 608
Nicaragua, 119, 197, 198, 422, 599, 878
Nickels, Greg, **594–596**
Nigeria, 694
Nobel Prize, 335, 369, 423
Nongovernmental organizations (NGOs), 228
Nonpolluting sources, of energy, 382
Nonviolent Peaceforce, 21
North American Free Trade Agreement (NAFTA), 438, 446, 580
North Branch Prairie Project, 623
North Branch Restoration Project, 623
North Cascades National Park, 415
North Cascades Scenic Highway, 271
Northern Forest Council, 68
Northwest Environment Watch (later Sightline Institute), 266
Northwood Manor landfill, 127
Norton, Bryan, **596–598**
Noss, Reed, **598–600**
Nuclear accident, 631–632
Nuclear fallout, 100, 192, 338, 554, 868
Nuclear power, 350
Nuclear power plants
    opposition to, 100
    workers' and community exposure to, 196
Nuclear war, 713
Nuclear waste disposal, 813
Nuclear Waste Management Policy Act, 829
Nuclear weapons policy, 712
Nuclear winter, 713
Nutrition education, 352
Nutrition Facts labels, 420
Nutrition labeling, 419

Nutrition Labeling and Education Act (1990), 420

Oakes, John, 810
Oasis Preserve International, 372
Oberholtzer, Ernest, 500, 513, 890
Occupational medicine, 557, 738, 739
Occupational Safety and Health Act (OSH Act; 1970, 1978), 578, 587
Occupational Safety and Health Administration (OSHA), 91, 92, 578
Occupational safety laws, 366
Oceanic Society, 632
Odum, Eugene, 288, **603–605**
Office of Government Ethics, 718
Office of Technology Assessment (OTA), 388, 719
Offshore wind energy farm, 750
Oglala Lakota (Sioux), 795
Oglala Sioux, 896
O. Henry Memorial Prize, 250
Ohio Canal, 271
Ohio River Valley, 789
Oil, 533
    drilling of, 124, 364
    embargo, 240
    exploration, 522, 750
    global production of, 219
    pipeline, 159
    refinery, 250
    shale, 378
    spill prevention, 551
    transport of, 364, 551
Oil Depletion Protocol, 219
Oilfield waste treatment, 784
Oil Pollution Act (1990), 165, 551
Ojibwe, 114, 472
Ojito Wilderness, 717
Okeechobee Lake, 250
Oliver, Mary, **605–606**
Olmsted, Frederick Law, Jr., **609–610**
Olmsted, Frederick Law, Sr., **607–609,** 845
Olsen, Marilyn, 879, 880
Olson, Molly Harriss, **610–612**
Olson, Sigurd, **612–614**
Olympic Coast Alliance (OCA), 271
Olympic National Park, 253, 270, 271, 277
One Bryant Park, 199–200
Open Space Coordinating Council (COSCC), 810
Open Space Institute, 11, 651

Open Space Sales Tax, 811
OpeNYC, 99. *See also* PlaNYC
Oregon Student Public Interest Research Group, 578
Organically produced food, 379
Organic farming, 691–693, 758
Organization of Tropical Studies (OTS), 421
Organochlorine pesticides, 135
Organ Pipe Cactus National Monument, 576
Orme Dam, 751
Orr, David, **615–616**
Osborn, Fairfield, **616–618,** 915–918
*Our Plundered Planet*, 915–918
Outdoor Advertising Association of America, 432
Outdoor Recreation Institute (now Craighead Environmental Research Institute [CERI]), 210
Outdoor Recreation Resources Review Commission (ORRRC), 689
*Outside* Magazine, 502
Outstanding Biology Teacher Award, 227
Overbrook Foundation, The, 450
Overpopulation, effects of, 636
Overseas Development Council, 120
Owings, Margaret, **618–620**
Ozone hole, 765

Pacific Creek Redwoods State Park, 619
Pacific Environment & Resources Center (PERC; now Pacific Environment), 448
Pacific island, 192
Pacific Lumber, 483
Pacific Northwest, 252
Pacific Southwest Water Plan, 833
Packard, Steve, **623–625**
Palila bird, 780
Palmer, Paula, **625–627**
Palo Verde nuclear power plant, 751
Panos Institute, 17
Papago, 400, 575
Paper trade associations, 348
Pardisan Environmental Park, 531
Parkman, Francis, **627–629**
Parks
    public, 261
    urban, 256
Parque Nacional Santa Rosa, 422
Participatory Action Research (PAR), 626

Patents, 375
Paul Winter Consort, 875
Paul Winter Sextet, 875
Pawnee, 347
Payette National Forest, 378
Pay-per-drive car rental, 171
PCB (polychlorinated biphenyl) contamination, 53, 175
Peacock, Doug, **629–631**
Peak Oil, concept of, 219
Peanuts, 158
Pearson, T. Gilbert, 269
Peary, Robert, 485, 499
Pelican Island Wildlife Refuge, 701
Pendleton, Genevieve, 223
People of color
    exposure to toxics, 29–30
    funding for, 17
People of Color Environmental Leadership Summit (Washington, D.C.; 1991), 17, 18, 127
People's Business Commission (now Foundation on Economic Trends, The), 675
People's League for Action Now (PLAN), 811
Peregrine falcons, 135
Peregrine Fund, 136
Perez Prize, 38
Perkins, Jane, **631–632**
Permanent Wild Life Fund (PWLF), 397, 398
Personal Sustainability Project, 854
Peru, 837
Peruvian Guano Administration Company, 837
Pesticide Education Center, 556, 557
Pesticides, 404, 437, 593, 778
    awareness of, 557
    health effects and, 588
    workers health and, 557
Peterson, Roger Tory (Bugs Peterson), **633–634**
Peterson, Russell, **635–636**
Peter Warshall and Associates, 847
Pew Fellowship in Conservation and the Environment, 599
Pew Scholarship on Conservation and Environment, 575
Peyote, 728
PG&E power company, 117
Pilgrim, Agnes, 517
Pilot whale, 740
Pinchot, Gifford, 109, 141, 245, 246, 304, 308, 397, 434, 499, 512, 608, **637–639**

Pine Ridge Reservation, protection from environmental threats, 795–796
Pioneer Award, 531
Pioneer Precaution Award, 642
Pittman-Robertson bill (1937), 223
Plains Indians, 161
Planetariat, 75
Planet Drum Foundation, 75, 76
Planned Parenthood Federation, 837
"Plant materials centers" projects, 418
Plants, 517
    breeding, 417
    medicinal properties of, 640–641
    native, 516, 548, 664
    protection of, 664
    species, 343
PlaNYC, 99
Plotkin, Mark, **639–641**
Pluma National Forest, 517
Plum Creek International and Champion, 508
Plutonium safety violations, 753
*Pneumococcus*, 262
Pneumonia, study of, 262
PNM, 493
Poaching, 250, 279, 553, 559, 849
Poetry, 605, 606
Poetry Society of America's Shelley Memorial Prize, 606
Point Lobos League, 619
Political reform, 829
Pollan, Michael, **642–643**
Pollution, 321
    control of, 570, 571
    and public health, 18
    *See also* Air pollution; Greenhouse gas; Water pollution
Polychlorinated biphenyl (PCB), 352, 737
Polyvinyl chloride (PVC) plastic, 195
Pontchartrain Lake, 297
Popper, Deborah, and Frank Popper, **643–647**
Population biology, 767, 872
Population control, 370
    policy for, 371
Population growth
    problems due to, 57
    and resource degradation, 371
    study for food supply to, 120
Post Carbon Cities, 219
Post Carbon Institute, 217, 219, 220
Postel, Sandra, **647–649**

Pough, Richard, **649–652**
Powell, John Wesley, **652–654**
Powell, Lake, 473, 474, 475, 853
Powers, Joshua, 146
Premio Gaia Award, 575
"Presentation to the United Nations," 954–955
"Preserving Wildness," 83
Presidential Award, 527
Presidential Commission on Wildlife Restoration, 222
Presidential Medal of Freedom, 567, 570
President's Council on Sustainable Development (PCSD), 611
Prevention of Significant Deterioration program, 39
Pribilof Island, 398
Pribilof Islands National Maritime Wildlife Refuge, 544
Prince Mahidol Award, 588
Prince's Foundation, 243
Principles and Criteria for Natural Forest Management, 246
Principles of Environmental Justice, 946–947
Pritchard, Paul C., **654–656**
Private landholders, role in national conservation strategies, 88
Program on Corporations, Law and Democracy (POCLAD), 350
Progressive Los Angeles Network (PLAN), 339
Progressive Resources, Inc., 678
Project Pride, 432
Pryor, Cynthia, **657–658**
Public Broadcasting Service (PBS), 582, 713
Public education campaign, 376
Public Employees for Environmental Responsibility (PEER), 228, 230
Public Interest Communications (PIC), 504
Public Interest Program, 315
Public Interest Research Groups (PIRGs), 577
Public land activism, 97
Public lands policy, books on, 180–181
Public Media Center, 504
Public transit systems, 242
Public transportation, 243, 286
Public Welfare Foundation (PWF), 18
Puget Sound, 735

Pugsley Award, 261
Pulido, Laura, **658–660**
Pulitzer Prize, 9, 220, 222, 234, 253, 323, 481, 534, 605, 683, 874
Pulpwood, 244
Pushcart Prize VIII, 6
PVC (polyvinyl chloride) plastic, 195

Quayle, Dan, 668
Quetico-Superior area, 142, 613, 614

Race project, 17
Rachel Carson Award, 225, 588
Rachel Carson Council, Inc., 152
Rachel Carson Memorial Fund, 619–620
*Rachel's Environmental and Health Weekly*, 554
Racial justice. *See* Environmental justice; Environmental racism
Racial Justice, Commission for (CRJ; United Church of Christ), 174
Racism. *See* Environmental racism
Radioactive contamination, 869
Radioactive fallout and waste. *See* Nuclear fallout; Nuclear waste disposal
Radioactive materials, 754
Radio astronomy, 713
Radon Abatement Act, 851
RAID (Ridding Activism of Intimidation and Disruption), 50
Railroads & Clearcuts Campaign, 425
"Rainbow Warriors," 45
Raines, Howell, 747
Rain forest, 372, 786
  conservation, 442, 489, 639–641
  deforestation, 383
  *See also* Tropical rain forests
Rainforest Action Network (RAN), 232, 383
Rainforest Alliance, 248, 441, 442, 449–450, 866, 867
Rancho del Cielo program, 843–844
Randers, Jorgen, 941–945
Raptors, 28, 458, 459, 809
Rara Avis, 87
RARE II (Roadless Area Review Evaluation), 880
Rasmuson Foundation Award, 544
Raven, Peter, **663–665**
Raymond B. Bragg Award, 283
Reagan, Ronald, 28, 92, 118, 193, 372, 452

Reconnecting America, 243
Recreation, 141, 142, 148, 179, 180
Recyclable waste products, 348
Recycled building techniques, development of, 672
Recycling
  community programs for, 86, 347
  and composting, 72, 348
  depletable resources, of, 416
  facilities for, 349
  food scrap, of, 595
  postconsumer waste, of, 382
  solid waste, of, 30
Red Cloud, Henry, **665–667**
Red Cloud Renewable Energy Center, 665, 666
Redefining Progress, 447–448
Redwood forests, 233
  implications for clear-cutting of, 50
Redwood National Park, 233, 415, 503, 524
Redwood Summer, 54
Redwood Summer Justice Project, 483
*Reflections from the North Country*, 613
Regional ecology. *See under* Ecology
Regional Planning Association of America (RPAA), 62, 499, 566
Regional Transit Committee, 822
Re-greening of New York City. *See* PlaNYC
Reilly, William K., **667–669**
Reinhabitation, 75, 760
Reisner, Marc, **669–670**
Relocalization Network and Local Energy Farms, 219
Remote Access Chemical Hazards Electronic Library (RACHEL), 555
Renewable energy, 296, 309, 324, 384
  resources, 665, 666, 763
Renewing America's Food Traditions, 576
Reporter, 746
Reproductive systems, 184
Resource Conservation and Recovery Act (RCRA) (1976), 451, 718
Resource management, 832
Resources and Conservation Act, 416
Resources for the Future (RFF), 180

Reuters-IUCN Global Awards, 642
Reynolds, Michael, **670–672**
Richards, Ellen Swallow, **673–674**
Rich, Cliff, 219
Rich, Heather, 219
Rich/poor gap, 282
Ridding Activism of Intimidation and Disruption (RIDE), 50
Ridesharing. *See* Car-sharing
Rifkin, Jeremy, **675–677**
Right Livelihood Award
  1983, 492
  1987, 477
Ringo, Jerome C., **677–679**
Rio Grande ecosystem, 93
Ríos, Albina Ruíz, 258
Riparian reserves, 304
Ritter, Bill, Jr., **679–681**
River basin, 787
River development projects, 474
Riverkeeper Project, 224
River of Words Project, 474
R. J. Margolis Award, 509
Road building, 301, 330, 483, 774
Roadless Area Review Evaluation (RARE II), 880
Robbins, John, **682–684**
Robert Marshall Award, 614, 636
Robert Wood Johnson Foundation award, 694
Robin, Vicki, **684–686**
Rockefeller Brothers Fund, 120
Rockefeller Foundation, 60
Rockefeller, John D., Jr., **686–688**
Rockefeller, Laurance, **689–691**
Rockford Female Seminary (Illinois), 14
Rockwood Leadership Program, 232
Rocky Flats Nuclear Weapons Plant, 23
  illegal incineration at, 801
  protests at, 800, 821
Rocky Flats Truth Force (RFTF), 800
Rocky Mountain Biology Laboratory, 184
Rocky Mountain Institute (RMI), 490, 491–492
Rocky Mountain Peace and Justice Center, 24, 800–801
Rocky Mountains, 22, 89, 231, 266, 509, 652, 653, 757, 780
Rodale, Robert, **691–693**
Rodman Dam, 149
Rolfes, Anne, **693–695**
Rollins Environmental Services, 298

Rolston, Holmes, III, **695–697**
Roosevelt, Franklin D., 222, 409, **697–699**
Roosevelt, Teddy, 390
Roosevelt, Theodore, 346, **699–701**, 731
Rosenfeld, Arthur H., **702–703**
Ross Lake National Recreation Area, 271
Ross, Tom, 963–978
Roszak, Theodore, **703–705**
Round River Conservation Studies, 630
Rubber plantations, 729
Ruby Mountains, 378
Ruether, Rosemary Radford, **705–706**
Rural water and sewage treatment plants, 240
Russell Sage Foundation, 269
Rutgers' Presidential Award, 646
Rwanda, 302, 303

Safe Drinking Water Act (1974, 1986, 1996), 125, 850, 895
"Safe Harbor" Agreements, 66
Safina, Carl, **709–712**
Sagan, Carl, **712–714**
Sahara Desert, 511
Sale, Kirkpatrick, **714–716**
Salmon migration, 804–805
Salt Creek Corridor, 437
Saltwater Institute, The, 169
SalvaNATURA, 868
Samuelson, Dan, 27
Sanctuaries, preservation of, 649–650
Sandoval, Arturo, **716–718**
San Francisco, 474
Sanibel Island, 223
San Isabel National Forest, 142
Sanitation, 14, 402, 529, 608, 673, 845, 846
San Joaquin River, 8
San Joaquin Valley (Calif.), 35
Sanjour, William, **718–719**
San Juan National Forest, 757
San Pedro River, 786
Santa Ana Mountains, 395
Santa Barbara Declaration of Environmental Rights, 582
Santa Barbara Oil Spill, 582
Santa Cruz Predatory Bird Research Group, 593
Santa Rosa Island, 12
Sargent, Charles Sprague, 344, **719–721**

Sauk and Fox tribal council, 812
Savannah River Ecology Laboratory, 604
Save EPA (now Environmental Safety), 258
Save Ourselves, 298
Save-the-Redwoods League, 260
Sawhill, John, **721–723**
Schlickeisen, Rodger, **724–725**
Schneider, Stephen, **725–727**
Schultes, Richard Evans, **728–730**
Schurz, Carl, **730–732**
Schwarzenegger, Arnold, **732–733**
Science and Planning in Conservation Ecology (SPICE), 600
Scientific agriculture, 844–845
Scientific Committee on Problems of the Environment (SCOPE), 858–859
Scientific Fellow of the Wildlife Conservation Society, 600
Scientific forest management, 637–639
Scouting movement, 745
Seabirds, 709, 710
Seafood, 711, 740
Sea level and coastal wetlands, 815
Seal hunt, campaign to oppose, 848
Sealth, Chief (Seattle), **734–735**
Sea otters, 619, 620–621
Sea Shepherd Conservation Society, 848, 849
Seaside Park, 608
Seaside Prize, 243
Seattle/King County Board of Health, 594
Sea turtles, 145–147, 711
Sebastopol (Calif.), 220
Second Nature, 642
*Secret Language of Snow, The*, 869
Sectionalism, 823
Sector Schultes, 729
Securities and Exchange Commission (SEC), 252
Seed Savers Exchange (SSE), 854, 855, 856
Seed Savers International, 856
Seeds of Change, 36, 37
Seeger, Pete, **736–738**
Selikoff, Irving, **738–740**
Seo, Danny, **740–741**
Service Employee's International Union (SEIU), 631
Sessions, George, 234, **742–743**
Seton, Ernest Thompson, **743–746**

Seton, Grace Gallatin, 745
Seventh Generation constitutional amendment, 114
Sewage runoff, 711
Sewerage system, 845
Shabecoff, Philip, **746–748**
Shamanic traditions, 639–641
Shamans and Apprentices Program, 639–640
Shapiro, Andrew L., **748–750**
Sharks, 710
Shawnee Mission Environmental Science Laboratory, 227
Shawnee Mission North High School, 226
Shawsheen River, 228
Shepard, Paul, 233
Shuey, Chris, **750–753**
Sick building syndrome, 526
Sierra Club, 225, 233, 234, 261, 283, 300, 314, 391, 503, 523, 524, 538, 562, 564, 583, 646, 663, 779
  John Muir Award, 16, 187, 525, 570
  Kings Canyon, 116
  National Park Service, 7
  protests to U.S. nuclear testing, 848
  publications of, 548, 555
  wilderness preservation, 894
Sierra Nevada Conservancy, 732
Sierra Student Coalition, 853
Sigurd F. Olson Nature Writing Award, 614
Sigurd Olson Environmental Institute, 614
Silkwood, Karen, **753–754**
Simplicity Forum, 685
Siskiyou National Forest, 301, 329
Sitting Bull, speech excerpt, 914
Sive, David, **754–756**
"Six Sins of Greenwashing™" 980–994
Sixth Annual Luminaria Award, 581
Small is Beautiful movement, 715
Small Planet Institute, 475, 477
SmartWood, 246, 449–450, 867
Smith, David, 380
Smith, Rocky, **757–758**
Smithsonian Institution, 12, 161
Snake River, 583
Sneed, Cathrine, **758–760**
Snyder, Gary, **760–762**
Social ecology, 101
Social entrepreneurs, 257

# Index

Social Investment Forum, 63
Social parasitism, cases of, 148
Social reforms, 14
Society for Animal Protective Legislation, 591
Society for Conservation Biology, 600
Society for Ecological Restoration (SER), 517
Society for the Preservation of National Parks, 187
Society of Conservation Biology, 279
Society of Environmental Journalists, 747
Sociobiology, 873
Soil conservation, 73, 228, 750
Soil Conservation Service, 410
Soil erosion, 73, 238, 750
 causes of, 418
Soil Erosion Service (later Soil Conservation Service), 73–74
Soil microbes, 262
Solar energy, 382, 493, 802–803
 use of, 401
Solar power, 749
Soleri, Paolo, **762–764**
Solid Waste Disposal Act (1965), 552
Solomon, Susan, **765–766**
Sombrero Marsh, preservation of, 811
Sophie Prize, 217
Soulé, Michael, **766–768**
Southern Christian Leadership Conference (SCLC), 174
Southern Rockies Ecosystem Project, 758
Southern Rural Women's Network, 17
South Platte River, 332, 757
Southwest Environmental Center (SWEC), 93–94
Southwest Research and Information Center (SRIC), 555, 750
Soviet Union, 192, 323, 415, 554, 876
Space exploration, 713
Spaceship Earth, 102, 103
Spain, 217
Spearfishing, 114
Special Weapons and Tactics (SWAT), 404
Species extinction, 469, 768
Speth, James Gustave, **769–771**
Spherical chamber, 70

Spirit in Action program, 20. *See also* Interfaith Solidarity Walks
Spirituality, 33, 81, 455, 538, 703, 807
Spotted owls, 228, 304, 305, 437, 785, 786
Standing Bear, Chief Luther, **771–772**
Starr, Ellen Gates, 14
Steel, William, **773–774**
Stegner, Wallace, 235, **775–776,** 919-924
Steingraber, Sandra, **776–778**
Sterling Forest, 11
Stockholm Convention, 289
Stone, Christopher, **779–780**
Stone-Manning, Tracy, **780–782**
Stonyfield Farm, 169
Stop Global Warming College Tour, 225
Stop Global Warming Virtual March, 224, 225
Stop the Poisoning (STP), 350
Storm King Mountain, 737, 755
 pump storage plant, 10–11
Stove project, 197–198
Strategic Arms Limitation Talks (SALT), 551
Strategic Defense Initiative, 457
Strategic open space parcels, 822
Strip mining, 163
Stuart Rebellion, 744
Subra, Wilma, **783–785**
Suburbanization, 29, 659
Suckling, Kierán, **785–787**
Sulfur-dioxide emissions, 464
 copper smelting, 445–446
Sunken Forest, 810
Sunshine Farm Research Program, 418
Superfund bill (1980), 335
Superfund legislation, 154
Superfund ombudsman, 719
Superfund sites, 22, 23, 125, 799
Supersonic transport aircraft (SSTs), 504
Surface Mine Control & Reclamation Act (1977), 264
Surface Transportation Policy Project (STPP), 241, 242, 243
Surinam, 553, 640, 641
Susanka, Sarah, **787–789**
Sustainability, 447
 energy efficiency, 490
 forest management, 106
 waste-reduction effort, 26

Sustainable Agriculture Network (SAN), 450, 868
Sustainable architectural design, 199
Sustainable development, 243, 295, 389, 500, 502, 525, 580
 projects, 770
 transportation, 170
 urban areas, 30
Sustainable Development of Ecotourism Web Conference, 502
Sustainable Growth Initiative, 749
Sustainable Seas Expeditions, 275, 276
Sustainable Seattle, 685
Sustainable South Bronx (SSBX), 155–156
Sustainable tourism, formal operational criteria for, 88
Swamp and Overflowed Lands Act (1850), 250
Swamp habitat, 332
Swearingen, Terri, **789–791**
Swedish Biodiversity Centre, 208
Swope Park, 226, 227
Szilard Award, 702

Taiwan, 470
Takelma Intertribal Project, 517
Tallgrass Prairie National Preserve, 656
Tall, JoAnn, **795–796**
Tamminen, Terry, 733, **797–799**
Taxidermy, 166, 397
Tchozewski, D. Chet, **799–802**
TEA-21 legislation, 243
Teamsters Union, 173
Tektite project, 275
Television, 5, 37, 45, 71
Tellico Dam, 335
Templeton Prize, 697
Tennessee River, 596
Tennessee Valley, 144
Tennessee Valley Authority (TVA), 39, 596, 699
Terra Alpha Technology acknowledgment award, 672
Teton River, 28
Tewa, Debby, **802–804**
Texas Clean Air Cities Coalition, 545
Theodore Roosevelt National Memorial Park, 260
Theory of evolution of species, 344
Third Scientific Assessment Report (TAR), 505
Thomas Jefferson Medal, 531

# INDEX

Thompson, Chief Tommy Kuni, **804–806**
Thoreau, Henry David, 292, **806–809**, 862, 863, 907-909
Thorne Ecological Institute, 810, 811
Thorne Films, Inc., 809, 810
Thorne Natural Science School, 810
Thorne, Oakleigh, II, **809–811**
Thorpe, Grace, **812–814**
Threatened species protection, 207, 209, 400, 864
Three Gorges project, 474
Tidepool (now Sightline Daily), 509
Tides Foundation, 801
Tidwell, Michael, **814–816**
Tiger conservation efforts, 471
Timber
    certification program, 247
    extraction, 244, 378, 437
    harvesting, 245
    industry, 391, 437
Tobacco, 157, 192, 337, 594, 798, 850
Tobay wildlife sanctuary, 837
Tohono O'odham, 400, 401, 575, 576, 579, 580, 847
Tokar, Brian, **817–818**
Tolba, Mostafa, 859
Tompkins, Douglas, 234, **819–820**
Tom's of Maine, 167, 168, 169
Toor, Will, **821–822**
Tortuguero beach, 145, 147
Tourism. *See* Ecotourism; Recreation
Toxic emissions, 789
Toxic Substances Control Act (1976), 552
Toxic waste contamination, 21, 23, 325, 778, 784
    in Love Canal, 122
    in Shelby, 799
Toxic waste problem, 451
Trade Record Analysis of Flora and Fauna in Commerce (TRAFFIC), 312
Traditional ecological knowledge (TEK), 518
Transcendentalist movement, 290
Transportation, 764. *See also* Automobiles
Transportation Justice Equity Platform, 286
Trappers Lake, 142
Trapping rights, 167
Traverse Area Community Currency Corporation, 550
Tree Claim Act, 142

Tree Corps, 760
Tree Media Group, 237
TreePeople, 491
Tree planting, 198, 385
Trees Foundation, 393, 394
Tree sitting, 393
Tree spiking, 880
TREES (Training, Extension, Enterprises and Sourcing) program, 248, 450. *See also* Rainforest Alliance
Trees, Water & People (TWP), 197–198, 665–666
Tribal land, 400
Tribal Sovereignty Program (later Seventh Generation Fund), 374
Trillium Asset Management Corporation, 63
Tropical deforestation, 488–489
Tropical dry forests, 422
"Tropical Forests, Interdependence and Responsibility" conference, 449
Tropical rain forests, 144
    deforestation of, 469
    loss of biodiversity in, 442
    medicinal plants growing in, 206
    public concern about destruction of, 488
    *See also* Ecotourism
Tuberculosis, 738
Tuna industry, dolphin slaughter by, 469, 470
Tuolumne River, 434
Turk, Rowena Unger, 227
Turner Family Foundation, 825, 826
Turner, Frederick Jackson, **823–824**
Turner, Ted, **824–826**
Turtles, sea, 145, 146, 149, 231, 279, 710, 711
Twinkie tax, 420
Two Forks dam, 332, 757
Tyler Ecology Award, 604
Tyrothricin, 263

Udall Center for Studies in Public Policy, 411
Udall, Morris, **829–831**
Udall, Stewart, 308, 431, 612, 614, 829, **831–833**
Uinta Basin, 376
Uinta Mountain, 376
Uinta River, 379
Underwater exploration, 275

Union Asbestos and Rubber Company (UNARCO), 738
Union Carbide, 79, 85
Union of Concerned Scientists (UCS), 225, 456–457, 925, 948–951
Union organizing, 528
United Auto Workers (UAW), 100
United Farm Workers (UFW), 172, 173, 404, 659
United Nations Charter for Nature, 849
United Nations Children's Fund (UNICEF), 683
United Nations Conference on Environment and Development (UNCED). *See* Earth Summit (Rio de Janeiro 1992)
United Nations Development Program, 649
United Nations Earth Summit, 315
United Nations Educational, Scientific and Cultural Organization (UNESCO), 580
United Nations Environmental Program (UNEP)
    Environmental Leadership Award, 589
    Global 500 Honor Roll, 525
    Gold Medal Award, 620
United States Army Corps of Engineers, 250
United States Biological Survey (USBS; now United States Fish and Wildlife Service [USFWS]), 47, 68, 223
United States Climate Action Partnership, 464
United States Climate Emergency Council, 816
United States Conference of Mayors, 594
United States Department of Agriculture (USDA), 575
United States Department of Commerce, 655
United States Department of Energy, 616, 702
United States Department of Fish and Wildlife (USDFW), 240
United States Forest Service (USFS), 142, 228, 499, 599, 607, 608, 637, 638, 698, 701
    Global Change Program, 597

# INDEX

Roadless Area Initiative of, 879, 880
United States Geographical and Geological Survey, 653
United States Geological Survey (USGS), 652, 654
United States Housing Act (1937), 61
United States Man and the Biosphere Program (U.S. MAB), 580
United States Mayors Climate Protection Agreement, 595
United States-Mexico border. *See* Mexico-U.S. border
United States-Mexico La Paz agreement Annex 4. *See* La Paz agreement
United States National Parks movement, 15
United States Peace Corps, 228
United States Postal Service (USPS), 53, 79
United States Public Health Service, 240
United States Public Interest Research Group (U.S. PIRG), 578
United States Sanitary Commission, 608
United Workers Organizing Committee (UFWOC), 404
Upjohn Corporation, 463
Uranium Impact Assessment Program, 750
Uranium mining, 750
Urban and industrial sanitation, importance of, 673
Urban city parks, 610
Urban environment, 198, 314
  revitalization of, 29
Urban Environmental Conference, 112
Urban gardening project, 176–177
Urban Habitat, 29, 30, 286
Urban landscapes, 439, 764
Urban planning, 61–62, 333, 610, 764
  Mcharg, Ian role in, 530, 531
  Mumford, Lewis role in, 565
Urban social wilderness, 9
Urban sprawl, 29, 80, 128, 295, 425, 763, 767, 821
Urban Underground (or Planners for a Democratic Society), 334, 338

Utah Public Lands Management Act (1995), 870

Vascular botany, 328
Vaux, Calvert, 256
Ventana Wilderness Sanctuary, 593
Vermilion Association to Protect the Environment, 298
Video-Active Productions, 195
Village Earth, 666
Vincent, LaDuke, 472
Viruga Mountains, 303
Vogt, William, 281, **837–838**
Voigt decision, 113
Volunteers in Service to America (VISTA), 232, 716
Volvo for Life Environmental Award, 784

*Walden*, 907–909
Wallace, Henry, 222
Walt Disney Company, 124
Walter, Martin **841–843**
W. Alton Jones Foundation, 185
Warburton, Barbara, **843–844**
Waring, George, **844–846**
Warshall, Peter, **846–847**
Wasatch Forest, 378
Wasatch Mountains, 399
Washington, Booker T., 157
Washington, D.C., 223
Waste disposal, 371
Waste incineration, 340, 791
Waste reduction, 26, 64
Waste Technologies Industries (WTI), 452, 789
Water conservation, 160, 357, 411, 416, 737
Water cycle, 250
Water development, public scrutiny of, 379
Water Keeper Alliance, 459
Water management, 379, 669
Water pollution, 11, 38, 203, 237, 271, 315, 346, 445, 895
  caused by mining activity, 96
Water quality, 14, 125, 737
  impact of mining on, 658
  in rural communities, 418
  standards and regulations, 895
  and wildlife habitat, 46
Water Quality Act (1965), 570, 571, 588, 589
Water resource
  management, 669–700
  projects, 412
Water rights, 35, 847, 865

Watershed Hero Award, 265
Watershed protection, 247, 459
Water supply, 376
Water use, 787
Watson, Paul, **847–849**
Waxman, Henry, **850–852**
Weather conditions, 324, 387
Weminuche Wilderness Area, 757
Werbach, Adam, **852–854**
Western Ancient Forest Campaign (WAFC; now American Lands Alliance), 438
Western Lake Erie Basin Conservation Program, 66
Western Lands Project, 97–98
Western religious settings, 81
Western Slope Energy Research Center (WSERC), 184
West, Paul, 5
Wetlands, 220, 222
  ecology, 250
  erosion, 319
  preserve, 749
  restoration, 319
Weyerhaeuser Recycling, 348
Whales, 482, 740, 741, 761, 848, 876
Whealy, Diane, and Kent Whealy, **854–856**
Wheelock College, 17
Whistle-blowing
  among public employees, 228
  of national environmental laws, 23
White Earth Land Recovery Project (WELRP), 472
White, Gilbert F., **857–859**
Whitehead, Alfred North, 182
White House Forest Conference, 304
White, Lynn, Jr., **859–861**
White Mountain National Forest, 499
White River, 378
Whitman, Walt, 130, **861–863**
*Whole Earth* publications, 549, 846, 847
Wichita Mountains Wildlife Refuge, 398
Wild and Scenic Rivers Act (1968), 112, 210
Wilderness
  conservation of, 629
  designation, 377, 581
  importance of, 627, 628
Wilderness Act (1964, 1974), 111, 116, 234, 308, 416, 568, 570, 612, 890, 894

# INDEX

Wilderness Bill (1956), 111, 132, 614
Wilderness Foundation, award of, 525
"The Wilderness Letter," 919–924
Wilderness preservation, 889–890
  national program for, 894
Wilderness Society, The (TWS), 109, 111, 252, 499, 512, 513, 589, 612, 890, 893, 894
Wilderness Watch, 880
Wild Forever (grizzly bear recovery project), 864, 865
Wildfowl habitat restoration, 220, 222, 223
Wild lands preservation, 478, 847
Wildlands Project, 766
Wildlife Australia, 610
Wildlife conservation, 223
Wildlife management, 223, 521–522, 568, 575, 597, 599
Wildlife preservation, 397
Wildlife refuge, 223
Wildlife Society, award of, 144
Wildlife-Wildlands Institute (now Craighead Wildlife-Wildlands Institute, Inc.), 210
Wildness, 83, 161, 201, 346, 806
Wild Rivers Act, 588, 589
Wild Rockies Conservation Award, 230
Willcox, Louisa, **864–866**
Wille, Chris, **866–868**
William G. Anderson Award, 583
William O. Douglas Wilderness, 253
Williams, Terry Tempest, **868–870**
Willie Nelson Biodiesel, 590
Wilson, Diane, **871–872**
Wilson, Edward O., 312, **872–874**
Wilson, Pete, 404
Wilson, Woodrow, 16

Wind turbines, 750
Winter, Paul, **874–877**
Wobblies, 252
Wolf, Hazel, **877–879**
Wolke, Howie, **879–881**
Wolves
  behavior, 484
  reintroduction of, 94
Women Donors Network, 232
Wood certification programs, 246
Woodcraft Indians, 745
Woodland restoration, 280
Woodrow Wilson Award, 536
Woodrow Wilson Fellowship Foundation, 227
Woods Hole Research Center, 882
Woodwell, George, **881–883**
Wootton, Timothy, 288
Worker's health and safety, 92
Working Families Win project, 438
"World Alert," 45
World Bank, 216, 364
World Bank Task Force of Biological Diversity, 553
World Conservation Union, 553, 610, 636
World Economic Forum, 324
World Ecotourism Summit (2002), 502
World Energy Modernization Plan, 324
"World Futuristics" course, 227
*World On Fire*, 550, 551
World Scientists' Warning to Humanity, 948–951
Worldwatch Institute (WI), 120, 447
World Wildlife Fund (WWF), 312, 553, 599, 618, 634, 641, 667
Worster, Donald, **883–885**
Writers Corps, 155

X-rays, harm of overexposure to, 85
Ya-ka-ama Indian Development and Education Corporation, 517
Yale School of Forestry and Environmental Studies, 611
Yard, Robert Sterling, 16, 131, 519, **889–890**, 893
Yellow Dog Watershed Preserve (YDWP), 657, 658
Yellowstone ecosystem, 864
Yellowstone National Park, 161, 688
  grizzly bears in, 209–210
  movement to oppose pollution from mining, 864–865
Yosemite National Park, 7, 8, 15, 187, 277, 608, 742
Yosemite Valley, 608. *See also* Hetch Hetchy Valley
Young, Roy, 348
Young Woman's Christian Temperance Union, 528
*Your Money or Your Life*, 685
Youth for Environmental Sanity, 683
Youth Venture, 259

Zahniser, Howard, **893–895**
Zech, Fredrich, 7
Zero-base budgeting, 153
Zero Cut, 390, 391
Zero Population Growth, 182
Zipcar, 170–171
*Zoboomafoo*, 461, 462
Zone System, 7
Zoos, 617
Zwick, David, **895–896**

## About the Authors

ANNE BECHER and JOSEPH RICHEY are a husband and wife team who have specialized in writing, researching, editing and translation for more than 20 years. Together they've worked on the bilingual Spanish/English literary magazine *The Underground Forest/La Selva Subterranea*. Becher co-authors *The New Key to Costa Rica* (Ulysses, since 1986). She authored the first edition of *American Environmental Leaders* (ABC-CLIO, 2000), and a reference book, *Biodiversity* (ABC-CLIO, 1998). Richey was a contributing editor to *Earth Prayers* (Harper & Row, 1991), *Prayers for a Thousand Years* (HarperCollins, 1998), and Martha Honey's *Ecotourism and Sustainable Development* (Island Press, 1999). More recently, he edited *Ed Dorn Live* (University of Michigan Press, 2007). The Richey-Bechers have two children, Jacob and Flora, and live in Boulder, Colorado.